⟨ **W9-BHA-427**

ENCYCLOPEDIA OF MODERN MEXICO

David W. Dent

The Scarecrow Press, Inc.
Lanham, Maryland, and London
2002

SCARECROW PRESS, INC.

Published in the United States of America
by Scarecrow Press, Inc.
A Member of the Rowman & Littlefield Publishing Group
4501 Forbes Boulevard, Suite 200, Lanham, Maryland 20706
www.scarecrowpress.com

4 Pleydell Gardens, Folkestone
Kent CT20 2DN, England

British Library Cataloguing in Publication Information Available

Library of Congress Cataloging-in-Publication Data Available

Dent, David W.
  Encyclopedia of modern Mexico / David W. Dent.
    p. cm.
  Includes bibliographical references.
  ISBN 0-8108-4291-2 (cloth : alk. paper)
  1. Mexico—History—20th century—Encyclopedias. I. Title.
F1234 .D364 2002
972.08'2'03—dc21   2002003316

CONTENTS

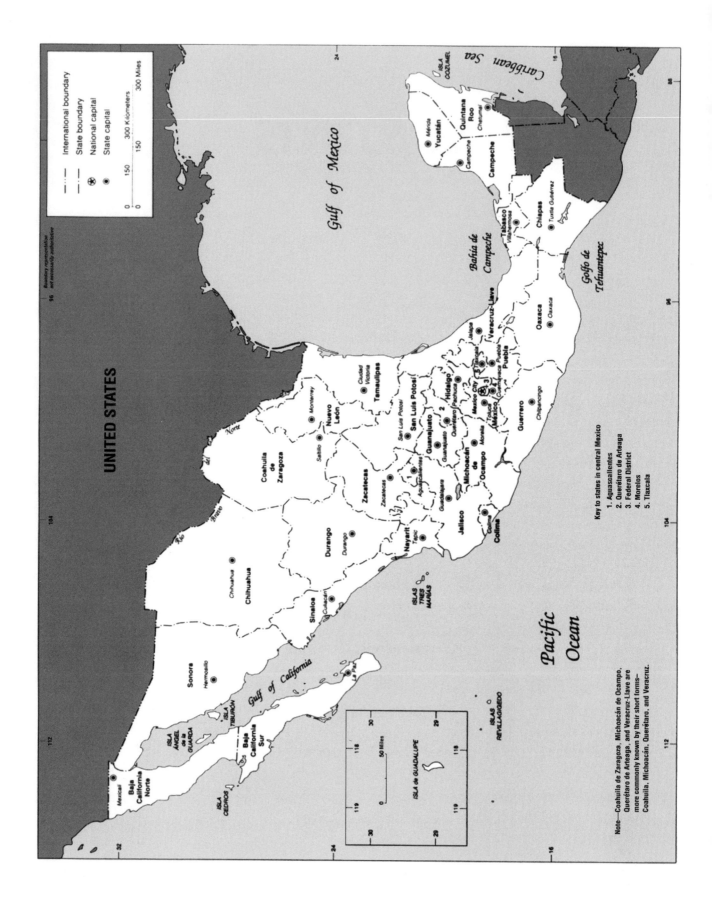

PREFACE

The *Encyclopedia of Modern Mexico* is designed to serve as a reference tool for anyone seeking a better understanding of contemporary Mexico—a major player in the Western Hemisphere and a country of growing importance to the United States. It contains information that captures the dramatic transformation that has taken place in Mexico since World War II, emphasizing the key events, individuals, institutions, procedures, controversies, and policy dilemmas that have determined the course of Mexican history from the presidency of Lázaro Cárdenas (1934–1940) to the beginning of the new millennium under President Vicente Fox (2000–2006). The past 60 years represent a critical phase in Mexican development—perhaps the most important in its long history—characterized by "the miracle" of dramatic economic growth and political stability (1940–1969), followed by a topsy-turvy period after 1970. During this turbulent period, Mexico's leadership struggled to correct a system—inherited from the 1940s—beset with corruption, economic inequalities, sharp ethnic and regional divisions, lack of democratic accountability, and serious tensions with Washington. By the 1980s, the highly centralized corporatist political model faced a legitimacy crisis of major dimensions. For years it had stressed the needs of business,

industry, and a select group called the Revolutionary Family or Coalition while largely ignoring the needs of the majority of the population.

While Mexico has managed to overcome some of the legacies from the past in confronting a plethora of pressing economic, social, and political problems, the "revolution" is still incomplete and full of new challenges and developmental dilemmas, particularly after the unprecedented transition of power from the ruling Partido Revolucionario Institucional (PRI) to the Partido Acción Nacional (PAN), which is expected to bring major changes to Mexico's political institutions. After such a tumultuous era, Mexico's future is far from certain; however, Mexico's transformation in the 21st century will require a better understanding of what transpired—for better or worse—during and after World War II.

This reference book contains over 200 entries that provide essential information for anyone interested in a basic cultural, political, and economic knowledge of modern Mexico. Mexico today is far more complex than what is reported on television programs and in newspapers and magazines (dominated by stories emphasizing crime, rebellion, corruption, and cocaine) in the United States and Mexico. Those who think of Mexico as only a rural, antientrepreneural, traditional, authoritarian, and poor country have overlooked the profound transformations that are under way. After the Mexican Revolution, Mexico made great strides in creating a common national identity, an effective and legitimate political apparatus, and a more just and prosperous economy than what existed before 1910. Although Mexico has made serious efforts to become more modern, prosperous, stable, and democratic, it is still troubled by forces that hinder its political and economic development, particularly the deep divisions between rich and poor, north and south, mestizo and Indian, and urban and rural. The economic transformation of Mexico since 1940 is impressive, but the results of the economic and political reforms are uneven and in some places counterproductive and harmful. For example, the corruption that became deeply rooted in the fabric of society during the 1940s has not been eliminated, despite efforts to create a political and economic system that is moral and just. According to exit poll interviews, corruption associated with the ruling party was the single most important issue to voters who chose Vicente Fox over Francisco Labastida and others in the 2000 presidential race.

Each entry in the encyclopedia offers readers an opportunity to "rethink" and "reinterpret" their perceptions (and misperceptions) of Mexico, Mexicans, and Mexican Americans. Thematically, most of the entries in this book fit into the following categories: (1) actors, filmmakers, and performers; (2) composers and musicians; (3) literature, writers, and educators; (4) communications media and journalists; (5) popular culture, rituals, and national and gender identity; (6) artists and architects; (7) economic and foreign policy; (8) industry and economic development; (9) geographic regions and ecology; (10) religion and politics; (11) diplomats, politicians, and heads of state; (12) political parties and organizations; (13) revo-

lutionary leaders and guerrilla organizations; and (14) political and economic conflicts.

What is the best way to use this reference book? The entries contained in the *Encyclopedia of Modern Mexico* are designed to draw the reader's attention to aspects of Mexico that are often neglected or not well understood in the United States, particularly its people, culture, customs, government, economy, late-20th-century history, party system, communications media, and public rituals. The reader will *not* find entries devoted to science, medicine (folk and modern), archeology, law, aviation, sports (with the exception of baseball), banking and finance, cuisine, mining, folk art, and nongovernmental organizations. There was not enough space to expand the entries to include these topics and others, regardless of their importance. A special effort was made to include current references with each entry—mostly in English but also some published in Mexico in Spanish—that will assist readers who seek further information on the subject.

In each entry, I highlight the history, achievements, and creations of the Mexican people. This is not a book about Chicanos/Latinos or Mexican Americans—although they are numerous and their achievements have been substantial—but the reader will find a few entries devoted to prominent Mexicans who spent a good part of their creative lives in the United States, Mexican Americans, and cultural concepts that are important to understanding modern Mexico. The reader should note that cross-references in the entries are designated with boldface type. A detailed index is included to assist the reader in tracking down important names, concepts, and events that are not included as separate entries. In many ways, the index is the most complete guide to the whole reference book and should be used as one of the major tools of this work. The selected bibliography includes current books on a variety of subjects of importance to understanding modern Mexico is published during the last 15 years, and there is also a comprehensive list of online resources of value for gaining more information on Mexico today.

There are over 50 photos—mostly from the Organization of American States, *Proceso*'s photo archive in Mexico City, AP/World Wide, Photofest, the Benson Latin American Collection at the University of Texas–Austin, and production stills provided by Carl J. Mora—in this reference book. Others came from my own collection or were donated by friends and colleagues. Each one is included to provide a visual companion to important entries and includes a caption in English to help place the photo in its proper context.

Although the *Encyclopedia of Modern Mexico* was created and written by a single author, it would not have been possible to cover such a wide range of topics dealing with modern Mexico without the assistance of friends, colleagues, and librarians. Over a span of three years, I visited five libraries known for their excellent collections on modern Mexico: the Library of Congress (Hispanic Division) in Washington, D.C.; the Benson Latin American Collection at the University of Texas–Austin; the Zimmerman Library at the University of New Mexico–Albuquerque; the Hayden Library at Arizona State University in Tempe; and the Social Sciences and Humanities Library and U.S.–Mexican Studies Center at the University of California–San Diego. For their valuable assistance during my visits to these fine libraries, I would like to thank Everett Larson (chief reference librarian, Hispanic Division, Library of Congress), Barbara A. Tenenbaum (Hispanic Division, Library of Congress), Ann Hartness (Benson Latin American Collection), Russ Davidson (curator of Latin American and Iberian Collections at the University of New Mexico), Orchid Mazurkiewicz (reference librarian/Latin America and Iberia area specialist, Hayden Library), and Karen J. Lindvall-Larson (Latin American Studies librarian at UCSD).

Academic colleagues were also instrumental in assisting me with this project. Tom Mullen of Dalton State College sent me a number of important books on Mexico and served as the "chief" of my clipping service, providing me with valuable information on a wide variety of contemporary subjects, and as a consultant on key entries dealing with film, actors, and directors. Charles F. Andrain, colleague and former professor (now retired) from San Diego State University, tracked down biographical information and enhanced my stay in San Diego with his hospitality. Larman C. Wilson shared some of his comprehensive files on the *Chamizal* conflict and the Zapatista uprising in Chiapas. Ann Mulrane of the Hispanic Division of the Library of Congress was supportive in locating hard-to-find books on numerous topics. Roderic Ai Camp offered his expertise on conceptualizing some of the entries and in fine-tuning the timeline. Andrew Wood provided valuable assistance with several entries dealing with cinema and music, offering important comments and corrections. Carl J. Mora let me use his production stills from the golden age of Mexican cinema and helped clarify the entries dealing with film stars and the post-1945 history of the film industry. J. Paul Breeding helped prepare some of the photos from my collection for this book. Fran Rothstein read the entries on machismo, feminism, and homosexuality, offering important commentary and clarifications for my draft copies. Tom Ward, Paul Collingson-Streng, Donald E. Shultz, and Sandra Messinger Cypess helped to clarify and enrich numerous entries with their expertise on modern Mexico. At Towson University the Faculty Development Office and the dean of the College of Liberal Arts were generous in providing financial assistance to acquire the numerous photographs used to illustrate many of the entries throughout the encyclopedia.

I also want to offer special thanks to four Mexicans whose assistance and generosity made this a more interesting, enjoyable, and valuable research project: Alejandro Junco (owner of *El*

Norte in Monterrey), Salvador González "Chava" (political cartoonist), Ulises Castellanos (photo archivist at *Proceso*), and María Elena Rico Covarrubias for granting the rights to use artwork by Miguel Covarrubias.

In no way are any of the above-mentioned individuals to be held responsible for the selection of entries, the interpretations of certain subjects, or the limitations and flaws found in this volume, which are entirely my own. If the *Encyclopedia of Modern Mexico* provides the reader with a better understanding of the economic, political, and cultural transformations now under way in Mexico, it will have achieved it major purpose.

ABBREVIATIONS AND ACRONYMS

AB	Asamblea de Barrios
ABBY	American Booksellers Book of the Year
AC	Alianza Cívica
ACPC	Association of Coffee Producing Countries
AI	Amnesty International
BAW	Border Arts Workshop
BIP	Border Industrialization Program
CD	Corriente Democrática
CIA	Central Intelligence Agency
CIHMA	Centro de Investigaciones Históricas de los Movimientos Armados
CNC	Confederación Nacional Campesina
CNDH	Comisión Nacional de Derechos Humanos
CNOP	Confederación Nacional de Organizaciones Populares
CONASUPO	Compañía Nacional de Subsistencias Populares
CONCAMIN	Confederación de Cámaras Industriales de los Estados Unidos Mexicanos
CONCANACO	Confederación Nacional de Cámaras Comerciales
CROM	Confederación Revolucionaria de Obreros y Campesinos Mexicanos
CT	Congreso del Trabajo
CTAL	Confederación de Trabajadores de América Latina
CTM	Confederación de Trabajadores de México
DEA	Drug Enforcement Administration
D.F.	Distrito Federal
DFS	Directorate of Federal Security
DINA	Diesel Nacional
ECLAC	Economic Commission for Latin America and the Caribbean
ENAH	Escuela Nacional de Antropología e Historia

ENP	Escuela Nacional Preparatoria	**INI**	Instituto Nacional Indígena
EPA	Environmental Protection Agency	**INS**	Immigration and Naturalization Service
EPR	Ejército Popular Revolucionario	**IPN**	Instituto Politécnico Nacional
EVRP	Ejército Villista Revolucionario del Pueblo	**IRCA**	Immigration Reform and Control Act (1986)
EZLN	Ejército Zapatista de Liberación Nacional	**ISI**	Import Substitution Industrialization
FAP	Federal Arts Project	**ITESM**	Instituto Tecnológico y Científico de Monterrey
FBI	Federal Bureau of Investigation	**LAFTA**	Latin American Free Trade Association
FDN	Frente Democrático Nacional		
FLN	Frente de Liberación Nacional	**MPPDA**	Motion Picture Producers and Distributors of America
FONATUR	Fondo Nacional de Turismo		
FTAA	Free Trade Area of the Americas	**NAFTA**	North American Free Trade Agreement
GAFE	Grupos Aeromóviles de Fuerzas Especiales	**NEA**	National Endowment for the Arts
GAO	General Accounting Office	**OAS**	Organization of American States
GATT	General Agreement on Tariffs and Trade	**OCIAA**	Office of Coordinator of Inter-American Affairs
GDP	Gross Domestic Product		
IBWC	International Boundary Water Commission	**OPEC**	Organization of Petroleum Exporting Countries
IFE	Instituto Federal Electoral	**PAN**	Partido Acción Nacional
IMC	Instituto Mexicano de Cafeteros	**PARM**	Partido Auténtico de la Revolución Mexicana
IMET	International Military Education and Training		
IMF	International Monetary Fund	**PCD**	Partido Centro Democrático
IMP	Instituto Mexicano de Petróleo	**PCM**	Partido Comunista Mexicano
IMSS	Instituto Mexicano de Seguro Social	**PDM**	Partido Democrático Mexicano
		PEM	Partido Ecológico Mexicano
INAH	Instituto Nacional de Antropología e Historia	**PEMEX**	Petróleos Mexicanos
INCIME	Instituto Mexicano de Cinematografía	**PFCRN**	Partido Frente Cardenista de Reconstrucción Nacional
INEGI	Instituto Nacional de Estadística Geografiae Informática	**PLM**	Partido de Liberal Mexicano
		PMS	Partido Mexicano Socialista

PMT	Partido Mexicano de los Trabajadores
PNR	Partido Nacional Revolucionario
PP	Partido Popular
PPS	Partido Popular Socialista
PRD	Partido de la Revolución Democrática
PRI	Partido Revolucionario Institucional
PRM	Partido Revolucionario Mexicano
PRONASOL	Programa Nacional de Solidaridad
PSP	Partido Socialista Popular
PST	Partido Socialista de los Trabajadores
PSUM	Partido Socialista Unificado Méxicano
PT	Partido de Trabajo
PVEM	Partido Verde Ecológico Mexicano
SEDESOL	Secretaría de Desarrollo Social
SEDUE	Secretaría de Desarrollo Urbano y Ecología
SELA	Sistema Económico Latinoamericano
SEP	Secretaría de Enseñanza Pública
SOA	School of the Americas
TELMEX	Teléfonos de México
TFE	Tribunal Federal de Electoral
TI	Transparency International
TLC	Tratado de Libre Comercio
TSM	Telesistema Mexicana
UN	United Nations
UNAC	Unión Nacional Agricultores Cafeteros
UNAM	Universidad Nacional Autónoma de México
UNESCO	United Nations Education, Science, and Culture Organization
UNS	Unión Nacional Sinarquista
WHISC	Western Hemisphere Institute for Security Cooperation
WOLA	Washington Office on Latin America
WPA	Works Progress Administration
WTO	World Trade Organization

TIMELINE: MEXICO SINCE 1910

1910–1917 Mexican Revolution.

1916 Francisco "Pancho" Villa invades the United States and raids town of Columbus, New Mexico.

1917 Constitution of 1917 is promulgated.

1919 Emiliano Zapata is assassinated.

1923 Pancho Villa is assassinated.

1926–1929 Cristero rebellion.

1929 Official political party is formed under banner of the Partido Nacional Revolucionario (PNR).

1930 Estrada Doctrine is announced by foreign minister Genaro Estrada.

1934–1940 Lázaro Cárdenas presidency; characterized by socialist reforms and nationalization.

1938 Mexican petroleum industry is nationalized, leading to the formation of Petróleos Mexicanos (PEMEX).

1938 PNR is reorganized and named Partido Revolucionario Mexicano (PRM).

1939 Partido Acción Nacional (PAN) is founded by Manuel Gómez Morín and others.

1940 Leon Trotsky is assassinated in Mexico City by one of Stalin's secret agents.

1940–1946 Manuel Ávila Camacho presidency; import substitution industrialization is started.

1942 Mexico declares war on Axis powers and enters World War II; *bracero* agreement is signed.

1944 *Bracero* program begins.

1945 Mexico participates in World War II by sending troops to fight in the Philippines.

1945 Chapultepec Conference on war and peace is held in Mexico City.

1946 Ruling party is renamed Partido Revolucionario Institucional (PRI).

1946–1952 Miguel Alemán presidency.

1947 Presidents Truman and Alemán exchange visits to each other's capital cities.

1947 *María Candelaria*, starring Dolores del Río and directed by Emilio Fernández, wins first prize at Cannes Film Festival.

1950 Television arrives in Mexico City with first station in Latin America.

1950–1952 New campus is built for National Autonomous University of Mexico (Universidad Nacional Autonoma de México, UNAM), including art and architecture by Mario Pani, Juan O'Gorman, and others.

1952 "Operation Wetback" leads to deportation of illegal Mexican workers in the United States.

1952–1958 Adolfo Ruiz Cortines presidency; beginning of "stabilizing development" model.

1953 Women are granted right to vote, but cannot choose a president until 1958.

1954 Frida Kahlo dies.

1955 Commercial television broadcasting begins.

1955–1956 Fidel Castro prepares his insurrection against Cuban dictator Batista in Mexico.

1957 Diego Rivera dies.

1958–1964 Adolfo López Mateos presidency.

1960 CBS television documentary, "Harvest of Shame," shows extent of poverty among Mexican migrant farm workers in the United States.

1960 David Alfaro Siqueiros is imprisoned for "social dissolution" and remains in prison until 1964.

1962 President Kennedy visits Mexico and proclaims that goals of his Alliance for Progress are identical with those of Mexican Revolution.

1962 Mexico refuses to join the United States, and most of rest of Latin America, in expelling Cuba from the OAS.

1963 *Chamizal* dispute over border territory is resolved, paving the way toward resolution of other border disputes with the United States.

1964 *Bracero* program is terminated.

1964–1970 Gustavo Díaz Ordaz presidency; government begins to face growing political crises.

1965 Border Industrialization Program is created by Mexican government; first *maquiladoras* established.

1968 Massacre of hundreds of students and workers at Tlatelolco Square by police/military.

1968 Olympic Games are held in Mexico City.

1969 President Nixon meets with Díaz Ordaz to inaugurate La Amistad Dam in northern Mexico.

1970 Lázaro Cárdenas dies in Mexico City.

1970–1976 Luis Echeverría presidency; "shared development" begins with a larger state role in the economy and greater emphasis on distributive policies; foreign policy activism and "Mexicanization" investment policies sour relations with Washington.

1973 Eugenio Garza Sada, head of Monterrey Group, is murdered.

1974 National Population Council and a network of family planning clinics are founded to curb Mexico's high population growth.

1974 Passage of Equal Rights Amendment for women.

1976–1982 José López Portillo presidency; substantial oil revenues help expand Mexican economy and lead to massive borrowing and debt crisis.

1977 Electoral reform is initiated to reduce voter apathy and growing criticism of country's one-party system.

1978 Proportional representation is introduced into the Chamber of Deputies through formal legislative reform.

1979 Pope John Paul II visits Mexico and speaks out against leftist liberation theology.

1979 Fernando Valenzuela signs contract to play baseball with Los Angeles Dodgers.

1979 Mexico breaks relations with Nicaraguan dictator Anastasio Somoza Debayle and refuses to admit the Shah of Iran.

1981 New oilfields are discovered in Gulf of Campeche; Mexico becomes world's fourth-largest oil producer.

1981 Octavio Paz wins the Premio Cervantes.

1982 Mexican economy nears bankruptcy with $83 billion debt and 100 percent devaluation of peso; economic crisis weakens Mexico's freedom to differ with Washington over economic and international issues.

1982 Private banks are nationalized.

1982–1988 Miguel de la Madrid presidency; oil revenues decline and economic conditions worsen; president is forced to implement stabilization and neoliberal restructuring programs; promises of a "moral renovation" prove disappointing.

1983 Contadora Group is formed to solve Central American crisis; gradual shift toward a less anti-American foreign policy begins.

1985 Earthquake devastates Mexico City, sparking citizens' movements promoting democratic reforms.

1985 DEA agent Enrique Camarena is murdered in Guadalajara, straining U.S.–Mexican relations.

1985 Electoral reforms expand size of Chamber of Deputies.

1986 Mexico joins General Agreement on Tariffs and Trade; petroleum prices crash, putting additional burdens on development initiatives; privatization of industries begins with a boon to politically connected, wealthy investors.

1986 Immigration Reform and Control Act (IRCA) is enacted by the United States to stem flow of illegal immigration.

1987 Democratic Current is formed among dissident PRI members, including Cuauhtémoc Cárdenas; it becomes the Frente Democrático Nacional (FDN) to contest 1988 presidential elections.

1987 Carlos Fuentes wins the Premio Cervantes.

1988 Programa Nacional de Solidaridad (PRONASOL) is established to reduce poverty and increase political loyalty to President Salinas and the PRI.

1988 Ernesto Ruffo Appel, first opposition party PAN governor, is elected in Baja California, Norte.

1988–1994 Carlos Salinas de Gortari presidency; controversial election and accusations of fraud lead to massive protests throughout the country.

1989 Partido de la Revolución Democrática (PRD) is established, succeeding FDN coalition led by Cuauhtémoc Cárdenas.

1990 Presidents Bush and Salinas issue joint statement in support of negotiations for future free trade agreement.

1990 Octavio Paz is awarded Nobel Prize in Literature.

1990 DEA–sponsored abduction of Dr. Humberto Álvarez-Machaìn in Mexico poisons U.S.–Mexican relations.

1991 President Salinas negotiates free trade agreement with Chile; large PRI plurality in midterm elections restores power to ruling party in Congress.

1991 Laws are changed to allow for greater religious freedom, altering fiercely anticlerical 1917 Constitution.

1991 *Como agua para chocolate* (Like water for chocolate) becomes the most successful foreign film distributed in the United States.

1992 Major changes in Article 27 of Constitution aim to promote foreign and domestic investment in agricultural production.

1992 Diplomatic relations established with Vatican.

1993 North American Free Trade Agreement (NAFTA) is approved by legislatures of Canada, United States, and Mexico.

1994, January 1 NAFTA goes into effect; Zapatista uprising in Chiapas begins.

1994, March 23 Luis Donaldo Colosio, PRI candidate for president, is assassinated in Tijuana.

1994, December Zedillo government is forced to devalue peso, leading to collapse of Mexican economy with severe international repercussions.

1994–2000 Ernesto Zedillo presidency; initiates political reforms and anticorruption campaign.

1995 Clinton administration helps negotiate $50 billion international loan package for Mexico, including $13.5 billion portion from the United States.

1995, February Raúl Salinas arrested for masterminding 1994 murder of José Francisco Ruiz Massieu.

1996 Changes in election laws seek to level electoral playing field by placing elections institute under supervision of nine-member "independent" council.

1996 Zapatista rebels and Mexican government agree to San Andrés Accords, but negotiations stall over conflicting claims of compliance.

1996 New guerrilla force—Ejército Popular Revolucionario (EPR)—emerges in state of Guerrero.

1996 Carlos Salinas leaves Mexico and settles with family in Dublin, Ireland.

1997 President Clinton travels to Mexico to discuss drug trafficking, immigration, and trade matters.

1997, July 6 National elections result in major gains for political opposition, breaking PRI monopoly on political decision making for first time; PRI loses control of lower house of Congress, two governorships, and mayoralty of Mexico City.

1997 Amado Carrillo Fuentes—Mexico's top drug dealer—dies while undergoing surgery to alter his appearance in order to avoid capture.

1997 Prominent labor leader Fidel Velázquez dies after leading CTM for 50 years.

1997, December 22 Acteal massacre kills 45 Indians in Chiapas.

1998, April 19 Octavio Paz dies.

1998, October 2 Mexico City's government, now in hands of opposition for first time, declares official day of mourning in honor of victims of Tlatelolco massacre in 1968.

1998, November CONASUPO is closed and government subsidy on corn tortillas terminated.

1998, November World Resources Institute (WRI) declares Mexico City most dangerous location for children under five years of age due to high pollution levels.

1999, January Raúl Salinas found guilty and sentenced to 50 years (later reduced to 27 years) in prison for masterminding assassination of Ruíz Massieu in 1994, considered most important criminal verdict in modern Mexico; pope visits Mexico.

1999 President Clinton visits Mexico to discuss drugs and trade with President Zedillo, their 10th one-on-one meeting since 1994; Mexico is certified as ally in war on illegal drugs despite considerable dismay in the U.S. Congress over Mexico's drug-fighting efforts.

1999, April 20 Tens of thousands of students begin 10-month protest at UNAM over proposed tuition hike and fears of privatization.

1999, May PRI approves single open presidential primary, ending autocratic system of *dedazo* used to pick previous 10 Mexican presidents; Mexican government issues first-time travel advisory about dangers of visiting Houston, Texas, where three Mexicans were killed by police in a two-year period.

1999, September 12 Vicente Fox becomes PAN candidate for president.

1999, September 15 Mario Ruiz Massieu, former Mexican deputy attorney general, commits suicide while under house arrest in New Jersey.

1999, September 28 Opposition parties fail in efforts to unite behind a single presidential candidate, increasing chances of PRI victory in 2000.

1999, October Carlos Fuentes receives Mexico's highest civilian award for distinguished service.

1999, November 3 Bishop Samuel Ruiz, a vocal defender of Indian rights in Chiapas state, resigns.

1999, November 7 Francisco Labastida Ochoa wins landslide victory over three rivals in PRI's first presidential primary.

2000, January Over 40 foreign tourists are ordered to leave Chiapas on grounds of "political interference."

2000, February After month of dueling plebiscites between students and administrators, federal police invade university and arrest striking UNAM protesters, allowing university to open after 10-month impasse.

2000, March President Zedillo negotiates free trade agreement with European Union.

2000, July 2 PAN opposition candidate Fox wins presidential race, ending PRI's 71-year period of rule.

2000, August President-elect Fox visits with outgoing President Clinton to discuss bilateral issues, including proposals to create a common North American market and preparation for open borders between the two nations.

2000–2006 Vicente Fox presidency; brings to a close Mexico's idiosyncratic style of democracy in which PRI and government were synonymous and self-perpetuating in power; early policy efforts focus on recreation of government without a state party, making government more accountable and less corrupt, and jump-starting the economy with more foreign investment, jobs programs, tax reform, more aid for small farmers, and peace talks with Zapatistas.

2001, February President George W. Bush travels to Mexico to meet with President Fox to discuss binational issues.

2001, March Subcommander Marcos and other Zapatista leaders leave on two-week "Zapatour" from jungles of Chiapas to Mexico City to lobby for political reforms, including constitutional changes for indigenous rights.

2001, April U.S. Senator Jesse Helms (R-N.C.), chairman of Senate Foreign Relations Committee and longtime critic of Mexico, visits Mexico City to discuss immigration, drugs, and foreign policy with President Fox and members of Mexican Congress.

2001, April Mexican Congress approves legislation granting new autonomy and antidiscrimination rights to indigenous population; leaders of National Indigenous Congress reject new law as too restrictive in its protection of Indian communities.

2001, May *Amores Perros* (Love's a bitch) becomes most successful Mexican film in the United States since *Like Water for Chocolate* in early 1990s.

2001, September 6 President Fox urges joint session of U.S. Congress to grant legal status to millions of Mexicans, citing cultural and economic benefits they bring to the United States; President Bush endorses Fox's immigration proposals.

2001, September 11 Simultaneous suicide attacks on New York and Washington, D.C., by terrorists associated with Osama bin Laden's Al Qaeda network have a profound impact on Mexico and U.S.–Mexican relations.

2001, November 18 Two top U.S. Democrats—Tom Daschle and Richard Gephardt–tour central Mexico to reenergize bilateral talks on immigration reform and to build support among the large number of Latino voters in the United States.

INTRODUCTION TO MODERN MEXICO

Modern Mexico is a complex nation with a history of authoritarian rule, foreign intervention, class and ethnic conflict, economic dependency, diplomatic blunders, and a constant struggle for greater equality and social justice. Since the middle of the 19th century, when Mexico fought a war with the United States and lost more than half of its territory, and the five-year period of French occupation in the 1860s, Mexican leaders have fought valiantly to retain a strong sense of nationhood in the shadow of the United States. Twentieth-century Mexico is the product of the Mexican Revolution (1910–1917) and its aftermath, the overbearing presence of the United States, and the search for a development strategy that will help solve the deeply rooted economic and social problems that still plague the Mexican people. Over the past several decades, multiple forces within and outside Mexico have been pushing the country and its leadership in the direction of greater democracy and a neoliberal economy emphasizing privatization, export-driven trade, and foreign investment.

While there are many who note the existence of a significant transformation—political, economic, and cultural—that is now under way in Mexico, with positive benefits for many in the process, there are others who argue that Mexico is not progressing in ways that augur well for the majority of the population. The Pacific Council on International Policy published *Mexico Transforming* in February 2000—the result of a binational study group made of individuals of different professions, political backgrounds, and generations from Mexico and the western United States—that describes a profound transformation that is currently under way south of the border:

> Mexico today is a very different country from what Mexico was twenty, fifteen, or even ten years ago. At the turn of the [twentieth] century, Mexico has competitive political parties, increasingly fair electoral procedures, independent media and public opinion, vibrant civic institutions, separation of powers and countervailing authority by different branches of government, considerable devolution of public authority, market-responsive and internationally competitive industries, strong pressures to respond to major regional and ethnic inequities, and broad acceptance of its fruitful integration with the United States. None of these statements were true a generation ago. (p. 33)

While no one can be sure of how effectively Mexico will meet the challenges of a global economy, pluralist politics, and the strains of a technological revolution, it is nevertheless a highly optimistic report on Mexico's future. The report is thoughtful and balanced, and its binational character lends credence to its findings. But it may also be too sanguine in its description of Mexico's transition from authoritarianism to pluralist democracy and its ability to restore sustained economic growth and improve socioeconomic equality, particularly in the distribution of wealth, income, and services. Whatever the case, the political, economic, and social alterations involved in Mexico's 21st-century transformation will present new challenges for Mexico and its "distant" neighbor, the United States.

After more than 70 years of operating a centralized, authoritarian corporatist state and efforts to confront deep social and economic problems, Mexico reached the dawn of a new millennium with a presidential election on July 2, 2000, that upset the world's longest-ruling political party, giving the Partido Acción Nacional (PAN) the opportunity to bring seismic changes to its governing institutions and the daily lives of its people. In the 1940s, Mexico's economy was heavily protected and inward-looking, based largely on a powerful state apparatus tied to the production and distribution of goods and services. Mexico's political economy has changed dramatically since World War II with a development strategy that is now more open, more internationally oriented, and more receptive to direct foreign investment. Mexico's population has increased fivefold, from a population of 20 million in the 1940s to over 100 million in 2000. Mexico now has the world's 12th-largest economy, trades heavily with the United States, and is an important player in Latin America and the Caribbean region, as well as international organizations. Since becoming part of the North American Free Trade Agreement (NAFTA) in 1994,

Mexico's economy is heavily dependent on the export of manufactured products—color televisions, computer keyboards, refrigerators, automobiles, and auto parts—to the United States, and the United States has come to rely on legal and illegal immigrants from Mexico to fill important gaps in the U.S. labor market. As Mexico sheds its revolutionary heritage and opens its economy to a more competitive and technological world, it finds that it is becoming more dependent on what happens in the United States and elsewhere, particularly Europe and Asia.

Mexican–U.S. relations have been greatly influenced by a long land border that has intertwined the two nations in intense conflict as well as periodic collaboration on bilateral issues—immigration, trade, drug trafficking, crime, environmental degradation, and energy—of importance to both governments. Mexico has had more impact on the United States than any other Latin American or Caribbean country because of 19th-century conflicts such as the 1846–1848 war with Mexico (the only Latin American country with whom the United States has been formally at war), a long border that stretches from Tijuana to Texas, the millions of immigrants from Mexico (more than any other Latin American country), two-way trade (Mexico is now the second-largest U.S. trading partner), and growing social and cultural ties. Mexico's third-largest source of income after petroleum and tourism comes from the money (more than $8 billion a year) that expatriates living in the United States send home to relatives and friends. In Dalton, Georgia, a major carpet manufacturing center, community leaders have made concerted efforts to assimilate Mexican immigrants, including the recruitment of instructors from Mexico to teach bilingual school classes.

The creation of NAFTA in 1994 and the international bailout of Mexico after the peso devaluation in 1995 demonstrated how closely tied Mexico is to the United States. No American president (or presidential candidate) can afford to ignore Mexico, given its economic, cultural, and political impact on the United States. With over $70 billion in American investments, $240 billion in bilateral trade flows, over 10 million tourists from the United States who flock to Mexican resorts every year, and some 350,000 Americans living in Mexico, the United States has good reason to worry about political upheaval and economic uncertainty south of the border. Despite these growing ties, Americans are surprisingly ignorant of their southern neighbor, often blind to what is happening in Mexico or misinterpreting or distorting the important political and economic transformations currently under way.

Mexico has been in the process of transforming itself to meet the challenges of democratization, globalization, and a technological revolution while leaving behind outdated patterns, rules, and rhetoric that once served Mexican society in a different era. Yet there are many Mexicos that have been left out of the profound changes that the country has undertaken in the past 20 years. The stability and legitimacy of the Partido Revolucionario Institucional (PRI) found itself in jeopardy by the 1990s as political crises and economic uncertainty began to overwhelm the Revolutionary Family, or ruling elite. After several decades of economic setbacks and public resistance to Mexico's rather unique system of governing, the state has made various adjustments to this challenge, often using a mixture of repression, concessions, constitutional-legal changes, heavy doses of revolutionary rhetoric, and even acknowledgment of the system's failures. As the PRI's grip on power continued to slip, raising questions about a non-PRI president, top officials in Washington faced the difficult task of anticipating what it might be like to deal with a more democratic Mexico, one in the hands of an opposition party for the first time since the 1920s. While Mexico has been particu-

larly sensitive to intrusions on its sovereignty and independence from the United States, powerful sectors of Mexican society are increasingly receptive to closer ties with the United States and global integration. The anti-gringo sentiment that was once common throughout Mexico during the Cold War has given way to less anti-Americanism, particularly in the geographical areas closest to the United States. President Vicente Fox (2000–2006) strongly supports NAFTA and has pledged greater cooperation with the United States in the drug war and the war on terrorism.

Before 1980 Mexicans were highly supportive of the political institutions and procedures that evolved from the Mexican Revolution and its aftermath. These generally supportive beliefs and attitudes, however, did not carry over to government performance and perceptions of government bureaucrats and politicians, many of whom were viewed as elitist, self-serving, venal, and corrupt. Over the past 20 years, Mexicans have become far less tolerant of corruption and more cynical and distrustful of the police, politicians, and government bureaucrats; they are less hesitant to criticize the system and increasingly blame their personal economic predicament on the failures of government performance. Mexicans today are more optimistic about their ability to affect election outcomes and are less likely to see an opposition victory as too risky or damaging to the country's economic prospects. The PAN victory in the 2000 elections makes Mexico's current political direction unclear. With political power increasingly in the hands of non-PRI bureaucrats, Mexico faces the 21st century with many unknowns.

What remains certain is that Mexico's growing links to the United States—particularly the border states of California, Arizona, New Mexico, and Texas—require a better informed and more refined understanding of Mexico's dilemmas and prospects. Politicians, business leaders, union representatives, students, and others in the United States need a better appreciation of Mexico as it begins the new millennium. The tough problems that continue to plague Mexico—and indirectly the United States—such as personal insecurity, poverty, gross inequities, human rights violations, pervasive corruption, drug trafficking, and democratic accountability can easily contribute to negative impressions of Mexicans and Mexican Americans, often exacerbated by xenophobic politicians and others with little understanding of our 100 million neighbors in Mexico.

Mexico's cultural achievements since 1940 have contributed to its recognition as a world center in literature, cinema, art, and architecture. The prevailing view of the government and heads of state as "bad" stands in stark contrast to the pride that Mexicans express in their artists, architects, and writers. Carlos Fuentes, Octavio Paz, and Juan Rulfo are recognized as the most important prose writers in 20th-century Mexico, and each has received numerous awards for his literary talents and accomplishments. Paz received the Nobel Prize for Literature in 1990 and is considered one of the most outstanding poets of Latin America. Rulfo's *Pedro Páramo* (1955)—part of a genre of novels concerned with Mexican history and the revolution—became one of the best known of all Mexican novels, a masterful blend of modern experimental techniques with Mexican folklore and traditional culture. Laura Esquivel's *Como agua para chocolate* (1989)—a popular novel (and later an award-winning film directed by Alfonso Arau) that outsold those of her male contemporaries—established her as one of Latin America's best-known women writers. Prose writers such as Elena Garro, Poniatowska, and Rosario Castellanos started their careers in journalism before publishing important feminist works of fiction. Poniatowska pioneered "new journalism" in Mexico, blending journalism and literature in her literary works, particularly her

vivid testimonial writing that has criticized the ruling party.

Mexico has also produced some of the world's outstanding easel painters, muralists, filmmakers, movie stars, comedians, and diplomats. The Big Three of Mexican muralists—Diego Rivera, José Clemente Orozco, and David Alfaro Siqueiros—who dominated the art world in the 1920s and 1930s continued to craft their masterpieces after World War II. All three completed commissioned works of art in the United States, helping to spread their talent beyond Mexico. Their large and politically charged murals helped define a nation undergoing dramatic change after the Mexican Revolution, didactic impressions of Mexico past and present. Frida Kahlo, third wife of artist Diego Rivera, gained an international reputation for her wrenching self-portraits, becoming an icon of the feminist movement after her death in 1954.

The golden age of cinema flowered in the 1930s and continued to produce some of Mexico's best films until a decline in film production set in after 1955. With outstanding producers such as Emilio "El Indio" Fernández, Alejandro Galindo, and Fernando de Fuentes and a star system that included Dolores del Río, María Félix, Pedro Armendáriz, Jorge Negrete, and Pedro Infante, Mexico made outstanding contributions to the world of cinema and cinematography. They were followed by a new generation of filmmakers—Arturo Ripstein, Alfonso Arau, and Pedro Estrada—who helped restore the stature of Mexican films after the hiatus that occurred between 1960 and 1985. Mario Moreno ("Cantinflas"), often considered the Charlie Chaplin of Mexico, captured the essence of being Mexican in his films and humorous nightclub acts.

Mexico is also the home of outstanding diplomats and statesmen, including Alfonso García Robles, winner of the 1982 Nobel Peace Prize for bringing to fruition the Treaty for the Prohibition of Nuclear Weapons in Latin America. Luis

Quintanilla was a towering figure in Mexican diplomatic circles from 1922 to 1960, serving as ambassador in numerous diplomatic posts and as ambassador to the Organization of American States from 1945 to 1958.

The *Encyclopedia of Modern Mexico* seeks to provide information that is easily accessible, accurate, relevant, and up-to-date on contemporary Mexico. Emphasizing the period since 1940, it is designed to be a ready-reference, short-entry encyclopedia that will meet the critical information needs of students and educators—high school, community college, college, and university—and the general public on matters of vital interest to the United States and Mexico. More than 200 entries are devoted to the people, institutions, concepts, and events that have helped shape Mexico's transformation over the past 60 years. As a reference tool, the *Encyclopedia of Modern Mexico* offers the reader valuable information and a better understanding of the important changes and challenges now under way in Mexico.

THE ENCYCLOPEDIA

Acteal Massacre ☀ In a carefully planned attack against Zapatista rebels on December 22, 1997, 45 unarmed men, women, and children were massacred in the small village of Acteal in Chiapas state by soldiers from the Mexican Army Airborne Special Forces Groups (Grupos Aeromóviles de Fuerzas Especiales, GAFE), a paramilitary group trained by the U.S. Army Special Forces. An additional 25 were seriously wounded before the carnage stopped. Public security forces were alerted to the paramilitary violence by villagers, but they refused to intervene. Acteal was not an isolated or spontaneous outburst; it was part of an ongoing political struggle in Chiapas—the poorest part of Mexico and home of numerous indigenous groups—that has been growing since the 1994 uprising of the Zapatista Army of National Liberation (Ejército Zapatista de Liberación Nacional, EZLN).

The proliferation of paramilitary groups in Chiapas is part of a strategy of controlling rebellious populations while reducing the visibility of direct government repression. To win the "hearts and minds" of the civilian population, the "low-intensity warfare" combines a mixture of repression, violence, and civic campaigns in southern Mexico. The objective of the Mexican military and the numerous paramilitaries is to dismantle all civilian groups that support, or are suspected of supporting, the EZLN. U.S. support of such nefarious activities, often disguised as part of the war on drugs, comes through the training of Mexican military officers and personnel in the United States. In 1996 and 1997 Mexico received more U.S. assistance through the International Military Education and Training (IMET) program than any other Latin American country. In 1997 it ranked first among Latin American military officers in attendance at the School of the Americas (renamed the Western Hemisphere Institute for Security Cooperation by the U.S. Congress in 2000).

Acteal was attacked at the beginning of the **coffee** harvest, in a year when prices were expected to be high, to deprive dissident communities of the chance to sustain their livelihood. Since the massacre in December 1997, intervillage conflict has created an atmosphere of suspicion and fear that dominates the Chiapas region. One year after the massacre at Acteal, tensions still ran high between the remaining survivors (mostly Tzotzil Indians) and progovernment villagers and Mexican troops stationed nearby. At the first anniversary of the massacre, 4,000 rebel supporters marched through Acteal shouting, "Chiapas is not a barracks; army get out!" while government helicopters buzzed the demonstrators in a show of aerial authority. During a yearlong investigation of the massacre, most of the suspected killers were identified as supporters of Mexico's ruling party, the **Partido Revolucionario Institucional (PRI)**, while the victims belonged to a group that sympathized with the **Zapatista rebellion in Chiapas**. After almost two years of delay and denials, in September 1999 a former PRI mayor and 23 other people were sentenced to 35 years in prison for their part (intentional homicide and illegal use of firearms, according to the judge) in the Indian massacre.

The few who remain in Acteal continue to be harassed and dispossessed of their small parcels of land by troops and supporters of the government. Chiapas remain a thorn in the side of the ruling party. Without a peaceful solution to the conflict over land, the rights of indigenous groups, and the growing disparity between Mexico's poverty-stricken south and more prosperous regions elsewhere (particularly the northern border region), winning the 2000 presidential election would be more difficult. Moreover, with a significant military presence in Chiapas, ongoing confrontation between Indian groups sympathetic to the Zapatistas and **mestizo** or white landowners, armed paramilitary groups claiming self-defense, and tension between evangelical Christians and Catholics, it seems obvious that the Mexican government needs to devote more attention to rural development programs and the needs of indigenous communities. *See also* Guerrilla Movements and Counterinsurgency; Ruiz García, Samuel; Subcommander Marcos.

SUGGESTED READING

George A. Collier, with Elizabeth Lowery Quarantiello, *Basta: Land and the Zapatista Rebellion in Chiapas,* rev. ed. (Oakland, Calif.: Food First Books, 1999); Neil Harvey, *The Chiapas Rebellion: The Struggle for Land and Democracy* (Durham, N.C.: Duke University Press, 1999); NACLA Report, *The Wars Within: Counterinsurgency in Chiapas and Colombia*, March-April 1998; Antonio Turok, *Chiapas: The End of Silence* (New York: Aperture, 1998); John Womack, ed., *Rebellion in Chiapas: An Historical Reader* (New York: New Press, 1999).

Aguascalientes. *See* Geographical Regions.

Alemán Valdés, Miguel (1900–1983) ☀ As Mexico's first postwar president (1946–1952), Miguel Alemán represented a significant shift in political power from older revolutionary generals to a new generation of younger professional politicians in Mexico. With a bevy of young college-educated politicians in his cabinet, he pushed state-supported industrialization, closer ties with the business community, modifications in the government-controlled dominant party (Partido Revolucionario Institutional, PRI), and the depoliticization of the military. By the time he left office in 1952 he had created one of the two most powerful political recruitment groups (*camarillas*) in Mexican politics, one that would influence political decision making for decades.

Born in the small village of Sayula, Veracruz, Alemán was the son of a farmer and merchant who served as a general in the **Mexican Revolution**. He completed his primary and secondary studies in his home state of Veracruz before entering the National Preparatory School in Mexico City in 1920. While attending the National School of Law, he came under the influence of some of Mexico's best-known intellectuals at the time, including **Manuel Gómez Morín, Vicente Lombardo Toledano,** and **Daniel Cosío Villegas.** It was at the National University that he

President Miguel Alemán, 1948. Credit: General Secretariat of the Organization of American States.

sharpened his leadership skills and formed a tight-knit group of friends to help each other advance socially and politically, a precursor to the *camarilla* of friends he would create while president.

After graduating in 1928, he spent a few years practicing labor law before entering the national political arena. His energetic and popular political career (first as senator and then as governor) in Veracruz attracted the attention of presidential candidate Manuel Ávila Camacho, who, once elected, appointed him secretary of government (i.e., security) from 1940 to 1945. Ávila Camacho handpicked Alemán to succeed him (using an established presidential prerogative called *dedazo*) and in 1946 Alemán was elected president of the Mexican Republic, the first civilian president since

Francisco I. Madero in 1913. He symbolized a new generation of leaders interested in expanding business activity with foreign capital and domestic policies designed to promote the growth of Mexican-owned industrial enterprises. Mexican politics moved further to the right as government expenditures largely ignored agrarian reform and the rural sector, except for agricultural credits and technology directed at commercial farmers rather than *ejidatarios* (communal farmers). As a result, income inequality and rural poverty increased while Mexico moved ahead with economic modernization programs.

Alemán expanded the powers of the presidency by reducing the power of the military, reorganizing and expanding the base of the official party, and initiating economic development strategies that would benefit the middle and upper classes at the expense of the poor. Recruitment for the dominant party shifted from the army and bureaucracy to graduates from the **Universidad Nacional Autónoma de México (UNAM)**. By altering the nature of political recruitment—emphasizing the importance of educational and bureaucratic contacts—Alemán and his friends were now in a position to apply their capitalist convictions to the industrialization of Mexico. With substantial economic assistance from the United States, President Alemán poured his energies into public works projects to serve the needs of the new industrialists in Mexico. As the hunger for land increased, the Alemán presidency started several large dams to create the energy for electrification and help in the manufacture of artificial fertilizers to improve the often depleted tropical soils. Alemán's ambitious projects were designed to help modernize the Mexican economy by providing resettlement space, food, and industrial goods for the rapidly growing population. The young president once boasted that he wanted "all Mexicans to have a Cadillac, a cigar, and a ticket to the bullfights" to symbolize the Alemán era—an impossible dream if there ever was one.

Recognizing the growing importance of women to Mexico, Alemán established a Feminine Commission within the newly organized party to gain the support of Mexican women and made known his position that women should have full political rights. However, after his election in 1946 President Alemán disappointed many women with his lackluster efforts to advance equal political rights for women. The task of granting women full political equality would pass to Alemán's handpicked successor, **Adolfo Ruiz Cortines**, who would submit woman suffrage proposals to Congress as soon as he took office in late 1952. One year later Mexican women were granted full political equality by the Mexican Congress and in 1958 women voted for president for the first time in Mexican history. The suffragette cause was advanced by **Amalia Castillo Ledón**, one of the founders of the Mexican Women's Alliance (Alianza de Mujeres de México) in 1952.

Miguel Alemán also cemented closer relations with the United States by assuring Washington that communists would not be included in his government, including the friends of Marxist labor leader Vicente Lombardo Toledano. His emphasis on industry and large-scale agricultural projects brought U.S. corporate and banking leaders to Mexico in search of economic opportunities south of the border. Despite nationalist rhetoric and distrust of the United States, Alemán accepted U.S. president Harry Truman's invitation to visit Washington. In turn, President Truman traveled to Mexico City in 1947 and laid a wreath on the monument to the "boy cadets" (*niños héroes*) who died fighting invading U.S. troops in the **Mexican American War** (1846–1848). In exchange for supporting the United States in the early years of the Cold War and using the Mexican military to put down labor strikes, Alemán was rewarded with bank loans and U.S. confidence in its southern neighbor.

The Alemán years were profitable for Mexico's well-to-do and their foreign partners, but this was not the case for the working class and rural subsistence farmers. It was an era dominated by powerful Mexican businessmen beholden to Alemán and his economic development policies that favored a network of friends with money to invest, making the Alemán years one of the most probusiness administrations in Mexican revolutionary history. The fictional title character in Carlos Fuentes's best-known novel—*La muerte de Artemio Cruz* (The death of Artemio Cruz)—bears a striking resemblance to Miguel Alemán; the son of a Veracruz landowner, Artemio is able to acquire immense power as a tyrannical and corrupt business magnate with a close network of friends and relatives.

Although Mexico signed the Rio Treaty in 1947, Alemán refused U.S. military assistance during the Korean War. It would have obligated Mexico to interfere in neighboring states when the United States feared "democratic" institutions were in danger of collapse, a violation of its commitment to the principle of nonintervention. The ***bracero* program** was extended under President Alemán, allowing landless Mexicans to legally migrate to the United States in search of work. The Truman administration spent $20 million to eradicate foot-and-mouth disease and by purchasing Mexican pesos helped strengthen the currency. With a treasury filled with wartime credits from the United States, Mexico's government spent lavishly on a modernized railway system and miles of improved roads. With better communication and transportation, over 400,000 U.S. tourists visited Mexico in 1952, spending hundreds of millions of vacation dollars south of the border. To meet the growing demand for competent technical and administrative personnel, Alemán spent generously on the new campus of UNAM, an architectural masterpiece adorned with murals and mosaics by Mexico's most talented artists. He also built a polytechnic institute and regional universities, sent civil servants abroad to acquire advanced skills, and invited foreign specialists to Mexico to provide professional advice.

The Mexican economy expanded rapidly after World War II, but most of the prosperity was directed at the middle and upper classes, not the rural subsistence farmers. With low taxes, subsidized electricity, and high rates of profit, Mexican and foreign capitalists enjoyed an ideal climate for making large sums of money as the industrial sector boomed. **Corruption** at the highest levels also tainted the Alemán years; President Alemán and several of his friends became millionaires and purchased prime pieces of real estate. Together with Emilio Azcárraga Vidaurreta and other powerful businessmen in Monterrey, Alemán established a private television network (**Televisa**) that provided slanted broadcasts aimed at undermining the power of labor unions and socialist ideas while always presenting a friendly view of the United States. The selection of Adolfo Ruiz Cortines, an honest and noncontroversial career civil servant, to be Alemán's successor in 1952 was based in large part on the political damage caused by the rampant corruption during the Alemán years. The scars left by Alemán—outrageous corruption and uneven economic development—would continue to plague Mexican politics for decades.

With a huge following among Mexico's business elite, Alemán became the leader of the right wing of the PRI after his term ended and later headed the National Tourism Board until his death in 1983. The family's influence in telecommunications and politics continues with the involvement of the ex-president's son, Miguel Alemán Velasco, a key figure in Mexican television and a brief candidate for the PRI nomination for president in 2000. *See also* Foreign Policy.

SUGGESTED READING

Frank Brandenburg, *The Making of Modern Mexico* (Englewood Cliffs, N.J.: Prentice-Hall, 1964); Roderic Ai Camp, "Alemán Valdés, Miguel," in Barbara A. Tenenbaum, ed., *Encyclopedia of Latin American History and Culture*, vol. 1 (New York: Scribners, 1996); Camp, *Mexico's Leaders: Their Education and Recruitment* (Tucson: University of Arizona Press, 1980); Enrique Krauze, *Mexico: Biography of Power: A History of Modern Mexico, 1810–1996* (New York: HarperCollins, 1997); Stephen R. Niblo, *Mexico in the 1940s: Modernity, Politics, and Corruption* (Wilmington, Del.: Scholarly Resources, 1999); Joseph B. Treaster, "Miguel Alemán of Mexico Is Dead; Was President from 1946–1952," *New York Times*, May 15, 1983.

Alianza Cívica ☀ One of many nongovernmental organizations that grew out of the popular movements that emerged after 1989. Formed in 1994 to help unify and coordinate the growing prodemocracy movement, the Civic Alliance (Alianza Cívica, AC) was headed by Sergio Aguayo, a leading intellectual and **human rights** activist who modeled the organization after the civil rights movement in the United States. The Civic Alliance received funds from the U.S. government, primarily the affiliates of the National Endowment for Democracy (NED), reducing the visibility of Washington's diplomatic support for electoral activities (mostly official observer/witness delegations) in Mexico. Prior to the 1994 election, it recruited hundreds of election observers to watch 5,000 polling places throughout the country. Although Ernesto Zedillo won the 1994 presidential elections by a comfortable margin, the Civic Alliance observed a range of electoral irregularities and fraud in the process of voting. In addition to media bias and the illegal use of government funds to support the PRI, the Civic Alliance found the use of strong-arm tactics by the ruling party to leverage a PRI advantage. The Civic Alliance played a critical role in the 1997 and 2000 elections, monitoring the fairness and honesty of the electoral process. *See also* Electoral System/Elections.

Anti-Americanism. *See* Foreign Policy; Gringo; Intervention; Mexican American War.

Arango, Doroteo. *See* Villa, Francisco "Pancho."

Arau Incháustegui, Alfonso (1932–) ☀ One of Mexico's leading film producers, directors, and actors. Alfonso Arau has won six Ariel Awards (the equivalent of an Academy Award in the United States) for his cinematic talent. During his early years as an actor, he played a series of Mexican stereotypes—wild, dirty, and savage-like—in popular films such as Sam Peckinpah's *The Wild Bunch* in 1969. He is best known for his adaptation of his wife **Laura Esquivel's** best-selling novel, *Como agua para chocolate* (Like water for chocolate) to the screen, and more recently for directing *A Walk in the Clouds* (1995) starring Keanu Reeves, Aitana Sánchez-Gijon, Anthony Quinn, and Angelica Aragón. Arau achieved international recognition for the sensuality and magical realism he created in *Like Water for Chocolate* (1992), a movie that became the most successful foreign film distributed in the United States until the success of *Crouching Tiger, Hidden Dragon* in 2000–2001. *Like Water for Chocolate* was honored as the Mexican entry in the foreign film category for the 1993 Academy Awards and remained in some markets for over a year. His film *Mojado Power* (1979) holds the U.S. record for the highest grossing film ever to play in the Spanish-language theater circuit.

Born in Mexico City to a family with roots in Spain (his grandfather was from Barcelona and his grandmother from San Sebastián), Arau attended public schools at the direction of his father (a Mexico City dentist) so that he could "learn to love Mexicans and to be patriotic," and he attended private schools to mingle with the wealthy who would later run the country. After his early schooling he became an accomplished tap and ballet dancer, singer, and comic. He studied drama with Seki Sano, a legendary theatrical director at the **Universidad Nacional Autónoma de México (UNAM)**, learning the skills of actor and director. Alfonso Arau moved to Havana, Cuba, in 1958 where he became the star of his own television variety show, "El show de Arau," until 1964. The next year he left for Paris with his family and took pantomime classes with Marcel Marceau and added to his knowledge of acting and directing through a friendship with Alejandro Jodorowsky. Before returning to Mexico in 1968, Arau attended the University of California–Los Angeles (UCLA) film school. Many of Arau's films were influenced more by Hollywood than by his European experience, which was not the case with many of his contemporaries such as **Arturo Ripstein**, Felipe Cazals, and others.

With the Mexican film industry in turmoil in the late 1960s, Arau found it difficult to apply his many talents to the industry he loved. To survive, he returned to acting and television, eventually gaining recognition through his successful films in the early 1970s, including *Calzonzín inspector* (1973), winner of two Ariel Awards. As an actor, Arau appeared in Peckinpah's classic western *The Wild Bunch*, starred in Jodorowsky's cult film *El Topo*, and appeared in *Romancing the Stone, Three Amigos, Posse,* and *Used Cars.*

Until the early 1990s, Arau worked mainly as an actor; however, his real talent lay in film directing. After directing the successful *Like Water for Chocolate* (1992) and *A Walk in the Clouds* (1995), Arau made *Picking up the Pieces*, released in 1999. *A Walk in the Clouds*, a remake of an Italian film by Alejandro Blasetti, was a huge financial success; it cost $19 million to make but earned Twentieth Century-Fox $110 million in 1995, the most lucrative film made in that year. His success as a director helped him produce five Hollywood films between 1995 and 2000. Arau brings a deep sense of passion and soul to his films, and he loves to tell a story that contains romance, sensuality, and tra-

Movie still of Alfonso Arau (center) in *Calzonzin inspector* (1973).

ditional values. Most of Arau's current work seems to be aimed at the mainstream American audience, moreso than his earlier work in Mexican **cinema**.

SUGGESTED READING

Carl J. Mora, *The Mexican Cinema: Reflections of a Society, 1896–1988*, rev. ed. (Berkeley: University of California Press, 1989); Charles Ramírez Berg, *Cinema of Solitude: A Critical Study of Mexican Film, 1967–1983* (Austin: University of Texas Press, 1992).

Architecture. *See* Barragán, Luis; Universidad Nacional Autónoma de México (UNAM).

Aridjis, Homero. *See* Environment and Ecology.

Armendáriz, Pedro (1912–1963) ☀ Premier Mexican actor during the so-called golden age of Mexican **cinema**. Pedro Armendáriz was the favored movie star of director **Emilio "El Indio" Fernández** and cinematographer **Gabriel Figueroa**. His acting career began in 1935 and by the end of his career he had appeared in dozens of film productions, both Mexican and foreign. Most of his roles typified the official nationalism of the period associated with the *indígena* genre of Fernández and Figueroa. His most notable films during the 1940s involved romantic, often historical, stories set in rural Mexico in which he portrayed Indians and **mestizos**. Although he was born in Churubusco (later becoming the name and site of Mexico's leading film studio), Mexico City, Armendáriz spent his youth in San Antonio, Texas; later he attended California Polytechnic Institute where he completed his studies and then worked as a journalist before returning to Mexico in 1934. The following year Armendáriz made his film debut in *Rosario*—just as sound production was being introduced in Mexican studios—and over the next 30 years appeared in more than 70 films, both Mexican and foreign productions. His striking screen presence made him the leading male film personality of the nation, and he appeared with **María Félix** and **Dolores del Río**, award-winning stars of Mexican film in the golden age.

Armendáriz's filmmaking career involved a complex relationship between the cinematic nationalism associated with Fernández and Figueroa, state-sponsored cinematic nationalistic ideology, Hollywood filmmakers, and the U.S. government. In *Soy puro mexicano* (1942), directed by Fernández, Armendáriz appears as a patriotic *mestizo* bandit in an attempt to stress the importance of *mestizaje* as the dominant symbol of Mexico. By portraying Mexican nationalism as antifascism, the movie was designed to improve U.S.–Mexican relations at a time when the Mexican people were displeased with the country's wartime alliance with Washington. The cinematic nationalism of many of Armendáriz's films—with heavy use of Mexican history and indigenous culture—was created to offer the masses passionate performances that would mask the growing conservative political and socioeconomic policies fostered by the state. His most memorable films in this genre include *Flor silvestre* and *María Candelaria* (1943), *Las abandonadas* (1944), and *Enamorada* and *La perla* (1946). In many of these films of political turmoil, **corruption**, **macho** heroics, patriarchy, and tragic love, he played opposite Dolores del Río.

The popular *La perla*, based on John Steinbeck's original script, was released in the United States in 1948 as *The Pearl*, a film that helped him make the bridge to Hollywood film stars and directors. From 1947 *(The Fugitive)* until his last film in 1963, he worked with John Ford, Figueroa, and Fernández and starred with his frequent Mexican film partner, del Río. In Hollywood, he worked with actors such as John Wayne, Henry Fonda, and Susan Hayward. His box office popularity in international films did not prevent him from making more Mexican movies, including his portrayal of **Pancho Villa** in Ismael Rodríguez's 1950s episodic trilogy of the guerrilla leader and revolutionary hero. His final film, the 1964 James Bond thriller, *From Russia with Love*, was barely completed as "Pete" Armendáriz (by now a part of John Ford's Hollywood stock company) was in continual pain from terminal cancer. Shortly after film production was completed, he committed suicide by a single gunshot to his heart while being treated in a Mexico City hospital. His son, Pedro Jr., followed in his father's footsteps as a film and television actor, although with considerably less success.

SUGGESTED READING

Seth Fein, "Armendáriz, Pedro," in Michael S. Werner, ed., *Encyclopedia of Mexico: History, Society, and Culture*, vol. 1 (Chicago: Fitzroy Dearborn, 1977); John King, *Magical Reels: A History of Cinema in Latin America* (London: Verso, 1990); Carl J. Mora, *The Mexican Cinema: Reflections of a Society, 1896–1988*, rev. ed.

(Berkeley: University of California Press, 1989); Andrew G. Wood, "One Hundred Years of Cinema: Redefining *Mexicanidad,*" *UC Mexus News*, Summer 1998.

Arreola, Juan José (1918–2001) ☀ Juan José Arreola was part of a generation of outstanding Mexican writers and poets that included **Juan Rulfo,** Antonio Alatorre, Rodolfo Usigli, José Revueltas, and **Octavio Paz.** Arreola was best known for his colorful short stories that used fantasy worlds to tell tales of self-discovery and the frustration that many Mexicans felt after the **Mexican Revolution.** Arreola was also influenced by 19th-century Russian writers and numerous French writers while he studied at the Instituto Francés de América Latina in 1945–1946. Arreola was born in Zapotlán (now Ciudad Guzmán), Jalisco, where he grew up with little education (he never finished elementary school) and worked at an assortment of poorly paid jobs until he moved to Mexico City at the age of 18. There he met literary and artistic figures who were crucial to his literary development. From 1936 until his death at the age of 83, he moved back and forth from Mexico City to Guadalajara. As a struggling writer, he faced periods when he would accept any job—secondary school teacher, book binder, cub reporter—that enabled him to survive financially.

Juan José Arreola's literary career took off in 1943 with a well-received short story in *Eos,* a popular Mexico City magazine. A number of key scholarships enabled him to study in Paris and at the **Colegio de México** in Mexico City, experiences that helped consolidate his ideas as a writer and poet. On his return from Paris after **World War II,** he helped redefine Mexican literature with *Varia Invención* (Diverse inventions), a collage of poetry and prose that led to the creation of a separate genre named after the book's title. From someone who taught himself to read and write, Arreola eventually became a professor at the Facultad de Filosofía y Letras at **Universidad Nacional Autónoma de México (UNAM),** an internationally recognized

writer, a director of literary programs, and a contributor to several cultural programs on radio and television. His literary style, influenced by the works of Rulfo, opened new ways of thinking about self-discovery, love, parody, physical decline, and human behavior. All of the ideas built into his literary style focused on Arreola's insistence that brevity and intellectual rigor prevail over the tendency of some literary artists to elaborate at great length on their thoughts and problems.

Throughout his lifetime Juan José Arreola published 15 books of short stories and one novel, *La Feria,* and received numerous literary prizes and honors. In 1976 he won Mexico's National Linguistics and Literature Prize and later the Juan Rulfo Prize for Latin American and Caribbean Literature. Other outstanding awards include the Premio Xavier Villarrutia, the Premio Azteca de Oro, and the Premio Nacional de Letras. The French government recognized his work and named him an officer of arts and letters. Before his death, Arreola provided television commentary during the 1994 World Cup in Mexico City. Arreola left a legacy of rigor and precision in his writing style, something he often attributed to his early life in rural Jalisco.

SUGGESTED READING
Emmanuel Carballo, *Protagonistas de la literatura mexicana* (Mexico, D.F.: Secretaría de Educación Pública, 1986); "Juan José Arreola, 83, Mexican Writer," *New York Times,* December 10, 2001.

Article 27 of Mexican Constitution. *See* Constitution of 1917.

Authentic Party of the Mexican Revolution. *See* Partido Auténtico de la Revolución Mexicana (PARM).

Automobile Industry ☀ Mexico's automobile industry has developed in four stages since its inception in the 1920s: assembly plants (1926–1962), import substitution manufacturing (1962–1969), export promotion of finished vehicles (1969–1981), and the globalization of the economy (1982–). As of 2000, the Mexican automobile industry (parts and assembled vehicles) ranked second in export industries, behind **Petróleos Mexicanos (PEMEX)**, the national oil company. The current automobile industry in Mexico is the result of economic crises and the interaction among government economic policies, multinational management—particularly the big five automakers: Ford, General Motors, Chrysler, Nissan, and Volkswagen—and Mexican owners of auto parts companies. Since the severe economic crisis of 1982, the automobile industry has expanded and diversified, particularly in northern Mexico close to the U.S. border. All of

Ford Motor Company Assembly Plant, Mexico City, 1954. Credit: General Secretariat of the Organization of American States.

Volkswagen's New Beetle cars are manufactured in Mexico and shipped to various ports of entry for sale in the United States.

The first auto factories were put in place to serve the domestic market beginning in the 1920s, when Mexican subsidiaries of Ford Motor Company (1926) and General Motors (1936) opened assembly plants in Mexico City. In 1938 Auto-Mex joined the Chrysler Corporation to assemble and sell cars in Mexico. In 1952 the government's Diesel Nacional (DINA) truck manufacturing corporation joined with Fiat of Italy to jointly produce passenger cars, later shifting the DINA partnership to Renault of France. A decade later, Toyota of Japan and Volkswagen of Germany received authorization to produce vehicles in Mexico.

Domestic automobile production began in 1962 with a new phase of import substitution industrialization (ISI) policies—a strategy of using high tariffs to protect the Mexican market from direct foreign imports—designed to broaden the range of local production and remedy the trade deficit. In a move to offset Mexico's trade imbalance (vehicles and parts amounted to 11 percent of Mexico's total imports), the Mexican government decreed (as of September 1, 1964) that the local content of automobiles made in Mexico had to be at least 60 percent of the direct costs of production, restricted the import of assembled vehicles and foreign raw materials, and placed a quota system on each firm. The 1964 decree achieved some success in higher production and employment, but multinational corporations soon became the sole owners of the auto assembly industry and the trade deficit did not improve.

To remedy this economic dilemma, the government issued a new decree in 1969, shifting from import substitution to export promotion, believing that increased export earnings could be used to finance the expansion of the sagging internal market. In 1973, after nearly four years of emphasizing automobile exports, exports increased to over $40 million worth of cars exported outside the country, mostly to the United States. Nevertheless, balance of trade problems continued and Mexican firms found it increasingly difficult to compete with the multinational corporations, which had significant production advantages. As the market share of foreign-owned companies increased after 1962, the Mexican government decided to intervene again in 1977, issuing a new decree requiring auto manufacturers in Mexico to increase their exports and rely more heavily on auto parts made in Mexico if they intended to remain in the country. One result of the 1977 law was to force the big five automakers to invest in engine factories, now a major part of the Mexican automobile export industry.

The general crisis in the Mexican economy in 1982, characterized by a dramatic drop in oil prices, two devaluations of the Mexican peso, and out-of-control inflation forced the **de la Madrid** administration to act again. This time, faced with increased internal demand because of the previous oil boom and a rising trade deficit fed by the auto industry, the Mexican government decided to reverse this trend by increasing the local content of vehicles assembled in Mexico. After 1982 more engine factories were built, and investment in new plants produced a more vibrant automobile industry geared heavily to exports via multinational corporations.

Today the Mexican automobile industry operates in a global environment, dependent on economic strategies devised by foreign firms faced with a competitive international environment, high labor costs relative to other world regions, and Mexican auto parts companies that often find it difficult to satisfy the growing industry with the volume and quality of parts the industry requires. Further dependency is the result of a weak state apparatus, unable to fully control the operation of the automobile industry or the key decisions made by multinational corporations.

SUGGESTED READING

Douglas C. Bennett and Kenneth E. Sharp, *Transnational Corporations versus the State: The Political Economy of the Mexican Auto Industry* (Princeton: Princeton University Press, 1985); Jorge Bustamante, Clark Reynolds, and Raúl Hinojosa-Ojeda, eds., *U.S.–Mexico Relations: Labor Market Dependence* (Stanford: Stanford University Press, 1992); Juan Carlos Moreno, *Mexico's Motor Vehicle Industry in the 1980s* (Geneva: International Labor Office, 1988); John P. Tuman and John T. Morris, eds., *Transforming the Latin American Automobile Industry: Unions, Workers, and the Politics of Restructuring* (Armonk, N.Y.: Sharpe, 1998); Francisco Zapata, "Automobile Industry," in Michael S. Werner, ed., *Encyclopedia of Mexico: History, Society, and Culture*, vol. 1 (Chicago: Fitzroy Dearborn, 1997).

Ávila Camacho, Manuel (1896–1955) ☀ Prominent military figure and president (1940–1946) whose term of office coincided with a noticeable shift to the right in Mexican politics and a concerted effort to improve relations with the United States and other foreign powers. As the candidate of the Partido de la Revolución Mexicana (PRM, later to become the PRI), Ávila Camacho's electoral success was marked by violence, irregularities in voting, and accusations of fraud. The election was marred by riots and protests against the tainted election and many people were killed before the winner was declared. With his political legitimacy in question, President Ávila Camacho began his term of office seeking national reconciliation at home and made numerous efforts to mend diplomatic relations with the Soviet Union, Great Britain, and the United States. During his six years in office he abandoned some of President **Lázaro Cárdenas**'s land reform programs, made a strong effort to eradicate illiteracy and poverty, and began early efforts to promote Mexico's industrialization.

Manuel Ávila Camacho was born into a family of middle-class ranchers in Teziutlán, Puebla, and grew up during the period in Mexican history that witnessed the end of the Porfiriato (the long period of rule by Porfirio Díaz) and the **Mexican Revolution** (1910–1917). After studying accounting at the National Preparatory School in Mexico City, he joined Venustiano Carranza's constitutionalist faction and fought in the revolution. Until his executive branch appointments in the administration of Lázaro Cárdenas (1934–1940), Ávila Camacho served in the Mexican military, eventually rising to brigadier general in 1929. In 1933 he was appointed undersecretary of war and navy. In order to heal the divisions in the **Revolutionary**

President Manuel Ávila Camacho. Credit: Benson Latin American Collection, University of Texas at Austin.

Family, Cárdenas chose the moderate Ávila Camacho to succeed him as president in 1940, a maneuver designed to pacify conservatives worried about his radical reform programs. After an election marred by fraud and violence, Ávila Camacho assumed the presidency at a crucial time in Mexico's history.

With **World War II** on the horizon, Ávila Camacho faced the difficult task of bringing together divergent groups split between conservative Catholic and free market forces on the one hand and socialists, anticlericalists, and advocates of state-directed economic development on the other. Recognizing the need for stability and harmonious relations with the United States, Ávila Camacho generally favored the conservative wing of the revolutionary coalition, pushing a series of policies that attempted to heal the wounds in Mexican society left by the revolutionary policies of Cárdenas. His presidency concentrated on taming some of the revolutionary fever built up during the Cárdenas years, particularly Mexican anti-Americanism and negative attitudes toward the Church. By rebuilding agricultural and industrial productivity that had suffered under Cárdenas, Ávila Camacho helped expand the middle class. He also made major changes in the areas of social welfare in order to bring about national reconciliation. In 1941 Ávila Camacho replaced the Marxist **Vicente Lombardo Toledano** with **Fidel Velázquez** as head of the powerful **Confederación de Trabajadores de México (CTM)**, a move that pleased the business community. In order to mollify the demands of organized workers, many of whom suffered from price increases and strike bans during the war, President Ávila Camacho established the country's first government-run health system (the Instituto Mexicano de Seguro Social, IMSS) in 1943. Ávila Camacho also deserves credit for the creation of the **Confederación Nacional de Organizaciones Populares (CNOP)** and for removing the military from Mexican politics through the elimination of the military sector from the dominant party, reducing its share of the budget and forcing many revolutionary generals into retirement.

The Ávila Camacho presidency marked the beginning of a new probusiness phase in Mexican development, one that was more interested in capitalist production and growth than the redistributive policies of Cárdenas during the 1930s. His administration embarked on industrialization programs favoring big business, including tax incentives, tariff protection, and cheap labor. A government-owned bank—Nacional Financiera—was created and industrialists formed the Cámara Nacional de la Industria de Transformación (CANACINTRA). By the time he left office in 1946, President Ávila Camacho had laid the foundation for Mexico's import substitution policies that would last for the next four decades. Public investment in industrial projects increased from 5 percent of total public investment to 11 percent during his six years in office, and Mexico's national income tripled while Ávila Camacho was president.

The war years helped improve U.S.–Mexican relations as President Ávila Camacho broke diplomatic relations with the Axis powers and cooperated closely with Washington. According to La France (1997, 116–17), "Mexico shut down fascist operations and German and Italian businesses within its territory, modernized its army with Lend-Lease funds, sent an air force squadron to fight in the Pacific theater, sold strategic war materials to the United States at guaranteed prices, and sent laborers (*braceros*) to work on farms and in factories north of the border." To solidify Mexico's wartime cooperation further, President Ávila Camacho mended diplomatic relations with Great Britain and the Soviet Union and agreed to compensate U.S. oil companies for property expropriated by Cárdenas in 1938. To demonstrate that Mexico was fully united in time of war, Ávila Camacho arranged to bring the previous six presidents of Mexico to the

National Palace to link arms as a sign of national unity. World War II served twin purposes for Mexico: it helped to improve relations with the United States and contributed to the rapid acceleration of its economic development.

The Mexican film industry blossomed under Ávila Camacho as wartime reductions in film-making in the United States and Europe helped catapult Mexican stars into international fame. **Dolores del Río** returned to Mexico from Hollywood to play romanticized Indian roles in films directed by **Emilio "El Indio" Fernández** . The United States, recognizing the opportunity to promote the war with entertainment propaganda, organized Hollywood assistance to expand production of films in Mexico. U.S.–Mexican collaboration helped broaden the Mexican film industry and attracted international acting talent and persuaded famous Mexican stars to return from Hollywood to work in Mexico City's thriving studios.

After turning over power to **Miguel Alemán** in 1946, Ávila Camacho retired to private life in Veracruz and spent most of his time running his ranch until his death in Mexico City at the age of 58. Although he was not well known before he became president in 1940, Ávila Camacho left many important legacies, including the beginning of major changes in the interpretation of the Mexican Revolution by postwar members of the Revolutionary Family.

SUGGESTED READING

Roderic Ai Camp, *Mexico's Leaders: Their Recruitment and Education* (Tucson: University of Arizona Press, 1980); Enrique Krauze, *Mexico: Biography of Power: A History of Modern Mexico, 1810–1996* (New York: HarperCollins, 1997); David G. La France, "Avila Camacho, Manuel," in Michael S. Werner, ed., *Encyclopedia of Mexico: History, Society, and Culture* (Chicago: Fitzroy Dearborn, 1997); Michael C. Meyer and William L. Sherman, *The Course of Mexican History*, 5th ed. (New York: Oxford

University Press, 1995); Juana Vázquez-Gómez, *Dictionary of Mexican Rulers, 1325–1997* (Westport, Conn.: Greenwood, 1997).

Azcárraga Milmo, Emilio ("El Tigre") (1930–1997) ✷
Mexican television broadcasting pioneer who became a billionaire through his aggressive business practices, autocratic style, and close ties with the ruling party and the **Revolutionary Family**. Azcárraga's imaginative and daring demeanor and physical appearance (he possessed a distinctive shock of white hair that formed a stripe on the top of his head) earned him the nickname of "El Tigre" (the tiger). He attended Culver Military Academy in Indiana where he completed high school, but chose not to attend a university, a practice that changed in the 1950s as Mexican leaders realized the importance of university training, either in Mexico or the United States or both. From the age of 21 when he joined his father's (Emilio Azcárraga Vidaurreta) communications conglomerate as a salesman, he helped build the family's radio and television network into the largest media empire in the Spanish-speaking world. After his father died in 1972, Azcárraga took over as chairman of the board and renamed the family company **Televisa**—the world's largest producer of broadcast programming in Spanish, whose television programs are seen throughout Latin America and in Spain. In 1996 Televisa reported $1.5 billion in revenues.

Emilio Azcárraga became known for his ability to find talented young performers who he trained to act in soap operas and variety shows. Many that he trained became Mexican stars at Televisa studios, but they had to maintain strict loyalty and obedience to Azcárraga or their acting careers were seriously jeopardized. He maintained a tall wooden chair in his office in downtown Mexico City that was designed to intimidate those he wished to reprimand and belittle. Those who had to sit in the chair were unable to touch the ground with their feet, and many felt like children submitting to the demands of a higher authority.

Despite a personal fortune estimated by *Fortune* magazine at $2 billion in 1996, there was no sense of noblesse oblige in Azcárraga's core philosophy. He often referred to Mexico as a nation of poor people with little hope for economic and social improvement. In Azcárraga's view, "Television has the obligation to entertain those people [in the middle and lower classes], to take them away from their sad reality and difficult future" (Preston 1997). He also believed that rich people are not "clients of television" because they rarely go out and buy anything.

A strong believer in the politics of patronage and power, Azcárraga felt the government deserved his unconditional support since successive presidents helped him preserve his near-monopoly and unchallenged control over Mexican television until the early 1990s. With control over 85 percent of Mexico's television audience and 90 percent of all advertising, Televisa presented extremely supportive news coverage in return for new licenses for local stations, tax breaks and indirect subsidies, and other material benefits. In return for government favors that allowed him to mold public opinion and amass a fortune, Azcárraga supported **Partido Revolucionario Institucional (PRI)** candidates and policies without criticism and suppressed news about the political opposition on Televisa's nightly newscasts. It was a cosy relationship based on trust, personal connections, and mutual political benefits. Azcárraga served as an informal adviser to six Mexican presidents and made generous financial contributions to the ruling party.

The symbiotic relationship between the government and business expanded during the administration of **Carlos Salinas de Gortari** (1988–1994). President Salinas, pressured to resolve the **debt crisis** and improve Mexico's economy, resorted to a stream of privatization schemes—including the telecommunications industry—that presented unprecedented opportunities for Mexico's wealthy to become even richer. The creation of Mexican billionaires became a growth industry during the Salinas years. When Salinas took office in late 1988, Mexico had only one billionaire; by the time President Salinas finished his term of office, Mexico had 24, including Emilio Azcárraga. At a private banquet held in early 1993 at the home of former finance minister **Antonio Ortíz Mena** to raise funds for the 1994 PRI electoral campaign, Mexico's billionaires gathered to discuss how they could help the ruling party win the next election. Faced with a serious challenge from the left, President Salinas joined the gathering to emphasize the importance of financial backing from the business community. Major contributions were needed to save the PRI from electoral disaster and to continue the bounty offered from the new political economy. One of the participants suggested that a figure of $25 million each was an appropriate contribution from each businessman, a return on the wealth gained from the recent privatization of state enterprises. While others were debating the amount of the contribution and the appearance of impropriety if the news of the secret meeting leaked to the press, Azcárraga offered to up the ante by donating $50 million, arguing that Mexico's billionaires owed a huge debt of gratitude to the government for the wealth they had accumulated over the past six years. By the time the banquet was over, Mexico's 30 wealthiest businessmen had pledged an average of $25 million apiece for a total of $750 million for the PRI electoral campaign. However, news of the dinner meeting soon leaked to the press and all the participants rescinded their earlier commitments.

Emilio Azcárraga also pursued business ventures in the United States—mainly television stations in the Southwest—until he was forced to sell them on antimonopoly grounds in 1986. Televisa continues to prosper through its 20 percent ownership of Univisión Communications, Inc., a producer of Spanish television programming in the United States. Once described by *Forbes* magazine as the richest man in Latin America, Emilio Azcárraga died of cancer at the residence he maintained in Miami at the age of 66. His son, Emilio Azcárraga Jean, now runs the company but has altered Televisa's policy of ignoring opposition parties by allowing the network to grant equal access to political parties beginning with the 2000 presidential election. *See also* Communications Media.

SUGGESTED READING

Claudia Fernández and Andrew Paxman, *El Tigre: Emilio Azcárraga y su imperio Televisa* (Mexico, D.F.: Grijalbo, 2000); Marjorie Miller and Juanita Darling, "The Eye of the Tiger: Emilio Azcárraga and the Televisa Empire," in William A. Orme, Jr., ed., *A Culture of Collusion: An Inside Look at the Mexican Press* (Miami: North-South Center Press, 1997); Andres Oppenheimer, *Bordering on Chaos: Guerrillas, Stockbrokers, Politicians, and Mexico's Road to Prosperity* (Boston: Little, Brown, 1996); Julia Preston, "Emilio Azcárraga Milmo, Billionaire Who Ruled Mexican Broadcasting, Is Dead at 66," *New York Times*, April 18, 1997.

Azuela, Mariano (1873–1952) ☀ Physician, soldier, and writer best known for his novels about the **Mexican Revolution**, popular rebellion, and the agonies of social life. Azuela's formal accomplishments in the art of novel writing—a direct style, story shifts, fast tempo, vivid description, and brilliant recreations of peasant vernacular—made him a towering figure in the modernization of Mexican literature. His most celebrated works include *Los de abajo* (1916), *Las moscas* (1918), *Domitilio quiere ser diputado* (1918), and *Las tribulaciones de una familia decente* (1918), all novels about the revolution completed between 1915 and 1920. Between

1918 and 1923, Azuela became so disheartened by the lack of attention conferred on him by literary critics and readers that he stopped writing novels. To remedy this situation, he turned to avant-garde methods in his novels, using stylistic and structural techniques rarely seen in Mexican fiction writing before 1932. Azuela continued to write until the time of his death in 1952, but the last two decades did not produce his best writing. During Azuela's lifetime of writing, he produced many novels, short stories, and several plays and biographies. His works covered a wide range of topics that were written to illustrate the magnitude of change taking place in Mexico at the time.

Born to a middle-class family in Lagos de Moreno, Jalisco, Azuela first studied for the priesthood but left the seminary in 1889. He then moved to Guadalajara to study medicine and after finishing his degree returned to his hometown to practice medicine and continue writing. Unable to adjust to village life, he turned to his literary interests, became embroiled in the revolutionary turmoil of the time, and eventually moved to Mexico City. A keen observer of Mexican life and politics, Azuela also admired the 19th-century works of European masters of romanticism and realism, often adding his own techniques to portray characters in terms of physical and moral degradation. His most famous novels were written during the revolutionary phase of Mexican history, often aimed at his own need to better understand the revolutionary experience from the viewpoint of the common man. His first novel of the Revolution, *Los de abajo*, was written while he served for several months as a surgeon with the rebel army of **Pancho Villa**. In *Los caciques* (1917), he treats the exploitation of the underclass by unscrupulous political bosses, or **caciques**, as a cause of the revolution raging across Mexico at the time.

As the initiator of the novel of the Mexican Revolution, Azuela broke new ground by breaking with European writing and Spanish American

Modernismo to create a genre of fiction writing emphasizing the common man's perceptions of social issues and concerns. As a novelist who offers the reader a sense of the true spirit of the Mexican Revolution, his heroes are either the exploited underclass or members of the well-to-do who, as a result of the revolution, come to realize that social justice and hard work are important traits. His literary themes emphasizing the betrayal of the Mexican Revolution, the damaging effects of urban life, and unrelenting attacks on Mexico's *nouveaux riches* gave Mexico's younger fiction writers inspiration for confronting some of the same moral degeneration witnessed by Azuela during the first half of the 20th century. He was awarded the Premio de Letras by the Ateneo Nacional de Ciencias y Artes in 1940 and helped found the Colegio Nacional in 1943 in an effort to further the study of art and languages in Mexico. Azuela died in Mexico City on March 1, 1952.

SUGGESTED READING

George R. McMurray, "Mariano Azuela, 1873–1952," in Verity Smith, ed., *Encyclopedia of Latin American Literature* (Chicago: Fitzroy Dearborn, 1997); Max Parra, "Azuela, Mariano," in Michael S. Werner, ed., *Encyclopedia of Mexico: History, Society, and Culture,* vol. 1 (Chicago: Fitzroy Dearborn, 1997).

Baja California (Norte and Sur). *See* Geographical Regions.

Ballet Folklórico de México (Folkloric Ballet of Mexico) After the **Mexican Revolution**, a nationalist trend in music and dance emerged, spearheaded by **José Vasconcelos**, secretary of public education. Nationalist dance emphasized choreography that reflected Mexican reality. In 1949 Amalia Hernández founded the Modern Ballet of Mexico, which created a number of folkloric dance works. Three years later, after years of working on folk or indigenous types of dances for theatrical presentation, Hernández founded the Folkloric Ballet of Mexico. She had studied Spanish dance and participated in numerous Mexican modern dance movements. With only eight women dancers, Hernández's group presented a weekly television program and toured European capitals with support from Mexico's Department of Tourism. By 1959, with the help of President **Adolfo López Mateos**, the group was elevated to professional status and became a member of the national theater. At the Paris Festival of Nations in 1962, the Ballet Folklórico won several prizes for performances.

The success of the Ballet Folklórico de México is due in large part to the thematic and choreographic skills of Hernández, an accomplished director who travels extensively to research original dances, costumes, and local cultures in order retain the original meanings of the dances. She always reconstructs them, however, in order to sharpen their impact on contemporary audiences around the world. Some of the more popular dances in the theatrical presentations are renditions of ancient Aztec and Mayan ceremonial rites, stagings of traditional festivals and celebrations, and important themes from Mexican history. With more than 200 members, the current Ballet Folklórico de México has both resident and touring companies that alternate performances at the Palacio de Bellas Artes in Mexico City. It is a production that is known worldwide for its skillfully choreographed and theatrically colorful spectacles celebrating the history of Mexican folk music and dance. The Ballet Folklórico has inspired other folkloric groups, created by government agencies, universities, primary schools, and even trade unions.

SUGGESTED READING

Gabriela Aguirre Cristiani, ed., *El Ballet Folklórico de México de Amalia Hernández* (Mexico, D.F.: Fomento Cultural Banamey, 1994); Taryn Benbow-Pfalzgraf, ed., *International Dictionary of Modern Dance* (Detroit: St. James, 1998); Selma Jeanne Cohen, ed., *International Encyclopedia of Dance* (New York: Oxford University Press, 1998); Donald Duncan, "Doña Amalia's Ballet Folklórico de México," *Dance Magazine* (November 1963).

Banda. *See* Music (Popular).

Barragán, Luis (1902–1988) ☀ Mexico's greatest architect of the 20th century. Luis Barragán's major contribution to the construction of buildings and garden landscapes was to reconcile international modernism with the Mexican regional styles he remembered from his youth. Barragán's architecture did not involve skyscrapers; many of his best-known works are private residences and their gardens, often with "Persian" or "Islamic" features, including running water, compartmentalized spaces, and rectilinear planes. Ironically, Barragán—trained as an engineer and self-taught as an architect and a landscape designer—worked in isolation from the architectural mainstream and even developed a suspicion of architectural education, despite the fact that other architects such as Le Corbusier and Mies van der Rohe had an impact on him.

Luis Barragán was born in Guadalajara, Jalisco, in 1902 to a family of builders and cattle ranchers. As a youth in Jalisco, Barragán learned to elicit regional images that would later appear in his designs. Barragán's creativity combines his admiration for poets, philosophers, painters, and sculptors with his ability to borrow from diverse sources while creating something in the end that seems to owe little to others. On a journey to Europe in the early 1930s he was influenced by a visit to the Alhambra's intriguing garden spaces in Spain and by the French painter and landscape architect Ferdinand Bac, best known for his garden designs. After moving to Mexico City in 1936, Barragán's architecture underwent a transformation, becoming more in tune with the new modernism in vogue at the time. Barragán returned to a more regional site-specific aesthetic by the end of **World War II**, focusing on a housing development in the El Pedregal section of Mexico City.

Barragán's best-known works combine pre-Columbian visions and styles, Mexican vernacular and monastic architecture, Mediterranean traditions, and Islamic and Japanese gardens—a masterful synthesis of multiple artistic traditions and styles, both regional and universal. The buildings that exhibit his synthetic eclecticism include the Jardines del Pedregal (1945–1950); Antonio Gálvez's house in San Ángel (1955); the chapel for the Capuchinas Sacramentarias del Purísimo Corazón de María (1952–1955); Satellite City Towers, designed in collaboration with Mathías Goeritz (1957); Las Arboledas residential subdivision (1958–1961); Los Clubes, a residential estate (1963–1964); and Francisco Gilardi's house in Mexico City (1976).

Barragán was not alone in his attempts to bring local vernacular tradition into modern architecture; Enrique del Moral, **Juan O'Gorman,** and others united functionalist architecture with an awareness of local building materials and landscapes. Ricardo Legorreta learned from Barragán's works but preferred factory complexes and hotels, elaborate monumental projects inserted into urban contexts. His design of the Centro Banamex in Monterrey, Nuevo León, incorporates spaces that are arranged around plazas and patios with light penetrating the building through small windows similar to North African architecture. During the **Carlos Salinas** administration, Legorreta was commissioned to design the Escuela Nacional de Artes Plásticas, a distinctly round building that recalls the Caracol at the Mayan temple of Chichen Itza, a multidomed structure of the San Francisco Monastery at Cholula, and the Great Mosque at Córdoba, Spain.

Luis Barragán died in Mexico City in 1988 and soon afterward his monumental achievements in architecture were honored by an exhibit of his works at the Palacio de Bellas Artes.

SUGGESTED READING

María Fernández, "Architecture: Twentieth Century," in Michael S. Werner, ed., *Encyclopedia of Mexico: History, Society, and Culture*, vol. 1 (Chicago: Fitzroy Dearborn, 1997); William Stockton, "Barragán's Eloquent Architecture," *New York Times*, January 9, 1986; "Barragán, Luis," *Encyclopedia of World Biography*, 2d ed. (Detroit: Gale Research, 1998).

Barzón, El ☀ A nationwide debtor's organization created in 1993 to assist middle-sized farmers, small business owners, and individual citizens who found it difficult to compete with cheaper imports and growing indebtedness due to the collapse of the peso and the subsequent increase in interest rates on their commercial and business loans. El Barzón (the yoke) started as a union of indebted farmers in western Jalisco seeking to prevent bank foreclosure on their farms, but it soon spread to the urban middle class areas as well. As more and more producers defaulted due to skyrocketing interest rates and depressed agricultural prices, the Barzonistas became more militant—

Poster expressing outrage over corruption of the Salinas administration, Mexico City, 1995. "Carlos Salinas to Jail: Help with Your Signature." The "crimes" listed beside his photo include, from top to bottom: traitor to the fatherland, genocide with radioactive milk, ripoff thief, narco-president, and neoliberal. Credit: Donald Windler.

including protest marches, civil disobedience, legal challenges, and bank boycotts—attracting large numbers of followers throughout Mexico. Overwhelmingly middle class and with no apparent ties to political parties, it has rejected the old corporatist design of the government; by the end of 1995 El Barzón claimed to have 4.5 million members in 300 affiliated groups across the country. The explosion of such social protest movements as El Barzón and the Zapatistas suggest that the public is growing weary of the neoliberal reforms and is becoming less tolerant of the ruling party's **corruption** scandals and the rhetoric of future prosperity.

Recognizing the seriousness of the middle-class element of El Barzón, the Zedillo administration agreed to the Debtor's Aid Program in 1995, which included measures to postpone foreclosures and limit interest rates affecting most credit card holders for at least one year. While El Barzón's demands led to the government's response and helped stabilize the political situation, President **Ernesto Zedillo**'s initiative also raised the costs to the Mexican government and banks holding potentially bad loans. By pumping billions of pesos into the banking industry, the Mexican government placed a higher priority on monetary stabilization than on assisting the large numbers of debtors throughout the land. The efforts of El Barzón illustrate the fact that political activity is increasingly taking place through a multiplicity of nonparty channels, often with ties to a variety of international social movements and organizations. As the Mexican economy began to improve at the macroeconomic level after 1997, however, the recovery failed to translate into significant benefits for the majority of the Mexican population. *See also* Debt Crisis.

SUGGESTED READING

Denise Dresser, "Treading Lightly and without a Stick: International Actors and the Promotion of Democracy in Mexico," in Tom Farer, ed., *Beyond Sovereignty: The Collective Defense of Democracy in Latin America* (Baltimore: Johns Hopkins University Press, 1996); Heather Williams, *Planting Trouble: The Barzón Debtors' Movement in Mexico* (La Jolla: Center for U.S.–Mexican Studies, University of California–San Diego, 1996).

Baseball ✳ The origins of baseball (**béisbol**) in Mexico vary according to geographical region, social class, and relations with the United States and the Caribbean. In the Yucatán Peninsula the sport was introduced by Cuban workers in the 1860s. American influence contributed to the appearance of baseball in Mexico's northern frontier cities like Monterrey and Chihuahua, where industrial and railroad workers from the United States and Mexico came into daily contact in the late 19th century. After the defeat of the French in 1867 and the early efforts at modernization under Porfirio Díaz in the 1870s, teams of railroad workers brought baseball to northern Mexico, where its popularity now far surpasses other sports such as soccer and basketball. One of the first Mexican baseball games was played in the late 1870s in Nuevo Laredo. Sailors from U.S. ships also helped turn Mexico into a baseball-loving country. In contrast to the beginnings of baseball in the Caribbean, where the popularity of baseball was based on the hope of somehow humiliating the North American imperialists after years of military intervention, baseball in Mexico began as a sport of the elite interested in the virtues of physical vigor and true competition. During the 1910–1917 Revolution, baseball was used as a propaganda tool by Felipe Carrillo Puerto, a socialist leader from Mérida, Yucatán, who believed that baseball could serve as a symbol for the transformation of Mexico's political culture from one of individualism into collectivism.

Today Mexico has the largest organized baseball system in Latin America, boasting 25 teams nationwide, one consisting of a Mexican League of 15 teams and a 10-team Mexican Pacific League. With the exception of **Fernando Valenzuela,** who pitched for the Los Angeles Dodgers in the 1980s, Mexico, unlike the Dominican Republic, Cuba, or Puerto Rico, is not recognized in the United States as a baseball powerhouse. The reason for this is due in large part to the fact that Mexico—unlike other Latin American or Caribbean countries that treat their baseball talent as a resource to be exported to the highest bidder in the United States—strives to keep its best players at home. The professional sports industry in Mexico requires a U.S. ball club desiring to obtain a Mexican player to purchase the player's contract outright. This usually means a steep sum to compensate for future gate revenues that would be lost to the player who migrates northward. The first Mexican to play in the major leagues was Baldamero Mela "Mel" Almada, an infielder who started with the Boston Red Sox in 1933. Since that time over 50 Mexican players have been drafted by U.S. baseball teams, including big-name successes such as Rubén Amaro, Jorge Orta, Cy Acosta, Aurelio "Señor Smoke" López, Teodoro "Teddy" Higuera, Vinny Castilla, and Valenzuela, hero to the large U.S. Hispanic population in the early 1980s. Some of the best Mexican baseball talent, however, including Hector Espino who holds the Mexican home run record, chose to remain in Mexico due to a combination of national pride and the high price tags on Mexican players.

Despite their longing to play baseball in the major leagues, life in the United States was not easy for Latino baseball players, whether from Mexico, Puerto Rico, Cuba, or the Dominican Republic. Latins in the United States, particularly those with dark skins and limited facility in the English language, confronted arrogance, racial stereotypes, and discrimination. Early Hollywood films such as *Tony the Greaser* (1911), *Barbarous Mexico* (1913), and *Bordertown* (1935), depicting Mexicans as unsavory, hot-tempered, and villainous, helped reinforce negative attitudes toward Mexican ballplayers in the United States that lasted for generations.

As more Mexican players cross the border to play in the major leagues, and as U.S. teams travel to Mexico to play both Mexican and U.S. teams, the physical separation and ethnic hostility that once characterized the past have started to decline. The two baseball games that were played by the Baltimore Orioles and the Cuban National Team (one game in Havana and the other in Baltimore)

in 1999 served to increase the awareness of quality baseball among Latin players. Major League Baseall officials in the United States announced in May 1999 that Mexicans would be able to vote for the 1999 All-Star baseball players, a first for baseball fans south of the border. Mexican fans received approximately 6 percent of the votes (5 million ballots), but the only Mexican on the ballot was Colorado Rockies third baseman Vinny Castilla. Mexican fans obtained their ballots at Oxxo convenience stores and at distributors of Carta Blanca beer, both owned by Femsa.

Within the next five years it is possible that a more authentic "World Series of Baseball" will be played, with professional teams from Mexico joining the National or American Leagues along with U.S., Canadian, and Japanese players. Commercial broadcasters and team owners have come to realize the monetary value of *béisbol*'s growing Latino audience and have made important strides to make Hispanics feel more at home in the major leagues: most have programs designed to ease the way for Spanish-speaking players, most major league teams broadcast their games in Spanish, and the growing Latino populations in major league cities have helped players feel more at "home" in the United States.

SUGGESTED READING

William H. Beezley, "The Rise of Baseball in Mexico and the First Valenzuela," *Studies in Latin American Popular Culture* 4 (1985); Alan M. Klein, *Baseball on the Border: A Tale of Two Laredos* (Princeton: Princeton University Press, 1999); Michael M. Oleksak and Mary Adams Oleksak, *Béisbol: Latin Americans and the Grand Old Game* (Grand Rapids, Mich.: Masters, 1991); Samuel O. Regalado, *Viva Baseball! Latin Major Leaguers and Their Special Hunger* (Urbana: University of Illinois Press, 1998).

Beer Industry ✳ Although Mexico ranks ninth among the top 20 brewing nations of the world and second in the Western Hemisphere behind the United States, beer drinking is not as celebrated in Mexico as it is in Germany, the United States, and the United Kingdom. Today the Mexican beer industry is dominated by the Big Three—Cuauhtémoc, Moctezuma, and Modelo—with each brewery located in a different **geographical region**. Before the arrival of the Spanish, the Aztecs and Mayas developed their own techniques for brewing beer, using maize or corn instead of barley to create an amber beverage called *tesguino*. Within the first 50 years of the Spanish conquest, the king of Spain set up a commercial brewery in Mexico, the first in the New World. By the time of independence in the early part of the 19th century, the number of breweries in Mexico was growing, thanks to the talents of German and Swiss settlers who immigrated to the region.

Mexico's first large-scale brewery—Cuauhtémoc in Monterrey—was established in 1890 by a German brewmaster who introduced Vienna-style beers, one of which won Grand Prize at the Chicago International Beer Exposition in 1893. Today the Cuauhtémoc brewery produces quality Pilsner-style beers, including the popular Carta Blanca, Tecate, and Bohemia brands, sold throughout Mexico, the United States, Canada, and Europe. Cuauhtémoc also has a one-third holding in Mexico's only "independent" brewery, Yucateca, which produces the pale Montejo and a highly hopped brew called León Negra, both popular on the Yucatán peninsula.

The second brewery—Cevecería Moctezuma in Veracruz—produces the Vienna-style Dos Equis, popular in the United States, and a seasonal dark lager called Nochebuena (Christmas Eve) with a higher alcoholic content.

The last of the Big Three is Modelo, in Mexico City, which brews a *clara* (clear or light) lager, Victoria, one of the national best-sellers and a popular beverage among the Mexican working class. Cevecería Modelo was founded in 1925 and is now Mexico's biggest brewing company, dominating more than 70 percent of Mexico's beer exports with its popular Corona brand. With a growing beer export market in the United States and Europe, Modelo's production exceeds all but five American breweries and all of Canada's breweries. Its brilliant marketing strategy—a clear bottle, served with a lime to add tropical flavor, and television ads aimed at attracting college students with fond memories of spring break in Cancún or Cabo San Lucas—has made Corona Extra the number one imported beer in the United States, having surpassed Heineken in 1998. To keep its successful beverage flowing, Grupo Modelo, Corona's Mexican manufacturer, is now building what business executives say will be Latin America's largest brewery, located in the state of Zacatecas.

Mexican beers, often light and of moderate alcoholic content, are popular throughout the country. The consumption of beer is actually encouraged by the Mexican government, based on the quenching quality of the beverage. Under a 1931 law, beer is not classified as an intoxicant because of its low alcoholic content (it is limited by law to 5 percent by volume). This means that brewers may label their products *la bebiba de moderación* to reinforce a particular drinking mood. Mexican beer is generally served in two ways, at room temperature (*al tiempo*) or chilled (*fria* or *helada*), and is popular among Mexicans of all social classes. Some **macho** beer drinkers opt for greater alcoholic potency by creating what is called a *submarino*, a glass of **tequila** submerged inside a chilled glass of beer, a dangerous combination for beer drinkers of any nationality.

SUGGESTED READING

Michael Jackson, ed., *The World Guide to Beer* (Philadelphia: Running, 1987); Stuart A. Kallen, *The Complete Idiot's Guide to Beer* (New York: Alpha, 1997); Gregg Smith, *Beer* (New York: Avon, 1995); Rick Wills, "The King of Imported Beers," *New York Times,* May 28, 1999; Heather Wood, *The Beer Directory: An International Guide* (Pownal, Vt.: Storey, 1995).

Border. *See* U.S.–Mexican Border/Boundary.

Bracero Program ☀ Migratory workers from Mexico have been coming to the United States for centuries to provide labor on large farms and ranches, railroads, factories, and small shops, often at the urging of the U.S. government and labor-starved businesses. After the **Mexican Revolution** of 1910 and the outbreak of World War I in 1914, hundreds of thousands of documented Mexican workers entered the United States. In 1921 the U.S. Congress passed laws restricting **immigration** and established the U.S. Border Patrol to control cross-border population flows. Efforts to establish quotas to prevent too many Mexicans from crossing the border were largely ineffectual. Agricultural workers were in such demand that they were exempted from the restrictions during the 1920s. Once the Great Depression hit the United States in 1929, however, Mexican workers were deported and U.S. government efforts were made to deter them from returning to the United States illegally.

The demand for Mexican labor increased again with the outbreak of **World War II** and U.S. youth out of the country to fight the war. With large segments of the U.S. population needed for the war effort, American businesses began vying for Mexican workers to fill the void. To solve this problem, in 1942 the U.S. government—under pressure from U.S. agricultural leaders—signed the International Agreement of Migratory Workers with Mexico to legalize the importation of Mexican *braceros* (*bracero,* from *brazo,* Spanish for "arm," can be translated loosely as "farm-hand") to work seasonally on farms and ranches. Farmers who employed Mexican migratory workers cared little about written contracts, working conditions, or a fair wage; in many cases *braceros* were treated worse than Italian and German prisoners of war held captive in northwestern farm labor camps. Between 1942 and 1964, 4.8 million *braceros* legally entered the United States to work, while approximately 5 million undocumented workers were apprehended during the same period. Most of the *braceros* worked on farms (picking lettuce, cotton, and sugar beets) and ranches in the Southwest, particularly Texas, California, Arizona, and New Mexico and in Arkansas. Smaller numbers worked in the Pacific Northwest, harvesting fruit and potatoes in Washington, Oregon, and Idaho. Under the rules of the *bracero* program, 10 percent of the Mexican worker's wages were withheld and entrusted to the Mexican government, to be returned to workers from a savings account when they returned to Mexico. However, very few *braceros* received this money—estimated at $150 million—and many have now concluded that corrupt banking officials in Mexico pocketed the funds. In 1999, under pressure from Mexican unions to uncover the missing money on behalf of ex-*braceros* and their survivors (many now living legally in western states), Mexican bankers began an investigation but have been unable to find the missing retirement account since the bank no longer exists and most of the records were destroyed. The pressure to rectify the *bracero* repayment blunder would be greater if the *braceros*—mostly poor and elderly—who had participated in the program (only 20,000 ex-*braceros* and their survivors have been located) had more political clout.

By the early 1960s, the program came under fierce attack because of the mistreatment of Mexican workers by their employers in the United States, charges from organized labor that *braceros* depressed wages and contributed to unemployment among U.S. farm workers, and a television documentary ("Harvest of Shame") that presented the poverty and despair of migratory workers. The sympathy of the liberal Kennedy and Johnson administrations toward the demands of organized labor and the public outcry over slave-like working conditions forced termination of the program in 1964.

Since the *bracero* program ended in the 1960s, the influx of Mexican workers has continued—despite increasing mechanization—with millions of Mexicans coming to the United States to work during the harvest season or full-time when demand permits. By 1986 there were so many Mexicans living permanently (but illegally) in the United States that the U.S. Congress passed the Immigration Reform and Control Act of 1986 (IRCA), allowing some 3 million of them to become American citizens. Often touted as a solution to illegal immigration by American conservatives, IRCA did not have any significant effect on the flow northward. Although there have been many critics of the *bracero* program—on both sides of the border—the majority of migratory workers who have entered the United States since the mid-1800s have done so because of demands from the U.S. government and American businesspeople. By replacing the American workforce that went into industry during and after World War II, millions of *braceros* contributed to agricultural expansion and high levels of farm production that otherwise would not have occurred. The influx of migrant farm workers from Mexico is a key reason for the success of agriculture in the United States.

In a last-ditch effort at immigration control in the 1990s, the U.S. Congress gave some thought to the possibility of another *bracero*-like program (driven by a booming U.S. economy and low unemployment), apparently ignorant of the fact that the earlier program *increased* illegal immigration to the United States and harmed Mexican–U.S. relations. Mexico would be receptive to a temporary worker agreement, but it would differ from the *bracero* program since it would require worker rights, guaranteed housing, and clear pay guidelines. The **Vicente Fox** administration, in a series of (Mexican) proposals to change U.S. immigration policy, is trying to improve the lives of Mexicans who cross the border by allowing more Mexicans to enter the United States legally, increasing the number of permanent visas the United States allots to Mexico, and creating a new guest worker program that would guarantee decent working conditions.

SUGGESTED READING

Kitty Calavita, *Inside the State: The Bracero Program, Immigration, and the I.N.S.* (New York: Routledge, 1992); Kitty Calavita, "Bracero Program," in Michael S. Werner, ed., *Encyclopedia of Mexico: History, Society and Culture*, vol. 1 (Chicago: Fitzroy Dearborn, 1997); Richard B. Craig, *The Bracero Program: Interest Groups and Foreign Policy* (Austin: University of Texas Press, 1971); Erasmo Gamboa, *Mexican Labor and World War II: Braceros in the Pacific Northwest, 1942–1947* (Austin: University of Texas Press, 1990); Juan Ramón García, *Operation Wetback: The Mass Deportation of Mexican Undocumented Workers in 1954* (Westport, Conn.: Greenwood, 1980); Peter Neil Kirstein, *Anglo over Bracero: A History of the Mexican Worker in the United States from Roosevelt to Nixon* (San Francisco: R. & E. Research Associates, 1977); David R. Maciel, "Braceros, Mojados, and Alambristas: Mexican Immigration to the United States in Contemporary Cinema," *Hispanic Journal of Behavioral Sciences* 8 (1986).

Bullfighting ☀ The practice of bullfighting was introduced by Spanish conquerors of Mexico in the early 16th century. The first official bullfight, or *corrida*, took place in 1529 to celebrate the feast of St. Hippolito, the day that modern Mexico City (then Tenochtitlán, the capital of the Aztec empire) was conquered by Fernando (Hernán) Cortés in 1521. Until the 18th century, bullfights were chaotic affairs as bullfighters (usually nobles) fought ferocious bulls on horseback, rather than on foot, a practice that developed later. During the 1700s *corridas* changed in form and style, gradually developing into a professional, popular, and lucrative sport. The sport was standardized in rit-

Matador with cape inciting the bull to charge during the final part of a bullfight in Mexico City, 1970. Credit: General Secretariat of the Organization of American States.

ual, and bullrings were constructed to house the spectacle. The first permanent *plaza de toros* (bullring) was built in Mexico City in 1788, and the popularity of the *corrida* spread rapidly to other Mexican cities. Bullfighting declined immediately after independence and was revived by the Mexican government after 1829 to provide profits for the state. President Benito Juárez attended bullfights and his wife organized bullfights as fund-raisers during the French occupation, but after the expulsion of French troops from Mexico, Juárez prohibited bullfighting. The prohibition was rescinded in 1887; with the exception of President Carranza's banning of bullfights (1916–1920) during the **Mexican Revolution**, no recent president has dared to ban the sport. Techniques of bullfighting improved in the 20th century, and a few world-class *torreros* (bullfighters) became superstars in Mexico and Spain. Mexico's great bullfighters—Rodolfo Gaona y Jiménez (1888–1975), Fermín Espinosa Saucedo, Pepe Ortíz, Carlos Arruza (1920–1966), and Bernardo Gaviño—have helped contribute to the sport's popularity in Mexico.

As new styles and techniques emerged—some imported from Spain—bullfighting changed from a rather static event into one with more fluid motion. Bulls are smaller and faster and have more stamina, and there is a more exciting pace to the spectacle. There are 225 permanent bullrings and over 500 improvised ones in Mexico; the Plaza de México in Mexico City is the world's biggest bullfighting arena with a seating capacity of 50,000. Most bullfights take place on Sunday and start promptly at 4:30 P.M. with a series of formal ceremonies and rituals before the bull (often weighing over 1,100 pounds) and *torero* meet in the middle of the ring to begin the fight. Although it resembles a cruel and unfair contest to some spectators (the bull almost always dies), many bullfighters are killed, crippled, and gored numerous times in the course of their career. In addition, a bull that puts up a good fight against impossible odds can be *indultado,* pardoned and allowed to retire to a pasture where he will spend the rest of his life.

The drama of the bullfight is divided into three separate acts, each giving the *torero* an opportunity to prove his skills with daring passes, working ever closer to the horns. *La hora de la verdad* (the moment of truth) occurs when he plunges his sword between the bull's shoulder blades, severing the artery to the heart or puncturing its lung. The *torero*'s reward for the kill—depending on how the judges rank the quality of his performance—is to receive parts of the bull's dead body: one ear, two ears, two ears and the tail if the performance is extraordinary, and sometimes even the hoof of the dead bull. A team of mules will drag the bull around the ring if the animal has fought with customary courage. Meanwhile, the fight ends with the *torero* walking around the ring in triumph. A bullfighter who performs badly will provoke the crowd to shout obscenities and *Sin vergüenza!* (for shame!). Rude fans have been known to throw cups of their urine at a *torero* to indicate extreme

displeasure at the poor performance. Depending on his rank, a Mexican bullfighter will earn from $3,000 to $10,000 per *corrida* and fight 20 to 30 times per year.

As a sport based on ritual sacrifice, the typical bullfight can be seen as a contest of two types of authority, the physical and animalistic authority posed by the bull versus the more subtle authority in the hands of the matador. There is also the sexual symbolism of the struggle, with the bull representing the masculine figure and the actions of the matador symbolizing feminine qualities. A few women have become bullfighters, but they do not equal men as skilled fighters. The Mexican cultural model emphasizes the masculinity of the *torero*, a valiant male engaged in an effort to demonstrate his sexuality, although his costume (*traje de luces*, suit of lights) is considered by some to be nonmasculine, and many of his gestures toward the bull suggest nonmale behavior. Nevertheless, for most aficionados, a good *torero* must be *muy macho* (extremely masculine) and possess *cojones* (literally, balls), an essential quality of maleness and masculinity. *See also* Machismo.

SUGGESTED READING

Barnaby Conrad, *Encyclopedia of Bullfighting* (Boston: Houghton Mifflin, 1961); José E. García, "Bullfighting," in Michael S. Werner, ed., *Encyclopedia of Mexico: History, Society, and Culture,* vol. 1 (Chicago: Fitzroy Dearborn, 1997); Gary Marvin, *Bullfight* (New York: Basil Blackwell, 1988); Sergio Rivero, *Tauromaquía Mexicana: Imágen y pensamiento* (Mexico, D.F.: Fernández Cueto, 1994).

Buñuel, Luis (1900–1983) ✳ Spanish-born iconoclast, moralist, and avant-garde surrealist movie director and naturalized Mexican citizen who worked in Spain, France, Mexico, and the United States between 1929 and 1974. Buñuel made over 20 films in Mexico between 1946 and 1964, many of which were critical of Mexican politics and society. His first films were made in Paris with Salvador Dalí, masterpieces of surrealist **cinema** that created a scandal but made both of them famous among the European avant-garde. His films often used provocative scenes and shocking images (such as a young woman's eye being slit by a razor blade) to express his ideology and obsessions: religion, sexual desire, marginalized individuals, and middle-class morality. The iconoclastic features of his films—caustic, witty, Marxist, and irreverent—brought severe criticism, and some (e.g., *Viridiana,* 1961) were banned in Spain because they were too blasphemous.

Born in Calanda, Spain, he was the oldest of seven, the son of landowner Leonardo Buñuel, one of the many Spaniards who went to Cuba at the time of the Spanish American War. He returned shortly thereafter, and Luis Buñuel was educated at the University of Madrid, where he befriended Dalí and Federico García Lorca, as well as other future Spanish intellectuals. His interest in moviemaking brought him to Paris in 1925 where he studied film and worked as an assistant to well-known French filmmakers. He returned to Spain in the 1930s, producing antifascist documentaries and dubbing American films for Paramount and Warner

Publicity photo of Luis Buñuel (seated at left) and movie crew for *Ensayo de un crimen* (1955), one of the Spanish director's many Mexican films.

Studios. While working for the Republican government of Spain during the Civil War, he was sent to Hollywood in 1938 to act as a technical adviser on pro-Loyalist American films. After it became clear that Francisco Franco was winning the war, Buñuel remained in the United States, where he worked on anti-Nazi projects for the Museum of Modern Art in New York and the U.S. Army during **World War II**. Failing to advance his career in Hollywood, Buñuel moved to Mexico in 1946, directing 21 films between 1947 and 1962. It was during the postwar years in Mexico that he was the most prolific, producing popular melodramas and more personal works that contributed to his international reputation.

Of his Mexican films, the most notable were melodramas (*Susana*, 1950; *La Hija del Engaña*, 1951), comedies (*El Gran Calavera*, 1950 [The great madcap]), and dramatic adaptations (*Robinson Crusoe*, 1952). The commercial success of *El Gran Calavera* made it possible for Buñuel to make his masterpiece, *Los Olvidados*, a stark and realistic portrayal of the effects of poverty and repression on slum children in Mexico City, which earned him the prize for best direction and the International Critic's Prize at the Cannes Festival in 1951. Although his first Mexican film, *Gran Casino* (1946), was a musical starring **Jorge Negrete** and Argentina's Libertad Lamarque, it did not succeed at the box office.

Many of Buñuel's Mexican films deal with the legacy of colonialism, the failures of capitalism, patriarchy, and the absurdities of social and sexual repression. His surrealistic images and tactics often included references to animals and insects, dreamlike visions and other irrational states of mind, and the exaggeration of absurdities. According to Hershfield (1996, 122), "The surrealists were revolutionaries of sorts, using humor, sex, and scandal as weapons to fight what they perceived to be the cultural, social, and political decadence of bourgeois society." In films such as

Susana, Buñuel challenged traditional notions of female sexuality and the sacrosanct Mexican family by carrying melodramatic convention to extremes and deliberately exaggerating absurdities. Buñuel believed that he could make a political statement in his films by provoking his audience to react with moral outrage against social repression characterized by conservative values of propriety and restraint. He also appropriated parodic strategies in his films, something that Mexican audiences were familiar with in a cultural form called *la vacilada,* or grotesque melodrama, as illustrated in the **Day of the Dead** celebrations every year in early November. After leaving Mexico in 1962, Buñuel continued to maintain his long-standing reputation for integrity and courage in the face of those who were offended by his films that offered biting criticism of various social institutions, especially the Church, his favorite target. "Thank God I am still an atheist," he was quoted as saying to those who questioned his ideas and motives. Luis Buñuel died in Mexico City in 1983.

Buñuel is often the only name that comes to mind when Mexican filmmaking is mentioned. He found Mexico a stimulating artistic environment for his style of filmmaking, and during the late 1950s and early 1960s he helped keep international attention on Mexican films while the creativity of **Emilio Fernández** and **Alejandro Galindo** declined in an era of tiresome melodramatic formula pictures. Ironically, few Mexican directors tried to emulate Buñuel's style, and his impact on the Mexican film industry was negligible. Nevertheless, he became one of the best-known filmmakers outside of Mexico, especially to non-Mexicans in the United States.

SUGGESTED READING

Francisco Aranda, *Luis Buñuel: A Critical Biography*, trans. and ed. David Robinson (New York: Da Capo, 1976); Luis Buñuel, *My Last Sigh*, trans. Abigail Israel (New York: Knopf, 1983); Peter B. Flint, "Luis Buñuel Dies at 83; Filmmaker for 50 Years," *New York Times*, July

31, 1983; Joanne Hershfield, *Mexican Cinema/Mexican Woman, 1940–1950* (Tucson: University of Arizona Press, 1996); Virginia Higgenbotham, *Luis Buñuel* (Boston: Twayne, 1979); Ephraim Katz, *The Film Encyclopedia*, 3d ed. (New York: HarperCollins, 1998); John King, *Magical Reels: A History of Cinema in Latin America* (London: Verso, 1990); J. H. Matthews, *Surrealism and Film* (Ann Arbor: University of Michigan Press, 1971); Joan Mellen, ed., *The World of Luis Buñuel: Essays in Criticism* (New York: Oxford University Press, 1978); Ginette Vincendeau, ed., *Encyclopedia of European Cinema* (New York: Facts on File, 1995); Linda Williams, *Figures of Desire: A Theory and Analysis of Surrealist Film* (Berkeley: University of California Press, 1981).

Caciquismo A form of local and regional leadership based on a Mexican form of political bossism, often focused on the expansion of wealth and power. Caciques (political strongmen or bosses) can also be found in the organizational makeup of political parties and **labor** unions. *Cacique* is an Indian word for chieftain, someone with absolute—almost theocratic—authority that could be exercised without compromise or bargaining with opponents. For example, the conservative dinosaurs *(dinosaurios)* within the **Partido Revolucionario Institucional (PRI)** have generally had a hand in party candidate selection, although this cacique-like power seems to be dwindling with the abolition of the *dedazo* in 1999 and the first defeat of a PRI presidential candidate in 2000. Many peasants in rural communities and within the *ejidos* are exploited by village caciques who maintain tight control over access to government agencies and largesse. Mexican federalism has taken the operational form of cacique domination, often thwarting the exercise of power from the center. During the Porfirian era and the 1910–1917 period of revolution, many of the small and large regional caciques possessed their own troops, arms, and interests, often imposing their own law on defenseless towns under their control. For example, the last attempted coup in Mexican politics occurred in 1938, when the cacique of San Luis Potosí, Saturnino Cedillo, took up arms against President **Lázaro Cárdenas** using his own paramilitary forces in an effort to counter the advance of *ejidos* and other collectivist experiments.

Beginning in the 1940s, charisma and authority of political leaders no longer rested with a cacique (as a person), but rather with the position itself. The institution of the presidency—beginning with **Miguel Alemán**—grants enormous power to the individual who assumes the role for six years. After his tenure is over, the power of the president declines dramatically, leaving him stripped of the ability to reward, punish, and distribute income through thousands of key positions. While there are fewer caciques in the traditional sense of the word, *caciquismo* as a form of leadership can still be found in pockets of authority within Mexico's paternalistic and semiauthoritarian political culture. *See also Personalismo.*

SUGGESTED READING

Enrique Krause, *Mexico: Biography of Power: A History of Modern Mexico, 1810–1996* (New York: HarperCollins, 1997).

Camacho Solís, Víctor Manuel (1946–) ✳ A powerful and ambitious politician from the Federal District who served as head of the Department of the Federal District (1988–1993) and peace commissioner to Chiapas after the **Zapatista rebellion** in 1994. The son of a prominent military officer, Camacho Solís was born in the Federal District, attended schools there, and in 1970 earned an economics degree from the National School of Economics, **Universidad Nacional Autónoma de México (UNAM)**. He earned a master's degree from Princeton University in 1972, then returned to Mexico and taught various subjects at the **Colegio de México**, the National Teachers College, and UNAM in the late 1980s. While a student at UNAM he was close friend of Emilio Lozoya and **Carlos Salinas de Gortari**.

Camacho joined the **Partido Revolucionario Institucional (PRI)** in 1965, eventually working his way to the top position as secretary-general of the ruling party in 1988. Through his friendship with Carlos Salinas de Gortari, Camacho became the leading precandidate for the PRI presidential nomination in 1993 before he was edged out by President Salinas's selection of **Luis Donaldo Colosio** the following year. While Camacho was foreign minister in early 1994, he threatened to quit over Salinas's handling of the turbulent events in Chiapas. After a tense meeting with Salinas in which he offered to resign his post as foreign minister to take on the task of resolving the Chiapas crisis, the president appointed him as the government's peace negotiator there. After winning praise for his work to bring about a peace settlement with Zapatista rebels, Camacho considered running against Colosio as an independent for the presidency in 1994, but he withdrew from the race shortly before Colosio's assassination. After being accused by some PRI members of being involved in the Colosio killing, he maintained a low profile before quitting the party in 1995. In November 1995 he published

Ruptura sin cambio, in which he explained his political philosophy. The failure of the main opposition parties to form an alliance against the PRI in 1999 led Camacho to declare himself a candidate for president of his **Partido Centro Democrático (PCD)** in late November of that year. He countered critics of his decision to run by saying that a Camacho candidacy would help form an opposition alliance by serving as a liaison with dissident members of the ruling party and building bridges with other parties through the development of common policies of reform.

SUGGESTED READING

Roderic Ai Camp, *Mexican Political Biographies, 1935–1993,* 3d ed. (Austin: University of Texas Press, 1995); Andres Oppenheimer, *Bordering on Chaos: Guerrillas, Stockbrokers, Politicians, and Mexico's Road to Prosperity* (Boston: Little, Brown, 1996).

Camarena Salazar, Enrique (1947–1985) ✳ U.S. government official responsible for fighting the drug war in Mexico in the 1980s, whose torture and murder in 1985 quickly led to a deterioration in collaborative efforts to stop illicit drugs from coming into the United States. After U.S. Drug Enforcement Administration (DEA) officials successfully ended the flow of cocaine through Miami in the early 1980s, Colombian drug traffickers pursued new routes to the American market through Puerto Rico and northern Mexico. As the illicit **drug trade** expanded along the border and in other states, **corruption** of Mexico's public officials—politicians, high-ranking police officers, and members of the military—also increased. To fight Mexico's drug problem, DEA agents joined hands with the Mexican army and members of the Mexican Federal Judicial Police and raided marijuana fields in San Luis Potosí, Zacatecas, Sinaloa, and Chihuahua. In retaliation for these raids, the narcotics cartel of Guadalajara planned a series of attacks on Americans working with Mexican authorities.

One of the early targets of Mexico's drug kingpins was Enrique Camarena, a DEA agent working on assignment in Mexico in February 1985 who was kidnapped and then tortured and murdered. After his body was discovered one month later, investigations into the murder were carried out on both sides of the border, each arriving at different conclusions about who was responsible for the tragedy. Mexican officials claimed that Guadalajara drug kingpin Rafael Caro Quintero was behind the murder; the DEA investigation blamed high-ranking Mexican officials for the crime, including Rubén Zuno Arce, an influential business executive and relative of former Mexican president **Luis Echeverría**, and members of Mexico's political elite, for carrying out a coverup of the sordid affair. When Mexican officials refused to allow DEA agents to take part in the investigation or view relevant evidence in the case, relations between the United States and Mexico soured as the United States pursued numerous retaliatory measures, including detailed inspections of all vehicles crossing the border from Mexico into the United States. The death of Camarena led to a public outcry in the U.S. Congress, which passed punitive legislation enabling the president to cut off financial aid to any country unwilling to actively pursue narco-traffickers. Efforts to avenge the murder of Camarena through DEA-sponsored actions (Operation Intercept II and Operation Leyenda) created a crisis in U.S.–Mexican relations and made Mexican officials painfully aware of the DEA's penchant to "go it alone" in the pursuit of drug traffickers inside Mexico.

U.S.–Mexican relations deteriorated further when DEA agents hired bounty hunters with instructions to kidnap Dr. Humberto Álvarez-Machaín, a Mexican physician suspected of being involved in the Camarena case, smuggle him across the border, and then turn him over to U.S. law enforcement officials. This DEA-sponsored abduction infuriated Mexicans who felt that the failure to seek extradition of Álvarez-Machaín was a clear demonstration of Washington's disregard for Mexican sovereignty. The Camarena assassination and the Álvarez-Machaín abduction brought to light the differing perceptions of the illicit drug trade and how to combat it. Washington tended to see Camarena's brutal murder as indicative of the widespread corruption pervading the Mexican law enforcement system. Many Mexicans, on the other hand, considered the DEA's decision to have Álvarez-Machaín kidnapped rather than seek extradition a major threat to their national sovereignty and further evidence of an overbearing attitude among U.S. officials. Mexico's resentment intensified when the U.S. Supreme Court ruled in 1993 that it was constitutional for U.S. authorities to kidnap a foreign criminal suspect and bring him to the United States for trial. While the Reagan administration viewed the Álvarez-Machaín case as a victory against terrorism and drug trafficking, Mexican authorities responded by terminating the activities of all DEA agents and interrupting years of close binational cooperation on drug matters. In order to gain greater cooperation from Mexico, Washington announced that it would not abduct kidnap suspects from foreign soil in the future.

After many court trials in the United States and Mexico, 19 Mexican citizens were eventually indicted for the abduction, torture, and murder of DEA agent Camarena. Caro Quintero, a key figure in the Guadalajara drug cartel, was arrested and convicted for crimes connected to drug trafficking. According to U.S. officials, he was part of La Familia, a drug trafficking group with four major heads, each in charge of a particular drug-export operation. However, the Camarena case did not erase the beliefs in the United States of high-level **corruption** and noncooperative attitudes among Mexican authorities, and the lingering resentment of U.S. antidrug strategies in Mexico. Although views of the major problem of illicit drugs tended to focus on the supply side of the issue, the heavy demand for drugs in the United States and Europe received considerably less press and legislative attention.

SUGGESTED READING

Bruce M. Bagley, ed., *Drug Trafficking Research in the Americas: An Annotated Bibliography* (Miami: University of Miami, North-South Center, 1997); Andrew Berenson, "An Examination of the Rights of American Bounty Hunters to Engage in Extraterritorial Abductions in Mexico," *University of Miami Inter-American Law Review* (Winter 1999); Paul Ganster, "Enrique Camarena," in Barbara A. Tenenbaum, ed., *Encyclopedia of Latin American History and Culture*, vol. 1 (New York: Scribners, 1996); Andreas Lowenfeld, "Kidnapping by Government Order: A Follow-up," *American Journal of International Law*, July 1990; William Dirk Ratt, *Mexico and the United States: Ambivalent Vistas* (Athens: University of Georgia Press, 1992); María Celia Toro, *Mexico's "War" on Drugs: Causes and Consequences* (Boulder, Colo.: Lynne Rienner, 1995); LaMond Tullis, *Handbook of Research on the Illicit Drug Traffic: Socioeconomic and Political Consequences* (Westport, Conn.: Greenwood, 1991).

Camarilla ☀ Group politics is a distinctive feature of Mexican government. A political clique or network (frequently referred to as a *camarilla)* determines who gets to the top of the Mexican power structure. The structural basis of Mexican *camarillas* is a mentor–disciple (patron–client) relationship, but membership is not exclusive since all successful politicians belong to several *camarillas*. These vertical groupings, or interlocking chains of clientage relationships, come together at the presidency, the supreme patron. *Camarillas* lie at the heart of an elaborate process of alliance building that occurs over a long period of time, often among aspirants to the presidency at the cabinet level. Each new president has his own *camarilla*, and during the presidential transition there is a frantic reshuffling of officeholders as other *camarillas* strive to gain authority over policy making in key areas. The essential bond in all *camarillas* is personal loyalty to the *camarilla* leader, not political ideology. What this means in Mexican politics is that the ruling elite is less likely to be responsive and accountable to the general public and the various groups that make up the corporatist arrangement of the **Partido Revolucionario Institucional (PRI)**. As Cornelius (2000, 486) points out, "Fervent, unquestioning loyalty and service to one's immediate superior in the PRI-government apparatus is the only promising route to upward political mobility." While it is possible to shift from one *camarilla* to another, particularly from one that is "losing" to one that is "winning," joining the "wrong" *camarilla* can be damaging to one's political career.

The most significant *camarillas* in Mexico today can be traced back to **Lázaro Cárdenas** and **Miguel Alemán**, presidents of Mexico who formed large *camarillas* based on ideology, personal characteristics, kinship, education (particularly at the **Universidad Nacional Autónoma de México, UNAM**), and professional merit. According to political scientist Roderic Ai Camp (1999, 118), "Cárdenas's personal camarilla spawned four successive generations of camarillas, accounting for at least 144 national officeholders." President **Carlos Salinas** managed to build an extremely large *camarilla*, alliances based on many members of the traditional ruling party political class as well as **técnicos** in the government bureaucracy. However, **Ernesto Zedillo**, a dark-horse candidate for the presidency in 1994 only possessed a small and narrow *camarilla*. The lack of clientage alliances proved to be a liability for him in mobilizing support for the various policy choices he sought to implement during his *sexenio*.

SUGGESTED READING

Roderic Ai Camp, *Politics in Mexico: The Decline of Authoritarianism*, 3d ed. (New York: Oxford University Press, 1999); Wayne A. Cornelius, "Politics in Mexico," in Gabriel A. Almond and G. Bingham Powell, eds., *Comparative Politics Today: A World View* (Boston: Little, Brown, 2000); Joy Langston, *The Camarillas: A Theoretical and Comparative Examination of Why They Exist and Why They Take the Specific Form They Do* (Mexico, D.F.: Centro de Investigación y Docencia Económicas, 1993).

Campa, Valentín. *See* Communism and Mexican Communist Party (Partido Comunista Mexicano, PCM).

Campeche. *See* Geographical Regions.

Cantinflas (1911–1993) ☀ Mario Moreno Reyes, better known as Cantinflas, was an extremely talented actor and comedian who achieved international recognition for his on-screen epitomization of a unique comic persona, the *peladito*. As defined by Cantinflas, the *peladito* is a symbol of Mexico itself, a member of the **mestizo** underclass—a streetwise itinerant citizen or bedraggled underdog who always, in the end, manages to endure his tribulations. Unlike Charlie Chaplin, the English-speaking equivalent of the Mexican comedian, Cantinflas never exhibited any form of leftism in his bawdy act. According to Stavans (1998, 35), Cantinflas was everybody's favorite rascal, someone who "symbolizes the rough-and-tumble slap-dash in poor barrios, the treacherousness of the

Publicity photo of Mario Moreno ("Cantinflas").

illiterate, the vitality of the dispossessed, the obscenity of working-class people." Over a half century, from 1939 to 1981, Cantinflas made 49 films, each one a huge box office success, that earned him a personal fortune estimated at $25 million. Chaplin himself is reported to have said, after viewing one of Cantinflas's movies: "He's the greatest comedian alive!" His most successful box office hits—*Ahí está el detalle* (1940) and *Ni sangre, ni arena* (1941)—came early and were always based on the formula of the *peladito* confronting the powerful and, with his verbal gymnastics, always getting the best of them.

Cantinflas was born in a poor neighborhood in Mexico City, the son of a postal worker and the sixth of 13 children. A born entertainer, as a child he earned small change by charming passersby with his rapid-fire jokes, dancing, and wordplay. While still a teenager, he worked as a bullfighter, shoeshine boy, taxi driver, and successful boxer before running away to join a *carpa*, an itinerant sideshow where the down-and-out could watch slapstick comedy and circus acrobatics. It was in the *carpa* that he polished his acting and comedy skills and acquired his stage name. A master at the art of combining gibberish, double-talk, mispronunciation, and wild exaggeration, during one performance a heckler shouted, "En la cantina tú inflas!" ("In the cantina you talk big"), a phrase he found so engaging that he contracted the words to Cantinflas, which he adopted as his only stage name. His signature act—amazing demonstrations in which he sounded like he was saying something important without actually saying anything at all—resembled a combination of Red Skelton and Danny Kaye. The ultimate satirist, Cantinflas loved to make fun of the **macho** husband, the abusive priest, the virginal female, the naive **gringo**, and the powerful *político*. He often portrayed politicians in an unfavorable light using his tongue as a weapon of ridicule. In his most popular skits, he

satirized the rhetorical tendency of Mexican politicians to engage in something called *pura palabrería,* the excessive usage of catchwords and phrases that say either nothing or very little. His international popularity contributed to the inclusion of his name as a verb (*cantinflear,* which means to talk incessantly and say nothing), as a noun (*cantinflesco,* which refers to someone who talks a lot but says nothing), and as an adjective (*cantinfleado,* which means dumb or stupid) in major dictionaries.

Cantinflas became famous for his wealth and philanthropy after his successful box office hits made him a millionaire. He became one of Mexico's most active philanthropists. In his mature years he is reported to have distributed $175,000 every year to the homeless who would wait outside his door on his birthday. He built apartment houses and supported more than 250 destitute families in a Mexico City slum called Granjas. Cantinflas also raised funds for charity by appearing at dozens of benefit performances every year. The most successful of these annual performances—adopted from Mike Todd's *Around the World in 80 Days*—was a comic **bullfighting** burlesque in the Plaza de México, Mexico's largest bullring. With such a fortune and his close connections with high-ranking officials of the **Partido Revolucionario Institucional (PRI)** (and some claim with members of Mexico's various drug cartels), Cantinflas often had to explain that his extreme wealth had nothing to do with **corruption** or **drug trafficking**.

The *peladito* that Cantinflas played to such perfection went through a metamorphosis during his lifetime. While his early achievements and image were endorsed by the Mexican government under the assumption that his humorous skits would make the masses happy and less likely to upset the status quo, around the time of the 1968 **Tlatelolco massacre** the ruling party was more interested in a modernized symbol of Mexico than the shrewd country bumpkin that Cantinflas epitomized. When Cantinflas died from lung cancer in 1993, the *peladito* he had symbolized for so many years had long ceased to be a positive element of Mexican national identity. *See also* Cinema.

SUGGESTED READING

Roger Bartra, *The Cage of Melancholy: Identity and Metamorphosis in the Mexican Character* (New Brunswick, N.J.: Rutgers University Press, 1992); Albin Krebs, "Cantinflas, Mexican Comic Actor and Philanthropist, Is Dead at 81," *New York Times,* April 22, 1993; Carlos Monsiváis, "Cantinflas and Tin Tan: Mexico's Greatest Comedians," in Joanne Hershfield and David R. Maciel, eds., *Mexico's Cinema: A Century of Film and Filmmakers* (Wilmington, Del.: Scholarly Resources, 1999); John Mraz, "Moreno Reyes, Mario (Cantinflas)," in Michael S. Werner, ed., *Encyclopedia of Mexico: History, Society, and Culture,* vol. 2 (Chicago: Fitzroy Dearborn, 1997); Jeffrey M. Pilcher, *Cantinflas and the Chaos of Mexican Modernity* (Wilmington, Del.: Scholarly Resources, 2000); Ilan Stavans, *The Riddle of Cantinflas: Essays on Hispanic Popular Culture* (Albuquerque: University of New Mexico Press, 1998).

Cárdenas del Río, Lázaro (1895–1970) ☀ Military figure in the **Mexican Revolution** and a popular postrevolutionary leader who was president of Mexico from 1934 to 1940. As president, Cárdenas initiated numerous changes in Mexico during a time of postrevolutionary turmoil and ferment. Like many of Mexico's leaders after the Mexican Revolution, Cárdenas believed that Mexico needed a strong, centralized state to maintain control over the social and political forces unleashed by the revolution. The highlights of his six-year presidency (*sexenio*) include an extensive agrarian reform program, the seizure and nationalization of foreign-owned oil companies, and the creation of a powerful corporatist party structure that tied peasant, labor, and popular sectors to the governing apparatus. After choosing General **Manuel Ávila Camacho** as his successor in 1940, Cárdenas held several positions within the government and became the unofficial leader of the left, or progressive, wing of the dominant party. He was particularly vocal in his opposition to U.S. **intervention** in the hemisphere during the Cold War and spoke out frequently on behalf of nonintervention and peace throughout the world before his death on October 19, 1970.

Cárdenas was born of mixed white and Tarascan Indian ancestry in Jiquilpán de Juárez, Michoacán, on May 21, 1895. He was the oldest son of a shopkeeper and was forced to work hard to succeed in Mexican society at the time. Prior to the 1910 Revolution, he worked in the local jail.

President Lázaro Cárdenas. Credit: Benson Latin American Collection, University of Texas at Austin.

When Francisco Madero's revolt broke out in the north, he released his prisoners and together they joined the *maderistas* (followers of Madero) in their effort to rid Mexico of the dictator Porfirio Díaz. From 1911 until 1928, Cárdenas rose through the ranks of the revolutionary armies, reaching the rank of brigadier general in 1924. Prior to his election as president in 1934, he served as governor of Michoacán (1928–1932), actively supporting land reform programs of benefit to landless peasants; leader of the governing party; minister of the interior; and secretary of war and marine. His agrarian reform programs antagonized the traditional landed elite, many of whom were tied to President Calles, who wished to end agrarian reform in order to appease commercial landowners and increase agricultural investment and production. Nevertheless, with the help of his agrarian faction within the dominant party, Cárdenas emerged from the nominating convention as presidential candidate with a radical six-year plan to reform Mexico.

As president, Cárdenas's support of labor and peasant groups, including support for strikes, antagonized business and commercial groups who worried about the consequences of a politically powerful **labor** force. Labor conflicts afforded Cárdenas the opportunity to push harder for socialist reforms established in the **Constitution of 1917.** The labor disputes on the cotton estates in the north-central regions of Coahuila and Durango led to the decision of the Cárdenas government to transform the large landed estates as collective *ejidos* or village cooperatives. The Cárdenas government distributed more land to peasants than all of his predecessors: 4.5 million acres were distributed to 800,000 peasant farmers over a span of six years. The expropriation of large landed estates and their conversion into collectives provoked resistance among landowners, who hired mercenaries to reverse Cárdenas's socialist policies.

In a dispute among Mexican workers demanding a collective contract, higher wages, and better benefits in the U.S.- and British-owned petroleum companies, Cárdenas refused to allow the foreign companies to defy the Mexican Supreme Court's ruling supporting the workers and expropriated their holdings. The nationalization of foreign-owned petroleum companies resulted in a massive outpouring of support for Cárdenas and helped expand the role of the state as a major economic actor in key industries previously under foreign control. The oil companies were outraged over what Mexico had done and pressured their respective governments to reverse the expropriation measures. The British broke diplomatic relations and the United States demanded immediate indemnification, boycotted Mexican petroleum exports to the United States, and embargoed the export of petroleum equipment to Mexico. Some companies called Cárdenas a communist and demanded that the United States intervene to put an end to revolutionary reforms. President Roosevelt resisted these demands, however, often citing his Good Neighbor Policy pledge of nonintervention and the need for hemispheric harmony given the threat of war in Europe. Under President Cárdenas, Mexico was successful in expanding its political and economic sovereignty by taking advantage of opportunities generated by the events leading up to **World War II**, often outmaneuvering U.S. and European diplomats on matters of importance to Mexico's growing economy.

Despite the conflicts engendered by the Cárdenas reforms, Mexico made significant strides in developing a more healthy economy. Government investments in roads, highways, and agricultural irrigation helped promote business growth, and the emergence of dozens of new financial institutions helped bolster sustained economic development. The collective *ejidos* achieved levels of productivity that rivaled private sector agriculture. Over the next three decades the agricultural sector was able to satisfy the food needs of the growing urban sector and assist with industrialization programs through exports of agricultural products.

During the final years of the Cárdenas administration, the reforms that caused tensions among business groups and conservative members of the government were checked and President Cárdenas decided to restructure the government party on a **corporatist** basis. By incorporating four sectors or constituencies—labor, peasant, popular, and the military—into the dominant party, he hoped the new sectoral structure would provide greater input into the new party, which was now called the Party of the Mexican Revolution—Partido de la Revolución Mexicana (PRM). Faced with the task of choosing a successor in 1940, Cárdenas picked General Manuel Ávila Camacho, a less controversial and more conservative candidate than the one favored by the progressive groups within the party, who expected to continue the Cárdenas-era reforms. The choice of Ávila Camacho was ratified at a nominating convention in which the various sectors within the party were allowed little input. With government party control of the electoral process, Ávila Camacho won a highly suspect election in 1940, ushering in a pattern of tight political control and dominance that would continue for decades.

From 1942 to his death in 1970, Cárdenas held several governmental posts while assuming the leadership of the progressive wing of the governing party. The power and mystique of *Cardenismo* developed into a symbol of the ideals of the Mexican Revolution. His agrarian refoms and nationalization programs ultimately benefitted many of the groups that earlier had criticized the president for instituting government-sponsored initiatives. Industrial capitalists gained the most from the peaceful mobilization of workers and peasants, but the control of such groups from above through an authoritarian party apparatus angered some who disliked the unequal way the benefits of reform were distributed. While current interpretations of the Cárdenas era remain controversial due to conflicting assessments of the authenticity of postrevolutory reforms, President Cárdenas carried out a series of bold reforms that were unmatched by his predecessors in Mexico or other utopian reformers elsewhere in Latin America at the time. Although some tried to link Cárdenas's name with revolutionary violence as a means of political change, he counseled those involved in the student disturbances of October 1968 to end all forms of violence and seek reform by peaceful means. Today, Lázaro Cárdenas remains the greatest leader of Mexico's modern history. The anniversary of his birth (May 21) and his petroleum nationalization decree (March 18) are both national holidays. *See also* Cárdenas Solorzano, Cuauhtémoc.

SUGGESTED READING

Marjorie Becker, *Setting the Virgin on Fire: Lázaro Cárdenas, Michoacán Peasants, and the Redemption of the Mexican Revolution* (Berkeley: University of California Press, 1995); Nora Hamilton, *The Limits of State Autonomy: Post-Revolutionary Mexico* (Princeton: Princeton University Press, 1982); Adolfo Gilly, *El cardenismo: Una utopía mexicana* (Mexico, D.F.: Cal y Arena, 1994); Gilbert M. Joseph and Daniel Nugent, eds., *Everyday Forms of State Formation: Revolution and the Negotiation of Rule in Modern Mexico* (Durham, N.C.: Duke University Press, 1994); Alan Knight, "Cardenismo: Juggernaut or Jalopy?" *Journal of Latin American Studies* 26 (1994); Enrique Krauze, *El sexenio de Lázaro Cárdenas* (Mexico, D.F.: Clio, 1999); Friedrich E. Schuler, *Mexico between Hitler and Roosevelt: Foreign Relations in the Age of Lázaro Cárdenas* (Albuquerque: University of New Mexico Press, 1998); William C. Townsend, *Lázaro Cárdenas: Mexican Democrat* (Ann Arbor, Mich.: George Wahr, 1952); Juana Vázquez-Gómez, *Dictionary of Mexican Rulers, 1325–1997* (Westport, Conn.: Greenwood, 1997).

Cárdenas Solorzano, Cuauhtémoc (1934–) ☀ The son of Mexico's reformist president of the 1930s, **Lázare Cardenas.** Cuauhtémoc Cárdenas served as **Partido Revolucionario Institucional (PRI)** governor of Michoacán and later ran three times as a presidential candidate of a leftist movement made up of people disgusted with the lack of democracy within the governing party. In the mid-1980s, Cárdenas, along with **Porfirio Múñoz Ledo** (previously the president of the PRI and ambassador to the United Nations), created the Democratic Current (Corriente Democrático, CD), a faction demanding democratization of the ruling party. After their demands for democratic selection of the PRI presidential candidate were rejected, they were expelled from the party. One of the most influential figures on the Mexican left, Cárdenas is credited with running the most successful opposition campaign for president in 1988, a controversial election in which many claim he garnered more than his "official" 31 percent of the national vote, and with the subsequent creation of the **Partido de la Revolución Democrática (PRD)** in 1989. In July 1997 he was elected mayor of Mexico City by a landslide, the first opposition politician to gain the powerful position and the first mayor of the city to be popularly elected. As a three-time presidential contender (1988, 1994, 2000), he had to suffer the declining electoral strength of the PRD, a party he helped create but after a decade is losing to the **Partido Acción Nacional (PAN)**, a conservative party with growing strength throughout Mexico.

Born in Mexico City in 1934, the son of one of Mexico's greatest and most revolutionary presidents, Cuauhtémoc Cárdenas was named after the last Aztec prince to actively oppose the Spanish conquest. His schooling prepared him for a career in regional and urban planning. He earned a degree in civil engineering from the **Universidad Nacional Autónoma de México (UNAM)** in 1957, then continued his education in France and Germany where he specialized in regional and

Cuauhtémoc Cárdenas, PRD candidate for president in 2000. Credit: *Proceso*, photo by Germán Canseco.

urban planning. After his European studies, Cárdenas became a practicing engineer in 1960 and worked for the Río Balsas Secretariat of Hydraulic Resources from 1964 to 1969. Until 1970, he operated under his father's enormous shadow, engaged in various business enterprises and at the same time building his own foundation within the ruling party. Through his father, he came in contact with many important members of the Mexican elite, and from an early age he adopted much of his father's political views and objectives. Following a strategy initiated by his father, Cuauhtémoc Cárdenas tried to move the PRI toward the left by challenging its refusal to push for greater democraticization and the need to rekindle the egalitarian goals of the Revolution.

From 1967 to 1986 he became more active in the **Partido Revolucionario Institucional (PRI)** and national politics. He served for four years as senator in the National Congress from 1976 to 1980 before he was elected to a six-year term as governor of Michoacán, his home state.

By 1987 he became so dissatisfied with the PRI that he made a clean break, created the Democratic Current, and became the CD's presidential candidate in 1988; after the fraud-tainted 1988 presidential elections he helped found the PRD in 1989. From 1989 to 1993, he served as president of the PRD, a position that provided a springboard for his second presidential bid in 1994. Although his platform called for a populist-nationalist economic program, he lost a second time, finishing in third place. During his last two campaigns for the presidency, Cárdenas has criticized the **North American Free Trade Agreement (NAFTA)** for not protecting workers' rights and the environment more vigorously, although he agrees with the underlying premise for a free trade zone. Between his second presidential loss in 1994 and his third bid for the presidency in 2000, Cárdenas moderated his political position. Running on an anti-corruption platform, he was elected mayor of Mexico City in the July 1997 balloting, marking the first time the capital's chief executive was not appointed by the president. His stint as mayor of Mexico City (1997–1999) was a frustrating experience, as his plan to carve a huge base of support out of the city of 20 million people was thwarted by soaring street crime, continuing **corruption**, ubiquitous pollution, and widespread traffic congestion, among other things.

As of 1999, the PRD seemed ready to self-destruct as quarrels between Porfirio Múñoz Ledo and Cárdenas intensified, the PRD had to jettison its supposedly "democratic and transparent" national contest for its presidential candidate in 2000, and accusations of electoral fraud directed at the PRD damaged its anti-PRI image.

In the months preceding the July 2000 presidential elections, Cárdenas remained in third place, according to several polls, behind the PRI front-runner, **Francisco Labastida,** and his PAN challenger **Vicente Fox.** Recent electoral trends suggest that the PAN, a powerful conservative opposition party, has a better chance of becoming the beneficiary of the disillusionment with the ruling party than the fractured and disorganized PRD. In any case, Mexico is unlikely to become fully democratic until there is more unity and **democracy** inside the three major parties. While Cárdenas has learned the value of popular mobilization as a political tool, he has yet to capture enough electoral support to convince millions of Mexicans that the country's future should be placed in the hands of those who constitute the Mexican left. However, by the end of the 2000 presidential campaign, the Cárdenas candidacy seemed to have turned into a wild card that drew enough votes from the PRI to tip the presidential race in favor of Fox, the PAN candidate with two to three times the support of Cárdenas according to most polls at the time. Under the banner of the multiparty Alliance for Mexico, Cuauhtémoc Cárdenas finished the contest with 16 percent of the vote, approximately the same percentage gained by the PRD in the previous presidential election.

SUGGESTED READING

Adolfo Aguilar Zinser, *Vamos a Ganar: La pugna de Cuauhtémoc Cárdenas por el poder* (Mexico, D.F.: Oceano, 1995); John Ward Anderson, "Mexican Politics Draws Wild Card," *Washington Post,* June 6, 2000; Kathleen Bruhn, *Taking on Goliath: The Emergence of a New Left Party and the Struggle for Democracy in Mexico* (University Park: Pennsylvania State University Press, 1997); Jorge G. Castañeda, *Utopia Unarmed: The Latin American Left after the Cold War* (New York: Alfred Knopf, 1993); José Luis Trueba, *Cárdenas: Una biografía* (Mexico, D.F.: Times Editories, 1997).

Cardenista Front Party for National Reconstruction.
See Partido Frente Cardenista de Reconstrucción
Nacional (PFCRN).

Carrillo Flores, Antonio (1909–1986) ☀ Prominent
lawyer, banker, diplomat, and politician who played
a key role in the development of banking legislation
adopted by the government from the 1940s to the
1970s. Born in 1909 in Mexico City, Carillo attended
primary school there in addition to three years in
New York City. He received his law degree from the
**Universidad Nacional Autónoma de México
(UNAM)** in 1929 and later taught at the Law School
at UNAM from 1936 to 1952. As an adviser to several Mexican presidents, Carrillo helped shape banking, development, financial, and **foreign policies**
throughout this long career. He was secretary of the
treasury (1952–1958) under President **Ruiz
Cortines**, ambassador to the United States
(1958–1964) under President **López Mateos**, and
secretary of foreign relations (1964–1970) during the
Díaz Ordaz presidency. He was Mexico's ambassador
to the Soviet Union in 1982 before retiring from government service. Through his teaching and writing
on banking law, Carrillo trained several generations
of disciples and influenced the ebb and flow of
domestic and foreign policies during the Cold War.
His father was the distinguished Mexican composer
Julián Carrillo, and his brother, Nabor, has been
Mexico's leading expert in the field of nuclear energy.
Antonio Carrillo's son, Emilio Carrillo Gamboa, followed in his father's footsteps, distinguishing himself as legal scholar, director general of Teléfonos de
México (1982–1987), and ambassador to Canada.

SUGGESTED READING

Roderic Ai Camp, "Carrillo Flores, Antonio," in Barbara
A. Tenenbaum, ed., *Encyclopedia of Latin American
History and Culture*, vol. 1 (New York: Scribners, 1996).

Castañeda de la Rosa, Jorge (1921–1997) ☀ Career
diplomat and foreign minister who led Mexico

into a more assertive and independent posture
toward the United States by strengthening ties
to Cuba and Central America for three years
beginning in 1979. Castañeda's appointment as
secretary of foreign relations (foreign minister)
was made by President **José López Portillo**
when Mexico was attempting to gain greater
geopolitical power due to its newly discovered
petroleum reserves. While he admitted the
importance of Mexico's ties to the United States,
Castañeda rejected a **foreign policy** that placed
Mexico in a dependent position. A Mexican
nationalist to the core, Castañeda led a 1982
peace initiative aimed at reducing the tensions
between the Nicaraguan Sandinista government
and the United States, but the Reagan administration refused to cooperate with the plan and
it ultimately failed.

Jorge Castañeda was born in Mexico City on
October 21, 1921, the son of an affluent lawyer. He
earned a law degree from the **Universidad Nacional
Autónoma de México (UNAM)** in 1943 and then
entered the foreign service in 1950, later serving as
Mexican ambassador to Egypt (1962–1965) and
France (1982–1988). He also had appointments as
professor of law at the National School of Law and
professor at the **Colegio de México** (1966–1967;
1969–1970). He died of complications from diabetes
in 1997. His son, **Jorge G. Castañeda Gutman**, is an
author, professor of political science and international relations at UNAM, and foreign minister during the **Vicente Fox** administration (2000–2006).

SUGGESTED READING

Sam Dillon, "Jorge Castañeda, 76, Diplomat and
Foreign Minister for Mexico," *New York Times*,
December 12, 1997.

Castañeda Gutman, Jorge G. (1953–) ☀ Professor of
political science, economics, and international
affairs at the **Universidad Nacional Autónoma de
México (UNAM)** in Mexico City. Castañeda is best

Jorge G. Castañeda Gutman. Credit: *Proceso*, photo by Germán Canseco.

known for his intellectual pursuits, including his perceptive policy analysis and criticisms of the ruling party. He was born in Mexico City in 1953 to a family of well-known diplomats, his father serving as foreign minister in the **López Portillo** administration and ambassador to Egypt and France. The younger Castañeda earned a B.A. at Princeton University (1973) and a B.A., M.A., and Ph.D. (1978) from the University of Paris. Since 1982 he has been a professor of political science at UNAM and a visiting professor at the University of California–Berkeley (1991–1992) and Princeton University (1990–1994).

A prolific writer, Castañeda has published six major books since 1988 and dozens of essays in Mexican and U.S. magazines and newspapers. His 1988 book *Limits to Friendship: The United States and Mexico* (with Robert Pastor), appraising both similarities and differences between the neighboring countries, received excellent reviews; in the controversial *La herencia: Arqueología de la sucesión presidential en México* (1999), Castañeda examined the complex mechanisms of presidential succession of four ex-presidents—**Luis Echeverría**, José López Portillo, **Miguel de la Madrid**, and **Carlos Salinas de Gortari**. His views on Mexican–U.S. relations and Mexican **foreign policy** are often expressed as a regular contributor to the *Los Angeles Times* (editorial page), *Proceso* (Mexico City), *El País* (Mexico City), *Current History*, *Foreign Affairs*, *Foreign Policy*, *World Policy Journal*, and *Newsweek*. He was awarded a Carnegie Fellowship in 1985–1987 and a MacArthur grant in 1989–1991. In a move that surprised many left-leaning intellectuals toward the end of the 2000 presidential race, Castañeda joined the presidential campaign of **Vicente Fox** in an effort to defeat the governing party. After the Fox victory, Castañeda was named foreign minister, a position held by his father 20 years earlier. *See also* Castañeda de la Rosa, Jorge.

SUGGESTED READING

Jorge G. Castañeda, *La herencia: Arqueología de la sucesión presidential en México* (Mexico, D.F.: Editorial Alfaguara, 1999); Donna Olendorf, ed., *Contemporary Authors* (Detroit: Gale Research, 1994).

Castillo Ledón, Amalia Caballero de (1902–1986) ☀ Teacher, essayist, playwright, diplomat, and **feminist** who played a key role in advancing political rights for women in the 1940s and 1950s. Born in San Jeronimo, Tamaulipas, Amalia Castillo Ledón spent her early years studying humanities and received a graduate degree from the **Universidad Nacional Autónoma de México (UNAM)**. Between 1929 and 1970, she played a major role in promoting child welfare, education, and full political rights for women. Castillo Ledón was a key player in changing the Mexican Constitution in 1953 to provide equal political rights for women. She founded the Mexican Alliance for Women (Alianza de Mujeres de México) in 1953 and served as president of the Revolutionary Federation of Women. She also helped create several national organizations devoted to education, the protection of children, theater, and women's rights.

Castillo Ledón represented her government at numerous world conferences, in various international organizations, and as ambassador to several foreign governments between 1945 and 1970. She was adviser to the Mexican delegation at the San Francisco Conference in 1945, and the only Mexican woman representative at the **Chapultepec Conference** in 1945. After joining the Foreign Service in 1953, Castillo Ledón served as ambassador to Finland, Sweden, and Austria, as well as ambassador and head of the International Atomic Energy Organization (1964–1970). She was also active in the Inter-American Commission on Women, serving as Mexican delegate (1934–1944), vice president (1944–1949), and president (1949–1953). She became the first woman to address the Mexican Senate on women's suffrage and the first woman to be appointed to a subsecretary position in the Mexican cabinet (1958–1964).

SUGGESTED READING

Roderic Ai Camp, "Amalia Castillo Ledón," in Barbara A. Tenenbaum, ed., *Encyclopedia of Latin American History and Culture*, vol. 2 (New York: Scribners, 1996); Camp, *Mexican Political Biographies, 1935–1993*, 3d ed. (Austin: University of Texas Press, 1995); Ward M. Morton, *Woman Suffrage in Mexico* (Gainesville: University of Florida Press, 1962).

Castro, Fidel (1927–) ☀ Cuban revolutionary and president. After spending 15 months in prison for his role in the failed attack on the Moncada army barracks in Santiago, Cuba, to spark an uprising to topple the dictator Fulgencio Batista, Fidel Castro left for Mexico on July 7, 1955, where he joined other Cubans in exile. Mexico City was a popular place for leftists, anti-imperialists, and reformers from all parts of Latin America, and thousands of exiles fleeing European fascism provided the city with a highly politicized ambience. It was a cosmopolitan capital known for its radical artists—**Diego Rivera**, **José Clemente Orozco**, **Frida Kahlo**, **David Alfaro Siqueiros**, and others—who attracted an assortment of international spies, exiles, writers, and vagabonds. After the postrevolutionary consolidation of power by its ruling party, Mexico's **foreign policy** stood out for its opposition to Washington's support for dictators and its penchant for Cold War **interventionism**. It was the perfect environment to stage a revolution (although the logistics of getting trained revolutionaries from Mexico to Cuba by boat never bothered Castro) that would alter Cuba's historic dependence on the United States.

Castro's purpose in going to Mexico was to organize and train a rebel army that would return to Cuba to carry out a campaign of guerrilla warfare in the Sierra Maestra mountains, defeat the Cuban armed forces, remove the tyrant Batista, and proclaim a revolutionary government to replace the corrupt, venal, and unpopular dictatorship. In Mexico City Castro found veterans of the Moncada attack and others willing to sponsor his revolution, including Ernesto "Che" Guevara, a medical graduate of the University of Buenos Aires who had just left Guatemala after the CIA-backed overthrow of Jacobo Arbenz in 1954. The training in guerrilla warfare was facilitated by Colonel Alberto Bayo, a Cuban with international experience in the use of guerrilla tactics to fight fascist dictatorships. Using a farm called Santa Rosa on the outskirts of Mexico City, Colonel Bayo taught the young Cubans how to fire pistols, rifles, and machine guns; how to craft bombs for destroying enemy tanks; and how to maintain discipline and engage in jungle survival. The training lasted nine months but was interrupted by several arrests made by the Mexican police on charges of violating immigration laws by conspiring to overthrow a foreign government and of illegally possessing weapons. After spending several weeks in prison, Castro was released with the agreement that he and his comrades would leave Mexico.

Over the next several months Castro focused on raising money to bribe the Mexican police to keep their distance and to obtain a yacht to carry his band of revolutionaries to eastern Cuba to spark the revolution. After some searching, he found a 58-foot motorboat—the *Granma*—that he purchased from an American physician. The revolutionaries—crammed into a boat designed to carry eight passengers and crew—left Tuxpan on the Gulf of Mexico in the early morning of November 25, 1956, but their arrival was delayed by rough seas and a faulty engine. The landing was in fact a shipwreck in which their food, heavy weapons, and radio transmitter were lost before a battle was fought. Castro's invasion from Mexico was another setback in his effort to foment an insurrection: the plan to spark an uprising with the arrival of his one-yacht navy and revolts in several cities failed, leaving the revolutionaries no choice but to head for the sanctuary of the Sierra Maestra. Of the 82 men who left Mexico in late November 1956, only 12 escaped Batista's military and made it to the top of the mountain where Castro planned to continue *la lucha* (the struggle).

The short time Fidel Castro spent in Mexico was critical for those dedicated to the demise of the Cuban dictatorship: the training in guerrilla warfare proved invaluable as Castro's charisma became more apparent, and the formation of a revolutionary cadre (the 26 July Movement, or M-26-7) began to take shape. In slightly more than two years Batista had been defeated and the United States faced another Latin American revolution close to its southern border. After his victory Castro claimed that the **Mexican Revolution** served as his guide during the struggle to remove the tyrant Batista—one of the most significant events in 20th-century Latin America. The yacht *Granma* that was purchased in Mexico was eventually restored to its original condition and preserved in a glass building in Havana where the Museum of the Revolution is located. *See also* Cuba and Mexico; Gutiérrez Barrios, Fernando.

SUGGESTED READING

Jon Lee Anderson, *Che Guevara: A Revolutionary Life* (New York: Grove, 1997); Peter G. Bourne, *Fidel: A Biography of Fidel Castro* (New York: Dodd, Mead, 1986); Thomas G. Paterson, *Contesting Castro: The United States and the Triumph of the Cuban Revolution* (New York: Oxford University Press, 1994); Tad Szulc, *Fidel: A Critical Portrait* (New York: William Morrow, 1986); Hugh Thomas, *The Cuban Revolution* (San Francisco: Harper & Row, 1977).

Catholic Church. *See* Church and State.

Cervecería. *See* Beer Industry.

Chamizal **Conflict** ☀ The story of *el chamizal* ("the thicket") rests on conflicting claims to sovereignty over a tract of land located between El Paso, Texas, and Ciudad Juárez, Chihuahua, that lasted from 1864 until an agreement was reached in 1963. The meandering course of the Río Grande caused a parcel of land, originally on the Mexican side of the river, to shift to the U.S. side, changing the international boundary between the two countries. As the river changed course over the years and more people lived and worked in the affected area, numerous attempts at bilateral negotiations were carried out, but nothing was done to completely resolve the conflict until the 1960s.

Despite Mexico's concerns (first raised in 1867) and a formal claim in 1895, it was not until 1910 that the two governments agreed to arbitrate the dispute through the International Boundary Commission. After lengthy hearings, the commission awarded to Mexico an estimated two-thirds of the area south of the 1864 channel. Washington rejected the arbitral tribunal's settlement but offered to resolve the remaining differences through diplomatic channels. Due to the **Mexican Revolution**, future discussions were delayed until 1925. The *chamizal* dispute impaired the settlement of numerous bilateral issues and affected every U.S. president from 1925 until 1962, when President Kennedy and others in his administration decided to settle the dispute on the basis of the 1911 decision, ultimately leading to a final settlement. The length of time it took to iron out the conflicting claims over a small patch of land damaged U.S.–Mexican relations and undermined cooperative measures on other matters of importance to the two countries in the border region. By the time the treaty (Chamizal Convention of 1963) was signed and ratified by both countries in 1963–1964, the *chamizal* dispute had occupied the attention of government officials in the United States and Mexico for almost a century. The final agreement was helpful in removing a source of anti-American propaganda and served to mitigate fears about Washington's interest in acquiring more Mexican territory. *See also* U.S.–Mexican Border/Boundary.

SUGGESTED READING

Alan C. Lamborn and Stephen P. Mumme, *Statecraft, Domestic Politics, and Foreign Policy Making: The El Chamizal Dispute* (Boulder, Colo.: Westview, 1988); Sheldon B. Liss, *A Century of Disagreement: The Chamizal Conflict, 1864–1964* (Washington, D.C.: University Press of Washington, D.C., 1965); Liss, "Chamizal Conflict," in Barbara A. Tenenbaum, ed., *Encyclopedia of Latin American History and Culture*, vol. 2 (New York: Scribners, 1996); Jerry E. Mueller, *Restless River: International Law and the Rio Grande* (El Paso: Texas Western Press, 1975); Robert M. Utley, *The International Boundary: United States and Mexico: A History of Frontier Dispute and Cooperation, 1848–1963* (Santa Fe, N. Mex.: Department of the Interior, National Park Service, 1964); Larman C. Wilson, "The Settlement of Boundary Disputes: Mexico, the United States, and the International Boundary Commission," *International and Comparative Law Quarterly* (January 1980).

Chapultepec Conference (1945) ☀ International conference attended by the United States and 19 Latin American states (Argentina did not attend because it had not declared war on the Axis powers) from February 21 to March 8, 1945, at the Chapultepec Castle in Mexico City. Known as the Chapultepec Conference because of its location, its major purpose was to increase cooperation in order to hasten the end of **World War II** and to build a united inter-American front at the forthcoming United Nations Conference at San Francisco. Worried that the inter-American system was in danger of being dismantled or diminished in importance, the Chapultepec Conference adopted several resolutions aimed at the reorganization, consolidation, and strengthening of regional arrangements that had developed over the previous five and a half decades. One of the formal declarations at the conference was the Act of Chapultepec providing for a collective response against any aggressor from outside or inside the region. It expanded the Monroe Doctrine from a unilateral guarantee against intervention into a mutual security system, included provisions that would prohibit aggression by one American state against another, and called for negotiation of a treaty of reciprocal assistance, foreshadowing the creation of the Rio Treaty in 1947. Other resolutions included the Declaration of Mexico, reaffirming important inter-American principles and the need to consider problems of peaceful settlement of disputes, human rights, and postwar economic and social problems. Between the end of this conference in 1945 and 1948, two other conferences were held that approved the three major documents authorized at Chapultepec, the Rio Treaty (1947), the Charter of the Organization of American States (1948), and the American Treaty on Pacific Settlement (1948). The Chapultepec Conference showcased some of Mexico's diplomatic personnel and helped the nation develop a reputation as a key player in hemispheric affairs during the Cold War. *See also* Foreign Policy.

SUGGESTED READING

G. Pope Atkins, *Encyclopedia of the Inter-American System* (Westport, Conn.: Greenwood, 1997); David W. Dent, *The Legacy of the Monroe Doctrine: A Reference Guide to U.S. Involvement in Latin America and the Caribbean* (Westport, Conn: Greenwood, 1999).

Charros ☀ The tradition of horsemanship in Mexico can be traced to the early successes of the Spanish conquistadors in their campaign to conquer Mexico on behalf of Spain. The horse played a major role in overwhelming the Indian societies found in the New World. The first *charros* were members of the Spanish aristocracy, but the sport eventually spread to other social classes. Recognizing the advantages that horses gave them, the Spanish quickly decreed that Indians could not own, ride, or use horses in any way, a law that was rigorously enforced during the first century of the 300-year colonial period. The interest in horsemanship gradually developed into a virtual cult in which men developed a form of dress, lifestyle, and sport called *charrería,* the art and tradition of the *charro* or *charra.* Known for their unique style of riding and colorful outfits, *charros* influenced North America's first cowboys (known as *vaqueros*). They became famous during the **Mexican Revolution** because they made up a large part of the various rebel forces, particularly in northern Mexico. For example, **Pancho Villa** and **Emiliano Zapata** were accomplished *charros* who fought in the revolution.

Since the early 1920s hundreds of amateur *charro* clubs have been formed throughout Mexico and the United States. Today *charros* are mostly urban dwellers, unlike the earlier horsemen who remained in the countryside. Mexican *charro* clubs compete against each other in events called *charreadas* that resemble U.S. rodeos, except that in Mexico the skills of the *charro* are judged according to teams rather than individual riders. The popularity of *charrería* continues to grow, as evidenced by the thousands who watched concerts, rodeos, and parades at the First World Congress of Mariachi and Charrería held in Mexico City in March 2000.

Raúl Salinas de Gortari in *charro* outfit. Credit: *Proceso,* photo by Germán Canseco.

As **labor** leaders developed into corrupt strongmen in the 1940s and 1950s, the term *charro* came to be associated with union bosses linked to the ruling party, particularly the powerful unions made up of petroleum workers, miners and metal workers, and railroad workers. When **Fidel Velázquez**, head of the powerful **Confederación de Trabajadores de México (CTM)**, imposed the leadership of Jesús Díaz de León (whose nickname was "El Charro" because of his penchant for fancy *charro* clothes) on the militant National Railway Workers Union in 1948, the term *charrismo* was born and quickly spread throughout the labor movement. Now a Mexican code word, *charrismo* captures the violence, **corruption**, anticommunism, and antidemocracy that some argue typifies state-sponsored union leadership.

SUGGESTED READING

José Álvarez del Villar, *Men and Horses in Mexico: History and Practice of "Charrería,"* trans. Margaret Fischer de Nicolin (Mexico, D.F.: Ediciones Lara, 1979); Kathleen Mullen Sands, *Charrería Mexicana: An Equestrian Folk Tradition* (Tucson: University of Arizona Press, 1993); James Norman Schmidt, *Charro: Mexican Horsemen* (New York: Putnam, 1969); Richard W. Slatta, *Cowboys of the Americas* (New Haven: Yale University Press, 1990); John Wilcock and Kal Müller, eds., *Insight Guide: Mexico* (London: APA Publications, 1996).

Chávez, Carlos (1899–1978) ☀ Mexico's most distinguished composer, conductor, and music educator. Known for his classical compositions inspired by the country's Indian heritage, Chavez's compositions were also influenced by the folk music of Manuel Ponce, the **Mexican Revolution**, and an indigenous heritage from his maternal grandfather. Chávez and fellow composer Silvestre Revueltas fused native music and styles with European art music to produce a nationalistic music with international appeal.

After studying in Europe and the United States, Chávez returned to Mexico to begin a brilliant career as a conductor, pianist, and composer. While in New York in the early 1920s he had been influenced by American composers such as Aaron Copland and others, whose music he introduced in Mexico after he returned in 1928. While director of the National Conservatory of Music, he wrote *Sinfonía India* (Indian symphony, 1935) and *Xochipili-Macuilxochitl* (1940), both an attempted reconstruction of pre-Columbian music using Aztec instruments. Like the famous muralists of the 1920s and 1930s, Chávez wanted to influence the Mexican people with themes of cultural nationalism. In a didactic fashion, he composed

Carlos Chávez. Credit: General Secretariat of the Organization of American States.

two important works—*Llamadas* (1934) and *Obertura Mexicana* (1935)—that emphasized familiar Mexican songs. Chávez and his generation helped create a distinctive cultural identity for Mexico, often playing the same role for music as did the revolutionary muralists for pictorial art and the many others for literature. One of his first large-scale works, *El fuego nuevo* (The new fire, 1921), based on an ancient Aztec ritual, included numerous indigenous percussion instruments. It established his nationalistic image and confirmed his skills of bringing contemporary styles and techniques to pre-Hispanic themes.

Born in 1899 in Calzada de Catube near Mexico City, he started his music studies there and later studied piano with Pedro Luis Ogazón and harmony with Juan B. Fuentes and Manuel Ponce. With the presidency of Álvaro Obregón beginning in 1921, Chávez acquired access to the upper ranks of Mexican culture and politics, which allowed him to use these valuable connections to bring culture to the masses. Between 1923 and 1924 he made his first trip to New York City, where he found an audience responsive to his musical skills. By the late 1920s the quality of orchestral organizations and professional musicians in Mexico had reached deplorable levels. To remedy the situation, concerned musicians invited Chávez to reform the orchestra and modernize Mexican music. With improved funding from the government and private sources, Chávez founded the Symphony Orchestra of Mexico in 1928, served as its conductor for 21 years, and eventually turned it into a first-class national institution. From 1928 to 1934, he served as director of the National Conservatory in Mexico. As general director of the Instituto Nacional de Bellas Artes (1946–1952), he served the administration of President **Miguel Alemán** by encouraging the importance of quality music through his bold programming, compositions, and newspaper articles. During this time he composed numerous ballets, operas, and symphonies and trained some of Mexico's most active contemporary composers, such as Silvestre Revueltas and Blas Galindo.

As the Mexican music world lost interest in nationalistic themes, Chávez turned to neoclassicism and contemporary music during the last two decades of his career. After 1936 he spent more time in the United States, conducting performances of his best-known works with most of the major orchestras of the time. During his musical career, Chávez was more than just a productive composer and an esteemed music teacher; he also helped stimulate a higher level of understanding and appreciation of music in Mexico, emphasized the importance of indigenous culture, and contributed to a meaningful dialogue among musicians throughout the Americas. He continued to produce important symphonic works, piano pieces, and ballets until his death in Mexico City in 1978. *See also Indigenismo.*

SUGGESTED READING

Miguel Ficher, Martha Furman Schleifer, and John M. Furman, eds., *Latin American Classical Composers: A Biographical Dictionary* (Lanham, Md.: Scarecrow, 1996); Donal Henahan, "Carlos Chavez, 79, Composer, Is Dead," *New York Times,* August 4, 1978; Carol A. Hess, "Chávez y Ramírez, Carlos Antonio de Padua," in Michael S. Werner, ed., *Encyclopedia of Mexico: History, Society, and Culture,* vol. 1 (Chicago: Fitzroy Dearborn, 1997); Robert L. Parker, "Carlos Chávez," in Barbara A. Tenenbaum, ed., *Encyclopedia of Latin American History and Culture,* vol. 2 (New York: Scribners, 1996); Parker, *Carlos Chávez: Mexico's Modern-Day Orpheus* (Boston: Twayne, 1983); Robert Stevenson, *Music in Mexico: A Historical Survey* (New York: Crowell, 1952).

Chiapas. *See* Geographical Regions; Guerrilla Movements and Counterinsurgency; Zapatista Rebellion in Chiapas.

Chiapas Rebellion. *See* Zapatista Rebellion in Chiapas.

Chicanos ☀ Among the various Hispanic sub-groups—Mexican, Cuban, Puerto Rican, and others from Latin America and the Caribbean—living in the United States (whether U.S. citizens or not), Mexican Americans, or Chicanos, represent the largest of the Spanish-speaking minority population. An estimated 38 million people of Hispanic origin live in the United States, roughly 13 percent of the population; demographers predict that Hispanics will surpass blacks as the largest minority population in 2003. As of 2000, 64 percent of the Hispanic population in the United States was of Mexican origin, 11 percent Puerto Rican, and 5 percent Cuban. Over 60 percent of U.S. Hispanics are concentrated in 10 cities: Los Angeles, New York, Miami, San Francisco, Chicago, Houston, San Antonio, Dallas, San Diego, and McAllen, Texas. Although there are different terms for Mexican Americans depending on the borderland region—Latinos in California and Hispanos in New Mexico, for example—Chicano is the more inclusive word used for all those of Mexican descent.

The United States is the fifth-largest Spanish-speaking nation in the world, and the growing impact of Mexican culture in the United States can be observed in Spanish news periodicals, radio and television stations, and Mexican food and drink (tacos, enchiladas, tortillas, cervezas, and margaritas), **music** (salsa, ranchera, and norteño), language, baseball players (**Fernando Valenzuela**, Vinny Castilla), and films (*Como agua para chocolate*, [Like water for chocolate] and *Amores Perros*, [Life's a bitch]) from south of the border. Many of Mexico's best students—including those who have become president of Mexico in the past 30 years—attend prestigious U.S. graduate schools like Harvard, Yale, and Stanford. The Autonomous University of Guadalajara has more U.S. citizens studying to be doctors than does any medical school in the United States. More than half the kindergarten pupils in Los Angeles County are Chicanos and are exposed to a Chicano-relevant curriculum.

Recognition of the Mexican American vote has been increasing with each presidential election since the 1960s. Beginning with the election of President Ronald Reagan in 1980, Republicans have attracted Chicanos away from the Democrats by traveling to Mexico, arranging campaign stops in barrio neighborhoods with Mexican food and mariachi music, using Spanish-language television to broadcast campaign commercials, and pitching their campaign rhetoric in Spanish (usually limited and not very good) on issues of importance to Chicano voters in states with large numbers of Spanish-speaking citizens and electoral votes. Of the 435 members of the U.S. House of Representatives in 2000, only 20 were Hispanic, including Lucille Roybal-Allard, the nation's first Mexican American congresswoman, elected to represent California's 33rd Congressional District in 1992. In California, where 1.6 million Hispanics are registered to vote, 2000 presidential candidates George W. Bush and Al Gore both realized that attracting the Latino voter was the key to victory in the nation's most populous state.

Although some Chicanos trace their heritage to early encounters between the Spanish invaders and the indigenous populations of what would eventually become the American Southwest, most borderland Mexican Americans live in a microsociety created by international conflicts (the **Mexican American War** of 1846–1848, World War I, and **World War II**), railroad building, flight from the **Mexican Revolution** (1910–1917), and waves of migration to the United States in search of employment and a better life. While many Mexican Americans have been successful living in the United States, they have had to confront powerful political and economic forces controlled by Anglos. Caught between two worlds, Mexican Americans—despite gains in civil rights in the United States—still represent a marginalized population in the modern period. In Colorado, for example, Hispanics are four times more likely to be incarcerated for crimes than Anglos, according to a 1998 study of the criminal justice system. The **communications media** pay little attention to the Hispanic community in the United States, unless there is a story of tragedy involving undocumented Mexicans, drug gangs, and violence, or a national holiday or cultural event (**Cinco de Mayo, Day of the Dead**) that is celebrated on both sides of the border—but often poorly understood in the north.

Tired of repeated clashes with Anglos over property rights, religious freedom, and personal liberty, Chicanos launched a period of struggle in the 1960s and 1970s to achieve their own political, economic, and civil rights. Political organization and activism combined with strikes and protests that took place in Texas, California, and New Mexico. The Chicano movement emphasized self-determination, cultural pride in its heritage, and a crusade for justice. Militant Chicanos joined the Brown Berets in 1967, which eventually had chapters in 27 cities across the United States. Chicano movement leaders such as César Chávez, José Angel Gutiérrez, and Reies López Tijerina became popular heroes among Mexican Americans. Whether in politics or economics (U.S. Hispanic consumers spend hundreds of billions annually in the U.S. market), the growing Hispanic population will be a significant part of U.S. society in the 21st century, despite its minority status. *See also* Immigration; U.S.–Mexican Border/Boundary; *Pachcos*; *Pochos*.

SUGGESTED READING

Anuario Hispano-Hispanic Yearbook, 13th ed. (TIYM Publishing, 1999); Arlene Dávila, *Latinos Inc.: The Marketing and Making of a People* (Berkeley: University of California Press, 2001); Mario T. García, *Mexican Americans: Leadership, Ideology, and Identity, 1930–1960* (New Haven: Yale University Press, 1989); Rodolfo O. de la Garza and Harry Pachon, eds., *Latinos and U.S. Relations with Latin America* (Lanham, Md.: Rowman & Littlefield, 2000); Douglas Monroy, *Thrown among Strangers: The Making of Mexican Culture in Frontier California* (Berkeley: University of California Press, 1990); Carlos Monsiváis, "The Culture of the Frontier: The Mexican Side," in Stanley R. Ross, ed., *Views across the Border: The United States and Mexico* (Albuquerque: University of New Mexico Press, 1978); Robert Brent Toplin, ed., *Hollywood as Mirror: Changing Views of "Outsiders" and "Enemies" in American Movies* (Westport, Conn.: Greenwood, 1993).

Chihuahua. See Geographical Regions.

Church and State ☀ The Catholic faith plays an important role in Mexican society; it provides a foundation for many of its traditions and serves as a symbol of Mexican national identity. While Mexicans enjoy freedom of religion, approximately 75 percent are nominally Catholics. They have a high regard for clergy and the church as a social institution. According to political scientist Roderic Ai Camp, one of the reasons for studying Mexico is its rather unique church–state relationship, one that emerged from the anticlerical provisions of the 1917 Constitution into a modus vivendi, and finally a more cordial relationship by the end of the 20th century. The tremendous influence exercised by the Catholic Church during the long colonial period was radically altered with the restrictive provisions written into the **Constitution of 1917**. Those who wrote the document were determined to define clearly the separation of church from the state. In five major articles (3, 5, 24, 27, and 130) the new constitution denied the Catholic Church any legal standing, guaranteed that public education would be secular and humanistic, and forbade the clergy from participating in political life and from owning property.

Once these strict constitutional provisions were enforced by President Plutarco Elías Calles in the 1920s, the Church took the offensive, leading to a religious war (the Cristero rebellion) that lasted from 1925 to 1929. As a way of achieving a truce, the government relaxed its anticlerical restrictions. For the next three decades the Church was allowed to carry out its spiritual and pastoral activities in exchange for its remaining publicly silent about political and social issues. This modus vivendi began to dissolve in the 1980s as the church hierarchy became associated with the antigovernment opposition and more involved with the increasingly militant social movements in the north and among impoverished sectors in Chiapas and Oaxaca. After Vatican II and the meeting of Latin American bishops in Medellín, Colombia, in 1968, the Catholic Church expanded its activities in social and economic affairs, increased the role of the laity, and focused more on what the church called the "material condition of man."

With the declining legitimacy of the Mexican state and the ruling party after 1980, religious leaders began to maneuver for the restoration of the Church's legal place in Mexican society and diplomatic relations with the Vatican, or Holy See. During the presidency of **Carlos Salinas de Gortari**, the PRI decided to modernize church–state relations by appointing a personal representative to the Vatican. From the start of his administration in late 1988, President Salinas showed his determination to put an end to the situation that had been in effect for 50 years; by late 1991 he had sent to Congress initiatives for constitutional reforms to dramatically alter the existing church–state relationship. The Salinas proposals were bolstered by the 1990 visit of Pope John Paul II, a popular figure who was treated favorably by the media during his stay in Mexico.

Despite opposition from within the ruling party, the intellectual community, and non-Catholic churches, the reforms were quickly approved in 1992. These modifications included the legal existence of religious associations and the right of clergy of all faiths to vote (although many actually did before 1992), the right to provide religious instruction in private schools, the right of religious associations to own property, and the right to organize cultural demonstrations outside of churches. In September 1992 diplomatic relations were established between Mexico and the Vatican, and in 1993 the pope visited Mexico again, but for the first time in an official capacity. Nevertheless, some restrictions remained attached to the Constitution, leading to a serious confrontation a few years later over the topic of ecclesiastical participation in the political life of the nation.

The Church's role as an interest group is limited by antichurch rhetoric that permeates the education of each child in Mexico and the fact that the Church does not speak with a single voice on social and economic matters. Priests and bishops who represent rural, indigenous interests in poverty-stricken regions such as Chiapas and Oaxaca have taken a firm stand against electoral fraud, the Mexican military's harsh treatment of the indigenous community, and the absence of government resources in these impoverished areas. For example, before his retirement in 1999, Bishop **Samuel Ruiz** in Chiapas took a firm position in defense of the Indians, engendering both criticism and support within episcopal ranks. On the other hand, ideologically right-wing bishops in the north oppose the stand on local and indigenous matters by left-wing priests like Bishop Ruiz. Although church–state relations are generally good, the conflict in Chiapas and other regions has brought the Church into a serious conflict between indigenous peasants, **mestizo** ranchers, the government, the army, and various paramilitary groups. The Salinas reforms helped make the Church a more influential actor in Mexican politics, serving at times as a legitimate institution for the expression of the general public's frustrations with the government's policy failures, particularly in the realm of employment, crime, **corruption**, economic austerity measures, and **human rights** abuses. With increasing democratization over the past two decades, Protestantism has made significant advances in Mexican society, creating new challenges to the church–state dynamic. President **Vicente Fox** has altered the traditional role of the Mexican president by going to Mass and using the image of the **Virgin of Guadalupe** as a symbol of political strength.

SUGGESTED READING

Tom Barry, *Mexico: A Country Guide* (Albuquerque: Inter-Hemispheric Education Resource Center, 1992); Roberto Blancarte, *Historia de la iglesia católica en México, 1939–1987* (Mexico, D.F.: Fondo de Cultura Económica, 1992); Roderic Ai Camp, *Crossing Swords: Politics and Religion in Mexico* (New York: Oxford University Press, 1997); Camp, "Mexico," in Paul E. Sigmund, ed., *Religious Freedom and Evangelization in Latin America* (New York: Maryknoll, 2001); Camp, *Politics in Mexico: The Decline of Authoritarianism*, 3d ed. (New York: Oxford University Press, 1999); Guillermo Gakt Corona, *Ley y religión en México* (Guadalajara: Iteso, 1995).

Cinco de Mayo ☀ One of the important national observances on Mexico's civic calendar is May 5 (Cinco de Mayo), commemorating the defeat of French forces at the Battle of Puebla in 1862. The French **intervention** in Mexico was a bizarre and tragic affair—fraught with repression, violence, and guerrilla resistance—that served to elevate Mexican nationalism, opened the door to large-scale foreign investment, and ultimately helped legitimize the dictatorship of Porfirio Díaz (1876–1911). The French invasion and occupation of Mexico—originally sanctioned by Spain and Great Britain on the grounds that their nationals had just claims from economic damages arising out of the violence and chaos in Mexico at the time—was the most spectacular and dangerous challenge to the Monroe Doctrine yet encountered by the United States. However, the U.S. Civil War prevented the United States from intervening in Mexico to help drive out Emperor Napoleon III's forces.

The French forces came ashore at Veracruz with intentions of seizing Mexico City. In an ill-planned attack on the city of Puebla, 4,500 poorly armed Mexican soldiers defeated the 6,500 French invaders, who were attempting to install Archduke Maximilian as head of France's empire in Mexico. The victory was a stunning defeat for the French and a glorious victory for the Mexican defenders, and the Mexican military leaders who devised the winning battle plan became national heroes. The daring resistance by the Mexican commanders, in which some 460 French soldiers perished, soon became known as the Battle of Puebla, and Cinco de Mayo was born as a permanent national holiday.

The Mexican victory at the Battle of Puebla helped erase the humiliating memory of the 1848 defeat by the United States in the **Mexican American War** and became an important symbol of national pride and a new Mexican nationalism. It became the anniversary of a great event, woven into the national conscience through textbooks and parades. As one of the winning generals at the Battle of Puebla, Porfirio Díaz tried to legitimize his presidency by wearing his uniform and organizing military processions on the Cinco de Mayo. Every year on May 5, President Díaz took advantage of the popularity of elaborate processions—made up of bureaucrats and military personnel—to march through Mexico City in separate processions to lay wreaths upon the grave of Ignacio Zaragoza, the triumphant general at Puebla in 1862. Within a year the French returned in force, defeated the Mexicans at Puebla, and then marched to Mexico City for the final victory. During Maximilian's empire (1864–1867), Mexicans countered French parades and celebrations with their own civic demonstrations of the Battle of Puebla, beginning with Cinco de Mayo events in Puebla and Mexico City in 1865.

Cinco de Mayo, the defeat of the French in 1862, is still celebrated in Mexico, and is gaining popularity in the United States. In Mexico, the famous military victory is reenacted every year through sober celebrations and political pronouncements. Mexico's Cinco de Mayo features rifle- and machete-toting Mexican "soldiers" in broad-rimmed straw hats, firing at French "invaders" wearing elaborate red-and-blue uniforms. In the United States, Cinco de Mayo is heavily promoted by the **beer industry** and the makers of salsa, margaritas, and **tequila** as a Latino version of St. Patrick's Day, a time to party with lots of drinking and dancing. Over the past 40 years, the Cinco de Mayo holiday has evolved into a major cultural event for **Chicanos** in the United States determined to preserve their culture and language in dominant Anglo society.

SUGGESTED READING

June Behrens, *Fiesta: Cinco de Mayo* (Chicago: Children's Press, 1978); María Cristina Urrutia, *Cinco de Mayo: Yesterday and Today* (Toronto: Douglas & McIntyre, 1999).

Cinema ☀ Mexico's film industry is a fascinating and important part of its 20th-century history. It is the product of talented actors, directors, cinematographers, and technicians, many of whom mastered their skills in Hollywood; government intervention designed to foster certain ideological and cultural themes in the industry; and the vicissitudes of U.S. **foreign policy**, particularly from the Good Neighbor period through **World War II**. Most of the early film productions were documentaries or travelogues, including epic stories of the **Mexican Revolution**. During the Mexican Revolution (1911–1917) **Pancho Villa** signed an exclusive contract with the Mutual Film Corporation, letting them film his guerrilla battles in the north, many of them staged and reenacted to maximize their visual impact. Once sound

motion pictures arrived in the 1930s, the film industry expanded dramatically with the creation of a star system (**María Félix, Dolores del Río, Pedro Armendáriz**, and others), film studios (Compañia Nacional Productora de Películas; Cinematográfica Latinoamericana S.A., CLASA), and movies with a variety of genres (family melodramas, historical epics, slapstick comedies, love stories, brothel-*cabareteras*, and others), each associated with noted directors.

Between 1935 and 1955, Mexican cinema became the world's dominant Spanish-language film industry, and these years are often called the golden age because of the quality and scope of its international impact. Although the rapid expansion of Mexican filmmaking sometimes appeared to threaten Hollywood's cultural and commercial hegemony, Mexican cinema never became completely autonomous, or radical, in the movies that it produced. It was a period of close collaboration between the Mexican government and the film industry, and at times mass media collaboration with the goals of U.S. foreign policy. The golden age was known for the development of a special generation of directors and cinematographers— **Emilio "El Indio" Fernández, Alejandro Galindo, Gabriel Figueroa**, and others—whose films were entertaining, popular, and often intelligent stories that could be enjoyed and appreciated by all family members. Their films were devoid of nudity or objectionable language and had minimum levels of violence.

The nationalistic orientation of Mexican cinema under President **Lázaro Cárdenas** (1934–1940) eventually gave way to closer collaboration with Hollywood studios and producers, but this contributed to more dependency on Hollywood's marketing-led production model of filmmaking. These vulnerabilities were compounded by World War II and U.S.–Mexican collaboration (often covert) on economic, military, and cultural matters. A number of prowar, antifascist propaganda films—*Soy puro mexicano* (1942), *Espionaje en el golfo* (1942), and *De Nueva York a Huipanguillo* (1943)—grew out of **Nelson Rockefeller's** government agency, the **Office of the Coordinator of Inter-American Affairs (OCIAA),** which organized Hollywood assistance in order to expand Mexican production. The war years also witnessed the production of some of the classic films of golden age cinema, including **Cantinflas**'s first big hit, *Ahí está el detalle* (1940); *Ay, Jalisco no te rajes!* (1941), starring **Jorge Negrete** and Gloria Marín; and the Fernández-Figueroa award-winning classic, *María Candelaria* (1943), featuring Dolores del Río and Pedro Armendáriz. The impressive performance of Río helped attract international talent to Mexico, boosted her image as the grande dame of Mexican cinema, and served as a catalyst for new types of films. At the same time urban settings became more prominent as the locus of national myth-making with the genre of film-making called *cabaretera*, featuring nightclub musical performances and stories of gangsters, prostitutes, and slum dwellers (made popular by film director Alejandro Galindo).

With the arrival in Mexico City of the Spanish expatriate filmmaker **Luis Buñuel** in the 1940s, Mexican cinema began to experiment with the pathology of urban poverty, comedies starring Cantinflas and his competitor, Tin Tan (Germán Valdés), and **immigration** themes. For example, in the controversial *Espaldas mojadas* (1953), the harsh conditions along the **U.S.–Mexican border** are portrayed vividly in order to discourage undocumented immigration to the United States. The iconoclastic Buñuel made *Los Olivadados* in 1950, a controversial film depicting the underside of Mexico City's contemporary development, which set the tone for some of his other movies made in Mexico during the 1950s and early 1960s. Many Mexicans criticized Buñuel's films because he was considered a Spaniard "visiting" Mexico, and his films that showed the underside of Mexico were hardly appreciated.

Despite the popularity of Buñuel and other filmmakers outside of Mexico, the postwar film industry experienced a decline because of competition with Hollywood, reduction in U.S. aid, new government regulations and censorship, artistic conservatism that restricted innovation, **labor** conflict, and oligopolistic exhibition and production practices. The postwar decline also contributed to the international migration pattern of some of Mexico's best film artists. For example, Pedro Armendáriz crossed over to Hollywood movies, María Félix left to make films in Europe, and Cantinflas applied his talent in Mike Todd's award-winning U.S. production *Around the World in Eighty Days* (1956). As the film industry declined in quality and profitability during the 1950s, the government stepped in to take over ailing studios in hopes of sparking a revival. However, the impact was inconsequential and the golden age of Mexican cinema came to an end, unable to compete with television and run by an industry stifled by inefficient state control over film production, neoliberal U.S. trade and communications policies of the Cold War, and the reactionary nature of Mexico's filmmakers. When Buñuel left for Europe in 1963, Mexican cinema suffered, but did not lose its international voice. Between 1958 and 1963, total Mexican film production dropped from 138 to 81, a sign that the glitter was gone from the golden era.

A new generation of filmmakers and critics emerged in the 1960s, determined to reverse the downward trend with a new cinema (Nuevo Cine), characterized by radically nationalist industrial practices, leftist ideological themes, and a new film culture. Influenced by the Cuban Revolution, the Nuevo Cine group was composed of mostly young, generally leftist critics, scholars, and aspirant filmmakers. Some of them became better known in subsequent years, including Salvador Elizondo, **Carlos Monsiváis**, Alberto Isaac, Jorge

Fons, Felipe Cazals, **Alfonso Arau,** and **Arturo Ripstein.** Often working with such literary luminaries as **Carlos Fuentes** and Gabriel García Márquez, the new cinema group achieved a degree of commercial success, but it was limited and mainly consisted of audiences of intellectuals, often non-Mexicans. The young filmmakers associated with the new cinema were bothered by the cultural influence of Hollywood and the **corruption** and inequities in Mexican society and anxious for a cinema that would deal realistically with Mexican life. Until the 1970s, the Mexican film industry was supported by the government and produced more than 100 movies per year, but since the 1980s economic setbacks have radically diminished government funds and the film industry has languished.

The travails of the Mexican film industry were addressed by the administration of **Luis Echeverría** (1970–1976), who tried to implement a radical change in government cinematic policies. In order to project a new image of Mexico in its film productions, he supported young and radical directors, appointed his brother to head the Banco Cinematográfico, and did not discourage controversial films such Cazals's *Canoa* (1975), a critique of the 1968 **Tlatelolco massacre;** Ripstein's *El castillo de la pureza* (1972); Arau's *Calzonzin inspector* (1973); and Galindo's *El juicio de Martín Cortés* (1973).

Closely responsive to the ebb and flow of Mexican politics, President **José López Portillo** reversed the film policies of his predecessor and named his sister head of the newly created Directorate of Radio, Television, and Cinema (DRTC), which encouraged the return of commercial production and more traditional films. The job of turning around the Mexican film industry in the 1980s was left to incoming President **Miguel de la Madrid** (1982–1988), a thankless task given the shape of the industry after the previous administration. He created the

Instituto Mexicano de Cinematografía (INCIME)— a state corporation—to make and promote quality films and appointed highly regarded filmmaker Alberto Isaac as its director. With Paul Leduc's *Frida* (1985), a moving story of the artist **Frida Kahlo** (wife of **Diego Rivera**), some degree of hope was restored to Mexican cinema. Isaac's efforts to restore the luster to the movie industry brought only limited success, however, as the popularity of Mexican television siphoned off talented actors and actresses who were growing disillusioned with the film industry.

The administrations of **Carlos Salinas** and **Ernesto Zedillo** ushered in an era of privatization as well-known film production companies were sold and privatized. Filmmakers also had to face serious political and economic uncertainties, particularly the **debt crisis** and peso devaluations, that raised doubts about adequate funding. The Council for Culture and the Arts was created in 1989, removing cinematic activity from the Dirección de Cinematografía, a unit that for decades operated under the Department of the Interior and was more concerned with security than art and culture.

The 1990s witnessed some revival in Mexican cinema with successful films coproduced with Spanish and American companies and with more women becoming filmmakers. In 1991 María Novaro directed *Danzón,* a popular Caribbean music-and-dance film with film star María Rojo. The most successful Mexican filmmaker in the 1990s was Alfonso Arau, a talented director who gained considerable fame in the international film market with *Como agua para chocolate* (Like water for chocolate, 1992), based on the **Laura Esquivel** novel of the same name. Arau, who had acted in some American films such as Sam Peckinpah's *The Wild Bunch,* turned to directing and soon made his way to Hollywood, where he made *A Walk in the Clouds* (1995) and *To Catch a Falling Star* and *Picking Up the Pieces,* both in 1999. The success of Mexican directors in Hollywood testifies to the continued vitality of Mexican cinema; however, it is also apparent that U.S.-made films on Mexican American themes have little to do with Mexican filmmaking.

The semiclandestine release of Luis Estrada's black comedy about Mexico's political machine, *Herod's Law* (*La ley de Herodes*, 1999), produced a scandal that helped revive interest in Mexican moviemaking. Driven by a younger generation of directors and producers with little allegiance to the state system, *Herod's Law* is the first film to offer a critical and comic portrayal of the **Partido Revolucionario Institucional**, calling the party by its name for the first time in a movie. Estrada's film takes place during the presidency of **Miguel Alemán**, but its present-day target is unmistakable: the PRI and its history of fraud, embezzlement, and ruthless treatment of all forms of opposition. *Herod's Law* (a reference to a governing principle that in more polite vernacular means "do it to them before they do it to you") weaves a tale of a small-town politician from the ruling party who becomes aware of the fact that corruption, extortion, and political murder can reap huge rewards. Film director Estrada says the film agency gave him complete freedom to make the film; however, after seeing the result, it tried unsuccessfully to talk him into delaying its release until after the July 2, 2000, presidential elections.

The new vitality in Mexican filmmaking is also attributable to Antonio Serrano's *Sexo, pudor y lágrimas* (Sex, shame, and tears), a movie released in 1999 that drew 5.4 million viewers and earned $12 million at the box office in six months, making it the most popular movie ever screened in Mexico, outgrossing Hollywood's *Star Wars: Episode I—The Phantom Menace*. In what some call a brilliant work for Mexican cinema, director Alejandro González Iñárritu captured the violence, passion, and grimy realism of Mexico City with *Amores perros* (Life's a bitch, 2000), a complex film that many feel will help jump-start the Mexican film industry.

Mexican cinema is now in a precarious situation, the result of domestic financial restraints and international competition, mostly from Hollywood. With Hollywood dominating Mexico's film market—limiting distribution opportunities for quality Mexican films—efforts to rebuild a film industry with a solid historical tradition and a bevy of talented film stars, filmmakers, and screen writers have been difficult. In a recent debate on the future of Mexican cinema and the influx of Hollywood films, Congresswoman María Rojo introduced a bill in the Mexican Congress in 1999 that would require theaters—which currently show mostly U.S. films—to set aside 30 percent of screen time for Mexican movies. The bill would also include a 5 percent tax on movie tickets to support a fund to rebuild the Mexican cinema industry—now ranking between 10th and 15th on the world export market. The current battle to revive the once glorious movie industry is the result of reduced government subsidies, and the dramatic influx of Hollywood exports to Mexicoreduced the number of Mexican films from 120 in 1988 to only six in 1998. The debate has introduced a number of forces to support or oppose the Rojo bill, including **Carlos Fuentes** (for), and free-market business types, movie distributors, television, and the Mexican theater industry (against). With deregulation, movie chains like Cinemex, a $60 million business started in the early 1990s, have poured money into Mexican multiplexes featuring digital sound, new seats, and cappuccino counters. Arguing that the Mexican cinema is a cultural treasure, many directors, producers, and actors want a policy of government support to continue showing films that reflect Mexican reality, not the distorted version that comes from Hollywood films. In other respects, the issue is not whether a national cinema should exist, but who will foot the bill and how much independence will exist from those who control the purse strings of the film industry.

The **Chicano** population in the United States has increased demand for films in Spanish or in English that reflect Latino society and culture. In an attempt to meet this demand, U.S.-based film companies such as Latin Universe, New Latin Picture, and Twentieth Century-Fox released a number of films aimed at the Latino audience in the United States. These 1999–2000 releases included *Santitos* (an offbeat romantic comedy), *Luminarias*, and *El Norte* (1983; to be rereleased). However, Mexican American directors such as Edward James Olmos and Gregory Nava seem to prefer films that deal with cultural repression, exploitation, and the consequences of crime and drugs and other topics that Mexican directors such as Alfonso Arau tend to avoid. There are some Mexican filmmakers who are now interested in a kind of "border" cinema emphasizing commercially successful themes of sex, violence, and drugs that reflect the experience of recent Mexican immigrants to the United States. Given the growing size and diversity of the Latino community in the United States, it is difficult to market Chicano films to Cubans, Puerto Ricans, Dominicans, and even Central Americans living in the United States. While the level of production and vitality that existed during Mexico's golden age may be gone forever, the cinematic changes taking place on both sides of the border suggest that Mexican and Latino-focused North American cinema have a promising, albeit challenging, future.

SUGGESTED READING

Seth Fein, "Motion Pictures, 1930–1960," in Michael S. Werner, ed., *Encyclopedia of Mexico: History, Society, and Culture*, vol. 2 (Chicago: Fitzroy Dearborn, 1997); George Hadley-García, *Hollywood hispano: Los latinos en el mundo del cine* (Secaucus, N.J.: Carol, 1991); Joanne Hershfield and David R. Maciel, *Mexico's Cinema: A Century of Film and Filmmakers* (Wilmington, Del.: Scholarly Resources, 1999); David R. Maciel, *El Norte: The U.S.–Mexican Border in Contemporary Cinema* (San Diego: Institute for Regional Study of the Californias, San Diego University, 1990); Randall M. Miller, ed., *The Kaleidoscopic Lens: How Hollywood Views Ethnic Groups* (Englewood Cliffs, N.J.: Jerome S. Ozer, 1980); Carl J. Mora, "Mexican Cinema: Decline, Renovation, and the Return of Commercialism, 1960–1980," in Michael T. Martin, ed., *New Latin American Cinema*, vol. 2, *Studies of National Cinemas* (Detroit: Wayne State University Press, 1997); Mora, *Mexican Cinema: Reflections on a Society, 1896–1980* (Berkeley: University of California Press, 1980); Lorenza Muñoz, "Demand for Latino Films Is Growing," *Atlanta Journal-Constitution*, November 7, 1999; Lorenza Muñoz and Mary Beth Sheridan, "Mexico's Government Becomes the Reluctant Star of the Show," *Los Angeles Times*, March 7, 2000; Julia Preston, "Mexican Film Rediscovers Its Voice," *New York Times*, December 16, 1999; Elissa J. Rashkin, *Women Filmmakers in Mexico: The Country of Which We Dream* (Austin: University of Texas Press, 2001); Mary Beth Sheridan, "Not Showing: Mexican Movies," *Denver Post*, November 16, 1998; Ann Marie Stock, ed., *Framing Latin American Cinema: Contemporary Political Perspectives* (Minneapolis: University of Minnesota Press, 1997); Robert Brent Toplin, ed., *Hollywood as Mirror: Changing Views of "Outsiders" and "Enemies" in American Movies* (Westport, Conn: Greenwood, 1993); Allen L. Woll, *The Latin Image in American Film* (Los Angeles: Latin American Center, University of California, 1977).

Civil–Military Relations ☀ When compared with other Latin American governments, Mexico's has been a bastion of political stability since the creation of the ruling party in 1929. Since the 1930s all of Mexico's presidents have completed their term of office and turned power over to their elected successor while avoiding the military takeovers so common elsewhere in the region. While there have been cycles of economic crises (debt repayment, peso devaluations, and bank defaults), assassinations of top leaders (civil and religious), disruptive strikes, and several guerrilla insurgencies since the 1960s, the regime has not collapsed and the military has remained in the barracks. The military's relationship to the government is different from that of other groups in Mexico in that it does not operate as a separate political actor. Instead, the Mexican military functions as part of the government and subordinates its interests to civilian authorities in exchange for public recognition and material rewards. How did this unique feature of Mexican government come about?

The success of the **Mexican Revolution** of 1910–1917 marked a turning point in civil–military relations and role of the armed forces. The **Constitution of 1917** assigned responsibility over the armed forces to the executive, and the revolutionary elite managed to dislodge the military from the core of political power. Career officers who exercised tremendous power for most of the 19th century were replaced by citizen soldiers who had taken up arms in the insurrection. From 1917 until 1946, all of the nation's presidents had started their political careers by serving in the revolutionary army. Nevertheless, there was a concerted effort by Mexican presidents in the 1920s and 1930s to reduce the army's political influence. When he created the corporate structure of Mexico's government in the 1930s, President **Lázaro Cárdenas** incorporated the military into the recently established government party, thus putting an end to the presidential succession conflicts that so frequently sparked military revolts. The last president with a military background was **Manuel Ávila Camacho** (1940–1946). The danger of military control over the party was reduced even further by the withdrawal of the military from the corporate structure in 1940.

By 1950, the armed forces had been disciplined, unified, and subordinated to civilian authority, thereby ushering in a stable pattern of civil–military relations. All of this was made possible through a semiauthoritarian form of government, a common ideological framework for pursing national goals, military representation within the ruling party, and a recognition that some of Mexico's security resulted from its geographical proximity to its superpower neighbor to the north. Today, the total armed forces number approximately 180,000 (active) with a 300,000-man reserve force. The army is the dominant service, outranking the navy and air force with a combined force of 135,000 men in uniform, more than double the number in the other two branches.

Through a variety of techniques, successive presidents reduced the military's influence in the political process. Until the 1990s, each successive government reduced the military's share of the national budget, averaging 2–3 percent per year. Military spending per capita in Mexico is now one of the lowest worldwide. However, with turmoil in Chiapas and other regions, President **Ernesto Zedillo** has had to increase military expenditures to 5 percent annually and also the overall size of the armed forces. While the civilian leadership was gradually reducing the size and influence of the military, at the same time it was creating stronger and more legitimate political institutions, including the party system and the powers of the presidency. To better control the military and reduce its coup-making potential, civilian leaders established several military schools to train officers in the most professional manner possible. As political scientist Roderic Ai Camp (1999, 132) points out, "One of the most important themes in the curriculum of the schools is respect for authority, for one's superior officer, and for the commander in chief, the president." Unlike the U.S. military, the Mexican military has the primary responsibility to operate as an internal police force during times of crisis, not national defense defined as fighting foreign wars. The Mexican military has been called on to settle contentious strikes, subdue and control guerrilla insurgencies, and carry out the government's anti–**drug trafficking** campaign.

As a result of rising crime, **corruption**, and drug-related violence, the government created the National Public Security Council in 1996, thereby increasing the military's role in domestic public security matters. The Mexican government has encouraged military control over civilian police forces as a means of fighting drug lord influence and corruption among the police. Recognizing the importance of building political support in rural areas, the Mexican army has engaged for some time in *labores sociales*, a broad range of civic action, public works, and service delivery missions. As the military is increasingly called upon to handle guerrilla organizations now operating in various parts of Mexico, the military may resort to more autonomy from the state and a much higher price for its continuing subservience to the party in power and government institutions. The growing militarization of Mexico—motivated by the battle against drug dealers and left-wing guerrilla groups—has spawned rumors of military coups (one in 1995 and another in 1996) and closer relations between the Mexican military and the U.S. Defense Department, the Drug Enforcement Agency (DEA), and other police agencies.

After the **Zapatista uprising in Chiapas** in 1994, the Mexican military created secret files (discovered by the press in March 2000) on more than 200 Mexican newspaper reporters, TV interviewers, leading intellectuals, opposition politicians, and foreign correspondents whom they judged to be excessively critical of the military. While there is no indication that the Mexican military took action against these "enemies," whose coverage of the Zapatistas (a **guerrilla movement** with a successful media campaign conducted by their charismatic, Internet-friendly chief, **Subcommander Marcos**) was considered negative, the secret dossiers raise serious questions about how much the armed forces are willing to accept democratic

reforms and a free press.

The stability in civil–military relations during the Cold War that occurred for reasons discussed above has not been without tensions, both domestic and international. The military's role in the student uprising and **Tlatelolco massacre** in 1968, several counterinsurgency campaigns in the 1960s and 1970s, electoral surveillance, drug-related corruption within the ranks, and the Zapatista revolt in Chiapas have brought tensions in civil–military relations. As the military is called upon to reduce the turmoil associated with organized group demands on civilian authorities, and as the hegemony of the dominant party declines, the Mexican military has been exposed to criticism from many parts of society and the international community. The military has been accused of being overly repressive in dealing with opposition forces, including the need to respect **human rights,** and less accountable than it should be as an agent of the state. Although President **Vicente Fox** has admitted that police officers and soldiers use torture to obtain information and confessions from subjects and that Mexican judges accept such treatment of suspects, ending this unjust practice will require a major overhaul of the criminal justice system.

The once secure civil–military pact that enabled the official party to perpetuate itself in power is now in jeopardy. As the political framework that allowed the PRI to maintain its hegemony begins to unravel, combined with a decline in the power of the presidency and central authority, military concerns are likely to intensify. Although Mexico has not been a coup-prone country since 1940, there is ample evidence that further democratization will require greater attention to the mechanisms needed to foster strong civilian leadership and control of the armed forces. Clearly, democratic consolidation has not reached the point where one can rule out a breakdown of serious proportions if the old ties between the military and civilian authority begin to unravel. In the event of a concerted attempt by the military to remove a civilian government, the U.S. Pentagon has promised military assistance to Mexico, including troops. *See also* Communications Media; Democracy and Democratization.

SUGGESTED READING

Martin Edward Anderson, "Civil–Military Relations and Internal Security in Mexico: The Undone Reform," in Riordan Roett, ed., *The Challenge of Institutional Reform in Mexico* (Boulder, Colo.: Lynne Rienner, 1995); Bruce Michael Bagley and Sergio Aguayo Quezada, eds., *Mexico: In Search of Security* (New Brunswick, N.J.: Transaction, 1993); Roderic Ai Camp, *Generals in the Palacio: The Military in Modern Mexico* (New York: Oxford University Press, 1992); Camp, *Politics in Mexico: The Decline of Authoritarianism*, 3d ed. (New York: Oxford University Press, 1999); David F. Ronfeldt, *The Modern Mexican Military: Implications for Mexico's Stability and Security* (Santa Monica, Calif.: Rand Corporation, 1985); Mónica Serrano, "The Armed Branch of the State: Civil–Military Relations in Mexico," *Journal of Latin American Studies* 27 (1995); Stephen J. Wager, "The Mexican Military Approaches the Twenty-First Century: Coping with a New World Order," in Donald E. Schultz and Edward J. Williams, eds., *Mexico Faces the Twenty-First Century* (Westport, Conn.: Praeger, 1995); Stephen J. Wager and Donald E. Schultz, "The Zapatista Revolt and Its Implications for Civil–Military Relations and the Future of Mexico," in Schultz and Williams, *Mexico Faces the Twenty-First Century*; David Ronfeldt, ed., *The Modern Mexican Military: A Reassessment* (La Jolla: Center for U.S.–Mexican Studies, University of California–San Diego, 1984).

Clouthier del Rincón, Manuel (1934–1989) ☀ A key member of the right-of-center **Partido Acción Nacional (PAN)**, prominent businessman, and presidential candidate in 1988. Manuel Clouthier was a bitter critic of the ruling **Partido Revolucionario Institucional (PRI)** and a tireless campaigner for his party's efforts to become a more unified movement to compete in Mexican elections. As a candidate of the free-market PAN, the charismatic Clouthier represented the "neo-*panista*" wing of the party, strong in the northern business sector and supported by the conservative Monterrey industrialist group. In the fraud-ridden 1988 presidential election, Clouthier placed third with 17.1 percent of the vote, behind the winner **Carlos Salinas de Gortari** of the PRI with 50.4 percent of the vote and **Cuauhtémoc Cárdenas** of the leftist National Democratic Front (FDN) with 31.2 percent.

Born in Culiacán, Sinaloa, on June 13, 1934, the descendant of French immigrants, Manuel Clouthier grew up knowing life on both sides of the border. He attended high school in San Diego, California, before going to the Monterrey (Nuevo León) Technical Institute (ITESM), where he played American-style football and majored in agricultural engineering. In his home state of Sinaloa, he became a wealthy grower and exporter of tomatoes, chilis, and rice and a leader in many agricultural and business organizations. He ran for governor in 1986 but lost to the Sinaloa PRI in a contest that Clouthier supporters claim was tarnished by widespread fraud in the ruling party. Clouthier gained national attention as president of the Mexican Employers' Federation council (1978–1980) while building a base of support within the PAN, mainly in the north.

Despite a disappointing third-place finish in the 1988 presidential race, Manuel Clouthier continued to criticize the PRI for being **corrupt**, fraudulent, and undemocratic, arguing that its continued rule (since 1929) was preventing Mexico from realizing its economic and political potential. A rousing stump speaker known for his puns and jokes, Clouthier's campaign efforts helped the PAN make history with the victory of Ernesto Ruffo as governor of Baja California in 1989. At the age of 55, he was killed in a suspicious automobile accident in Sinaloa while on the way

Manuel Clouthier, PAN candidate for president in 1988. Credit: *Proceso*, photo by Germán Canseco.

to Mazatlán to meet with Ruffo, the governor-elect of Baja California that he had campaigned for and helped become the first opposition party governor in Mexican history.

SUGGESTED READING

Enrique Nanti Fernández, *El Maquío Clouthier: Bibliografía, 1934–1989* (Mexico, D.F.: Planeta, 1998); "Manuel Clouthier, Who Sought Mexican Presidency, Dies in Crash," *New York Times*, October 2, 1989.

Coahuila. *See* Geographical Regions.

Cocaine. *See* Drug Trade/Trafficking.

Coffee ☀ After Brazil and Colombia, Mexico has become Latin America's third largest coffee exporter. The high quality of *café de altura* (coffee beans grown at elevations over 3,300 feet) has put coffee in first place among agricultural exports in Mexico. Among Latin American coffee producers, Mexico now ranks second to Brazil in coffee exports to the United States, the world's largest consumer of coffee. The best Mexican coffee is grown in tropical mountainous zones with warm climates and abundant precipitation and vegetation. Mexico's coffee farms exhibit a diversity of types of

production, from large *fincas* to small indigenous landowners and communal village plots. However, all producers are subject to climatic change, diseases, and the vicissitudes of the global marketplace. Over 90 percent of Mexican coffee is grown in eight states (Veracruz, Chiapas, Oaxaca, Puebla, San Luis Potosí, Guerrero, Nayarit, and Hidalgo), mostly on medium to large estates, collectively employing millions of Mexicans. The production of coffee in Mexico today is characterized by extreme inequality between small and large producers: over two-thirds of Mexico's coffee producers are poor, indigenous families in isolated mountain regions, mostly in southern Mexico. Unlike the wealthy producers who operate large farms (2 percent of the producers hold over 33 percent of the most productive land), the small producers live in extreme poverty, hampered by poor transportation, ancient technology, and little access to credit.

As coffee production experienced setbacks from world price fluctuations, the decade-long turmoil from the **Mexican Revolution**, and the reduction in prices from the Great Depression in the 1930s, large producers formed regional associations to defend their interests, banding together in 1949 to form the National Agricultural Union of Coffee Producers (UNAC). As the international market for coffee revived after the depression years, the Mexican government decided to take a more interventionist role to improve production for export. President **Miguel Alemán** (1946–1952) founded the National Coffee Commission in 1949 in an effort to introduce modern technology, improve cultivation, and take a more assertive approach in defense of coffee prices on the world market. Under the presidency of **Adolfo López Mateos** (1958–1964), the Mexican Coffee Institute (IMC) was created to promote the development of coffee cultivation and promotion, both nationally and internationally.

Today, the major agribusiness producers are facing a number of problems tied to the transition to a free-market economy and the affects of globalization. Under the neoliberal economic policies of President **Carlos Salinas**, the IMC started to privatize some of its storage and processing centers. With privatization and the globalization of coffee production, Mexican producers faced new challenges and problems. Small producers were forced to abandon their *fincas*, large producers remained closely tied to important multinationals such as General Foods and Nestlé, and both had to deal with a drop in coffee prices due to the collapse of the international quota system. Since coffee prices peaked in the early 1980s, the world price for a pound of coffee has declined by more than 50 percent. While the Salinas administration responded with its antipoverty **Programa Nacional de Solidaridad (PRONASOL)** to solve the problems of the small coffee producers, many could not compete effectively due to heavy indebtedness and the lack of sufficient credit and technical assistance. In response, coffee producers united to form independent grassroots organizations and organized demonstrations to defend their interests. As Mexico's most important agricultural export faces the repercussions from globalization—bringing impoverished indigenous populations in contact with worldwide economic competition—both producers and consumers are faced with many uncertainties and economic and political consequences that are difficult to predict. Although Mexico is not a member of the worldwide Association of Coffee Producing Countries (ACPC), it is a sympathetic nonmember and normally follows the coffee cartel's efforts to cut production in order to increase coffee prices per pound.

In addition to the global efforts of international organizations to stabilize coffee prices, foreign sympathizers of the small coffee growers and Zapatista rebels have stepped in to help some Chiapas farmers get better prices for their coffee by buying and selling their beans directly to the U.S. consumer, thus bypassing the Mexican middlemen who pay coffee farmers considerably less. In January 2000, Kerry Appel—owner of the Denver-based Human Bean Company and Café Zapatista—and 11 other U.S. citizens were expelled from Chiapas for "interfering in domestic politics." At the Café Zapatista in Denver, a cup of coffee is advertised as being made from "natural, pesticide free, shade grown, fair trade coffee [beans] from the Indigenous Communities in Resistance in the highlands of Chiapas, Mexico." Starbucks Corporation, in an effort to respond to consumer concerns that growing coffee is damaging to the rain forest, has been successful in supporting Mexican coffee farmers who grow shade-grown beans. The environmental benefits from this marketing strategy have also been profitable, as the demand for Mexican premium-priced coffee has increased considerably over the past several years.

SUGGESTED READING

Laure Waridel, *Coffee with Pleasure: Just Java and World Trade* (Montreal: Black Rose, 2001).

Colegio de México, El ☀ A small public university dedicated to graduate-level research and instruction in the social sciences and humanities. The brainchild of writer **Alfonso Reyes** and historian **Daniel Cosío Villegas**, El Colegio de México was founded in 1940 with the help of the federal government, the Bank of Mexico, the **Universidad Nacional Autónoma de México (UNAM)**, and the Fondo de Cultura Económica. For years its alumni have occupied top positions in the Mexican government and in other universities.

In its early years the school consisted of many renowned Spanish scientists and intellectuals exiled in Mexico as a result of the Spanish Civil War in the 1930s. It is funded by a wide variety of sources, including the Ford, Rockefeller, and other foundations, UNESCO, and the Mexican government. The college offers three-year master's and five-year doctoral programs in the social sciences and humanities. It publishes a number of important journals such as *Historia Mexicana*, *Foro Internacional*, *Estudios Demográficos y Urbanos*, and *Estudios Económicos*. Cosío Villegas was El Colegio's director until 1966 when he was replaced by Víctor Urquidi, an economist. El Colegio's current president is Andrés Lira González. The school has 180 teachers and researchers and approximately 250 students. Its library, named after cofounder Cosío Villegas, has approximately 710,000 volumes available to graduate students and the general public. With the publication of multivolume works on Mexican history and the **Mexican Revolution**, luminaries at the school have led the way in modern academic historiography and policy analysis. Its modern campus and facilities are located in Colonia Pedregal de Santa Teresa, south of Mexico City.

Colima. *See* Geographical Regions.

Colosio Murrieta, Luis Donaldo (1950–1994) ☀
Presidential candidate of the governing **Partido Revolucionario Institucional (PRI)** in the 1994 presidential election until he was assassinated on March 23, 1994, as he was leaving a campaign rally in Tijuana, Baja California. Born to a prominent ranching family in Magdalena de Kino, Sonora, on February 10, 1950, Colosio advanced rapidly in a political career after studying economics at the Monterrey Technical Institute and earning a master's degree in urban economic and regional development from the University of Pennsylvania.

The spark that launched his political career was a trip—which he won for obtaining the best grades in high school—to Mexico City where he met and shook hands with then-president **Adolfo López Mateos**. After his studies in Monterrey and the United States, he became active in national politics, serving as congressman, senator, and head of

Luis D. Colosio. Credit: *Proceso*, photo by Germán Canseco.

the PRI. During the **Carlos Salinas** presidency, Colosio became director of **Programa Nacional de Solidaridad**, the government's popular program for welfare, social services, and basic infrastructure (roads, water, and electricity) in low-income rural areas. Although he was not the most charismatic candidate that Salinas could have chosen, Colosio fit the mold of the new technocratic elite that Salinas admired. His success in managing Salinas's 1988 presidential campaign earned him the personal endorsement of the president to become the PRI presidential candidate in 1993. In naming Colosio as the PRI precandidate, Salinas chose one of Mexico's young, highly educated **technocrats** (*técnicos*), thus ensuring that the next administration would continue his policies.

Colosio's assassination while campaigning on the streets of Tijuana traumatized Mexico and raised questions about Mexico's stability and the viability of its political and economic institution. No politician of Colosio's rank had been murdered in Mexico since 1928. After the death of Colosio, the ruling party chose the uncharismatic **Ernesto Zedillo** to be its 1994 presidential candidate.

Six months after Colosio's death another leading PRI politician, party secretary general José Francisco Ruiz Massieu, was murdered in Mexico City. The deaths of Colosio and Ruiz Massieu spawned a outbreak of conspiracy theories in which many Mexicans suspected either conservative members of the PRI—many of whom found Colosio too receptive to democratic reform—or **drug traffickers** (or possibly both) as prime suspects in the murders. Less than three weeks before he was killed, Colosio had criticized Mexico's concentration of power in the hands of a few and promised to end the authoritarianism in Mexican politics. In trying to distance himself from President Salinas, he had described Mexico as an impoverished Third World country and promised to carry out plans to implement democratic reforms and separate the government from the dominant party. The government-appointed special prosecutor in charge of the investigation of Colosio's death fueled speculation of a conspiracy by claiming that there had been a "concerted action" to carry out the murder plot while at the same time claiming to have found a lone assassin—Mario Aburto Martínez—who confessed to the crime. Numerous suspects were detained, including three of Colosio's security guards and the PRI official who hired them, but government investigators let them go weeks later, citing lack of evidence against them. With growing suspicion of a wider plot than the single, deranged gunman put forth by President Salinas, Zedillo reopened the investigation in hopes of proving that Colosio was a victim of a conspiracy that included the military and police/security agents.

The assassination of Colosio had a negative effect on the **Revolutionary Family** and the pres-

idential succession system that had served Mexico's elite since 1934. If Colosio had been elected president, he would have reversed a trend in which his recent predecessors all came from Mexico City. The fact that Colosio had been a congressman, senator, and president of the PRI altered the concentration of power in the hands of a close-knit technocratic elite that began with **Miguel de la Madrid** in 1982. Colosio's assassination revealed the resistance of sectors within the PRI to the unorthodox way in which Salinas picked his successor, in effect breaking the circulation among elites at the top. The closeness of Colosio's murder and the indigenous uprising in Chiapas three months earlier heightened the sense of despair among the revolutionary elite and contributed to growing political instability.

SUGGESTED READING

Roderic Ai Camp, "Luis Donaldo Colosio Murrieta," in Barbara A. Tenenbaum, ed., *Encyclopedia of Latin American History and Culture*, vol. 2 (New York: Scribners, 1996); Camp, *Mexican Political Biographies, 1935–1993*, 3d ed. (Austin: University of Texas Press, 1995); Enrique Estrada Barrera, *Colosio: Candidato de la unidad y la esperanza: Diario de campana* (Mexicali, B. C.: Estrada Editores, 1999); Howard Handelman, *Mexican Politics: The Dynamics of Change* (New York: St. Martin's, 1997); Andres Oppenheimer, *Bordering on Chaos: Guerrillas, Stockbrokers, Politicians, and Mexico's Road to Prosperity* (Boston: Little, Brown, 1996); Juana Vázquez-Gómez, *Dictionary of Mexican Rulers, 1325–1997* (Westport, Conn.: Greenwood, 1997).

Communications Media ☀ Newspapers, magazines, radio, and television are important parts of Mexican politics and society. While the constitution guarantees freedom of expression, there is a constant debate inside Mexico as to the level of press freedom. Freedom of the press depends in large part on the medium. Until recently, the most strictly controlled media were radio and television programming, both subject to strict supervision by the dominant party. Overall, the broadcast media are more important because approximately 75 percent of all Mexicans rely on television for their major source of news compared with about 10 percent who read newspapers. Book publishing is the most open and free, but some censorship still exists. Since the 1970s, the print media have shown signs of becoming more independent and responsive to issues and arguments that challenge government policy, although parts of the press remain docile and collusive.

Mexico's current transition to a more open and democratic system has created a new role for the media since the 1970s: journalists are younger and more professional, vigilant, and critical of public officials and government policies than in the past; television stations are becoming more private, competitive, and less arrogant, offering more inclusive and fair-minded coverage of elections; political campaigns now include public opinion polling, debates, and more open criticism of the president (and ex-presidents and family members) and the ruling party, the **Partido Revolucionario Institucional (PRI)**; and the intellectual community has increasingly sought new channels in the print and broadcast media to reach a larger audience and express controversial political and social subjects.

The dominant medium of mass communication in Mexico is television, the major source of news for over three-quarters of all Mexicans. In 1995 Mexico was estimated to have 13.1 million television sets (149 per 1,000 population) and five major stations: Canal 11, Canal 22, Multivisión, Televisa/Eco/Galavisión, and TV Azteca. Television broadcasting is dominated by the networks of **Televisa**, a $9 billion conglomerate that accounts for more than 80 percent of the nation's television audience and carries 90 percent of all advertising.

Until 1997, under the powerful control of its pro-PRI owner, **Emilio Azcárraga Milmo**, Televisa

effectively functioned as a public relations firm for the Mexican government. With Televisa's monopoly and tightly controlled government networks, there was little televised campaign coverage of opposition candidates and the ruling party rarely got unfavorable stories. For example, a study of 1994 campaign coverage on the nightly news program *24 horas* (24 hours) and *Hechos* (the major news program of the much smaller competing network, Televisión Azteca) revealed the huge bias in favor of the PRI. Another PRI advantage in electoral contests is the popularity of *24 horas* news anchor Jacobo Zabuldovsky, considered by some to be almost as popular as the Mexican president.

However, in 1997, under pressure from poor ratings and the demands of the semiautonomous Federal Electoral Institute, television stations were obligated to provide more inclusive and fair-minded coverage of political parties, politicians, and the issues. Although the playing field is far from level, opposition candidates are now on more equal footing, but close television coverage does not always translate into an advantage for all competitors. As Dresser (1998, 237) points out, "Media access [in the July 1997 election for mayor of Mexico City] magnified the virtues of good candidates and the vices of bad ones. Via television, radio, and the press, political competition reached people's homes and psyches, and thus undermined the PRI's arguments that opposition candidates were Antichrists." With new reforms and greater competition for viewers (and ratings), Mexican television has changed considerably since the 1994 and 1997 elections. For example, television coverage of the three major candidates was more balanced and less interested in the need to please the Mexican president and his ruling party. Televisa, the largest broadcast network, did not back any candidate in 2000 and its current owner, Emilio Azcárraga Jean, insisted that he favored "whoever wins," adding that "democracy is very, very good business" (quoted in Preston 2000).

Although Mexico was the first country in the Americas with a printing press in 1536 and its newspaper tradition began 150 years before its independence from Spain in 1821, the print media—newspapers and magazines—have nowhere near the audiences today compared with television. While several print publications have considerable influence because they offer more independent political analysis and are read by Mexico's professional and cultural elite, the struggle for a free press continues in a political environment in which numerous forms of government control and domination persist. For example, publications such as *Proceso*, *La Jornada*, and *El Financiero* have responded to controversial issues—drug **corruption**, post-electoral violence, and **human rights** abuses—with more critical and negative coverage of the president, the Catholic Church, and the military than in the days prior to the democratic opening of the 1980s. For years, Mexican journalists adhered to the maxim that news organizations cannot criticize or adversely portray three "untouchable" groups or figures: the armed forces, the president, or the **Virgin of Guadalupe**. Although change is under way, the media still play a subservient role in Mexico, content to engage in reporting that helps to legitimize one party or another, or to enhance communication between members of the political elite. Change-oriented journalists continue to work in Mexico, but critical reporting on sensitive subjects is still in its infancy.

In 1995 Mexico was estimated to have 292 daily newspapers with a combined circulation of roughly 10,231,000. Of the 25 major newspapers throughout the country (see table 1), over half are located in Mexico City. Magazines are important communications media in Mexico City as well, although they tend to have a smaller circulation and are targeted to a selective readership (see table 2). *See also* Junco de la Vega, Alejandro.

Table 1. Major Daily Newspapers in Mexico, by City and Circulation, 1995

Newspaper	City	Total Circulation
Diario de Chihuahua	Chihuahua, Chihuahua	50,000
Diario de Guadalajara	Guadalajara, Jalisco	60,000
Diario de Monterrey	Monterrey, Nuevo León	75,000
Diario de Morelos	Cuernavaca, Morelos	47,000
Diario de Xalapa	Jalapa, Veracruz	40,000
Diario de Yucatán	Mérida, Yucatán	65,000
Díctamen de Veracruz	Veracruz, Veracruz	38,000
El Economista	México, D.F.	35,000
El Financiero	México, D.F.	135,000
El Heraldo de México	México, D.F.	180,000
El Nacional	México, D.F.	27,000
El Norte	Monterrey, Nuevo León	125,000
El Sol de México	México, D.F.	76,000
El Universal	México, D.F.	142,000
Excelsior	México, D.F.	200,000
La Jornada	México, D.F.	120,000
La Prensa	México, D.F.	300,000
Noreste	Culiacán, Sinaloa	30,000
Noticias de Oaxaca	Oaxaca, Oaxaca	25,000
Novedades	México, D.F.	230,000
Ocho Columnas	Guadalajara, Jalisco	48,000
Reforma	México, D.F.	100,000
Siglo 21	Guadalajara, Jalisco	34,000
The News	México, D.F.	35,000
Uno Mas Uno	México, D.F.	80,000

Source: World Media Handbook (New York: United Nations, 1995), 188–92.

SUGGESTED READING

Ilya Alder, "The Mexican Case: The Media in the 1988 Presidential Election," in Thomas E. Skidmore, ed., *Television, Politics, and the Transition to Democracy in Latin America* (Baltimore: Johns Hopkins University Press, 1993); Tom Barry, ed., *Mexico: A Country Guide* (Albuquerque, N. Mex.: Inter-American Hemispheric Resource Center, 1992); Denise Dresser, "Post-NAFTA Politics in Mexico: Uneasy, Uncertain, Unpredictable," in Carol Wise, ed., *The Post-NAFTA Political Economy: Mexico and the Western Hemisphere* (University Park: Pennsylvania State University Press, 1998); Elizabeth Fox, ed., *Media and Politics in Latin America: The Struggle for Democracy* (Newbury Park, Calif.: Sage,

Table 2. Major Periodicals in Mexico City, 1995

Periodical	Major Interest	Frequency	Circulation
Época	General	Weekly	39,300
Este País	General	Monthly	14,000
Impacto	General	Weekly	115,000
Proceso	General/Political	Weekly	200,000
Siempre	General	Weekly	100,000
Tiempo	General	Weekly	15,000
Visión	General	Bimonthly	246,000
Debate Feminista	Women	Quarterly	2,000
Etcetera	Sociopolitical	Weekly	n.a.
Expansión	Business	Bimonthly	27,000
FEM	Women	Monthly	5,000
México Desconocido	Cultural	Monthly	74,000
Nexos	Sociopolitical	Monthly	23,500
Quehacer Político	Political	Weekly	90,000
Rescate Ecólogico	Environment	Monthly	20,000
Revista Mexicana de Comunicación	Media	Monthly	6,000
Voz y Voto	Political	Monthly	n.a.
Vuelta	Literary	Monthly	15,000

Source: World Media Handbook (New York: United Nations, 1995), 190–91.

1988); Murray Fromson, "Mexico's Struggle for Press Freedom," in *Communication in Latin America: Journalism, Mass Media, and Society* (Wilmington, Del.: Jaguar Books on Latin America, 1996); P. Dale Gardner, *Communication Development in Venezuela and Mexico: Goals, Promises, and Reality* (Columbia, S.C.: Association for Education in Journalism and Mass Communication, 1988); Sallie Hughes, "The Pen and the Sword: Mexican Mass Media Coverage of the Armed Forces, 1986–1996" (paper presented at the Congress of the Latin American Studies Association, Chicago, September 25, 1998); "Mexico: Free to Be Bad," *The Economist,* March 11, 2000; Michael Nelson Miller, *Red, White, and Green: The Maturing of Mexicanidad, 1940–1946* (El Paso: Texas Western Press, University of Texas at El Paso, 1998); William A. Orme Jr., ed., *A Culture of Collusion: An Inside Look at the Mexican Press* (Miami: University of Miami, North-South Center Press, 1997); Robert N. Pierce, *Keeping the Flame: Media and Government in Latin America* (New York: Hastings House, 1979); Julia Preston,

"Mexican TV, Unshackled by Reform, Fights for Viewers," *New York Times,* June 7, 2000; Michael Brian Salwen and Bruce Garrison, *Latin American Journalism* (Hillsdale, N.J.: L. Erlbaum, 1991); Cris Villarreal Navarro, "Televisa, Telecracy of Mexico" (master's thesis, University of Texas, 1993).

Communism and Mexican Communist Party (Partido Comunista Mexicano, PCM) ☀ While various forms of communist ideology and communist parties have had a considerable impact on politics, **guerrilla movements**, and the arts, communism has failed to create a mass base or a significant electoral presence in modern Mexico. Mexican communism has come in different varieties—Trotskyist, Marxist-Leninist, anarcho-syndicalist, Eurocommunist, revolutionary nationalist—but its main protagonist until its dissolution in 1981 was the Mexican Communist Party (Partido Comunista Mexicano, PCM). From its inception in 1919, the PCM played a significant role in the formation of peasant and **labor** unions and opposition political parties and in helping to mold Mexico's political culture. From 1920 to 1940, the PCM became deeply involved with the cultural aspects of the **Mexican Revolution,** recruiting the "red" muralists—**Diego Rivera, David Alfaro Siqueiros,** and **José Clemente Orozco**—writers, academics, and others. It was a symbiotic relationship that developed slowly between the Mexican left and the cultural life of the nation. The PCM gained additional strength with the election of **Lázaro Cárdenas** (1934–1940) and the vast peasant and labor mobilization that occurred during his presidency. In its effort to push the Mexican Revolution to the left by developing a solid base among key unions, the PCM had to make concessions to the ruling party and the opportunism within the rank and file that would ultimately weaken the movement. The PCM published several newspapers and journals, including *El Machete,* but its membership never reached more than 40,000. It was characterized by its close links with the **Soviet Union** and its national organization was considered Stalinist in ideological orientation.

From 1940 until the final years of its existence, the PCM suffered from a series of mistakes, leading to a rapid decline in membership and political prestige. From a peak of 30,000 members in 1940, the PCM membership dropped to 10,000 in 1945, and by 1960 there were fewer than 2,000 party members. After the Hitler–Stalin pact, the beginning of **World War II,** and the assassination of **Leon Trotsky** in Mexico City in 1940, PCM membership declined and in 1946 could not meet the minimum requirements of the labor code. With the creation of the Worker and Peasant Party and the Popular Party in the 1940s, PCM membership declined even further. For the first two decades after World War II, the small base of the PCM consisted of urban intellectuals, teachers, students, and a few industrial unions located in Mexico City, Oaxaca, and Guerrero.

The anticommunism of the **Alemán** administration (1946–1952), the formation of other communist parties, government repression, and the loss of key party organizers eroded much of what the PCM was at an earlier time in its history. The Alemán government was denounced as a "government of national betrayal" in 1949, leaving PCM leadership to search for a new vision reflecting the tremendous changes in Mexican society. At the behest of new party leadership, the PCM rejected the ideology of the Mexican Revolution for the first time, built new organizations to challenge official and semiofficial peasant federations such as the Confederación Nacional Campesina, and claimed that the process of repeated efforts to reinvigorate the revolution from above was now over. A period of radicalization energized the left after the bloody repression of the student movement in 1968, but it was short-lived and by the mid-1970s the notion of armed struggle and confrontation with despotic presidential leadership ceased to be a viable option for the left. The demise of the guerrilla stage of Mexican communism, compounded by the deepening economic crisis in the late 1970s, prompted a return to the electoral path for some kind of leftist coalition that would help revive the movement. At the same time its membership changed significantly, with new members coming from the ranks of intellectuals, university teachers, and other educational sectors.

While the changing composition and ideology (the PCM adopted a Eurocommunist position during the late 1970s) offered new hope for the left, the party continued to experience only limited success in local and national politics. In an effort to build ties with other sections of the left, the leadership of the PCM decided that it would dissolve itself in 1981 and create a more unified socialist party that included other political parties on the left. Under a new name—Partido Socialista Unificado Mexicano (PSUM)—the Mexican left reflected a fusion of the old PCM with four other parties.

At the end of the 20th century, the main opposition party on the left is the Party of the Democratic Revolution (**Partido de la Revolución Democrática, PRD**), led by **Cuauhtémoc Cárdenas**, a heterogeneous coalition of PRI defectors, ex-Communists or Marxists, former members of the Mexican Socialist Party, and leftist activists and victims of repression unleashed after the 1968 **Tlatelolco massacre**. As the largest left-of-center party (it is ideologically neither communist nor socialist), the PRD is interested in preserving and reformulating the major tenets of the tradition of revolutionary nationalism—anti-imperialism, strengthening economic and political sovereignty in the wake of free trade and globalization, and reaffirming the direct authority of the state in economic matters. Electorally, the PRD has been a disappointment since its founding in 1989. Unable to engage its potential constituency throughout Mexico, it has watched its percentage of the national vote decline and support for the right-wing **Partido Acción Nacional** (PAN) grow into Mexico's largest opposition force to the ruling party. *See also* Electoral System/Elections; Foreign Policy.

SUGGESTED READING

Barry Carr, "Communism and Communist Parties," in Michael S. Werner, ed., *Encyclopedia of Mexico: History, Society, and Culture*, vol. 1 (Chicago: Fitzroy Dearborn, 1997); Carr, *Marxism and Communism in Twentieth-Century Mexico* (Lincoln: University of Nebraska Press, 1992); Arnoldo Martínez Verdugo, ed., *Historia de Comunismo en México* (Mexico, D.F.: Grijalbo, 1985); Karl M. Schmitt, *Communism in Mexico: A Study of Political Frustration* (Austin: University of Texas Press, 1965).

Compañía Nacional de Subsistencias Populares (CONASUPO) ☀ In an effort to counter the rising discontent and growing political unrest—peasant land invasions, more militant trade unionism, and student protests—from a development path that seemed to ignore the problems of poverty and inequality, Mexican presidents began to address some of these issues with mild land reform measures and the inauguration of CONASUPO in 1961. To balance the problem of the floundering peasant economy while at the same time encouraging agro-industrialization, CONASUPO was charged with regulating grain and oilseed markets and providing important subsidies for basic foods such as rice, sugar, and tortillas. For decades it served as the mainstay of various government welfare programs aimed at alleviating poverty and bolstering the sagging legitimacy of the government and ruling party. However, by the 1990s CONASUPO was increasingly viewed as a costly and unfortunate drain on limited government resources. Although CONASUPO survived the initial structural economic reforms of the **Carlos Salinas** administration, such as the privatization of hundreds of state enterprises or parastatals, public opinion in favor of keeping the food distribution agency public was not enough to prevent its termination in 1997 after years of **corruption** scandals and fiscal mismanagement. An investigation of possible embezzlement at the agency by **Raúl Salinas de Gortari**, the brother of the former president, was halted by President **Ernesto Zedillo** in 1995. *See also* Hank González, Carlos.

Confederación de Cámaras Industriales de los Estados Unidos Mexicanos (CONCAMIN) ☀ Unlike Mexican **labor**, which is represented at least nominally by a single umbrella organization, the business community is organized into a number of specialized employer associations. One of the oldest and most powerful is CONCAMIN (Confederation of Industrial Chambers of the United States of Mexico), formed in 1918 as a public autonomous institution under Articles 73 and 123 of the **Constitution of 1917**. All businesses above a certain size are required to join the Chambers of Industry, but they typically are not highly active and are not regarded as the best channel for communicating with government officials. In most cases, Mexico's private industry and commerce is controlled by "groups" or holding companies that are dominated by a small number of linked families who hold key managerial positions and control much of the capital.

CONCAMIN includes manufacturing industries and has approximately 126,000 affiliated businesses throughout Mexico. Unlike its counterpart CONCANACO (**Confederación Nacional de Cámaras Comerciales),** which is organized regionally, CONCAMIN is organized by industry—iron and steel, cement, shoes, and so on—and is composed of 75 industrial chambers that can vote in the organization. It also includes 42 industrialist associations that can affiliate by either industrial sector or by region. Employer organizations such as CONCAMIN, which must deal with the state on a wide range of economic and political issues, consist of different ideological tendencies. CONCAMIN tends more toward moderation and negotiation with the government on matters of regulation, ownership of the economy, exports, and democratization of the political system. The Confederation of National Chambers of Commerce (CONCANACO) tends toward a more "radical" position, offering forceful resistance when the state has tried to expand its powers over the business sector.

Since the 1980s, employer organizations such as CONCAMIN have become more active in the political process, often calling for important economic, political, and social changes in Mexico. They have spurred the drive toward greater democratization and have called for a "social market economy" to promote greater individual freedom as well as the social agenda of the Catholic Church. With the advent of neoliberal reforms pushing for greater privatization of state enterprises, large corporations and the financial sector have been the principal beneficiaries of these changes. The **North American Free Trade Agreement (NAFTA)** has also increased the power of export-oriented industries over those more closely tied to the domestic market.

SUGGESTED READING

Roderic Ai Camp, *Los empresarios y la política en México* (Mexico, D.F.: Fondo de Cultura Económica, 1996); Matilde Luna, "Employer Organizations," in Michael S. Werner, ed., *Encyclopedia of Mexico: History, Society and Culture,* vol. 1 (Chicago: Fitzroy Dearborn, 1997); Cristina Puga, *México: Empresarios y poder* (Mexico, D.F.: Miguel Angel Porrúa and UNAM, 1993).

Confederación de Trabajadores de México (CTM) ☀
As part of the "**labor** sector" of the **Partido Revolucionario Institucional (PRI),** the CTM has been Mexico's most important labor union since it was organized in 1936 by **Vicente Lombardo Toledano** along the lines of the American CIO (Congress of Industrial Organizations). It emerged out of a period of tremendous divisions in the Mexican labor movement, when tensions were high due to the efforts to mobilize workers influenced by fascism and popular front alliances between communist and bourgeois democratic parties in Europe and Latin America. With close to 500,000 members—miners, factory workers, petroleum workers, and transport workers—the CTM provided the backbone of support for many of President **Lázaro Cárdenas**'s policies, including the nationalization of the foreign-owned oil companies in 1938. More than any other corporatist segment of the ruling party at the time, the CTM has come to play a central role in government policy and the economy.

In its early years the CTM adopted a strong anticapitalist platform, using the slogan "for a classless society" to recruit new members, reduce tensions among Mexican workers, and unify the international labor movement. From 1941 until his death in 1997, the CTM's secretary-general was **Fidel Velázquez Sánchez**, a corporatist labor leader par excellence. He ruled Mexico's largest labor union for more than 50 years, vigorously defending the PRI and its corporatist political structure. During the last decade of his rule he became increasingly critical of the government's neoliberal economic policies and their impact on workers and working conditions. As long as labor **corporatism** was firmly entrenched in the Mexican political system, Velázquez's power was secure.

Over the years the comfortable arrangement between the government and the CTM began showing signs of weakening. From 1970 until 1982 the Mexican government faced increasing problems with its policies of maintaining national economic development and political stability. With growing social and political unrest in the 1960s and 1970s, the role of the CTM also was questioned. After the economy collapsed in 1981–1982, the pillars of labor corporatism began to crumble as the CTM faced harsh criticism from the Mexican state, disgruntled employers, dissident labor unions, and its own rank and file. To make matters worse, Fidel Velázquez and the CTM leadership proved incapable of responding to the nation's economic crisis. Despite the CTM's formal alliance with the state, Mexican presidents, beginning with President **Miguel de la Madrid**, tried to marginalize the labor confederation as they attempted to implement a new model of economic development based on fiscal austerity, privatization, trade liberalization, and the export of manufactured goods. Under these economic reforms, the CTM lost the clout it once had and its power faded along with its leader's. With challenges to CTM control of the labor movement increasing during the last two decades of the 20th century, workers began mobilizing around core economic issues—skyrocketing unemployment and declining levels of wages and benefits aggravated by the government's structural adjustment initiatives—and taking the daring step of voting against PRI candidates in local and national elections. While the future of labor relations with the Mexican state is yet to be determined, there is little doubt that the Mexican government will have to devise a less corporatist arrangement than the one that has been in effect since the 1930s.

SUGGESTED READING

Javier Aguilar García, "Confederación de Trabajadores de México (CTM)," in Michael S. Werner, ed., *Encyclopedia of Mexico: History, Society, and Culture*, vol. 1 (Chicago: Fitzroy Dearborn, 1997); García, ed., *Historia de la CTM, 1936–1990*, 2 vols. (Mexico, D.F.: UNAM, 1990).

Confederación Nacional Campesina (CNC) ☀
Formed in 1935 by President **Lázaro Cárdenas** to deradicalize the peasantry, the National Peasant Confederation became one of the pillars of the newly created **corporatist** structure, made up of agricultural wage workers, sharecroppers, and similar occupations. Since the National Revolutionary Party (PNR) was renamed the Party of the Mexican Revolution (PRM) in 1938, the peasant sector has been dominated by the CNC, made up mostly of *ejidatarios* (farmers whose land had been provided as part of the national agrarian reform program). Although the CNC is the largest **labor** organization in Mexico, its members are isolated and poorly organized, lack political experience, are dominated by the **Partido Revolucionario Institucional** (PRI), and since the 1940s the union has done a poor job of representing the interests of peasants. It is clearly the weakest of the corporatist links to the PRI, since small farmers are included in the popular sector of the PRI, diluting further the clout of rural farmers. With agrarian reform and the demobilization of the peasant sector, the CNC has uncritically supported government agricultural policy, even during times when its members were affected adversely. Despite a muted political

voice on agricultural policy, the CNC has been one of the most dependable sources of support for the PRI election machine, heavily dependent on the state for credit, irrigation, seeds, fertilizers, and other fundamental needs of farmers in Mexico. Until recently, the PRI's rural machine received a significant portion of the peasant vote; however, the **Partido de la Revolución Democrática (PRD)** has made considerable progress in gaining more of the peasant vote with the growing disenchantment with the government over the private sector focus of agricultural policy and the popularity of the **Zapatista rebellion in Chiapas.** Mexico's greatest postrevolutionary project—land reform—became a boon to the ruling party and its political agenda, but agriculturally the program has been a disaster for the 3 million *ejidatarios* stuck with small plots and a lack of modern technology. During the past decade, the plight of the rural farmer has been compounded by free trade competition from U.S. farmers and—with the exception of a few new pilot projects for the *ejidos*—the declining interest in the small rural farmer in Mexico City.

Confederación Nacional de Cámaras Comerciales (CONCANACO) ☀ Mexico's commercial sector is primarily represented by the Confederation of National Chambers of Commerce, the oldest (founded in 1917) and largest of the employer organizations. With approximately 500,000 affiliated businesses, the CONCANACO is organized regionally and represents commerce, service, and tourism industries throughout Mexico. Unlike its counterpart **Confederación de Cámaras Industriales de las Estados Unidas Mexicanos. (CONCAMIN)**, it has a more "radical" ideological tendency when it comes to negotiating with the government. Under the leadership of CONCANACO and other small and medium business associations, calls for an active industrial policy have been put forth in published documents challenging the Mexican government to foster the conditions for greater economic competition and a stronger voice for business concerns in public policy making.

SUGGESTED READING

Matilde Luna, "Entrepreneurial Interests and Political Action in Mexico: Facing the Demands of Economic Modernization," in Riordan Roett, ed., *The Challenge of Institutional Reform in Mexico* (Boulde, Colo.: Lynne Rienner, 1995).

Confederación Nacional de Organizaciones Populares (CNOP) ☀ President **Manuel Ávila Camacho** created the CNOP in 1943 as a third sector of the Partido Nacional Revolucionario (PNR) for bureaucrats, professionals, housewives, merchants, and others in Mexico's growing middle class. What President **Lázaro Cárdenas** did for the peasants and workers, Ávila Camacho did for others who had been left out of the party structure. It quickly became a major political force within the dominant party, overshadowing the **labor** and peasant sectors in overall policy making. Unionized public-sector employees are the most important actors in the CNOP, mostly school teachers and white-collar workers in the state bureaucracy. In addition, other occupations such as commercial farmers, owners of small businesses, street vendors, shoeshine men, and mariachi musicians belong to associations that are affiliated with the CNOP.

The decision to alter the sectoral organization of the ruling party in 1943 has generated several interpretations about its origins and purpose. Some argue that the formation of the CNOP was designed to demobilize labor while expanding the sectoral reach of the party to the growing number of disgruntled workers among Mexico City's middle-class residents. Others feel that the genesis of the CNOP was rooted in the need to counter the growing political opposition, including the creation of the **Partido Acción Nacional (PAN)** in 1939, by including a wide variety of groups that were forgotten by the ruling party elites. By emphasizing middle-class values—protection of private property, legal rights for professionals, credit and financial support for small industries, cooperation with foreign capital, and rent control—the CNOP hoped to appeal to the country's "popular middle classes." Founded on principles of nationalism and patriotism at a time of international turmoil, the CNOP was also designed to include ex-military personnel, giving the military a connection to the ruling party. Although the CNOP often suffered from legitimacy problems due to its diversity and contradictory demands on public policy, it helped to buffer the ruling party from opposing forces such as state workers, former members of the military, and the urban middle class.

Although the CNOP is relatively small, with less than four million members, and has a very heterogenous membership, most of its members have more education and substantially greater political skills than the other sectors of the **Partido Revolucionario Institucional**. The popular sector is more political in its orientation than the other two sectors, which are mainly economic organizations. There is a close connection between membership in the CNOP and PRI deputies in the Chamber of Deputies, with members holding approximately 50 percent of the seats. With growing intrasectoral conflicts, the power of the CNOP began to wane, prompting efforts by party leaders to question the value of such a complex organization. Since the **Carlos Salinas** presidency (1988–1994), the role of the CNOP in national policy making was reduced in an effort to experiment with new sectoral federations that would help offset the growing electoral strength of the PAN and the growing number of middle-class environmental and social movements. As long as the PRI maintains its essential **corporatist** design, it will need to have some way of effectively embracing the segments of the population that make up the popular middle-class sector.

SUGGESTED READING

Diane E. Davis, "New Social Movements, Old Party Structures: Discursive and Organizational Transformations in Mexican and Brazilian Party Politics," in William C. Smith and Roberto P. Korzeniewicz, eds., *Social Change and Economic Restructuring in Latin America* (Boulder, Colo.: Lynne Rienner, 1996); Miguel Osorio Marbán, *El sector popular de PRI: La escencia de la nación* (Mexico, D.F.: Coordinación Nacional de Estudios Históricos, Políticos, Sociales, 1994); William P. Tucker, *The Mexican Government Today* (Minneapolis: University of Minnesota Press, 1957).

Confederation of Industrial Chambers of the United States of Mexico. *See* Confederación de Cámaras Industriales de los Estados Unidos Mexicanos (CONCAMIN).

Confederation of National Chambers of Commerce. *See* Confederación Nacional de Cámaras Comerciales (CONCANACO).

Confederation of Workers of Mexico. *See* Confederación de Trabajadores de México (CTM).

Constitution of 1917 ☀ Mexico's current basic law is the product of the **Mexican Revolution** of 1910–1917, which replaced the 1857 constitution of reformer Benito Juárez. Like the constitution of the United States, a federal system divides powers between the federal government and individual subnational administrative units called states, and there is also a separation of powers in which executive, legislative, and judicial functions are both shared and divided. Those who wrote the Mexican constitution of 1917 superimposed North American ideas of federalism and liberty on top of unwritten values of **personalism** and authoritarianism. The first reflects the political ideal of **democracy** and limited government; the second indicates the reality of Mexico's political tradition, concentrating considerable power in the hands of the president. In its completed written form, the

1917 consitution was a nationalistic document based on socialist principles, particularly in the areas devoted to the rights of **labor**, agriculture, and management and the restrictions on foreign ownership and property; it was also a basic law that contained the written aspirations of millions of Mexicans for social justice, **human rights**, and security after a decade of chaos, violence, and instability. It was drafted and approved at an assembly gathered in Querétaro, rather than Mexico City, by President Venustiano Carranza from 1916 to 1917.

The constitutional convention that met in Querétaro was composed of mostly young middle-class individuals who either supported the conservative Carranza or the more progressive forces of Alvaro Obregón. None of the 220 individuals who participated in the deliberations represented **Pancho Villa** or **Emiliano Zapata**; however, they shared the anti-American nationalism that developed from the punitive expeditions carried out by U.S. military forces in the north, and the need to break up the large landed estates as advocated by Zapata and others.

The *obregonistas* wrote the social and economic sections of the constitution, especially Articles 27, 33, 123, and 130. Article 27 evoked the spirit of Zapata and his followers, who called for the alteration in the ownership of the large landed estates. In addition to the breakup of the haciendas, it restricted the right of foreigners to acquire real estate and mineral resources, affirmed the principle of nationalization, and asserted the legal right to expropriate private property. Article 33 stated that foreigners could be extradited without a trial, and Article 123 guaranteed workers an eight-hour day and the right to unionize and strike. When hundreds of foreigners descended on the state of Chiapas to express admiration and support for the Zapatistas in 1999–2000, the **Ernesto Zedillo** administration applied Article 33 of the Constitution and they were expelled from Mexico

for interfering in its domestic affairs. Article 130 guaranteed freedom of worship while prohibiting priests from criticizing the government or the constitution. Article 27 was the most troubling for the United States—given the fact that it owned most of Mexico's petroleum resources—and if interpreted retroactively, it constituted a major threat to U.S. oil interests in Mexico.

It took more than 20 years for the right conditions to occur to fully implement Article 27. On March 18, 1938, President **Lázaro Cárdenas** issued a decree nationalizing the British- and American-owned oil fields, including the important properties of Standard Oil. It was a day of celebration for Mexicans and clearly a loss to corporate America. Reflecting the concerns of petroleum companies, American newspapers lashed out at the Mexican president in editorial opinions and reports of the event, calling him a "communist" and a serious threat to U.S. security interests. Although pressured to **intervene** in Mexico to reverse the expropriation decision, President Franklin Roosevelt stuck to his Good Neighbor pledge of nonintervention and the dispute was finally settled years later through diplomatic channels and binational negotiations.

The *carranzistas* wrote the less spectacular portions of the 1917 constitution in the area of government powers, particularly the efforts to strengthen the presidential system over the parliamentary system as originally conceived in the 1857 constitution. The federal executive was given expanded powers while in office: the president did not have to respond politically to the Congress and was free from prosecution while in office, except for legal transgressions, betrayal of his country, and severe crimes. A vice president was left out of the executive arrangement, and the president possessed the powers to nominant and remove cabinet members and those responsible for public agencies that participate within the administration. The president is the predominant power when it comes to the Mexican military and the conduct of international relations, similar to the status prescribed by the U.S. Constitution. The anti-reelection principle that emerged from the revolution was incorporated in the Constitution of 1917 so that the Mexican president is restricted to a single six-year term of office (*sexenio*). The president's control of national political life was enhanced during the long period of PRI rule by the fact that the incumbent president was in charge of the dominant party when in power and not the reverse.

The Constitution of 1917 is not a static document setting forth rules, powers, rights, and procedures; its 136 articles have been reformed through 102 decrees since 1921, with only 38 articles from the 1917 Constitution still in their original form. The Revolution helped create a greater sense of constitutionalism in Mexico, providing legitimacy for a document with a set of ideas that established the goals, political concepts, and procedures of Mexican society after 1920. While its more radical economic, social, and political provisions are often perceived as being observed more in abeyance than reality, it remains an important document that influenced the political values of successive generations. *See also* Corporatism.

SUGGESTED READING

Manuel González Oropeza, "Constitution of 1917," in Michael S. Werner, ed., *Encyclopedia of Mexico: History, Society, and Culture*, vol. 1 (Chicago: Fitzroy Dearborn, 1997); Sergio Elías Gutiérrez, *La Constitución Mexicana al final del siglo XX*, 2d ed. (Mexico, D.F.: Las Lineas del Mar, 1995); W. Dirk Ratt, *Mexico and the United States: Ambivalent Vistas* (Athens: University of Georgia Press, 1992).

Contadora Group. *See* De la Madrid Hurtado, Miguel; Foreign Policy.

Corporatism ☀ A central characteristic of Mexico's political structure with roots in Catholic social the-

ory. A corporatist society tends to be elitist, patrimonial, authoritarian, and statist. Mexican corporatism is a formal–legal arrangement in which selected economic groups/interests are organized into vertical functional associations that can be controlled and managed by the government or state. As an ideology, corporatism differs from Marxist socialism by rejecting class struggle, a stateless society, individualism, and pluralist **democracy**, while retaining the concept of private property, state control of the economy, and authoritarian leadership. As the dominant political structure of the 20th century, corporatism has endowed Mexican leaders with considerable political power and extraordinary policy flexibility. As Grayson (1998, 2) points out, "When [corporatism] performs well, the government acts as a gyroscope—balancing competing corporatist interests by integrating them into the state apparatus."

Mexico's corporatist structure was largely devised by President **Lázaro Cárdenas** in the 1930s. With a political initiative designed to protect the interests of the ordinary worker and peasant, his original intent was to create umbrella organizations loyal to the government. By absorbing various interest groups—peasants, **labor**, the military, and middle-class professional groups—into a government-sponsored political party, the central government was able to create a system of political reciprocity: in return for official recognition and association, these groups could then expect protection from their natural political enemies and special consideration for their interests on behalf of the state. With a system of corporatist representation, the state enhanced its ability to manipulate various groups in the state's own interest, although the structure that Cárdenas created ended up serving the interests of the middle classes and the wealthy rather than the downtrodden.

Toward the end of the 20th century, Mexico's corporatist structure began to erode due to neoliberal economic policies, free trade initiatives, and increasing electoral competition from the right and left, thereby reducing the resources the ruling party was able to offer to various groups. Thus the mass organizations and well-controlled political representation so important to Mexican presidents from Cárdenas to **Carlos Salinas** have been worn away as the power of the state slips and citizens look for other ways of making effective demands on the political system and its elites. While it may be premature to argue that pluralism has replaced corporatism as Mexico's governing ideology, the PRI defeat in 2000 clearly weakened the ability of the state to manipulate various groups in society as it once did.

SUGGESTED READING

Roderic Ai Camp, *Politics in Mexico: The Decline of Authoritarianism*, 3d ed. (New York: Oxford University Press, 1999); George W. Grayson, *Mexico: From Corporatism to Pluralism?* (Fort Worth, Texas: Harcourt Brace, 1998).

Corridos ✺ As a narrative ballad or story-song genre, Mexican *corridos* are part of a tradition that has influenced the course of Mexican history over the past century. The *corrido* has functioned as an expressive art form throughout Mexico; it is a vibrant living ballad tradition, one that is created and performed in response to homespun events that touch local communities. The *corrido* folk tradition first became popular during the **Mexican Revolution**, which created events and heroes—such as **Pancho Villa** and **Emiliano Zapata**—who were ideal subjects for national balladry. Following the revolution, the artistic elite—among them **Frida Kahlo, Diego Rivera, José Clemente Orozco, David Alfaro Siqueiros,** and **Carlos Chávez**—imbued with a new spirit of Mexican nationalism, drew inspiration from the powerful *corrido* narratives and applied them to their pictorial, poetic, and musical expressions of the nation.

The early *corridos* that dealt with heroes and political events eventually changed to more controversial ballads as they glamorized the lives of bandits, outlaws, and smugglers of illegal immigrants. *Narcocorridos* became popular in the early 1970s after Los Tigres del Norte recorded "Contrabando y Traición" and "Camelia la Tejana." In the 1980s and 1990s Los Tigres moved away from their *narcocorridos* and began writing songs of Mexican pride and the plight of poor immigrants facing discrimination in America. Today the paradigm for the typical *corrido* is the hero of the Revolution, someone who has taken up arms against an abusive and illegitimate government, leaving vague or unstated the often violent or barbaric activities for which they were responsible.

The origins, functions, and contemporary meaning and consequences of *corrido* lyrics have spawned interesting debates and controversies, many of which help drive the continuing popularity of this form of artistic expression. One of the debates centers on whether the *corrido* is of European origin or is a form of narrative poetry and song indigenous to Mexican cultures. Another controversy surrounds the inherent functions of the *corrido*: is the story-song a kind of oral newspaper, spreading word of catastrophe and violent confrontations, or is the purpose of the ballad not to inform but to commemorate events already widely known to the public?

At the heart of most ballads is a genre called the *corrido trágico,* with its evocation of heroes confronting scenes of mortal danger or loss of life. This means that lyrics often include violent encounters between antiheroes and those in positions of authority. *Corridos* with braggadocio-filled tales of the **drug trade** and outlaws, or ballads that portray the government in an unflattering way, have sparked a negative reaction from various publics in which *corridos* have been banned from radio play lists. Thus the contemporary *corrido* is designed to express the views of the underdogs (*los de abajo*). *Corrido* heroics typically represent a revolutionary fighting the power of the state, a drug trafficker hoping to become wealthy in a flash, a borderlander (*fronterizo*) who resists the encroachment of the *americanos*, or a villager who stands up against the intrusion of state or national authorities.

The *narcocorrido* boom that started in the early 1970s has grown into one of the most popular **music** styles in the Latino market, both in the United States and Mexico. A large segment of this growing market are drug-trafficking ballads played to polka or waltz rhythms. The Nashville of narco-corrido is Sinaloa, where many of Mexico's drug traffickers are headquartered, and the birthplace of Los Tigres and other artists who write and sing bawdy *corridos*. Elijah Wald keeps track of *corridos* on current events that appear and adds them to his website (Corrido Watch). After the terrorist attacks on the United States on **September 11, 2001**, Wald detailed the words of two popular *corridos* on the subject. In "El terror del siglo" (The terror of the century), José Guadalupe Paredes sings of the disaster and the cowardly terrorists who have surrounded the world with danger. In a more controversial corrido, "El corrido de bin Laden, el error de la CIA," Rigoberto Cárdenas Chávez sings of the search for Osama bin Laden, but blames the CIA for much of his training, "the American government's biggest mistake."

SUGGESTED READING

Ramiro Burr, *The Billboard Guide to Tejano and Regional Mexican Music* (New York: Billboard Books, 1999); John Holmes McDowell, "Corridos," in Michael S. Werner, ed., *Encyclopedia of Mexico: History, Society, and Culture*, vol. 1 (Chicago: Fitzroy Dearborn, 1997); Sam Quiñones, "Narco Pop's Bloody Polkas," *Washington Post*, March 1, 1998; Ilan Stavans, "Trafficking in Verse," *Nation*, January 7/14, 2002; Elijah Wald, *Narcocorrido: A Journey into the Music of Drugs, Guns, and Guerrillas* (New York: HarperCollins,

2001); Wald, "Corrido Watch," www.elijahwald.com/corridowatch.htm; Eric Zolov, *Refried Elvis: The Rise of the Mexican Counterculture* (Berkeley: University of California Press, 1999).

Corruption ☀ Various forms of fraud and corruption have plagued Mexican society and politics throughout its history. Graft and corruption were the driving forces behind the **Mexican Revolution** (1910–1917), and since the 1980s, drug cartels have corrupted Mexico's law enforcement system. Numerous cases detail how the federal police have collaborated with drug traffickers by taking part in abductions, beatings, and killings. During Mexico City's 1985 earthquake, thousands of buildings and houses collapsed in less than three minutes, while older buildings survived the quake with little damage; an investigation discovered that greedy developers, engineers who lied in their calculations, inspectors who grew rich by looking the other way, and unscrupulous bureaucrats who authorized poor construction in unstable areas contributed to the areas that received the most damage. In 1999 the U.S. Federal Bureau of Investigation (FBI) accused ex-president **Carlos Salinas de Gortari** (living in self-imposed exile in Ireland since 1995) of benefiting from the surge in illicit **drug trafficking** during his administration (1988–1994) and the existence of an incestuous relationship between senior *priístas* (members of the ruling party, PRI), organized crime, and powerful drug gangs throughout Mexico. Using a false name, **Raúl Salinas de Gortari**, brother of the ex-president, spirited away over $100 million into foreign bank accounts from protection money received from the drug cartels and kickbacks (one of Raúl's nicknames was "Mr. Ten Percent") from those who made huge sums from privileged access to the privatization of state enterprises that occurred while his brother was president.

Although a slippery concept that carries multiple definitions and interpretations in public life, corruption—flagrant abuse of the public trust in the pursuit of private gain—undermines the legitimacy of democratic systems, fosters disrespect for the integrity of the judicial process, and contributes to the loss of significant sums of money for corporations and governments when contracts are lost due to the nonpayment of bribes. Corrupt practices associated with tax collection often deny the government the necessary revenue to deal adequately with a plethora of development projects. Among industrial nations, Mexico has one of the lowest rates of tax collection, a lowly 11 percent of gross domestic product. The Organization of American States (OAS) adopted the Inter-American Convention against Corruption in 1996, an international legal code outlawing cross-border bribery and the "illicit enrichment" of public officials that many hope will help in the investigation of bribery charges and the expedition of extradition procedures among the member states. Although Mexico is one of the 34 participating members of the OAS, this multilateral treaty has not been in effect long enough to measure its impact on reducing corruption in Mexico. Some argue that public (and media) outrage at the more blatant cases of corruption in recent years is more likely to reduce corruption than an international legal instrument.

Mexico is still considered a corrupt place in which to do business. According to a 1999 corruption index (derived from surveys performed by international lending agencies and others and published by Transparency International [TI], a Berlin-based group devoted to fighting corruption worldwide), Mexico ranked medium-high (61st out of 99 countries ranked) in the level of corruption associated with its business environment. Corrupt practices that affect the business community include collusion on public contracts, sharing insider information, harassment and intimidation, contributions to political campaigns, and kickbacks for lucrative government decisions.

Of course, the corrosive affects of corruption are not restricted to the business world; corruption also affects the political culture and the common citizenry, who have little respect for government agencies and their representatives. Indeed, most Mexicans believe corruption to be the most important obstacle to achieving full **democracy**. Transparency Mexico discovered in a 2001 study that Mexico City residents must pay bribes for almost one-quarter of the government services they receive. The most frequently paid bribes are given for car-related services such as avoiding traffic tickets and for retrieving an impounded automobile or truck. Despite President **Vincente Fox**'s "no more bribes" campaign, most Mexicans see little change in the ethos of police officers, public clerks, and other government officials. Because of slow and cumbersome public bureaucracies, many Mexicans find paying bribes a convenient way of dealing with their government.

What causes individuals to engage in corrupt political and business practices? Several reasons stand out in Mexico: Elaborate bureaucratic rules and requirements—multiple papers, stamps, signatures, and visits to multiple points in the chain of authority—contribute to the use of bribes to cut through the thicket of red tape. Most civil servants—police, customs officials, antinarcotics police, building inspectors, and those who work in government ministries—work for subsistence wages and in deplorable conditions; many see bribe taking as a means of survival. The act of winning an election is often seen as an economic bonanza for the winners, combined with the expectation that elected officials will dip into the public treasury with impunity. The bounty associated with public office is captured by the phrase "Un político pobre es un pobre político" (a politician who is poor is a poor politician), heard often in Mexican political circles. The difficulty of rooting out corruption is compounded by the fact that journalists and others who attempt to investigate politically sensitive topics—police corruption and misconduct, election fraud, money laundering, **human rights** violations, and drug trafficking—are often harassed, physically attacked, or murdered. Between 1970 and 1988, 51 Mexican journalists were murdered due to their investigations and stories of official corruption and other misdeeds. During his first year in office, President Fox spoke out against government corruption on a regular basis, appointed a new federal customs chief with instructions to clean up one of Mexico's most corrupt agencies, and made known his intentions to carry out threats to dismiss government officials suspected of acts of extortion and for collaborating with criminals. The use of torture by police officers to extract confessions is part of a corrupt labyrinth that has existed in Mexico's justice system for centuries. The longstanding impunity associated with officials who break the law contributes to the lack of faith most Mexicans have in their current system of justice and tax collection.

SUGGESTED READING

Wayne A. Cornelius, Judith Gentleman, and Peter H. Smith, eds., *Mexico's Alternative Political Futures* (La Jolla: Center for U.S.–Mexican Studies, University of California–San Diego, 1989); Eduardo A. Gamarra, "Transnational Criminal Organizations in Mexico," in Tom J. Farer, ed., *Transnational Crime in the Americas* (New York: Routledge, 1999); Walter Little and Eduardo Posada-Carbó, eds., *Political Corruption in Latin America and Europe* (New York: St. Martin's, 1996); Juan Miguel de Mora, *Ladrones en el gobierno: Mexico, la corrupción,* 2d ed. (Mexico, D.F.: Editores Asociados Mexicanos, 1979); Stephen D. Morris, *Corruption and Politics in Contemporary Mexico* (Tuscaloosa: University of Alabama Press, 1991); Lorenza Muñoz and Mary Beth Sheridan, "Mexico's Government Becomes the Reluctant Star of the Show," *Los Angeles Times,* March 7, 2000; "Murder, Money, and Mexico," *Frontline* video (Alexandria, Va.: PBS Video, 1997); Jorge Nef, "Government Corruption in Latin America," in Gerald E. Caiden, O. P. Dwivedi, and Joseph Jabbra, eds., *Where Corruption Lives* (Bloomfield, Conn: Kumarian Press, 2001); Andrew Wheat, "Mexico's Privatization Piñata," *Multinational Monitor* (October 1996).

Cosío Villegas, Daniel (1898–1976) ✳ Monumental figure in the intellectual history of modern Mexico whose intellectual pursuits spanned many professional areas, from history and economics to politics, journalism, and diplomacy. Casío Villeges developed a capacity for critical analysis of culture, society, and history that made him a legend in shaping the trajectory of Mexican development from the efforts at reconstruction after the **Mexican Revolution** to the promotion of **democracy**, economic and social justice, and greater respect for individual liberties in the post–**World War II** period. After receiving his bachelor's degree in law in 1925, he continued his academic studies at Harvard University, the University of Wisconsin, Cornell University, the London School of Economics, and the École Libre des Sciences Politiques de Paris. Most of his intellectual stimulus came from university students and professors in Mexico whose teaching and research contributed to his pioneering efforts in economic policy, international relations and diplomacy, critical analysis of history and governments, and educational reform.

In an effort to expand the academic study of Mexico's social realities, Cosío Villegas founded the school of economics at the **Universidad Nacional Autónoma de México (UNAM)**, the Casa de España (a research institute for Spanish exiles displaced by the Spanish Civil War), **El Colegio de México** (where he taught and produced many

Daniel Cosío Villegas. Credit: General Secretariat of the Organization of American States.

famous disciples), and the publishing house Fondo de Cultura Económica. He was also instrumental in the creation of several important academic journals in Mexico: *El Trimestre Económico*, *Historia Mexicana*, and *Foro Internacional*. He devoted the last decades of his life to the critical study of Mexican history and the evolution of power and politics in Mexico beginning in the 19th century. With a team of historians and economists, Cosío Villegas produced *Historia moderna de México*, considered a classic reference work devoted to the

historiography of 19th-century Mexico. His interest in dissecting the inner workings of Mexican government and politics resulted in a caustic study entitled *La crisis de México* (1947), a work that marked a turning point in his political thinking.

Always the professional who defended "liberty over political deal making," Cosío Villegas claimed that "the intellectual is a man who turns all answers into questions" (Yankelevich 1997, 356). Unfortunately, his death in 1976 prevented him from applying his rigorous professional analysis to

Mexico's troublesome social and political realities that beset the country during the last two decades of the 20th century. During the presidency of **Luis Echeverría** (1970–1976), he was given the National Prize in Letters for his intellectual and cultural contributions to modern Mexico.

SUGGESTED READING

James W. Wilkie and Edna Wilkie Monzón, "Daniel Cosío Villegas," in *Frente a la Revolución Mexicana: 17 protagonistas de la etapa constructiva, Entrevistas de historia oral*, vol. 1 (Mexico City: Universidad Autónoma Metropolitana, 1995); Pablo Yankelevich, "Cosío Villegas, Daniel," in Michael S. Werner, ed., *Encyclopedia of Mexico: History, Society, and Culture* (Chicago: Fitzroy Dearborn, 1997).

Covarrubias, Miguel (1904–1957) ☀ Although he was born in Mexico, Miguel Covarrubias spent many years in the United States, developing a reputation as a painter, scholar, and caricaturist. Known in Mexico and the United States as "El Chamaco" (the kid) for his youthful artistic creativity, Covarrubias developed his characteristic style by drawing figures from the world of theater and high fashion in 1920s New York. His talent as a graphic artist and caricaturist landed him jobs with New York magazines such as *Vanity Fair* and the *New Yorker*; he also played an active part in the political and intellectual life of the city, working with Langston Hughes and other members of the Harlem Renaissance. After he married dancer "Rosa" Cowan Rolando, the couple went on a round-the-world travel venture that sparked a lifelong interest in anthropological studies. With stops in many of the exotic spots of Pacific Asia, Covarrubias and his wife developed a mutual interest in writing and illustrating books about the Pacific basin. Assisted by a Guggenheim grant, Covarrubias spent a year in Bali in 1934 and wrote *Island of Bali* (1937), an appealing book that he illustrated with his wife's photographs and some of his own creative drawings of the island.

After returning to Mexico, Covarrubias developed an interest in ethnography, particularly the indigenous cultures of the Isthmus of Tehuantepec in southern Mexico. During the 1940s, he moved back and forth between New York and Mexico City. He curated exhibits of Mexican art for the Museum of Modern Art in New York, published *Mexico South: The Isthmus of Tehuantepec*, and helped spur an interest in Mexican anthropology, museography, and archeology. While at the National School of Anthropology and History (Escuela Nacional de Antropología e Historia, ENAH) between 1943 and 1947, he served as the first head of museography, curated exhibits of Mexican masks and Indian art of North America, taught courses on pre-Hispanic and primitive art, and painted an ethnographic mural.

Carlos Chávez named Covarrubias chair of the dance department at the National Institute of Fine Arts (Instituto Nacional de Bellas Artes) in 1950, where he designed costumes and theatrical sets for the well-known ballets that were performed at Bellas Artes in the early 1950s. According to art scholar Adriana Williams (1996, 296), "He possessed a rare intuitive ability to capture and synthesize at a glace the essentials of character or situation, as demonstrated by his famous caricatures for *Vanity Fair* and his illustrations for his first books." After leaving the National Institute of Fine Arts, he published a two-volume study of indigenous art, *The Eagle, the Jaguar, and the Serpent*. The first volume appeared in 1954 and the second was published shortly after his death in 1957.

SUGGESTED READING

Antonio Saborit, "Covarrubias, Miguel," in Michael S. Werner, ed., *Encyclopedia of Mexico: History, Society,*

Miguel Covarrubias drawing of *Tehuana—Mexican Belle*. Credit: Art Collection, Harry Ransom Humanities Research Center, University of Texas at Austin.

and Culture, vol. 1 (Chicago: Fitzroy Dearborn, 1997); Bennett Schiff, *A Caricaturist Who Brought the Stars Right Down to Earth* (Washington, D.C.: Smithsonian Associates, 1984); Adriana Williams, *Covarrubias* (Austin: University of Texas Press, 1994); Williams, "Covarrubias, Miguel," in Barbara A. Tenenbaum, ed., *Encyclopedia of Latin American History and Culture* (New York: Scribners, 1996).

Cuba and Mexico ☀ Since the Spanish American War of 1898, the island of Cuba has been of crucial importance to Mexico. Its geographical location—strategically situated between the United States (less than 100 miles from Key West) and one of the main entrances to the Gulf of Mexico—has given Cuba a special place in Mexican–Cuban relations. Between 1917 and 1959, Cuba's close ties to the United States put Mexico at odds with Cuba, resulting in mostly informal contacts and obvious differences in diplomatic behavior in the Organization of American States (OAS) and the United Nations.

Fidel Castro's insurrection against the dictator Fulgencio Batista offered a brief opening for closer Mexican–Cuban friendship, largely because Castro used Mexican soil to prepare and launch his revolution and after his victory his reforms and ideology appeared to be more nationalist than socialist. Castro's land reform and his nationalization of foreign assets (mostly property controlled by the United States) provided the Mexicans with positive memories of similar policy initiatives put forth by President **Lázaro Cárdenas** in the 1930s. The whole intellectual spectrum of Mexico cheered Castro's triumph over Batista. The new intellectual generation, including writer **Carlos Fuentes,** came to believe that Cuba represented the wave of the future, a living argument for socialism and collectivism in contrast to the Protestant individualism represented by the United States. However, early enthusiasm for the young Cuban *barbudos*

(bearded ones)—and declarations of solidarity and support for the Cuban revolution by ex-president Cárdenas and President **Adolfo López Mateos** (1958–1964)—soon vanished under the pressure of U.S. **intervention** and hostility.

After the Bay of Pigs invasion (1961) and the Cuban Missile Crisis (1962), López Mateos realized that he needed to mollify two groups that espoused opposite agendas in Mexico: leftists and nationalists who wanted stronger government support for Castro's Cuba on the one hand, and conservatives and foreign investors who urged the Mexican government to join the United States in condemning the Castro regime on the other. While both groups found common ground with Mexico's need to defend Cuba's national sovereignty in the face of U.S. **intervention**, the Mexican government faced a difficult balancing act among a variety of ideological groups at home and its historic dependency on the United States for trade and financial aid. According to Enrique Krauze (1997, 654), a writer and one of Mexico's leading advocates of democratic reform, "The [Mexican] government had to find a reasonable balance between the American Goliath and the Cuban David supported by the Russian Goliath."

The American government never faced such a policy dilemma after Castro came to power. With no need to appease the American left, and with a wealthy and vocal community of Cuban exiles in Miami with connections in Washington, domestic politics (including the large number of electoral votes in key states where exiles reside) became the major factor in the tenacity of a more than 40-year-old policy of punitive economic sanctions against the ailing regime.

Mexico's relations with Cuba offer a revealing example of how politics at home influences **foreign policy.** To keep the spirit of the revolution alive, PRI-dominated governments often exploited Cuba's revolutionary experience in order to placate the Mexican left and divert attention from unprogressive, and unpopular, domestic policies. Many members of the Mexico's intellectual elite believed that the values inherent in the Cuban revolution could be used to resuscitate the **Mexican Revolution**, viewed by some in the 1960s as a cadaver. Mexico has consistently opposed the U.S. trade embargo against the island nation and adamantly refuses to bow to U.S. coercion to adhere to the dictates of the Helms-Burton Law to "strangle" Cuba economically. After the Cuban Missile Crisis, when the United States and the rest of the Latin American and Caribbean states voted to expel Cuba from the OAS, the Mexican government steadfastly refused to sever diplomatic ties with Cuba and criticized the United States during this tense period of Cold War bluster.

Since the 1960s, Mexico has been attempting to reintegrate Cuba into the inter-American system by helping to persuade the OAS to lift its sanctions against Cuba in 1975; not joining in U.S. pressures against the island; creating a Latin American Economic System (SELA), a group that included Cuba but excluded the United States; refusing to bow to the extraterritorial dictates of Helms-Burton; and engaging in high-level diplomatic contacts on a frequent basis. The Mexican government's domestic exploitation of Cuba's revolution in order to claim greater legitimacy at home does not mean that Cuba is allowed to meddle in Mexico's internal affairs. What the relationship means is that in return for its cordial foreign policy, the government in Mexico City expects Cuba to stay out of Mexican domestic politics, whether the subject is **human rights**, social justice, inequality, poverty, crime, or **corruption**. Once Castro is no longer at the helm, Mexico will be forced to adjust its rhetoric and policies—domestic and foreign—toward a Cuba without Castro. Whatever future modifications take place in the formulation of Mexican foreign policy, they will have to consider the important symbolism of the Mexican Revolution, Mexico's previous struggles against foreign intervention, and the preponderant influence of the United States.

The most sensitive issue in Mexico's relationship with Cuba is human rights, particularly the treatment of dissidents who oppose the dictatorship. Although President **Vicente Fox** has taken a strong stand against human rights violations in Mexico, he has not deviated from Mexico's longstanding practice of abstaining when anti-Cuba resolutions come before the United Nations Human Rights Commission. In Castro's view, the real offense against human rights is the decades-old embargo against the island by the United States, not the manner in which governments treat enemies of the regime. *See also* Estrada Doctrine.

SUGGESTED READING

Jürgen Buchenau, "Mexico as a Middle Power: A Historical Perspective," in Thomas M. Leonard, ed., *Perspectives on Inter-American Relations in the Twentieth Century* (Tuscaloosa: University of Alabama Press, 1997); Enrique Krauze, *Mexico: Biography of Power*, trans. Hank Heifetz (New York: HarperCollins, 1997); Edward L. McCaughan, *Reinventing Revolution: The Renovation of Left Discourse in Cuba and Mexico* (Boulder, Colo.: Westview, 1997); Laura Muñoz, ed., *México y Cuba: Una relación historica* (Mexico, D.F.: Instituto Mora, 1998); Mario Ojeda, *Alcances y límites de la política exterior de México* (Mexico, D.F.: Colegio de México, 1976); Olga Pellicer de Brody, *México y la Revolución Cubana* (Mexico, D.F.: Colegio de México, 1972); Josefina Z. Vázquez and Lorenzo Meyer, *The United States and Mexico* (Chicago: University of Chicago Press, 1985).

Day of the Dead *(Día de los Muertos)* ☀ On the night between November 1 and 2, Mexicans celebrate the Day of the Dead, an elaborate and unique ritual that combines All Saints Day, All Souls Day, and Halloween. It is a tradition that has been practiced in Mexico and Central America for more than 3,000 years. Spanish Catholic priests persuaded the newly conquered Aztecs and other indigenous groups to shift the dates of their death cult festivals to match All Saints and All Souls Day, an act that helped solidify Spanish domination in the Americas. Celebrated in every region and by all social classes and ethnic groups, *Día de los Muertos* is based on the belief that lost love ones can communicate with the living if the correct rituals are followed. One is supposed to provide a meal—supplemented with skull-shaped sugar candies and *pan de muerto* ("bread of the dead")—on the graves of the deceased in order to lure the departed back to the world of the living, at least for that night. As Mexican writer **Carlos Fuentes** (1997, 12) points out, "Life in Mexico foresees death; it knows that death is the origin of all things. The past, the ancestors, are the sources of the present."

Throughout Mexico, family members erect home altars, usually made of wooden tables decorated with offerings (*ofrendas*) of candles, food, flowers, and drink, especially items the deceased was known to enjoy. Most of these altars include bread, fruit, sugar, and *mole*; **beer**, **tequila**, and other liquor; and pictures of the deceased and various saints. It is important that family members make nighttime visits to the graves of the departed. As relatives spend the night waiting to hear from their loved ones, they frequently gorge themselves and get a little drunk waiting for signs

that those from beyond have returned. In urban Mexico, mourners may pay musicians to sing at the grave sites of the departed. Mexican children have long used the occasion to request that passersby provide them with *mi muertito* (my little dead one), any sweet or food item the individual is willing to surrender. Today, children stroll through city streets and grave sites carrying small plastic jack-o'-lanterns, begging for *mi Halloween*, which usually means a small coin or sweet treat.

Punishment is said to await family members who neglect the dead during this costly two-day celebration. This belief contributes to the large outlay of energy and money made by family members. At the same time, the holiday provides a boost to local economies through the sales of sweets, flowers, and candles. The Catholic Church celebrates special masses for the occasion, ones that honor the souls of the departed and certain causes designated each year by the pope and the parish priest. This uniquely Mexican folk ritual is a fusion of pre-Conquest and Roman Catholic ceremonial practices. It is one of Mexico's richest and most interesting rituals devoted to the theme of death and the afterlife. However, the iconography of death tends to be lighthearted and humorous, involving lively drawings of animated skulls and skeletons found in bakeries, supermarkets, and candy stores.

The Day of the Dead is a uniquely Mexican expression of death, ridicule, humor, and color. The annual November celebration has long been used to ridicule politicians and public figures. This is usually done with a *calavera* or skull molded from sugar, chocolate, and amaranth seed. Candy *calaveras* are often whimsically decorated, including the names of a living person to whom the item is presented as a gift. The term *calavera* also refers to a form of satirical poetry used to poke fun at the privileged and wealthy, showing that the well-to-do and powerful are no better than the rest of society. According to Brandes (1997, 393), "The *calavera* is a brilliant social leveling mechanism. It, together with the rest of the humor and whimsy that characterize the Day of the Dead, is unique to Mexico."

Today, the Day of the Dead competes with Halloween, driven by the desire of powerful commercial establishments like Sanborns and Superama to sell masks, candy, costumes, and jack-o'-lanterns throughout Mexico. Many Mexicans resent this trend because of Halloween's association with the United States. However, many **Chicanos** in the United States have Day of the Dead celebrations, particularly in California, Arizona, New Mexico, and New York, as recently arrived Mexicans use the ritual to express and reinforce their Mexican identity. It is not uncommon for *ofrendas* in the United States to display Mexican and American flags. Those who have lived in the United States for longer periods have taken an interest in the celebration as part of a growing interest in their "roots" south of the border. Unlike Halloween, which depicts spirits as evil tricksters, the Day of the Dead teaches Mexicans that dying is part of the cycle of life and is not to be feared. Despite apprehension that the spread of American pop culture into Mexico will wipe out traditional rites such as *Día de los Muertos,* the death cult festivity is still strong in many places.

SUGGESTED READING

Stanley Brandes, "Day of the Dead," in Michael S. Werner, ed., *Encyclopedia of Mexico: History, Society, and Culture,* vol. 1 (Chicago: Fitzroy Dearborn, 1997); Barbara Brodman, *The Mexican Cult of Death in Myth and Literature* (Gainesville: University Presses of Florida, 1976); Elizabeth Carmichael and Chloë Sayer, *The Skeleton at the Feast: The Day of the Dead in Mexico* (Austin: University of Texas Press, 1992); Robert V. Childs and Patricia B. Altman, *Vive tu recuerdo: Living Traditions in Mexican Days of the Dead* (Los Angeles: Museum of Cultural History, 1982); Carlos Fuentes, *A New Time for Mexico* (Berkeley: University of California Press, 1997); Jennifer Merin with Elizabeth Burdick, *International Directory of Theatre, Dance, and Folklore Festivals* (Westport, Conn.: Greenwood, 1979); Patrick Oster, *The Mexicans: A Personal Portrait of a People* (New York: William Morrow, 1989).

De la Madrid Hurtado, Miguel (1934–) ☀ Mexico's seventh postwar president (1982–1988). De la Madrid faced a nation on the brink of economic collapse—rapidly increasing inflation, a reversal in economic growth, high rates of unemployment, capital flight, and massive external debt—when he assumed the presidency in December 1982. With the country in a full-scale economic depression and the legitimacy of the presidency battered by poor management and increasing amounts of graft and **corruption**, President de la Madrid decided to pursue a conservative strategy with emphasis on economic austerity measures. In political matters, he stressed the importance of political stability at home and cautious accommodation with Mexico's powerful northern neighbor, the United States.

As the value of the Mexican peso to the U.S. dollar sank to all-time lows, President de la Madrid was forced to accept austerity prescriptions from the International Monetary Fund (IMF) and World Bank, as well as greater U.S. influence in Mexican affairs. He doubled the price of gasoline and instituted a general austerity to reverse the economic downslide, and he made efforts toward a "moral renovation" campaign to alleviate the crisis and restore confidence at home and abroad. With a burgeoning foreign debt, declining world oil prices, and economic turmoil, illegal **immigration** to the United States increased dramatically, leading to further tensions over increased flow of migrants into the U.S. labor market. With a leadership style that emphasized pragmatism and tolerance of political dissent, de la Madrid moved away from the populist and demagogic method of governing of his two predecessors.

Under de la Madrid, the government made concerted efforts to eliminate corruption, particularly in the oil and teachers unions, but his anti-corruption drive was hampered by the economic crisis and the pervasiveness of corruption itself. Although he and his advisers criticized the corrupt practices of their predecessors and spoke of a moral renovation, there was a tremendous gap between de la Madrid's lofty rhetoric and policy application. Despite the arrest of top officials who had served during the **López Portillo** administration, de la Madrid's own government was by no means free of graft and bribery. Many failed to see anything resembling a "moral" reconstruction, given the deterioration of **human rights** conditions and the declining importance of civil liberties. His mishandling of the rescue and relief efforts in Mexico City after the 1985 earthquake that killed upwards of 20,000 residents and destroyed thousands of buildings provoked the wrath of citizens and the development of numerous popular opposition movements. Mexico's declining oil prices and the resource demands for post-earthquake reconstruction left de la Madrid's administration with little hope of making much economic and social progress during his presidency.

Miguel de la Madrid was born to a well-to-do family in Colima in 1934, although he grew up and attended schools in Mexico City. The son of Miguel de la Madrid Castro (a lawyer and government employee who was killed by wealthy landowners because of his defense of peasant rights) and Alicia Hurtado, he attended private schools until he entered the National Law School, from which he graduated with honors in 1957. At the National Law School de la Madrid studied

under José López Portillo, creating a friendship that catapulted him into the presidency several decades later. He attended Harvard University in the mid-1960s and earned a master's degree in public administration, thus becoming the first Mexican president with an advanced degree or a foreign degree. On returning to Mexico, he taught at the National University and began work at the Bank of Mexico, where he developed important political contacts. These were developed further when he moved to **PEMEX** as assistant director of finance and later as assistant secretary of credit in the treasury department. Once President López Portillo appointed him secretary

President Miguel de la Madrid. Credit: *Proceso*, photo by Germán Canseco.

of programming and planning in 1979, he had the inside track for selection as the **PRI** candidate for president in 1981.

Mexico's economic slump in the early 1980s put severe restrictions on Mexican **foreign policy** initiatives, eventually forcing Mexico to bend to U.S. policy in Central America and to adopt measures accelerating the integration of the Mexican and U.S. economies. Mexico's heavy debt burden reduced its ability to continue assisting the Sandinistas in Nicaragua and forced it to bow to the dictates of foreign investors and the international lending community, pushing Mexico further in the direction of neoliberal economics and closer ties to the United States. Mexico joined the Contadora Group (made up of Colombia, Panama, and Venezuela) in 1983 so that it could extricate itself from the burdens of the Central American **debt crisis** while at the same time somewhat satisfying members of the Mexican left that it opposed President Ronald Reagan's hard-line agenda by participating in an honorable search for a peaceful solution.

As Mexico expanded its share of the production and transshipment of illicit drugs to the United States, U.S. government agencies attacked Mexican officials as being inept, corrupt, and cowardly in avoiding the roots of the problem. After the murder of U.S. drug agents in Mexico in 1985 and 1986, President de la Madrid became the first Mexican president to label **drug trafficking** as a national security issue and "an affair of state." In response to the frustration of trying to work with Mexican officials, the Reagan administration demanded that Mexico allow U.S. law enforcement officials to carry guns and make arrests inside Mexico. Mexico rejected this arrogant attitude and intrusion on its national sovereignty but nonetheless offered to cooperate with the United States in intercepting illicit drug shipments. Despite the recognized need for cooperation, Mexico refused to budge on its belief that the destructive nature of the drug problem originates with the voracious appetite for drugs in the United States.

Mexico's economic turmoil after 1982 produced a dramatic increase in undocumented **immigration** to the United States that further complicated bilateral relations. Soon a diverse anti-immigration alliance developed in the United States determined to stop illegal immigration to the United States from Mexico. The Reagan administration recognized the domestic political value of making immigration a focal issue, beefing up border patrols and demanding that Mexico do more to stem the flow to "El Norte." The U.S. Congress debated several versions of an immigration reform bill before the controversial Immigration Reform and Control Act (also known as Simpson-Rodino, the last names of its sponsors) was passed in 1986. The winning alliance of conservative Senator Jesse Helms along with the AFL-CIO and the United Farm Workers of America designed the legislation to grant amnesty to all undocumented workers with at least two years of continual residence in the United States, combined with harsh penalties on employers who hire new arrivals without proper immigration papers. The debate—often with strong racist overtones—and new legislation upset many Mexicans who argued that undocumented workers are a boon to U.S. employers because of the low wages paid to Mexicans and the frequent human rights violations and indignities suffered by many Mexicans in the United States. President de la Madrid tried to walk a fine line between a strong defense of the civil rights of Mexican citizens and the legal right of the United States to determine its own immigration policy.

By the end of the de la Madrid administration, Mexico was well on its way to ending its postrevolutionary model of state-mediated capitalism, creating a more competitive and conflictual political system, and adopting a foreign policy more closely tied to the United States. This neoliberal course of economic development may not last forever, but

Miguel de la Madrid will be remembered for his efforts to guide Mexico away from the brink of economic collapse. When the time came for President de la Madrid to pick his successor, he chose a young neoliberal economist trained at Harvard—**Carlos Salinas de Gortari**—who shared a great deal of the faith of the United States in the advantages of free trade and minimizing the role of the state in the economy. Nevertheless, the emerging rift between the old *políticos* and young **technocrats** developed into a major fault line in the Mexican political system. After de la Madrid left office in 1988, President Salinas made him director of the Fondo de la Cultura Económica, a publicly funded publishing firm.

SUGGESTED READING

John Bailey, *Governing Mexico: The Statecraft of Crisis Management* (New York: St. Martin's, 1988); Roderic Ai Camp, "Madrid Hurtado, Miguel de la," in Barbara A. Tenenbaum, ed., *Encyclopedia of Latin American History and Culture*, vol. 3 (New York: Scribners, 1996); Jorge G. Castañeda, *La herencia: Una arqueología de la sucesión presidencial en México* (Mexico, D.F.: Editorial Alfaguara, 1999); Wayne A. Cornelius, *The Political Economy of Mexico under de la Madrid: The Crisis Deepens, 1985–1986* (La Jolla: Center for U.S.–Mexican Studies, University of California–San Diego, 1986); Timothy P. Kessler, *Global Capital and National Politics: Reforming Mexico's Financial System* (Westport, Conn.: Praeger, 1999); Stephen D. Morris, *Political Reformism in Mexico: An Overview of Contemporary Mexican Politics* (Boulder, Colo.: Lynne Rienner, 1995).

Debt Crisis ☀ Mexico's postwar record of government-directed economic growth produced an annual rate of 6–7 percent growth in the gross domestic product between 1940 and 1970 that was impressive by any standard of economic achievement. Even with population growth factored into the equation, per capita gains remained at about 3.5 percent annually, and the rapid growth did not trigger high levels of inflation. Few Latin American countries have experienced such impressive levels of economic growth over such a long period of time. Yet, despite its achievements, Mexico's postwar economic boom was seriously flawed: the benefits of growth were unevenly distributed; the model of import substitution industrialization (ISI) produced economic inefficiencies, balance of payments problems, and monetary instability; and the persistence of poverty and income inequality generated serious political protest movements aimed at undoing the economic injustices. All of these forces contributed to the debt crisis that Mexico faced in the early 1980s. When President **Luis Echeverría** took office in 1970, the public sector's external debt was $4.2 billion; by the time President **José López Portillo** left office 12 years later, the debt had risen to $85 billion, the second largest in the developing world.

In the search for renewed prosperity and stability, Presidents **Miguel de la Madrid** (1982–1988) and **Carlos Salinas de Gortari** (1988–1994) reversed decades of economic nationalism and state economic intervention. The debt crisis was compounded by the unexpected fall in petroleum prices in the early 1980s. In 1982 the Mexican government announced that it could no longer meet its foreign debt obligations, helping spread the crisis (sometimes called the "tequila effect") throughout Latin America. In Mexico the debt crisis necessitated painful austerity programs and generated high levels of inflation and unemployment, as well as declining living standards, that Mexicans had not encountered since the 1930s. Presidents de la Madrid and Salinas opened the country to foreign imports and investment, promoted industrial exports, joined the **General Agreement on Tariffs and Trade** (GATT) in 1986, and championed Mexican membership in the **North American Free Trade Agreement** (NAFTA) in 1994, leading to greater financial dependency on the United States and a peasant uprising in Chiapas by a group calling itself Zapatistas.

Although many Mexicans initially considered President Salinas a savior who had resolved the debt crisis, brought inflation under control, and restored a modest amount of economic recovery, he underestimated Mexico's large balance of payments problems and refused to devalue the peso, leaving an economic mess for his successor, **Ernesto Zedillo**. Once President Zedillo was installed in office, the value of the peso plunged again, foreign capital fled, the stock market took a nosedive, and Mexico was again faced with a deep depression. During his last year in office, President Zedillo claimed in a New Year's speech that Mexico had finally left the 1994–1995 peso crisis behind, urged citizens to go to the polls in July 2000, and told his audience, "We Mexicans are living in full democracy" in an effort to applaud his political reforms. *See also* Zapatista rebellion in Chiapas.

SUGGESTED READING

Jorge G. Castañeda, *The Mexican Shock: Its Meaning for the United States* (New York: New Press, 1995); Sudarshan Gooptu, *Debt Reduction and Development: The Case of Mexico* (Westport, Conn.: Praeger, 1993); Howard Handelman, *Mexican Politics: The Dynamics of Change* (New York: St. Martin's, 1997); Nora Lustig, *Mexico: The Remaking of an Economy*, 2d ed. (Washington, D.C.: Brookings Institution, 1998); Riordan Roett, ed., *The Mexican Peso Crisis: International Perspectives* (Boulder, Colo.: Lynne Rienner, 1996).

Dedazo ☀ The staying power of Mexico's one-party system in which the **Partido Revolucionario Institucional (PRI)** managed to remain in power for over 70 years was largely the result of an unwritten prerogative of the sitting president to designate his successor, impose him as the PRI's sole candidate, and ensure that he prevailed in the national vote for president. This rather remark-able feature of presidential succession meant that while there were times when the president consulted with other PRI power brokers before appointing a successor, the selection process was essentially a one-person decision. Because the incumbent president chose his successor (and other officials) by "pointing his finger" at them, the process of presidential recruitment came to be known as the institution of *dedazo* (Spanish for finger or toe is *dedo*), or the fingering. Since the PRI presidents maintained close control over virtually all stages of the succession process, elections were considered meaningless exercises in "democratic" selection. Despite the **corporatist** features of the party system, there is no evidence that the leaders of the **labor**, agrarian, and popular sectors have been able to impose a PRI candidate for president.

The institution of the *dedazo* as a method of candidate selection began to change in the 1980s and 1990s, as critics charged that PRI authoritarianism denied Mexican voters a voice in determining who would be president of the country would and opposition parties began to gain electoral strength. As the crisis in the PRI deepened after the 1988 election and economic and financial problems continued, PRI politicians worried that without significant reforms, Mexico would be unable to meet the challenges of the 21st century. The first PRI candidate to advocate putting an end to the "finger system" was **Luis Donaldo Colosio**, but his plan fizzled when he was assassinated—reportedly ordered by PRI hard-liners—at a campaign rally in March 1994. **Ernesto Zedillo** was chosen by outgoing president **Carlos Salinas de Gortari** to replace Colosio, promising in the final months of the campaign to end the *dedazo* by "cutting the finger off" and using a different method of selection.

After winning the presidency in 1994, Zedillo worked to fulfill his campaign promise of getting rid of the *dedazo* system and replacing it with a primary election that would take place in early

November, nine months before the general election. During its first presidential primary in 1999, the PRI spent over $9 million in an effort to avoid the perception of a rigged, fraudulent, and undemocratic process of presidential selection. While the *dedazo* no longer exists, cynics claim that President Zedillo, despite repeated denials during the primary campaign period, engaged in behind-the-scenes efforts to make sure that his former interior secretary, **Francisco Labastida,** won the party's nomination over two former governors and a former party leader.

Is the *dedazo* finally dead after 71 years of one-party rule? The combination of President Zedillo's decision to dispense with the *dedazo* in 1999 and the election of PAN candidate **Vicente Fox** in 2000 would seem to signal that the ability of Mexican presidents to perpetuate one-party rule through the use of "fingering" as a mechanism of political recruitment no longer exists. In any case, it remains to be seen whether Mexico's political and economic reforms have leveled the playing field for opposition parties and candidates that compete in future elections. The transition from an oligarchy of those in the **Revolutionary Family** to a more authentic **democracy** may not be complete, but the recent defeat of the PRI brings Mexico closer than ever before to a pluralist form of rule.

SUGGESTED READING

M. Delal Baer, "Mexico's Coming Backlash," *Foreign Affairs* (July-August 1999); Jorge G. Castañeda, *La herencia: Arqueología de la sucesión presidencial en México* (Mexico, D.F.: Editorial Alfaguara, 1999); Boye Lafayette De Mente, *NTC's Dictionary of Mexican Cultural Code Words* (Lincolnwood, Ill.: NTC, 1996).

Del Paso, Fernando (1935–) ☀ One of a group of Mexican writers who have produced experimental novels that avoid established rules and traditions by emphasizing imaginary narrations.

By relying on colossal verbal constructions in his works, del Paso often rejects the simple answers offered by historiography, preferring to associate history with allegory, fantasy, and imagination. However, most of his novels make for exacting reading and require active involvement by the reader.

Born in Mexico City in 1935, Fernando del Paso spent more than 10 years in advertising before taking his plunge into the literary world in 1958. He attended the **Universidad Nacional Autónoma de México (UNAM)** and studied biology and economics. With a grant from the Mexican Writer's Center in 1964–1965, he produced his first novel, *José Trigo*, which was awarded the Xavier Villaurrutia Prize in 1966. After receiving a grant from the Guggenheim

Political cartoon by Salvador González ("Chava") following primary victory of PRI candidate Francisco Labastida in November 1999. Titled "New Tricks," the November 8, 1999 caricature shows President Zedillo being asked "Who did you vote for, Dr.?" by a member of the press situated on a stage named "New PRI." With a smile and gesture with his gigantic index finger, the president answers "For the rule by fingering." Credit: Salvador González and *El Norte,* November 8, 1999.

Foundation, he moved to London, where he exhibited his drawings and finished his second novel, *Palinuro de México* (1977), for which he received numerous prizes, including the Rómulo Gallegos International Novel Prize (1977). Since returning to Mexico in 1992, he has been director of the **Octavio Paz** Library in Guadalajara. In his writings he has turned to a new kind of autobiography—in which he serves as an intermediary for another great writer to recount his life story—and crime fiction. In *Palinuro en la escalera* (1992), del Paso's story includes a colorful cast of international characters: Ernesto "Che" Guevara, **Francisco "Pancho" Villa**, Jonathan Swift, Ho Chi Minh, and Latin American literary figures such as Rubén Darío and others.

SUGGESTED READING

Fernando del Paso, *Yo soy un hombre de letras: Discurso* (Mexico, D.F.: Colegio Nacional, 1996); Robin W. Fiddian, "Palinuro de México: A World of Words," *Bulletin of Hispanic Studies*, April 1981; Ilan Stavans, "Fernando del Paso," in Verity Smith, ed., *Encyclopedia of Latin American Literature* (Chicago: Fitzroy Dearborn, 1997).

Del Río, Dolores. *See* Río, Dolores del.

Del Río, Eduardo (1934–) ☀ One of Mexico's few cartoonists to achieve international fame, producing popular comic books and editorial cartoons under the pen name "Rius." Eduardo del Río grew up to be a rebel and powerful voice for the Mexican left, at one point boasting he had been fired by almost every newspaper he worked for. Using a strong, clear, and simple ink line, Rius turned some of his cartoons into a new comic book called *Los Supermachos,* featuring a naive but politically rebellious Indian. By using a comic-book style and quirky political humor, Rius acquired a reputation, and a

voice, for his secular-left perspective on Mexican political life.

Born in Zamora, Michoacán, in 1934, Eduardo del Río was the son of a shopkeeper who died shortly after Eduardo was born. After moving to Mexico City, his mother sent him to a Catholic seminary to avoid the "socialist" education then in vogue at public schools. However, while growing up in Mexico City, he rejected most of his formal education—and any kind of authority—preferring to express himself through his caricatures. His early career was influenced by the work of Saul Steinberg and Abel Quezada, two cartoonists who emphasized spare linear drawings with large amounts of blank space on the page. There are also elements of the cartoon drawings of José Guadalupe Posada— perhaps Mexico's best-known cartoonist of the first half of the 20th century—in Rius's cartoons, which often mocked the Church and landowning elites through skeleton motifs.

As his politics moved further to the left, Rius began to extend his political critique to a whole spectrum of topics that composed the Mexican counterculture of the 1960s and early 1970s— student activism, birth control, the **Mexican Revolution**, **corruption**, superpower politics, and vegetarianism. He joined a Marxist study group, visited Cuba, and participated in the 1961 Literacy Brigade; he also joined the Mexican **Communist** Party (PCM) for a few years. He devoted much of his artistic work to the Mexican student movement, Marxism, and the Cuban revolution, including the widely distributed *Cuba para principiantes* (Cuba for Beginners) in 1966. Between 1966 and 1995, he published 85 books, many of which have managed to stay in print for long periods of time (unlike most books published in Mexico that disappear after their initial print run).

After years of focusing his artistic endeavors on comic books such as *Los Supermachos* and *Los*

Agachados, in 1980 he turned to writing and drawing *infolibros* (informational books), often tackling controversial subjects—from human sexuality and **foreign policy** hypocrisy to the myth of the **Virgin of Guadalupe**—in a witty and didactic fashion. In a 1976 cartoon in *Los Agachados*, Rius captures Mexico's domestic policy–foreign policy paradox—sympathy for leftist movements outside of Mexico but not at home. A Mexican political leader pontificates that his country will restore diplomatic relations with Spain (then ruled by the fascist Francisco Franco) only after the dictatorship is deposed and **democracy** established, to which the Spanish general responds: "In Mexico?" As one of the most important expressions of the Mexican left, Rius continues to produce popular books and drawings that reach a large audience, although the majority of his followers are in urban Mexico.

SUGGESTED READING

David William Foster, *From Malfada to Los Supermachos: Latin American Graphic Humor as Popular Culture* (Boulder, Colo.: Lynne Rienner, 1989); Harold Hines and Charles Tatum, *Not Only for Children: The Mexican Comic Book in the 1960s* (Westport, Conn.: Greenwood, 1992); Eduardo Rius, *Rius para principiantes* (Mexico, D.F.: Grijalbo, 1995); Anne Rubenstein, "Del Río, Eduardo (Rius)," in Michael S. Werner, ed., *Encyclopedia of Mexico: History, Society, and Culture*, vol. 1 (Chicago: Fitzroy Dearborn, 1997).

Democracy and Democratization ☀

Mexican interest in democratization can be traced back to efforts at political liberalization in the 19th century and the antidictator reform efforts associated with the **Mexican Revolution** (1910–1917). Instead of a pluralistic democracy, Mexican elites created a strong corporatist system in the 1930s based on a dominant party and government-controlled organizations (particularly the **labor**

and peasant sectors). The authoritarian aspects of **corporatism** have eroded slowly over the past 20 years with a movement toward further democratization, as domestic and international forces have pressured Mexico to transform its political system into a more pluralistic society. By improving the quality of elections, curtailing government **corruption**, providing for broader group representation, making the party system more competitive, and striking a greater balance between presidential and other institutional bases of power, Mexico is more democratic than at any time in its modern history. Yet how democratic is Mexico today?

Political scientists, policy makers, journalists, and others have spent the past 50 years judging and analyzing the degree of democracy in Mexico. The apparent paradox between Mexico's formal democratic rules and structures and the reality of its unique and long-lasting one-party-dominant system has confounded analysts and commentators, who have yet to reach a consensus on the degree of democracy in the current system. Using a panel of distinguished area specialists, Russell Fitzgibbon developed a reputational survey method of measuring Latin American democracy that has been used on 20 countries since 1945, including Mexico. With a wide range of economic, social, and political variables, the panelists placed Mexico in third place (tied with Chile) in its cumulative democracy rankings between 1945 and 2000, behind Costa Rica and Uruguay. In the 2000 survey data Mexico ranked sixth, behind Brazil, Argentina, Chile, Uruguay, and Costa Rica. While somewhat puzzling to critics of the Mexican political system, Mexico's third-place overall ranking comes from scoring relatively high on some of Fitzgibbon's indicators: civilian supremacy over the military, regular elections, lack of ecclesiastical dominance, internal unity, and political maturity.

The paradox of residual authoritarianism and formal democracy lies at the core of Mexican politics today. It is a unique hybrid system that combines political liberalism with its own brand of authoritarianism, although it appears to be gradually moving toward a more pluralistic model. Compounding the assessment of Mexican democracy is the diversity of terms (or adjectives) that were used by scholars who studied Mexico during the period of PRI dominance: one-party democracy, semidemocracy, selective democracy, and partial democracy. Those who emphasized the authoritarian features of Mexican politics labeled the system with one or several of the following terms or concepts: perfect dictatorship, semiauthoritarian, hegemonic one-party, inclusionary authoritarianism, technocratic populism, or electoral bureaucratic authoritarianism.

Judging Mexico by stricter standards of democracy reveals that until the 2000 presidential election, the process of voting was far from perfect. Voting was sometimes fraudulent and unfair with most of the electoral advantages in the hands of the ruling party; executive–legislative relations were skewed in favor of the Mexican president, despite the fact that the legislature has become more representative and less of a rubber stamp than in the past. Moreover, civil and **human rights** are not as well protected as one would expect in a fully democratic polity (*see* appendix A).

The democratic and authoritarian features of Mexico's political system continue to change as economic and social modernization advance and increasing international pressures are put on the country's elites to discard the residual features of authoritarianism. Since 1988, Mexico has made a more serious effort to make elections more fair and competitive. As of 1999, 10 of Mexico's 31 states were in the hands of the opposition. In preparation for the 2000 election, President **Ernesto Zedillo** dispensed with the *dedazo* ("finger pointing"), the presidential mechanism for picking 10 consecutive presidents, and instead relied on a national primary. During the 2000 primary campaign, PRI hopefuls adopted some features of U.S. election campaigns,

including candidate debates, negative TV commercials, hiring U.S. pollsters and media consultants such as James Carville and Douglas E. Schoen, and appearing on popular TV programs in an effort to appeal to a younger audience. Some of the important opposition parties have followed suit in an effort to gain legitimacy and more effectively challenge the monopoly once held by the PRI. The historic defeat of the PRI candidate, **Francisco Labastida**, in 2000 suggested that a new political order—one with less corporatism and more democratic pluralism—may finally be in the making.

The traditional model of corporatist representation is beginning to break down with the growth of independent unions, cooperatives, and other groups outside the old system of rule. President **Carlos Salinas** revised the Mexican **Constitution of 1917** to give the clergy and the Catholic Church greater political rights. PRI dominance (in the 1950s and 1960s it won the presidency with close to 90 percent of the vote) has ended, as it only managed to capture 37 percent of the national vote in 2000. As a result of electoral reforms in 1990, 1993, 1994, 1996, and 1999, Mexican elections are now more honest, transparent, and fair contests at the polling booths. Former president Zedillo deserves credit for putting in place a number of initiatives aimed at creating a more democratic political system. Emphasizing the importance of democracy and the rule of law, President Zedillo initiated multiparty talks on political reform, the devolution of power from the executive to Congress and Mexico's 31 states, greater accountability through unscripted press conferences, and judicial review, allowing the constitutionality of new laws to be challenged in the supreme court.

While Mexico's democratization is mainly the product of domestic forces, it has also been prodded by Washington policy makers. As one of the pillars of U.S. foreign policy, democracy promotion has been applied to Mexico through government efforts to cultivate positive relations with opposition parties, providing election observers, and supporting expanded political participation by all elements of Mexican society. All these efforts have not as yet instilled greater faith in democratic institutions—judicial systems, legislatures, political parties, and even the presidency—as large numbers of ordinary Mexicans in recent polls still express negative views of democracy. The U.S. government's public statements and actions regarding democracy in Mexico from 1980 to 2000 were designed to nudge government efforts at reform, but without upsetting the stability, and longevity, of the ruling party.

Has Mexico consolidated a democratic system that will operate the government during the 21st century or will the Mexican paradox continue? The forces that gnaw at the foundations of meaningful political change have not disappeared, despite numerous electoral reforms implemented since 1989. Perhaps what is most needed in Mexico is a political culture that is more democratic in its outlook. The severe gap that separates the Mexican rich from the poor continues to widen as the middle and lower classes have been battered by declining incomes and government policies that have removed much of the safety net that once existed. The richest 10 percent of Mexicans receive more than 40 percent of total income, whereas the poorest 40 percent get only 13 percent. The rise of technocratic presidents over the past 20 years has put more emphasis on political stability, economic reform, and popular support for carrying the burden of neoliberalism. The ruling PRI, by emphasizing solidarity and harmony under government tutelage and dividing the right–left opposition with political reforms, was able to delay the march toward greater democratization until the July 2, 2000, election. As Mexicans prepared to vote in the 2000 election for president, opposition parties were unable to unify (or create a coalition candi-

date) in any significant manner. Nevertheless, Mexican voters felt confident enough to choose the change offered by PAN candidate **Vicente Fox** rather than sticking to the old politics under the PRI system of governing.

Throughout its 71-year rule, the PRI developed into a formidable organization for winning elections at all levels of society, holding on to the presidency, and dominating the whole state apparatus. Besieged, corrupt, and prone to elaborate cover-ups of official wrongdoing, the PRI government elite seemed more interested in playing a "reformist game" than a democratic one that would allow serious change from below. For years the PRI faced a major governing dilemma because of the contradiction between the desire for administrative and fiscal decentralization and the fear that this kind of reform would only strengthen the power of local bosses (*caciques*) or the opposition. Obviously, the paradox of Mexican politics will take time to fully resolve. While some have characterized the 2000 elections as a major political earthquake and a turning point toward greater democracy, Mexico still faces the negative consequences of a political culture with remnants of authoritarian and antidemocratic features that can be traced to the long period of a corporatist, one-party-dominant system that governed for most of the 20th century. If President Fox is successful in his efforts to expand democracy during his *sexenio*, some Mexican scholars believe this will make it easier to deal with issues of joint U.S.–Mexican concern and help transform Fox into a key figure in the democratization process now under way for the rest of Latin America. What role will Washington play in this transformation? In Mazza's (2001, 154) assessment of the U.S. role in recent Mexican democratization, "The United States will likely not want to rock the boat of a new Fox government by questioning their difficult process of deconstructing PRI rule." *See also* Electoral System/Elections.

SUGGESTED READING

Roderic Ai Camp, "Province versus the Center: Democratizing Mexico's Political Culture," in Philip Kelly, ed., *Assessing Democracy in Latin America: A Tribute to Russell H. Fitzgibbon* (Boulder, Colo.: Westview, 1998): 76–92; Jorge G. Castañeda, *La herencia: Arqueología de la sucesión presidential en México* (Mexico, D.F.: Editorial Alfaguara, 1999); John H. Coatsworth, "The United States and Democracy in Mexico," in Victor Bulmer-Thomas and James Dunkerley, eds., *The United States and Latin America: The New Agenda* (Cambridge, Mass.: Institute of Latin American Studies, University of London/David Rockefeller Center for Latin American Studies, Harvard University, 1999); Wayne A. Cornelius, *Mexican Politics in Transition*, 5th ed. (La Jolla: Center for U.S.–Mexican Studies, University of California–San Diego, 2000); Wayne A. Cornelius, Todd A. Eisenstadt, and Jane Hindley, eds., *Subnational Politics and Democratization in Mexico* (La Jolla: Center for U.S.–Mexican Studies, University of California–San Diego, 1999); Dan A. Cothran, *Political Stability and Democracy in Mexico: The "Perfect Dictatorship"?* (Westport, Conn.: Praeger, 1994); Nikki Craske, "Another Mexican Earthquake? An Assessment of the 2 July 2000 Elections," *Government and Opposition*, (Winter 2001: 27-47); Jorge I. Domínquez and Alejandro Poiré, eds., *Toward Mexico's Democratization: Parties, Campaigns, Elections, and Public Opinion* (New York: Routledge, 1999); Daniel C. Levy and Emilio Zebadúa, *Mexico: The Struggle for Democratic Development* (Boulder, Colo.: Westview, 1998); Arend Lijphart and Carlos Waisman, *Institutional Design in New Democracies: Eastern Europe and Latin America* (Boulder, Colo.: Westview, 1996); Jacqueline Mazza, *Don't Disturb the Neighbors: The U.S. and Democracy in Mexico, 1980–1995* (New York: Routledge, 2001); Stephen Morris, *Political Reformism in Mexico: An Overview of Contemporary Mexican Politics* (Boulder, Colo.: Lynne Rienner, 1995); Eric Olson, "So Close and Yet So Far: Mexico's Mid-term Elections and the Struggle for Democracy," Washington Office on Latin America, June 1997; Guy Poitras, "Mexico's Problematic Transition to Democracy," in Kelly, ed., *Assessing Democracy in Latin America*: 63–75; Andrew Reding, "Mexico: The Crumbling of the 'Perfect Dictatorship,'" *World Policy Journal* (1991): 255–88; Jesús Silva-Herzog Márquez, *El antiguo régimen y la transición en México* (Mexico, D.F.: Planeta Joaquín Mortiz, 1999); Beth Sims, *Foreign Support for the Mexican Democratization Process: Focus on the U.S. Agency for International Development and the National Endowment for Democracy* (Albuquerque, N. Mex.: Resource Center Press, 1993).

Díaz Ordaz, Gustavo (1911–1979) ☀ Mexico's fourth postwar president (1964–1970), known for his authoritarian style of administration and resistance to democratic reforms during a time when Mexico managed to maintain accelerated economic growth with low inflation. Although he continued the successful efforts of his predecessors to promote industrialization by substituting domestic manufactures for imported, Díaz Ordaz's political failures—the **Tlatelolco massacre** at the Plaza de las Tres Culturas, using the 1968 **Olympic Games** for propaganda purposes, and opposing the **democratization** of the PRI—during his *sexenio* (six-year term) produced a crisis in the presidency and the dominant party that sent shock waves of discontent inside and outside Mexico. A conservative reformer with a penchant for order, his power base originated from the clientelist network (*camarilla*) of former president **Miguel Alemán Valdés**.

Díaz Ordaz was born at the beginning of the **Mexican Revolution** in Ciudad Serdán, Puebla. His father was a government employee whose forefathers included Spanish conquistador and historian Bernal Díaz del Castillo; his mother, Sabina Bolaños Cacho, was a schoolteacher with stern and pious habits. It was a poor family that had to face numerous hardships as Díaz Ordaz was growing up. Considered ugly by many of his peers, he compensated by taking his studies seriously, dressing well, cultivating an attractive speaking style, and displaying an incredible capacity to retain large amounts of information. He was educated at the Universities of Oaxaca and Puebla, graduating in law in 1937. His career path to the presidency involved decades of public service, holding important government posts first in Puebla's government (1932–1943) and then in the federal government (1943–1970). After being selected as the PRI presidential nominee by outgoing president **Adolfo López Mateos** in 1963, he went on to win the 1964 presidential election with, allegedly, 90 percent of the vote. He was the last president to have served previously in Congress (as federal deputy and senator) until **Vicente Fox** won the 2000 election.

Díaz Ordaz's conservative domestic policies stressed industrial development and the pursuit of foreign capital. His administration, unlike those of his successors, was blessed with modest inflation and a stable peso, due in large part to his brilliant finance minister, **Antonio Ortíz Mena.** Mexico achieved agricultural self-sufficiency under his administration for the first (and last) time, while at the same time distributing more than 22 million acres of land to peasants (*campesinos*). His administration expanded educational opportunities and made substantial improvements in Mexico's infrastructure, building dams and the subway transportation system in Mexico City. Mexico's economic progress was once defined by Ortíz Mena as "stabilizing development," a reference to dramatic economic growth, low inflation, and a stable currency.

The magnitude of Mexico's domestic problems after 1965 led President Díaz Ordaz to conduct a less activist foreign policy than López Mateos had. A more conservative president than his predecessor, Díaz Ordaz pursued a **foreign policy** that minimized global diplomacy over matters closer to home while cultivating a close relationship with Washington. He became the first president to visit

Central America, opposed U.S. **intervention** in the Dominican Republic in 1965, and tempered Mexican relations with **Fidel Castro**'s Cuba. He worked to improve bilateral relations with the United States, addressing problems of **immigration**, termination of the *bracero* agreement, and the promotion of the Border Industrial Program making the Mexican north the major area for *maquiladoras*, the assembly-for-export plants along the border.

The defining event in the presidency of Díaz Ordaz was the Tlatelolco uprising and massacre of workers and students in Mexico City in 1968 just prior to the **Olympic Games**, the first to be staged in a Third World country. The government became enmeshed in a conflict with a student–worker movement demanding the broadening of civil liberties, cancellation of the expensive Olympics, and an end to the use of the Games for propaganda purposes. Concerned that the activism of students and workers was the product of an international **communist** conspiracy aimed at the heart of Mexico, President Díaz Ordaz became convinced he had to apply maximum force to maintain order so that Mexico could successfully host the Olympic Games. As demonstrations mounted prior to the scheduled October games, a desperate and authoritarian government responded with considerable military force. Students called for a demonstration on October 2, 1968, at the Plaza de las Tres Culturas in the Tlatelolco neighborhood of Mexico City. It was met with government tanks, snipers, and armed soldiers. With between 5,000 and 10,000 people in the plaza, the military opened fire on the demonstrators, leaving hundreds of students and bystanders dead. The carnage lasted for over an hour; the games would proceed on schedule.

The repercussions from this event alienated intellectuals as well as members of the military, who said it gave the armed forces a negative image. It produced a generation of new leaders

President Gustavo Díaz Ordaz and U.S. President Richard Nixon, inaugurating La Amistad Dam, 1969. Credit: General Secretariat of the Organization of American States.

who began to question the Mexican economic and political model. The Mexican presidency suffered a tremendous loss of prestige, and Díaz Ordaz left the presidency in 1970 a disgraced figure whose economic successes meant little to most Mexicans. The disarray left by the events of 1968 divided the **Revolutionary Coalition,** leaving Díaz Ordaz more latitude in picking his loyal minister of government, **Luis Echeverría,** to succeed him in 1970. When his handpicked successor tried to appoint him ambassador to Spain in 1977, however, the former president was forced to decline the offer because of the public outcry it generated around the country. Díaz Ordaz then withdrew from public view until his death two years later.

SUGGESTED READING

Roderic Ai Camp, "Díaz Ordaz, Gustavo," in Barbara A. Tenenbaum, ed., *Encyclopedia of Latin American History and Culture,* vol. 2 (New York: Scribners, 1996); Enrique Krauze, *Mexico: Biography of Power: A History of Modern Mexico, 1810–1996,* trans. Hank Heifetz (New York: HarperCollins, 1999); Harold Dana Sims, "Gustavo Díaz Ordaz," in Michael S. Werner, ed., *Encyclopedia of Modern Mexico* (Chicago: Fitzroy Dearborn, 1997); Juana Vázquez-Gómez, *Dictionary of Mexican Rulers, 1325–1997* (Westport, Conn.: Greenwood, 1997).

Distrito Federal, D.F. *See* Geographical Regions.

Drug Certification. *See* Drug Trade/Trafficking.

Drug Trade/Trafficking ☀ The drugs that flow from Mexico—cocaine, marijuana, heroin, and methamphetamine—to satisfy the voracious appetite for illicit substances north of the border represent a significant threat to the security of the United States. They pose serious political and economic costs to Mexico by producing high levels of **corruption,** economic distortions, crime and violence, **human rights** violations, and ultimately a threat to the

legitimacy of the state in dealing with these matters. In a 1999 report on U.S.–Mexican counternarcotics activities published by the U.S. General Accounting Office (GAO), Mexico ranked as one of the largest centers for narcotics-related business in the world, the major transit country for cocaine entering the United States, and a major hub for money laundering or the recycling of drug proceeds. Mexico has several drug trafficking organizations that are far more powerful and dangerous than the ones that once existed in the Colombian cities of Medellín and Cali prior to the 1990s.

Mexico has been the center of the illicit production of and commerce in drugs since the beginning of the 20th century, when the United States banned the importation of opium and cocaine. As a result of these restrictions, drug smuggling became a lucrative activity in Mexico and most of the American drug market went underground. The laws enacted to prohibit drugs and alcohol in the United States had a direct impact on Mexico, in effect creating a profitable market for narcotics in the United States and providing a huge incentive for Mexicans to devise ways to ship drugs into the United States. During the 1910s and 1920s—long before the "war on drugs" was declared by U.S. and Mexican presidents in the 1970s and 1980s— Mexican exports of opium, heroin, and marijuana to the United States flourished despite public and private efforts to halt the flow of illicit drugs northward. By the 1930s, Mexican and American smugglers were using the northern border region as a place to conduct illegal transactions. There were times when the U.S. demand for drugs such as opium and heroin was so great that Mexico had to import these drugs from other sources and then reexport them into the United States. The federal governments in Mexico and the United States enacted numerous antidrug laws prior to **World War II,** but they could not be enforced with any degree of effectiveness. Instead, attempts to prohibit the drug trade led to more lucrative markets, official corruption, and the death of numerous officials employed to put an end to the illicit drug business.

By the 1940s, the cultivation of marijuana and opium poppies supplied a thriving drug trade that was well established in northern Mexico, largely to the U.S. market. In contrast to its drug-producing neighbors to the south, there are four factors that make Mexico unique: (1) Mexico is the only country in the Americas that produces significant amounts of opium poppy and heroin, but has almost no domestic market for these drugs; (2) Mexican drug traffickers have no symbiotic relationship with ideological or guerrilla organizations whose goal is to change the existing political order; (3) opium growing is relatively recent in Mexico and even though it is illegal (in contrast to Bolivia where coca growing is legal), it is mostly grown on unowned land for extra cash, not as a subsistence crop as in the Andes; and (4) Mexico has more resources and has shown a greater ability (largely at the behest of Washington) to develop a counterdrug infrastructure, although this has yet to prove effective in the drug war.

Most of the illicit drugs—heroin and marijuana—produced in Mexico are destined for the U.S. market, not for consumption in Mexico. A 1990 study demonstrated that the prevalence of drug consumption in Mexico was far less (one-tenth) than in the United States and one of the lowest in the Americas. Mexicans are firmly convinced that the illicit drug problem originated in the United States, with one of six Americans consuming illegal drugs. Comedian Jay Leno, host of NBC's "Tonight Show," uses drug consumption among high public officials (Bill Clinton, Al Gore, and George W. Bush) and others as a source of humor, delivering one joke after another on the "casual" use of drugs in his nightly monologue.

Between 1945 and 1980 the major burden of fighting the illicit drug trade was left up to Mexican authorities, mainly the military; however, antidrug campaigns that were devised dur-

ing this period had limited success in interrupting the flow of drugs. The heavy demand for marijuana in the United States during the 1960s converted Mexico into the most important foreign supplier of marijuana for the American market. By the early 1970s, Mexico was supplying over 80 percent of the heroin and marijuana available in the United States. Most of the cocaine consumed in the United States originated in Colombia, Peru, and Bolivia, but Mexico was becoming an important conduit for the South American drug by the 1970s. As Mexico emerged as a major source of drug trafficking activity in the Americas, the U.S. government became more interested in organizing joint efforts to halt the flow of drugs. Following Operation Intercept in 1969—an exercise in coercive diplomacy based on a meticulous inspection of cars and individuals that slowed border crossing to a crawl—the U.S. government started to get more serious about drug trafficking. After years of pressure from Washington, Mexico started a major antidrug campaign in 1975, worried about the growing power of drug cartels and the autonomy of its own law enforcement programs.

The cultivation of illicit drug crops—marijuana, opium poppies, and coca leaf—and transshipment to the United States expanded greatly throughout Latin America after the economic tragedies of the early 1980s.

In Mexico, the flow of illegal drugs to the United States created powerful drug cartels and increased U.S. involvement in combating drug production and trafficking inside Mexico. Beginning with President Nixon's creation of the U.S. Drug Enforcement Agency (DEA) in the early 1970s, drug trafficking has become a troublesome and sensitive issue for the United States and Mexico. By the 1990s the major locus for combating the drug trade was along the Mexican border, not in the Andean countries where most of the world's coca leaf is grown and processed into cocaine. (Dent, 1999, 275)

Growing evidence of close ties between drug traffickers and Mexican law enforcement authorities has not diminished the inflow of drugs or improved Mexico's image in the United States. According to 1999 drug trade estimates, 66 percent of cocaine available in the United States comes from Mexico, 30 percent of heroin used in the United States originates in Mexico, and marijuana seizures from Mexico increased from 102 tons in 1991 to close to 750 tons in 1998.

The extent of drug-funded official corruption in Mexico in 1996–1999 has generated skepticism among U.S. legislators and antidrug officials about Mexico's level of commitment to combatting drug trafficking and related corruption. For example, the arrest of three Mexican army officers in 1997 underscored how deeply the drug traffickers have penetrated Mexico's governmental institutions and the military. General Jesús Gutiérrez Rebollo—the head of Mexico's antidrug agency—was arrested in 1997 for protecting drug traffickers while amassing $500 million between 1990 and 1996. Between 1997 and 2001, Mexico arrested six generals on charges of being in the pay of drug traffickers, a small but significant sign of progress.

Carlos Salinas de Gortari's older brother, Raúl, is in jail on murder and corruption charges—which he continues to deny—linked to Mexico's drug trade. Secret cables sent to Washington by the American Embassy in Mexico show that U.S. officials had obtained evidence of close ties between **Raúl Salinas** and narcotraffickers as early as 1991. In January 1999 Raúl Salinas was found guilty and sentenced to 50 years in prison (later reduced to 27 years) by a Mexico City judge for masterminding the assassination of José Francisco Ruiz Massieu in 1994, considered the most important criminal verdict in modern Mexico.

In a successful 1998 undercover sting operation (Operation Casablanca), U.S. Customs officials captured 26 Mexican bankers involved in the laundering of drug funds. It is difficult to gauge the impact of drug-related corruption on Mexico's political system, but according to one U.S. estimate, Mexican drug traffickers spend as much as $6 billion a year to suborn public officials at all levels of government. The principal agency for drug control is the attorney general's office, but in the 1990s the Mexican military has been increasingly involved in crop eradication, interdiction, and destruction of secret landing strips.

> Mexico's number one cocaine trafficker (until his death in 1997 while undergoing radical plastic surgery to mask his identity) was Amado Carillo Fuentes, commonly known as "Lord of the Skies" for his use of aging Boeing 727s to fly Colombian cocaine into Mexico for reexport to the United States. At one time Carillo Fuentes allegedly employed General Gutiérrez Rebollo, before he was arrested in 1997. (Dent, 1999, 275)

The failure of the United States and Mexico to stem the flow of drugs and disrupt Mexico's drug gangs is most apparent along the **U.S.–Mexican border**, where family-based cartels operate in major cities, principally Tijuana and Ciudad Juárez. Despite the long history of drug trafficking along the border and the most sustained and costly fight ever waged against a single drug mafia, the six Arellano Félix brothers of Tijuana have evaded capture. One of the brothers, Ramón Arellano Félix, became the first Mexican drug trafficker to make the FBI's 10 most wanted list in 1997, but he is still on the loose despite the use of hundreds of drug enforcement authorities and millions of dollars spent. Thomas Constantine, former head of the DEA, admitted after leaving office, "It's just not working," an expression of the frustration among policy makers involved in the fight. The inability of any binational effort to capture this notorious gang of traffickers is a glaring symbol of the failure of American and Mexican governments to disrupt Mexico's most powerful gangs. Mexico's counternarcotics efforts have not been without some merit—the implementation of currency and suspicious transaction reporting requirements and a few key arrests—but as of 1999 no major drug trafficker had been extradited to the United States, money-laundering prosecutions and convictions were minimal, corruption remained a major impediment to antidrug efforts, and most drug traffickers in Mexico continued to operate with impunity.

In a move to tighten the noose around drug cartel leaders and their collaborators, the U.S. Congress passed the Foreign Narcotics Kingpin Designation Act in 1999. Its aim is to empower the U.S. Treasury Department to provide a yearly list of world drug "kingpins" in an effort to locate and impose sanctions against the most notorious drug cartels. In the first designation in June 2000, the Mexican kingpin list included six traffickers (out of a worldwide list of 12) who are under indictment in the United States for drug trafficking: Benjamin Alberto Arellano Félix and Ramón Arellano Félix (Tijuana Cartel) and Rafael Caro Quintaro, Luis Ignacio Amezcua Contreras, José de Jesús Amezcua Contreras, and Vicente Carrillo Fuentes (Juárez Cartel).

To further complicate U.S.–Mexican relations, Mexico must be judged every year on the merits of its antinarcotics efforts by the U.S. Congress, a highly partisan and hypocritical process called "certification." Despite a new Mexican initiative called "a total war against the scourge of drugs," the magnitude of the task remains Herculean in scope and dedication for authorities on both sides of the border. Every year Mexico goes through a ritual known as the "February surprise," in which the government unveils a new and bold antidrug

initiative prior to the March certification decision. At the certification ritual in Washington in March 2000, the Clinton administration "fully certified" Mexico as a reliable partner in the drug war despite heavy criticism on Capitol Hill that Mexico has failed to arrest any major traffickers in the past few years, has suspended lie detector tests for antidrug agents, and has failed in a string of failed extradition attempts. So far Mexico has never been decertified (which would mean a cut in U.S. aid), but it is sensitive to the constant criticism it receives from Washington for its "failed" antidrug efforts while nothing seems to be done about the poor U.S. record in halting the consumption of drugs among its citizenry. During the electoral campaign in 2000 candidate **Vicente Fox** said that "certification is more than an affront to Mexico and to other countries. It is a sham that should be denounced and cancelled."

In recognition of the need to improve U.S.–Mexican relations, members of the Congressional Hispanic Caucus visited Mexico in early 2001 to gain firsthand knowledge of the drug trade and to assess the effect of the annual drug certification process. On returning from their two-day visit to Mexico, the Hispanic members of Congress said they were committed to ending the U.S. drug certification ritual or changing it into a binational process of review in which the United States would submit to a review of its own antidrug effort. On his first visit to Mexico in April 2001, Senator Jesse Helms indicated he was in favor of suspending the certification program.

While many observers of the drug trade applaud efforts to legislate a more effective, fairer process of measuring national efforts to curb the flow of illicit drugs, it is not clear what impact such legislation is likely to have on the "war on drugs." In the 2001 Hollywood movie *Traffic*, disturbing images of middle-class teenage drug addiction, outgunned and befuddled U.S. counternarcotics agents, and corrupt Mexican drug officials have increased the need to rethink the most effective way of dealing with both the *supply* of drugs from Latin America and the *demand* for them in the United States and elsewhere.

With large amounts of U.S. resources devoted to the fight against terrorism in 2001–2002, U.S.–Mexican counternarcotics efforts have dropped dramatically. U.S. Coast Guard seizures declined by 70 percent during this period, as special agents formerly working on the drug war shifted to sky marshal surveillance aboard U.S. flights. Many money laundering investigators moved from tracking billion-dollar drug trafficking deals to the Osama bin Laden money trail. *See also* Foreign Policy.

SUGGESTED READING

Sam Dillon, "A Fugitive Lawman Speaks: How Mexico Mixes Narcotics and Politics," *New York Times,* December 23, 1996; Kate Doyle, "The Militarization of the Drug War in Mexico," *Current History* (February 1993); Tim Golden, "Mexican Gang Is Still on Loose Despite Search," *New York Times,* January 10, 2000; Guadalupe González and Marta Tienda, *The Drug Connection in U.S.–Mexican Relations* (La Jolla: Center for U.S.–Mexican Studies, University of California–San Diego, 1989); Jerome H. Jaffe, ed., *Encyclopedia of Drugs and Alcohol*, vol. 2 (New York: Simon & Schuster, 1995); Elizabeth Joyce, "Packaging Drugs: Certification and the Acquisition of Leverage," in Victor Bulmer-Thomas and James Dunkerley, eds., *The United States and Latin America: The New Agenda* (Cambridge, Mass.: Institute of Latin American Studies, University of London/David Rockefeller Center for Latin American Studies, Harvard University, 1999); Peter A. Lupsha, "Drug Lords and Narco-Corruption: The Players Change but the Game Continues," in Alfred W. McCoy and Alan A. Block, eds., *War on Drugs: Studies in the Failure of U.S. Narcotics Policy* (San Francisco: Westview, 1992); Robert E. Powis, *The Money Launderers: Lessons from the Drug Wars: How Billions of Illegal Dollars Are Washed through Banks and Businesses* (Chicago: Probus, 1992); Roberto Steiner, "Hooked on Drugs: Colombian–U.S. Relations," in Bulmer-Thomas and Dunkerly, eds., *The United States and Latin America;* María Celia Toro, *Mexico's "War" on Drugs: Causes and Consequences* (Boulder, Colo.: Lynne Rienner, 1995); U.S. General Accounting Office, *Drug Control: Update on U.S.–Mexican Counternarcotics Activities* (Washington, D.C.: General Accounting Office, March 1999); *US/Mexico Bi-National Drug Strategy* (Washington, D.C.: U.S. Office of National Drug Control Policy Information Clearing House, 1998).

Durango. *See* Geographical Regions.

Echeverría Álvarez, Luis (1922–) Mexico's fifth postwar president (1970–1976). Echeverria began his administration during economic decline and a political crisis of substantial proportions. He also brought several personal and political liabilities to the presidency that were compounded by his mismanagement of public finances: First, he had never been elected to political office, making him a maverick among other successful presidential candidates. Second, as minister of government under **Gustavo Díaz Ordaz**, Echeverría was held responsible for the tragic **Tlatelolco massacre** at the Plaza de las Tres Culturas in 1968. Third, with the **Revolutionary Coalition** divided over who should succeed Díaz Ordaz, President Echeverría took office without the strong base of party support that his predecessors had benefited from. The selection of Echeverría to succeed Díaz Ordaz was based largely on his bureaucratic merits, not his governmental experience and close ties to elite groups that emerged in the aftermath of the revolution. His was the first Mexican government to be controlled by **technocrats** (*técnicos*), many with postgraduate degrees rather than career politician (*políticos*).

President Echeverría tried to overcome these handicaps by building a consensus among the revolutionary elite by stressing economic growth and social justice, or "shared development," instead of the previous emphasis on stabilizing development. Calling himself a "leftist" president, he tried to distance his administration from that of his predecessor with populist rhetoric and programs and recruited many young intellectuals, economists, and political activists who had been part of the student movement of 1968. Echeverría believed that the solution to his and Mexico's problems lay in expanding the role of the state in the economy and increasing public sector spending. By advocating a statist development strategy popular among dependency theorists in Latin America at the time, he believed that Mexico could achieve both greater independence from industrialized countries and substantially greater social justice. However, the economic boom under way since 1940 came to an abrupt halt under Echeverría. Unemployment doubled, the public debt increased over 550 percent, inflation leaped from 3 percent to 22 percent, and the peso went through another devaluation during Echeverría's six-year term.

Echeverría's policies angered Mexico's business leaders, spawned student protests and widespread peasant-led land invasions, and contributed to the emergence of **guerrilla movements** in various parts of Mexico. As president, however, he maintained a hard line against such groups, using widespread repression and counterinsurgency campaigns to silence the opposition. As if economic deterioration and financial chaos were not bad enough, the **corporatist** political apparatus that had guaranteed the **PRI** a monopoly on the levers of political power since the 1930s broke down. After being warned by several prominent Mexican demographers of the negative impact of Mexico's high population growth rates (some estimated that, unless policies changed, Mexico would have close to 150 million inhabitants by 2000), President Echeverría established the National Population Council to control population, along with a network of government clinics to assist with family planning. With government assistance and changing attitudes about birth control among Mexican women, family size began to shrink dramatically, almost overnight. Today women in Mexico are giving birth to far fewer children than before (the number of children per woman is currently 3.1, less than half of what it was in 1950), but the population continues to grow and is expected to reach more than 112 million in 2010.

Luis Echeverría was born in Mexico City in 1922 and studied abroad (in Chile, Argentina, France, and the United States) before he graduated from the law school at the **Universidad Nacional Autónoma de México (UNAM)** in 1945. He met his future wife, María Esther Zuno, at the home of **Diego Rivera** and they were married in the same year. He joined the PRI the following year and became a rising star in the party bureaucracy. Prior to his handpicked nomination for president by President Díaz Ordaz in 1969, he managed his predecessor's presidential campaign and served as secretary of the interior. Echeverría was the last

President Luis Echeverría. Credit: *Proceso*, photo by Germán Canseco.

president with ties to the Mexican military, having married the daughter of a general and former governor of Jalisco and serving as the private secretary to a general who was head of the ruling party. His use of the Mexican military for counterinsurgency campaigns and his tolerance of paramilitary groups seemed to reinforce the belief of some in the importance of these ties for presidential decision making. His wife was known for championing equal rights for women and domestic social and cultural programs while she was first lady.

President Echeverría's **foreign policy** continued Mexico's traditional emphasis on nationalism and anti-imperialism, an effort designed to divert attention from his economic and political troubles at home. Paradoxically, while he applied hard-line measures against Mexican leftist groups—guerrillas, terrorists, and student activists—in Monterrey, Chihuahua, Culiacán, Puebla, Tlaxcala, and Mexico City, he strongly supported the socialist president of Chile, Salvador Allende, and **Fidel**

Castro's Cuba. After the CIA-backed coup against Allende in 1973, Echeverría welcomed refugees from Chile and gave asylum to those fleeing many harsh military regimes in Latin America at the time. In international organizations, Mexico adopted a Third World strategy that often clashed with U.S. interests. He promoted UN resolutions that revised the Law of the Sea definition of offshore territorial claims and a Charter of Rights and Duties of States. Mexico voted for the UN resolution that equated Zionism with racism, a decision that ultimately led many Jewish groups to boycott Mexico's tourist resorts.

After a computer study determined the optimum site for creating a new, world-class beach resort on a narrow sand strip on the Yucatán Peninsula, construction began in Cancún during the presidency of Luis Echeverría. The first hotels opened in 1972 and the number of tourists visiting the area now surpasses the port city of Acapulco on the west coast. To overcome the problem of extensive poor areas surrounding the resort, Cancún was constructed so that everyone working in the hotel zone had access to decent housing and safe drinking water.

The widespread repression characterized by **human rights** violations during Echeverría's administration contributed to a wave of abductions of industrialists, politicians, and prominent people, including the U.S. consul in Guadalajara and the president's father-in-law. In response to personal criticism in the editorial pages of *Excelsior*, one of Mexico City's highly regarded newspapers, Echeverría retaliated by having the publisher of the newspaper fired. The leftist journal *¿Por Qué?* was forced out of business on similar grounds. There were rumors that Echeverría was plotting a military coup d'état, and the erosion of the president's legitimacy made the presidential succession process tense as power shifted to **José López Portillo**, the PRI presidential winner in 1976.

After his term of office, Echeverría kept a low profile that included an attempt to create a Third World University and appointments to several ambassadorships, including to UNESCO and Australia. Many politicians and business leaders continue to blame him for Mexico's economic plight and the damage done to the monopoly of power once enjoyed by the ruling party. In December 1995 he was accused of orchestrating charges against former president **Carlos Salinas**, then under fire due to a **corruption** scandal of his own.

"In the final accounting," according to political scientist Howard Handelman (1997, 43), "Echeverría's administration has been judged a tremendous failure." During his term in office, Echeverría was the butt of jokes that mocked him as an ignoramus or dolt. Much of the humor concentrated on his alleged *pendejismo*, or doltishness: A future Mexican president arrives in heaven and is shown the clocks that mark the times that pre-vious presidents were guilty of a *pendejada* (a gross stupidity). He observes those of his predecessors, which move at a moderate pace. When he asks to see the Echeverría clock, they tell him, "Oh, *Señor presidente*, it's being used as a fan in the gambling room."

SUGGESTED READING

Jorge G. Castañeda, *La herencia: Arqueología de la sucesión presidential en México* (Mexico, D.F.: Editorial Alfaguara, 1999); Howard Handelman, *Mexican Politics: The Dynamics of Change* (New York: St. Martin's, 1997); Stephen D. Morris, *Political Reformism in Mexico: An Overview of Contemporary Mexican Politics* (Boulder, Colo.: Lynne Rienner, 1995); Susan Kaufman Purcell, "Mexico," in Howard J. Wiarda and Harvey F. Kline, eds., *Latin American Politics and Development*, 5th ed., rev. (Boulder, Colo.: Westview, 2000); Samuel Schmidt, *The Deterioration of the Mexican Presidency: The Years of Luis Echeverría* (Tucson: University of Arizona Press, 1991); Juana Vázquez-Gómez, *Dictionary of Mexican Rulers, 1325–1997* (Westport, Conn.: Greenwood, 1997).

Ejército Revolucionario Popular (ERP). *See* Guerrilla Movements and Counterinsurgency.

Ejército Zapatista de Liberación Nacional (EZLN). *See* Guerrilla Movements and Counterinsurgency; Zapatista Rebellion in Chiapas.

Ejido ☀ With agricultural resources increasingly concentrated in a few hands by 1910, demands for agrarian reform and cries of "land and liberty" provided a catalyst for the **Mexican Revolution** (1910–1917). Prior to the revolution, millions of rural Mexicans were dispossessed of their land and condemned to debt peonage and slavery on the large haciendas. Out of this situation came the idea of the *ejido*, a parcel of land granted by the Mexican state to peasant-farmers living in rural areas.

The *ejido* as a concept of land ownership has its origins in the Aztec form of land tenure and Spanish feudal institutions. The legal foundation of the modern-day *ejido* is based on Article 27 of the **Constitution of 1917**, which recognized three types of property: private, *ejido*, and communal. The land—a mixture of grazing, forest, and agriculture—is communally controlled in each *ejido*, with the state in charge of its tenure and sale. The communally owned land cannot be sold or otherwise transferred outside the community.

Although Article 27 addressed the problem of landless peasants in ways that no previous Mexican government had dared to confront, the expansion of agrarian reform measures was not a top policy priority until the presidency of **Lázaro Cárdenas** in the 1930s. His administration distributed more than double the area disbursed by all other Mexican governments combined since the revolution. Most of the *ejidos* were created in the Yaqui valley of Sonora, the sugar growing regions of Sinaloa, the Laguna cotton district, and the henequén farms of Yucatán. The agrarian reform initiatives carried out by Cárdenas continued after 1940, but never with the zeal displayed by those in the Cárdenas administration. By the end of his administration, half of the rural land—over 50 million acres—had been distributed to the peasantry. Despite the rhetoric of radical agrarian reform, some critics of the government's agrarian reform argue that the real purpose of the *ejido* system was to suppress peasant revolts, preserve the hegemony of landlords and capitalists, and help institutionalize the new regime. As Markiewicz (1993, 8) points out, "The results of cardenismo demonstrate that under capitalism, even a government sympathetic to the peasantry cannot fundamentally improve the circumstances of those who till the soil."

After 1940, land distribution slowed as the **Ávila Camacho** administration began to withdraw financial and legal support of agrarian reform measures and shift its resources in favor of agricultural development projects and wartime collaboration with the government of the United States. By the time **Miguel Alemán** became president in 1946, agrarian reform was considered antithetical to economic development and opposition hopes for a cardenista-style revival appeared dim. However, beginning in the 1960s, *ejido* lands increased as federal land was distributed and nonagricultural activities were incorporated under the *ejido* system. The last Cárdenas-type distribution took place under President **Luis Echeverría** (1970–1976), as more land was distributed and further agrarian legislation expanded the range of activities within the *ejido*. The distribution of land practically came to a halt during the 1980s, as consecutive presidents announced the lack of available land for distribution, and *ejido* development began to emphasize modernization and productivity rather than land distribution.

As of 1991, less than one-third (31 percent) of rural land was devoted to *ejido* and communal land tenure, employing 7.3 million people in mostly agricultural activities devoted to basic crops such as corn, beans, wheat and rice. Although *ejidos* vary greatly in terms of size and agricultural activity from one geographical region to another, close to 60 percent of *ejido* plots average only 5.5 acres, but others are often irrigated and engaged in commercial agriculture. For rural farmers with little income and few resources, the *ejido* farm remains the basic unit for those who grow crops for self-consumption and small amounts of cash.

Under the banner of neoliberal reform, President **Carlos Salinas** decided to change the existing *ejido* system, convinced by his market-oriented advisers that most *ejiditarios* (members of the cooperative) could not become competitive in the new global economy, and opposed substantial public spending to sustain them. In 1992, Article 27 was amended by the Mexican Congress to permit—but not compel—the private sale of *ejido* lands. The new *ejido* law put an end to one of the Revolution's greatest achievements, an unthinkable move decades earlier, arguing that with outside investment and a more open land market, production would increase for the domestic and export market. In essence, the new *ejido* law terminated the government's constitutional obligation to redistribute land to the peasantry, thereby officially terminating one of the basic tenets of Article 27 of the Constitution. In addition, *ejiditarios* were now permitted to sell their plots and use them as collateral for loans and to enter into joint ventures with foreign investors, who can legally own up to 49 percent of the farm.

The Salinas initiative was praised by the business community, the Catholic Church, and conservative politicians on the right, but peasant organizations, indigenous communities, and politicians on the left almost unanimously declared the reforms a catastrophe for *ejiditarios*, agricultural workers, and the rural poor. The media reported both a rush to speculate in ejidal lands and resentment among those most affected by the government's decision. While critics of the law have argued that great harm will come to the rural sector by allowing outsiders and richer villagers to buy out poorer farmers, the impact of the new *ejido* reform has been limited, as much of the land where *ejidos* exist is of poor quality and lacks irrigation. In areas where *ejido* lands contain valuable forest timber, corrupt and unscrupulous village leaders have allowed logging companies to cut valuable trees for their own personal gain. This problem has been particularly acute in the state of Guerrero, where serious deforestation has led to countermeasures by peasant ecologists to halt pine forest destruction and protect watershed land.

As the main institution of Mexican agrarian reform (the *ejido* peasant community) begins to disappear, the Mexican government now believes that increased private and foreign investment in agriculture (and the rest of the economy) will generate enough prosperity to make the *ejido* obsolete and

stifle peasant discontent and revolts. Today the traditional linkage between the state and the *ejido* system has ended, and Mexican farmers can no longer count on the degree of government intervention in *ejido* life that once prevailed, but the prospects for peasant families in a world of economic liberalization and privatization remain problematic.

SUGGESTED READING

Kirsten Appendini, "*Ejido*," in Michael S. Werner, ed., *Encyclopedia of Mexico: History, Society, and Culture*, vol. 1 (Chicago: Fitzroy Dearborn, 1997); Wayne A. Cornelius and David Myhre, eds., *The Transformation of Rural Mexico: Reforming the Ejido Sector* (La Jolla: Center for U.S.–Mexican Studies, University of California–San Diego, 1998); Billie de Walt and Martha N. Rees, *The End of Agrarian Reform: Past Lessons, Future Prospects* (La Jolla: Center for U.S.–Mexican Studies, University of California–San Diego, 1994); Gareth A. Jones, "Dismantling the *Ejido*: A Lesson in Controlled Pluralism," in Rob Aitken et al., eds., *Dismantling the Mexican State?* (New York: St. Martin's, 1996); Dana Markiewicz, *Ejido Organization in Mexico, 1934–1976* (Los Angeles: UCLA Latin American Center, 1980); Markiewicz, *The Mexican Revolution and the Limits of Agrarian Reform, 1915–1946* (Boulder, Colo.: Lynne Rienner, 1993); Gerardo Otero, *Farewell to the Peasantry? Political Class Formation in Rural Mexico* (Boulder, Colo.: Westview, 1999); Laura Randall, ed., *Reforming Mexico's Agrarian Reform* (Armonk, N.Y.: Sharpe, 1996); Richard Snyder and Gabriel Torres, eds., *The Future Role of the Ejido in Rural Mexico* (La Jolla: Center for U.S.–Mexican Studies, University of California–San Diego, 1998).

Electoral System/Elections ☀ The presidential system outlined by the **Constitution of 1917** established the basis for suffrage and elections, although there have been numerous changes in the process of electing public officials since that time. Officials are elected to office by plurality vote in direct popular elections (see table 3), with no reelection for governors or presidents and no immediate reelection for seats in the federal and state legislatures. In the 1917 Constitution, suffrage was not universal. For example, all married men 18 years and older and all unmarried men 21 years and older were able to vote, but women and single men under 21 years of age were not. Between 1947 (municipal elections) and 1953 (federal elections, including president of the republic), women—married or unmarried—were given the right to vote, but eligible females had to wait until 1958 to vote for president. In 1969, the age limit for all Mexican voters was lowered to 18 years.

The president is elected for a six-year term (*sexenio*), as are senators in the upper house of the national legislature. Beginning in 1991, one senator from each state is elected in the midterm elections; the other senators have terms that run concurrently with the president's. *Diputados* in the lower house (Chamber of Deputies) are elected through a combined process of single-member districts and multimember districts on the basis of proportional representation for three-year terms. This means that 300 *diputados* are elected on the first-past-the-post rule, usually favoring the **Partido Revolucionario Institucional (PRI)**, and 200 are chosen in five *national* multimember districts, a process that allows for greater opposition representation in Congress.

At first, control over elections was given to authorities at the municipal and state levels; however, beginning in 1946, the registration of political parties and the process of running elections (registration, conduct, and certification of results) came entirely under federal control. The 1946 reforms also specified that only registered parties may nominate candidates for public office who appear on the ballot. Unregistered parties may form, but they are not allowed to compete in elections. To be active in the electoral process, parties must be registered (they must present a party platform), issue a regular party publication, have a national executive committee that holds a national assembly meeting, and demonstrate electoral support in two-thirds of the federal "entities" (states, territories, and the Federal District). To be nationally registered, political parties must poll 1.5 percent of the national vote in federal elections. They can also demonstrate support by holding state assembly meetings with a requisite number of meetings and attendees. Parties that fail to secure permanent registration must compete on a "conditional registration" basis pending future voting returns.

During the early 1990s, there were six political parties that managed to acquire the necessary votes to compete electorally: the **PRI**, the **PAN**, the **PRD**, the **PFCRN**, and the **PPS**. By the time the 1997 congressional elections were over, the same number of parties were nationally registered, but the **PFCRN** and the **PPS** were replaced by the **PVEM** and the **PT**.

Mexico's long history of one-party rule and the absence of clean and fair elections have contributed to a political culture in which over 70 percent of Mexicans express little faith in their political parties, even though close to 60 percent said (in a 1995 study of voter attitudes by the National Democratic Institute for International Affairs, a U.S.-based election-monitoring organization) they were "very" or "somewhat" interested in politics.

Electoral reforms in 1989–1990, 1993, and 1994 created a Federal Code of Electoral Procedures and the Federal Electoral Institute (IFE), an independent institution that is constitutionally separate from the secretary of *gobernación* but has close ties to the executive branch of government. They also increased the number of senators from each state and the Federal District from two to four, set limits on the number of seats a party can have in the Chamber of Deputies, and restructured the General Council of the IFE by creating a special prosecutor to investigate electoral crimes and a provision that allows external audits of voting procedures and foreign observers to witness Mexican elections. The **Alianza Cívica** (Civic Alliance), a non-governmental election watchdog group that was founded in 1994, is active in monitoring the electoral process.

With all these changes in rules and procedures, Mexico's elections have improved since the fraud-tainted 1988 presidential election in which **Carlos Salinas** was announced the winner under questionable electoral circumstances. Nevertheless, numerous trouble spots remain—making elections less legitimate than they should be—including the limited powers of the newly created federal election authority to control campaign expenditures, equal access to the media, threats of intimidation, violations of ballot secrecy, and routine efforts by local party bosses to induce voters to support the ruling party by handing out goods of all sorts at campaign rallies. However, as the power of the PRI as a vote-getting machine gradually declined after 1988, elections became more volatile and unpredictable, often the result of decreasing party loyalty and more crossover votes driven by anti-PRI sentiment. Much of the electorate's anger in 2000 was provoked by one economic crisis after another followed by chronic government austerity measures (most of which were seen as having little effect on promoting economic growth and reducing poverty) and bureaucratic **corruption** tied to party, judicial, and police organizations.

The **communications media** play an important role in Mexico's elections, traditionally favoring the PRI in their news coverage. While some improvements have been made since the 1988 presidential election, there is still evidence of bias in favor of the PRI among major media such as **Televisa** and TV Azteca, the principal commercial TV networks. The IFE is responsible for monitoring media coverage of elections, although it has no authority to regulate the media to offer equitable access to the media for all political parties. Instead, the IFE must limit itself to supervising unfair bias in the coverage of candidates and the purchase of airtime by candidates. Although measuring bias is the more thorny of the regulatory issues, monitoring airtime purchases by candidates requires substantial personnel and bureaucratic procedures. The IFE also oversees the candidate debates and the publication of opinion results prior to voting. Existing regulations mandate that no information may be published about the campaigns during the four days preceding the election, and the publication of opinion poll results within eight days of the federal elections is also prohibited. Nevertheless, the ability of the Mexican voter to make an accurate personal judgement on the candidates and issues is still compromised by distortions brought about by a myriad of manipulations of the electoral system.

With recent changes in the Mexican electoral map, the conduct of presidential elections is beginning to look like the electoral process in the United States: the leading parties are spending millions in television advertising to sway voters, high-level political consultants (James Carville for the PRI, Dick Morris for the PAN) were hired in 2000 to run a U.S.-style campaign, several televised debates are being used to "democratize" the electoral process, and down-and-dirty campaign rhetoric has become the stock-in-trade of candidate discourse. Although the 2000 elections were the first to be organized by a fully autonomous agency (the IFE), it remains to be seen how far Mexico's **democracy** will advance now that the last PRI president, **Ernesto Zedillo**, has left office on December 1, 2000.

While Mexicans living in the United States cannot vote by absentee ballot, opposition candidates have tried to woo the 7–10 million expatriates because of the vast amount of money they send home every year and the broad influence they have over family and friends south of the border. Prior to the July 2, 2000, presidential elections, **Vicente Fox** and **Cuauhtémoc Cárdenas** made several campaign stops in the United States,

Table 3. Presidential Election Results, by Candidate, 1934–2000

Year	Candidate	Valid Votes	Percentage of Votes
1934	Lázaro Cárdenas (PRI)	2,225,000	98.19
	Antonio Villarreal	29,395	1.07
	Adalberto Tejeda	16,037	.70
1940	Manuel Ávila Camacho (PRI)	2,476,641	93.89
	Juan A. Almazán	151,101	5.72
	Rafael Sánchez Tapia	9,840	.37
1946	Miguel Alemán Valdés (PRI)	1,786,901	77.90
	Ezequiel Padilla (PAN)	443,357	19.33
	Enrique Calderón	33,952	1.48
	Other	29,337	1.27
1952	Adolfo Ruiz Cortínes (PRI)	2,713,419	74.31
	Miguel Henríquez Guzmán	579,745	15.87
	Efraín González Morfín (PAN)	285,555	7.82
	Vicente Lombardo Toledano (PP)	72,482	1.98
1958	Adolfo López Mateos (PRI)	6,767,754	90.43
	Luis H. Álvarez (PAN)	705,303	9.42
	Other	10,346	.13
1964	Gustavo Díaz Ordaz (PRI)	8,368,446	88.82
	José González Torres (PAN)	1,034,337	10.98
	Other	19,402	.20
1970	Luis Echeverría Álvarez (PRI)	11,970,893	86.02
	Efraín González Morfín (PAN)	1,034,337	13.98
1976	José López Portillo (PRI)	16,727,993	100.00
1982	Miguel de la Madrid (PRI)	16,748,006	70.90
	Pablo Emilio Madero (PAN)	3,700,045	15.70
	Arnoldo Martínez Verdugo (PSUM)	821,995	3.50
	Ignacio González Gollaz (PDM)	433,886	1.80
	Candido Díaz Cerecero (PST)	342,005	1.50
	Rosario Ibarra de la Piedra (PRT)	416,448	1.80
1988	Carlos Salinas de Gortari (PRI)	9,604,905	50.36
	Cuauhtémoc Cárdenas (FDN)	5,376,946	31.12
	Manuel J. Clouthier (PAN)	3,288,523	17.07
	Gumersindo Magaña (PDM)	198,854	1.04
	Rosario Ibarra de la Piedra (PRT)	79,294	.42
1994	Ernesto Zedillo Ponce de León (PRI)	17,336,325	48.77
	Diego Fernández de Cevallos (PAN)	9,222,899	25.94
	Cuauhtémoc Cárdenas (PRD)	5,901,557	16.60
	Cecilio Soto González	975,356	2.74
	Jorge González Torres	330,381.93	

Year	Candidate	Valid Votes	Percentage of Votes
2000	Vicente Fox Quesada (PAN)*	18,335,458	42.07
	Francisco Labastida Ochoa (PRI)		35.07
	Cuauhtémoc Cárdenas (PRD)**		16.05
	Víctor Manuel Camacho Solís (PCD)		1.09
	Gilberto Rincón Gallardo (PDS)		1.01

Sources: George W. Grayson, ed., *Prospects for Mexico* (Washington, D.C.: Foreign Service Institute, U.S. Department of State, 1988); James W. Wilkie, ed., *Statistical Abstract of Latin America* (Los Angeles: UCLA Latin American Center Publications, 1998), 34:254.

*The Fox campaign was called the Alliance for Change and involved the support of the Mexican Green Ecologist Party (PVEM).

**The Cárdenas campaign was called the Alliance for Mexico and involved the support of the Labor Party (PT), Social Alliance Party (PAS), Convergence for Democracy (CD), and Party of the Nationalist Society (PSN).

urging Mexicans to lobby family members in Mexico to vote against the PRI. The continuing ability of PRI candidates to engage in voting fraud and corruption—illegally stuffed ballot boxes, lost ballot boxes, and voter coercion—to benefit the party means that the electoral playing field is still not level. Nevertheless, the opposition's strong challenge to the ruling party in 2000 was the result of the reformed electoral code and the creation of the new and independent IFE. With the IFE in complete control of the electoral process, the 2000 presidential election was the first to be conducted free of executive branch control, greatly diminishing the PRI's use of the crude old-style techniques of election manipulation of the past. The thousands of foreign observers—including former U.S. president Jimmy Carter—who were on hand for the 2000 elections were almost unanimous in their praise for the high turnout of Mexican voters and the depth of the government's commitment to hold free and fair elections. *See also* Dedazo.

SUGGESTED READING

Sergio Aguayo Quezada, "Electoral Observation and Democracy in Mexico," in Kevin Middlebrook, ed., *Electoral Observation and Democratic Transitions in Latin America* (La Jolla: Center for U.S.–Mexican Studies, University of California–San Diego, 1998); Charles D. Ameringer, ed., *Political Parties of the Americas, 1980s to the 1990s: Canada, Latin America, and the West Indies* (Westport, Conn.: Greenwood, 1992); John Ward Anderson and Molly Moore, "How to Vote Twice in Mexico," *Washington Post*, May 27, 2000; Roderic Ai Camp, ed., *Polling for Democracy: Public Opinion and Political Liberalization in Mexico* (Wilmington, Del.: SR Books, 1996); Wayne A. Cornelius, "Politics in Mexico," in Gabriel A. Almond and G. Bingham Powell, eds., *Comparative Politics Today: A World View*, 6th ed. (Glenview, Ill.: Scott, Foresman/Little, Brown, 2000); Nikki Craske, "Another Mexican Earthquake? An Assessment of the 2 July 2000 Elections," *Government and Opposition*, (Winter 2001); Jorge I. Domínguez and James A. McCann, *Democratizing Mexico: Public Opinion and Electoral Choices* (Baltimore: Johns Hopkins University Press, 1996); George W. Grayson, *A Guide to 2001 Gubernatorial and Local Elections in Mexico* (Washington, D.C.: Center for Strategic and International Studies, 2001); Eric Olson, *So Close and Yet So Far: Mexico's Mid-term Elections and the Struggle for Democracy* (Washington, D.C.: Washington Office on Latin America, 1997); Mónica Serrano, ed., *Governing Mexico: Political Parties and Elections* (London: Institute of Latin American Studies, University of London, 1998); Washington Office on Latin America (WOLA), "Overview of Critical Issues," *Mexico Election Monitor 2000* (February 2000).

Emigration. *See* Immigration.

Environment and Ecology ☀ Mexico faces a widely acknowledged environmental crisis that is rooted in its import substitution development strategy adopted after **World War II** and exacerbated by the more recent transition to free market policies, a peso crisis, and the reduction of available resources to protect the environment because of the imperative of economic competition in a global marketplace. In addition to these broad changes in the international political economy and shifts in public policy, concern for the environment and ecological preservation have been transformed into an area for state intervention and public mobilization, both Mexican and foreign.

Mexico's environmental crisis is visible throughout the country: massive oil spills, deforestation, health hazards from border assembly plants, toxic waste dumping, pipeline explosions, and water and air pollution of staggering proportions. According to recent government studies, almost every stream and river in Mexico is polluted, the result of years of neglect, contamination, and the lack of resources to maintain water treatment facilities. Mexicans living in the nation's capital must put up with some of the world's worst pollution, open sewers, urban congestion, mounds of garbage, and undrinkable water. The New River (Río Nuevo), which flows from the border city of Mexicali into the California desert, is listed by the U.S. Environmental Protection Agency (EPA) as one of North America's most polluted—raw sewage, industrial waste, trash, and agricultural runoff.

As Mexico's population grows and becomes more urban, environmental degradation becomes an ongoing problem with the depletion of natural resources combined with increasing pressures from trading partners, international lending agencies, and environmentalists to develop some strategy to confront the crisis. Paradoxically, Mexico

has made some impressive achievements with respect to conservation, mitigation, and environmental legislation; however, the environmental crisis continues, leaving in its wake a huge gap between environmental policy and practice. Clearly, there is a connection between macroeconomic policies designed to move Mexico's economy forward and development imbalances and accelerated ecological decline. Recent efforts to create a new economy and handle the demands of globalization have come with substantial social, economic, and environmental costs.

Environmental policy initiatives did not get under way until the 1970s, when international concern over the impact of industrialization and the depletion of nonrenewable energy resources on the global resource base generated demands for change. The Mexican government passed its first environmental legislation in 1971, but environmental enforcement languished because effective regulatory authority was lacking. As rising levels of smog engulfed Mexico City and other major cities, President **Miguel de la Madrid** established the first cabinet-level environmental agency, the Ministry of Urban Development and Ecology (Secretaría de Desarrollo Urbano y Ecología, SEDUE). But as the economy deteriorated, the commitment to environmental protection remained largely symbolic and unenforceable.

A more integral ecological approach was tried in 1988 with a comprehensive law aimed at the goal of continuing economic development but based on environmental sustainability. During the **Carlos Salinas** administration, SEDUE was replaced with the Ministry of Social Development (Secretaría de Desarrollo Social, SEDESOL) in an effort to respond to international environmental concerns and to improve policy implementation under growing domestic pressure from organized groups concerned with the environment. By the time President Salinas left office in late 1994, Mexico had improved its conservation and protective efforts, but the government's strategy seemed to be aimed more at satisfying the international financial community and the United States than an authentic attack on the depth of Mexico's environmental and ecological difficulties.

Over the past 20 years, the major efforts to deal with Mexico's environmental predicament have been in Mexico City (extreme urban pollution) and in cleaning up the **U.S.–Mexican border** region. Mexico City, the world's largest megacity, has the "honor" of being the world's most polluted urban center. According to the World Health Organization and other international organizations, the poor air quality standards are the result of thousands of industries, service facilities, and over three million motor vehicles that clog the streets of the capital city on a daily basis. As a result of climatological and topographic factors, Mexico City suffers from pollutant emissions—sulfur dioxide, ozone, carbon monoxide, nitrogen dioxide, and lead—as well as other contaminants (fecal dust and airborne particles) that produce chronic respiratory illnesses, heart disease, gastrointestinal infections, child development disorders, and hepatitis.

The Salinas administration tried to tackle these problems by regulating vehicle emissions and introducing lead-free gasoline and a traffic revision system, as well as a program called *un día sin auto* (a day without a car), mandating that drivers leave their cars at home one day a week in an effort to curb traffic and ozone pollution. Using comprehensive pollution control programs for the urban core of Mexico City, the government was able to make some headway in achieving its environmental goals. While Mexico City remains badly polluted, the city has made significant progress in reducing its air pollution in the 1990s, due in large part to an aggressive antismog program. Officials reported that 1999 was the cleanest year of the decade, with airborne pollutants triggering emergencies on just five days, compared with close to 180 early in the decade. With tougher laws and more determined enforcement, Mexico City's smog is decreasing, but changing behavior and implementing programs to improve air quality remain major challenges for those in change of environmental and ecological policies. The more serious environmental issue for the citizens of the nation's capital is the lack of drinking water, with roughly one out of eight Mexicans lacking easy access to drinking water.

The U.S.–Mexican border region is an environmental disaster zone, with heavily polluted rivers, hazardous waste dumps, air pollution, and water tables contaminated by chemicals and toxins. With growth rates twice the national average, the arid border region is fighting an uphill battle to reverse the environmental impact of rapid and uncontrolled urban and industrial expansion. The first comprehensive border environmental accord between the United States and Mexico was not signed until 1983. Since that time binational efforts to confront the massive environmental problems along the border have increased, but there has been little progress in reversing environmental degradation. The environmental side agreements that came with the **North American Free Trade Agreement** did not improve the situation, despite claims that a free trade agreement would improve conditions on both sides of the border.

Some of Mexico's worst environmental degradation is associated with agriculture and forestry. The crisis in the countryside is the result of neglecting the subsistence farmer and emphasizing export crops to generate income rather than to meet basic food needs. Agricultural modernization has been devastating to the tropical rain forests of southeastern Mexico, where millions of acres of land have lost their forest cover due to logging and mechanized agriculture. Some see the 1992 law to end land redistribution and permit the legal sale or rental of *ejido* plots as a disaster for the environment.

Current environmental policy involves a set of policies aimed at sustainable development, an approach that pursues economic growth to meet human needs while at the same time protecting the environment. This difficult balancing act has generated a heated debate between those who argue that protecting the environment is simply too costly and those who call for a more radical approach of slow growth for the sake of a healthy environment and protected ecosystems. Nevertheless, promoting sustainability constitutes a direct challenge to neoliberalism, and some see solving other social and economic problems as deserving a greater degree of government and private sector attention.

Under pressure from Mexican and foreign environmentalists (including the U.S.-based National Resources Defense Council), in March 2000 the Mexican government canceled plans with the Mitsubishi Corporation of Japan to build an enormous salt plant at Laguna San Ignacio, a serene lagoon on the coast of Baja California where gray whales are known to give birth every year. Unable to dismiss the complaints of foreign environmentalists as interfering in their national affairs, the Mexican government discovered it cannot ignore the transnational effects of sustained pressure to force governments and corporations to respect nature. In 2001, the U.S.-based Grupo de los Cién Internacional spearheaded an international campaign to prevent the building of a new Mexico City airport in Lake Texcoco, arguing that the location would endanger both air travelers and a prime bird habitat. Mexico has refused to agree to recent debt-for-nature swaps carried out in other Latin American countries because it considers such initiatives a threat to its sovereignty and territorial integrity.

Mexico's best-known environmentalist is Homero Aridjis, a poet and longtime member of the prodemocracy movement that helped defeat the PRI in 2000. He helped spark the beginning of the environmental movement in 1985 by gathering over 100 artists and intellectuals to petition the government to do something about the horrendous smog over the capital city. Since that effort

he has succeeded in getting the government to remove lead from gasoline, protect monarch butterflies, prohibit the slaughter of sea tortoises, and offer sanctuaries for gray whales along the Baja California peninsula. *See also* Partido Verde Ecológico Mexicano (PVEM).

SUGGESTED READING

Tom Barry, ed., *Mexico: A Country Guide* (Albuquerque, N. Mex.: Inter-Hemispheric Education Resource Center, 1992); Marilyn Gates, "Ecology," in Michael S. Werner, ed., *Encyclopedia of Mexico: History, Society, and Culture*, vol. 1 (Chicago: Fitzroy Dearborn, 1997); Lawrence A. Herzog, ed., *Shared Space: Rethinking the U.S.–Mexico Border Environment* (La Jolla: U.S.–Mexican Studies Center, University of California–San Diego, 2000); Rodolfo Lacy, ed., *La calidad del aire en el Valle de México* (Mexico, D.F.: Colegio de México, 1993); Daniel Lapis Acuña et al., *La salud ambiental en México* (Mexico, D.F.: Universo Veintiuno, 1987); Julia Preston, "In Mexico, Nature Lovers Merit a Kiss from a Whale," *New York Times*, March 5, 2000; Mark J. Spalding, ed., *Sustainable Development in San Diego–Tijuana: Environmental, Social, and Economic Implications of Interdependence* (La Jolla: U.S.–Mexican Studies Center, University of California–San Diego, 2000); Tim Weiner, "Mexico Grows Parched, with Pollution and Politics," *New York Times*, April 14, 2001.

Escuadrón de Pelea 201 (201st Combat Squadron) ✵
A unit of Mexican volunteer fighter pilots, trained in the United States and attached to the U.S. Air Force to fight in the Pacific War during **World War II**. After German submarines sank several Mexican tankers in the Gulf of Mexico and under pressure from Washington, Mexico declared war on the Axis powers in 1942, and the United States and Mexico became formal allies. Through the lend-lease policy, the Mexican armed forces were modernized and expanded, but only the air force saw action during the war. This arrangement marked the first military

alliance between the two nations. It sealed a historic reconciliation after the lingering petroleum expropriation dispute and set the stage for an era of good feelings throughout the war years. Mexico and the United States developed joint defense arrangements, although the United States provided the bulk of military assistance funds. For example, U.S. aid helped Mexico develop a special air wing (the Mexican Expeditionary Air Force) of three squadrons: the 201st Combat Squadron (Escuadrón de Pelea 201); the 202d, a replacement training squadron; and 203d, a primary training squadron. The 300 men who composed the air wing were trained in the United States and later saw combat in the Philippines.

The Mexican flying and ground crews underwent training in Texas in 1944, forming the Escuadrón de Pelea 201 in early 1945 with 25 P-47 fighter planes. After the air squadron reached Clark Field in the Philippines, the Mexican pilots performed reconnaissance, ground attack, and close air support operations against Japanese forces in the Philippines and Formosa until Japan's surrender in August, losing nine pilots in action. The Escuadrón de Pelea 201 also created a native mascot to motivate its war effort, a green and maroon bird with black face and yellow beak, yellow spurs, and a green pistol in each claw. The pistol-packing bird—named "Pancho Pistolas"—symbolized a flying *charro* and inspired combat missions against the Japanese in Asia.

In addition to the 300-member combat squadron of Mexican pilots, some 6,000 Mexican citizens voluntarily joined the U.S. armed forces, although some put the numbers much higher. Although there was some discrimination against Mexicans and Mexican Americans during the war, it was relatively marginal. Some Hispanics advanced rapidly in rank, the most notable being MG (Major General) Pedro del Valle, MG Terry de la Mesa Allen, and MG Elwood R. Quesada.

SUGGESTED READING

John M. Andrade, *Latin American Military Aviation* (Leicester, England: Midland Counties Publications, 1982); James F. Dunningham and Albert A. Nofi, *The Pacific War Encyclopedia*, vol. 2 (New York: Facts on File, 1998); Donald Fisher Harrison, "United States–Mexican Military Collaboration during World War II" (master's thesis, Georgetown University, 1976); "Mexico's Squadron 201," video (Harlingen, Texas: KMBH-TV, 1993); María Emilia Paz, *Strategy, Security, and Spies: Mexico and the U.S. as Allies in World War II* (University Park: Pennsylvania State University Press, 1997).

Esquivel, Laura (1950–) ☀ One of Latin America's best-known female writers. Esquivel achieved fame for her novel *Como agua para chocolate* (Like water for chocolate), the second best-selling novel in Mexico in 1989. After being translated into English to coincide with release of the film of the same name directed by **Alfonso Arau**, the novel spent a considerable period on the *New York Times* best-seller list for 1993. Arau's screen adaptation of his (now ex-) wife's novel was a huge international success; it won 18 international awards, achieved the highest box office takings in the United States of a foreign language film in 1993, and boosted sales of Esquivel's book worldwide.

Laura Esquivel was born in Mexico City in 1950 and later worked as a schoolteacher. Before she achieved fame as a novelist, she wrote books for children and produced numerous filmstrips. The phenomenal success of her first novel—*Like Water for Chocolate* (1989)—and the mass appeal of the film adaptation a few years later can be attributed to various factors: the emphasis on a romantic rural past in a time of rapid and unsettling urbanization; the portrayal of a lasting love affair in an age of dysfunctional families; the reclamation of traditional notions of gender roles (femininity and the art of cooking); a feeling of perceived cuisine authenticity and Mexican culture at a time when Tex-Mex restaurants and fast-food franchises like Taco Bell are gaining popularity in the United States and Europe; a narrative formula and cast of characters whom readers either applaud or hiss as in a soap opera or pantomime; and the sensual and romantic aspects of "magical realism" that make the film sparkle. *Como agua para chocolate* is a love story rooted in an extremely traditional and conservative ideology that prevailed among the landed elite of revolutionary and postrevolutionary Mexico. Based on a rather innocent and conventional storyline, it is a recipe for romantic success with plenty of culinary metaphors—and humor, sentimentality, and exaggeration—woven into the love affair between Tita and Pedro, her childhood sweetheart. As Shaw (1997, 118) emphasizes, "Tita's sole desire in life is to marry Pedro, rear his children and provide husband and children with delicious food." For her entertaining and award-winning novel, Esquivel was named Mexican Woman of the Year in 1992 and awarded the ABBY (American Booksellers Book of the Year) in 1994, the first for an author who was a non–U.S. citizen.

SUGGESTED READING

Deborah A. Shaw, "Laura Esquivel," in Verity Smith, ed., *Encyclopedia of Latin American Literature* (Chicago: Fitzroy Dearborn, 1997); Barbara A. Tenenbaum, "Why Tita Didn't Marry the Doctor; or, Mexican History in *Like Water for Chocolate*," in Donald F. Stevens, ed., *Based on a True Story: Latin American History at the Movies* (Wilmington, Del.: Scholarly Resources, 1997).

Estrada Doctrine ☀ A recognition policy formulated by Mexican Foreign Minister Genaro Estrada in 1930 in response to the need for legitimacy experienced by governments that come to power through revolution. His principle of diplomatic recognition challenged the Tobar Doctrine, a formula based on the theory that governments can put an end to revolutions by not giving them the satisfaction of formal recognition, arguing instead that a new government which has political control of a state should *automatically* be recognized. Mexico's difficulty in obtaining diplomatic recognition from Washington during and after its own revolution produced a sympathy for the plight of other revolutionary governments.

The Estrada Doctrine argued that diplomatic recognition should be de facto, accepting the government in actual control, and not based on political considerations inherent in the selective application of de jure, or legal, recognition of the government. Despite the enthusiastic reception that Estrada's principle received among Latin Americans, the United States has continued to base its recognition policy on political and national interest considerations. Since the 1930s the Tobar Doctrine has increasingly given way to the recognition theory contained in the Estrada Doctrine, although the United States is still convinced that some form of collective **intervention** by friendly states can put an end to civil strife, ethnocide, and military takeovers.

Mexico's application of the Estrada Doctrine became evident after **World War II** when it recognized revolutionary governments in **Cuba**, Guatemala, Nicaragua, and Grenada. However, Mexico's refusal to recognize Franco's dictatorship in Spain illustrates how difficult it is to be wholly principled in **foreign policy**, regardless of the importance attached to the Estrada Doctrine. Beginning in the late 1980s, Mexico began to distance itself from its traditional practice of recognition of governments contained in the Estrada Doctrine by making an open statement against Panama's General Noriega. By the end of the **Ernesto Zedillo** administration, it was clear that Mexico had moved closer to the United States on numerous bilateral issues, particularly the noneconomic ones such as drugs and immigration. Nevertheless, Mexico has remained steadfast on its opposition to U.S. efforts to bring down the **Castro** government in Cuba through tightened restrictions on trade and other matters. When Jesse

Helms, conservative chairman of the U.S. Senate Foreign Relations Committee and the most outspoken Mexico basher in Congress, visited Mexico City in April 2001, Mexicans speculated that the meeting had more to do with urging President **Vicente Fox**'s government to condemn Cuba's **human rights** record than to signal his approval of Mexico's new president and government.

SUGGESTED READING

Guadalupe González, "Foreign Policy Strategies in a Globalized World: The Case of Mexico," in Joseph S. Tulchin and Ralph H. Espach, eds., *Latin America in the New International System* (Boulder, Colo.: Lynne Rienner, 2001); Larman C. Wilson and David W. Dent, *Historical Dictionary of Inter-American Relations* (Lanham, Md.: Scarecrow, 1998).

Félix Güareña, María de los Angeles (1914–) Famous actress in the 1940s and 1950s. María Félix starred in 47 films, often under the direction of distinguished filmmaker **Emilio "El Indio" Fernández**. Beginning with her first film, *El peñón de las ánimas* (1942), Félix created an image of a woman with power and self-sufficiency, not the female prototype of a submissive and self-denying mother. As a Mexican femme fatale, she appeared in scenes that depicted her as a wild woman, filling the screen with her beauty, forceful presence, and scandalous poses. She costarred often with movie idols **Pedro Armendáriz**, **Pedro Infante**, and **Jorge Negrete**; made films in Europe and the United States; posed for a painting by **Diego Rivera**; and had various poets dedicate verses in her name.

Born in Alamos, Sonora, at the beginning of World War I, María Félix moved with her family to Guadalajara, Jalisco, when she was a young student. With her dynamic personality and beauty, she became very popular and attractive to men in her community. After a short marriage and divorce (a scandal in provincial Jalisco), she left town for Mexico City, where she began a successful career in acting. The film that established her screen persona as a vamp who takes away men's strength was *Doña Bárbara* (1943), directed by Fernando de Fuentes; after that movie she became known as "La Doña." According to Tuñón Pablos (1997, 480), "Her love affairs and marriages, in particular to **Agustín Lara** and Jorge Negrete, added to her image as a woman who would let nothing hinder her rise to stardom."

Unlike **Dolores del Río,** who chose to make her fame in Hollywood, María Félix moved to Europe and made numerous films in Spain, France, and Italy between 1948 and 1955. After this international phase of her film career, she returned to Mexico and continued to play starring roles in a variety of films, although she never fully shed her "wild woman" stereotype. In the 1970s she appeared in the telenovela "La constitución" but did not return to the big screen. Toward the end of her career she attributed her popularity to "someone who feels good in their own skin" all the while playing the role of "the triumphant Mexican who doesn't get duped by anyone" (Tuñón Pablos 1997, 480). She received an Ariel Award (the equivalent of an Oscar) for *Enamorada*

Movie still of María Félix in *Doña Bárbara* (1943).

(1946), *Río Escondido* (1948), and *Doña Diabla* (1950). In 1986 she was awarded a special Ariel recognizing her lifetime contribution to Mexican **cinema**. According to film scholar David Maciel (1996, 549), "Félix is a living legend and symbol of Mexican beauty, femininity, and strength, and is arguably the greatest screen presence of twentieth-century Mexican cinema."

SUGGESTED READING

David Maciel, "Félix, María," in Barbara A. Tenenbaum, ed., *Encyclopedia of Latin American History and Culture* (New York: Scribners, 1996); Enrique Serna, ed., *María*

Félix: Todas mis guerras (Mexico, D.F.: Clio, 1993); Paco Ignacio Taibo, *María Félix: 47 pasos por el cine* (Mexico, D.F.: Planeta, 1985); Julia Tuñón Pablos, "Félix Güareña, María de los Angeles," in Michael S. Werner, ed., *Encyclopedia of Mexico: History, Society, and Culture*, vol. 1 (Chicago: Fitzroy Dearborn, 1997).

Feminism ☀ Feminist thought and mobilizing activity can be traced to the last decade of the 19th century. The early advocates of feminism battled to elevate the status of wife and mother, as well as the position of females within the family, and expand women's freedom in a **macho** society, *not* to achieve equal rights. The right of women to exercise political power was considered desirable but achievable only in the long term.

Many women participated in the **Mexican Revolution**, but few were interested in equal rights and suffrage for women. Despite the socialist provisions in the **Constitution of 1917**, members of the various factions that wrote the document denied women the right to vote and exercise their influence through political action. Beginning in the 1920s, women founded organizations with ties to women's groups in the United States and pushed for improvement in the social, economic, and political status of women. However, Mexican women found it difficult to stay united on the themes that had the most impact on women, eventually splitting into conservative and left-wing feminists. During the 1930s women's political organizations and activity were oriented to the popular sectors and included demands of workers and peasant women (*campesinas*). Women associated with the **Partido Revolucionario Institucional (PRI)** were angry at President **Lázaro Cárdenas** for reneging on his campaign promise to engineer a change in the Constitution to provide equal rights for women.

The power of the women's movement declined during **World War II** and the early years of the **Miguel Alemán** administration. The civic rights of women were established in 1953, due in large part to the determination of **Amalia Castillo Ledón**, leader of the suffragette cause. With the same rights as men, Mexican women voted for the first time at the state level in 1955 and for president in 1958. On two occasions, women have run for the presidency, but with little success. Rosario Ibarra de Piedra was the first female candidate for president, running as a candidate for the Revolutionary Workers Party in 1981–1982 and 1987–1988. Cecilia Soto campaigned for the Labor Party in 1994, a candidacy that was discredited by evidence that the government was backing her in an effort to split the opposition vote.

Rosario Robles, a member of the left-of-center **Partido de la Revolución Democrática (PRD)** and the first female mayor of Mexico City (taking office in 1999), has been at the forefront of efforts to improve the rights of women. The rise of Mayor Robles and others after 1998 seems to be part of a recent boom of women actively involved in the upper reaches of political power, including Amalia García (president of the PRD), Dulce María Sauri Riancho (president of the PRI), Rosario Green (foreign minister), Julia Carabias (environment minister), María de los Ángeles Moreno (president of the Senate). Although no woman ran for president of Mexico in 2000, the decline of authoritarian politics has caused political parties of all stripes to recognize the importance of women, as both voters and leaders in high-profile political positions. Unfortunately, this has not been the case in corporate Mexico, where men occupy the highest positions in the world of business and finance.

The expansion of educational opportunities for women in the 1960s and the women's liberation movement in the United States had a major influence on the revival of feminism in Mexico. By the 1970s the demands for equal rights that defined feminism during the first half of the 20th century were replaced with criticism of inequality in the workplace, sexuality, and domestic work. Despite the growing awareness of the social and moral consequences implicit in women's lack of rights, feminism appealed to only a few, mostly university-educated middle-class women and those with Marxist ideas. Efforts to eliminate the inequality of men and women under the law were bolstered by the 1975 World Women's Conference in Mexico City and the UN declaration of the International Year of Women. As a result, the government initiated a series of legal reforms to eliminate certain kinds of discrimination.

After 1975, feminists rallied around political issues that shaped the movement for decades. At the top of the list was voluntary maternity, sexual harassment, violence against women, legalization of abortion (still banned altogether by the penal code), contraception, rape and incest, and the rights of gays and lesbians. Despite setbacks in bringing about legal reforms, feminism flourished with the formation of women's organizations, feminist magazines (the first edition of *Fem* was published in 1976), and the growing legitimacy of feminist ideas in Mexico's traditionally male-dominated culture. One of the many successful groups is Diversa, a national feminist organization founded by Patricia Mercado to push legislation on women's rights, including the decriminalization of abortion.

Mexico's feminist movement is still dominated by middle-class women with a high level of formal education, but recent efforts to reach the popular sectors have been gaining ground. Despite the relative absence of women in positions of political power, women have joined the movement to clean up the political process by attacking fraud and offering ways to make the system more **democratic**. Feminist ideas and women's equality still lag as salient issues among a majority of Mexicans, but there is a growing awareness of the need to improve the status of women throughout Mexico, as evidenced by the attention devoted to women in academia, government, diplomacy, advertising, and the media. *See also* Guillén y Sánchez, Palma.

SUGGESTED READING

Gabriela Cano, "Feminism," in Michael S. Werner, ed., *Encyclopedia of Mexico: History, Society, and Culture*, vol. 1 (Chicago: Fitzroy Dearborn, 1997); Altha J. Cravey, *Women and Work in Mexico's Maquiladoras* (Lanham, Md.: Rowman & Littlefield, 1998); Heather Fowler-Salamini and Mary K. Vaughn, eds., *Women of the Mexican Countryside, 1850–1990* (Tucson: University of Arizona Press, 1994); Kristine Ibsen, ed., *The Other Mirror: Women's Narrative in Mexico,*

1980–1995 (Westport, Conn.: Greenwood, 1997); Lashawn R. Jefferson, *Mexico: No Guarantees: Sex Discrimination in Mexico's Maquiladora Sector* (New York: Human Rights Watch, 1996); Marta Lamas, "The Mexican Feminist Movement and Public Policy-Making," in Geertje Lycklama À Nijeholt et al., eds., *Women's Movements and Public Policy in Europe, Latin America, and the Caribbean* (New York: Garland, 1998): 113–26; Anna Macías, *Against All Odds: The Feminist Movement in Mexico to 1940* (Westport, Conn.: Greenwood, 1982); Victoria E. Rodríguez, *Women's Participation in Mexican Political Life* (Boulder, Colo.: Westview, 1998); Cynthia Steele, *Politics, Gender, and the Mexican Novel, 1968–1988: Beyond the Pyramid* (Austin: University of Texas Press, 1992); Lynn Stephen, *Women and Social Movements in Latin America: Power from Below* (Austin: University of Texas Press, 1997); Julia Tuñón, *Women in Mexico: A Past Unveiled,* trans. Alan Hynds (Austin: University of Texas Press, 1999); María Elena de Valdés, *The Shattered Mirror: Representations of Women in Mexican Literature* (Austin: University of Texas Press, 1998); Teresa Valdes and Enrique Gomariz, eds., *Latin American Women: Compared Figures* (Santiago, Chile: Instituto de la Mujer–Spain, FLACSO, 1995).

Fernández Romo, Emilio ("El Indio") (1903–1986) ☀

Mexico's leading film director during the golden age of Mexican **cinema**. Inspired by the social meaning of cinema, El Indio (the Indian) made 41 films, many with **Dolores del Río** and **Pedro Armendáriz**, that attempted to locate the essence of Mexico in its indigenous population. Many of his best films were made in the 1940s, a period that epitomized the golden age of Mexican cinema. Fernández's films emphasized the symbolic importance of land as the wellspring of nationhood and the rural drama with Indian women, **mestizo** political bosses, and desert vegetation. According to Hershfield (1996, 52), "Fernández maintained that his purpose as a filmmaker was to glorify Mexico, to counteract the thrust of

Publicity photo of Emilio "El Indio" Fernández, golden age director who helped place Mexican cinema on the world stage.

Hollywood's influence on Mexican films, and to articulate and make sense of the past in order to reconstitute what he saw as the authentic Mexican national identity."

Born in 1904 in El Hondo, Coahuila, Emilio Fernández's views were shaped by the **Mexican Revolution** during which he rose to the rank of captain. After the revolution he turned his attention to acting and filmmaking, in both Hollywood and Mexico. In Hollywood during the 1920s he worked as a dancer and actor, mostly secondary roles in cowboy action films. He was influenced by the work of Sergei Eisenstein, a film director who focused on the social meaning of cinema. The high levels of unemployment due to the Great Depression in the United States contributed to his deportation to Mexico in 1933. After returning to Mexico, he began his career in the film industry there, first as an actor and then as a film director. One of his first starring roles was in *Janitzio*

(1934), an *indigenista* ("Indianist") film directed by Carlos Navarro that portrayed Mexico's Indians as poor but pure, simple, and honorable.

After playing lead roles in the 1930s, El Indio shifted to directing in 1941. The most important period of Fernández's directing career came during the 1940s when he put together a blockbuster team including **Gabriel Figueroa** (cinematographer), Dolores del Río and **María Félix** (two of Mexican cinema's major stars), Pedro Armendáriz (a leading man who appeared in two of his earlier films), and Mauricio Magdaleno (scriptwriter). In an effort to dramatize Mexico's Indian past and **mestizo** present in order to create a more authentic national identity, El Indio revived the *indigenista* genre with *Flor Silvestre* (1943), *María Candelaria* (1943), *La Perla* (1946), *Enamorada* (1946), *Maclovia* (1948), and *Río Escondido* (1948). *María Candelaria*, starring Río and Armendáriz, won top awards at the Cannes Film Festival of 1946. As a result of the tremendous success of his early films, he quickly acquired a unique influence in the Mexican film industry and was soon recognized internationally for his directing talent.

After 1948, El Indio's career began to decline as the success of his earlier films did not adapt well to the new interests of the public, and he often repeated themes and obsessions from previous efforts. His films were low-budget affairs that relied on production formulas that tried to cut costs at the expense of creativity and quality. After making *Pueblerina* (1948), *La malquerida* (1949), *Víctimas del pecado* (1950), *Acapulco* (1951), and *El mar y tú* (1951), his well-earned career as a film director and actor began to fade, damaging the prestige of Mexican **cinema** in the process.

Known as the father of the golden age of Mexican cinema, Fernández stamped his films with a distinct nationalist tone inspired by the Mexican muralists—he often showed the great works of architecture, painting, and sculpture from all historical periods—and the visual style of the Russian director Eisenstein, whose work infused social meaning into celluloid. His films focused on the symbolic importance of land as the source of nationhood and progress. He was also influenced by the U.S. cinema, having codirected *El fugitivo* (The fugitive) with John Ford. While most of his cinematic efforts focused on rural Mexico where the revolution, race, social class, and exploitation were ever present, he also filmed some urban dramas and comedies in the later part of his career.

El Indio's public image emerged from his own personality and deep interest in portraying himself as the authentic Mexican macho. According to film scholar Julia Tuñón Pablos (1997, 488), "His films attempt to find the essence of what is Mexican in a series of folkloric stereotypes, and he considered himself to be an authentic representative." He liked to dress in elaborate *charro* costumes, display a violence that he thought virile, and extol the virtues of *Mexicanidad* (Mexicanness).

SUGGESTED READING

Joanne Hershfield, *Mexican Cinema/Mexican Woman, 1940–1950* (Tucson: University of Arizona Press, 1996); Joanne Hershfield and David R. Maciel, eds., *Mexico's Cinema: A Century of Film and Filmmakers* (Wilmington, Del.: Scholarly Resources, 1999); Carl J. Mora, *Mexican Cinema: Reflections of a Society, 1896–1982* (Berkeley: University of California Press, 1982); Paco Ignacio Taibo, *El Indio Fernández: El cine por mis pistolas* (Mexico, D.F.: Joaquín Mortiz-Planeta, 1991); Julia Tuñón, "Between the Nation and Utopia: The Image of Mexico in the Films of Emilio 'Indio' Fernández," *Studies in Latin American Popular Culture* 12 (1993); Julia Tuñón Pablos, "Fernández Romo, Emilio (El Indio Fernández)," in Michael S. Werner, ed., *Encyclopedia of Mexico: History, Society, and Culture*, vol. 1 (Chicago: Fitzroy Dearborn, 1997).

Figueroa Mateos, Gabriel (1907–1997) ✳

Cinematographer known for his vivid panoramas of rural Mexican landscapes, dramatic cloud-laced skies, and the faces of stoic and beautiful Indians. Figueroa made over 200 films for leading directors, both Mexican and American, including **Emilio Fernández**, John Ford, John Huston, and **Luis Buñuel**. He won international acclaim for his pictures of Mexican revolutionaries and bandits in wide-brimmed sombreros framed by large cactus and vast desert horizons with threatening clouds. A master of color, light, and shadows, Figueroa filmed *The Fugitive* for Ford in 1946 and *The Night of the Iguana* (for which he received an Academy Award nomination) in 1966 for Huston. Figueroa filmed several of Buñuel's best-known movies, including *Los Olividados* and *Exterminating Angel*. He received the National Arts Prize in 1977, Mexico's highest award for artistic achievement.

Gabriel Figueroa's parents died while he was very young and he spent his youth in the care of relatives. He turned to still photography to earn a living but soon shifted to moving pictures, learning the craft during its technological infancy. In the late 1930s he spent time in Hollywood and learned how to create foreboding shadows and a melancholy ambience from cinematographer Greg Toland, a close associate of Orson Welles. On his return to Mexico he formed a cinematic group that included director Fernández and his favorite stars, **Dolores del Río, Pedro Armendáriz,** and **María Félix,** to make movies that depicted rural Mexico as rife with cowboy violence and hot-blooded romance. Such films as *Flor silvestre* (Wild Flower), dealing with the meaning of the **Mexican Revolution**, and the dilemmas of Indians in *María Candelaria* were major achievements. They won important prizes at film festivals and helped establish a European market for the Mexican **cinema**. Despite the prestige that Fernández gained from *María Candelaria*, the film was criticized for depicting a stereotypical image of Mexico as a rural land of stoic and attractive Indians. The portrayal of Indians in a positive light bothered media mogul **Emilio Azcárraga**, who boycotted the movie and refused to show it in his Alameda Theater.

Gabriel Figueroa was drawn into politics and ideological conflicts through **labor** union battles in Mexico and contacts with several Hollywood actors and filmmakers who fled to Mexico during the anticommunist McCarthy hysteria in the United States. After **corrupt** leaders gained control of the union with which Mexican cinematographers were affiliated, Figueroa joined with comedian **Cantinflas** to form a new union. During the 1950s Figueroa was blacklisted in the United States due to his Hollywood "connections" and friendships with radical Mexican painters like **Diego Rivera** and other giants of the arts. After the success of *The Fugitive* he was offered a three-year contract by John Ford but had to turn it down because the U.S. government refused to let him enter the country to work. Forty years later he suffered the same fate when John Huston invited him to make *Prizzi's Honor* in 1983. He was so repulsed by the script of *Rambo: First Blood Part 2* that he refused an offer to shoot the Sylvester Stallone film, even though it was to be made in Mexico. At the time of his death in 1997, President **Ernesto Zedillo** issued a statement saying that "we have lost the photographer who did the most to enhance and project Mexico's cinema."

Recent film scholarship has focused on the films produced by Emilio Fernández and cinematographer Gabriel Figueroa during the era of Mexico's golden age (1935 through the 1950s) with an interest in **feminism**, political symbolism, and national identity. Considered one of the best cinematographers in the world, Figueroa created striking camera angles that displayed the lyrical interplay of shadow and light and the power of the natural landscape. His life work is a reminder of how dramatic black-and-white images can be in the hands of a master cinematographer. In addition to many international prizes for cinematography, Figueroa received more awards from the Mexican film academy than any single performer or filmmaker.

SUGGESTED READING

Joanne Hershfield, *Mexican Cinema/Mexican Woman, 1940–1950* (Tucson: University of Arizona Press, 1996); Joanne Hershfield and David R. Maciel, eds., *Mexico's Cinema: A Century of Film and Filmmakers* (Wilmington, Del.: Scholarly Resources, 1999); John King, *Magical Reels: A History of Cinema in Latin America* (New York: Verso, 1990); Carl J. Mora, *Mexican Cinema: Reflections of a Society, 1896–1988*, rev. ed. (Berkeley: University of California Press, 1989); Chon A. Noriega and Steven Ricci, eds., *The Mexican Cinema Project* (Los Angeles: UCLA Film and Television Archive, 1994); Paulo Antonio Paranaguá, ed., *Mexican Cinema*, trans. Ana M. López (Bloomington: Indiana University Press, 1997); Julia Preston, "Gabriel Figueroa Mateos, 90; Filmed Mexico's Panoramas," *New York Times*, April 30, 1997; Charles Ramírez Berg, *Cinema of Solitude: A Critical Study of Mexican Film, 1967–1983* (Austin: University of Texas Press, 1992); Ramírez Berg, "Figueroa's Skies and Oblique Perspective: Notes on the Development of the Classical Mexican Style," *Spectator* (Spring 1992).

Filmmaking. *See* Cinema.

Flag of Mexico (*la bandera Mexicana*) ☀ The design in the center of the Mexican flag is derived from the Aztec legend of Tenochtitlán ("Cactus Rock"), the center of Aztec life that is now Mexico City. According to the legend, the Aztecs could not settle until they located a cactus plant on an island in a lake. The sacred spot would also have an eagle holding a snake in its beak. The wandering Aztecs found this place in 1325 and then built their empire, which was later conquered by the Spaniard Hernán Cortés in 1521. The present colors of the flag—green, white, and red—date back to a national emblem that was created at the Iguala convention of 1821. The vertical tricolor was introduced in November of the same year, representing independence (green), religion (white), and unity (red) with the white center section having a represention of an eagle holding a snake on top of a cactus. It included a crown above the eagle and cactus symbol because for the first year of independence Mexico was an empire, not a republic. The present form of the flag was made official on September 17, 1968.

The **Partido Revolucionario Institucional (PRI)** uses the colors of the Mexican flag in its logo and on ballots, one of the many advantages it enjoys at the polls. After opposition political parties sued the PRI to give up the national colors on grounds of unfair electoral competition, Mexico's highest elections court ruled in February 2000 that the PRI could not be forced to give up the tricolor advantage it has maintained in every election since the 1930s.

SUGGESTED READING

E. M. C. Barraclough and W. G. Crampton, eds., *Flags of the World,* 2d ed. (London: Frederick Warne, 1981); Carol Shaw, *Flags: A Guide to More Than 200 Flags of the World* (Philadelphia: Running, 1994).

Foreign Policy ☀ The framework of Mexico's postwar foreign policy is based on both domestic and international considerations, particularly the need to retain a strong sense of national self-identity in the shadow of the United States. Mexico's leaders must rely on nationalist symbols to legitimize their authority in terms of protecting Mexican sovereignty and independence. Since the **Mexican American War (1846–1848)**, there has been an important antiforeign (mainly anti–United States) and nonintervention focus to Mexican foreign policy. U.S. ownership and exploitation of Mexico's

oil and mining resources began during the time of Porfirio Díaz, and continual U.S. military **intervention** during the **Mexican Revolution (1910–1917)** added to the antiforeign legacy. Ending foreign control became an important part of the **Constitution of 1917**, implemented during the 1930s with the nationalization of the assets of foreign oil companies and during the Cold War through the support for other Latin American revolutions sparked by foreign dominance and exploitation. As a result, Mexico has placed great emphasis on international law, particularly the principles of nonintervention and sovereignty spelled out in the Charters of the United Nations and the Organization of American States (OAS). The 1930 **Estrada Doctrine** was formulated by Mexican foreign minister Genaro Estrada to remove all political considerations from the process of granting or withholding diplomatic recognition of foreign governments, even revolutionary ones. Given the difficulties in obtaining diplomatic recognition from the United States during its own revolution, Mexico has always supported other revolutionary governments in the Americas, often in opposition to strictly political and national interest (security) components of U.S. recognition policy. For most of the 20th century, the antiforeign legacy required that Mexican presidents criticize, or not appear too cooperative with, the United States. The support for the **North American Free Trade Agreement (NAFTA)**, spearheaded by President **Carlos Salinas**, represented a major departure from this tradition.

Since 1946, the contours of Mexican foreign policy have changed according to domestic and international forces. After **World War II**, the Cold War, rapid urbanization and industrialization, and increasing ties with the United States and other world regions have influenced the formulation and implementation of Mexican foreign policy. In the mid-1940s, with the United States no longer needing as many Mexican workers and resources

President Harry Truman visiting Aztec pyramids in Mexico City, 1947. Credit: General Secretariat of the Organization of American States.

and the end of the war, Mexican presidents turned away from relying on the export of raw materials to pay for imported industrial goods to government-assisted import substitution industrialization programs combined with a protectionist trade policy. New protectionist tariffs on imported manufactured goods helped to create joint industrial ventures that were of particular benefit to the Monterrey Group, a cartel of rich industrialists in Nuevo León. U.S.–Mexican relations improved during the **Miguel Alemán** administration (1946–1952) as Mexican demand for U.S. imports increased and Presidents Truman and Alemán

made diplomatic calls to each other's capital in 1947. Alemán normalized relations with Mexico's wartime enemies—Germany, Italy, and Japan—by returning confiscated property to its former owners and reestablishing diplomatic relations.

The rapid industrialization and dramatic economic growth of the 1950s (sometimes called the "Mexican Miracle") influenced Mexican foreign policy by providing solid support of the United States on the Cold War, anticommunism, and related issues. Mexico supported the United States in the United Nations and the OAS after World War II, with the one exception over Guatemala in

1954. At the Inter-American Conference held in Caracas, Venezuela, in March 1954, Mexican diplomats objected to the U.S.–sponsored anti-communist resolution (aimed at the Jacobo Arbenz regime in Guatemala) by introducing countermeasures to weaken the resolution. Once these were defeated, to avoid the wrath of the United States, Mexico chose to abstain on the final vote, along with Costa Rica and Argentina. After the CIA-backed overthrow of Arbenz three months later, President **Ruiz Cortines** said nothing in protest, angering both business leaders and the nationalist left inside Mexico.

The shortcomings of the Mexican Miracle in the early 1960s contributed to a more assertive foreign policy, beginning with the presidency of **Adolfo López Mateos** (1958–1964). The new president managed to maintain cordial relations with the United States while at the same time opening up new economic and political partnerships with countries in Europe, East Asia, and the Third World in an effort to stimulate foreign investment. Mexican foreign policy veered to a position more in line with the wishes of neo-*cardenista* politicians, joining the Nonaligned Movement and helping to found the Latin American Free Trade Association (LAFTA), an early effort to create a free trade area for Latin America, and expressing support for the revolution in **Cuba**. The early support for **Fidel Castro** did not last for more than a few years, as U.S. pressure on Mexico increased after the Bay of Pigs invasion in 1961. Mexico continued its support for the foreign policy principle of nonintervention and protection of national sovereignty, but U.S.–Mexican relations cooled considerably by the time President López Mateos left office in late 1964.

President **Gustavo Díaz Ordáz** (1964–1970) continued the outlines of foreign policy that he inherited from his predecessor, struggling to put concerns about economic development on the front burner while dealing with unpleasant bilat-

eral problems with the United States, particularly with regard to illegal **immigration** and trade issues. When domestic problems—middle class unrest over the economy, runaway population growth, and the demonstrations over the **Olympic Games** in 1968 that contributed to the **Tlatelolco massacre**—moved to center stage during the last two years of his administration, Díaz Ordáz was faced with far less activism in the foreign policy arena.

President **Luis Echeverría** inherited a volatile situation when he took office in late 1970. Determined to restore the legitimacy of the government and its tarnished international image, he embarked on an effort to put people to work through ambitious public projects, a neo-*cardenista* land reform program, and concerted efforts to take control of key industries. In the realm of foreign policy, Echeverría resumed his predecessor's travel diplomacy, visiting 36 countries during his *sexenio*. In defiance of the United States, he helped create the Latin American Economic System (SELA), a regional trade bloc that included Cuba while rejecting the United States and ameliorated Mexico's ties with numerous socialist and communist countries. In many respects, his foreign policy was a made-for-television program that emphasized photo opportunities, nationalist gimmicks (by handing out colorful guayaberas on his travels, he became the architect of "guayabera diplomacy"), and leftist rhetoric designed to placate those who agreed with his support of the socialist president of Chile, Salvador Allende. In the end, his carrot-and-stick foreign policy failed to reduce Mexico's dependence on the United States, quadrupled the debt of the public sector, and failed to generate much legitimacy, both domestically and internationally.

The discovery of significant new oil reserves in the Gulf of Mexico brought good economic news to the next president, **José López Portillo** (1976–1982). The first of a series of university-trained **tech-**

nocrats to occupy the presidency, the new president attempted a scaled-down version of Echeverría's populism and aggressive foreign policy nationalism. The Jimmy Carter administration recognized the growing importance of Mexico and, with the newly discovered oil, elevated Mexico to a "special relationship" in the Latin American policy of the United States. To make his mark in the area of foreign policy, López Portillo focused on the growing crisis in Central America, opposing many U.S. initiatives, breaking relations with Somoza's Nicaragua in support of the Sandinistas, and attempting to mediate the civil war in El Salvador. Mexico gained international respect for its Central American diplomacy, but its efforts were undermined by events at home, including the negative effects of a rapidly growing debt, massive **corruption**, and capital flight in astronomical proportions. As oil prices fell, Mexico declared in August 1982 that it could no longer pay the interest on its debt, sending a ripple effect throughout Latin America that was called the "tequila effect."

The large foreign debt, capital flight, a precipitous decline in real wages, and a currency crisis increased Mexico's dependency on international lending agencies, and the United States forced the incoming administration of **Miguel de la Madrid** (1982–1988) to adopt neoliberal economic policies, abandon populist economic rhetoric, and kowtow to the Reagan administration. By the time de la Madrid left office in late 1988, the postrevolutionary model of state-mediated capitalism was gone, as well as the more critical foreign policy initiatives of the past that displeased the United States. However, new problems related to **drug trafficking** and illegal immigration—both largely the result of Mexico's economic crisis and the demand for illicit drugs north of the border—generated more tensions between the United States and Mexico.

While the de la Madrid years were more cautious in foreign policy initiatives, particularly toward the United States, his successor, **Carlos Salinas de Gortari** (1988–1994), decided to pursue more radical and unprecedented moves to improve relations with the United States by cracking down hard on drug trafficking, cooperating with the United States on immigration, legalizing full foreign ownership of property, and negotiating a free trade agreement with the United States. NAFTA became the cornerstone of Mexican foreign policy, a radical departure from the principles of foreign policy established in the 1917 Constitution and respected by Mexican presidents for 60 years. Critics of this new relationship argued that Mexico had become an appendage of the United States with little recourse to protect its national sovereignty and the well-being of its citizenry. Selling NAFTA to Mexicans and Americans was not easy, but after a long and ferocious debate, the treaty was approved, Salinas was praised as a diplomatic wizard, and both countries settled in to enjoy what they thought would be the fruits of free trade. By the time NAFTA went into effect, President Salinas had less than a year left in his presidency, little time to handle the critics of his neoliberalism and a powerful indigenous uprising in Chiapas led by the Zapatista Army of National Liberation. Beyond his interest in integrating the Mexican and North American economies, Salinas tried to extend free trade arrangements with other Latin American countries and made overtures to Japan, Southeast Asia, and the European Community in hopes of attracting new investments to Mexico. The economic and political crisis that Salinas faced when he arrived in office still existed six years later when he left the presidency with a legacy of an overvalued peso, rampant corruption at the highest levels, and declining faith in the ability of the ruling party to reverse these trends through foreign policy initiatives.

President Salinas's successor, **Ernesto Zedillo** (1994–2000), was left with the same problem that faced earlier administrations: a Hobbesian choice between adopting nationalist rhetoric to shore up dwindling support at home or continuing to grant concessions to the United States on crucial bilateral matters. Although he began his administration declaring that the highest priority of his presidency would be "strengthening and fully exercising national sovereignty," after six years Mexican foreign policy had done little to remove itself from the influence the United States has over Mexico's leadership.

The prospects for a more cooperative relationship increased with the end of the PRI era and the election of **Vicente Fox** in July 2000. President-elect Fox promised a foreign policy that would enhance the friendly ties established under Zedillo, particularly the Mexican commitment to the battle against narcotics and the pursuit of economic policies that will reduce the incentives for jobless Mexicans to emigrate to the United States. During the 2000–2001 energy crisis in California, President Fox paid a visit to California and spoke with Governor Gray Davis about a cooperative energy policy. With an end to the quasi-authoritarian rule that persisted under 13 PRI presidents, Mexican foreign policy under PAN leadership is less strident when it comes to the revolutionary principles of nationalism, anti-interventionism, and the protection of national sovereignty. *See also* Cárdenas del Río, Lázaro; Debt Crisis; General Agreement on Tariffs and Trade (GATT); U.S.–Mexican Border/Boundary.

SUGGESTED READING

Guadalupe González, "Foreign Policy Strategies in a Globalized World: The Case of Mexico," in Joseph S. Tulchin and Ralph H. Espach, eds., *Latin America in the New International System* (Boulder, Colo.: Lynne Rienner, 2001); Rosario Green and Peter H. Smith, eds., *Foreign Policy in U.S.–Mexican Relations* (La Jolla: Center for U.S.–Mexican Studies, University of California–San Diego, 1989); Neil Harvey, ed., *Mexico: Dilemmas of Transition* (New York: St. Martin's, 1993); Gordon Mace and Jean-Philippe Thérien, eds., *Foreign Policy and Regionalism in the Americas* (Boulder, Colo.: Lynne Rienner, 1996); Jacqueline Mazza, *Don't Disturb the Neighbors: The U.S. and Democracy in Mexico, 1980–1995* (New York: Routledge, 2001); Robert A. Pastor and Jorge G. Castañeda, *Limits to Friendship: The United States and Mexico* (New York: Vintage, 1989); Clint E. Smith, *Inevitable Partnership: Understanding Mexico–U.S. Relations* (Boulder, Colo.: Lynne Rienner, 2000); Michael T. Snarr, "Mexico: Balancing Sovereignty and Interdependence," in Ryan K. Beasley et al., eds., *Foreign Policy in Comparative Perspective* (Washington, D.C.: Congressional Quarterly Press, 2001).

Fox Quesada, Vicente (1942–) ☀ A popular neopopulist governor of the state of Guanajuato and **Partido Acción Nacional (PAN)** presidential winner in 2000. Vicente Fox ran an unorthodox campaign that ousted the ruling party (**Partido Revolucionario Institucional, PRI**) after 71 years of uninterrupted state-party domination. By rejecting the party's leadership in favor of a grassroots effort built around a group separate from PAN called "Friends of Fox," Fox outsmarted his opponents and helped orchestrate an unprecedented transfer of power, perhaps the most dramatic since the **Mexican Revolution**. With a 60 percent turnout, Fox won with 43.4 percent to only 36.9 percent for his ruling party opponent, **Francisco Labastida**. In comparison with 1994, this electoral outcome represented an increase of nearly 16 percent for PAN and a 14 percent decrease for the PRI.

Vicente Fox was born July 2, 1942, in León, the son of a wealthy Guanajuato farmer of Irish descent and a Spanish-born mother. It was here that he built a political career and established himself in a variety of export businesses. He studied business administration at the Jesuit-run Iberoamerican University in Mexico and then advanced management at Harvard University in the United States. His dynamic personality and business acumen helped him advance to the top of Coca-Cola Mexico, serving as president from

1975 to 1979. Fox was elected to Mexico's Congress as a member of PAN in 1988, but he lost his first bid for governor of his home state in 1991. To help him expand his assortment of business enterprises in 1979, he founded Grupo Fox, a conglomerate of agricultural (cattle raising, farming, animal feed, frozen vegetables) and manufacturing (footwear, cowboy boots) activities aimed at the export market. Most of his political career centered on legislative and executive positions in his home state of Guanajuato, including the governorship from 1995 to 2001. He took a leave of absence so that he could run for president in the July 2, 2000, elections. With promises of major change and the image of a charismatic sex symbol resembling the Marlboro Man, Vicente Fox represented an outsider's contempt for large bureaucracies and **corruption**—a new man for a new era in the minds of many Mexican voters.

With the reluctant backing of his own National Action Party (PAN), the endorsement of the small Green Ecologist Party, and the backing of some leftist intellectuals fed up with **Partido dela Revolución (PRD)** candidate **Cuauhtémoc Cárdenas**, Fox ran an aggressive campaign as the more down-home candidate of the Alliance for Change coalition against the stodgy and soft-spoken PRI hopeful, Francisco Labastida. More independent, more liberal, and less nationalistic than his conservative Catholic party on major economic and social issues, Fox started his campaign for the presidency more than two years before the election and without asking his party's permission. In polls conducted in October 1999, after a failed effort by opposition parties to form an alliance to offer a single candidate, Fox managed to pull within three percentage points (32 percent to 35 percent) of the two leading PRI candidates competing in the first-ever primary for the ruling party. After the PRI selected Labastida in a nationwide primary in November, Fox slipped behind the PRI frontrunner but remained close throughout the rest of the campaign. In the months leading up to the July 2000 election, polls showed Fox pulling within 3–5 percent of Labastida. Some polls showed Fox ahead as the election neared, and Labastida's advisers warned him weeks before the election that it was unlikely he could prevent a PRI defeat at the polls.

Fox rejected opposition efforts in mid-1999 to hold a primary to choose a single opposition candidate between him and Cárdenas, the former mayor of Mexico City and leader of the leftist opposition. He angered Catholics during the campaign by associating Mexico's Catholic clergy with the PRI, the party that had controlled Mexico for seven decades. However, Fox was not adverse to using religious symbolism to reinforce his populist image. On more than one occasion he "wrapped" himself in the Guadalupana, a flag bearing the image of the **Virgin of Guadalupe**, although this tactic did not work and he had to reiterate his belief in nonreligious education.

PAN candidate for president in 2000, Vicente Fox. Credit: Mexican Embassy, Washington, D.C.

During the 2000 election campaign, his support organization, Friends of Fox, grew to have six times as many members as the PAN itself. In contrast to Labastida, who enjoyed the help of the party machinery, Fox relied heavily on television. He had a more casual style than his PRI opponent, frequently appearing as a down-home hero dressed in an open shirt and and wearing cowboy boots (although he changed to a suit and tie as the election neared) and a "FOX" belt buckle. His campaign vernacular was loaded with negative (and slang-filled) remarks about the PRI, its candidate (he called Labastida a "sissy" and implied on several occasions he was a homosexual), and the need for change. The lower classes seemed more receptive to Fox's use of slang and profanity in campaign appearances, particularly when he attacked the ruling party; however, others despised Fox for running what they called a dirty and slanderous presidential race.

During the campaign Vicente Fox portrayed himself as a dynamic modernizer, promising to spur economic growth, push a "revolution in education" based on new investments in teachers and schools, generate over a million new jobs, revamp the rural sector by doubling aid to farmers and offering incentives to change to more profitable crops, and improve management of **government**. To convince voters of his populist reforms, he often pointed to his business experience (in a span of 15 years he rose from route supervisor to chief executive of Coca-Cola Mexico) and favorable record as governor of Guanajuato, having attracted major foreign investments. He also helped manage his family's footwear factories (a major industry in Guanajuato) before making a successful run for Congress in 1988, and an unsuccessful attempt at the governorship of Guanajuato in 1991 (he claims the PRI cheated him out of victory in this race).

With a slogan ("The change that suits you") aimed at voters reluctant to switch to the PAN over the well-known PRI, Fox employed a campaign strategy that he hoped would attract PRI voters and those who traditionally have voted for other opposition parties. His campaign rhetoric made frequent references to the **corruption**, age, and failures of the ruling party by using the Spanish word *ya!* (enough already!) to convince hesitant voters that it was time for the PRI to go. In a physical gesture of defiance to the ruling party, Fox's logo devised a hand with two fingers raised (and superimposed on the letter Y) that conveyed to the crowd both a V-for-victory and the Y-for-*ya* signal that seemed to suggest to some voters that he could actually beat the formidable PRI. Recognizing the importance of giving Mexican voters the impression that he could actually win, Fox told his campaign audience, "we're fighting a monster!" and that with support dwindling for the leftist opposition he was the only answer to Mexico's problems.

Fox's strength as an "independent" politician and charismatic businessman helped against his two less forceful and dynamic rivals in the presidential contest. In a last-minute effort to forge a campaign alliance between the right-of-center PAN and the left-of-center PRD, Fox failed to convince Cárdenas and his followers that they should join forces to prevent the opposition from being defeated again at the polls. Despite many campaign blunders, Vicente Fox proved to be a formidable candidate, dodging and weaving against everything the ruling party pitched his way, eventually handing the PRI its first defeat at the presidential level.

Once his presidency got under way in 2001, Fox's populist tendencies waned as he struggled to build broader support for his programs at home and abroad. After one year of his six-year term, President Fox has been slowly transformed from an impatient crusader against the evils of PRI rule into a frustrated leader whose campaign promises have been difficult to fulfill. When he took office on December 1, 2000, Fox promised a "revolution of hope" that would change Mexico into a prosperous, pluralistic, and modern democracy. He falsely predicted that the economy would grow at a healthy pace and his political legitimacy would allow him to successfully tackle the problems of crime, **human rights** violations, corruption, **guerrilla movements**, political reforms, an antiquated tax system, and the creation of a new partnership with the United States. President Fox hoped that he could shift Mexico from a quasi-authoritarian to a more democratic regime and establish a new activist **foreign policy** in which the principles of nonintervention and the supremacy of national sovereignty would be given less emphasis, in some cases even abandoned. In a spirit of transparency and political tolerance, President Fox's foreign minister, **Jorge G. Castañeda Gutman**, indicated that human rights observers, election monitors, foreign journalists, and Zapatista sympathizers would be welcome in Mexico. By 2002 many Mexicans were losing hope in Fox's "revolution."

The problems that Vicente Fox faces after one year in office are rooted in a sluggish economy and a hostile Congress, compounded by the terrorist attacks on the United States, several domestic human rights cases, and his inability to follow through on bold promises made early in his presidency. With a public that is doubtful about Fox's ability to carry through on his reform promises, there is a growing image of indecisiveness under pressure that has eroded his standing with the average citizen. After receiving favorable reviews on his four-day state visit with President George W. Bush in early September 2001, Fox was perceived to have fumbled in his reaction to the events of **September 11, 2001**, and the way in which he handled the murder of Mexico's leading human rights lawyer, Digna Ochoa y Placido, on October 19. After weeks of agonizing over Mexico's proper response to the terrorist attacks on the United States and the U.S.-led war on terrorism, President Fox paid a hastily arranged visit to President Bush to try to repair the diplomatic

damage. Fox took three days to publicly condemn Ochoa's killing, generating further criticism of his commitment to human rights. Fox was criticized by environmental and human rights groups for the false imprisonment of the two environmental activists—Rodolfo Montiel and Teodoro Cabrera—whom Ochoa had defended in the past and for failing to protect those who engage in such legal activity at high risk. Three weeks after Ochoa's murder, Fox bowed to pressure from the human rights community and freed Montiel and Cabrera, reading a terse statement that said, "With these actions we show in deed the commitment of my government to the promotion and observance of human rights in our country." By the end of his first year in office, Fox's approval rating had dropped from 56 percent "strongly approving" to only 25 percent.

The drama of winning the 2000 election and ending the 71-year rule of the PRI did not translate into the ability to dominate the Mexican legislature, where the PRI continues to hold a majority of seats, and Fox's PAN refuses to blindly support their president. With less power than any president in generations, Fox's legislative proposals have stalled in Congress. Shortly after taking office, Fox allowed the Zapatistas to voice their concerns in person before the national Congress and then tried to push an Indian rights bill that would put an end to the **Zapatista rebellion in Chiapas**. After the bill was watered down by Panistas opposed to Fox's proposal, members of the Mexican Congress concluded that challenging the new president was not as difficult as they once thought. The worldwide economic slump has forced President Fox to scale back or eliminate his overhaul of the tax system and promises of new funds for education, health, local governments, and welfare. Despite promises to deal with human rights abuses, including the creation of a commission to investigate alleged crimes involving the military, Fox has been timid in pursuing accusations of torture by the military in order to bolster its role in the battle against **drug trafficking**. After one year of the Fox presidency it seems clear that the president will need to shake up his cabinet and forge an alliance with the PRI if he is serious about pushing his reforms through Congress.

Despite his fumbling response to the terrorist attacks on the United States, President Fox has had more success on the world stage, moving Mexico away from its traditional isolation toward a more active role in global affairs. After spending months traveling across Europe, Asia, and Latin America, he was able to gain Mexico a seat on the UN Security Council for the first time in two decades. The UN victory will help restore Fox's tarnished image at home and help him push for new strategies to deal with **immigration**, drug trafficking, guerrillas, organized crime, and trade disputes. According to Foreign Minister Castañeda, Mexico is interested in dealing with global conflicts through what he calls "preventive diplomacy," a growing need in the aftermath of the Cold War and current war on terrorism. For example, Mexico remains committed to a nonmilitary solution to the civil war in Colombia and a policy of normalization—trade, tourism, and investment—toward **Cuba**. In the aftermath of the terrorist attacks of September 11, 2001, Fox has had to down play his top priorities in dealing with the United States: a new guest worker program, more permanent visas, improved border safety, and the "regularization" of Mexican illegals in the United States. The U.S. public is widely unsympathetic toward a blanket amnesty for the estimated three million Mexican immigrants now living in the United States. With more than four years left in his presidency, President Fox has plenty of time to move beyond his "cheerleader in chief" role to one that includes fulfilling the promises he offered in his "revolution of hope." *See also* Electoral System/Elections.

SUGGESTED READING

John Ward Anderson and Molly Moore, "A Leap into the Unknown," *Washington Post,* July 4, 2000; "Beyond NAFTA: A Forum," *Nation,* May 28, 2001; Lucy Conger, "Mexico's Long March to Democracy," *Current History* (February 2001); Nikki Craske, "Another Mexican Earthquake? An Assessment of the 2 July 2000 Elections," *Government and Opposition* (Winter 2001): 27–47; Sam Dillon, "In Mexico's Election, the Race Is Real," *New York Times,* March 12, 2000; Vicente Fox, *A los pinos: Recuento autobiográfico* (Mexico, D.F.: Oceano, 1999); Robert S. Leiken, "With a Friend Like Fox," *Foreign Affairs* (September–October 2001); "A Year into His Term, Mexico's Fox Struggles," *Baltimore Sun,* December 1, 2001.

Fuentes, Carlos (1928–) ☀ One of Mexico's outstanding prose writers. Carlos Fuentes is known principally for his narrative writing—novels and collections of shorter fiction—although he is also famous for his essays and articles in international journals, plays, poetry, and movie scripts. Many of his recent novels were inspired by the agony of past tragedies and the hope that by putting the worst possible scenarios in his writing he could ward off disasters on the horizon. Since he wrote his first book, *Los días enmascarados* (1954), he has published over 20 novels and collections of shorter fiction and won almost every literary award available to Latin American authors, including the Premio Cervantes in 1988.

His short stories and novels often draw on elements of Mexico's rich mythical past in an effort to reinterpret present historical realities. For example, in his first major work, *La región mas transparente* (1958), he uses a variety of novelistic techniques—allegory, interior monologues, fragmented time sequences, lavish metaphors, and vibrant imagery—to tell a story in which colorful characters who are disillusioned with the **Mexican Revolution** intermingle with others who engage in

Aztec rituals dealing with human sacrifices in order to secure the survival of the human race. With a family saga in 20th-century Mexico City, his narrative style concentrates on characters—streetwalkers, indigenous peoples, and others—in search of their lost identities. In *La muerte de Artemio Cruz* (1962), perhaps his most accomplished work, Fuentes elaborates on many of the technical devices and subjects that later became characteristics of the Latin American "boom" in fiction writing. The new narrative style, characterized by a broader interest in Latin America and what Fuentes called "magic realism," soon became a trend as more and more writers associated with the "boom" (the literary resurgence in the years following the 1959 Cuban Revolution) added to the interest in the works of Latin American literary figures such as Gabriel García Márquez, Julio Cortázar, and Mario Vargas Llosa.

The son of a Mexican diplomat who fought against the U.S. invasion of Veracruz, Carlos Fuentes was born in Panama City on November 11, 1928. He spent his youth outside Mexico, in Ecuador, Brazil, Chile, and Argentina, with a six-year stay in Washington, D.C., from 1934 to 1940. While attending elementary school in Washington, he learned English, read the works of Mark Twain and Robert Louis Stevenson, and discovered the difficulty of being Mexican in the United States after the expropriation of American petroleum interests by the administration of **Lázaro Cárdenas** in 1938. At the age of 16 he returned to Mexico and finished high school at Colegio Francisco Morelos. In 1948 he earned a law degree from the **National Autonomous University of Mexico (UNAM)**, and also studied at the Institute of Advanced International Studies in Geneva. His childhood experience of living between two cultures, languages, and nations had a profound impact on his work as a novelist, political essayist, short-story writer, journalist, and social critic.

Coming of age at the beginning of the Cold War, and as a member of a diplomatic family with close contacts with the architects of Mexican **foreign policy** that emphasized nationalism and anti-imperialism, Carlos Fuentes became a dissident who opposed official policy in Mexico and criticized U.S. foreign policy toward Latin America. He entered the diplomatic corps in 1950, serving in posts that allowed him to form tight bonds with the world of the arts and literature. From 1950 to 1974, Fuentes represented Mexico in the International Labor Organization (Geneva), worked in the Ministry of Foreign Affairs, served as press secretary in the United Nations Information Center (Mexico City), married film star Rita Macedo in 1959 (divorced in 1966), married Silvia Lemus in 1973, and was a fellow at the Woodrow Wilson International Center for Scholars in Washington, D.C., in 1974. He served as Mexican ambassador to France in 1974–1977, after which he lectured and taught at numerous American universities, including the University of Pennsylvania, Columbia University, Princeton University, and Harvard University, where he has been professor of Latin American Studies since 1987.

Although Fuentes has attracted an international following and admiration for his literary work, his critics find his leftist ideology, anti-Americanism, pseudohistoricism, and critical commentary on Mexican political life unfortunate, disturbing, and hypocritical. The most prominent critic of Fuentes was **Octavio Paz**, a literary giant who disliked the support that Mexican intellectuals gave to the Cuban Revolution and its Cuban writers. Fuentes's admiration for **Fidel Castro** ran out in 1965, when the Cuban government launched a campaign against Chilean poet Pablo Neruda. Fuentes began to criticize Paz for his bourgeois reformism, leading to years of bickering over political and social matters. In the 1970s Fuentes continued his political writing with

Carlos Fuentes, flanked by his wife, Silvia Fuentes, while in Brazil to receive Latin Identity Award at the Literary Academy in Rio de Janeiro, Brazil, June 1999. Credit: AP/World Wide Photos.

several plays that offered caustic critiques of Mexico's authoritarian power structure. Nevertheless, he developed a close relationship with President **Luis Echeverría** and in 1975 was named ambassador to France.

Although Carlos Fuentes was denied permission to enter the United States in 1969 because of what the U.S. Department of State called "Communist sedition," during the late 1970s he began a gradual reconciliation with the United States. He remained a critic of U.S. Central American policy during the Reagan years, defending Latin American sovereignty and condemning U.S. **intervention** in numerous articles that

appeared in U.S. newspapers and magazines. To voice his concerns on these matters he wrote *Gringo Viejo* (1985), which subsequently was made into a Hollywood movie starring Jane Fonda and Gregory Peck. He also traveled widely to film *The Buried Mirror*, an examination of the cultural contributions of Spanish-speaking countries.

With the election of **Carlos Salinas de Gortari**, Fuentes returned to essay writing in Mexican newspapers and magazines, criticizing the president's neoliberal economic policies, political **corruption**, and a flawed foreign policy in which Mexico has given far too much to the United States. Fuentes is intensely aware of the historical relations between cultures in which he sees the impact of England, Spain, France, and the United States on the creation of Mexican identity. In his many novels, Fuentes articulates a vision of Mexico as a chaotic and fragmented nation whose indigenous past weighs heavily on the present, often symbolized as a country in a dismal state of political decay.

Carlos Fuentes is less outspoken in political matters now that the PRI has been defeated and **Vicente Fox** is president of Mexico. While Fuentes argues that Mexican **elections** and politics are now **democratic**, he is also convinced that Mexican society is far from a fully democratic society, particularly given the fact that Mexico faces huge burdens in dealing with extensive poverty, rampant corruption, and the lack of rule of law.

In October 1999, Fuentes was given Mexico's highest civilian award for his lifetime achievements. He does not appear concerned that he has never received the Nobel Prize in Literature, an honor that many feel he deserves, but seems content with the current Latin American winners of his generation, including his good friend Gabriel García Márquez.

SUGGESTED READING

Stephen Boldy, "Carlos Fuentes," in John King, ed., *Modern Latin American Fiction: A Survey* (London: Faber & Faber, 1987); Victor Manuel Durán, *A Marxist Reading of Fuentes, Vargas Llosa, and Puig* (Lanham, Md.: University Press of America, 1993); Wendy B. Faris, *Carlos Fuentes* (New York: F. Ungar, 1983); Alfonso González, *Carlos Fuentes: Life, Work, and Criticism* (Fredericton, N.B.: York, 1987); Charlene Helmuth, *The Postmodern Fuentes* (Lewisburg: Bucknell University Press, 1997); Kristine Ibsen, *Author, Text, and Reader in the Novels of Carlos Fuentes* (New York: Peter Lang, 1993); Ilán Semo, "Fuentes, Carlos," in Michael S. Werner, ed., *Encyclopedia of Mexico: History, Society, and Culture*, vol. 1 (Chicago: Fitzroy Dearborn, 1997); Kenneth M. Taggart, *Yáñez, Rulfo, y Fuentes: El tema de la muerte en tres novelas Mexicanas* (Madrid: Playor, 1983); Ginger Thompson, "Fuentes Finds His Powers Have a Will of Their Own," *New York Times*, January 31, 2001; Maarten Van Delden, *Carlos Fuentes, Mexico, and Modernity* (Nashville: Vanderbilt University Press, 1999); Raymond L. Williams, *The Writings of Carlos Fuentes* (Austin: University of Texas Press, 1998).

Galindo, Blas. *See* Chávez, Carlos.

Galindo, Héctor Alejandro (1906–1999) ☀ A major director who, along with **Emilio Fernández**, helped pioneer the growing film industry in Mexico in the 1940s and 1950s. Known in the Mexican film world as Don Alex, he was the first director to place his films in the streets, bars, and factories in the urban barrios of Mexico City. His movies often portrayed the hardship and heartbreak of working Mexicans: down-and-out boxers, bus drivers, prostitutes, accountants, gangsters, and fathers struggling to make a living—a film genre that made Galindo popular and famous in Mexican film circles. In his long career, he directed or wrote more than 70 films, receiving eight Ariels (the Mexican equivalent of the Oscar) and other honors for his cinematic craftsmanship. In one of his most famous films, *Campeón sin corona* (1945), a street kid climbs out of urban poverty through success in the boxing ring only to be defeated by a corrupt network of gangsters controlling the sport.

Alejandro Galindo was born in Monterrey, Nuevo León, in 1906, but his sensitivity to the problems and feuds of ordinary Mexicans only came after he left for Mexico City with his mother. Disgusted with the **cinema** he was exposed to in Mexico City as an adolescent, he decided to learn the trade by going to Hollywood in the 1920s. After entering the United States illegally, Galindo first worked as an office boy in Hollywood; he was subsequently employed by Metro-Goldwyn-Mayer and Columbia Pictures to write scripts for silent films and later for dubbing their talking films into Spanish. While working in the film industry in Los Angeles, Galindo took classes in drama and photography at the University of Southern California. The financial crash of 1929 forced the aspiring director to return to Mexico, where he applied what he had learned in Hollywood over the next 50 years.

Aware of the plight of the Mexican *bracero* in the United States during the 1940s, Galindo made *Espaldas mojadas* (1953), one of the early critiques of the exploitation of "wetbacks," or illegal Mexican workers, in the farms in the southwestern United States. Other noteworthy Galindo films include *Una familia de tantas* (1948), *Doña perfecta* (1950), and *El juicio de Martín Cortés* (1974). Despite his creativity and success in Mexican cinema, Don Alex never received the National Prize for the Arts, the country's highest honor bestowed on its artists. Consequently, at his death in 1999, he was denied a wake in the Palacio de Bellas Artes in Mexico City, an unjust decision that was protested by Galindo's family and others in the film community.

SUGGESTED READING

Joanne Hershfield and David R. Maciel, eds., *Mexico's Cinema: A Century of Film and Filmmakers* (Wilmington, Del.: Scholarly Resources, 1999); Julia Preston, "Héctor Alejandro Galindo, Mexican Film Director, 93," *New York Times,* February 10, 1999.

García Robles, Alfonso (1911–1991) ☀ One of Mexico's most important 20th-century diplomats and international legal experts. Alfonso García Robles earned a reputation as a specialist in nuclear disarmament during the Cold War. A passionate foe of weapons of mass destruction and a skilled negotiator on matters of detente and disarmament, he was awarded the 1982 Nobel Peace Prize along with Alva Myrdal. He received the Nobel as "not only a reward for almost twenty years of work on disarmament, but also vindication of the virtues of patient and methodical negotiation."

Born in Zamora, Michoacán, García Robles studied law at the University of Paris in 1936 and received a diploma from the International Law Academy at the Hague in 1938. The following year his government career began with a series of diplomatic posts and foreign assignments for the ministry of foreign relations. During his long career in foreign service, he served as Mexico's permanent representative to the United Nations Committee on Disarmament (1971–1975). From 1962 to 1964 he was the Mexican ambassador to Brazil, and from 1964 to 1970 he was state secretary in the Ministry of Foreign Affairs in Mexico City. During this time García Robles played a crucial role in establishing and implementing the agreement on a denuclearized zone in Latin America, which led to the 1967 Treaty for the Prohibition for Nuclear Weapons in Latin America (also known as the **Treaty of Tlatelolco**), his greatest achievement.

García Robles is the author of numerous books and articles on disarmament and maritime law, including Mexico's position on the law of the sea in the late 1950s, and different aspects of Latin American government. His long career in diplomacy and international relations culminated with his 1975–1976 appointment as foreign minister and subsequently the rank of ambassador emeritus in 1981. In 1999 his widow, Juanita García Robles, donated her husband's large collection of books to the University of Virginia library. As a critic of the arms race and a tireless advocate of détente during the Cold War, Alfonso García Robles helped Mexico become one of the foremost proponents of global disarmament, including the elimination of nuclear weapons and land mines, and multilateral efforts to curtail the illicit manufacturing and trafficking in firearms.

SUGGESTED READING

"Biography of Alfonso García Robles," www.nobel.se/peace/laureates/1982; Miguel Marín Bosch et al., *Armas nucleares, desarme y carrera armamentista* (Mexico, D.F.: Ediciones Gernika, 1985); Bettina Corke, ed., *Who Is Who in Latin America: Government, Politics, Banking, and Industry*, 2d ed. (New York: Decade Media, 1989); John T. McQuiston, "Alfonso García Robles Dies at 80; Shared Nobel for Atom Arms Ban," *New York Times*, September 4, 1991; Bernard S. Schlessinger and June H. Schlessinger, *The Who's Who of Nobel Prize Winners, 1901–1995*, 3d ed. (Phoenix: Oryx, 1996).

Garro, Elena (1920–1998) ☀ One of Mexico's best-known and most important "magical realists" in Latin American fiction writing. Garro's novels, plays, and stories exploring the clash between illusion and reality are central to the understanding of contemporary Mexican fiction, including recent writing by Mexican women. Although she lived for many years in Spain and France, her writing captures much of the essence of contemporary Mexican society, often using her hometown and childhood memories to provide detailed realistic descriptions of violence, sexual intimidation, and psychological torment along with nightmarish fantasies.

Her contributions to Mexican novel writing are devoted to many themes of importance to comprehending contemporary Mexican novel writing in general, and Mexican **feminist** writing in particular: the magical and the imaginative as they coexist with reality (*Los recuerdos del porvenir*, 1963); the development of characters that may simultaneously coexist in two historical periods (*La semana de colores*, 1964); the capriciousness, **corruption**, and opportunism associated with the drive for political power (*Felipe Ángeles*, 1979; *Y Matarazo no llamó*, 1991); and women who suffer the consequences of living in a male-dominated society (*Testimonios sobre Mariana*, 1981; *Reencuentro de personajes*, 1981). In other stories she depicts women as the victims of government persecution and exclusion, often in exile from their countries of origin (*Andamos huyendo Lola*, 1980; *La casa junto al río*, 1981). Novelist and literary critic **Carlos Fuentes** judged Garro's first book, *Los recuerdos del porvenir* (Recollections of things to come) one of the most significant Mexican novels of the 20th century. The technical and stylistic sophistication of her works has contributed to her popularity among Latin American women writers during the second half of the 20th century. Her pessimistic view of Mexican society and avant-garde writing style are visible in *Felipe Ángeles* (1979), a three-act play that is highly critical of the **Mexican Revolution** and its aftermath.

Born in Puebla, Mexico, in 1920, Elena Garro started her writing career as a journalist before she embarked on writing novels, short stories, and plays. While married to **Octavio Paz** (1937–1959) she wrote her first book—*Los recuerdos del porvenir* (1963)—a depressing and negative recreation of life in her hometown, for which she won the Villarrutia Prize. Her marriage to Paz brought her into a circle of intellectuals where her own radical ideas thrived, but eventually her views clashed with those of her artistic contemporaries. Shortly after her marriage to Paz, the couple moved to Spain to write about the Spanish Civil War. While living in Paris after **World War II,** they became part of a literary circle that included surrealist André Breton and Argentine poet Jorge Luis Borges. After her marriage ended, she lived in Paris until 1963, but the two famous Mexican writers never spoke to each other again.

Garro's rejection of the student protest and rebellion in the late 1960s—she called the student movement a "crazy adventure"—stirred open hostility and led to a split with Mexico's writers and intellectuals. Shortly after being rejected by Mexico's literary community, she left for New York and later moved to Paris, living in exile for 23 years before returning to her native land in 1991. Although she found Mexico a changed place—and painfully hard to accept—she continued her provocative and highly successful writing until her death from emphysema in Cuernavaca in 1998.

SUGGESTED READING

Anthony DePalma, "Elena Garro, a Mexican Literary Figure, Dies at 78," *New York Times,* August 25, 1998; Elena Garro, *First Love: And Look for My Obituary: Two Novellas,* trans. David Ungar (Willimantic, Conn.: Curbstone, 1997); Gabriela Mora, "A Thematic Exploration of the Works of Elena Garro," in Yvette Miller and Charles Tatum, eds., *Latin American Women Writers Yesterday and Today* (Pittsburgh, Pa.: Latin American Review Press, 1997); Patricia Rubio, "Elena Garro," in Verity Smith, ed., *Encyclopedia of Latin American Literature* (Chicago: Fitzroy Dearborn, 1997); Anita Stoll, ed., *A Different Reality: Essays on the World of Elena Garro* (Lewisburg: Bucknell University Press, 1990); Stoll, "Elena Garro," in Diane E. Marting, ed., *Spanish American Women Writers: A Bio-Bibliographical Source Book* (Westport, Conn.: Greenwood, 1990).

Garza Sada Financial Group or Family ☀ One of the most influential and extensive entrepreneurial families in Mexico with interlocking corporate interests in **beer,** glass, steel, petrochemical, bottling, and packaging. The original head of this powerful capitalist family was Isaac Garza Garza, the son of Jewish immigrants from Spain who settled in the region of Monterrey at the end of the 19th century. He married Consuela Sada Muguerza, the daughter of Francisco Sada Gómez, a prominent businessman. The closely knit Garza Sada family cultivated business partnerships with others (often related by marriage) that led to the establishment of a number of major firms devoted to brewing (Cervecería Cuauhtémoc, 1890), steel, glass, and paper packaging. Isaac's union with Consuela produced numerous children who took over the leadership of a number of interconnected corporations that became known as the Monterrey Group.

The Monterrey Group (based in the northern commercial-industrial city of Monterrey) is one of many holding companies dominated by a small number of linked families that control most of the capital and hold key executive positions in these firms. Although the group is not as tightly knit as it was before it broke up into several smaller groups in the 1970s, it continues to be a powerful force in the political and economic life of Mexico. Made up of approximately 200 families from Monterrey, the group produces about 25 percent of Mexico's industrial output. Unlike most of the private sector that supports the **Partido Revolucionario Institucional (PRI),** the Monterrey Group supports the **Partido Acción Nacional (PAN),** particularly after President **López Portillo's** bank nationalization in 1976. All of the conglomerates that make up the Monterrey Group rank among the top 50 firms in Mexico. The best-known of these groups is ALFA industrial group, founded by Bernardo Garza Sada, grandson of Isaac Garza Garza and son of Roberto Garza Sada. Other members of the family control the various holding companies located in Monterrey. Before Mexico's 1995 peso devaluation, *Forbes* magazine listed five branches of the Garza Sada and Garza Sepúlveda families as Mexican billionaires.

More than 100 years after the Garza and Sada families bonded and founded a number of firms, the offspring continue to be a powerful force among Mexican entrepreneurs, part of the economic elite who hold shares and serve as board members of major industrial firms, dominate the activities of interest groups, and manage most of the major industrial holding groups in Monterrey. Adrián Sada attended the notorious private fund-raising dinner of Mexican billionaires, a gathering of the superrich to pay back President **Carlos Salinas** for his economic policies (privatization, **NAFTA**, and less state regulation) that proved to be so beneficial to Mexican business tycoons.

SUGGESTED READING

Roderic Ai Camp, *Entrepreneurs and Politics in Twentieth-Century Mexico* (1989); Camp, "Garza Sada Family," in Barbara A. Tenenbaum, ed., *Encyclopedia of Latin American History and Culture*, vol. 2 (New York: Scribners, 1996); Paul B. Carroll, "Garza Sadas Build an Unrivaled Latin Empire," *Wall Street Journal*, December 11, 1995; Jesús Casla Francisco, *Don Eugenio Garza Sada* (Monterrey, N.L.: Gobierno del Estado de Nuevo León, 1994); Alex Saragoza, *The Monterrey Elite and the Mexican State, 1880–1940* (Austin: University of Texas Press, 1988); Menno Vellinga, *Economic Development and the Dynamics of Class: Industrialization, Power, and Control in Monterrey, Mexico* (1979); Andrew Wheat, "Mexico's Privatization Piñata," *Multinational Monitor* (October 1996).

Gender and Sexuality. *See* Feminism; Homosexuality; Machismo.

General Agreement on Tariffs and Trade (GATT) ☀ A multilateral trade organization founded by treaty in 1947 to advance the principle of free trade in the aftermath of **World War II**; GATT was eventually replaced by the World Trade Organization (WTO) in 1995. The major purpose of GATT was to reduce tariffs and nontariff barriers and to help create rules of conduct for world trade, particularly in countries with import-substitution industrialization (ISI) strategies of economic development. Until the 1970s, Mexico relied heavily on protective tariffs on industrial imports to benefit domestic manufacturers and therefore resisted joining the GATT arrangement. As Mexican economists and **technocrats** came to the realization that ISI was a contributing factor in Mexico's trade problems (primarily the shortcomings of economic protectionism and debt-led growth), the administrations of **Miguel de la Madrid** and **Carlos Salinas de Gortari** mounted an aggressive campaign to expand trade and investment with Europe and Asia and entered into free trade negotiations with several Latin American countries.

When President **José López Portillo** first raised the possibility of joining the GATT, he faced strong opposition from cabinet members, the intellectual community, and **labor** organizations who argued that joining GATT would put an end to the country's economic nationalism and give the United States a mechanism to control Mexico's oil riches. When the **debt crisis** and collapse of oil prices hit Mexico hard in 1982, the option of joining GATT resurfaced once again. As Mexico faced new drops in oil prices and continuing capital flight, public opposition to trade liberalization faded and Mexico finally joined the GATT in 1986. Until this decision was made, Mexico had one of the most protected economies in the world; however, by 1990 it had one of the most open.

After joining the GATT, Mexico proceeded to privatize major industries and services, lowered trade barriers, eliminated export permits, moved toward greater deregulation of the economy, and began pursuing a free trade agreement with the United States and Canada. The decision to join the

GATT in 1986 and the implementation of the **North American Free Trade Agreement (NAFTA)** in 1994 showed that Mexico was determined to discard its inward-oriented development model in exchange for a more vigorous export-driven economy.

While Mexican leaders argue that they had no choice but to liberalize trade and open the economy to greater foreign investment, critics maintain that by doing so Mexico has damaged the agricultural sector and put the environment and health standards at risk. All of these changes exposed Mexican industry to international competition for the first time, but in return the government expected an increase in export revenue, greater economic efficiency, and renewed possibilities for growth and job creation. While many see membership in GATT/WTO as a positive move to solve pressing economic problems, others find that Mexico's dependence on foreign capital and multinational corporate strategies is still a thorn in its newly devised political economy.

SUGGESTED READING

David R. Mares, "Explaining Choice of Development Strategies: Suggestions from Mexico, 1970–1982," *International Organization* (Autumn 1985); Luz María de la Mora, "General Agreement on Tariffs and Trade (GATT)," in Michael S. Werner, ed., *Encyclopedia of Mexico: History, Society, and Culture,* vol. 1 (Chicago: Fitzroy Dearborn, 1997); Luis R. Rubio, Cristina D. Rodríguez, and Roberto V. Blum, "The Making of Mexico's Trade Policy and the Uruguay Round," in Henry Nau, ed., *Domestic Trade Politics and the Uruguay Round* (New York: Columbia University Press, 1989); Dale Story, "Trade Politics in the Third World: A Case Study of the Mexican GATT Decision," *International Organization* (Autumn 1982).

Geographical Regions ☀ Mexico's regional diversity is reflected in its official name—the United Mexican States (Estados Unidos Mexicanos)—and in the rich cultural and historical traditions that make up the Federal District (Distrito Federal, D.F.) and the 31 states (see table 4). In 1845 Mexico's total land area in square miles was almost equal to that of the United States (1,712,000 versus 1,787,880), but the annexation of Texas (an independent nation at the time), Mexico's defeat in the **Mexican American War** (1846–1848), and the Mesilla Valley purchase (Gadsden Purchase) in 1853, reduced Mexico's total geographical area by 55 percent while the United States increased its total land area by approximately 47 percent. The tremendous loss of territory to the United States soured U.S.–Mexican relations for the next 100 years.

Since the turn of the century Mexico has experienced a huge shift in population from the countryside to its major cities, particularly Mexico City, Guadalajara, Monterrey, Ciudad Juárez, and Tijuana. Today, metropolitan Mexico City contains over 20 million people, roughly one-fifth of Mexico's total population of approximately 100 million. The relationship between the urban core of Mexico City and its surrounding area and the rest of Mexico remains a source of tension and conflict as urbanization continues at a rapid pace. From a country that was less than 10 percent urban in 1900, Mexico is now 72 percent urban (versus 75 percent in the United States). Political efforts at decentralization—diverting economic growth away from the capital—has had little success due in large part to the federal **government**'s refusal to yield more power to states and local governments. The following six regions (and Mexico City) define the geography of Mexico: Independent North, North Pacific, Central Breadbasket, Oil Basin and the Gulf Lowlands, Southern Mountains, and Chiapas and Yucatán.

The Independent North encompasses the states from San Luis Potosí to the **U.S.–Mexican border.** This region—Mexico's largest, with 41 percent of the national territory but only 18 percent of its population—includes the states of Chihuahua,

Table 4. Mexican States, Area and Population, 1997

State	Area (square kilometers)	Population	State Capital
Aguascalientes	5,589	900,551	Aguascalientes
Baja California	70,113	2,249,968	Mexicali
Baja California Sur	73,677	398,437	La Paz
Campeche	51,833	671,343	Campeche
Chiapas	73,887	3,851,555	Tuxtla Gutiérrez
Chihuahua	247,087	2,892,725	Chihuahua
Coahuila	141,571	2,225,752	Saltillo
Colima	5,455	502,887	Colima
Distrito Federal, D.F.	1,499	8,519,305	
Durango	119,648	1,454,979	Durango
Guanajuato	30,589	4,588,751	Guanajuato
Guerrero	63,794	3,049,167	Chilpancingo
Hidalgo	20,987	2,184,178	Pachuca
Jalisco	80,137	6,241,683	Guadalajara
México	21,461	12,198,634	Toluca
Michoacán	59,864	3,997,565	Morelia
Morelos	4,941	1,511,287	Cuernavaca
Nayarit	27,621	916,270	Tepic
Nuevo León	64,555	3,680,565	Monterrey
Oaxaca	95,364	3,420,659	Oaxaca
Puebla	33,919	4,875,158	Puebla
Querétaro	11,769	1,309,470	Querétaro
Quintana Roo	50,350	766,895	Chetumal
San Luis Potosí	62,848	2,275,205	San Luis Potosí
Sinaloa	58,092	2,478,535	Culiacán
Sonora	184,934	2,157,252	Hermosillo
Tabasco	24,661	1,824,104	Villahermosa
Tamaulipas	79,829	2,602,891	Ciudad Victoria
Tlaxcala	3,914	916,800	Tlaxcala
Veracruz	72,815	7,090,128	Jalapa
Yucatán	39,340	1,607,534	Mérida
Zacatecas	75,040	1,372,087	Zacatecas
Islands	5,073		
Totals			
	1,972,256	94,732,320*	

Source: México, Social, 1996–1998 (México, D.F.: Banco Nacional de México, 1998): 83.

*Population, 1999: 100,718,000 (est.)

Coahuila, Nuevo León, Tamaulipas, Durango, Zacatecas, and San Luis Potosí. It is dominated by the Mexican plateau, rugged mountains and vast regions of semidesert and mountainous terrain. The rugged beauty of northern Mexico has served as a backdrop for numerous Hollywood (and Mexican) films starring both American and Mexican actors. The North suffers from deficient rainfall, which means that any expansion of agriculture or population will require new irrigation systems. States such as Zacatecas have lost close to one-third of their population due to migration to the United States, but the population left behind has reaped the benefits of large amounts of remittances from relatives working in the farms and factories in the United States.

The border towns of the Independent North have been the target of the *maquiladora* program, started in 1965 to replace the *bracero* program. With over 3,000 factories employing more than a million workers, the North is the center of this assembly-for-export activity. As Mexico has moved toward a deregulated economy, multinational firms have located in the North to take advantage of cheap labor and trade benefits. Ford Motor Company opened an engine plant in Chihuahua City and an assembly plant in Hermosillo (Sonora). General Motors and Nissan have also opened similar plants. Multinational companies like IBM, Whirlpool, Kodak, and Caterpillar have invested in modern plants in hopes of creating a high-tech industrial zone in northern Mexico. The North is plagued by a plethora of border problems—air and water pollution, traffic congestion, crime, and **drug trafficking**—that have serious consequences for those living north of the border.

With wide vistas, large cattle ranches, and dispersed settlement clusters, the North has the feel of the American West. The people of the North are known for their political independence and conservatism, cowboy culture (*charros*, horses, rodeos, roundups, and lariats), and closer ties with the United States. Mexican businesspeople from the North are more likely to admire American business methods and marketing procedures than their counterparts in the rest of Mexico. It is not uncommon for the children of Mexico's well-to-do to attend a university in New Mexico, Texas, or Louisiana and then return to work in Mexico. Monterrey, Mexico's third largest city, is located in the North and serves as a commercial and industrial center, producing approximately 25 percent of Mexico's manufactured goods. The economic success of Monterrey is often attributed to the **Garza Sada family**, an enterprising clan that emigrated to Mexico from Spain in the 19th century. Government-sponsored programs to convert semiarid parts of the Independent North to irrigated oases through land reform, peasant cooperatives (*ejidos*), and improved technology have met with limited success. Anti-Americanism is less common in the North than in other parts of Mexico.

The North Pacific region includes the states of Baja California, Baja California Sur, Sonora, Sinaloa, and Nayarit. This region includes 21 percent of the total area of Mexico but is occupied by only 14 percent of the Mexican people. It is a region of deserts and the exceptionally rugged mountains of the Sierra Madre Occidental with elevations of 10,000 feet and above. The coastal lowland varies in width from less than 10 to more than 50 miles. With numerous dams—eight large ones were built after **World War II**—and adequate rainfall in some parts, particularly in the southern states of Sinaloa and Nayarit, Mexico has achieved self-sufficiency in certain foodstuffs and has a thriving farming-for-export focus in these states. This region of Mexico is the leading source of wheat and cotton. Tomatoes, melons, and other fruits and vegetables are grown to be shipped north to compete in the U.S. market. Commercial fishing and cattle raising are also important to this region; beef is important for the local economy and for export and large amounts of frozen or canned fish (tuna, shrimp, and sardines) make their way into the American market. Millions of Americans visit the border towns each year and a growing number of **tourists** are attracted to beach communities such as Mazatlán, La Paz, Cabo San Lucas, and Puerto Vallarta. The railroad journey from the city of Chihuahua to Los Mochis on the Gulf of California is a major tourist attraction for those interested in Mexico's Copper Canyon. The state of Sinaloa is the center of opium production and is plagued with drug-related killings and kidnappings.

Sonora is known for the sport of **baseball** and the development of excellent players who compete in the Mexican and American leagues. The most celebrated and talented Mexican ballplayer from that area is **Fernando Valenzuela**, a left-handed pitcher with a tricky screwball from a small town near Navajoa. Valenzuela grew up playing in the Mexican leagues before he was spotted by a talent scout for the Los Angeles Dodgers in 1979. His pitching talent earned him millions of adoring fans (and numerous professional awards as a pitcher and hitter) throughout Mexico and among Mexican Americans living in the United States during the 1980s.

The Central Breadbasket comprises the states of Aguascalientes, Jalisco, Guanajuato, Querétaro, Hidalgo, Michoacán, México, Distrito Federal, Morelos, Tlaxcala, and Puebla, 14 percent of the national territory and 50 percent of the Mexican population. This region is one of the traditional centers of Mexico's Indian population and the main area of food production. These states account for nearly 20 percent of all agricultural land, with small farmers producing large amounts of maize, beans, and chilies for the local and national economy. Before the **Mexican Revolution** (1910–1917) large estates run by powerful landowners dominated the valleys where wheat and sugar cane were grown. Poor farmers were left with small plots on the poorer soils of the surrounding higher ground. After the revolution, the better areas in the flat lands were partially redistributed and irrigated, creating a mixture of collective (*ejido*) and private farms that became the basis of modern agricultural development in the region. One of the most productive areas is the lowland region around Guanajuato that is watered by the Lerma River. The large wheat fields of the past have given way to fresh produce (broccoli, cauliflower, and snow peas) that is sold to multinational packing plants owned by Bird's Eye, Green Giant, and Del Monte Foods for export to the U.S. market. Other fields are devoted to agricultural activities aimed at the large domestic urban markets in the population centers in the central region.

The Central Breadbasket contains other important commercial and industrial enterprises. Guadalajara, Mexico's second largest city, is the center of food distribution, textile manufacturing, and a growing number of high-tech industries devoted to electronics and computers. León is the home of an important tanning industry and is Mexico's shoe production center. **Automobile** plants can be found in Toluca, Cuernavaca, and Puebla. The remote valleys and suburbs of the larger cities in this region contain commercial communities devoted to tourism, traditional crafts such as pottery, lacquered boxes, copperware, and woolens. The craftspeople who produce these items—often combining ancient artistic traditions and modern techniques—are supported by government programs intended to improve the standard of living in outlying areas, thus minimizing the flow of migrants to the larger cities.

The Oil Basin and Gulf Lowlands region includes the states of Veracruz, Tabasco, and Campeche, an arc of forested and lightly settled lowlands facing the Gulf of Mexico. These three states represent 8 percent of the total territory and 10 percent of the nation's population. With great reserves of petroleum and natural gas, this region is the source of Mexico's greatest wealth. Oil pipelines connect the major centers of petroleum production in the Gulf Coast region to the United

States as well as to Mexico City on the central plateau and across the Gulf of Tehuantepec to Salina Cruz. The petroleum industry (nationalized since 1938) has become a source of Mexican nationalism—and controversy—with recent policies of privatization and deregulation. Exploration and production are controlled by **Petróleos Mexicanos (PEMEX)**. Working in tandem with the numerous oil refineries in this region of Mexico are several giant petrochemical complexes where fertilizers and fibers are produced. The wet tropical lowlands of the Gulf Coast region is also important for growing maize (corn), bananas, cacao, **coffee**, rubber, tobacco, rice, vanilla, and other spices. Because of adequate rainfall, yields of the major crops are high and profitable.

The Southern Mountains region includes the states of Colima, Guerrero, Oaxaca, and Chiapas (treated separately with the Yucatán). It is a region that includes 8 percent of Mexican territory, with 7 percent of the total population. With less than 20 percent level land, this is a region of rugged mountains, verdant valleys, dramatic coastlines and seaside resorts, and architectural treasures that draw millions of tourists to Mexico. Because of its remote terrain, it has long been a refuge for bandits and guerrillas, as well as home to mostly Mixtec and Zapotec Indians, subsistence farmers who try to survive by growing corn on steep mountain slopes. Guerrero has more insurgent groups than any other Mexican state. The economic growth of the Southern Mountains region is hindered by the lack of transportation, rough topography, and marginal government interest in developing a more diverse economic base.

Most of the economic growth and benefits occurs along the Pacific Coast, where a new coastal highway links a growing number of government-planned tourist resorts. In addition to the old colonial port of Acapulco, this part of Mexico has spent billions of dollars developing the expensive resorts of Puerto Vallarta, Manzanillo, Zihuantanejo, Ixtapa, Puerto Escondido, and Huatulco. With fancy hotels, restaurants, beachfront activities, and modern international airports, this part of the Mexican economy depends on tapping the North American tourist market during the cold winter months north of Mexico. The two contrasting activities and cultures—subsistence peasant farmers and wealthy North American tourists—rarely come in contact with one another, which may serve the needs and interests of both communities. Reports of pollution, crime, guerrilla insurgencies, and decaying infrastructure have been a source of concern for Mexican officials worried that without a healthy tourist industry, Americans and Canadians may not venture south of the border to spend time and money. Although outside of the tourist region, Guerrero is also faced with serious deforestation from national and international lumber and timber companies.

The peripheral areas of Chiapas and the Yucatán Peninsula contain the southern states of Chiapas, Yucatán, and Quintana Roo. With 8 percent of the territory and 6 percent of the population, this is a region of traditional Mayan communities; rural poverty; a booming tourism industry in the coastal resorts of Cancún and Cozumel Island; coffee, cacao, and cotton production; refugees from Guatemala and El Salvador; and a strong resistance to central government authority. The new city of Cancún, created in 1972 to service the tourist industry in Yucatán, is joined with other old colonial towns of Mérida and San Cristóbal de las Casas within the states of this region. The wealth generated from the hordes of workers in the tourism industry in Yucatán provides remittances to family members in the remote network of villages that dot the region. Much of the growth in Mérida is due to the government's decision to expand the *maquiladora* program of assembly-for-export in areas beyond the northern border cities. More than 50 *maquiladoras* have been built in the Mérida suburbs for the conversion of sisal (henequin) plants into natural fibers, the conversion of soybeans (imported through the port of Progreso) to oil for the domestic market, and apparel assembly for export to the United States.

This southern region of Mexico is also rich in archaeological treasures, forests with valuable hardwoods, and natural habitats. Environmentally conscious tourists from Mexico and other parts of the world have tried to introduce environmentally sensitive planning to the preservation of the region's heritage as more and more tourists are attracted to the beauty of the area. The Chiapas region is the home of numerous Indian communities that have become part of the Ejército Zapatista de Liberación Nacional (EZLN) seeking greater autonomy from the national government that has neglected the area while investing in tourism, border industries, commercial enterprises, and light industry in other parts of Mexico. Until his retirement in 1999, Bishop **Samuel Ruiz** was one of Chiapas' major defenders of Indian rights and often the subject of harsh criticism from the government and conservatives for his relentless efforts on behalf of the downtrodden. President **Vicente Fox** of the PAN has tried to meet many of the demands for major reform in Chiapas, but he has been thwarted by conservative members of Congress, both within his own party and among those in the **Partido Revolucionario Institucional (PRI)**.

The heart of Mexico from the time of the Aztecs to the present is Mexico City, arguably the largest city in the world and one of the noisiest and most polluted cities on earth. In 1997 the population of the Federal District (Distrito Federal) was estimated at 8,520,900, that of the surrounding area at about 18 million. Since World War II there has been an exodus from the rest of the country to the nation's capital, creating a growth rate (an influx of up to 700,000 people a year has been reported) and set of urban problems of staggering proportions: unemployment, squatter settlements, choking pollution, horrendous traffic congestion, respiratory diseases,

violent crime, **corruption**, lack of schools, severe water shortages, and the lack of wastewater treatment facilities. One large squatter settlement (Nezahualcóyotl) has close to 2 million in population and others continue to proliferate despite the government's inability to provide the necessary services demanded by the residents of these urban slums that spread for miles, often without paved streets, running water, or electricity. When the **Partido Revolucionario Institucional** was in power, it controlled the water supply and used water as a political tool, linked to political alliances, favors, and votes.

Many people—locals and visitors—have a love-hate relationship with the nation's capital. It is a place of enormous intensity, energy, and artistic and culinary activity combined with chaos, crisis, corruption, crime, and pollution. Over the past decade criminal activity of all sorts has captured the headlines of the national and international press. While there is no doubt that crime is a real factor for those who live in the city, there is also an element of sensationalism, particularly on the part of Mexican television stations, which for years presented a somewhat wholesome view of daily life. Crime in the capital manifests itself in many ways, from petty thieves to pirate cabdrivers, but most associate the rise in serious crime with Mexico's chronic economic crises, the efforts to create a more open and pluralist political apparatus, the tremendous disparity in income among the social classes, and global criminal networks involved in drugs and money laundering. Nevertheless, Mexico City is the political, economic, communications, cultural, entertainment, financial, and transportation center of the country, which means that it serves as a magnet for population flows, regardless of its urban problems and dismal future prospects. Mexico City is full of street performers, giving the city a circus atmosphere where people perform a variety of acts—juggling, gymnastics, fire-eating, people who roll on broken glass, and those who construct human pyramids—in exchange for money from the passersby. Mostly jobless, the street performers in Mexico City often stake out a popular intersection to put on their stunts. Others make a living by parading down busy streets with rubber masks that resemble well-known world figures such as Osama bin Laden, George W. Bush, and **Fidel Castro**. The best time to visit Mexico City is during the end-of-year holiday season, known in Mexico as the *Fiestas Navideñas*, from the Fiesta of Our **Virgin of Guadalupe** on December 12 through the Day of the Three Wise Men *(Día de los Reyes)* on January 6.

SUGGESTED READING

Jonathan R. Barton, *A Political Geography of Latin America* (New York: Routledge, 1997); Edgar W. Butler, James B. Pick, and W. James Hettrick, *Mexico and Mexico City in the World Economy* (Boulder, Colo.: Westview, 2000); Diane E. Davis, *Urban Leviathan: Mexico City in the Twentieth Century* (Philadelphia: Temple University Press, 1994); "Emerging Mexico," *National Geographic* (August 1996); Preston E. James, *Latin America*, 5th ed. (New York: Wiley, 1986); Kent Klich, *El Niño: Children of the Streets, Mexico City* (Syracuse: Syracuse University Press, 1999); José Luis Lezama, "Mexico," in Gerald Michael Greenfield, ed., *Latin American Urbanization: Historical Profiles* (Westport, Conn.: Greenwood, 1994); Eric Van Young, ed., *Mexico's Regions: Comparative History and Development* (La Jolla: Center for U.S.–Mexican Studies, University of California–San Diego, 1992); Peter M. Ward, *Mexico City*, rev. ed. (Chichester, U.K.: Wiley, 1998); Tim Weiner, "Mexico Grows Parched, with Pollution and Politics," *New York Times*, April 14, 2001.

Gómez Morín, Manuel (1897–1972) ✸ One of the founders of the **Partido Acción Nacional (PAN)** in 1939. Manuel Gómez Morín was an intellectual and major figure in Mexican finance. His major contribution to modern Mexico was as an opposition leader, the prime mover in the creation of one of the two major independent political movements toward **democracy** in the 20th century.

Gómez Morín was born in the small mining town of Batopilas, Chihuahua. His father was a successful miner and prominent figure in the community. After finishing school in his hometown, Manuel Gómez Morín moved to Mexico City and carved out a career in legal studies and public life. As a professor at the National School of Law, Gómez Morín was influential in the creation of a generation of distinguished intellectuals and public figures such as Alfonso Caso, **Vicente Lombardo Toledano**, and many others.

Gómez Morín's political life began in 1919 with positions in government agencies concerned with banking and finance; he helped found the Federal Reserve Bank of Mexico in 1925 and served as its first director until 1929. After assisting **José Vasconcelos**'s failed presidential bid, he retired from public life and devoted his time to his academic career in law and administration, serving as rector of the National University in 1933 and 1934. Gómez Morín then went into private law practice and made a number of wise financial investments in corporations that he helped create before returning to party politics.

Disenchanted with the direction of government policies under the socialist president **Lázaro Cárdenas**, Gómez Morín and Efraín González Luna founded the PAN in 1939. The PAN's struggle to create a viable alternative to the dominant party consisted of demonstrating its democratic organization and procedures: open discussion, financial accountability, freedom of the vote, and party decisions by majority vote. However, during the first decade of the PAN's existence, its democratic credentials were questioned due to the closeness between its members and the Catholic hierarchy, the sympathy of many members toward fascist governments and parties in Europe, and its initial lack of enthusiasm for Mexico's participation in **World War II**. While the leadership of PAN comes mostly from right-wing intellectuals and financiers, the bulk of its membership is derived from the middle classes of the capital and provinces, particularly in the northern border states. Until the surprising presidential victory of **Vicente Fox** in the 2000 presidential elections, the PAN served as Mexico's major opposition party, except for a short period from 1988 to 1994 when the left-of-center **Partido de la Revolución Democrática (PRD)** eclipsed the PAN in voter strength.

Manuel Gómez Morín spent his final 30 years as a financier and lawyer in Mexico City before his death in 1972.

SUGGESTED READING

Roderic Ai Camp, "Gómez Morín, Manuel," in Barbara A. Tenenbaum, ed., *Encyclopedia of Latin American History and Culture,* vol. 3 (New York: Scribners, 1996); María Teresa Gómez Mont, *Manuel Gómez Morín: La lucha por la libertad de Catedral* (Mexico, D.F.: Universidad National Autónoma de México, 1996).

Gómez-Peña, Guillermo (1955–) ☀ Writer and experimental performing artist. Guillermo Gómez-Peña uses the border region as a malleable metaphor from which to confront the narrow conceptualizations of "national culture" and what it means to be an "American." Through intercultural performances—radio, poetry, essays, television, on-site performances, newspapers, and art institutions—his main objective is to be an "artist-shaman" who exorcizes cultural boundaries by dramatizing them and bringing them face-to-face with his audience (Bright 1997, 605).

Born in Mexico City in 1955, Gómez-Peña began doing experimental performances on the streets of Mexico City in the 1970s while studying at the university. He moved to California in 1978, where he founded the Poyesis Genética with other students at the California Institute of the Arts. At first Poyesis was a troupe dedicated to culturally pluralistic and interdisciplinary performances; after years of experimentation and regroupings, it evolved into the Border Arts Workshop (BAW) in 1985. After years of working in groups, Gómez-Peña left the BAW in 1990 to emphasize solo performances, mostly in the United States and Mexico, but also internationally. To draw attention to his philosophy of conceptualizing changing cultural conditions and relationships, he designed three basic strategies: (1) performance as "intercultural intervention," with frequent use of the **U.S.–Mexican border** as a metaphor; (2) "performance diplomacy" aimed at understanding and information exchange; and (3) "cross-cultural/interdisciplinary collaboration" between performing artists of different cultural, regional and national backgrounds (Bright 1997, 604).

Using multiple forms and strategies for communicating ideas, Gómez-Peña tries to create a world where the fears of cultural differences and transnational migration disappear when the audience is challenged to engage in critical self-examination and historical reflection. His radio essays appear often on National Public Radio in the United States. In one segment on the fear of **immigration**, he asked his listeners to respond mentally to a psychological test measuring "Mexicophobia." He considers this unfortunate mental state "a psychosomatic condition created by xenophobic politicians and sleazy reporters with the sole objective of distracting you from your real problems." A self-described migrant provocateur, Guillermo Gómez-Peña uses life along the border to make his case for a borderless future for the United States and Mexico. He currently resides and performs in San Francisco.

SUGGESTED READING

Brenda Jo Bright, "Gómez-Peña, Guillermo," in Michael S. Werner, ed., *Encyclopedia of Mexico: History,*

Society, and Culture, vol. 1 (Chicago: Fitzroy Dearborn, 1997); Guillermo Gómez-Peña, *Dangerous Border Crossers: The Artist Talks Back* (New York: Routledge, 2000); Gómez-Peña, *Temple of Confessions: Mexican Beasts and Living Santos* (New York: Powerhouse, 1996); Gómez-Peña, *Warrior for Gringostroika: Essays, Performance Texts, and Poetry* (Saint Paul, Minn.: Graywolf, 1993).

Gorostiza Acalá, José (1901–1973) ☀ Outstanding poet and diplomat. José Gorostiza and his playwright brother Celestino were major figures in *Los Contemporáneos*, a loose group of poets and intellectuals that included such writers as **Jaime Torres Bodet**, Antonio Caso, and **José Vasconcelos**. As a key figure in the lively literary scene of the 1920s, he wrote insightful essays and poetry that helped bring Mexican poetry to the world stage. Interestingly, his reputation and literary achievements rest on a single work, *Muerte sin fin*, his 1939 poem that is considered one of the finest in the Spanish language.

Born in 1901 to a middle-class family in Villahermosa, Tabasco, José Gorostiza spent his youth moving around Mexico in the period before and during the **Mexican Revolution**. Once the family settled in Mexico City, he came under the influence of well-known writers and poets that would later be of benefit in his diplomatic and cultural-bureaucratic career. He developed an interest in Eastern mysticism, philosophical discourse, and literary theory, subjects that he applied to his personal poetics.

After publishing *Canciones para cantar en las barcas* in 1925, he launched a career in which he served as a diplomatic and cultural representative in various government agencies around the world and in the United Nations. While working in the Ministry of Foreign Relations in the administration of **Lázaro Cárdenas** (1934–1940), he wrote his most important work, *Muerte sin fin* (1939), a long poem in which the central image

of a glass of water serves as a metaphor for the self, soul, and mind. According to Bennett (1997, 611), "The 'endless death' of the title refers to the consciousness of death, the fundamental fact of human life and mind." With elegant diction and a marvelous use of paradox and self-reflection, the poem has been widely studied by numerous scholars who have approached it from entirely separate perspectives. There is still much speculation as to why Gorostiza virtually stopped writing poetry after *Muerte sin fin* was published. A stylistic perfectionist, some critics have speculated that either the nature of the poem (representing the end of poetry writing for him), the changing political and cultural atmosphere after 1940, or his desire to engage in more tangible activities contributed to his decision to put an end to his poetry. In any case, he continued to write insightful literary essays while serving as ambassador in some foreign land or a post in the Ministry of Foreign Relations. Gorostiza's work influenced other Mexican literary figures, especially **Octavio Paz** and other writers who dominated the modern period. Prior to his death in Mexico City in 1973, he won the National Literary Prize in 1968.

SUGGESTED READING

John M. Bennett, "Gorostiza, José," in Michael S. Werner, ed., *Encyclopedia of Mexico: History, Society, and Culture*, vol. 1 (Chicago: Fitzroy Dearborn, 1997); Juan Gelpí, *Enunciación y dependencia en José Gorostiza* (Mexico, D.F.: Universaidad Nacional Autónomo de Mexico, 1984); Octavio Paz, *Children of the Mire*, trans. Rachel Phillips, rev. ed. (Cambridge: Harvard University Press, 1991).

Government, Mexican National ☀ Mexico's form of government is designed to provide a separation of powers between the three branches of government—executive, legislative, and judicial—combined with elements of federalism whereby power is divided between the central (or federal) government and 31 administrative divisions called states, plus one federal district to govern the capital known as the Distrito Federal. Mexico's government is guided by the **Constitution of 1917,** which incorporates the essential features of representative **democracy**, including federalism, separation of powers, a bicameral congress, and a Bill of Rights. Although the constitutional design resembles that of the United States, power is weighted in favor of the president, who is elected by popular vote for a single six-year term of office (known as the *sexenio*) with no chance for reelection. There is no vice president, which means that in the case of removal or death, a provisional president would be elected by Congress to perform the president's duties until a new election can be held.

This presidential system means that the president is chief of state, head of government, and chief of the armed forces. The Constitution gives the president the power to appoint his cabinet (with the consent of the Senate) of 21 members, including 17 ministries or secretariats and four presidential assistants, and, until 1997, the power to appoint the governor (now mayor, an elected position) of the Federal District. In addition to the nominating powers of the president, he also has constitutional authority to nominate and remove cabinet heads and other federal employees. Despite recent governmental reforms, political power is still highly centralized in the executive branch and the office of the presidency.

The most powerful cabinet posts—often the source of recruitment of future presidents—are those of finance, interior (*gobernación*), planning and budget, and commerce and industry. From the 1930s to the 1990s all nominated presidential candidates of the ruling party (**Partido Revolucionario Institucional, PRI**) were cabinet members, and until its first primary in 1999, the president handpicked the next PRI presidential candidate from his cabinet. Until the victory of the right-of-center **Partido Acción Nacional (PAN)** in 2000, the PRI

worked hand in glove with the government and built a political machine that produced 13 consecutive presidents of the nation. Current president **Vicente Fox** (2000–2006) was a businessman and state governor (of Guanajuato) before his election in 2000, not a member of the previous president's cabinet, as was the case for more than 70 years.

The bicameral National Congress (Congreso de la Unión) consists of the Senate (Cámara de Senadores) and the Chamber of Deputies (Cámara de Diputados). Until 1994, the Senate contained two senators from each state and the Federal District (a total of 64); since that time, 64 additional seats have been added, half assigned to the political party with the second highest vote count in each state in 1994, and the remaining 32 as national proportional representation seats in 1997, for a total of 128 senators. The Chamber of Deputies has 500 members, 300 of whom are elected on the basis of roughly equally populated legislative districts, while the remaining 200 are distributed among the political parties based on proportional representation. The 200 deputies that are selected from party lists based on proportional representation reflect the growing demands to increase the opposition's representation in the legislative arena.

Legislators in both chambers cannot be reelected to consecutive terms of office: deputies serve for three-year terms corresponding to each half of the presidential *sexenio*; senators serve six-year terms, with half the Senate renewed by direct election every three years. Without the possibility of reelection, there is little in the way of seniority in Congress and, until 1997, the legislative branch was tightly controlled by the PRI, whose members accounted for more than 90 percent of all district seats. Until the 2000 elections, when the balance of power shifted toward the Mexican Congress, legislative independence was undermined by the fact that each PRI legislator was beholden to the party's leadership and indirectly to the president of Mexico. In order to carry out his legislative reforms, President Fox was forced to bargain and compromise with Congress, something none of his predecessors had to do.

After a coalition of opposition parties, led by the PAN and the **Partido de la Revolución Democrático (PRD)**, took control of the Chamber of Deputies in the 1997 elections, the role of the legislative branch in the governmental decision-making process changed dramatically, altering executive proposals and debating policy issues in a much more contentious environment. During the 1997–2000 legislative period, the PRI controlled 239 seats (out of 500) in the Chamber of Deputies and 77 seats (out of 128) in the Senate, in contrast to the PAN (121 and 33, respectively) and the PRD (55 and 16). In the 2000 elections, the PAN won 223 Chamber of Deputies seats while the PRI won 209 and the PRD 68.

Despite significant gains in the number of opposition legislators, voting on controversial legislation and constitutional amendments requires a united front, including a two-thirds majority in each chamber to approve constitutional amendments. With restricted funds available to congressional staff and limited expertise due to term limits, the legislature remains in a weaker policy-making position compared to the executive. Nevertheless, Mexico's legislature serves as a training ground for future political leaders, a major source of political patronage, and a conduit for upward mobility for some from working-class backgrounds or the provinces and for women. Although women's entry into the legislature has been slow, by 1994 Mexico had 11.8 percent women senators and 13.8 percent deputies, one of the highest percentages in Latin America.

The judicial branch is structurally patterned after that of the United States, with local and federal courts based on a mixture of U.S. constitutional theory and Roman civil law. At the highest level of the judicial system is the Supreme Court of Justice (Corte Suprema de Justicia), made up of 11 judges, appointed for terms up to 15 years with the consent of the Senate. The Supreme Court then appoints circuit and district judges and magistrates. The Supreme Court has a president, usually a close associate of the president of the nation, elected by the membership of the court each year. It is the president's prerogative to appoint his attorney general, as well as other officials of the prosecutor's office. The power of the judicial branch in Mexico is limited by its quasi-independence from the other branches of government, the absence of life terms, and, particularly at the lower court levels, decisions that are often tainted by political appointments, **corruption**, and a general lack of respect for legal authority. Efforts were made to overcome these weaknesses in the legal process during the administration of **Ernesto Zedillo**, including the arrest and conviction of **Raúl Salinas de Gortari** (the ex-president's brother) on charges of murdering a PRI official and the appointment of an opposition party attorney general. Although the imprisonment of President **Carlos Salinas**'s brother is unprecedented in Mexico's legal system, the rule of law remains an elusive goal as noted cases of corruption repeatedly appear throughout the nation's criminal justice and drug enforcement agencies.

Mexico's political system and governing structure is not an easy one to classify, particularly given the changes in executive–legislative relations over the past decade and the more recent defeat of the PRI, the world's most entrenched political machine, after more than seven decades of continuous rule. While it is clear that Mexico is in some type of transition from presidential authoritarianism to a more democratic form of government, the first alternation of presidential power in 2000 moves Mexico into unknown governmental terrain. According to Adolfo Aguilar Zinser, an independent senator and Fox campaign adviser, "This is our first constitutional transition of power since the Aztecs. We have never transferred power from one group to another by peaceful means. Either you killed your enemy or organized a revolution; you didn't just win in a fair game" (quoted in Moore and Anderson 2000, A1). *See also* Revolutionary Family or Coalition.

SUGGESTED READING

Tom Barry, ed., *Mexico: A Country Guide* (Albuquerque, N. Mex,: Inter-Hemispheric Education Resource Center, 1992); Roderic Ai Camp, *Politics in Mexico: The Decline of Authoritarianism*, 3d ed. (New York: Oxford University Press, 1999); Wayne A. Cornelius, "Politics in Mexico," in Gabriel A. Almond and G. Bingham Powell, eds., *Comparative Politics Today: A World View* (Glenview, Ill.: Scott, Foresman/Little, Brown, 2000); Wayne A. Cornelius and Ann L. Craig, *The Mexican Political System in Transition* (La Jolla: Center for U.S.–Mexican Studies, University of California–San Diego, 1991); George W. Grayson, *Mexico: From Corporatism to Pluralism?* (Fort Worth, Texas: Harcourt Brace, 1998); Molly Moore and John Anderson, "Mexican Power Shift Stirs Wide Celebration," *Washington Post,* July 4, 2000; George Philip, *The Presidency in Mexican Politics* (New York: St. Martin's, 1992); Victoria Rodríguez, "Centralizing Politics versus Decentralizing Policies in Mexico," in Menno Vellinga, ed., *The Changing Role of the State in Latin America* (Boulder, Colo.: Westview, 1998).

Gringo ☀ The word *gringo* refers to any American or English-speaking Caucasian and is used by Mexicans of all social strata; however, it is also a word with multiple meanings and interpretations on both sides of the border. The word's derivation has two explanations that can be traced back to the war with Mexico in the 1840s. During the **Mexican American War** (1846–1848), U.S. soldiers marching through northern Mexico often sang the old ballad "Green Grow the Rushes, Oh!" After hearing this so often, Mexicans began identifying the song with Americans but shortened "Green Grow" to *gringo*. The second explanation—a more plausible one to many—is that *gringo* comes from an old word meaning "gibberish" that was used to describe anyone who spoke poor Spanish. After the invasion of Mexico in the 1840s and the influx of foreigners (particularly North Americans) into the country thereafter, the word soon became a part of the national vocabulary.

For the first hundred years the word *gringo* carried a distinct derogatory connotation; however, by the 1970s the negative references declined as Mexicans became less antagonistic toward their neighbors to the north, and North Americans began using *gringo* in a more neutral sense. The word *gringo* is still a slang term—to be avoided in business and formal settings—that is used in casual reference to English-speaking non-Mexicans. **Chicano** communities in the United States sometimes use the term *agringado* or *agringada* to refer to Mexican Americans who have lost most of their Mexican cultural heritage and integrated into the white Anglo culture of the United States. Mexicans also use the term *gabacho* (an adaptation of the word *gabacha* "apron") for Anglo-Saxon foreigners because Mexican men noticed how often foreign men helped their wives in the kitchen and around the house, something a Mexican male would never do. The word *gabacho* carries a more negative connotation than *gringo* in today's Mexico. .

SUGGESTED READING

Boye Lafayette De Mente, *NTC's Dictionary of Mexican Cultural Code Words* (Lincolnwood, Ill.: NTC, 1996); Don H. Radler, *El Gringo: The Yankee Image in Latin America* (Philadelphia: Chilton, 1962).

Guadalajara. See Geographical Regions.

Guadalupe, Virgin of. *See* Virgin of Guadalupe.

Guanajuato. *See* Geographical Regions.

Guerrilla Movements and Counterinsurgency ✹ A constant presence in Mexico, the result of internal wars and foreign **intervention** reaching back to the 19th century. Between the **Mexican American War** (1846–1848) and the beginning of the Díaz dictatorship in the 1870s, foreign armies encountered guerrillas inside Mexico. Modern Mexico was born in a violent struggle early in the 20th century called the **Mexican Revolution**. In that conflict, Mexican peasants (Indian and non-Indian) played a major role in the rebellion and the postrevolutionary reform programs that were carried out as a result of the rural mobilization of 1910 to 1917. While the Mexican **government** managed to create a successful state-peasant alliance in the 1930s—a major pillar of the **corporatist** state—the inequalities in economic development, **corruption**, extreme poverty, long-term failure of agricultural policy, slow pace of political reforms, and gradual form of militarization (accompanied by closer ties with the U.S. military and police agencies) to deal with social turmoil and guerrilla warfare indicate the seriousness of Mexico's social, economic, and political problems.

As Mexico has entered the 21st century, new guerrillas symbolize Mexico's malaise and the legacy of earlier struggles by guerrilla leaders like **Emiliano Zapata, Francisco "Pancho" Villa**, Ruben Jaramillo, Genaro Vázquez, Lucio Cabañas, and others. The Center for the Historical Investigation of Armed Movements (El Centro de Investigaciones Históricas de los Movimientos Armados, CIHMA) identified from 14 to 17 guerrilla groups operating in Mexico, but most are too small to do much more than fax inflammatory documents about armed insurrection and guerrilla ideology to local newspapers. The election of **Vicente Fox** as president in 2000 does not seem to have had much impact on reducing the size or numbers of the armed insurgencies operating throughout Mexico.

There are currently two major guerrilla movements operating in various parts of Mexico:

Ejército Zapatista de Liberación Nacional (EZLN), which led the Chiapas rebellion in 1994, and the Ejército Revolucionario Popular (ERP), which appears to be descended from the Party of the Poor with deep roots in Mexico's 20th-century tradition of armed peasant insurrection that reaches back to Zapata. While the EZLN is strongest among indigenous Mayan Indians in Chiapas, with perhaps 2,000 followers (it also claims to have 400 branches throughout Mexico), the ERP is much smaller with an estimated membership of some 50–200 followers. Nevertheless, since its emergence in 1995, its leftist guerrilla units have carried out armed skirmishes in six states: Chiapas, Oaxaca, Guanajuato, Guerrero, México (the state), and Tabasco. There have even been reports of ERP military action in the heart of Mexico City, particularly the fashionable La Condesa district.

While the response to the **Zapatista rebellion in Chiapas** has been a combination of establishing a strong Mexican Army presence in the area and what seems like an elusive search for peace negotiations with the EZLN leadership, the more radical and violent ERP has born the brunt of a government effort to rid Mexico of their presence. Echoes of old **communist** and leftist ideologies serve as motivators for reform and social justice. The ERP believes that small "foco" guerrilla groups can spark an authentic revolution among the oppressed (as Ché Guevara advocated in the 1950s and 1960s), eventually leading to the creation of socialism through the centralization of political and economic power in the hands of a single revolutionary communist party, in this case the ERP. Although the ERP once called on the Mexican people to rise up and overthrow the **Partido Revolucionario Institucional (PRI)**, so far its appeals have found little response due in large part to the group's history of violent attacks on the left and opposition throughout Mexican civil society (**human rights** groups, nongovernmental organizations, and others). The goals of the ERP, as stated in a 1996 manifesto, include: (1) the removal of the "illegitimate" Mexican government and the foreign forces that support it; (2) the restoration of popular sovereignty; (3) the implementation of serious economic, political, and social change; (4) the creation of fair international relations; and (5) the punishment of those guilty of crimes against the people. The Mexican police and army have characterized the ERP as a Marxist group made up of bandits, criminals, and terrorists and continues to pursue a policy of using army patrols to weaken and eventually eliminate them on national security grounds.

The EZLN, led by **Subcommander Marcos,** emerged in the state of Chiapas in 1994 in opposition to the implementation of the **North American Free Trade Agreement (NAFTA).** Since that time it has been surrounded by the Mexican Army, has engaged in on-and-off peace talks with the Mexican government, and has tried to create a mass organization throughout Mexico which would serve as a potent mechanism to bolster their case for reforms. In a span of five years, the EZLN managed to build a remarkable social base among the Indian peasants of Chiapas, some of Mexico's youth and intellectuals, and supporters around the world sympathetic to the plight of indigenous populations in an age of globalization. The EZLN's legitimacy is enhanced by its more peaceful and less violent approach to change, its use of the Internet to build a broad base of support, and the general fascination with its non-Indian, charismatic, ski-masked leader, Subcommander Marcos. Despite these remarkable achievements, the popularity of its proposals and the general dissatisfaction with the once-ruling PRI and its neoliberal economic programs, the EZLN has failed to become a **democratic** movement or vehicle to succeed in the current Mexican political environment. After the Zapatistas were given safe passage to travel from Chiapas to Mexico City in 2001 to bring their message to

Congress, namely the passage of the **San Andrés Accords,** they traveled to the capital in a caravan that brought more than 200,000 people to greet them in the Zócalo. Some 300 Italian communists also participated in what the press called the "Zapatour."

Unlike the guerrilla bands of the past, the current insurgent groups cover their heads with hoods of one style or another to protect their identities and so are called *encapuchados*, or hooded ones, by most Mexicans. The EZLN prefers the black woolen balaclava helmets popularized by Subcommander Marcos; the ERP wears cloth masks with ill-cut eye holes reminiscent of the Ku Klux Klan in the United States. While there appear to be more guerrilla organizations in Mexico than at any time since the 1970s, the ability of these insurgents to spread the message of revolt (and serious reform) beyond a few is quite limited.

SUGGESTED READING

Ian F. W. Beckett, *Encyclopedia of Guerrilla Warfare* (Santa Barbara, Calif.: ABC-CLIO, 1999); Kathlyn Gay and Martin K. Gay, *Encyclopedia of Political Anarchy* (Santa Barbara, Calif.: ABC-CLIO, 1999); Neil Harvey, *Rebellion in Chiapas: Rural Reforms, Campesino Radicalism, and the Limits to Salinismo* (La Jolla: U.S.–Mexican Studies Center, University of California–San Diego, 1994); Dan La Botz, "Mexico: Armed Rebellion and Militarization: A Nation at a Turning Point," *Mexican Labor News and Analysis*, September 2, 1997; John Ross, *Rebellion from the Roots: Indian Uprising in Chiapas* (Monroe, Maine: Common Courage, 1995).

Guillén Vicente, Rafael Sebastián. *See* Subcommander Marcos.

Guillén y Sánchez, Palma (1898–1981) ☀ A prominent academic and foreign diplomat who was Mexico's first female to represent her country as envoy and foreign minister. Born in Mexico City in 1898, Guillén grew up in a world of political upheaval, cultural and artistic innovation, and tremendous social and economic inequalities. During the first 15 years of her academic career, she was highly regarded on campus and cultural circles in the nation's capital as a talented university professor who taught philosophy, psychology, and literature.

Between 1920 and 1935 Guillén held academic posts at the Escuela Normal de México, Escuela Nacional Preparatoria de México, and the **Universidad Nacional Autonoma de México (UNAM)**, specializing in a wide range of fields from psychology and literature to ethics and epistemology. It was during this period of postrevolutionary transformation that she spent a considerable amount of time in Europe, working on a number of educational assignments for the Ministry of Education and various institutes associated with the League of Nations.

Through her travels and work in public education, she came to know President **Lázaro Cárdenas**. Guillén's distinguished record in public education and her left-wing ideology so impressed President Cárdenas that he appointed her to several diplomatic posts in Venezuela and Colombia. After a cool reception from Colombian conservatives, concerned with her progressive ideas, she requested a transfer to a northern European, preferably Scandinavian, country in 1936. She was soon appointed to a diplomatic post (special envoy and minister plenipotentiary) in Denmark and developed an interest in advanced social legislation and methods of corporate organization. Her diplomatic mission was cut short as the Mexican foreign service needed a delegate to the League of Nations in Geneva.

Although she was never a career foreign service officer, her prestige in educational circles and the full support within the Cárdenas administration enabled her to continue her diplomatic activities in Europe. By 1942 she was assigned to the Mexican embassy in Havana, **Cuba**, although her stay was a brief one. She left diplomatic life in 1943 and returned to academic pursuits until 1952. After a short assignment as cultural attaché at the Mexican embassy in Rome in 1952–1953, she again left the Mexican foreign service and devoted the rest of her life to academia, including work with the influx of Spanish exiles in Mexico at the time. Her success in education and diplomacy helped expand opportunities for Mexican women interested in diplomatic service at a time when few women could aspire to such career goals. She died in Mexico City in 1981 at the age of 83. *See also* Feminism.

SUGGESTED READING

Roderic Ai Camp, *Mexican Political Biographies, 1935–1993*, 3d ed. (Austin: University of Texas Press, 1995); Carlos Fernández Dittman, "Guillén y Sánchez, Palma," in Michael S. Werner, ed., *Encyclopedia of Mexico: History, Society, and Culture*, vol. 1 (Chicago: Fitzroy Dearborn, 1997).

Gutiérrez Barrios, Fernando (1927–2000) ☀ Mexico's chief of secret police and a fearsome figure in the once dominant **Partido Revolucionario Institucional (PRI)**. As the nation's longtime spymaster, Gutiérrez Barrios worked for six presidents, maintaining secret dossiers on Mexico's important figures. Later he became a leading politician, one of the "dinosaurs" or party hard-liners whose mission was to perpetuate the dominance of the ruling party. As a secret police official in the 1950s, Gutiérrez Barrios was responsible for the arrest of **Fidel Castro**, then illegally in Mexico preparing to overthrow the dictator of **Cuba**, Fulgencio Batista. However, in a display of moral relativism, the Mexican secret police official and the Cuban revolutionary struck a deal in which Castro was cleared of all charges and subsequently set free, one of Castro's many strokes of luck in his rise to power. Throughout his career, either as part of the secret police or as a government official, Gutiérrez Barrios was known as a suave and sophisticated man who supervised the arrest, torture, and murder of hundreds of opponents of the ruling party. During the Cold War, he worked closely with the CIA's Mexico City office, sharing information and assisting its search for **communists** and Latin American revolutionaries.

Fernando Gutiérrez Barrios was born in Veracruz, Veracruz, in 1927, the son of a military officer and businessman. After graduating from the Heroic Military College in the late 1940s, he rose to power through the Federal Security Police, becoming director during the troublesome administration of **Díaz Ordaz** (1964–1970). While official secrecy continues to obscure the incident, many Mexican historians claim Gutiérrez Barrios was a key figure in planning the massacre of student protestors gathered on Tlatelolco Plaza on October 2, 1968. From 1970 to 1982, he served as undersecretary of government and then as secretary of government during the first four years (1988–1992) of the presidency of **Carlos Salinas de Gortari**. In the former position, he tapped the telephones of thousands of political figures, particularly left-wing groups involved in antigovernment protests. As secretary of government under Salinas, Gutiérrez Barrios commanded the entire security apparatus, a position that made him the second most powerful figure in Mexico.

In his final years Gutiérrez Barrios served as governor of Veracruz (1986–1988) and at his death in October 2000 he was a senator from the same state. Prior to his death, he watched the PRI lose the presidency, having spent most of his life helping to guide and perpetuate the party in power. Nevertheless, Gutiérrez Barrios was chosen to oversee the PRI's first presidential primary in 1999 and to ensure the integrity of the ballot in 2000, paving the way for the first **democratic** transition of power in modern Mexico. *See also* Tlatelolco Massacre.

SUGGESTED READING

Roderic Ai Camp, *Mexican Political Biographies, 1935–1993*, 3d ed. (Austin: University of Texas Press, 1995); Tim Weiner, "Fernando Gutiérrez, 73, Head of Secret Police in Mexico," *New York Times*, November 1, 2000.

Guzmán, Martín Luis (1887–1976) ☀ An active participant in the political and military struggles of revolutionary Mexico and Spain during the first half of the 20th century. Martín Guzmán is best-known for *El águila y la serpiente* (1928)—a fusion between journalism and literature—and *Memorias de Pancho Villa* (1951), a powerful work on the violent phase of the upheaval known as the **Mexican Revolution**. Having personally experienced the fighting in the north under **Pancho Villa**, he applied his travels and firsthand experiences to the creation of stylistically refined novels of the revolutionary period. His political views and activities during times of turmoil often forced him to flee his native land; he was exiled in Spain (1915–1916; 1924–1936) and the United States (1916–1920), where he continued his journalistic activities. His early contacts with the intellectuals who participated in the *Ateneo de la Juventud* (including **Alfonso Reyes, José Vasconcelos**, and Pedro Henríquez Ureña) helped establish valuable friendships that later contributed to his career in journalism and academia.

Born in Chihuahua, Chihuahua, the son of an army colonel, Martín Guzmán studied in Mexico City and received a law degree from the National School of Law in 1909. After the start of the Mexican Revolution, he joined the forces of Francisco Madero to fight against Victoriano Huerta; later he joined the staff of General Álvaro Obregón, moved to Ciudad Juárez, and served under General Francisco "Pancho" Villa. His close proximity to Villa was reflected in the aforementioned *Memorias de Pancho Villa* and *El águila y la serpiente*, an autobiographical account of the revolution.

Between 1915 and 1919 Guzmán traveled abroad, writing and teaching in Paris, Madrid, New York, and Minneapolis. His political activities in the early 1920s eventually drove him into exile in Madrid, where he edited and wrote for newspapers and magazines. It was in Spain that he wrote he *El águila y la serpiente*, a gripping novel of the revolution with its many short and expressive scenes that give the reader a sense of almost cinematic style. He continued to publish in Spain until shortly before the Spanish Civil War, when he returned to Mexico at the invitation of President **Lázaro Cárdenas.**

Back in Mexico, Guzmán continued his writing, founded the magazine *Tiempo,* served as its director (1942–1976), and cofounded with **Adolfo**

López Mateos and Pascual Gutiérrez Roldán the publishing house that is today Librería Cristal. Once López Mateos became president in 1958, he named Guzmán president of the National Commission on Textbooks, a position he held from 1959 to 1976. The winner of the National Prize in Literature in 1958, Guzmán continued to write novels and serve in government posts until his death in Mexico City in 1976.

SUGGESTED READING

Emilio Abreu Gómez, *Martín Luis Guzmán* (Mexico, D.F.: Empresas, 1968); Héctor Perea, "Guzmán Franco, Martín Luis," in Michael S. Werner, ed., *Encyclopedia of Mexico: History, Society, and Culture,* vol. 1 (Chicago: Fitzroy Dearborn, 1997).

Hank González, Carlos (1927–2001) ☀ A billionaire and traditional power broker, one of Mexico's most powerful men. Together with his two sons, Jorge and Carlos Hank Rhon, known as "Grupo Hank" in Mexico, the Hank family makes up a powerful business-political trinity whose clout enables them to pull political and economic strings that dwarfs those with ordinary political authority. A personification of Mexico's political businessman, Carlos Hank González was famous for coining the phrase "A politician who is poor is a poor politician." All members of the Hank family have been investigated for various criminal activities, including money laundering, rigged gambling operations, murder, and ties to Mexican drug cartels—a situation that has worried governments in both the United States and Mexico.

Born in Tiangustenco de Galeana, México, to a Mexican mother and a German father who was a military officer first in the German army and later in the Mexican army under General Amaro, Carlos Hank used his home state of México as a foundation for advancing his political and business careers. After receiving a teacher's diploma from the Superior Normal School of Mexico (Mexico City) with specialties in biology and history, he taught in the primary and secondary schools between 1941 and 1951. Once a teacher who sold candy to supplement his income, Don Carlos is now among the most powerful men in Mexico.

After joining the **Partido Revolucionario Institucional (PRI)** in 1944, Hank participated in numerous party conventions before becoming mayor of Toluca. As he worked his way up the ruling party's ladder of power, he occupied increasingly influential bureaucratic jobs with the help of his personal and party connections. As director general of the multimillion-dollar Mexican state food agency (**Compañia Nacional de Subsistencias Populares, CONASUPO**) during the presidency of **Gustavo Díaz Ordaz**, Hank expanded CONASUPO retail stores for the poor throughout Mexico, selling food and consumer essentials at considerably reduced prices. CONASUPO's major purpose was to provide low-cost food for the masses, but while it set fairly decent prices for crops such as corn and sorghum, it worked hand in glove with transnational corporations such as Ralston Purina and Anderson Clayton to the detriment of Mexican farmers and consumers. A disciple of **Adolfo López Mateos** and Alfredo del Mazo, Hank parlayed key positions in the federal government with business investments in banking and transportation, including the ownership of Taesa airlines, horse racetracks, and vast real estate holdings.

With a large catalog of powerful political contacts, Hank became governor of the state of México (1969–1975), a congressman (1958–1961), secretary of both agriculture (1990–1994) and tourism (1988–1990) under president **Carlos Salinas de Gortari**, and mayor of Mexico City (1976–1982). While he was mayor of Mexico City, Hank speculated in real estate and made sure that companies he owned were rewarded with contracts to provide vehicles and construct highways for the city government. During the **López Portillo** administration, Hank purchased a luxury mansion in New Canaan, Connecticut, for $1 million, one of several pieces of property that stirred the wrath of many Mexicans.

As one of the widely known leaders of the "dinosaur" faction of the ruling party, Hank's power expanded during the 1980s and 1990s as government policies favored those in the upper ranks of the business community. Some believe that Hank handpicked Carlos Salinas to be the

PRI's presidential candidate in 1988; in return the young president helped Hank and his family amass tremendous wealth and power. Worried about the possibility of a PRI maverick becoming president in 1994, Hank opposed Salinas's handpicked candidate, **Luis Donaldo Colosio.** Many of the old guard were offended at Colosio for calling for more electoral transparency and a shift in economic policy that would have improved the lives of the poor and dispossessed. To shore up his power base after winning the presidency in 1994, **Ernesto Zedillo** turned to Carlos Hank González, leader of the Grupo Atlacomulco, for key personnel to fill his inner circle and solidify his ties to the private sector and the *dinosaurios.*

The Hank family is alleged to have close ties with the Arellano Félix group (also known as the Tijuana Cartel), one of the three major border drug cartels. While Carlos, the current patriarch of the Hank family, seems untouchable and will probably remain so, the younger Hank Rhon, Jorge, seems more of a loose cannon in the network of family power. A collector of exotic animals and endangered species from around the world (he calls this activity his only vice), he teamed up with David Ibarra to create Reino Aventura, a popular animal park near Mexico City (it was later sold to **Televisa**), whose main attraction, Keiko the whale, later became a star in the popular film *Free Willy.* Jorge Hank Rhon owns Agua Caliente, a Tijuana racetrack alleged to be a vehicle for money-laundering and other profitable operations. With the creation of the **North American Free Trade Agreement (NAFTA)**, the Grupo Hank has made efforts to expand its financial empire to the United States, particularly in real estate, banking, and gambling ventures.

The Federal Reserve Board in the United States has cited Carlos Hank Rhon for violating banking regulations, questioning some of his self-funded loans from U.S. banks to Grupo Hank's businesses and the shuffling of large amounts of money to cover questionable banking transactions. His conflict with the Federal Reserve centered on his ownership of Laredo National Bancshares, a company that the Fed alleged he used to benefit his father and other business associates. Although Carlos Hank Rhon denied the charges, in May 2001 he agreed to pay the American government $40 million and leave his post as chairman of the bank's board of directors. In the meantime, the Grupo Hank keeps expanding the family business, claiming the accusations emerging on both sides of the border are false, regardless of the information gathered by the Drug Enforcement Agency, the FBI, the Customs Service, the CIA, and Interpol, among others.

Before his death from prostate cancer in August 2001, Carlos Hank González was worth an estimated $1.3 billion; however, many believe his wealth to be substantially higher. *See also* Revolutionary Family or Coalition.

SUGGESTED READING

James Austin and Gustavo Esteva, eds., *Food Policy in Mexico: The Search for Self-Sufficiency* (Ithaca: Cornell University Press, 1987); Jamie Dettmer, "Family Affairs," *Insight*, March 29, 1999; Douglas Farah, "Prominent Mexican Family Viewed as Threat to U.S.," *Washington Post*, June 2, 1999; Jonathan Fox, *The Political Dynamics of Reform: State Power and Food Policy in Mexico* (Ithaca: Cornell University Press, 1991); Joaquín Herrera, *Hank: Las élites del power en México* (Mexico, D.F.: Parmon, 1997); José Martínez, *Las enseñazas del profesor: Indagación de Carlos Hank González, lecciones de poder, impunidad y corrupción* (México, D.F.: Editorial Oceano de México, 1999); Julia Reynolds, "The NAFTA Gang," *El Andar* (Summer–Fall 1999); Reynolds, "When Prohibition Meets Free Trade: Wealth, Power and Intimidation in Mexico," *NACLA Report on the Americas* (July/August 2001); Felipe Ruanova Zarate, *Hank: El sello de la impunidad* (Mexico, D.F.: Editorial Posada, 1995).

Hidalgo. *See* Geographical Regions.

Hispanics. *See* Chicanos.

Homosexuality ☀ Since the time of the Aztecs, there has been ambivalence, prejudice, and hypocrisy regarding homosexuality in Mexico. Despite the deep-rooted culture of **machismo**, there is a surprising amount of male bisexuality that exists side by side with heterosexual behavior. Having sex with another man may not be seen as homosexual as long as the "active" partner displays macho behavior during the sex act. Homophobia derives from contempt for the effeminate homosexual, particularly among men. While negative attitudes and prejudice still exist, defining "homosexuality" depends on a lot more than a male–male sexual relationship.

The Aztecs were the most hostile toward homosexuals, often executing transvestites and males who engaged in anal sex. However, in the Veracruz region of Mexico, Hernán Cortés noticed that homosexuality was widely practiced and generally accepted. With the arrival of the Spaniards, negative attitudes toward homosexuals were reinforced by the cult of the male (machismo) that served a colonial power determined to subjugate the native population by emphasizing the values of warfare, conformity, and male aggressiveness. Attitudes toward women were also influenced by the Aztec ideal of the passive female and Spanish machismo, including the early acceptance of prostitution and mistresses for males who could afford these sexual practices. Inside Mexican culture, a sharp dichotomy emerged between the idealized views of women as virtuous and asexual mother (or wife) and as sexual temptress (prostitute or mistress). The former is embodied in the **Virgin of Guadalupe**, a brown-skinned religious symbol created as an asexual substitute for the Aztec's native god of fertility (Tonantzín); the latter is symbolized in La **Malinche** (Doña Marina), the mistress/companion to Spanish conqueror Hernán Cortés, who came to personify betrayal and promiscuity. Because she served as his adviser and later bore him a son, she is also considered a traitor as well as the mother of the **mestizo** race. In Mexican cultural history, La Malinche also symbolizes the untrustworthy sexual nature of women. Mexican men are raised to expect wives to be like their mothers, dutiful to the image of the Virgin; except for a procreative role, Mexican women are expected to be submissive, show self-sacrifice toward the home and children, and show little concern for sexual fulfillment. After independence from Spain, homosexuality between consenting adults was decriminalized, following the Napoleonic Code, but hostility and ambivalence toward homosexuals continued to dominate the culture.

The entrenched cultural prejudice against homosexuals is not equal between homosexual partners in modern society: the partner who assumes the dominant (often described as *activo*, or "active") male role in an act of homosexual intercourse is less vulnerable to hatred because he is perceived to have retained his manhood in the process, whereas the partner who assumes the traditional female role (often referred to as *pasivo*, or "passive") is considered debased and truly "homosexual" in the context of Mexican culture. The strongly negative attitudes toward transvestites, with their outward display of femininity, grows out of the code of machismo and the lower social status assigned to women. In a *machista* culture it is particularly offensive to witness a male who voluntarily gives up his maleness to adopt female mannerisms and the sexual role of a woman. This explains why transvestites have been subject to physical attacks and murder, often by (male) authorities charged with maintaining law and order or with their complicity. Between 1990 and 1995, more than two dozen homosexuals (mostly transvestites) were murdered in Chiapas, Guadalajara, Nayarít, Chihuahua, and the Federal District. While these are the more violent and repressive areas of Mexico, other parts of the country are more tolerant, particularly when homosexuals remain hidden. However, few prosecutions have been made, even in cases where domestic **human rights** groups have managed to publicize and document serious violations by Mexican authorities. Further discrimination results from widespread misconceptions about the spread of the HIV virus and AIDS.

Given the traditional social construct used to define male homosexuality—a dominant role that is more acceptable than a passive one—it becomes more difficult to imagine sex between two women when there are only two types of women as defined by the culture: virgins and prostitutes. The female counterpart to machismo is called *marianismo*, being like the Virgin Mary. Traditionally, female identity in Mexico did not exist outside of these two opposing roles in society. Since lesbians are far less visible in Mexico and the word *homosexual* is used to refer to men only, they are less likely to encounter the same level of problems that men face in a male-dominated society. Lesbians have been able to make some inroads in the political system. The first openly homosexual member of Congress is Patricia Jiménez, a **Partido de la Revolución Democrátia (PRD)** member of the Chamber of Deputies.

The counterculture era and the homosexual rights movement in the United States had a marked impact on Mexico's gay and lesbian communities, particularly after the **Tlatelolco massacre** in 1968. In response to mistreatment of homosexuals and the rather vague laws and ordinances that are designed to prohibit and punish homosexual acts, homosexuals have started to form organizations to defend homosexual rights. In Mexico City, Super Gay has emerged to unite the gay community, often leading gay pride parades and media events calling for justice, legal protection for homosexuals, and measures to end homophobia in Mexico. The only major political party to defend the rights of homosexuals is the PRD. The former ruling party the **Partido Revolucionario Institucional (PRI)** has never taken a formal position on homosexuality, preferring to treat the issue as something best left to the discretion of consenting adults. The political party that is the most hostile to homosexuality is the center-right **Partido Acción Nacional (PAN)**, in part because of its close association with the Catholic Church; some of its leaders have taken public stands describing homosexuality as degenerate, abnormal, sick, or immoral. With most of their support from the extreme left, Mexican homosexuals have difficulty cultivating a broad base of support for their cause.

The most active gay communities in Mexico are in the capital, Mexico City, and Tijuana, a large border community that is influenced by cross-cultural fertilization from its U.S. border city opposite, San Diego. Puerto Vallarta, a thriving tourist center on the Pacific Coast, also attracts a large number of gay visitors from Mexico and abroad.

While machismo continues to be strong and prejudices against homosexuals persist, there are signs that a greater acceptance of **feminism** and gay and lesbian lifestyles is occurring in Mexico. Traditional machismo is not as strong as it once was, and the social taboos against homosexuals are gradually being broken. Moreover, as opposition parties gain greater power and more attention is paid to the protection of human rights, people will develop a greater awareness of safe sex practices and the prevention of the spread of HIV/AIDS. The status of women will improve throughout Mexico, and patriarchal machismo will no longer be the norm in Mexican society. Yet the government has not undertaken a national campaign to develop solutions for the serious problems faced by gays and lesbians in Mexico. There are few openly gay politicians in Mexico.

Although there is an astonishing range of slang words for homosexual in Mexico, the most common is *maricón*. Other words that are considered more derogatory include *joto* (the letter *J*, because gay inmates at Mexico City's federal jail were once isolated on J block), *puto*, and *mariposa*.

SUGGESTED READING

Katherine Elaine Bliss, "The Sexual Revolution in Mexican Studies: New Perspectives on Gender, Sexuality, and Culture in Modern Mexico," *Latin American Research Review* 36, no. 1 (2001); James Carrier, *De Los Otros: Intimacy and Homosexuality among Mexican Men* (New York: Columbia University Press, 1995); "Living the Vida Loca," *Economist*, December 18, 1999; Ian Lumsden, *Homosexuality, Society, and the State in Mexico* (Toronto: Canadian Gay Archives, 1991); Elena M. Martínez, *Lesbian Voices from Latin America: Breaking Ground* (New York: Garland, 1996); Sylvia Molloy and Robert Irwin, eds., *Hispanisms and Homosexualities* (Durham: Duke University Press, 1998); Stephen O. Murray, ed., *Latin American Male Homosexualities* (Albuquerque: University of New Mexico Press, 1995); Andrew Reding, "Mexico: Treatment of Homosexuals," *World Policy* (November 1997); Anthony G. Rominske, "Homosexuality," in Michael S. Werner, ed., *Encyclopedia of Mexico: History, Society, and Culture*, vol. 1 (Chicago: Fitzroy Dearborn, 1997); Claudia Schaefer, *Danger Zones: Homosexuality, National Identity, and Mexican Culture* (Tucson: University of Arizona Press, 1996).

Human Rights ✳ The legal history of Mexico is closely connected with the protection of human rights. After independence in 1821, individual rights were protected by the Constitution of 1824 and expanded in the Constitution of 1857. The **Constitution of 1917** became the first to establish the protection of social rights. The principles of peace, social justice, and nonintervention that dominated postrevolutionary **foreign policy** contributed to Mexico's support for the League of Nations and later its endorsement of the United Nations Charter in 1945. In 1948 it endorsed the

Universal Declaration of Human Rights and the American Declaration of Human Rights, the former drafted by the United Nations and the later by the Organization of American States (OAS), the regional counterpart to the United Nations. "By the mid-1990s, Mexico was a party to 38 binding international human rights treaties and conventions, designed to protect the full range of human rights: individual, civil, political, social, economic, and cultural, as well as the rights of minorities" (Acosta 1997, 659). Nevertheless, the human rights declared in various international treaties rarely have been upheld by Mexican courts.

The complex political and economic issues facing the country mean that the protection of human rights has always been a constitutionally desired aim more than a reality in modern Mexico. The protection of human rights has been compounded by an authoritarian political system that has abused human rights and often shielded the perpetrators from prosecution. Human rights violations such as torture, imprisonment on political grounds, disappearances, and the mistreatment of indigenous and rural populations are committed at all levels of government, but the most common perpetrators have been members of the security forces, rural *caciques* (or their hired gangs tied to the drug war), and paramilitary groups. With the passage of the **North American Free Trade Agreement (NAFTA)** in 1993, Mexico proceeded to modify its constitution, in some cases actually curtailing social and individual rights.

The documented abuse of human rights after the suspect 1988 presidential election did not stop the United States from going ahead with efforts to approve NAFTA in 1992–1994. Furthermore, Mexico's human rights organizations, particularly the National Commission for Human Rights (Comisión Nacional de Derechos Humanos, CNDH), are hampered because their powers are severely limited since they are not legally independent of the executive and judiciary. The major

national nongovernmental organizations devoted to the protection of human rights have fought an uphill battle to improve the right to life, social justice, and security. However, with an ill-trained and underpaid police force, torture, disappearances, and criminal activity have reached staggering proportions. With close to 80 percent of the federal judicial police engaged in criminal activity, as well as a growing tendency to rely on the military for public security, the defense and protection of human rights have grown into a social movement in Mexico. By the mid-1990s, civil organizations devoted to human rights protection numbered close to 250, the largest number of nongovernmental organizations in the country.

In response to criticism by human rights groups such as Americas Watch and Amnesty International, Mexico created CNDH in 1990 to improve the nation's image abroad. The creation of CNDH was almost simultaneous with the beginning of NAFTA negotiations, a recognition that continual human rights violations could jeopardize trade relations with the United States. To remedy the major weakness of CNDH, largely its limited prosecutorial powers and lack of independence, in 1992 a system of 32 state-sponsored human rights commissions was created to function in each of the Mexican states and the Federal District.

Until the **Zapatista rebellion in Chiapas** in 1994, the official commissions made some progress in addressing the human rights complaints throughout the nation. However, the issue of human rights and social justice returned to the national stage with the events in Chiapas where hundreds were killed, arbitrarily detained, tortured, and forced to confess to members of the security forces that were sent to the region. After the nongovernmental human rights community—both Mexican and international—visited the area, large demonstration marches occurred in Mexico City demanding a negotiated settlement, and the

Catholic Church stepped in to rally behind the Mayan rebels and called for peace talks, President **Salinas** announced a cease-fire initiative. In its 1999 report on the human rights situation in Mexico, Amnesty International (1999) found that "torture, extrajudicial executions, 'disappearances' and arbitrary detentions are widespread and the perpetrators frequently act with impunity." After publishing a proposal calling for a human rights ombudsman for Mexico's armed forces, General José Francisco Gallardo Rodríguez was arrested and convicted of nonpolitical offenses, and he remains in jail, a political prisoner according to Amnesty International. President **Vicente Fox** has vowed to put an end to the impunity that police officers and soldiers have when it comes to the use of torture to extract confessions from subjects, and has appointed a special ambassador on human rights to stamp out the practice.

The increase in human rights violations along the border—where hundreds of Mexican migrants have been victims of abuses by immigrant traffickers and U.S. Border Patrol agents—has raised concerns along the northern border. With an active human rights community demanding more attention to issues of justice and **democracy** and greater concern among inter-American organizations about the importance of observing human rights, Mexico has made some progress in recent years in legitimizing the impor-

tance of individual rights, regardless of who they are in Mexican society. Yet many of the causes of human rights violations are systemic and occur throughout the nation, particularly in the southern states of Chiapas, Oaxaca, and Guerrero, where **guerrilla movements** are present along with paramilitaries and the Mexican Army. *See also* Acteal Massacre.

SUGGESTED READING

Mariclaire Acosta, "Human Rights," in Michael S. Werner, ed., *Encyclopedia of Mexico: History, Society, and Culture,* vol. 1 (Chicago: Fitzroy Dearborn, 1997); Americas Watch, *Human Rights in Mexico: A Policy of Impunity* (New York: Human Rights Watch, 1990); Amnesty International, *Mexico: Under the Shadow of Impunity* (London: AI, 1999); Tom Barry, ed., *Mexico: A Country Guide* (Albuquerque, N. Mex.: Inter-Hemisphere Education Center, 1992); Edward L. Cleary, *The Struggle for Human Rights in Latin America* (Westport, Conn.: Praeger, 1997); Comisión Nacional de Derechos Humanos, *Informe Anual: Mayo 1995—Mayo 1996,* 2 vols. (Mexico, D.F.: CNDH, 1996); Eric Olson, *The Evolving Role of Mexico's Military in Public Security and Antinarcotics Programs* (Washington, D.C.: Washington Office on Latin America, 1996); Partido de la Revolución Democrática, Human Rights Commission, Parliamentary Group, *The Political Violence in Mexico: A Human Rights Affair* (Mexico, D.F.: Congreso de la Unión, 1992).

Ibarra de Piedra, Rosario. *See* Feminism.

Immigration ☀ One of the many constants in U.S.–Mexican relations is immigration, a salient

issue for both countries, but one often distorted for political purposes and poorly understood by citizens on both sides of the border. When asked about their perceptions of Mexico prior to the

North American Free Trade Agreement (NAFTA), slightly more than one-third of Americans agreed that immigration is the most important issue in regard to Mexico. However, more than 75 percent felt that Mexico's economic problems affecting the U.S. economy was the most important issue to the bilateral relationship. Immigration and its consequences—cultural, economic, and political—are deeply rooted in U.S.–Mexican relations, but only in recent years has the United States undertaken formal and comprehensive efforts to prevent the flow of Mexican immigrants northward. Faced with limited opportunities in the Mexican economy, many Mexicans perceive vast economic opportunities in the United States, where labor shortages—especially of unskilled workers—spur impoverished Mexicans to venture north in search of work. This has been a fact of life since the mid-1800s, and U.S. policy has fluctuated between efforts to encourage Mexican immigration and attempts to control it through various measures. The result has been measurable economic gains for both countries, although not always equal and recognized as such.

Since **World War II**, legal immigration has gone hand in hand with flows of undocumented or illegal Mexican migrants, although getting accurate figures on the numbers of people who come to the United States without official permission is difficult. The impact of cheap Mexican labor on the American economy is obvious, whether in fast-food restaurants, farms, hotels, poultry and hog processing plants, garment and carpet factories, and gardening/landscape companies. The continuing debate over immigration presents profound challenges to leaders on both sides of the border in the 21st century—particularly in the few states that contain most of the population of Mexican origin.

The strategy of tightening controls at ports of entry to reduce the size of the illegal immigrant population contributes to the appearance of success by creating the image of a more secure and orderly border; however, the overall deterrent effect has been limited as the economic push to open borders clashes with law enforcement efforts to close the border to "undesirable" population flows. The heated immigration debate often fails to take into account the fact that nearly half of all illegal immigrants in the United States entered *legally* as tourists or students, then decided to overstay their visas. Moreover, evaluating border policing solely in terms of deterrence may be only part of what governments state as their policy goals. As Andreas (1999, 20) points out, "This neglect of visa overstays is . . . revealing [because] the symbolic importance of border control trumps the stated policy goal of reducing the size of the illegal immigrant population." By claiming to be "winning" the war against illegal immigration through stricter policies, governments can also reinforce territorial identities while projecting an image of state authority and legitimacy, regardless of whether border policies are working or not.

According to the 2000 U.S. census, the Latino population increased 46.7 percent over 1990. Census projections show that by the end of 2002, Latinos will have passed black non-Latinos as the largest minority group in the United States. Among Latinos, the Mexican American segment counted for over 63 percent in 2000, with most of the **Chicano** population living in a few, mostly border, states. California alone counts for close to 50 percent of Chicanos, and close to 90 percent of all Chicanos live in six states: California, Texas, Arizona, New Mexico, Colorado, and Illinois.

Large numbers of Mexicans were admitted as legal immigrants after the U.S. Congress passed the Immigration Reform and Control Act (IRCA) in 1986, the most important piece of legislation in decades. In an effort to balance the American economy's labor requirements with restrictions on future immigration, the IRCA allowed undocumented aliens who had migrated to the United States prior to 1982 to apply for an amnesty giving them legal resident status. To western agricultural interests in the United States, the legislation also offered amnesty to farm workers who had entered the country after the 1982 deadline, provided they had been employed in the United States for 90 days during a one-year period in 1986. To limit further immigration, the IRCA intensified border patrols and introduced employer sanctions against hiring any undocumented worker who had entered the United States since the beginning of 1982. Despite its sweeping provisions and bureaucratic protections, the IRCA's record has been disappointing, as millions of eligible illegal residents failed to apply, out of fear or lack of knowledge of the law. Nevertheless, the continued prevalence of illegal workers in the United States demonstrates the colossal failure of the 1986 legislation intended to stem illegal immigration with tough new sanctions against U.S. employers, including heavy fines and prison terms. Stepped up Immigration and Naturalization Service (INS) efforts to force the dismissal of illegal workers only covers a small fraction (44,474 in 1999) of the 1.5 million annual apprehensions at the **U.S.–Mexican border.**

In 1996 the INS estimated that there were 5 million illegal immigrants (of all nationalities) in the United States, with over half living in two states, California (2 million) and Texas (700,000). The INS predicted that the number of illegal immigrants will grow by 275,000 a year, particularly in the top 10 states that receive the bulk of Latino immigrants: California, Texas, New York, Florida, Illinois, New Jersey, Arizona, Massachusetts, Virginia, and Washington.

From the Mexican perspective, the most extreme proposals for limiting immigration are offensive because they are perceived as unrealistic, counterproductive, or even racist. Mexico sees emigration to the United States functions as a crucial pressure valve and economic benefit, relieving unemployment and defusing political discontent at home while providing large amounts in remittances

from Mexican workers in the United States. Mexican authorities are constrained by the lack of resources and political will to control the outflow of illegal immigrants from south of the border. Still, the reality of a 2,000-mile border, **corruption** among Mexican border authorities, and the absence of resources have hampered a solution from Mexico's side. The ambivalence toward the immigration issue in the United States has not made it easier for Washington to deal with undocumented workers in a successful way, particularly when U.S. taxpayers believe that illegal immigration depresses wages, imposes a financial burden on the public, and takes jobs away from American workers. More important for a solution to the immigration issue is a recognition of the need for greater government cooperation and a cooling of inflammatory rhetoric on both sides of the border.

Once a "hot-button" issue in U.S. elections, anti-immigrant rhetoric has been transformed into a warm political *abrazo* (a hug or embrace) by both Republicans and Democrats alike. Both Al Gore and George W. Bush courted the Hispanic vote with their campaign proposals in 2000 and purported an ability to speak Spanish, recognizing that this potential voter pool may provide swing votes in the four states— California, New York, Texas, and Florida—which have large Latino populations and, taken together, account for half the electoral votes needed to win the presidency. Some economists, corporate executives, and the influential Federal Reserve chairman, Alan Greenspan, believe that the record economic boom in the United States during the 1990s would not have been possible—or lasted very long—without the influx of immigrants to fill millions of American jobs. In any case, there is no doubt that attitudes toward immigrants, control/limitation efforts through legislation, and the potential value of the Hispanic vote for winning U.S. elections will continue to ebb and flow with the economic, political, and demographic trends in the United States. *See also Bracero Program*; Foreign Policy.

SUGGESTED READING

Peter Andreas, "Borderless Economy, Barricaded Border," *NACLA Report on the Americas* (November–December, 1999); Max J. Castro, ed., *Free Markets, Open Societies, Closed Borders? Trends in International Migration and Immigration Policy in the Americas* (Miami: North-South Center Press, 1999); Leo R. Chávez and Rebecca G. Martínez, "Mexican Immigration in the 1980s and Beyond: Implications for Chicanas/os," in David R. Maciel and Isidro D. Ortíz, eds., *Chicanas/Chicanos at the Crossroads* (Tucson: University of Arizona Press, 1996); Wayne A. Cornelius and Philip L. Martin, *The Uncertain Connection: Free Trade and Mexico–U.S. Migration* (La Jolla: Center for U.S.–Mexican Studies, University of California–San Diego, 1993); Peri Fletcher, *La Casa de mis sueños: Dreams of Home in a Transnational Mexican Community* (Boulder, Colo.: Westview, 1999); Steven Greenhouse, "Politicians Embracing Immigrant Population," *New York Times*, March 15, 2000; John Mason Hart, ed., *Border Crossings: Mexican-American Workers* (Wilmington, Del.: Scholarly Resources, 1998); Susanne Jonas and Suzie Dod Thomas, eds., *Immigration: A Civil Rights Issue for the Americas* (Wilmington, Del.: Scholarly Resources, 1998); José Limón, *American Encounters: Greater Mexico, the United States, and the Erotics of Culture* (Boston: Beacon, 1999); David R. Maciel and María Herrera-Sobek, eds., *Culture across Borders: Mexican Immigration and Popular Culture* (Tucson: University of Arizona Press, 1998); Marcelo M. Suárez-Orozco, ed., *Crossings: Mexican Immigration in Interdisciplinary Perspectives* (Cambridge: Harvard University Press, 1998); Sam Howe Verhovek, "Illegal Immigrant Workers Being Fired in I.N.S. Tactic," *New York Times*, April 2, 1999.

Immigration Reform and Control Act (IRCA). *See* Immigration.

Import Substitution Industrialization (ISI). *See* Automobile Industry; General Agreement on Tariffs and Trade (GATT).

Indians. *See* Mestizo and *Mestizaje*; Zapatista Rebellion in Chiapas.

Indigenismo ☀ One of the dominant themes in Mexican history is the ideology of *indigenismo* (indigenism), the attempt to define and defend indigenous groups from the Conquest forward. Mexico's large indigenous population has generated an interest in the cultures of native peoples and various methods of defending and protecting them against the oppression by the majority and other forces. Many times, indigenous policies have implied assimilating native cultures into the mainstream of Mexican society. Early indigenists such as Bishop Bartolomé de Las Casas and Bernardino de Sahagún wrote historical propaganda to convince people of the civilized nature and importance of Indians. Paradoxically, Benito Juárez, Mexico's first Indian president, supported legislation in the 1850s that exacerbated the poor condition of indigenous communities by expropriating communal lands in an effort to expedite capitalist development.

While the colonial period was known for its paternalistic treatment of Indian peoples, it took the revolutionary political movements of the early 20th century to generate the intellectual forces of *indigenismo* in Mexico. *Indigenismo* became part of the **Mexican Revolution** and government policy under President **Lázaro Cárdenas** in the 1930s. Intellectual policy makers such as **José Vasconcelos** advocated pro-Indian policies that would help bring Indians into national life through education, economic development, and social change. Pro-Indian policies and rhetoric have been part of government programs since the time of Cárdenas, although critics of these efforts argue that they are paternalistic, disingenuous, and largely ineffective.

The officially proclaimed respect for the nation's Indian heritage after the Revolution—symbolized in the murals of **Diego Rivera**, **David Alfare Siqueiros**, **José Clemente Orozco,** and others—was more of an ideology designed to undermine Indian culture and eventually integrate Mexico's Indians into the national and international economy than one designed to alleviate the plight of the indigenous population. As an ideology of the procedure of integration, *indigenismo* became institutionalized in 1936 with the creation of the Department of Indian Affairs, which 12 years later was incorporated into the National Indigenous Institute (INI). The INI estimates that there are approximately 8–10 million indigenous persons in Mexico, located in 13 states labeled "eminently indigenous": Oaxaca, Chiapas, Quintana Roo, Campeche, Guerrero, Hidalgo, Nayarit, Puebla, San Luis Potosí, Veracruz, Yucatán, the state of México, and Michoacán.

Mexican *indigenismo* has had its most important impact in anthropology, archeology, architecture, literature, **cinema,** and the arts. Since the 1930s, concerted efforts have been made (with government financial assistance) to reconstruct pre-Hispanic monuments, portray Indians as part of the national heritage, and defend their interests during periods of intense political and economic change. Mexicans like to tell foreigners that Mexico City has public statues honoring the Aztec chief Cuauhtémoc, but none for his Spanish conqueror, Hernán Cortés. Novels such as *El Indio* (1935) by **Gregorio López y Fuentes** and *El resplandor* (1937) by Mauricio Magdaleno are classic examples of the ideals of Cardenismo's efforts to improve the plight of the indigenous population through programs of integration. Muralists and painters such as Rivera and Orozco depicted Indian life both past and present in their works, while at the same time attacking clerical, capitalist, military, and class exploiters. Architectural styles that reflect pre-Hispanic traditions include the Anáhuacalli Museum, designed by Rivera; **Juan O'Gorman**'s house (built in 1958 but since destroyed); and the Central Library at University City, covered with mosaics that depict Indian cosmology.

In many ways indigenism is the factor that best distinguishes Mexicans from people in the United States, as the Indian component appears constantly in the history and legends of the nation, from the plight of La **Malinche** to the struggle of those who followed **Emiliano Zapata** in hopes of a better life. In contrast to the genocide and isolation of indigenous groups in the United States and Canada, Mexico's policy of inclusion has been a major factor in Mexican national identity and the creation of the **mestizo** race.

Since the Mexican Revolution, there has been an acceleration of efforts to assimilate the indigenous population into a **mestizo** culture. As a result, the proportion of Indians in the national population has dropped from 45 percent in 1910 to somewhere less than 10 percent by the end of the 20th century. The *indigenismo* that was popular in the 1930s and 1940s has given way to other means—electoral politics or revolutionary struggle—of achieving social justice and higher social status for Indians. Indian activism is alive in Mexico, where a number of national organizations exist to promote economic development, **human rights,** sound ecological practices, and the preservation of indigenous culture. With increasing **democratization** and globalization, Mexico's indigenous movement has become more internationalized and concerned with issues of autonomy and independence. Yet Mexico's indigenous population still suffers from neglect, racism, dependency, and oppression, a sign that government programs and constitutional changes, rhetoric, and cultural attention have not been sufficient to solve one of Mexico's most pressing problems. In response, indigenous peoples are now more likely to resist government policies through organization and ethnic mobilization strategies in an effort to achieve the rights of autonomy, dignity, equality, and difference.

SUGGESTED READING

Marie-Chantal Barre, *Ideologías indigenistas y movimientos indios* (Mexico, D.F.: Siglo XXI, 1983); Alan Knight, "Racism, Revolution, and Indigenismo: Mexico, 1920–1940," in Alan Knight, ed., *The Idea of Race in Latin America, 1870–1940* (Austin: University of Texas Press, 1990); Charles Ramírez Berg, "The Indian Question," in Michael T. Martin, ed., *New Latin American Cinema*, vol. 2, *Studies of National Cinemas* (Detroit: Wayne State University Press, 1997); Julio C. Tresierra, "Mexico: Indigenous Peoples and the Nation-State," in Donna Lee Van Cott, ed., *Indigenous Peoples and Democracy in Latin America* (New York: St. Martin's, 1995); Greg Urban and Joel Scherzer, eds., *Nation-States and Indians in Latin America* (Austin: University of Texas Press, 1991); Luis Villorio, *Los grandes momentos del indigenismo en México* (Mexico, D.F.: Ediciones de la Casa Chata, 1979); José Eduardo Zárate Hernández, "*Indigenismo* and Ethnic Movements," in Michael S. Werner, ed., *Encyclopedia of Mexico: History, Culture, and Society*, vol. 1 (Chicago: Fitzroy Dearborn, 1997).

Infante, Pedro (1917–1957) ☀ Film actor and singer. Pedro Infante became a legend of Mexico's golden age of **cinema** through his portrayals of singing *charros*, boisterous and **macho** personalities that captured Mexico's postwar tension about its identity and relations with the United States. An extremely versatile actor and talented nightclub singer of *bolero* songs, Infante emerged as the leading symbol of popular culture during the 1940s and 1950s. As one of the premier *ranchera* singer/actors, Infante popularized hundreds of *rancheras* and *boleros*, including his signature hits "Cien años" and "Amorcito corazón," and starred in 59 movies, almost always cast as the hopeless romantic, the bold hero, the sexy singer, or the tough macho with a heart.

Born in Mazatlán, Sinaloa, to a lower-middle-class family—his father was a music teacher and performer—Infante worked a variety of jobs while singing informally in various town squares. He began performing professionally in 1937 with a small musical group based in Culiacán. At the urging of his first wife, María Luisa León, he moved to Mexico City, where he joined thousands of other Mexicans anxious to benefit from the nation's industrial expansion; it was also a vibrant time for the entertainment industries that were helping shape the national and international image of Mexico as a center of film and music. Infante found work with radio station XEB and then began playing local clubs, including a regular act at the Hotel Reforma, home of Mexico City's best nightclub acts, as well as the main venue for major movie producers and directors. With his growing fame among recently arrived radio fans, he made his first recording, "El soldado raso," in 1943 with Discos Peerless, the only record label for which he ever recorded. His early hits were from the great songwriters of the day, including Cuco Sánchez, Rubén Fuentes, and José Alfredo Jiménez. He was credited with introducing the *bolero-ranchero* style into Mexican pop **music** in the 1940s.

Pedro Infante's long film career began in 1942 with a supporting role in *La feria de las flores*, directed by Ismael Rodríguez and starring Antonio Badú. By 1943, his career was well under way in all of mass media as a key figure in helping define Mexico's transformation from a rural-agricultural society to an urban and industrial nation. Infante's films helped ease the tensions created by postwar socioeconomic development. He often portrayed the warmhearted, womanizing, and boisterous singing *charro*, as in *Los tres García* (1946) and *Los huastecos* (1948), in which he plays three roles in one of his masterful screen performances. His versatility on the screen, unique among Mexican movie stars of the golden age, earned him shared top billing with **Jorge Negrete** in *Dos tipos de cuidado* in 1952, a comparison of two types of macho stereotypes: Pedro Malo played by Infante and Jorge Bueno played by Negrete.

Many of Infante's films in the 1950s took more urban forms, reflecting the dramatic growth and modernization of Mexico City as well as the growing Americanization of the nation's capital. As Fein (1997, 703) points out, "In these movies, as in the los García movies, the figure of a U.S. feminine love object as a personification of the United States inverted Mexico's real-life economic and political dependence on its northern neighbor." In a nightclub scene in *A toda máquina* (1951), he parodies Frank Sinatra (his singing/acting U.S. counterpart) as he flatters his American *gringa* object of his desire. Infante's film career seemed to improve with age; he earned best actor Ariels, for *La vida no vale nada* (1954) and for his penultimate film, *Tizoc* (1956), in which he costarred with **María Félix** in a historical epic about the Mayan civilization. *Tizoc* won the 1958 Ariel for best film and a posthumous Golden Bear Award for best actor for Infante at the 1958 Berlin film festival.

Pedro Infante's off-screen life was full of daring adventures and scandalous macho episodes with women, wives and mistresses alike. The negative publicity that followed his love affairs and divorces did not diminish audience interest in his personal life, no matter how offensive to some in the audience. During the 1950s he developed a love for motorcycles and a passion for flying, obtaining his pilot's license and eventually purchasing several airplanes. Known as "Capitán Cruz" by his friends, he was involved in two air crashes before his third, fatal accident in Mérida, Yucatán, while on the way to Mexico City to negotiate a divorce from his wife. Although Infante's death was untimely, occurring at the height of his popularity in 1957, it reflected his penchant to live life to the fullest. His image as a fun-loving singing *charro* outlived Mexico's golden age. As one of the leading film icons of postwar Mexican popular culture, Pedro Infante was commemorated annually with officially sanctioned public ceremonies in Mexico City throughout the rest of the 20th century.

SUGGESTED READING

Seth Fein, "Infante, Pedro," in Michael S. Werner, ed., *Encyclopedia of Mexico: History, Society, and Culture* (Chicago: Fitzroy Dearborn, 1997); Gustavo García, *No me parezco a nadie: La vida de Pedro Infante* (Mexico, D.F.: Clio, 1994); José Ernesto Infante Quintanilla, *Pedro Infante: El máximo ídolo de México (vida, obra, muerte, y leyenda)* (Mexico, D.F.: Ediciones Castillo, 1992); Carl J. Mora, *The Mexican Cinema: Reflections of a Society, 1896–1988* (Berkeley: University of California Press, 1989).

Institutional Revolutionary Party. *See* Partido Revolucionario Institucional (PRI).

Intervention ☀ Since Mexico achieved independence from Spain in 1821, its historical development has been affected by foreign involvement and military intervention, including by Spain, Britain, France, and the United States. However, Mexicans are most concerned with U.S. interference in the country's internal affairs. Mexicans are taught that from the early 19th century, the United States has had designs on Mexico, either by acquiring territory or by seeking to change something in Mexico to better suit U.S. interests and wishes. As late as 1986, when polled as to the most negative aspect of the United States, Mexicans replied by saying drug addiction, nuclear weapons, and interventionism, in that order.

Between 1836 and 1920 the United States intervened with military force at least 15 times to protect its interests. Since the **Mexican Revolution** (1910–1917), the United States has developed and used a variety of indirect and nonmilitary techniques for exerting and maintaining its influence.

In retaliation for repeated U.S. intervention during the revolution, **Francisco "Pancho" Villa** and his ragtag army invaded Columbus, New Mexico, in 1916, the only time the United States has experienced an armed invasion of its territory from Latin America. To make sure that the United States had secure access to Mexican oil resources, U.S. military planners developed Special Plan Green in 1920 calling for possible invasion in the event of problems in the oil fields or along the border. The U.S. plan for an invasion of Mexico lasted until 1942, when Mexico joined the United States as an ally in the war effort.

It was not uncommon until 1940 for some domestic faction in Mexico to welcome U.S. involvement in hopes of securing recognition, arms, or funding for their own purposes. From 1940 until the late 1980s Mexican political factions respected an unwritten rule not to seek or welcome American involvement in domestic matters. Mexican political leaders opposed instances of U.S. intervention in Latin America, from the CIA-backed overthrow of Jacobo Arbenz in Guatemala in 1954 to the use of over 20,000 ground troops to remove Panamanian dictator General Manuel Noriega in 1989. Mexico never had Peace Corps volunteers and refused to accept U.S. aid under the Alliance for Progress program in the 1960s. Currently, Mexico refuses to support UN-sponsored actions that involve intervention of one sort or another in places such as Iraq and opposes the punitive aspects of the U.S. Helms-Burton Law aimed at undermining foreign investment in **Cuba.**

At the National Museum of Intervention in Mexico City, Mexican national identity is reaffirmed largely in terms of a response to U.S. intervention and aggression. Mexican schoolchildren are taught that the United States is always trying to take something away from Mexico and that the intervention theme is still relevant in modern Mexico. U.S. intervention is not seen by the majority of Mexicans as an altruistic advocacy of noble causes, whether done in the name of stability, **democracy**, **human rights**, economic growth, reduction in poverty, or the elimination of illicit **drug trafficking.** However, anti-Americanism in Mexico has been more of a response by political elites who need an issue to generate political support than a negative feeling that permeates the Mexican population.

In order to claim its heritage as a revolutionary regime and protector of the social and economic advances for workers and peasants, members of the Mexican elite constantly invoke the principles of national sovereignty, independence, and nonintervention. The size of the U.S. diplomatic mission, business community, and press corps in Mexico also serves to remind Mexicans of what they see as a monolithic and overpowering involvement in Mexico's domestic affairs. U.S. Congressional hearings that probe Mexico's failings (e.g., drug trafficking, money laundering, crime, and **corruption**) and the annual drug certification ritual (critics would say "charade") serve to inflame Mexican feelings of resentment and are often interpreted as another form of intervention. The Drug Enforcement Agency (DEA) has been involved in Mexican affairs for decades and often acts with impunity inside Mexico. The United States has also resorted to the threat of intervention, meaning that if Mexico acts in ways that are detrimental to American interests, then some form of reprisal from Washington will be forthcoming.

Beginning with the presidency of **Carlos Salinas de Gortari** in late 1988, Mexico began to reverse its historic antipathy toward U.S. involvement in Mexico in order to push a series of economic and political reforms deemed beneficial to Mexico, including the passage of the **North American Free Trade Agreement (NAFTA)** and allowing the National Endowment for Democracy to oversee the 1994 presidential elections, won by **Ernesto Zedillo**. Texas governor George W. Bush indicated during the 2000 U.S. presidential campaign that he wanted Mexico to be a regional partner with the United States in implementing its Latin American policy, an idea that runs strongly against the tradition in Mexican **foreign policy** to avoid interference in the affairs of foreign states. While the principle of the sovereign equality of states and nonintervention in the domestic affairs of states has been the basis for international law for centuries, efforts are now under way among international organizations to create new guidelines for humanitarian intervention to prevent genocide, violent mass ethnic expulsions, or other serious human rights violations. Given Mexico's historical sensitivity to intervention, this trend against traditional notions of sovereignty is disturbing to policy makers in Mexico City. *See also* Mexican American War; Estrada Doctrine.

SUGGESTED READING
David W. Dent, *The Legacy of the Monroe Doctrine: A Reference Guide to U.S. Involvement in Latin America and the Caribbean* (Westport, Conn.: Greenwood, 1999); Robert A. Pastor, *Whirlpool: U.S. Foreign Policy toward Latin America and the Caribbean* (Princeton: Princeton University Press, 1992); Robert A. Pastor and Jorge G. Castañeda, *Limits to Friendship: The United States and Mexico* (New York: Knopf, 1988); Carlos Rico, "The Future of Mexican–U.S. Relations and the Limits of the Rhetoric of 'Interdependence,'" in Carlos Vásquez and Manuel García y Griego, eds., *Mexican–U.S. Relations* (Los Angeles: UCLA Latin American Center Publications, 1983); Larry Rohter, "Just Forget the Alamo! Ponder Yankees' Sins," *New York Times*, September 28, 1990.

Jalisco. *See* Geographical Regions.

Jarabe Tapatío The national folk dance of Mexico, originating in the state of Jalisco. The *jarabe* was adopted as the main representative of Mexican musical folklore during the nationalist movement in the arts beginning with the revolutionary period and continuing through the 1930s. Also known as the "Mexican hat dance," it involves a man in a *charro* suit and a woman in a *china poblana* dress; both dance separately with vigorous foot stomping, all the time closely circling the man's large *sombrero*. It is a popular folk dance performed throughout the country that evokes warm feelings of pride in Mexican national identity.

SUGGESTED READING
Gabriel Saldívar, *El jarabe: Baile popular Mexicano* (Mexico, D.F.: Talleres Gráficos de la Nación, 1937).

Jaramillo, Rubén. *See* Guerrilla Movements and Counterinsurgency.

Journalism. *See* Communications Media; Junco de la Vega, Alejandro.

Junco de la Vega, Alejandro (1949–) Journalist and newspaper publisher from Monterrey who became one of the prime movers in the development of independent and technologically sophisticated journalism throughout Mexico. Part of a well-known newspaper family in Monterrey, Junco de la Vega has been involved in the professionalization of journalism for young news reporters, the application of on-line news service, and the expansion of daily newspapers in Mexico City *(Reforma)*, Saltillo *(Palabra)*, and Guadalajara *(Mural)*. With ownership of dailies in Mexico's three largest cities, Junco's newspaper empire has flourished by providing independent and professional journalism, confident that he will succeed by fighting for the public's right to information without **government** intimidation or interference.

With a college degree in journalism from the University of Texas (1969), Junco worked in the family's newspaper business in Monterrey (*El Norte*, a morning paper, and *El Sol*, an afternoon paper) where he helped the newspaper's conversion to cold-type and offset printing in 1971. He inherited his family's newspaper in 1971 and became publisher in 1973 at the age of 24.

After *El Norte* demanded to know why President **Luis Echeverría** had not been more vigilant in solving the kidnapping and murder of one of Monterrey's most powerful business leaders in 1973, the president responded by trying to sabotage Junco's newspaper by cutting his newsprint supply and subsidizing one of his competitors in the city. Junco de la Vega refused to budge and Echeverría's vindictive campaign eventually collapsed, but the publisher of *El Norte* quickly realized that he needed to cut his ties to government-subsidized paper products if he was going to continue independent reporting. In the meantime, he broadened *El Norte*'s advertising base so that no private or government client contributed a large percentage of revenues. He then hired young reporters for his in-house training program and invited one of his Texas journalism professors to Monterrey to

Alejandro Junco de la Vega, 1997. Credit: Alejandro Junco de la Vega.

teach the aspiring news reporters everything from copy editing to newsroom ethics. His news staff are paid higher salaries than those at most Mexican newspapers, are forbidden to accept bribes or government "gifts," and are relieved of the obligation to sell advertising. In two decades *El Norte*'s staff increased from 17 editorial employees to 440.

Today, Junco de la Vega's *El Norte* is Latin America's most technologically advanced newspaper. In 1990 Junco expanded his newspaper operation into the delivery of electronic information to computer-based subscribers with a real-time financial information service that serves the financial community of Mexico and Wall Street. His emphasis on the professionalization of Mexican journalism and the modernization of publishing earned *El Norte* international awards, including the prestigious Maria Moors Cabot Award from Columbia University in 1991. By 1995 he had started a new venture on the electronic information world, launching an Internet strategy that has made the company the largest Internet access provider in Mexico as well as the most important content provider on the Internet in Latin America. His electronic commerce services include transactional networks, on-line banking applications, on-line payments, electronic advertising, and on-line shopping.

Junco de la Vega's most ambitious project was his decision to launch *Reforma* in an effort to compete with more than 25 other newspapers already publishing in Mexico City. Unlike most Mexico City dailies that act as obedient courtesans to powerful politicians and presidents in the nation's capital, *Reforma* revolutionized the politics of print (and broadcast) journalism in Mexico. To increase readership and challenge the competition, Junco de la Vega designed a visually dazzling paper, recruited dozens of respected columnists reflecting a broad spectrum of Mexican opinion, and broadened his coverage to attract readers from Mexico's fledgling middle class. More important to the startling success of *Reforma* was Junco de la Vega's decision to challenge Mexico City's newsstand monopoly (controlled by a **Partido Revolucionario Institucional (PRI)**-dominated union) and to increase street sales; he created his own independent distribution system so that his paper arrived at a subscriber's door far sooner than any of his competitors. *Reforma* also created the most important independent opinion polling unit in Mexico, publishing preelection poll results and doing periodic evaluations of President **Ernesto Zedillo's** approval ratings. Many consider

Reforma to be Mexico's most influential newspaper, offering coverage on controversial subjects and powerful individuals that until recently was unheard of by most newspapers in the capital.

As one of Mexico's most significant journalists, Alejandro Junco has gained further notoriety by expanding the number of dailies throughout the country, challenging the country's powerful political class, transforming Mexican journalism into a more professional undertaking, and changing the historic relationship between the media, the government, and the public. The renovating force behind Junco's burgeoning media empire is another sign of the gradual erosion of Mexico's authoritarian political tradition and the difficult steps needed to complete the country's **democratic** transition. He is also responsible for ushering in a new era in Mexican journalism that puts a high priority on professional standards, raising the cost of being corrupt, and providing space to stories and commentaries that are critical of the government and its leaders. *See also* Communications Media.

SUGGESTED READING

Ilya Adler, "The Mexican Case: The Media in the 1988 Presidential Election," in Thomas E. Skidmore, ed., *Television, Politics, and the Transition to Democracy in Latin America* (Washington, D.C.: Woodrow Wilson Center Press, 1993); John Ward Anderson, "Newspapers Chain Sets New Standards," *Washington Post*, June 23, 2000; Sam Dillon, "Lusty New Papers Take on the Powerful in Mexico," *New York Times*, January 3, 1999; Murray Fromson, "Mexico's Struggle for a Free Press," in Richard R. Cole, ed., *Communication in Latin America: Journalism, Mass Media, and Society* (Wilmington, Del.: Scholarly Resources, 1996); William A. Orme Jr., ed., *A Culture of Collusion: An Inside Look at the Mexican Press* (Miami: University of Miami, North-South Center Press, 1997).

Kahlo, Frida (1907–1954) One of Mexico's most significant artists and writers, known internationally for the wrenching self-portraits she painted in the 1930s and 1940s. The fascination with Kahlo's life and artistic endeavors has grown at a dramatic rate over the past 20 years, driven in large part by her strength and resilience in face of tragedy and physical pain, her difficult relationship with her husband, muralist **Diego Rivera**, and the creation of herself as a work of Mexican art. Today, her canvases—particularly the self-portraits and still lifes—command high prices in New York and London art markets. Forgers, recognizing the value of her paintings and the ignorance of Latin American works of art in the United States, have generated hundreds of fake paintings with her name.

Frida (most of her followers called her by her first name) was born in Coyoacán (now a suburb of Mexico City) to a German Jewish father of Hungarian descent and a Mexican Catholic mother of Spanish and Indian heritage. Her mixed ethnic background played a major role in the way she defined herself and as the subject of her own paintings. Kahlo was raised in the Catholic faith, attending church daily as a child, but she was atypical in her religious devotion, influenced in her early years by her nonreligious European father. Until the age of six she roamed the streets and played with neighborhood boys; from that time on her life was filled with illness (polio), operations (she was hit by a trolley car on the way home from school), and suffering that strengthened her resolve and fostered her strong personality. Kahlo's determination to overcome her handicaps gradually helped her

become an extrovert, constantly building friendships among public personalities. During the long periods of painful recovery from illness and the trolley car accident, she began to paint scenes of her world of pain, a theme that dominated Kahlo's works throughout her life. Over a span of 28 years she created 130 paintings, 30 drawings, and a few watercolors.

Frida Kahlo's early life was influenced by government efforts to integrate Mexican Indians into mainstream society after the Revolution (*indigenismo*) and Mexican muralists like Diego Rivera who presided over the Mexicanization of several art forms. In what became known as the Escuela de México (Mexican School), painters such as Rivera, **David Alfaro Siqueiros**, **José Clemente Orozco**, Jean Charlot, and others became part of a movement that produced avant-garde art based on ancient and indigenous artistic practices of Mexico.

Kahlo became an admirer of Rivera when he created a mural in her high school. After her accident, she met him at a party and from that time forward Rivero figured prominently in her life. Shortly after their encounter, they married, but it was a rocky relationship with periods of separation, divorce, and remarriage to each other between 1929 and her death in 1954. Although both marriage partners had lovers, Rivera's philandering became a source of pain and anger for Kahlo, who was 21 years younger than her husband. In the early years of the marriage Kahlo tried to please her husband by adopting his **communist** ideology and the nationalist rhetoric of the **Mexican Revolution** with its emphasis on Mexico's Indian past that dominated his murals.

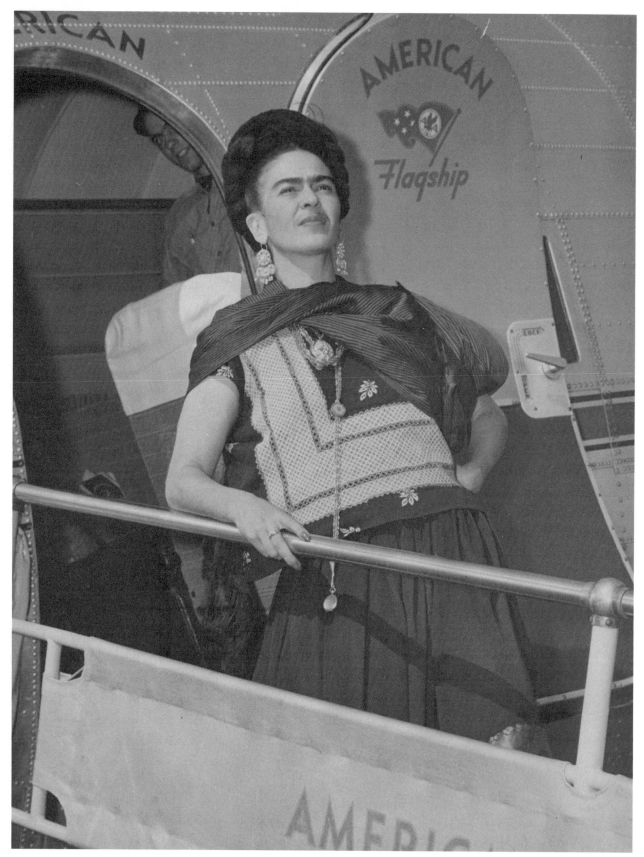

Frida Kahlo. Credit: Fotofest.

Diego Rivera's reputation as the most outspoken and respected of the Mexican mural painters opened the door for Kahlo to meet international artistic and political figures in Mexico and abroad, including **Tina Modotti**, Henry Ford, **Nelson Rockefeller**, **Leon Trotsky**, and Pablo Neruda. In 1930 they traveled to the United States, where Rivera had contracted to paint murals in San Francisco, Detroit, and New York. Kahlo continued to paint in the United States and produced some of her groundbreaking work between 1930 and 1933. In works such as *Portrait of Luther Burbank* (1931), *Frida and Diego Rivera* (1931), *Self-Portrait on the Border between the United States and Mexico* (1932), *My Dress Hangs There* (1932), *My Birth* (1932), and *Henry Ford Hospital* (1932), Kahlo expressed her disenchantment with the bourgeois, technologically advanced, and culturally deprived United States and graphic depictions of her miscarriage. She was determined to forge her own reputation as a respectable artist with her own style rather than simply following in Rivera's footsteps. The couple returned to Mexico in 1933 after Rivera's mural *Man at the Crossroads* at Rockefeller Center was destroyed when he refused to remove the controversial sketch of Lenin contained in the partially completed work.

Rivera encouraged her separate path and served as her most energetic supporter; he was instrumental in constructing her identity by bringing her a Tehuana outfit (brightly colored fabric made into embroidered blouses and long skirts worn by women in the Isthmus of Tehuantepec region) symbolizing the power of Tehuana women in Mexican society. Tehuana fabrics and jewelry soon became the source of Kahlo's empowerment and a symbol (and advertisement) of and for Mexico. The ability of Kahlo to embody the essence of Mexico in her art and dress makes her unique among Mexican artists.

Frida Kahlo was a strong believer in the Mexican mural tradition with its emphasis on history, politics, and imperialism but rejected this form in her painting. Her paintings emphasized first-person themes of human catastrophe and intense suffering, often constructed from pieces of her own life and that of everyday people. In many ways she represented the conflicting character of postrevolutionary Mexican identity in which religion, class, ethnicity, and gender clashed in so many ways. According to Bakewell (1997, 725), "Kahlo identified herself with the contradictions of her **mestizaje** and through the assemblage of disparate objects, through her identity with church and national icons, and through the exposure of her own fragmented materiality she constructed a subjectivity for herself." She was uncomfortable with her upper-middle-class status and tried to define her life within a range of gender and class identities. Her house was decorated with Mexican indigenous art and crafts rather than European and American imports so common among her class. As an art teacher in the 1940s she insisted on taking her students (her disciples were called Los Fridos) into the street to paint Mexican life as it appeared to most Mexicans, with scenes of poor barrios, local bars, churches, open-air food pavilions, and the like. Kahlo's popularity among many young painters and writers today is attributable to the frankness in her artistic imagery and rejection of the submissive role of women in Mexican culture. Through the use of the self-portrait, according to Bakewell (1997, 725), Kahlo "operationalized the psychology of being a woman as she did being a Mexican." After more than 20 years of artistic creativity, she received the National Prize of Arts and Sciences in 1946.

When Frida Kahlo died prematurely in 1954 at age 47, her casket was placed in state in the Palacio de Bellas Artes; mourners at her funeral included many prominent political figures, including former president **Lázaro Cárdenas**. As Lowe points (1997, 759) out, "Kahlo is primarily remembered for her obsessive rendering of herself, a pre-occupation that achieved worldwide recognition decades after her death." Her popularity continues to grow in the United States, particularly in the world of art and food in New York City; one of the new restaurants to open there, Café Frida, is offering authentic expressions of Mexican regional cooking to the wave of immigrants from Mexico and others who now live and work in the city.

SUGGESTED READING

Elizabeth Bakewell, "Kahlo, Frida," in Michael S. Werner, ed., *Encyclopedia of Mexico: History, Society, and Culture*, vol. 1 (Chicago: Fitzroy Dearborn, 1997); Holly Barnet-Sánchez, "Frida Kahlo: Her Life and Art Revisited," *Latin American Research Review* 3 (1997): 243–57; Erika Billiter, *The Blue House: The World of Frida Kahlo* (Seattle: University of Washington Press; Houston: Museum of Fine Arts, 1993); Malka Drucker, *Frida Kahlo* (Albuquerque: University of New Mexico Press, 1995); Haydee Herrera, *Frida: A Biography of Frida Kahlo* (New York: Harper & Row, 1983); Janet Kaplan, "Frida Kahlo: Life, Death, and Self-Creation," in Marjorie Agosín, ed., *A Woman's Gaze: Latin American Women Artists* (Fredonia, N.Y.: White Pine, 1998); Margaret A. Lindauer, *Devouring Frida: The Art History and Popular Celebrity of Frida Kahlo* (Hanover, N.H.: University Press of New England, 1999); Sarah M. Lowe, "Kahlo, Frida," in Delia Gaze, ed., *Dictionary of Women Artists*, vol. 2 (Chicago: Fitzroy Dearborn, 1997); Jack Rummel, *Frida Kahlo: A Spiritual Biography* (New York: Crossroad, 2000); Raquel Tibol, *Frida Kahlo: An Open Life*, trans. Elinor Randall (Albuquerque: University of New Mexico Press, 1993); Marta Zamora, *Frida Kahlo: The Brush of Anguish*, trans. Marilyn Sode Smith (San Francisco: Chronicle Books, 1990).

Krauze Kleinbort, Enrique (1947–) ☀ One of Mexico's most popular historians and intellectuals, known for his essays and prize-winning books on Mexican history (including the **Mexican Revolution**) and biographies of political personalities. Born in 1947 in the Federal District, Krauze studied industrial engineering at the **Universidad Nacional Autónoma de México (UNAM)** before receiving his doctorate in history

from the **Colegio de México** in 1974. After receiving his doctorate, he worked as a research professor at the Colegio de México (1976–1978) and as a writer for *Vuelta* (1976–1981), a prestigious intellectual journal run by **Octavio Paz**, becoming coeditor in 1982. From the mid-1970s to the present, he has written numerous books, articles, and essays, including *Caudillos culturales de la revolución mexicana* (for which he was awarded the 1976 Premio Magda Donato) and *Biografías del poder* (1987), a collection of fascinating portraits of key figures in the history of Mexico during the 20th century that served as the basis of a television series of the same name. This book was later translated into English as *Mexico: Biography of Power: A History of Modern Mexico, 1810–1996* (1997). A similar work, *Siglo de caudillos, 1810–1910* (1994) became a best-seller in Mexico and in Spain, where it won the Premio Comillas, an important literary prize in that country.

Krauze is an intellectual disciple of Nobel Prize winner Paz and **Daniel Cosío Villegas**. His Guggenheim fellowship award for 1979–1980 allowed him to advance his intellectual pursuits and journalistic interests. One of the leading advocates of democratic reform in Mexico, Enrique Krauze has written articles for the *New York Times*, *Dissent*, the *Wall Street Journal*, *Time*, and the *New Republic* on contemporary politics and economic problems in Mexico. He has also written or edited other books on **democracy** in Latin America and intellectual history in Mexico, including a collaborative work on Cosío Villegas, one of Mexico's best-known liberal historians and writers. Krauze still lives in Mexico City, where he focuses on intellectual history, biography, and political commentary.

SUGGESTED READING

Roderic Ai Camp, "Krauze, Enrique," in Barbara A. Tenenbaum, ed., *Encyclopedia of Latin American History and Culture* (New York: Scribners, 1996).

Labastida Ochoa, Francisco (1942–) One of several top **Partido Revolucionario Instituticional (PRI)** leaders who sought the Mexican presidency in 2000. Francisco Labastida emerged from a field of four candidates in the ruling party's November 1999 primary to win with 55 percent of the vote against his three rivals: Roberto Madrazo (29 percent), Manuel Bartlett (6 percent), and Humberto Roque (4 percent). However, eight months later he lost the presidential race to **Vicente Fox**, winning only 36 percent of the vote for the PRI, the lowest in its more than 70-year domination of Mexican politics.

Labastida was considered one of the PRI's old-guard leaders, and his primary win was a sign that the PRI had returned to selecting presidential candidates who previously held public office and were experienced in areas of taxation, finance, and budgetary planning. In Mexico's **technocrat**-politician debate, Labastida managed to steer a middle road in which many of his supporters described him as a pragmatic, nonideological politician more than a technocrat or gray politician. His opponents emphasized his affiliation with the PRI, pointing to his deep establishment credentials (he served in the administrations of six presidents, was elected governor of Sinaloa, and was ambassador to Portugal) with close ties to the *dinosaurios*, the old-guard faction of the ruling party that resisted many reform efforts after 1980. By stressing the importance of improving the economy and public safety, Labastida's strategy was to overcome the negative perceptions of his ties to the old-guard members of the PRI. In dealing with the United States, Labastida said during the campaign that he would seek a better understanding on contentious binational issues, and an expanded the NAFTA, to include an agreement on temporary workers.

After years of criticism for its autocratic conduct, the PRI decided in 1999 that a primary election held before the general election would demonstrate that the party is becoming more democratic and politically legitimate. Labastida announced in April 1999 that he would resign from his cabinet position as interior secretary to seek the nomination in the party's primary on November 7. Throughout the primary campaign, political experts claimed that Labastida was the preferred candidate of incumbent president **Ernesto Zedillo**, although he consistently denied this. In the primary, Labastida won 55 percent of the 9 million votes cast, an electoral showing that

PRI presidential candidate in 2000, Francisco Labastida. Credit: *Proceso*, photo by Germán Canseco.

won 273 of the 300 electoral districts throughout the country. Despite Labastida's decisive victory over closest rival Roberto Madrazo, questionable campaign practices—using government funds to solicit votes, intimidating Madrazo supporters, and other irregularities—reminded some of the durability of old PRI tricks involving electoral manipulation and intimidation.

Part of an aristocratic family that played a major role throughout Mexican history, Francisco Labastida was born in Los Mochis, Sinaloa, the son of a prominent surgeon. His deep interest in the political process may be inherited from ancestors who fought in the war for independence and during the French **intervention** in the 1860s; Labastida's grandfather was a well-known senator, governor, and member of the constituent assembly that wrote the **Constitution of 1917**. Francisco Labastida moved to Mexico City after his primary studies, earning an economics degree from the National School of Economics at the **Universidad Nacional Autónoma de México (UNAM)** in 1964. He did postgraduate work in economics, education, and planning at the UN Economic Commission for Latin America and the Caribbean (ECLAC) in Santiago, Chile. In an interview with the *Los Angeles Times* in January 2000 he claimed that his ECLAC education helped him see the need for improving the plight of poor people in his country.

After returning to Mexico City, Labastida taught at UNAM and worked his way up the bureaucratic ladder through various **government** positions, mainly in the areas of finance and planning. After serving as undersecretary of programming in the Planning and Budget Department (1979–1982) and as secretary of government properties (1982–1986), he served for six years as the governor of Sinaloa state. While governor, he claimed success in fighting the drug cartels in his state. As secretary of the government (*gobernación*) in the Zedillo administration, Labastida

took credit for dealing with the ongoing crisis in Chiapas by passing legislation that incorporated 85 percent of the provisions in the **San Andrés Accords** and directing more public spending to education and literacy programs, as well as building more schools, health centers, and roads in rural Chiapas.

After months of campaigning against a fractured opposition, a contest marred by mudslinging, profanity, and personal attacks, Labastida failed to carry the PRI to victory in the July 2, 2000. His unsuccessful campaign surprised many of his supporters, since he was helped by his close association with the incumbent president, local and state PRI officials, union bosses who poured valuable funds and other kinds of support into his campaign, the split vote among the major opposition parties, and millions of older, semiliterate rural voters who still admire the PRI for its pork-barrel politics. Throughout the presidential campaign, Labastida strongly identified himself with **Luis Donaldo Colosio**, the assassinated presidential candidate in 1994 and one of the PRI's heroes (and avoided mention of ex-president **Carlos Salinas de Gortari**). After his defeat, Labastida declared that Mexican citizens had made a political decision that must be respected and, despite the loss, asserted that the PRI is still alive, fully capable of recovery despite its historic setback at the polls in 2000. *See also* Electoral System/Elections.

SUGGESTED READING

Roderic Ai Camp, *Mexican Political Biographies, 1935–1993*, 3d ed. (Austin: University of Texas Press, 1995); Sergio Muñoz, "Francisco Labastida, Mexico's Mystery: A Patrician and His Party Lobby for the Poor," *Los Angeles Times*, January 30, 2000; Julia Preston, "The Elite's Choice Heads to Victory in Mexico Primary," *New York Times*, November 8, 1999; Mary Beth Sheridan, "Mexico's Ruling Party Loses Presidency in Historic Election," *Los Angeles Times*, July 3, 2000.

Labor ☀ Since the establishment of one-party rule in 1929, Mexico's organized labor movement has been closely tied to the government and the **Partido Revolucionario Institucional (PRI)**. Before the Revolution and the creation of the **corporatist** system, labor conflicts remained isolated incidents and were muted by a dictatorship that prohibited the growth and organization of a militant labor movement. Despite advanced labor laws (established in the **Constitution of 1917** and federal labor statutes) that guarantee a minimum wage, an eight-hour day, the right to strike, worker's compensation, and liberal maternity-leave benefits, current labor practices often violate both the intent and letter of the these legal provisions. Labor unions are more likely to serve the interests of their powerful leaders and PRI operatives than the true interests of workers.

Labor unions made considerable gains during the presidency of **Lázaro Cárdenas** with the creation of the **Confederación de Trabajadores de México (CTM)**, a corporatist arrangement that was beneficial to the state and union members. While the CTM attained its privileged position under the aegis of President Cárdenas, corporatist unions made relatively little progress in developing effective representation or any sense of internal democracy.

Until the early 1970s, the labor sector made substantial advances in political clout and economic strength. However, the unions that emerged from the 1968 student movement were more independent than the powerful CTM and demanded that President **Luis Echeverría** (1970–1976) grant them official recognition, a practice that had been severely restricted before the 1970s. As the new unions gained strength and began to challenge the corporatist unions, President Echeverría changed his mind and started to implement measures that would stifle the growth in independent unions.

The economic crisis that began with the 1982 **debt crisis** was a major blow to the labor movement, suddenly faced with IMF-modeled austerity policies that sent wages spiraling downward while government services and benefits were cut drastically. In an effort to stem the alarmingly high inflation (over 160 percent), President **Miguel de la Madrid** (1982–1988) approved a "Pact of Solidarity" between big business and the PRI labor and peasant sectors. By freezing wages and putting the government in charge of future wage increases, the **technocrats** in charge of the government began to centralize state economic agencies and push toward a new political economy based on neoliberal economic principles. President **Carlos Salinas de Gortari** (1988–1994) continued the antiworker (and anti-inflation) policies of his predecessor as labor unions struggled to retain gains made prior to the 1980s.

Mexican labor is one of three official pillars of the dominant political party, the Institutional Revolutionary Party (PRI). The CTM represents industrial workers, the **Confederación Nacional Campesina (CNC)** represents peasants or small farmers, and the amorphous popular sector is represented by the **Confederación Nacional de Organizaciones Populares (CNOP)**. The CTM is part of the Labor Congress (Congreso del Trabajo, CT), a large umbrella organization that groups all major labor confederations, including those not affiliated with the PRI as well as industrial unions that are not part of the CTM. The large size of the CT allows for some diversity of opinion within the labor movement. However, the decision-making process within the CTM and CT is secret, making leadership selection rather mysterious and labor demands dependent on the wishes of the PRI and big business. In the end, it is a symbiotic relationship, but it is the power of the state in deciding the outcome of labor demands that counts most. Since **World War II**, the state–labor relationship has contributed to a decline in the number of strikers, meaning that labor activism has been restrained in favor of "national unity," a recognition that encouraging private investment and containing labor demands best serve the interests of the state and its economic development efforts.

While the official unions tend to be tightly controlled and passive in their demands, this is not the case with independent unions, found in both the private and public sectors. Private sector unions tend to dominate industries associated with **automobiles**, aviation, and metalworking segments of the economy; in the public sector, independent unionism exists in various institutions of higher learning such as the **Universidad Nacional Autónoma de México (UNAM)**. The independent unions are more militant in their demands for higher wages and greater democracy within the decision-making process. By challenging the subordinate behavior of the official union leadership, independent unionism has been a new and progressive force in the labor movement.

With greater competition inside the labor sector, leaders of the official unions have responded by becoming more active in the promotion of worker interests. As Mexico experiences a decline in the authoritarian features of its political system and the corporatism that has been in place for close to 70 years begins to erode, the close ties between organized labor and state will be increasingly challenged. With the death in 1997 of **Fidel Velázquez**, strong-arm leader of the CTM, and the growing support of independent unions, official unions will find it more difficult to limit worker demands in the future. If this occurs, it will signify a major alteration in the basic operation of the Mexican political system, a change that "would contribute to the elimination of the Mexican paradox of mobilization without conflict and conflict without mobilization" (Zapata 1997, 697).

The current labor movement is the victim of the overall economic crisis that has plagued Mexico for the past 20 years, neoliberal economic policies, and the unwillingness of labor bosses to defend worker's interest in the face of challenges from a new political economy based on exports and global integration. The current crisis in the labor movement is compounded by declining membership, high unemployment or underemployment, corrupt *charristisa* union bosses, and a "crisis in corporatism." With cheap labor one of Mexico's primary comparative advantages in the new global economy, political leaders are not inclined to make major concessions to labor's wage demands in an era of free trade and regional integration. *See also Charros*; Lombardo Toledano, Vicente.

SUGGESTED READING

James D. Cockcroft, *Mexico's Hope: An Encounter with Politics and History* (New York: Monthly Review Press, 1998); Ruth Berins Collier and David Collier, *Shaping the Political Arena: Critical Junctures, the Labor Movement, and Regime Dynamics in Latin America* (Princeton: Princeton University Press, 1991); Kevin J. Middlebrook, *The Paradox of Revolution: Labor, the State, and Authoritarianism in Mexico* (Baltimore: Johns Hopkins University Press, 1995); Fred Rosen, "The Underside of NAFTA: A Budding Cross-Border Resistance," *NACLA Report on the Americas* (January–February 1999); Francisco Zapata, "Industrial Labor, 1940–1996," in Michael S. Werner, ed., *Encyclopedia of Mexico: History, Society, and Culture*, vol. 1 (Chicago: Fitzroy Dearborn, 1997); Zapata, "Social Concertation in Mexico," in Tiziano Treu, ed., *Participation in Public Policy Making: The Role of Trade Unions and Employer's Associations* (Berlin: Walter de Gruyter, 1992).

Labor Party. *See* Partido de Trabajo (PT).

Lara, Agustín (1897–1970) ☀ Musician, actor, and composer of over 500 compositions who developed a reputation as one of Mexico's most prolific and talented singer/songwriters. His signature hits—known worldwide—included "Granada," "Noche de Ronda," "María Bonita," and "Solamente una vez." He developed a love for the port city of

Veracruz, and this tropical location stimulated some of his best songs, including "Veracruz," a *bolero* that became the unofficial state anthem. He was one of Mexican radio's early stars, as well as a popular performer in theaters, clubs and concert halls.

Born in Mexico City in 1897, Lara grew up in a family that wanted him to be a medical doctor like his father, but his musical talents took him in other directions. After being introduced to the piano at an early age, Lara left home to develop his musical talent by playing in various "nightspots" and living a bohemian and romantic lifestyle. It is unclear what he did during his mid-teens, except that it was reported that he was forced to attend a military academy after his father yanked him out of a bordello he was working in. Later, while working in the bordello/clubs and cafes in the neighborhood along Santa Maria la Redonda street (later renamed for **Lázaro Cárdenas**), he made friends with other established musicians, expanded his repertoire to include numerous musical styles, and began creating his own compositions. His love of life, as well as his dashing and suave demeanor, attracted many beautiful women, leading to four marriages and many other romances during his long career. His unsuccessful marriages and divorces produced some of his best songs, including the classic "María Bonita" about the breakup of his marriage to actress **María Félix**, who left him for **Jorge Negrete**.

During the 1930s and 1940s, Lara acted in several films and provided the **music** for many others during the golden age of **cinema**. By 1950 he was a successful international star of Mexican film and music with a lavish lifestyle to prove it. From 1950 to the mid-1960s he continued to perform in films, toured, played in theaters and nightclubs, and appeared on many radio and television shows. He traveled to Spain to sing and watch **bullfights** and on several occasions was showered with Spanish appreciation for his music, particularly the songs "Granada," "Sevilla,"

"Murcia," "Toledo," and "Madrid," named in honor of Spanish cities. Spain's dictator, Francisco Franco, gave him a home in Granada to express his gratitude for these songs.

As Mexicans developed new tastes in music during the 1960s, Lara spent less time in the limelight and more time relaxing and enjoying the good life with his friends at his house in Veracruz. He died of a heart attack in October 1970, after complications from a fractured hip. His funeral was attended by thousands of adoring fans who had been inspired by his music. Agustín Lara was unmatched by any other composer of his time for his extraordinary production of popular songs.

SUGGESTED READING

Ramiro Burr, *The Billboard Guide to Tejano and Regional Mexican Music* (New York: Billboard Books, 1999); Carlos Monsiváis et al., *Todo lo que usted quiere saber sobre Agustín Lara* (Mexico, D.F.: Editorial Continedo, 1993); Andrew Grant Wood, "Lara, Agustín," in Michael S. Werner, ed., *Encyclopedia of Mexico: History, Society, and Culture*, vol. 1 (Chicago: Fitzroy Dearborn, 1997).

Liberation Theology. *See* Church and State; Ruiz García, Samuel.

Lombardo Toledano, Vicente (1894–1968) ☀ The father of Mexican Marxism, an intellectual, politician, and labor leader who believed that the **Mexican Revolution** could act as a model for all of Latin America. Lombardo Toledano was born in Teziutlán, Puebla, to a family with Italian ancestry. His Italian Mexican father was mayor at one time and his sisters married leading figures in Mexican intellectual and political life. After finishing his preparatory studies, he earned a law degree and a master's degree from the National University. Before he became interim governor of Puebla in 1923, he worked as a professor and founded a night school program for working-class students. On two occasions (in 1924–1928 and 1964–1966), Lombardo Toledano served in the Chamber of Deputies. However, it was his **labor** union activism that made him a key figure in Mexican politics from the 1930s to the 1960s.

Known to his followers as the "Maestro," Lombardo Toledano worked to build a close alliance between the state and labor and peasant organizations. He was firmly convinced that this **corporatist** arrangement would allow the central **government** to pursue economic policies of benefit to the urban and agrarian masses. He founded the **Confederación de Trabajadores de México (CTM)** in 1936, which would become the labor hub of the new corporatist structure of the ruling party.

An active member in Mexico's first national labor organization—the Regional Confederation of Mexican Workers (Confederación Revolucionaria de Obreros y Campesinos Mexicanos, CROM)—Lombardo developed a life-long interest in working-class politics. However, he broke with the CROM, a staunchly anticommunist organization, in 1932 and declared himself a "non-Communist Marxist." After visiting the Soviet Union in 1935, he confirmed his Marxism and developed an interest in the idea of the popular front. Interestingly, Lombardo's growing identification with the Soviet state did not make him an automatic ally of the Mexican **Communist** Party, an organization he criticized for its lack of intellectual depth and poor understanding of Mexico's political reality. Prior to **World War II**, Comintern and Soviet support for Lombardo's increasingly antidemocratic and anticommunist policies helped reverse a move by the Mexican Communist Party to withdraw its support from the CTM, founded in 1936 by Lombardo.

Lombardo Toledano created the Confederation of Latin American Workers (Confederación de Trabajadores de América Latina, CTAL) in 1938 (with the support of President **Lázaro Cárdenas**) and then as its director during the 1940s promoted antifascist and progressive labor organizations throughout Latin America on the basis of popular front principles. His decision to create a new united-front party—the Partido Popular (PP, or Popular Party)—in the late 1940s stemmed from his disgust with the government and his interest in the idea of a popular front party that would challenge both the newly founded **Partido Acción Nacional (PAN)** and the more conservative elements within the **Partido Revolucionario Institucional (PRI)**. Recognizing the importance of not expressing open defiance of the ruling party, Lombardo and his PP (which changed its name in 1960 to the **Partido Popular Socialista, PPS**) consistently supported the PRI, while always distinguishing between the old-guard members of the party and the president himself. The relationship between Lombardo's PP and the PRI (and its labor affiliates such as the CTM) was not a warm embrace because the ruling party felt that the PP would threaten its mass base and corporate power structure.

The inability of the Popular Party to expand beyond its narrow base was due in large part to Lombardo's authoritarian leadership style, his almost unconditional support for the PRI, and his opposition to union reform movements, including efforts to change the heavy-handed influence exercised by *charros*, or authoritarian labor bosses. Lombardo lost the support of students and many workers when he denounced the student-led revolts of 1968, calling them "subversives" and "enemies" of the state. As students led the movement toward a more serious critique of the Mexican state based on the antiauthoritarianism of the new left, Lombardo and his followers continued to represent a positive view of the state, often glorifying its progressive nationalizing and anti-imperialist pretensions years after the radical reformism of the Revolution had run its course. As Carr (1997, 756) points out, "Of all the currents within Mexican Marxism, it was Lombardismo that was most intimately bound up with the image and practice of the caudillo, the authoritarian populist."

The legacy of Vicente Lombardo Toledano's revolutionary nationalism continued long after his death in 1968. Despite his subservience to the PRI regarding electoral politics, Lombardo and his PP/PPS managed to cultivate a substantial following among Mexican intellectuals during the 1950s and 1960s that has yet to be destroyed. For example, many of his followers—particularly among rural workers and peasants—still find wisdom in *Lombardismo*, although those involved in popular struggles have often disagreed quite forcefully with the Maestro's message. The enduring attraction of Lombardo's ideas can be seen in the events surrounding the 1988 presidential campaign, when the neo-*Cardenista* opposition presented a serious challenge to the dominant party that ultimately led to the emergence of the center-left Party of the Democratic Revolution (**Partido de la Revolución Democrática, PRD**) in 1989, two decades after the death of the key left-wing ideologue of the Mexican Revolution.

SUGGESTED READING

Roderic Ai Camp, "Lombardo Toledano, Vicente," in Barbara A. Tenenbaum, ed., *Encyclopedia of Latin American History and Culture*, vol. 3 (New York: Scribners, 1996); Barry Carr, "Lombardo Toledano, Vicente," in Michael S. Werner, ed., *Encyclopedia of Mexico: History, Society, and Culture*, vol. 1 (Chicago: Fitzroy Dearborn, 1997); Carr, *Marxism and Communism in Twentieth-Century Mexico* (Lincoln: University of Nebraska Press, 1992); Enrique Krauze, *Caudillos culturales en la revolución mexicana*, 6th ed. (Mexico, D.F.: Siglo XXI, 1990); Robert P. Millon, *Mexican Marxist: Vicente Lombardo Toledano* (Chapel Hill: University of North Carolina Press, 1966); Martín Tavira Urióstegui, *Vicente Lombardo Toledano: Rasgos*

de la lucha proletario (Mexico, D.F.: Partido Popular Socialista, 1990).

López Mateos, Adolfo (1909–1969) ☀ President of Mexico (1958–1964) whose term coincided with **labor** and student conflicts, the rise of **Fidel Castro** in **Cuba** and the Cuban Revolution, state-sponsored economic development programs, and the beginning of the diversification of Mexico's international relations. The election of Adolfo López Mateos (secretary of labor during the presidency of **Adolfo Ruiz Cortines**) in 1958 broke with the tradition of always choosing the secretary of government as president and began a period in which a postrevolutionary generation of politicians moved into the elitist **Revolutionary Coalition**. López Mateos became the only candidate to win the presidency as secretary of labor.

López Mateos was born in Atizapán de Zaragoza, México state, to a prominent dentist who died when he was quite young. His mother moved the family to Mexico City, and López Mateos attended the Colegio Francés, then moved to Toluca to complete his secondary and preparatory studies. After receiving his law degree from the **Universidad Nacional Autónoma de México (UNAM)** in 1934, he began a career of political activism in which he worked in various government-party, labor, and educational positions. His early political activities, combined with keen oratory skills that he would use later to resolve labor disputes and build support for his cause, helped him advance rapidly within the ruling party. According to Mexican historian **Enrique Krauze** (1997, 626), "He would be the first genuine orator in the history of the modern Mexican presidency." After participating in the failed presidential campaign of **José Vasconcelos** in 1929, López Mateos left the political arena for a time before deciding to link up with the National Revolutionary Party from 1931 to 1933. During the presidency of **Lázaro Cárdenas** (1934–1940), he worked as a labor rep-

President Adolfo López Mateos. Credit: Benson Latin American Collection, University of Texas at Austin.

resentative and served in the secretariat of public education. His close association with **Miguel Alemán Valdés** led to his selection as a candidate for the Senate from his home state in 1946 and secretary of the ruling party in 1951, organizing the successful 1952 presidential campaign of **Adolfo Ruiz Cortines**. He was rewarded for his party-campaign efforts with the position of secretary of labor, a post he used to win the presidential office in 1958 through his skillful management of labor disputes in favor of the government.

In the area of domestic policy, López Mateos pursued a moderate economic path to development, touting the slow, steady enlargement of the economy and the stabilization of the ailing peso. His appointment of **Antonio Ortíz Mena** as treasury secretary began an unprecedented period of economic growth that lasted through two presidential administrations. Part of the economic growth that occurred during his presidency was achieved through the suppression of the Mexican working class and antigovernment rebellions in the countryside. The railroad, teachers, oil workers, and telegraph unions repeatedly clashed with the government, confrontations that often resulted in their imprisonment on charges of "antisocial behavior." The prisons bulged with opponents of the regime, including the last living member of Mexico's famous muralists, **David Alfaro Siqueiros**. Nevertheless, the economic expansion helped produce a growing middle class and greater state participation in the economy through new investments and the opening of new opportunities for local industries. López Mateos nationalized the electricity industry, created the Institute of Social Security and Social Services of State Employees to help the marginalized sectors of society, founded the National Institute for the Protection of Children, and pushed for greater budgetary attention to education, including the distribution of free school textbooks at the primary school level. He renewed the revolutionary emphasis on land reform—in part to repel the threat posed by ex-president Lázaro Cárdenas's praise for the distributional aspects of the Cuban Revolution—distributing more land to *campesinos* than all of his predecessors except Cárdenas.

After the rather insular years of President Ruiz Cortines, López Mateos tried to diversify Mexico's foreign relations. He made many foreign tours in search of commercial markets and invited several foreign heads of state and other foreign dignitaries to visit Mexico. Citing the principles of nonintervention and national sovereignty, President López Mateos expressed support for the Cuban Revolution, in defiance of the hostile U.S. policy toward Castro's government. He opposed the ill-fated Bay of Pigs invasion, refused to join the United States and most of the rest of Latin America in severing relations with Castro's regime, and rejected the resolution to expel Cuba's government from the Organization of American States (OAS), thus continuing the importance of independence in Mexico's **foreign policy**. Despite these differences over Cuba, Mexico's relations with the United States remained cordial under Presidents Eisenhower and Kennedy, and López Mateos managed to negotiate an end to the long-standing **Chamizal Conflict** with the United States over a small piece of border land. President Kennedy and his wife visited Mexico in 1962 and was received by adoring crowds. To further bolster Mexico's image abroad, López Mateos was the prime mover in bringing the 19th Olympic Games to Mexico in the late 1960s.

By the time his *sexenio* ended, López Mateos was able to pass a favorable economic and political situation to his handpicked successor, **Gustavo Díaz Ordáz**, in 1964. After leaving the presidency López Mateos was named president of the Olympic organizing committee. After two years in a vegetative state due to a brain aneurysm, he died prematurely at age 60, one of Mexico's more popular presidents in life and death.

SUGGESTED READING

Héctor Aguilar Camín and Lorenzo Meyer, *In the Shadow of the Mexican Revolution: Contemporary Mexican History, 1910–1989* (Austin: University of Texas Press, 1993); Frank Brandenburg, *The Making of Modern Mexico* (Englewood Cliffs, N.J.: Prentice-Hall, 1964); Roderic Ai Camp, "López Mateos, Adolfo," in Barbara A. Tenenbaum, ed., *Encyclopedia of Latin American History and Culture,* vol. 3 (New York: Scribners, 1996); Enrique Krauze, *Mexico: Biography of Power: A History of Modern Mexico, 1810–1996* (New York: HarperCollins, 1997); Juana Vázquez-Gómez, *Dictionary of Mexican Rulers, 1325–1997* (Westport, Conn.: Greenwood, 1997).

López Portillo y Pacheco, José (1920-) ☀ Mexico's sixth postwar president (1976–1982). José López Portillo presided over the shift from import substitution industrialization economics to "shared development," emphasizing privatization and export-oriented growth. These programs were designed to share the wealth by assisting rural farmers while reducing the quick profits of Mexican industrialists. With the discovery of new oil reserves in the Gulf of Campeche, López Portillo tried to create more wealth for the few who already had it and share the added wealth with the masses.

López Portillo's presidency started with a search for ways to appease the urban middle class and bring about a moral regeneration for the country, but it ended up plagued with public spending extravaganzas, nepotism, and **corruption**. He named his son assistant minister of programming and the budget, often referring to him as "the pride of my nepotism," and appointed his young and beautiful mistress minister of **tourism**. He also named his sister, Margarita López Portillo, to head the government agency in charge of radio, television, and **cinema**. Not satisfied with the content of Mexican films, she decided to eliminate almost all state-sponsored film production, leaving the production, exhibition, and distribution of films to the private sector. It was a tragic period for Mexico's best filmmakers, with some directors forced to work for the private sector doing soap operas and others giving up altogether and never directing another film. Throughout his administration, President López Portillo's desire for power and his need to display macho dominance clearly outpaced his ability to conduct the affairs of state.

López Portillo was born on June 16, 1920, in Mexico City to a distinguished Guadalajara family that traces its roots back 400 years to a small village in Spain. His father, José López Portillo y Weber, was an engineer and prominent historian until his death in 1974. López Portillo attended state-run schools in Mexico City, including the **Universidad Nacional Autónoma de México (UNAM)**. He traveled to Chile with **Luis Echeverría** to study law at the University of Santiago, sealing a friendship that continued for decades. From the time he received his law degree from UNAM in 1950 until his appointment to minor positions in the presidency of **Adolfo López Mateos,** he showed little interest in politics,

President José López Portillo. Credit: *Proceso,* photo by Germán Canseco.

a trait attributed to his wealthy and aristocratic background.

While his childhood friend and classmate Luis Echeverría went immediately into politics, López Portillo became a professor of politics at UNAM, where he taught courses in political science, law, and public administration, and practiced law. Until President Echeverría appointed him secretary of the treasury in 1973, López Portillo's career languished in relatively unimportant political posts. Because of his lack of political experience and the fact that no finance minister had made it to the presidency in this century, López Portillo was considered a long-shot candidate for the presidency in 1976. President Echeverría's unexpected selection of his former classmate raised suspicions that he might try to maintain political influence after leaving office. However, after being handpicked by Echeverría as the **Partido Revolucionario Institucional (PRI)** choice for president in 1976, López Portillo's strong personality soon dispelled rumors of this form of political influence.

The legitimacy of the PRI's governing ability was marred by the fact that López Portillo was forced to run unopposed because every opposition candidate boycotted the election. With the country in political crisis by the time he assumed office in late 1976, López Portillo confronted a host of political and economic crises, beginning a long cycle of national problems that lasted well into the 1990s. His silence after winning the July 4, 1976, election and the growing uncertainty in the ability of López Portillo to reverse the economic slide of his predecessor's administration prompted rumors of a military coup or an organized attempt by Echeverría to retain power. Promising less populism and demagoguery, President López Portillo began his term emphasizing efficiency, organization, and increased productivity in both the government and private sectors in an effort to repair the damaged relations with the alienated business leadership. He ended his term by nationalizing the domestically owned banking industry, blaming the private sector and greedy bankers for Mexico's economic mess.

López Portillo's domestic difficulties were so immediate that the new president put less emphasis on **foreign policy** and abandoned former president Echeverría's campaign for a "new world economic order." Nevertheless, he continued to emphasize the basic principles—nonintervention and national sovereignty—of Mexico's foreign policy. He maintained an "open door" policy for Latin American leftist exiles, particularly those seeking asylum from dictatorships in Argentina, Chile, and Uruguay. López Portillo supported the Sandinistas in Nicaragua and the right of Panamanians to complete sovereignty over the Canal Zone. He was also sympathetic to the aims of the guerrilla opposition movement in El Salvador.

After his *sexenio* expired, López Portillo retired from public life and began living abroad (largely because of his unpopularity), devoting his time to writing his memoirs (*Mis tiempos: Biografía y testimonio político*, 1988) and works of fiction dealing with pre-Hispanic Mexican history.

SUGGESTED READING

Jorge G. Castañeda, *La herencia: Arqueología de la sucesión en México* (Mexico, D.F.: Editorial Alfaguara, 1999); Daniel Levy and Gabriel Székely, *Mexico: Paradoxes of Stability and Change*, 2d ed. (Boulder, Colo.: Westview, 1987); José López Portillo, *Mis tiempos: Biografía y testimonio político* (Mexico, D.F.: Fernández, 1988).

López y Fuentes, Gregorio (1892–1966) ☀ Journalist and novelist best known for *El Indio* (1935), a dramatic demonstration of the misery and exploitation of Indians in the wake of the **Mexican Revolution**. Born in Veracruz, López y Fuentes grew up with farmhands and Indians and developed an intense understanding of the plight of the rural poor. He studied to be a teacher in Mexico City but soon realized that he wanted to devote his life to writing. In his efforts to depict the specific reality of Mexico, López y Fuentes placed his narratives in rural areas that included new heroes of the national epic: poor farmers, revolutionary soldiers (both female and male), and Indians. In *Campamento* (1931), his first important novel, López y Fuentes takes the reader through a number of sketches of what occurs among various groups of revolutionary soldiers in a camp at night. He portrays the role of **Emiliano Zapata** and the nature of the agrarian revolution in *Tierra* (1932), a dramatic portrayal of the conflict between powerful and ruthless landowners (backed by corrupt politicians, the military, and the Catholic Church) and peasants struggling to survive in wretched poverty. In his most famous novel, *El Indio* (1935), the plight of the indigenous populations reflects the ideals of the reforms of President **Lázaro Cárdenas,** in which Indian traditions and customs are poetic and pure, victims of an evil society. He continued to write books of fiction that depict the lives of peasants, Indians, and rural migrants until his death in 1966 at the age of 74. *See also Indigenismo.*

SUGGESTED READING

John S. Brushwood, *Mexico in Its Novel: A Nation's Search for Identity* (Austin: University of Texas Press, 1966); Peter Standish, ed., *Dictionary of Twentieth-Century Culture: Hispanic Culture of Mexico, Central America, and the Caribbean* (Detroit: Gale, 1996).

Los Pinos. *See* Metropolitan Cathedral (Catedral Metropolitana), National Palace, and Los Pinos.

Machismo ☀ Mexico is well known for having a culture—brought to the Americas by Spanish soldiers during the 16th century—that extols manliness in all its manifestations. In its Mexicanized form, someone who is *muy macho* (a complete man) signifies courage, heroism, and a particular attitude toward women, life, death, and drinking alcoholic beverages. The number of Spanish men who had access to women of their own race was quite small during the colonial period, and this resulted in the sexual exploitation of indigenous women. The major characteristics of machismo, often referred to as the cult of virility, are exaggerated aggressiveness and intransigence in male-to-male relationships, along with sexual aggression and exploitation in male-to-female relationships.

However, in today's Mexican culture, machismo is a multifaceted trait with both positive and negative behaviors. The more exaggerated (and negative) forms are often attributed to the lower classes, while the more positive characteristics are associated with the upper classes. Machismo can also influence the legislative process, where male legislators tend to ignore key policy areas like education, health, and labor because they are considered "feminine issues." Mexican politicians are expected to be aggressive and intransigent, giving the impression of toughness in dealing with party adversaries and other opponents. The Mexican *charro*—the singing cowboy protagonist popular in golden-age Mexican **cinema**—represents a combination of machismo, exaggerated nationalism, sexuality, heroism, and honor, made famous in the box-office success of *Allá en el Rancho Grande* and other *charro* films of the 1940s and 1950s. Singing cowboy **Jorge Negrete** was known

as the consummate macho of Mexican movies during the golden age.

Someone who is called *muy macho* has learned to express his virility by completely dominating his wife and children, having sexual relations with any woman he wants, and refusing to let anyone question, disapprove, or attempt to interfere with his manhood. The term *machismo* is often considered a form of sexual discrimination in Mexico, since it sanctions male behavior over that of the female. The macho man never reveals his true feelings to anyone lest they somehow take advantage of him. A Mexican male who does not pay enough attention to his masculinity runs the risk of being referred to as impotent, bewitched, a **homosexual**, or a sissy. Maintaining manliness in Mexico is vital, as nonmasculine (or homosexual) behavior is ridiculed and condemned. Among lower-class men, bragging and refusing to take no for an answer are also symptoms of macho behavior, especially when they are drinking among male companions. Psychological studies of machismo reveal that fathers who abandon their families tend to have a negative affect on young male sex-role identification, often leading to patterns of exaggerated masculinity and antisocial behavior. Machismo is a contributing factor in the large number of illegitimate births, abortions, irresponsible fatherhood, spousal abandonment, and single motherhood in Mexico.

Mexican machismo is often considered an ambivalent practice of debasing and glorifying women. Some psychologists in Mexico argue that machismo is largely a reaction to the powerful Catholic veneration of the Virgin Mary (in Mexico this takes the form of worship of the "Indian"

Virgin of Guadalupe) and the vision of one's mother as a saintly person uncontaminated by eroticism. While the mother becomes the model for a wife, in real life the wife can never match the mother's perfection in the eyes of most Mexican men. Thus machismo in Mexico offers the paradox that men's efforts to reinforce and exaggerate their masculinity are often guided and controlled by a woman. When women are considered inferior and unworthy of respect—particularly among the country's poorly educated farmers and slum dwellers—family planning and contraception are unheard of, wife beating is widespread, and male virility depends on fathering as many children as possible, whether by a wife, a mistress, or other conquests the macho male has found in his day-to-day life. Mexican sexologists have written that machismo is the result of a deep-seated fear of latent homosexuality, stemming from the prevailing influence of the Catholic Church.

In recent years, some of the most acute manifestations of machismo have declined as Mexican women have made a concerted effort to remove or diminish the more harmful aspects of sexual aggression and overt machismo of Mexican men. During the administration of President **Luis Echeverría**, indirect efforts to combat machismo were carried out by a new birth control policy, as well as numerous programs to bolster the family unit and support women. Despite some legislative advances, Mexican law still favors men. For example, under the Mexican civil code a man can divorce his wife if she commits adultery, but a wife can only divorce an adulterous husband if the act took place in their home, if there is a public scandal, or if he insults her. Wife beating is illegal in Mexico, but it remains common throughout the country. In what recently has become a sort of "billboard war," Mexican women have mobilized opposition to the large billboards that have appeared in major cities showing blond models clad only in bra and panties. Protesting that the Vicky Form ads are degrading to women and invite more sexual aggression in a macho society, Mexican women have successfully used interest group politics to engineer political change at the local level. Within the past two decades, Mexican social commentators have noticed that patriarchal machismo has declined in many areas and that the gay and lesbian movement has had a slight impact on breaking the social taboos against questioning traditional views of machismo.

During the last week of the 2000 presidential campaign, the two leading candidates engaged in macho mudslinging by attacking each other's masculinity in television ads and stump speeches. However, this campaign rhetoric brought a strong negative reaction throughout the country, leading the two candidates (and their parties) to issue apologies and retractions in the news media. Until legislative and educational measures are taken to combat the negative affects of machismo and elevate the status of women, the Mexican family will continue to suffer from existing models of gender behavior. *See also* Feminism.

SUGGESTED READING

David T. Abalos, *The Latino Male: A Radical Redefinition* (Boulder, Colo.: Lynne Rienner, 2001); David D. Gilmore, *Manhood in the Making: Cultural Concepts of Masculinity* (New Haven: Yale University Press, 1990); Marvin Goldwert, *Machismo and Conquest: The Case of Mexico* (Lanham, Md.: University Press of America, 1983); Ray González, ed., *Muy Macho: Latin Men Confront Their Manhood* (New York: Anchor, 1996); Matthew C. Gutmann, *The Meanings of Macho: Being a Man in Mexico City* (Berkeley: University of California Press, 1996); Ian Lumsden, *Homosexuality, Society, and the State in Mexico* (Toronto: Canadian Gay Archives, 1991); Annick Prieur, *Mema's House, Mexico City: On Machos, Queens, and Transvestites* (Chicago: University of

Chicago Press, 1998); Darío Salaz, "Machismo: Cult of the Superman," *Mexican World* (February 1970); Violeta Sara-Lafosse, "Machismo in Latin America and the Caribbean," in Nelly P. Stromquist, ed., *Women in the Third World: An Encyclopedia of Contemporary Issues* (New York: Garland, 1998).

Madrazo, Carlos A. (1915–1969) ☀ An early effort to reform the **Partido Revolucionario Institucional (PRI)** came from within the ruling party by PRI president Carlos Madrazo, who tried unsuccessfully to introduce more grassroots control over the candidate selection process. While Madrazo was able to implement his reforms in seven states, his efforts were ultimately defeated by PRI conservatives and he was forced to resign by President **Gustavo Díaz Ordaz** in 1969. PRI *dinosaurios* blamed him for the 1968 student uprising, and when he was killed in a commercial plane crash in 1969, many suspected foul play among the party's elite. Madrazo's failure to reform the PRI from within, as well as the advancing rigidity and old age of the political system, led to the increase in political agitation, **labor** militancy, nongovernmental organizations, and even guerrilla warfare that have plagued Mexico since the 1970s. Until the drive to democratize the ruling party became more intense in the early years of the **Carlos Salinas** administration, Madrazo's efforts were reduced to nothing more than a traumatic memory. His association with the Mexican left made him a controversial figure in Mexican political circles.

Born in Villahermosa, Tabasco, in 1915, Carlos Madrazo received his early schooling in his home state before traveling to Mexico City, where he attended preparatory school and law school at the **Universidad Nacional Autónoma de México (UNAM)** in 1937. His legal background and interest in politics drew him to the ruling party and a lifelong career as a politician and political reformer. Associated with the progressive groups on the left, Madrazo began his career with an active role (he was a mesmerizing speaker) in student politics in Tabasco. He became a member of the Federation of Socialist Students of Tabasco in 1933–1935 and president of the Federation of Mexican Youth in 1939. Between 1943 and 1969, he was a federal deputy (1943–1946), president of the National Executive Council of the PRI (1954–1965), governor of Tabasco (1959–1964), and president of the PRI (1968–1969). While serving in the national Chamber of Deputies in the 1940s, he developed a friendship with Gustavo Díaz Ordaz, later president of Mexico (1964–1970).

Carlos Madrazo's early interest in leftist politics contributed to his determination to create more competition—internal elections, criticism, and self-criticism among different political currents and options—that characterizes a modern democratic party. Although he quickly gained the support of the young reformers within the PRI and achieved national attention with his fiery speeches against PRI stalwarts, he was never able to convince the old guard that his bottom-up reforms were necessary to revitalize the ruling party.

A controversial figure in modern Mexican political life, Madrazo's forceful battles to make the PRI more democratic and independent remain symbols of the struggles to transform the ruling party. His two sons—Carlos and Roberto—have both taken up where his father left off, using the PRI as a vehicle for climbing the ladder to political power in Mexico. Roberto Madrazo ran in the November 1999 PRI primary elections, winning 29 percent of the party vote while coming in second behind the winner, **Francisco Labastida**.

SUGGESTED READING

John Bailey, *Governing Mexico: The Statecraft of Crisis Management* (New York: St. Martin's, 1988); Roderic Ai Camp, *Mexican Political Biographies, 1935–1993*, 3d ed. (Austin: University of Texas Press, 1995); Raúl Cruz Zapata, *Carlos A. Madrazo: Biografía Política* (Mexico, D.F.: Editorial Diana, 1988).

Madrid Hurtado, Miguel de la. *See* de la Madrid Hurtado, Miguel.

Malinche, La (1495?–1527?), and Malinchismo ☀
Woman who served as interpreter for Hernán Cortés in his conquest of Mexico and later gave birth to a son by the famous conquistador. Born in Veracruz around 1495 to an Aztec governor, she was baptized Marina and given the nickname La Malinche. She is also known as Malintzin (in Nahuatl the termination *tzin* denotes nobility). As beautiful as she was intelligent, La Malinche is regarded by many as the major factor in Cortés's successful conquest of Mexico because she played a key role as an interpreter and adviser to the Spaniards, which enabled Cortés to easily capture and destroy the Aztec empire.

A controversial and long-lasting mythology has been constructed around La Malinche. Historians do not agree on many features of her biography, including her actual name and heritage, place and date of birth, and accounts of her life before the arrival of the Spaniards. Between the time she was given to Cortés in 1519 to the time she gave birth to her master's son, Martín Cortés, in 1524, she served as the conquistador's interpreter, guide, and companion. Although she was recognized as "legitimate" by Cortés, they

Malinche II, 1994. Lithograph by Tita Guizar Griesbach depicting Juan Xaramillo and La Malinche, Hernán Cortés and his wife, and the king and queen of Spain (top). Credit: Tita Guizar Griesbach.

never married, and during an expedition to Honduras between 1524 and 1526 Cortés married her to Juan Jaramillo. While married to Jaramillo, she had a daughter named María.

It is hard to overestimate the value of La Malinche's role in the conquest of Mexico by the Spaniards. In addition to her function as a translator of Indian languages—she spoke Nahuatl (the language of the Aztecs and many other cultures of central Mexico) and Maya (the language of the people from the Yucatán region)—Malinche possessed critical information about the Aztecs and the political systems of central Mexico that was indispensable to the formation of alliances with the traditional enemies of the Aztec empire. Her special linguistic skills and her close collaboration with Cortés gave him a tremendous advantage in dealing with the ill-fated indigenous groups.

The portrayal of La Malinche in Mexican folklore has changed over the centuries, offering insights into the development of Mexican nationalist ideologies. By some accounts La Malinche was portrayed as an intelligent and powerful woman commanding great respect. After all, couldn't she be considered the mother of the first **mestizo**? However, during the Independence period she became known as a prostitute, traitor, or scapegoat for centuries of colonization. The more recent focus on La Malinche's "willful betrayal" centers on her involvement in the events leading up to the Spanish massacre of the people of Cholula and her role in the interrogation of the last Aztec ruler, Cuauhtémoc, before the fall of Teotihuacán. As someone who sold out to foreign invaders, La Malinche was transformed into a negative character trait.

A *malinchista* is someone in Mexico who is considered to have been "corrupted" by foreign influence, such as speaking a lot of English and preferring objects that are foreign rather than Mexican. For example, a public official in Mexico who kowtows to Washington for the benefit of the United States may be called a *malinchista*. Linda Chávez, neoconservative president of One Nation Indivisible, one of several organizations in the United States behind the English Only movement, has been called "La Malinche" by **Chicanos** who favor bilingual education in schools.

The theme of *malinchismo* appears often in 20th-century literature. For example, La Malinche's betrayal identifies her with *la chingada* (the violated one) in **Octavio Paz**'s *El laberinto de la solidad* (1950). According to Paz, the alienation and solitude endured by the Mexican is the result of the initial betrayal, thus the openness of the female makes her suspect and open to attack while the male must be closed to protect himself from outside penetration or run the risk of being considered less than a man. Novelist **Carlos Fuentes** focuses on the encounter of Cortés and the Aztec monarch Montezuma II, mediated by La Malinche, in one of his best-known plays, *Todos los gatos son pardos* (All cats are gray, 1970). More recently, Mexican and Mexican American women writers and artists have sought La Malinche's redemption by arguing that as a slave she was not free to oppose Spanish control, the persistent misogynist perceptions so common in Mexican folklore are incorrect, and themes of strength and intelligence deserve greater attention in the historical literature.

La Malinche died at a young age in Mexico City, most likely from smallpox or some other disease brought to Mexico by European invaders. *See also* Feminism.

SUGGESTED READING

Roger Bartra, *The Cage of Melancholy: Identity and Metamorphosis in the Mexican Character*, trans. Christopher J. Hall (New Brunswick, N.J.: Rutgers University Press, 1992); Sandra Messinger Cypess, *La Malinche in Mexican Literature: From History to Myth* (Austin: University of Texas Press, 1991); Joanne Hershfield, *Mexican Cinema/Mexican Woman,*

1940–1950 (Tucson: University of Arizona Press, 1996); Miguel León-Portilla, ed., *The Broken Spears: The Aztec Account of the Conquest of Mexico* (Boston: Beacon, 1992); Fernanda Nuñez Becerra, *La Malinche: De la historia al mito* (Mexico, D.F.: Instituto Nacional de Antropología e Historia, 1996); José Rabasa, "Malinche," in Barbara A. Tenenbaum, ed., *Encyclopedia of Latin American History and Culture*, vol. 3 (New York: Scribners, 1996).

Maquiladoras ☀ The use of export-driven assembly plants was started in the 1960s to relieve mass unemployment along the border caused by the termination of the **bracero program** in 1964. As part of the Border Industrialization Program (BIP), a bilateral effort was made to solve the problem of industrial growth in the border region. With the consent of the Mexican and American governments, foreign companies were allowed to establish a factory in one of the *maquilas,* or work processing zones. The original meaning of the word *maquila* goes back to colonial Mexico, when a portion of grain, flour, or oil was kept by the miller in exchange for his services. A *Maquiladora* was the place where the milling was done and the finished product was called *maquila.* Attracted by the promise of cheap Mexican **labor** (mostly young females), in 1965 the *maquila* industry established the first "in-bond" or "twin" plants to assemble goods for export to the U.S. market.

Beginning in 1965, *maquiladoras* could be 100 percent foreign owned and customs procedures were eased to promote industrial parks, first along the **U.S.–Mexican border** and later in the interior. Globalization of the world economy has made it possible to divide manufacturing processes into those that are capital- and technology-intensive and those that are labor-intensive. Taking advantage of the Mexican law allowing machinery, components, and supplies to be imported duty-free as long as the finished product is exported and of the cheap Mexican labor, the *maquiladora* option created a large magnet for United States, Japanese, and Southeast Asian manufacturers to become more profitable and competitive. Despite the **debt crisis**, depression, and the devaluation of the peso, *maquiladora* assembly plants continue to spiral upward in border cities such as Tijuana, Ciudad Juárez, Mexicali, Matamoros, Reynosa, and others. The *maquiladoras* are a paradox of Mexican development since they continue to grow at a phenomenal rate (30 percent in 1995) while the rest of the Mexican economy overall shrinks (–6.9 percent in 1995).

As of 2001, 3,600 *maquiladoras*—including such U.S. corporate giants as Dell Computer, Ford Motor, General Electric, and United Technologies—were operating in Mexico, an export industry that in 2000 was growing at a rate of 14–15 percent a year. Japanese companies with in-bond plants along the border include Canon, Casio, Kyocera, Matsushita, Pioneer, and Toshiba. There are also numerous Korean companies, including Lucky-Goldstar and Samsung. Altogether, the *maquiladoras* employed more than 1.3 million people in 2001, many of whom have migrated north from the poorer interior to find work at an average daily wage of $10.00.

From the beginning, *maquiladoras* have been economically, politically, and socially controversial. North American critics claim they undercut American industry by exporting jobs to Mexico and making it possible for U.S. industries to produce cheaper goods in Mexico and then import them back to the United States to sell at cheaper prices than local companies can afford. The main reason for cheaper labor in Mexico is that *maquiladoras* employ young girls and women (mostly unmarried with only a basic education) to work long hours doing tedious tasks. Many Mexicans were highly critical of the first *maquiladoras* because of the low wages and unsafe working conditions. After facing more and more competition from incoming plants, employers altered their approach and started paying higher wages, improving the workplace, and offering better benefits. Despite these improvements, workers still complain of health problems, sexual harassment, and other forms of discrimination. Young women in such a large workforce live in constant danger of violence, including murder, rape, and intimidation. **Environmentalists** have accused the *maquiladoras* of polluting the air and soil in the vicinity of their plants and dumping harmful chemicals into streams and rivers along the border. Serious infrastructure and social problems have been created by the massive influx of workers who have moved north in search of jobs, only to be forced to live in slums or *colonias* on the outskirts of cities such as Tijuana, Reynosa, Acuña, and Ciudad Juárez. Others argue that *maquiladoras* have not produced significant transfers of technology and are not well integrated with the Mexican economy.

Despite the criticisms of the *maquila* sector, they are large, increasingly diversified, and successful (particularly for the transnational corporations), and they are not likely to be dismantled in an age of increasing globalization and free trade. Moreover, proponents of *maquiladoras* point to numerous benefits of the growing export-driven assembly plants, including job creation, technology transfer, worker satisfaction, and increased amounts of foreign exchange for the Mexican economy. Any future effort to measure the impact of the *maquiladoras*, in the United States or Mexico, is bound to be subject to an emotional debate over issues that are complex and difficult to measure with any degree of empirical precision. With thousands of well-paid U.S. business executives and their families relocating to border cities like Laredo, Brownsville, and McAllen—and commuting to their jobs across the border—it easy to see how some reap the rewards of living in two worlds while millions live in a squalid grid of dirt streets, substandard housing, schools, health clinics, and pollution. *See also* Geographical Regions; North American Free Trade Agreement (NAFTA).

SUGGESTED READING

Altha J. Cravey, *Women and Work in Mexico's Maquiladoras* (Lanham, Md.: Rowman & Littlefield, 1998); David W. Eaton, *Transformation of the Mexican Maquila Industry: The Driving Force behind the Creation of a NAFTA Regional Economy* (Tucson, Ariz.: National Law Center for Inter-American Free Trade, 1997); Kathryn Kopinak, *Desert Capitalism: Maquiladoras in North America's Western Industrial Corridor* (Tucson: University of Arizona Press, 1996); Leslie Sklair, *Assembling for Development: The Maquila Industry in Mexico and the United States* (La Jolla: Center for U.S.–Mexican Studies, University of California–San Diego, 1993).

Marcos, Subcomandante. *See* Subcommander Marcos.

Mariachis. *See* Music (Popular).

Massacre of Tlatelolco. *See* Tlatelolco Massacre.

Mata, Eduardo (1942–1995) ☀ One of Mexico's most celebrated symphonic directors and composers. Eduardo Mata built a career in music that brought him fame and fortune on both sides of the border. Born in Mexico City in 1942, Mata began his music studies with Rodolfo Halffter at the National Conservatory of Music from 1954 to 1960; from 1960 to 1965 he took lessons in composition and conducting with **Carlos Chávez.** He studied conducting at the Berkshire Center in Tanglewood, Massachusetts, in 1964, before starting his conducting career with the Guadalajara Symphony Orchestra that same year. Two years later Mata became music director and conductor of the Orquesta Filarmónica of the **Universidad Nacional Autónoma de México (UNAM)** in Mexico City, a position he held until 1975. In 1975–1976 he became director of the National Symphony in Mexico City while directing international music festivals in the nation's capital. He then moved to the United States, where he was conductor and musical adviser to the Symphony Orchestra of Phoenix, Arizona (1970–1978) and music director of the Dallas Symphony Orchestra (1977–1994). Beginning in 1989 he served as the principal guest conductor of the Pittsburgh Symphony. Mata recorded numerous top-quality albums with some of the world's leading symphonic orchestras. His many awards include the Golden Lyre Award (Mexico, 1974), the Elías Sourasky Prize in the Arts (Mexico, 1975), the Mozart Medal (conferred by the President **Carlos Salinas** in 1991), and the White House Hispanic Heritage Award (conferred by President George H. W. Bush in 1991). Until he was killed in a January 1995 plane crash near Mexico City, Eduardo Mata was one of Mexico's most accomplished conductors and one of the most prominent Hispanic Americans in the United States.

SUGGESTED READING

Miguel Ficher, Martha Furman Schleifer, and John M. Furman, eds., *Latin American Classical Composers: A Biographical Dictionary* (Lanham, Md.: Scarecrow, 1996).

Media. *See* Communications Media.

Mestizo and *Mestizaje* ☀ One of the important legacies of the 300-year Spanish colonial experience is the term *mestizo,* used commonly in Mexico to refer to persons of mixed white European and Indian descent. The assimilation of indigenous people into mestizo culture is referred to as *mestizaje,* and it can include racial mixing between Spaniards (or in more modern times other Europeans) and the Indian populations.

Unlike most British colonists who came to North America with their entire families in pursuit of a new life, Spaniards often left their women behind. Thus it was only a matter of months after the Spanish conquistadors set foot on Mexican soil that the first mestizo (Spanish Indian) was born. With large numbers of illegitimate mestizos, the two terms (*illegitimate* and *mestizo*) were often used

interchangeably, and pejoratively, during the colonial period in Mexico. Although the majority of Mexico's 100 million people are considered mestizos, there are still a large number of Indians, from the Tarahumaras in the north to the Mayans in the south. Figures from the National Indigenous Institute (INI) put the Indian population, consisting of more than 50 Indian groups, somewhere between 8.7 and 12 million, speaking 68 languages and living in over 44,000 communities throughout Mexico.

Mexican folklore attributes the first mestizo birth to La **Malinche,** or Doña Marina, an Aztec woman given by her parents to Hernán Cortés and later reviled as someone who betrayed her race. However, in more recent feminist literature, the role of La Malinche has been revised to stress that what she did was not a traitorous act but one over which she had little control.

In the Spanish colonial caste system of ranking racial groups, mestizos were positioned above blacks and Indians but considered a subspecies under Spaniards and creoles (Spaniards born in the New World). Until the 19th century, mestizos were considered to have a stigma attached to them because of their mixed-race status and often found it difficult, if not impossible, to achieve leadership positions in society. The social status of mestizos began to improve with the independence movement (1810–1821) and the effort by Mexican intellectuals to praise the strength and patriotism of the mestizo, based on the premise that the mixed-blooded population of the Americas composed a superior blend of cultural and genetic factors.

The **Mexican Revolution**—led mostly by mestizo revolutionary military and political leaders—helped create a mythology of a whole national identity based on the fusion of the great European (Spanish) heritage with the rugged and praiseworthy Indian races of pre-Columbian Mexico. As head of the Ministry of Public Education (SEP) in the 1920s, philosopher **José Vasconcelos** championed the mestizo—what he called in his best-known essay, "La raza cósmica" (1925), a superior fifth race (a combination of Spanish and Indian descent) that will confront the Anglo-Saxon race in the future. He was the prime mover behind Mexico's official Indian policy, or **indigenismo**, placing a great deal of faith in education to form a mestizo nation by celebrating racial miscegenation. Those who were the victors in the revolutionary struggle wanted to prevent the outbreaks of violence and chaos that characterized the past by building a new national (mestizo) identity that represented the future. According to Lewis (1997, 839), "Once Mexicans felt that they shared a common heroic past, common obligations as citizens, and a common destiny, it was thought [by the revolutionary leaders], they would subsume their local, regional, clientelist, class, and a lasting peace could be achieved." Proponents of _mestizaje_ believed that it would help overcome national differences and achieve political hegemony. However, over the past three decades indigenous groups have begun to challenge the commonly held assertion that _mestizaje_ represented the only authentic Mexican.

After building a nation on the foundation of _mestizaje_ for most of the 20th century, it was not easy to shift from mestizo revolutionary nationalism to a nonmestizo national identity. However, in 1992 President **Carlos Salinas**, in response to pressures from national and international human rights observers, helped to amend Article 4 of the **Constitution of 1917** to read: "The Mexican Nation has a pluricultural composition, originally based on its indigenous peoples. The law will protect and promote the development of their languages, cultures, . . . customs, resources and . . . social organization and will guarantee their members effective access to the jurisdiction of the state." While the constitutional language would suggest a serious recognition of the Indians' claim to Mexican national identity, the Salinas reform remains more symbolic than legally binding. The

recent indigenous uprisings in the heavily populated Indian states would seem to suggest that those who are still in charge of the postrevolutionary state are still committed to a Mexico that reflects _mestizaje_ rather than one with a pluricultural composition.

The multicultural composition of Mexico makes it difficult to determine one particular mestizo physiognomy. Since the term _mestizo_ has multiple meanings and interpretations, it is hard to use it to denote racial characteristics (e.g., "Indian-looking") only. There is a mestizaje culture associated with a way of life, character, language, and so on. What this means in Mexican society is that mestizo status suggests not only a particular racial component but also a cultural, political, and economic distinction. There are also basic differences between the attitudes of Indians and mestizos in modern Mexico. In general, the Indian tends to be stoic and accept things passively, while believing that one must come to terms with life and the universe; the mestizo is determined to dominate things and control life. The Indian is community oriented and capable of subjugating his ego; the mestizo is aggressively individualistic and glories in his vibrant personality and the feeling that comes from being _muy macho_, someone with guts and bravado who bows to no one. Although mestizo Mexicans make up about 60 percent of the national population, they are more likely to think of themselves as simply "Mexicans" rather than a racial blend of Spaniards and Indians. Nevertheless, according to Slick (1997, 542), "It is in Mexico where the mestizo and _mestizaje_ are most heralded."

SUGGESTED READING

Jane Hindley, "Toward a Pluricultural Nation: The Limits of Indigenismo and Article 4," in Rob Aitken et al., _Dismantling the Mexican State?_ (New York: St. Martin's, 1996); Alan Knight, "Race, Revolution, and Indigenismo: Mexico, 1910–1940," in Richard Graham, ed., _The Idea of Race in Latin America_ (Austin:

University of Texas Press, 1990); Stephen E. Lewis, "Mestizaje," in Michael S. Werner, ed., *Encyclopedia of Mexico: History, Society, and Culture*, vol. 2 (Chicago: Fitzroy Dearborn, 1997); Sam L. Slick, "Mestizo," in Verity Smith, ed., *Encyclopedia of Latin American Literature* (Chicago: Fitzroy Dearborn, 1997); John Wilcock and Kal Müller, eds., *Insight Guides: Mexico* (Boston: Houghton Mifflin, 1996).

Metropolitan Cathedral (Catedral Metropolitana, National Palace, and Los Pinos) ☀ The Metropolitan Cathedral, considered to be the largest church in the Americas, is located on the north side of the Zócalo in the historic center of Mexico City. It was started in 1525 but some 50 years later was demolished to make way for the present structure, which took 240 years to complete. The exterior represents a mixture of architectural styles, from baroque to neoclassical. Adjoining the cathedral is El Sagrario (Sacristy), a parish church with a Churrigueresque facade that was originally built to house vestments and sacred relics. Both structures were damaged in the 1985 earthquake and are undergoing interior and exterior renovations.

Metropolitan Cathedral and National Palace. Credit: General Secretariat of the Organization of American States.

On the south side of the Metropolitan Cathedral is the National Palace (Palacio Nacional), the monolithic, ever-present symbol of state power. The palace's original structure was built with slave labor by Hernán Cortés on the site of Aztec emperor Moctezuma's palace. After being destroyed by anti-Spanish mobs in 1692, it was rebuilt and from 1698 to 1821 served as the official residence of the viceroys. The National Palace contains two government ministries—Treasury and Presidential Planning—and a museum honoring former liberal president Benito Juárez. However, the main attraction of the National Palace is the series of murals by **Diego Rivera** with scenes of major milestones in Mexican history.

Ironically, neither the Mexican president nor members of Congress use the National Palace. While the president resides in Los Pinos (the Mexican "White House")—located in Chapultepec Park—every year he returns to the National Palace on September 16 to proclaim (*El Grito Presidential*) once again the independence of Mexico from the main balcony of the *palacio*, a brief but emotional ceremony where everyone yells "Viva Mexico! Viva la independencia!" In an effort to change the aloof and authoritarian image of the Mexican president, President **Vicente Fox** opened Los Pinos to visitors and reduced the number of armed guards at the Mexican White House.

Mexican Air Squadron 201. *See* Escuadrón de Pelea 201.

Mexican Americans. *See* Chicanos; *Pachucos*; *Pochos*.

Mexican American War (1846–1848) ☀ American Westward expansion in the 1840s led to a war with Mexico, the only time the United States has declared war against a Latin American country. After the United States annexed Texas in 1845, the newly elected U.S. President James K. Polk wanted to acquire California, at the time a large province of Mexico. Worried about British and French designs on Mexico, President Polk at first tried to get Mexico to negotiate away its northwest territories, but the confused and disorganized Mexicans rejected all offers. With strong currents of anti-Mexican racism growing in the United States, Polk increased the pressure on Mexico until a minor provocation near the **U.S.–Mexican border** gave him the necessary justification to send U.S. forces into Mexican territory. Mexico was no match for the United States, since the nation was deeply divided politically and torn by strife; its army was poorly equipped and had little training for war. Many critics considered the war a shameless act of aggression to acquire more territory on behalf of the southern "slavocracy." The brutal and unjust nature of the war contributed to the highest desertion rate in U.S. military history. Fully 13 percent of the regular army and thousands of draftees left and did not return.

U.S. forces captured the coastal town of Veracruz, and General Winfield Scott led the attack on Mexico City in 1847. After a fierce three-week siege of the capital, the final battle of the war (a brutal massacre) took place at Chapultepec Castle, defended by a few Mexican troops and the now famous "boy heroes" (*los niños héroes*) who are reported to have fought bravely, jumping to their death from a parapet wrapped in the **flag of Mexico** rather than surrender to Scott's invading forces. The final *day* of the war killed 1,800 Mexicans and 450 Americans, culminating in the massacre of the boy cadets on the castle grounds.

The brutality of the war was also evident in the treatment of the San Patricio Battalion, an estimated 500 Irish soldiers who defected to the losing side. Survivors from the Battle of Churubusco were charged with defection and had their faces branded with D for defector; 52 San Patricios had ropes fastened around their necks by U.S. troops and were forced to watch the final bloody assault on Chapultepec hill. After being told by the U.S. Army that they could live only until the American flag was raised, signaling victory over the hapless Mexicans, they were hanged and left to die in the hot sun. In U.S. textbooks covering the war, the San Patricios are largely forgotten, while in Mexico the Irish immigrants to America are revered as war heroes along with the *niños héroes*.

American troops occupied Mexico City and did not leave until May 1848 after Mexico had ratified the onerous Treaty of Guadalupe Hidalgo, "which ceded to the United States 55 percent of Mexican territory (including present-day California, Arizona, New Mexico, Texas, and parts of Colorado, Nevada, and Utah). In return the United States paid Mexico $15 million and assumed responsibility for $3.5 million in claims against the Mexican government by U.S. citizens" (Dent 1999, 262–63). Nicholas Trist, U.S. State Department official and chief negotiator, later recalled how he felt as he signed the treaty ending the war: "Could those Mexicans have seen into my heart at that moment, they would have known that my feeling of shame as an American was far stronger than theirs could be as Mexicans. [The Treaty of Guadalupe Hidalgo] was a thing for every right-minded American to be ashamed of." The humiliating defeat traumatized the Mexican psyche, and there was deep resentment over imperialistic U.S. designs.

The war cost the United States $100 million and 15,000 lives (1,733 were deaths from battle; the others died of tropical diseases or simply disappeared), but many in Washington considered the price very low for what the United States had achieved: a vast amount of territory, valuable resources (including the discovery of gold in California in 1849), and a continental power base stretching from the Atlantic to the Pacific Oceans. (Dent 1999, 263)

Mexico lost more than 50,000 in the Mexican American War.

President Polk's imperialistic muscle-flexing confirmed the dogma of Manifest Destiny and established the Polk Corollary to the Monroe Doctrine, in effect restricting the transfer of territory from one foreign country to another in the Americas. By putting limits on Latin American sovereignty, the Mexican American War and Polk's interpretation of it helped spread Yankeephobia (anti-Americanism) and served as a precursor to the Big Stick policy of the United States 50 years later. After more than 150 years, the trauma of the war President Polk started in the 1840s is still very much alive in Mexico, where the event is known as the American **Intervention**. The brutal nature of the war and the harsh terms of the treaty ending the conflict contributed to further tensions between the United States and Mexico that continue to the present day.

Only two U.S. presidents—Harry Truman in 1947 and Bill Clinton in 1997—have paid anniversary visits to the scene of the final battle of the war where *los niños héroes* vainly defended Chapultepec Castle. Each visit was a simple ceremony with little fanfare (only the Clinton visit resulted in the playing of national anthems). Neither president uttered a word after placing a wreath near the monument and both quickly returned to the motorcade. Obviously, it is a difficult subject for any U.S. president to talk about; for the many Mexicans who climb the walkway to Chapultepec Castle, where bronze statues of *los niños héroes* stand as silent sentries, the Mexican American War still evokes strong emotions and bitter feelings toward the United States after more than 150 years. *See also* Foreign Policy.

SUGGESTED READING

Jack K. Bauer, *The Mexican War, 1846–1848* (Lincoln: University of Nebraska Press, 1992); David W. Dent, *The Legacy of the Monroe Doctrine: A Reference Guide to U.S. Involvement in Latin America and the Caribbean* (Westport, Conn.: Greenwood, 1999); Sam Dillon, "On Clinton Itinerary: Mexico City Counterpart of the

Alamo," *New York Times,* May 6, 1997; Cecil Robinson, ed., *The View from Chapultepec: Mexican Writers on the Mexican American War* (Tucson: University of Arizona Press, 1989).

Mexican Communist Party (Partido Comunista Mexicano, PCM). *See* Communism and Mexican Communist Party.

Mexican Counterculture ☀ Known as *la onda* (the wave, as in electronic broadcast waves) in Mexico, counterculture is connected with a generation of young writers who began to publish between the 1960s and 1970s. At first the term was used more narrowly to refer to a certain ambience associated with the hippie movement, but following the **Tlatelolco massacre** it came to represent modern communications, political protest, and avant-garde trends in literature, **music, cinema**, art, and fashion.

With a youthful and counterculture perspective on language and lifestyles of adolescents in urban settings, the new generation of writers rejected the narrow themes of Mexican nationalism found in previous generations and instead focused on formerly forbidden subjects such as drugs, hippie culture, rock music, sexual fantasies, and **homosexuality**. They adopted some of the techniques of well-known writers such as **Carlos Fuentes, Juan Rulfo,** and **Agustín Yáñez**—multiple narrative voices, shifting points of view, and fragmented nonchronological time—but were more interested in changing the nature and tempo of literary discourse. The most prominent writers of the *la onda* generation include **Gustavo Saínz,** José Agustín, María Luisa Puga, **Fernando del Paso,** and Salvador Elizondo, all born between 1932 and 1944 and key figures in spreading the counterculture to Mexico. Each of these writers represented a sharp break with the previous generation of Mexican writers.

While the counterculture in the United States railed against the war in Vietnam, racism, sex-

ism, and the dehumanization of everyday life in the wake of a growing globalization, in Mexico large numbers of young people fought against a closed and authoritarian political system that seemed to sanction an outdated nationalism, blatant class disparities, and the cultural drawbacks of **machismo**. It was a literature that aimed at middle-class youth identity by using music and colloquial language to escape from the oppressiveness of political authority and materialism.

The significance of *la onda* lay precisely in its ability to question authority by creating a sense of Mexican national identity distinct from that dictated by the **Partido Revolucionario Institucional** **(PRI)**. One of the broader legacies of *la onda* and the *jipiteca* (hippie) movement is that many of Mexico's middle-class youth now embrace the trappings of indigenous cultures (artisanal jewelry, indigenous fashions, long hair, and spending time in the countryside) in a kind of mix between "modern" and "traditional" Mexican culture. Despite efforts of the state to repress or coopt *la onda* since its inception, the depth and dynamism of the wave movement has been too powerful for the state to succeed with its own counterwave movement. *See also Indigenismo.*

SUGGESTED READING

David William Foster, *Mexican Literature: A History* (Austin: University of Texas Press, 1994); Anne Rubenstein, *Bad Language, Naked Ladies, and Other Threats to the Nation: A Political History of Comic Books in Mexico* (Durham: Duke University Press, 1998); Juan Serna, *Mexican Culture* (New York: Garland, 2001); Peter Standish, ed., *Dictionary of Twentieth-Century Culture: Hispanic Culture of Mexico, Central America, and the Caribbean* (New York: Gale, 1996); Richard Teichmann, *De la onda en adelante* (Mexico, D.F.: Editorial Posada, 1987); Eric Zolov, *The Rise of the Mexican Counterculture* (Berkeley: University of California Press, 1999).

Mexican Democratic Party. *See* Partido Democrático Mexicano (PDM).

Mexican Green Ecologist Party. *See* Partido Verde Ecológico de México (PVEM).

Mexican Revolution ☀ Modern Mexico is the product of a violent revolution that lasted from 1910 to 1920. It was the 20th century's first mass insurrection, preceding the Russian revolution by seven years. The event is usually spelled with a patriotic capital R in Mexico, meaning that the Revolution depicts both the fighting and turmoil between 1910 and 1920, as well as the ongoing or institutionalized social and economic reforms mandated by the **Constitution of 1917**. It was not as radical as many other 20th-century revolutions, but it was the first to overturn its traditional oligarchy made up of landowners, the Catholic Church, and the military and to remove foreign control over its economy. The causes of the Mexican Revolution are numerous, but the most important are foreign economic penetration, inequalities in land ownership, class struggle, local autonomy, and the lack of opportunity for upward mobility for a majority of the population.

The revolutionary forces that were unleashed by these developments directed their hatred on the aging regime of Porfirio Díaz, a friend of foreign investors and the oligarchy, who ignored the extreme poverty of the masses and ruled with an iron fist. Led by Francisco Madero and others, the revolutionaries' call for "effective suffrage, non-reelection, and a redistribution of the land" helped mobilize sufficient segments of the opposition to drive the dictator from power. Once in power, Madero emphasized political reform more than socioeconomic change, and this contributed to his assassination in 1913. Internal war and years of turmoil and instability followed with a process of musical chairs occurring among a series of civilian and military leaders, most of whom were later assassinated. Unlike other revolutions in Latin America, Mexico's lacked both a dominant leader and a unifying political party or movement. Thus, with the absence of a charismatic figure such as Cuba's **Fidel Castro**, the Mexican Revolution followed a more gradual and moderate course after the last successful military rebellion in 1920. With the creation of a one-party-dominant system in 1929—with "Revolution" attached to its name and the tricolor of the **flag of Mexican** as part of its logo—Mexico's political development followed a distinct **corporatist**-authoritarian path that brought political stability and economic growth, but at the price of **democratic** freedoms and effective competition.

Over time the Mexican Revolution has been the source of sharply differing interpretations of its essential trajectory, major flaws, programmatic successes, and even the meaning of the term *revolution* itself. The orthodox image of *La Revolución Mexicana* emphasizes the positive aspects of the popular revolution, its pantheon of heroes, and populist and progressive aspects of the regime that embodied all of its aspirations. Revisionist opinion offers a more negative view, emphasizing the corrupt, elitist, and hypocritical aspects of the revolution. With blunders such as the **Tlatelolco massacre**, neoliberal economic policies that have expanded trade and spawned dozens of billionaires, significant increases in poverty and economic inequality, and the deleterious effects of increases in crime and **drug trafficking**, the revisionist view seems to have gathered strength in recent years. While these two main paradigms may not be completely satisfactory to fully understand the Mexican Revolution, they remain a central feature of Revolutionary historiography. Moreover, the tendency to recognize "many" revolutions may be just as valid as the existence of "many" Mexicos in the kaleidoscope of forces that make up the national experience during the 20th century. In any case, the rhetorical power of the Revolution in everyday political discourse, and its constant usage in naming political parties, is not likely to end any time soon. *See also* Villa, Francisco "Pancho"; Zapata, Emiliano.

SUGGESTED READING

Thomas Benjamin, *La Revolución: Mexico's Great Revolution as Memory, Myth, and History* (Austin: University of Texas Press, 2000); Ilene V. O'Malley, *The Myth of the Revolution: Hero Cults and the Institutionalization of the Mexican State, 1920–1940* (New York: Greenwood, 1986); Andrew Wheatcroft, *World Atlas of Revolutions* (London: Hamish Hamilton, 1983).

Mexican Socialist Party. *See* Partido Mexicano Socialista (PMS).

Mexican Workers Party. *See* Partido de Trabajo (PT).

México (State of). *See* Geographical Regions.

Mexico and the Soviet Union ☀ Until the collapse of **communism** in 1989, "the Soviet Union's interest in Mexico stemmed from its long border with the United States, its revolutionary doctrine and heritage, certain economic advantages, and its tradition of one-party governments" (Dent 1999, 272). Mexico was the first country in Latin America to recognize the new Soviet government in 1924, but enthusiasm for its policies and actions declined to the point that in 1930 diplomatic relations with the USSR were broken off, not to be resumed until **World War II** (1942). The Mexican Communist Party (Partido Comunista Mexicana, PCM) was founded in 1919 (Mexico's oldest), and until its dissolution in 1981 had considerable influence in social movements, politics, and the arts. Nevertheless, communist doctrines and promises never captured a significant majority of Mexicans due in large part to national pride over the fact that the **Mexican Revolution** antedated the Russian one

by a number of years, the significance of revolutionary slogans and documents, and the antiforeign ideology that evolved from the outside manipulation of Mexican affairs before the revolution. According to Cline (1963, 178), "Communism is suspect of having no real Mexican roots." Other scholars argue that it is Mexico's **corporatist** tradition, with its emphasis on the elimination of the class struggle and the retention of private property, that has diminished the impact of Marxist socialism on Mexican society.

From the 1930s until the end of the Cold War, anticommunism played a role in domestic and **foreign policy**. Opponents of President **Lázaro Cárdenas** (1934–1940) alleged that he was under the influence of the PCM when he nationalized Mexico's petroleum industry in 1938 and allowed **Leon Trotsky** asylum in Mexico during the same year. While **labor** and student leaders—and many artists and writers—were often harassed during the Cold War because of their alleged communist ideology, Mexico maintained close and uninterrupted relations with the Soviet Union and **Cuba**. It allowed the Soviets to operate a large embassy in Mexico City staffed with diplomats, KGB spies, and military personnel—all this despite repeated scolding from Washington for what it considered a political heresy.

The Soviet embassy in Mexico City gained notoriety when it was discovered that Lee Harvey Oswald was in Mexico City for one week during the fall of 1963, inquiring at the Soviet embassy and the Cuban consulate about visas needed to go to the Soviet Union via Cuba. The U.S. Central Intelligence Agency (CIA) was aware of the visit to the Soviet embassy, including contact with a case officer involved with the KGB's division responsible for "sabotage and assassination." In recently declassified documents, investigators of President Kennedy's assassination found a tape of a phone call to the Soviet embassy in Mexico City by someone impersonating "Lee Oswald," leading to further speculation as to the possible source and motives for the caller, among other things, associated with the event.

SUGGESTED READING

Cole Blasier, *The Giant's Rival: The USSR and Latin America* (Pittsburgh: University of Pittsburgh Press, 1983); Howard F. Cline, *Mexico: Revolution to Evolution, 1940–1960* (New York: Oxford University Press, 1963); David W. Dent, *The Legacy of the Monroe Doctrine: A Reference Guide to U.S. Involvement in Latin America and the Caribbean* (Westport, Conn.: Greenwood, 1999); Deb Riechmann, "Voice on Tape Not Oswald's," *Denver Post,* November 22, 1999.

Mexico City (Distrito Federal, D.F.). *See* Geographical Regions.

Mexico City Conference. *See* Chapultepec Conference.

Mexico–U.S. Relations ☀ *See* Alemán Valdés, Miguel; Ávila Camacho, Manuel; Cárdenas del Río, Lázaro; de la Madrid Hurtado, Miguel; Díaz Ordaz, Gustavo; Echeverría Alvarez, Luis; Foreign Policy; Fox Quesada, Vicente; López Mateos, Adolfo; López Portillo Pacheco, José; Ruiz Cortines, Adolfo; Salinas de Gortari, Carlos; U.S.–Mexican Border/Boundary; Zedillo Ponce de León, Ernesto.

Mezcal. *See* Tequila.

Michoacán. *See* Geographical Regions.

Military. *See* Civil–Military Relations.

Modotti, Tina (1896–1942) ☀ Modernist photographer and political activist who devoted her short life to many causes—**communism**, antifascism, rights of the underclass, universal literacy—and used her photographic skills to express her radicalism. The pinnacle of her career occurred during the seven years (1923–1930) she spent in Mexico perfecting her style of a modernist aesthetic known as the "new vision" photography. In many ways, her provocative photographs depict the pains of modernization in a largely agrarian society. Mexico was crucial to Modotti's development: it reminded her of her native Italy, provided the motivation for her work in modernism and abstraction, and offered her many subjects of interest—indigenous cultures, folk art, and interesting architectural forms—for her camera's lens.

Tina Modotti was born in Undine, Italy, in 1896, the third child of a large, poor family. Her father's life centered on factory work and labor organizing. From an early age, she toiled in the local sweatshops, an experience that would help her identify with workers and farmers. At the age of 16, Modotti followed her father to San Francisco, where he hoped to find better work. She worked in a textile factory before starting an acting career in local amateur Italian theaters. In 1918, at the age of 22, she moved to Los Angeles with her new husband and made three films and modeled for a number of artists, including Edward Weston, who would become the greatest artistic influence of her life. In 1922, after the death of her husband, Modotti moved to Mexico City with Weston and they established a photographic studio together. Modotti assisted Weston in the studio, posed as his model (both nude and clothed), and learned the craft of photography from the master.

As Tina Modotti's photographic career evolved in the 1920s, she grew apart from Weston, beginning to use her photographic skills to express her radicalism. Weston left Mexico in 1926, but Modotti stayed behind to create some of her most daring compositions. Between 1927 and 1929, she became a formal member of the Communist Party and formed close friendships with **Diego Rivera** and **Frida Kahlo**, as well as the other Mexican muralists, who inspired her politically charged photography. She fell in love with Julio Antonio Mella, a Cuban revolutionary leader, while working for the Communist cause. At the peak of her artistic career in 1929, Mella was assassinated as he and Modotti were walking together one evening in Mexico City. Modotti was briefly blamed for the killing and smeared in the Mexican press. She began to lose interest in photography by 1930. In 1932, while living in Moscow, she gave her Leica camera to a young comrade as a gift, in effect putting an end to her short photographic career.

Inspired by the idea that art could educate and carefully crafted visual images could function as an agent for political and economic change, Tina Modotti's subjects were provocative and critical. She had strong political leanings and devoted a good part of her life to leftist causes in Mexico and Europe. Her *Worker Reading "El Machete"* (1927) shows a young worker reading, one of the unfulfilled promises of the **Mexican Revolution** and a goal of the Communist movement.

Her photographs became increasingly critical of government policies that failed to meet the objectives of the revolution, and in 1930 Modotti was branded an undesirable alien and deported from Mexico. For the next 12 years she hopscotched around Europe on a variety of political and humanitarian missions, working for the International Red Aid in Moscow, where she took on spy missions, wrote polemics, and helped build the Moscow subway. After working in a hospital and serving as a propagandist in the Spanish Civil War, Modotti returned to Mexico City in 1939, exhausted and demoralized. She died there of a heart ailment at the age of 46, although some suggested she was poisoned by Stalinists.

Making sense of the colorful traces she left behind has made Tina Modotti the subject of many studies focusing on her energetic life, revolutionary commitment, and artistic achievements.

In Mexico she pushed her new art of photography into experimental territory, emphasizing the lives of ordinary people who contributed to revolutionary Mexico and leftist revolutions that were shaping other parts of the world.

SUGGESTED READING

Patricia Albers, *Shadows, Fire, Snow: The Life of Tina Modotti* (New York: Clarson Potter, 1999); Pino Cacucci, *Tina Modotti: A Life* (New York: St. Martin's, 1999); Amy Conger, "Tina Modotti and Edward Weston: A Re-evaluation of their Photography," in *Edward Weston 100: Centennial Essays in Honor of Edward Weston* (Carmel, Calif.: Friends of Photography, 1986); Vicki Goldberg, "Going Modern in Mexico and Trying to Solve Life," *New York Times*, June 4, 1999; Margaret Hooks, *Tina Modotti: Photographer and Revolutionary* (San Francisco: Harper, 1993); Sarah M. Lowe, "Tina Modotti," in Delia Gaze, ed., *Dictionary of Women Artists*, vol. 2 (Chicago: Fitzroy Dearborn, 1997); Lowe, *Tina Modotti: Photographs* (New York: Abrams/Philadelphia Museum of Art, 1995).

Monsiváis, Carlos (1938–) ☀ Respected writer and cultural critic who is a regular contributor to *La Jornada*, *Proceso*, and *La Opinión*. Monsiváis is recognized as one of Mexico's leading journalists and cultural analysts. His authoritative and insightful essays, chronicles, and literary works often deal with the apparent hypocrisy of the classes in power: politicians, media elites, and significant cultural figures. Using satire and humor to demystify those in power, Monsiváis constantly attacks the lack of accountability and **corruption** of the ruling elites, whom he blames for Mexico's economic and cultural decline. He was profoundly influenced by the events of the **Tlatelolco Massacre** in 1968 and the antigovernment civil rights movements in the United States and Europe, and he serves as an independent voice for **democratic** change in Mexico and Latin America.

Carlos Monsiváis was born in a working-class neighborhood in Mexico City and still lives in the house where he was born. Unlike most Mexicans, he grew up in a household without siblings. His mother was a practicing Protestant in a Catholic country who influenced her son's views of the popular classes being left behind by the increasingly exclusionary Mexican nation-state. Monsiváis studied in the Department of Philosophy and Letters at **Universidad Nacional Autónoma de México (UNAM)**, but dropped out before finishing his work at the university. As he gained popularity as a literary critic, he was awarded honorary degrees from several universities in Mexico. From 1972 to 1987 he was director of *Siempre*'s literary and cultural supplement (*México en la cultura*). His major works include *Díaz de guardar* (1971), *Amor perdido* (1977), *Escenas de pudor y liviandad* (1981), and *Entrada libre* (1987). Between 1986 and 1996 he was awarded three major literary prizes: the Premio Jorge Cuesta (1986), the Premio Mazatlán (1989), and the prestigious Premio Xavier Villaurrutia (1996).

As a writer and critic, Carlos Monsiváis is an omnipresent figure in Mexican literary and media circles, and he retains a huge following among those who value his critical literary talents. As a prominent member of the post-1968 generation, he is firmly attached to the belief that "critical literacy is fundamental if a society wants to undergo a transformation in the name of social justice" (Klahn 1997, 939). *See also* Revolutionary Family or Coalition.

SUGGESTED READING

Ann Duncan, *Voices, Visions, and a New Reality: Mexican Fiction since 1970* (Pittsburgh: University of Pittsburgh Press, 1986); Linda Egan, *Carlos Monsiváis: Culture and Chronicle in Contemporary Mexico* (Tucson: University of Arizona Press, 2001); Norma Klahn, "Monsiváis, Carlos," in Michael S. Werner, ed., *Encyclopedia of Mexico: History, Society, and Culture* (Chicago: Fitzroy Dearborn, 1997); Laura Podalsky, "Consuming Passions: Popular Urban Culture in Mexico," *Studies of Latin American Popular Culture* 15 (1996).

Monterrey. *See* Geographical Regions.

Monterrey Group. See Garza Sada Financial Group or Family.

Morelos. *See* Geographical Regions.

Moreno Reyes, Mario. *See* Cantinflas.

Múñoz Ledo Lazo de la Vega, Porfirio (1933–) ☀ A key political figure since the 1970s who left the **Partido Revolucionario Institucional (PRI)** along with **Cuauhtémoc Cárdenas** to become one of the founders and leaders of the **Partido de la Revolución Democrática (PRD)** after 1989. With the help of electoral reforms, Múñoz Ledo was elected one of the first opposition senators in modern times and in 1993 became president of the PRD. Born in Mexico City in 1933, he graduated from the National School of Law and later obtained a law degree from the University of Paris. After teaching for several years, he entered public life as a member of the PRI, eventually working his way to key cabinet posts and president of the PRI in 1975. While serving as secretary of education (1976–1977), he was fired by President **José López Portillo**. Between 1979 and 1985 he served as Mexico's ambassador to the United Nations. After the opposition won control of the Chamber of Deputies in 1997, the deputies elected Múñoz Ledo, by then a prominent PRD politician, to be their leader until 2000. For the 2000 presidential election he switched parties again and ran as a candidate for the **Partido Auténtico de la Revolucion Mexicana (PARM)**. However, shortly before the July 2 election he dropped out of the race and gave his support to the leading opposition candidate, **Vicente Fox** of the right-of-center **Partido Acción Nacional (PAN)**.

Music (Popular) ✸ Mexican music is rich and varied, often quite danceable and melodic, and much more than mariachi—a form of band music from Jalisco dominated by strings and trumpets. The most popular style in Mexico today is the ensemble *banda* music, dominated by brass and percussion bands of up to 20 musicians playing everything from merengue and salsa to *ranchera* ballads and *norteño* polkas—all arranged for brass. Despite its close proximity to the United States, Mexico has made an effort to resist American rock, although it has gained popularity in recent years. Much of Mexican music today is hard to define since it often borrows from other parts of the world to create music that is more romantic, emotional, and danceable.

The most prominent styles of Mexican music include *cumbia mexicana*, *norteño* (with a wide range of forms, including **corridos**, conjunto, nortec, and narcocorridos), *ranchera*, mariachi, *banda*, *huapango* (with several regional variations), and a Mexican version of rock music called "rock en Español." Other regional styles of music (and instruments) can be found in Mexico, but one must venture into less traveled areas to enjoy the unique sounds that are rarely recorded for commercial use.

Cumbia mexicana fuses Colombia's most popular dance music with Mexican tones and was the most popular music in Mexico in the 1980s, until *bandas* arrived on the scene. The Mexican blend retains the flirtatious tone of Colombian *cumbia*, but played in Mexico it becomes more mellow, direct, and danceable. Mexican *cumbia* was popularized by Los Bukis, a band from Michoacán, whose album *Me volvi a acordar de ti* became the most popular Mexican record ever made. Another successful Mexican *cumbia* band is Sonora Dinamita, whose disc "Mi Cucu" includes lyrics full of double meanings. Mexican *cumbia* bands are also popular among the new Mexican **immigrant** communities in the United States, particu-larly in California and Texas where migrants cling firmly to the music they identify with back home in rural Mexico.

Norteño is accordion-led music from the north of Mexico and is known in the United States as "Tex-Mex." *Norteño* music is rooted in the *corrido* ballads of the 19th and early 20th centuries, typically about the battles between Anglos and Mexicans, the **Mexican Revolution**, common heroes and villains, catastrophic events, politics, current affairs, and romantic love. The accordion was introduced by Bohemian (Eastern European) immigrants who came to work in Mexican mines in the late 19th century. Along with the accordion came the polka, which was soon blended with the traditional duet singing of northern Mexico. By the 1930s a definitive *norteño* style of music had emerged with accordion, brass, and drums combined with lyric ballads that often treat the government as evil and everyday people who have the courage to stand up to the corrupt system as anti-heroes: small-time drug runners who bribe politicians, "wetback" immigrants, petty thieves, and other antiestablishment figures.

Groups such as Los Tigres del Norte, Los Cadetes del Norte, and Los Tucanes de Tijuana often draw on stories from the local papers and convert them into *norteño* hits. Los Tigres are the superstars of *norteño* music, mixing the familiar rhythms with *cumbias* while retaining the nasal singing style and *corrido* bawdiness. Los Tigres won a Grammy award, have been adopted by **Televisa,** and have made significant inroads into the market for Mexican music in the United States. Their recording *Corridos prohibidos* about Mexican low life and heroism is one of the most popular collections by one of the best *norteño* groups on both sides of the border. Los Tucanes offer *corridos* whose lyrics chronicle the daily lives and violent routines of Mexican **drug traffickers**, often punctuating their recordings with machine-gun fire and police sirens. The success of Los

Tucanes' music is rooted in admiration for the heroic drug trafficker in parts of Mexico where wealth, antiestablishment bravura, and intrepid entrepreneurial skills are considered important values. Their first hit, "Clave Privada" (Private pin), chronicled the growing use of beepers among drug wholesalers and their street salesmen in Mexico and the United States.

Although some abhor the violent backdrop of the *corridos*, many see drug traffickers as men of humble origins who cleverly defy the power structure in Mexico. These drug lord ballads (*narcocorridos*) are popular on both sides of the border, where themes of drugs, violence, and police perfidy are popular among Mexican and Mexican American working-class youth. The content and success of *narcocorridos* has helped generate a national debate over the effect of this kind of music on young people, particularly among Catholic Church leaders and members of the **Partido Acción Nacional (PAN).**

The popularity of Tex-Mex music in the United States was enhanced by a Texas singing sensation, Selena (Selena Quintanilla Pérez), until she was shot by one of her followers in 1995. Selena was well known for her *tejano* style of regional Mexican music, a form that gained tremendous popularity among **Chicanos** in the border states. When she died at age 24, she was as much a singing icon for Latinos in the United States as Elvis Presley was for rock 'n' roll fans at the peak of his career.

Ranchera music is characterized by melodramatic passion and joyous exclamations ("¡Ay ay ay ay ay!") by singer and audience. *Ranchera* tends to be pessimistic and nostalgic, the sorrow of a people who have been forced to leave their land and are now lost in a strange city or another country. Mexican American rocker Linda Rondstadt recorded a fine *ranchera* album (*Canciones de mi padre*) in 1987 with songs like "Los laureles," "Hay unos ojos," and "El sol que tú eres." The greatest

ranchera singer of all time, José Alfredo Jiménez, typified *ranchera* with his popular "La vida no vale nada" (Life is worth nothing). "His was a world where only the **tequila** bottle is faithful, where love is violent and jealous and where a man who dies in a duel is a man who has lived" (Broughton 1994, 544). *Ranchera* music blends various regional styles but is essentially an urban phenomenon and is clearly distinguished by the way singers (mostly female) stretch out the final note of the line and add a glissando, or sliding passage.

Mariachi music is a regional style of *ranchera* that grew out of the **mestizo** mix of indigenous and Spanish influences. Since the 1930s, it has been the most nationally famous folk-derived Mexican musical style, popularized by the rising radio and film industries during the golden age of **cinema**. At first the musicians used only string instruments; later trumpets were added for spark. The style was popularized by the mariachi bands who came originally from the state of Jalisco in western Mexico. Dominated by trumpets and various string instruments (violins, harp, and the enormous *guitarrón*, an acoustic bass guitar), mariachi bands were popular at wedding celebrations at the turn of the century. The name *mariachi* was formerly thought to have derived from the French word for wedding (*mariage*), based on the apparent notion that folk string ensembles had performed at weddings for the French imperialists who occupied Mexico in the 1860s. Recent documents uncovered by musicologists debunk this etymology, pointing to a much earlier use of the term for the popular string musicians.

The popularity of mariachi music evolved largely in response to the success of the commercial music industry in radio, cinema, recordings, and later television. However, many were drawn to mariachi bands because of the *charro* suit worn by the musical performers: tight pants, dark jackets with silver buttons and decorations, and wide-brimmed felt cowboy hats. Mariachi bands can be found all over Mexico in taverns and restaurants playing (in exchange for money, usually per song) an incredible range of popular songs on request. The golden era of mariachi was the 1940s and 1950s, when the music accompanied films with Mexican matinee idols like **Pedro Armendáriz**, **Pedro Infante**, and **Jorge Negrete** serenading their lovers. The king of mariachi since the 1940s has been Mariachi Vargas de Tecalitlán, the archetypal mariachi group that was chosen by Linda Ronstadt to accompany her *Canciones* album of *ranchera* songs. On December 12, mariachis are often invited to play at the annual Fiesta of Our Lady of Guadalupe (Festividad de Nuestra Senora de Guadalupe), a religious ceremony honoring the **Virgin of Guadalupe**, an Indian Madonna and patron saint of the Indians. They are also popular during **Cinco de Mayo** celebrations and often provide a powerful melodic flare to election campaigns in the United States when politicians are courting Latino voters in states with large Mexican American populations.

Banda music is now the most popular style of music in Mexico, having replaced the Mexican *cumbia* that was popular in the 1980s. It is a fusion of *norteño* style with the large brass bands that have played at village gatherings in Mexico for the last century. Dominated by brass and percussion, with an occasional guitar, *bandas* play *norteño* polkas, *ranchera* ballads, *cumbia*, merengue, and salsa (a form of dance music that evolved from classics found in many parts of the Caribbean). The most popular of these groups is Banda del Recodo, a fiery orchestra from Mazatlán, Sinaloa, that has contributed to the *banda* boom throughout Mexico. It has also brought a series of new dances, including the *quebradita*, a rollicking combination of *lambada*, polka, *cumbia*, rap, and rock 'n' roll. *Bandas* also dominate TV music programs in all parts of the country, except Mexico City, where *cumbia* and salsa are more popular.

Huapango music can be divided into several main regional types and is found mostly in the central Bajío region and along the Gulf Coast of eastern Mexico. The *huapango huasteco* is played on violin with several small guitars and is usually sung in falsetto. It is popular in the states from Tamaulipas to Hidalgo and Puebla. One of the best groups of this type of Mexican music is Los Camperos del Valles, a trio from San Luis Potosí. Another type of *huapango* is *veracruzano*, made famous by the Richie Valens's rearrangement of "La Bamba." The traditional *huapango veracruzano* is played on guitars, harp, and percussion, typically in Veracruz's seafood restaurants and taverns. One of the best known groups along the Veracruz coast is Los Pregoneros del Puerto, whose album *Music of Veracruz* features an enchanting series of songs dominated by harp and jarana guitars.

Recent trends in Mexican music suggest a revival of interest in folkloric music with performers dressed in colorful Indian clothes, old *corridos* and sad love songs, and a growing interest in rock music attuned to a Latino beat. In the United States, younger Latino artists are pioneering a new, adventurous kind of music called rock en Español, a mixture of hip hop and rock with merengue, salsa, punk, reggae, and more. The bilingual, Los Angeles–based band Ozomatli has issued a number of albums in this style that are gaining popularity, particularly across the border in Mexico. Another popular group from Mexico City, Café Tacuba, is known for its aggressively avant-garde sounds in a genre called "Alterna-Latin" and has been successful on tours of the United States.

With increasing numbers of Mexican Americans growing up with pride in their ethnicity, Mexican regional music is booming in the United States. At large sports arenas and coliseums from California to New York, concerts devoted to regional Mexican music—*corridos, tejano, narcocorridos*— are drawing packed crowds. Nationwide, Mexican folk music accounted for 52 percent of all Latin music sales, which total more than $600 million a year. The popular bands that play this music on both sides of the border have essentially taken music that some consider old-fashioned and made it hip and very popular because this genre of Mexican music always has a story that touches everyone.

SUGGESTED READING

Simon Broughton et al., eds., *World Music: The Rough Guide* (London: Rough Guides, 1994); Ramiro Burr,

The Billboard Guide to Tejano and Regional Mexican Music (New York: Billboard Books, 1999); Patricia W. Harpole, *Los Mariachis: An Introduction to Mexican Mariachi Music*, rev. ed. (Danbury, Conn.: World Music Press, 1991); Mireya Navarro, "Where Mexico (Not Salsa) Is King," *New York Times*, November 6, 2001; Dale A. Olsen and Daniel E. Sheehy, eds., *The Garland Encyclopedia of World Music*, vol. 2, *South America, Mexico, Central America, and the Caribbean* (New York: Garland, 1998); Sam Quiñones, "Narco Pop's Bloody Polkas," *Washington Post*, March 1, 1998; Juan Serna, *Mexican Culture* (New York: Garland, 2001).

Narcocorridos. *See* Corridos; Music (Popular).

National Action Party. *See* Partido Acción Nacional (PAN).

National Autonomous University of Mexico. *See* Universidad Nacional Autónoma de México (UNAM).

National Museum of Intervention (Museo Nacional de las Intervenciones) ☀ Government-owned museum established in 1981 to remind Mexicans of the importance of foreign **intervention** in their history. While numerous European countries come under attack in the graphic displays, the United States is the most heavily criticized for its seizure of Mexican territory during the **Mexican American War** (1846–1848), domination of Mexico's economy, and efforts to thwart the **Mexican Revolution** (1910–1917). Located

in the Churubusco section of Mexico City, exhibitions show the history of invasions along with Mexico's struggle for independence from Spain. The museum chronicles the exploits of private adventurers and foreign armies—chiefly from the United States and France—that have invaded Mexico over the past four centuries. The numerous displays include weapons, flags, and other war memorabilia presented in Spanish. Its library contains over 800 volumes devoted to the subject of intervention, conquest, invasions, and occupations by foreign powers. The museum is used to inform Mexican schoolchildren and their teachers of the importance of protecting *la patria* (the fatherland) from cunning foreigners determined to take advantage of Mexico and the rationale for supporting the principle of nonintervention in international relations. *See also* Foreign Policy.

SUGGESTED READING
Bettina Bartz, ed., *Museums of the World*, 6th ed., rev. and enl. (Munich: K. G. Saur, 1997); Larry Rohter, "Just Forget the Alamo! Ponder Yankees' Sins," *New York Times,* September 28, 1990.

National Palace. *See* Metropolitan Cathedral (Catedral Metropolitana), National Palace, and Los Pinos.

National Peasant Confederation. *See* Confederación Nacional Campesina (CNC).

National Public Subsidized Staple Products Company. *See* Compañía Nacional de Subsistencias Populares (CONASUPO).

National Solidarity Program (PRONASOL). *See* Salinas de Gortari, Carlos.

Nayarit. *See* Geographical Regions.

Negrete, Jorge (1911–1953) ☀ Film star who gained fame for his macho roles in Mexican movies during the 1930s and 1940s. Negrete provided star-quality performances as a singer and actor between 1933 and his premature death in 1953. One of the few truly great mariachi/*ranchera* singers, he was Mexico's first singing cowboy (*charro cantor*). He recorded some 200 songs and appeared in 38 movies, becoming one of the great stars of Mexico's golden age of **cinema** in the 1940s and early 1950s. His signature song was "Mexico, lindo y querido," although he had many hits such as "Paloma querida," "El hijo del pueblo," "Ella," and "Amor con amor se paga." Within a short time, Negrete became one of Mexico's biggest song and film celebrities, achieving the same international stature as film actor Rudolph Valentino and Argentine tango master Carlos Gardel.

Born in Silao, Guanajuato, to an upper-class family, Jorge Negrete grew up in Guanajuato and later in San Luis Potosí. His father served as a lieutenant colonel in the Mexican Army during the **Mexican Revolution,** which later helped him land a teaching job in Mexico City's German College. It was here that the young Jorge learned five languages and earned a college degree. Then he entered the Heroic Military College, reached the rank of lieutenant, and joined the Mexican Army. This did not last long, and he soon left to pursue his interest in opera singing, developing a magnificent tenor voice in the process. The popular interest in *ranchera* singing did not mix well with his operatic training, so he began to transform himself into a singer more suited to popular Mexican **music.**

Negrete started singing on the radio in Mexico City in 1933 and appeared in his first film in 1937. During the 1930s he sang with the Xavier Cugat band in New York and throughout Latin America and the Caribbean. It was in New York that he met his first wife, Elisa Christy, and developed an interest in establishing an organization to work on behalf of struggling actors. His reputation as a singing *charro*—one of the most popular types of film in Mexico—gained him notoriety and helped create a cult of personality for him and his movies. As the handsome and consummate macho, Negrete always played himself in films, the story driven by various forms of male bonding and rivalry. In a blend of **machismo** and Mexican nationalism, Negrete's films were full of scenes dominated by a cantina, a gunfight, a singing match between *charros*, and the consumption of large quantities of alcohol, apparently something indispensable for demonstrations of virility.

The artistic heart of Negrete's films was the song of the macho romantic. According to Mraz (1997, 1012), "The *charro* serenades his sweetheart outside her window, battles his rivals with guitars, sings of his sorrows over the cantina's table, or joins in a chorus on horseback." From *¡Ay Jalisco, no te rajes!* (1941), a popular movie hit that projected his *charro cantor* image worldwide, to *No basta ser charro* (1945) and his last film *El rapto* (1953) with film sensation (and third wife) **María Félix,** Jorge

Movie still of Jorge Negrete and Pedro Infante in *Dos tipos de cuidado* (1948), a film that typified the singing cowboy (*charro cantor*).

Negrete played the handsome, aloof, and omnipotent macho. Negrete's films treated women as sexist stereotypes, minor figures in comparison to the singing *charros*, their friends, and rivals. Considered the greatest of the cowboy singers of his time, Negrete captured the essence of *charro* cinema in the golden age before he died of cirrhosis of the liver in Los Angeles at the age of 42. Apparently he lived many of his film roles off-screen as well.

SUGGESTED READING

Ramiro Burr, *The Billboard Guide to Tejano and Regional Mexican Music* (New York: Billboard Books, 1999); John Mraz, "Negrete, Jorge," in Michael S. Werner, ed., *Encyclopedia of Mexico: History, Society, and Culture* (Chicago: Fitzroy Dearborn, 1997); Enrique Serna, *Jorge el bueno: La vida de Jorge Negrete* (Mexico, D.F.: Clío, 1993).

Norteño. *See* Music (Popular).

North American Free Trade Agreement (NAFTA) ☀
Comprehensive trade pact between the United States, Canada, and Mexico designed to gradually eliminate some barriers to the flow of goods and services among the three North American countries

over a 15-year period. The agreement was signed in October 1992, ratified in November 1993, and entered into force on January 1, 1994. By linking more than 360 million consumers in a $6 trillion market, NAFTA was designed to benefit people on both sides of the border.

The brainchild of President **Carlos Salinas de Gortari**, NAFTA reflected the growing interest in "free trade" throughout the Americas. Mexico's decision to negotiate NAFTA stemmed from its desire to secure market access for its exports, as well as gaining access to foreign capital with which to create jobs, stimulate economic recovery, and service its large public debt. NAFTA seemed the best strategy to promote its export-oriented economic model and gain market access guarantees. As a way of promoting economic integration, NAFTA is expected to create the largest single market in the world. NAFTA included side agreements intended to protect the **environment** and **labor** rights and made it possible for Mexicans to take advantage of new opportunities to work in the United States.

After eight years, NAFTA has produced both winners and losers. Large, innovative producers that have adapted to changing marketing conditions have prospered under NAFTA. Smaller producers wedded to old methods of doing business have been the losers. Although 1992 U.S. presidential candidate Ross Perot warned of a "giant sucking sound" of U.S. jobs moving to Mexico, the labor picture is more of a tossup with winners and losers on both sides of the border. The U.S.–Mexico Chamber of Commerce claims that 1.7 million export-related jobs have been created in the United States due in large part to NAFTA. Nevertheless, lower labor costs continue to lure more U.S. companies to move their operations to Mexico since the creation of NAFTA, including Zenith Electronics, Nintendo of America, Mattel, Sara Lee Knit Products, Vanity Fair, and Pendleton Woolen Mills. While wages for production workers in the United States have grown steadily since NAFTA's creation,

those of Mexican workers have declined, in part due to the 1995 economic crisis. Total two-way trade between the United States and Mexico has risen from $117.2 billion before NAFTA (1993) to $242.7 billion in 1998. After NAFTA, trade between the United States and Mexico increased by 6 percent, while trade with South America, Asia, and the European Union decreased. Mexico is now America's second largest trading partner after Canada. With Mexico's population approximately four times that of Canada's, Mexico may one day rank as the largest trading partner of the United States.

In a November 1999 poll, 65 percent of the Mexicans interviewed said that Mexico benefited at least somewhat from NAFTA, including 17 percent who indicated that the country had benefited "a lot." Those who criticize NAFTA are less concerned with polls and macroeconomic factors related to free trade and global competition than the negative impact of NAFTA on real wages, the environment, worker safety, meaningful employment, and the need for serious political reform. There is recent solid evidence that NAFTA contributed to the negligible growth in U.S. wages during the 1990s—despite high corporate profits and low employment—and that air pollution levels in Mexican industry have almost doubled since NAFTA's approval in 1994. Both supporters and critics of NAFTA approach the ongoing efforts to create a Free Trade Area of the Americas (FTAA) with polished rhetoric based on their studies and perceptions of the pros and cons of NAFTA. The vicissitudes of NAFTA are closely tied to the corporate search for places on the planet that offer low-wage benefits. For example, Mexico's manufacturing base—located mostly along the **U.S.–Mexican border** in the *maquiladora* export zones—is now shrinking due to the U.S. recession and the departure of factories lured into exaggerated claims of NAFTA-based integration with the United States and Canada. As wages have risen along the border, corporate manufacturers are now looking to China and elsewhere for the low-wage benefits that NAFTA once offered. While corporate globalization has proven to be a benefit to some parts of the economy where export production by foreign multinationals flourished, much of the Mexican economy is now suffering because of the basic flaws in the export-driven model of development. *See also* Foreign Policy; General Agreement on Tariffs and Trade (GATT).

SUGGESTED READING

M. Delal Baer and Sidney Weintraub, eds., *The NAFTA Debate: Grappling with Unconventional Trade Issues* (Boulder, Colo.: Lynne Rienner, 1994); Donald Barry, Mark O. Dickerson, and James D. Gaisford, eds., *Toward a North American Community? Canada, the United States, and Mexico* (Boulder, Colo.: Westview, 1995); Stephen Blank and Jerry Haar, *Making NAFTA Work: U.S. Firms and the New North American Business Environment* (Miami: North-South Center Press, 1999); Maxwell A. Cameron and Brian W. Tomlin, *The Making of NAFTA: How the Deal Was Done* (Ithaca: Cornell University Press, 2001); Jorge G. Castañeda, *The Mexican Shock: Its Meaning for the U.S.* (New York: Norton, 1996); Gustavo del Castillo and Gustavo Vega Cánovas, *The Politics of Free Trade in North America* (Ottawa: Centre for Trade Policy and Law, 1995); George W. Grayson, *The North American Free Trade Agreement: Regional Community and the New World Order* (Lanham, Md.: University Press of America, 1994); William Greider, "A New Giant Sucking Sound," *Nation*, December 31, 2001; Gary Clyde Hufbauer and Jeffrey Schott, *NAFTA: An Assessment* (Washington, D.C.: Institute for International Economics, 1993); Ann E. Kingsolver, *NAFTA Stories: Fears and Hopes in Mexico and the United States* (Boulder, Colo.: Lynne Rienner, 2001); John R. MacArthur, *The Selling of "Free Trade": NAFTA, Washington, and the Subversion of American Democracy* (Berkeley: University of California Press, 2001); Jacqueline Mazza, *Don't Disturb the Neighbors: The U.S. and Democracy in Mexico, 1980–1995* (New York: Routledge, 2001); Peter Morici, *Trade Talks with Mexico: A Time for Realism* (Washington, D.C.: National Planning Association, 1991); William A. Orme, Jr., *Understanding NAFTA: Mexico, Free Trade, and the New North America* (Austin: University of Texas Press, 1996); Manuel Pastor. Jr., "Mexican Trade Liberalization and NAFTA," *Latin American Research Review* (Summer 1994); Guy Poitras, *Inventing North America: Canada, Mexico, and the United States* (Boulder, Colo.: Lynne Rienner, 2001); Guy Poitras and Raymond Robinson, "The Politics of NAFTA in Mexico," *Journal of Interamerican Studies and World Affairs* (Spring 1994); Hermann von Bertrab, *Negotiating NAFTA: A Mexican Envoy's Account* (Westport, Conn.: Greenwood, 1997).

Nuevo León. *See* Geographical Regions.

Oaxaca. *See* Geographical Regions.

Office of the Coordinator of Inter-American Affairs (OCIAA) One of the most important events associated with radio broadcasting during **World War II** was the propaganda offensive aimed at Mexico by the U.S. Office of the Coordinator of Inter-American Affairs under the direction of

Nelson A. Rockefeller. The OCIAA was established to promote inter-American trade, counter Nazi propaganda in the Americas, and provide mutual understanding and cooperation through cultural programs between the United States and Latin America. The OCIAA used a combination of shortwave broadcasts, recorded radio programs, local broadcasts, and film productions to spread unprecedented quantities of pro-U.S. propaganda throughout Mexico and the rest of Latin America. By relying on key radio stations owned by **Emilio Azcárraga Milmo**, the OCIAA incorporated its propaganda into popular programs of Mexican **music** and dramatizations. In 1948, the OCIAA's Radio Division was transferred to the U.S. Department of State, where it became the Voice of America.

SUGGESTED READING

Ariel Dorfman and Armand Mattelart, *How to Read Donald Duck: Imperialist Ideology in the Disney Comic* (New York: International General, 1991); Seth Fein, "From Collaboration to Containment: Hollywood and the International Political Economy of Mexican Cinema after the Second World War," in Joanne Hershfield and David R. Maciel, eds., *Mexico's Cinema: A Century of Film and Filmmakers* (Wilmington, Del.: Scholarly Resources, 1999); Gerald K. Haines, "Under the Eagle's Wing: The Franklin Roosevelt Administration Forges an American Hemisphere," *Diplomatic History* 1 (1977): 373–88; Stephen R. Niblo, *The Impact of War: Mexico and World War II* (Melbourne, Australia: Latrobe University Institute of Latin American Studies, 1988); Niblo, *War, Diplomacy, and Development: The United States and Mexico, 1938–1954* (Wilmington, Del.: Scholarly Resources, 1995); María Emilia Paz, *Strategy, Security, and Spies: Mexico and the U.S. as Allies in World War II* (University Park: Pennsylvania State University Press, 1997); Donald W. Rowland, *History of the Office of the Coordinator of Inter-American Affairs* (Washington, D.C.: Government Printing Office, 1947).

O'Gorman, Juan (1905–1982) ☀ Painter and architect best known for his works that integrated art—especially mural painting—and architecture, a movement known in Mexico as *integración plástica*. Among O'Gorman's major works in Mexico City are murals and frescoes at the National Museum of Anthropology, the international airport, the Museum of National History in Chapultepec Castle, and the Central Library at *Ciudad Universitaria* (University City). The library at University City is a unification of art and architecture with a stone-and-glass mosaic that covers its massive tower. These polychrome mosaics incorporate and integrate pre-Columbian architectural forms and nativistic motifs, as well as images from great murals from the postrevolutionary period.

Born in Mexico City in 1905, Juan O'Gorman developed an early interest in drawing, form, and composition from his Irish English father, Cecil Crawford O'Gorman, a perfectionist portrait painter. He studied architecture at the **Universidad Nacional Autónoma de México (UNAM)**, where he came in contact with individuals who favored the simplicity and directness of functionalism that could be incorporated into the nationalistic and modern. O'Gorman's artistic achievements were influenced by Guillermo Zárraga (functionalism), Le Corbusier (functionalism and plasticity), Frank Lloyd Wright (organicism), **Diego Rivera** (sculptural mosaics), and **Frida Kahlo** (easel painting). His striking buildings with nativistic motifs, such as the central library illustrating the history of Mexico, attracted large numbers of foreign tourists who wrote the most about this form of architecture. Ironically, while his great building projects were highly nationalistic and provided the government with an important propaganda tool, the integration of art and architecture also helped expand **tourism**, making it Mexico's greatest source of income and increasing its dependence on the United States.

O'Gorman's designs were also influenced by his social beliefs and political ideology. As a member of

Library tower of the Central Library, National Autonomous University of Mexico, with stone mosaics, colored tiles, and frescoes created by Juan O'Gorman. Credit: General Secretariat of the Organization of American States.

the Mexican **Communist** Party, O'Gorman rejected conventional aesthetics in favor of socially oriented rationalism that was evident in the rather austere and featureless houses he designed, including the design of Rivera's house-studio complex (1929–1930), the Cecil O'Gorman house (1930–1931), and his own house (1931–1932), all located in the Pedregal de San Gerónimo residential district of Mexico City. Between 1935 and 1948, O'Gorman withdrew from architectural practice, mainly for ideological reasons, and focused on murals and easel painting. O'Gorman was one of many anti-Stalinist intellectuals and painters who initially defended **Leon Trotsky** before he was assassinated by a pro-Stalinist agent while living in exile in Mexico City. In 1963 the U.S. State Department denied O'Gorman a visa to visit the United States on the grounds that he was a communist. After weeks of protest—in Mexico and the United States—the Department of State reversed itself, and he was finally allowed to visit the United States.

O'Gorman became despondent because heart disease had curtailed his work and committed suicide in January 1982 at the age of 76. Juan O'Gorman left a magnificent artistic legacy, both in his architectural masterpieces and his outstanding smaller-scale paintings of urban life and imaginary landscapes.

SUGGESTED READING

"Juan O'Gorman, 76; Painter and Architect," *New York Times,* January 20, 1982; Jane Turner, ed., *The Dictionary of Art*, vol. 23 (New York: Grove Dictionaries, 1996).

Olympic Games (1968) ☀ Mexico's bid to host the 1968 Summer Olympics was accepted in 1963, but five years later the forces of international conflict, domestic protest, and violence had spread to Mexico City. Students and workers—angered by the huge government expenditures on preparations for the games and the authoritarianism of the **Díaz Ordaz** administration—clashed with government and local authorities over the wisdom of holding the sporting event. Mexico was the first Latin American country—or developing nation—to host such an event, and Mexico wanted the games to bolster its international image, thereby earning greater acceptance as a friendly place for **tourists** and a safe haven for foreign investors. The student movement of July–October 1968 threatened to interfere with those goals; furthermore, any prolonged instability would call into question the already flagging legitimacy of the ruling **Partido Revolucionario Institucional (PRI).**

To host the 5,531 athletes (4,750 males, 781 females) from 113 countries that would compete in the Games, Mexico built athletic facilities, housing projects, hotels, and a modern subway system to accommodate and impress visitors from around the globe. Mexican officials also planned a cultural Olympics to coincide with the sporting events, featuring international art, books, concerts, and plays. President Gustavo Díaz Ordaz spent more than $170 million on the games, hoping to reap a profit from the visiting teams and foreign tourists, an increase in tax collection, and a greater sense of national pride.

Although workers finished the facilities in time for the acclaimed event and the Olympics themselves went well, the events leading up to the Olympic Games damaged Mexico's image as the police and army attacked student protesters, killing hundreds of people in what became known as the **Tlatelolco Massacre** shortly before the games got under way. The pressure of the impending games and international focus on Mexico were a source of tremendous preoccupation for the government. When more than 10,000 demonstrators gathered in the Plaza of the Three Cultures (or Tlatelolco) for what was to be another protest against the regime, the government was not about to suffer the ill effects of such an unwanted event. Without warning, the protest movement was met by police and riot-control troops that retaliated with gunfire that left more than 300 dead and thousands wounded in the plaza. Many were jailed and the movement was crushed, but the massacre at Tlatelolco left a deep wound in Mexican society that would continue to influence the political culture. Ten days after Tlatelolco, Norma Enriqueta Basilio, a young hurdler, became the first woman to bring the Olympic torch into the arena to light the Olympic flame in Aztec Stadium to start the games.

Although there were doubts about Mexico's ability to fulfill its Olympic responsibilities and complaints about the city's high altitude and thin air, pollution, and lack of air movement, the Games proceeded with few glitches and mishaps.

In fact, the Games witnessed some remarkable feats, with the competing athletes matching or surpassing 24 world and 56 Olympic records. Mexicans cheered their 300-member squad of athletes, the largest in its history, who gave their country its best results ever: nine medals—three each of gold, silver, and bronze. Mexicans also took pride in conducting what were judged by some foreign observers as one of the best Olympic Games in the modern era. However, the benefits of the 1968 Olympic Games—increased spending, new housing units in two Olympic Villages, the numerous works of art created especially for the sporting event that were left for public enjoyment, and the inheritance of a technologically superior television and communication infrastructure—were overshadowed by the price of Tlatelolco and its aftermath on the stability of the governing system.

SUGGESTED READING

Joseph L. Arbena, "Mexico City 1968: The Games of the XIXth Olympiad," in John E. Findling and Kimberly D. Pelle, eds., *Historical Dictionary of the Modern Olympic Movement* (Westport, Conn.: Greenwood, 1996); Arbena, "Sport, Development, and Mexican Nationalism, 1920–1970," *Journal of Sport History* (Winter 1991); Christopher Brasher, *Mexico 1968: A Diary of the XIXth Olympiad* (London: S. Paul, 1968).

Onda, La. See Mexican Counterculture.

Organization of American States. *See* Foreign Policy.

Organization of Petroleum Exporting Countries (OPEC). *See* Petróleos Mexicanos (PEMEX).

Orozco, José Clemente (1883–1949) ☀ One of masters of Mexican *muralismo*, along with fellow artists **Diego Rivera** and **David Alfaro Siqueiros**. José Clemente Orozco devoted much of his life to the postrevolutionary program of teaching an extremely nationalist version of Mexican history to the illiterate masses. Although Orozco was considered a key figure in the muralist movement from the 1920s to the 1940s, his art portrays historical events and important figures differently from that of his competitors. For example, unlike the idealized version of Mexico's indigenous past and the revolutionary experience found in the Rivera murals, Orozco's murals and easel paintings portray the bleaker side of life and history, often reflecting his own painful experiences.

Born in Zapotlán del Grande (now Ciudad Guzmán) in the state of Jalisco, Orozco grew up in Mexico City and studied at the School of Agriculture (1897–1899), the National Preparatory School (1899–1908), and the Academy of San Carlos, National School of Fine Arts (1908–1914). Although he spent his early education training as an agricultural engineer, he soon gravitated to the world of art as a means to communicate to a much broader audience. In 1910 he was one of the six members of the Centro Artístico, directed by Dr. Atl, who tried unsuccessfully to obtain contracts to paint public murals. While enrolled at the Academy of San Carlos, he was influenced by the popular engraver, caricaturist, and illustrator José Guadalupe Posada, known for his graphic attacks on Porfirio Díaz at the beginning of the **Mexican Revolution**.

During his early years in Mexico City Orozco found work as a cartoonist and illustrator for Mexico City newspapers and for one of the revolutionary armies. A protégé of muralist Atl, he focused much of his early works on images of women, schoolgirls, and prostitutes—controversial subjects that did not go over well with the public. When Mexico City was occupied by **Pancho Villa**'s forces in 1914, Orozco and Atl, who had been appointed chief of propaganda by revolutionary chieftain Venustiano Carranza, fled to Orizaba and began publishing a pro-Carranza newspaper *La Vanguardia* in collaboration with other artists such as Siqueiros.

Although he did not participate in the revolution, Orozco witnessed the agony of the war from a peasant perspective. His illustrations for *La Vanguardia* often dealt with issues related to the civil war—political propaganda, the uselessness of violence, and the plight of the downtrodden—and helped confirm his negative views of the revolution. Although he was an early supporter of Carranza, the excesses of Carranza's forces in battle put him at odds with the revolutionary leader. After a critical caricature of President Carranza was published in 1915, Orozco was prevented from publishing and forced to live as an outcast in the poorest neighborhoods of Mexico City. He lost his left hand (and damaged his hearing and sight) in an accident, physical injuries that many believe contributed to his need to portray the history of Mexico as an interracial drama of conflict and anguish. After a large-scale exhibit of his works in 1916 was savagely panned by critics unaccustomed to such avant-garde paintings, he decided to leave Mexico for California in 1917 (and later New York) where he made a living doing portraits and working as a commercial artist.

After nearly three years in the United States, Orozco returned to Mexico in 1920 to work on larger-scale art forms that would address the emotional intensity of Mexico's calamitous revolutionary reality. However, his art was ignored until he was called on to paint the walls of the Escuela Nacional Preparatoria (ENP) by education minister **José Vasconcelos**. As part of the artistic renaissance in the 1920s, Orozco's frescoes at the ENP clearly rejected the idealized imagery used by other artists and gained him a reputation as a major Mexican artist.

In 1923 Orozco and fellow muralists Rivera, Siqueiros, and others helped found the Syndicate of Technical Workers, Painters, and Sculptors, a group that rejected "bourgeois individualism" and dedicated itself to the monumental art form that would make the "big three" of Mexican muralists world famous. Using allegorical images, dark colors (mostly dark browns, reds, and black), and geometric shapes, Orozco produced a series of caustic, caricature-like murals at the Preparatoria that many found too critical and offensive. One such mural—*Los ricos en banquete mientras los obreros pelean* (The rich at their banquet while workers quarrel 1923–1924), depicting Orozco's disillusionment with the state's betrayal of revolutionary ideals—caused a riot at the Preparatoria, during which many of the murals were seriously damaged. Following this incident all the muralists except Rivera were dismissed, although Orozco was allowed to finish his commission. Nevertheless, this period produced some of Orozco's best-known murals, including *Cortés and La Malinche* (1926), in which the Spanish conquistador and his Indian translator and guide are seated next to a prone dark-skinned figure symbolizing a subjugated race—the **mestizo** descendant of the conjugation of two distinct cultures. Between 1924 and 1927 he produced caricatures for *El Machete*, a worker newspaper that was later converted into a publication of the Mexican **Communist** Party.

Orozco (along with other prominent Mexican muralists) left for the United States in the late 1920s and was commissioned to produce more of his controversial frescoes. From 1930 until 1934, he produced a series of remarkable murals at Pomona College, California (1930); the New School for Social Research in New York City (1930); and Dartmouth College, New Hampshire (1932–1934). As an artist in residence at Dartmouth College, he painted *Epic of American Civilization*, a multipart mural located in the Baker Library. In this, one of his most important works, Orozco presents a number of panel/scenes that stretch from the pre-Columbian era to the modern period. In the panel titled "Hispano-America," an armed Mexican peasant stands straight, while surrounded by contorted figures of mainly foreign interlopers and exploiters. The controversial panel is not a polemic against foreign **intervention**; it suggests

that the heroic rebel would have been less suscep-
tible to external exploitation had he cared more
for education and political maturity.

After he returned to Mexico in 1934, Orozco
painted murals in Mexico City and Guadalajara. In
his murals at the Palacio de Bellas Artes (Mexico
City), as well as the Universidad de Guadalajara,
Palacio de Gobierno, and Hospicio Cabañas (all in
downtown Guadalajara), his themes refer to specific historical events or peoples, but he represented them as symbolic universal forces shaping
the human condition. Orozco's Guadalajara
murals offer a biting critique of political leaders, a
large image of Miguel Hidalgo, the religious leader
of Independence, and his most outstanding work,
Man in Flames, where on the ceiling of the main
dome of the Hospicio Cabañas he integrates his
mastery of human history and nature by portraying a Promethean figure of a man devouring himself by fire. His universal themes and vibrant
textured figures influenced future generations of
Mexican artists interested in making a break with
tradition. In the United States, José Clemente
Orozco and the other muralists had an impact on
well-known abstract artist Jackson Pollack, who
admired this style of Mexican painting.

Orozco helped found the National College in
1943, and three years later he was awarded the
National Prize in the Arts and Sciences. The Palace
of Fine Arts presented a retrospective exhibition
of his best works in 1946. He continued to paint
with emotional intensity during the 1940s, finishing his last complete work in 1949, a fresco in
the dome of the Legislative Chamber of the
Government Palace in Guadalajara. Orozco died
in Mexico City in 1949 and was buried at the
Panteón de Hombres Ilustres, the first artist to be
honored in this manner.

SUGGESTED READING

Albert I. Dickerson, *The Orozco Frescoes at Dartmouth*
(Hanover, N.H.: Dartmouth College Publications, 1934);
Renato González Mello, *Orozco: ¿Pintor Revolucionario?*
(Mexico, D.F.: UNAM, 1995); Mackinley Helm, *Man of
Fire: J. C. Orozco: An Interpretive Memoir* (Westport,
Conn.: Greenwood, 1959); Laurance P. Hurlburt, *The
Mexican Muralists in the United States* (Albuquerque:
University of New Mexico Press, 1989); Leslie Robinson,
"N.H. Murals Showcase Mexico Past," *Dallas Morning
News,* December 5, 1999; Desmond Rochfort, *Mexican
Muralists: Orozco, Rivera, Siqueiros* (London: Laurence
King, 1993); Peter Standish, ed., *Dictionary of
Twentieth-Century Culture: Hispanic Culture of Mexico,
Central America, and the Caribbean* (New York: Gale
Research, 1996); Mary Kay Vaughan, "Orozco, José
Clemente," in Barbara A. Tenenbaum, ed., *Encyclopedia
of Latin American History and Culture* (New York:
Scribners, 1996).

Ortíz Mena, Antonio (1908–) ☀ Treasury secretary under President **Adolfo López Mateos.** Known
for his legal-financial expertise, Ortíz Mena held
important positions in the federal bureaucracy
and banking. He was head of the Inter-American
Development Bank from 1971 through 1988. On
two occasions—in 1963 and 1969—he was considered as a possible precandidate for the **Partido
Revolucionario Institucional (PRI)** nomination
for president. Born in Parral, Chihuahua, to a
family of prominent political figures, Ortíz Mena
attended the National Preparatory School and the
National School of Law, where he became associated with the influential Generation of
1925–1928, a group that included political luminaries such as **Miguel Alemán, Antonio Carrillo
Flores,** Alfonso Noriega, and others. As a disciple
of President **Ruiz Cortines (1952–1958)** and the
uncle of President **Carlos Salinas (1988–1994),**
Ortíz Mena possessed important contacts that
helped advance his career in politics and business.
He served as director general of the Mexican
Institute of Social Security (1952–1958), a cabinet post in the Ruiz Cortines administration. His
long experience with the Inter-American

Development Bank helped him acquire the post of director general of Banamex, Mexico's largest bank, from 1988 to 1990. As part of the Salinas de Gortari family (he married Martha Salinas, Carlos Salinas's aunt), Ortíz Mena developed close ties to the **technocrats** who carried out the neoliberal reforms in the 1990s.

The growing ties between the business community and the ruling party were revealed in a widely publicized dinner party at Ortíz Mena's home in late 1993. At what the press called the "billionaire's banquet," 30 of Mexico's wealthiest businessmen met with top PRI officials to offer $750 million to bolster the PRI's ailing presidential campaign. The huge financial offer from the nation's billionaires was equal to more than 10 times the amount raised by U.S. presidential candidate Bill Clinton for the 1992 campaign. Although the offer was rescinded after the financial meeting was leaked to the press, the dinner meeting demonstrated a form of gratitude for the huge profits that some in the business community made from the massive privatization policies of the Salinas administration. *See also* Azcárraga Milmo, Emilio ("El Tigre").

SUGGESTED READING

Roderic Ai Camp, *Mexican Political Biographies, 1935–1993*, 3d ed. (Austin: University of Texas Press, 1995); Andres Oppenheimer, *Bordering on Chaos: Guerrillas, Stockbrokers, Politicians, and Mexico's Road to Prosperity* (Boston: Little, Brown, 1996).

Pachucos ☀ During **World War II** Mexican American youths (mostly between the ages of 13 and 18) began to form gangs and dress in garish clothes in order to assert their separate identity within the dominant Anglo society. The typical *pachuco* costume (zoot suit) included a wide-brimmed hat with a huge feather stuck in the brim, baggy pants, and a single-buttoned long jacket, usually light in color. In a determined effort to remain ethnically different, *pachucos* (also referred to as "zoot suiters"), concentrated in East Los Angeles, California, clashed with the growing sense of xenophobia among many Anglos. Between 1942 and 1943, racial tensions (inflamed by the Los Angeles press) led to riots between *pachucos* and U.S. sailors on short furloughs looking for a good time, particularly with young Mexican American girls (*pachucas*) who reminded them of prostitutes in Tijuana, Baja California. Finally, sailors and *pachucos* clashed in an act of macho rage, ripping the "zoot suits" off the *pachucos*, leading to more violence and arrests.

The Mexican comedian Tin Tan (Germán Valdés) played a *pachuco* in his movies and nightclub acts. His *pachuco* persona challenged **Cantinflas**'s *peladito* by appealing to transnationalized Mexican and Mexican American audiences. Because of the history and press coverage of *pachucos*, the term has taken on a derogatory meaning for those who have opted for practical assimilation over chauvinistic separation within the border region. **Carlos Monsiváis** wrote about the *pachuco* as a search for and creation of a new and radical identity, while **Octavio Paz** rejected this positive view, calling the *pachuco* a social aberration. *See also* Chicanos; *Pochos*.

SUGGESTED READING

Manuel G. González, *Mexicanos: A History of Mexicans in the United States* (Bloomington: Indiana University Press, 1999); David G. Gutiérrez, *Walls and Mirrors: Mexican Americans, Immigrants, and the Politics of Ethnicity* (Berkeley: University of California Press, 1999); Luis Hernández Palacios and Juan Manuel Sandoval, eds., *Frontera norte: Chicanos, pachucos, y cholos* (Mexico, D.F.: Universidad Autónoma Metropolitana, 1989); Manuel A. Machado, Jr., *Listen Chicano! An Informal History of Mexican Americans* (Chicago: Nelson Hall, 1978).

Padilla Peñalosa, Ezequiél (1890–1971) ☀ Diplomat and politician who played a key role in Mexican politics, jurisprudence, and inter-American relations from 1920 to 1970. Born in 1890 in Coyuca de Catalán, Guerrero, the son of an impoverished lawyer father and schoolteacher mother, Padilla grew up with an interest in law and education. His lively intelligence and excellent oratory skills helped prepare him for a career in law and diplomacy. He began his legal studies at the National School of Law, **Universidad Nacional Autónoma de México (UNAM)**, on a government scholarship, but completed his degree in 1912 at the Free Law School (Escuela Libre de Derecho), which he helped found with the help of other students. With a scholarship from the secretary of education, Padilla continued his legal studies at the Sorbonne in 1913–1914; after returning from Europe, he fought in the **Mexican Revolution**, first as a common soldier under **Emiliano Zapata** and later as part of the anti-Huerta forces of **Francisco "Pancho" Villa**. After Villa's defeat, Padilla fled Mexico for the United States, where he taught constitutional law at Columbia University and became a representative of the New York–based Latin American Supply Company in Mexico and Cuba. He returned to his native town in 1922 and started a long career in state and national politics. As secretary of public education (1928–1930), he developed important projects extending public education into rural areas.

Padilla's many diplomatic posts included minister to Hungary and Italy, ambassador to the United States, delegate to the United Nations, and secretary of foreign relations (1940–1945). During the war years he helped resolve a number of thorny bilateral issues with the United States, including a conflict over petroleum compensation and the external debt, and was instrumental in establishing the contracts that would regulate the emigration of workers involved in the **bracero** program. After German submarines sank two Mexican oil tankers in 1942, Padilla helped forge the **World War II** alliance with the United States, a first for Mexico and the United States.

After being a precandidate for the ruling party in 1945, Padilla emerged as a presidential candidate of the **Partido Democrático Mexicano (PDM)**. Despite a consistent ideology and program, he was unable to defeat ruling party candidate **Miguel Alemán** in the 1946 elections. He made a mild protest against what he saw as electoral fraud and manipulation, but his movement faded and he moved to the United States. In Dallas, Texas, Padilla tried to mobilize opposition forces to mount a rebellion against Alemán's pro–United States and capitalist economic policies, which he considered to be the basis for **communist** propaganda in Latin America. His attempts to forge a revolutionary group failed, and many years later he returned to Mexico and assumed a low-level position in the foreign service. He died in Mexico City in 1971.

SUGGESTED READING

Roderic Ai Camp, "Padilla Peñalosa, Ezequiél," in Barbara A. Tenenbaum, ed., *Encyclopedia of Latin American History and Culture*, vol. 4 (New York:

Scribners, 1996); Josephus Daniels, *Shirt-Sleeve Diplomat* (1947); Engracia Loyo Bravo, "Padilla, Ezequiél," in Michael S. Werner, ed., *Encyclopedia of Mexico: History, Society, and Culture* (Chicago: Fitzroy Dearborn, 1997).

Pani, Mario. *See* Chávez, Carlos.

Partido Acción Nacional (PAN) ☀ Center-right political party with a program based on Christian Democratic principles and the concept of solidarity. The PAN is essentially a conservative, proclerical, and probusiness party that favors limitations on the government's economic role in society. It has competed in congressional elections since 1943 and most presidential elections since 1952. From its founding in 1939 to its presidential victory in 2000, it functioned as the most viable opposition party to the **Partido Revolucionario Institucional (PRI)**, dependent on urban middle-class support, particularly in large urban centers, the northern border states, and Yucatán. With the exception of Mexico City, the PAN has been successful in most of the large urban centers in Mexico, including such PAN strongholds as Guadalajara, Chihuahua, Monterrey, Ciudad Juárez, and Tijuana. Despite some problems within its organization, the PAN possesses the most organizational strength and ideological coherence among the various parties that challenged the PRI. Unlike other political parties that made up the opposition during the long period of PRI rule, the PAN maintained its independence and was not considered a tool of the ruling party or the state. While the PAN is frequently considered to have spiritual ties to the social doctrine of the Catholic Church, the party's association with the church hierarchy is not as close as it might seem.

With the **Salinas** electoral reforms beginning in 1989, the PAN won its first governorship, and by the 1990s it had become the second most powerful political party in the country. Between 1989 and 1999, the PAN acquired electoral victories in more than 200 municipalities and governorships in seven states, including Baja California, when it was able to transfer power from one PAN governor to another in 1995, something that no opposition party had previously achieved. Between 1997 and 2000, the PAN held 24 percent of the seats in the Chamber of Deputies and 25 percent of the seats in the Senate. In the federal elections in 1997, the PAN received 27 percent of the votes nationwide.

Largely because of the fragmentation within the leftist opposition and the erosion of support for the PRI due to electoral fraud and manipulation, the National Action Party has helped make the Mexican political system more open and competitive. However, beginning with the decade of the 1980s, the PAN started to diversify, including a northern "radical" conservative faction called *neopanistas* who resisted the moderate traditionalist faction that was more inclined to work with the PRI for pragmatic reasons. Several of the *neopanista* entrepreneurs who became governors include Ernesto Ruffo, governor of Baja California (1989–1995), and Francisco Barrio, governor of Chihuahua (1993–1997).

Currently led by Luis Felipe Bravo Mena, the PAN nominated **Vicente Fox Quesada** as its presidential candidate for the 2000 elections. A former Coca-Cola executive, governor, and congressman from the state of Guanajuato, Fox emphasized a more open economy, improved education, and greater security in the presidential campaign. In the July 2, 2000, elections Fox won 43 percent of the popular vote, handing the PRI its first defeat at the presidential level, but his Alliance for Change coalition received only 38 percent of the ballots for Congress. Thus, Fox is the first president in Mexican history to take office with a plurality, but not a majority, of the national vote and must govern without a majority in Congress and a large number of state legislatures run by the opposition. In order to govern effectively, President Fox has been forced to bargain and compromise to get legislation passed, something that PRI presidents never had to worry about.

The PAN, like the PRI, has undergone changes in the method and locus of internal decision making. The PAN leadership lost control of their party nomination procedures when Vicente Fox began campaigning well in advance of the normal campaign period. As a result, the PAN was forced to change its candidate selection process from a party convention to selection by party members through a direct secret ballot. Now that the PAN has captured the presidency, it remains to be seen what role Fox will play in PAN's candidate selection process when his *sexenio* is over in 2006. *See also* Electoral System/Elections.

SUGGESTED READING

Soledad Loaeza, *Partido Acción Nacional: La larga marcha, 1939–1994: Oposición leal y partido de protesta* (Mexico, D.F.: Fondo de Cultura Económica, 1999); Kevin J. Middlebrook, ed., *Party Politics and the Struggle for Democracy in Mexico: National and State-Level Analysis of the* Partido Acción Nacional (La Jolla: Center for U.S.–Mexican Studies, University of California–San Diego, 2001); Victoria E. Rodríguez and Peter M. Ward, eds., *Opposition Government in Mexico* (Albuquerque: University of New Mexico Press, 1995).

Partido Auténtico de la Revolución Mexicana (PARM) ☀ The PARM was founded in 1954 by dissident members of the **Partido Revolucionario Institucional (PRI)** who were disenchanted with the dominant party's candidates and policies. The most well known among the founders were General Jacinto B. Treviño, a former minister of industry, and General Juan Barragán. Most ana-

lysts of Mexican party politics regard the PARM as a parastatal party—one that usually supports the PRI and its national candidates—but it has also been known to support candidacies of dissent members of the PRI as well. It is primarily a loose association of retired generals who advocate a moderate approach to the ongoing revolution, emphasizing the protection of private property and welfare programs, as well as increased government assistance to small farmers. Its greatest **electoral** strength has been in Tamaulipas, but it has also garnered significant support in Nuevo León, Jalisco, and the Federal District.

Beginning in 1958, the PARM has won a small number of seats in the Chamber of Deputies. After a brief period in the 1980s when PARM lost its official status due to a shortage of votes needed to retain its electoral registration, it nominated **Cuauhtémoc Cárdenas** as its own candidate in 1988. With Cárdenas at the head of the party ticket, PARM won 30 *diputado* seats in the election, but its support declined to 2.2 percent of the vote in the 1991 congressional elections. **Porfirio Múñoz Ledo**, former president of the PRI and the leftist **Partido de la Revolución Democrática (PRD)**, was the PARM candidate for president in 2000. He dropped out of the race two weeks before the election to support **Vicente Fox**, the leading opposition leader in the presidential campaign and the eventual winner of the tightly fought contest.

Partido Centro Democrático (PCD) ☀ The PCD was formed in 1997 and received its official registration in May 1999. It is led by **Manuel Camacho Solís**, former mayor of Mexico City, minister of foreign relations, and Chiapas peace negotiator under the **Carlos Salinas** administration. The PCD defines itself as a liberal republican party and was one of the main proponents of efforts to form an opposition alliance for the 2000 elections. After failing to acquire the ruling party's nomination to succeed President Salinas in 1994, Camacho Solís split with the **Partido Revolucionario Institucional (PRI)** to launch the PCD in 1997.

Partido Comunista Mexicano (PCM). *See* Communism and Mexican Communist Party (Partido Comunista Mexicano, PCM).

Partido de la Revolución Democrática (PRD) ☀ The Party of the Democratic Revolution was founded in 1989 after the controversial 1988 presidential elections. It is composed of former members of the Democratic Current (Corriente Democrático, CD) of the **Partido Revolucionario Institucional (PRI)** and the alliance of several leftist organizations, the most important of which was the **Partido Mexicano Socialista (PMS)**, a party with close ties to **communist** activists. Headed by Amalia García at the time of the 2000 election, the PRD for the third time chose **Cuauhtémoc Cárdenas** as its candidate for the presidency. It is currently Mexico's largest left-of-center political party.

Before 1988, Mexico's left was made up of political parties that for decades acted as a home for moderate socialists and an assortment of left-of-center politicians willing to collaborate with the government in exchange for a seat in Congress or other political favors. After the tumultuous presidential elections in 1988, the PRD was founded the following year to give a more coherent identity and formal organization to the broad coalition (Frente Democrático Nacional, FDN) that supported Cuauhtémoc Cárdenas in the previous election. The PRD is hampered by its diverse sources of support, drawing largely from voters who supported the political parties and successor movements to the Mexican Communist Party, the PMS, and the Partido Mexicano de los Trabajadores (PMT); leftist activists and victims of the government repression generated by the 1968 **Tlatelolco massacre** in Mexico City; and dis-

sident members of the ruling Institutional Revolutionary Party bothered by the neoliberal economic model and the absence of democratic reform being pursued by the **Miguel de la Madrid** government at the time.

Drawing on an extraordinary mixture of political personalities and a broad assortment of national grievances, the ideology of PRD members is difficult to pinpoint with any degree of accuracy. For example, it is not strictly a social democratic party, although a substantial number of its members believe in some form of socialism and in 1996 the PRD became a full member of the Socialist International. What interests the leaders and rank and file of the PRD is the attempt to preserve and reformulate the tradition of revolutionary nationalism, a tenet of leftist intellectual thought that reaches back to the goals and ideals of six years of reform under President **Lázaro Cárdenas** (1934–1940). Currently *Cardenismo* (PRD ideology) incorporates elements of economic sovereignty, anti-imperialism, and a preference for a strong state apparatus to guide economic policy.

Despite a progressive political platform calling for the **democratization** of Mexico's political system, an end to neoliberal economic policies, and orthodox responses to financial crises implemented by President **Ernesto Zedillo,** the PRD has not been able to gain electorally since the 1988 election. Cárdenas won 31 percent of the votes in 1988 but obtained only 17 percent in 1994, a rather dismal showing for the left against the PRI and the PAN. In an effort to reduce the dissension within its ranks, in 1996 the PRD became the first political party to select its leadership by direct vote of its members, while also granting the franchise to voters who opted to join the party on the day of the election. During the 1997–2000 period of the Mexican Congress, the PRD controlled 25 percent of the seats in the Chamber of Deputies and close to 12 percent in the Senate. By 2000, elected officials of the PRD at the state and local levels were governing close to one-fifth of the total Mexican population, and Cuauhtémoc Cárdenas had resigned from his position as mayor of Mexico to make his third run for the presidency. Despite a long campaign that stressed the need to establish honest government, end discrimination against women, reduce poverty and economic inequalities, and create jobs, the PRD was unable to make significant gains against the PRI and the center-right PAN party. In the 2000 election for president, the PRD again placed third and its share of the national vote slipped below its 1994 level to 15 percent.

The **electoral** weakness of the PRD stems from its inability to develop a credible alternative program of governance to the other major parties. The PRI enjoys a reservoir of electoral strength throughout the country, but PRD voters are concentrated in the states of Michoacán, the impoverished southern states of Guerrero, Oaxaca, and Chiapas, and the Mexico City metropolitan region. The most serious defect of the Mexican left, according to political scientist Wayne Cornelius (2000, 500), is "the lack of a strong, nationwide, local-level infrastructure that is not dependent on the personal charisma of Cuauhtémoc Cárdenas to mobilize PRD supporters." During the **Carlos Salinas** administration, the PRD suffered from serious conflicts with PRI bosses, with hundreds of PRD activists punished, intimidated, or murdered since the party was created. Carr (1997, 1054) explains the predicament as follows: "The PRI has always taken revenge on defectors [from the ruling party] and PRD officials claim that 'more than 350 PRD activists had been assassinated by the end of 1995.'" However, during the last half of the Zedillo administration, PRD–PRI relations improved considerably as substantial electoral victories, first in the 1997 mayoral race in Mexico City (won by Cárdenas himself), followed by gubernatorial victories by PRD candidates (mainly defectors from the PRI) in the states of Baja California Sur, Tlaxcala, and Zacatecas in 1998 and 1999 left the PRI with few alternatives but to cooperate with the leftist opposition. Nevertheless, the poor PRD showing in the 2000 elections does not augur well for either the political future of Cárdenas, the moral and spiritual leader of Mexican left, or the left's chances to gain the presidency in the near future.

SUGGESTED READING

Charles D. Ameringer, ed., *Political Parties of the Americas, 1980s to 1990s: Canada, Latin America, and the West Indies* (Westport, Conn.: Greenwood, 1992); Arthur S. Banks and Thomas C. Muller, eds., *Political Handbook of the World, 1998* (Binghamton, N.Y.: CSA Publications, 1998); Kathleen Bruhn, *Taking on Goliath: Mexico's Party of the Democratic Revolution* (University Park: Pennsylvania State University Press, 1997); Barry Carr, "Partido de la Revolución Democrática (PRD)," in Michael S. Werner, ed., *Encyclopedia of Mexico: History, Society, and Culture*, vol. 2 (Chicago: Fitzroy Dearborn, 1997); John Coggins and D. S. Lewis, eds., *Political Parties of the Americas and the Caribbean: A Reference Guide* (Detroit: Longman, 1992); Wayne A. Cornelius, "Politics in Mexico," in Gabriel A. Almond and G. Bingham Powell, eds., *Comparative Politics Today: A World View*, 6th ed. (Glenview, Ill.: Scott, Foresman/Little, Brown, 2000); Jorge I. Domínguez, James A. McCann, and Alejandro Poiré, eds., *Toward Mexico's Democratization: Parties, Campaigns, Elections, and Public Opinion* (New York: Routledge, 1999); Mónica Serrano, ed., *Governing Mexico: Political Parties and Elections* (London: Institute of Latin American Studies, University of London, 1998).

Partido Democrático Mexicano (PDM) ☀ Founded in 1971 as a successor to the Unión Sinarquista Nacional (USN), a neofascist and ultra-Catholic movement with a large following in the late 1930s, the PDM is a small right-wing conservative party that has registered a number of **electoral** victories at the municipal level since the early 1980s. After winning a few elections at the municipal level in 1983, it was awarded 12 chamber seats on a proportional basis in 1985, the high mark of its electoral history. Declaring that it would not seek alliances with other parties in 1988, it continued its decline until it lost all congressional representation, and its current status, in the early 1990s.

Partido de Trabajo (PT) ☀ The Labor Party is a moderate leftist political party composed of several grassroots organizations, mainly from the northern states of Durango and Chihuahua. The PT won 1.2 percent of the vote in the 1991 congressional **elections** and obtained its legal registration in the 1994 federal elections. In the August 1994 presidential election, Cecilia Soto González fought a vigorous campaign that pulled voters from the more established **Partido de la Revolución Democrática (PRD)** and gave her 2.7 percent of the national vote. The PT won 10 seats in the Chamber Deputies in 1994 and seven in 1997. The current national leader of the PT, Alberto Anaya, decided to back **Cuauhtémoc Cárdenas**, a three-time candidate for the PRD, in the 2000 presidential elections. The PT was part of the unsuccessful effort to form an Opposition Alliance for the 2000 elections.

Partido Frente Cardenista de Reconstrucción Nacional (PFCRN) ☀ The PFCRN has roots in the Partido Socialista de los Trabajadores (PST) and the events associated with the **Tlatelolco massacre** in 1968. The PST was founded in 1973 by Rafael Aguilar Talamantes and other leaders who had been imprisoned for their involvement in the 1968 student movement. The social base of the party was composed of university students, intellectuals, peasants, and urban squatters. It obtained official registration in 1978 but never won more than 12 seats in the Chamber of Deputies between 1979 and 1985. After gaining **electoral** strength between 1985 and 1988, it was renamed as the PFCRN in

1988 and supported **Cuauhtémoc Cárdenas** in that year's presidential election. However, the PFCRN suffered another electoral decline in 1991 when its number of congressional members fell from its high of 41 seats in 1988 to only 23 deputies. Although the PFCRN has voted with the **Partido de la Revolución Democrática (PRD)** in Congress, it reverted to its prior status as a parastatal party during the 1990s, aligning itself with the **Partido Revolucionario Institucional (PRI)** on various laws that it agreed with.

SUGGESTED READING

Charles D. Ameringer, ed., *Political Parties in the Americas, 1980–1990s: Canada, Latin America, and the West Indies* (Westport, Conn.: Greenwood, 1992).

Partido Mexicano Socialista (PMS) ☀ Founded in 1987, the PMS attempted to merge two of Mexico's principal leftist groups at the time, the Unified Socialist Party of Mexico (PSUM) and the Mexican Worker's Party (PMT), as well as three smaller parties with little following on the left. Until it dissolved in May 1989 and merged with the **Partido de la Revolución Democrática (PRD)** in that same year, it was the third largest political party in Mexico. Before its merger with the PRD, the PMS struggled to unite a fractious number of leftist parties and run PMT leader Herberto Castillo as the PMS presidential candidate in 1988. Shortly before the 1988 election, he withdrew in favor of the Frente Democrático Nacional's **Cuauhtémoc Cárdenas** to help maximize his electoral gain against the PRI; however, the ballots had already been printed, leaving the FDN with little to gain from the merger at the polls.

Partido Popular Socialista (PPS) ☀ The PPS is the first of the parastatal political parties, formed in 1948 (as the Partido Popular, PP) by **Vicente Lombardo Toledano**, when he split with the **Partido Revolucionario Institucional (PRI)** over some of its conservative tendencies. Known as the Popular Socialist Party since 1960, the PPS is Marxist in ideological orientation, seeks the establishment of a vague form of socialism in Mexico, and draws its support from intellectuals, students, and some **labor** elements close to Lombardo. Yet it has consistently belied its leftist credentials by being a "satellite" of the PRI, endorsing many of its candidates and winning a few seats of its own, but posing virtually no threat to the hegemony of the PRI. In 1976, the PPS secretary-general, Jorge Cruikshank, became the first opposition candidate to win a Senate seat since 1929, although he was charged with having a made a "deal" with the PRI to get it. The PPS strategy of siding with the PRI derives from its position that imperialism (particularly U.S. **intervention**) is Mexico's worst enemy and that the PRI has stood up to this threat by pursuing nationalist and revolutionary policies to counter it.

The PPS is a party suffering from **electoral** decline; between 1963 and 1985, the PPS backed every PRI presidential candidate and witnessed a slight increase in representation in Congress, but the party continued to decline at the polls. In 1979 it won fewer than 400,000 seats (2.6 percent of the total), and in 1982 it was only able to garner 1.9 percent of the total. It broke with the PRI over its choice of **Carlos Salinas** as its presidential candidate in 1988 and joined the National Democratic Front to support the coalition candidacy of **Cuauhtémoc Cárdenas.** In the 1991 congressional elections, none of the PPS candidates were directly elected, but it was awarded 12 seats in the Chamber of Deputies on a proportional basis. The party's decline continued in 1994, when it received only 0.5 percent of the presidential vote and later failed to win any congressional representation in 1994 and 1997, all of which suggest that the PPS is close to political death after more than 50 years of struggling to

offer a "progressive" program that would attract voters. *See also* Foreign Policy.

Partido Revolucionario Institucional (PRI) ☀ The PRI is the dominant political party that ruled Mexican **government** from 1929 until its defeat at the hands of **Vicente Fox** in the 2000 presidential election. At first called the National Revolutionary Party (PNR), it changed its name to the Party of the Mexican Revolution (PRM) in 1938 and then to its current name, Institutional Revolutionary Party, in 1946. Fashioned by revolutionary statesmen after the end of the **Mexican Revolution** (1910–1917), the ruling party was conceived as a mechanism for achieving a balance between stability and orderly change in a society plagued by regional battles among major political bosses and a plethora of small and unruly political parties. As the official party evolved, it broadened its representation by creating a **corporatist** structure in which the government assumed responsibility for specific private economic and social groups such as **labor** and farmer organizations. While dominating national politics, the PRI also left a small space for opposition political parties, but they operated at a severe disadvantage and were often coopted by the ruling party. Between 1929 and 2000, 13 consecutive PRI presidents governed Mexico. The entrenched power of the Institutional Revolutionary Party started to erode in 1988 when several opposition parties managed to make significant advances in eroding the **electoral** power of the dominant party.

Until the PRI was defeated in 2000, it stood as the world's longest-ruling political party; however, this period of domination was also accompanied by heavy criticism from those who resented its antidemocratic procedures and authoritarian tactics of maintaining a grip on Mexican politics. Although Mexican presidents are limited to a single six-year term of office (*sexenio*), until recently an elaborate system of party rules and rituals made it possible for the PRI to perpetuate itself in power. Of most importance was the president's prerogative to choose his own successor in what Mexicans called the *dedazo* (the act of tapping his finger on the shoulder of the chosen one), the widely accepted act of picking a presidential candidate from inside the ranks of the president's cabinet, usually 9–10 months before the next election. The outgoing president's handpicked successor would then be unveiled (*destapado*) to the public and a "campaign" would begin with highly orchestrated bus trips to the most remote corners of Mexico, where the central plazas would be filled with supporters waving PRI flags, often paid (with money and drink) to applaud and cheer the next president of the republic.

The tradition of Mexican presidents handpicking their successor ended in 1999, when the governing party approved a new system in which PRI candidates for president would be chosen in a nationwide presidential primary. Under the new rules, PRI politicians who want to run in the primary in November must resign their government positions, register as precandidates, and delay their campaign for the primary election until August 1, when the formal campaign begins. All registered precandidates must agree to take part in a public debate among all presidential contenders. To win the November primary, the PRI candidate must acquire a majority of votes in the largest number of Mexico's 300 electoral districts, instead of winning a simple majority of votes nationwide. All 58 million Mexicans with voting cards, regardless of party affiliation, are eligible to vote. Unlike the United States, the winner is not determined in a party convention but is formally sworn in as the PRI candidate two weeks after the November primary vote.

In addition to the nationwide primary system, the PRI established campaign spending limits and a committee to oversee fund-raising and spending. To ensure that the party's first primary vote was untainted by fraud, the PRI spent $9.2 million to demonstrate that it has evolved from an institution to keep carefully selected rulers in power into a more authentic **democratic** party. The more than 64,000 voting stations were each staffed by three party representatives, and each candidate could have his own representative. The voting process in 1999 also involved foreign and national election observers, further insurance that at the end of the voting there would be no complaints that the electoral process was unfair. The autocratic tradition that picked 10 successive presidential candidates since **Manuel Ávila Camacho** in 1940 ended with the 2000 election, putting a close to an undemocratic arrangement in which the PRI presidential candidate came directly out of the president's office.

While the PRI was in power, the party served as a channel in decision making for the least-influential groups in society, but it did not exercise policy-making authority over the political system. Most national elites until recently were members of the PRI, but the official party is under the thumb of the executive branch and thus not a major force as a policy vehicle. Despite years of opposition criticism of electoral fraud, the PRI displayed a remarkable ability to adapt and survive while continuing to legitimize its authority through the electoral process. Electoral reforms beginning in the 1970s helped expand political participation and allow for more opposition candidates to have a chance to obtain and exercise power. The structure of opportunity has changed for the political opposition, suggesting a major break from past presidential elections. For example, in 1994 the PRI controlled 89 percent of governorships, 60 percent of seats in the federal Chamber of Deputies, and 74 percent of seats in the Senate. Six years later the opposition held 34 percent of the governorships, 52 percent of the seats in the Chamber of Deputies, and 41 percent of Senate seats. The 1997 congressional elections resulted in the first defeat for the PRI, leaving control of the Chamber of Deputies in the hands of the opposition for the first time since 1913, and PRD stalwart **Cuauhtémoc Cárdenas** won the Mexico City mayoralty contest, the second most powerful position in Mexico.

While Mexico continues to strain under the pressure (internal and external) to democratize its procedures for recruiting and transferring power, there are also currents of structural political change that portend a more open and competitive system, one that is at odds with its authoritarian past and cynical political culture. With populist candidates like Venezuela's Hugo Chávez, who won the 1998 presidential election by attacking **corruption** and misrule of the two traditional parties, PRI stalwarts worried that the same fate would touch Mexico in 2000. The erosion of traditional-party dominance in Latin America is often attributed to the structural adjustments demanded by international financial institutions, thus making it more difficult for governments to maintain their grip on power through elaborate patronage networks. The patron–client advantages enjoyed by the PRI were gradually being eroded by a political culture in which the majority of citizens believe that politicians are in cahoots with the rich, corruption is rampant, and deal making the norm, as well as by the push for neoliberal reforms that reduced the size of the state apparatus. Recent electoral studies indicated that the Mexican voters mostly likely to leave the PRI at the time of the 2000 election were males, urban dwellers, and individuals with a high school education, especially if they believed the PRI government was primarily responsible for the country's economic decline. After being defeated in 2000, the PRI exploded into warring factions—mainly **technocrats** and traditionalists—and some analysts of the Mexican political scene argued that the PRI may soon be doomed to extinction. In an effort to maintain its political grip at the national and state levels, the PRI has retained its corpo-

ratist structure with linkages to major segments of society.

SUGGESTED READING

John J. Bailey, *Governing Mexico: The Statecraft of Crisis Management* (New York: St. Martin's, 1988); Roderic Ai Camp, *Politics in Mexico*, 3d ed. (New York: Oxford University Press, 1999); Wayne A. Cornelius, *Mexican Politics in Transition: The Breakdown of a One-Party-Dominant Regime* (La Jolla: Center for U.S.–Mexican Studies, University of California–San Diego, 1996); Luis Javier Garrido, "Partido Revolucionario Institucional (PRI)," in Michael S. Werner, ed., *Encyclopedia of Mexico: History, Society, and Culture*, vol. 2 (Chicago: Fitzroy Dearborn, 1997); Howard Handelman, *Mexican Politics: The Dynamics of Change* (New York: St. Martin's, 1997); Neil Harvey, *Mexico: Dilemmas of Transition* (New York: St. Martin's, 1993); Martin Needler, *Mexican Politics* (New York: Praeger, 1990); George Philip, *The Presidency in Mexican Politics* (London: Macmillan, 1992); Riordan Roett, ed., *The Challenge of Institutional Reform in Mexico* (Boulder, Colo.: Lynne Rienner, 1995); Monica Serrano, ed., *Governing Mexico: Political Parties and Elections* (London: Institute for Latin American Studies/Brookings Institution, 1998).

Partido Socialista Unificado Mexicano (PSUM). *See* Communism and Mexican Communist Party (Partido Comunista Mexicano, PCM).

Partido Verde Ecológico Mexicano (PVEM) ☀ The PVEM is the outgrowth of the National Ecologist Alliance (Alianza Ecologista Nacional), formed in 1984, and the Mexican Ecologist Party (PEM), which emerged in 1987. Mexico's "Greens" adopted their present name in 1987, when they formally entered the **electoral** arena as the Mexican Green Ecologist Party, bringing together members of the two previous green/ecologist groupings. In the 1991 elections the PVEM failed to obtain the minimum vote share necessary to gain full legal status as a political party. The poor showing in the 1991 elections led to a severe internal crisis during which the leader of the party removed its directors in Mexico City. Since its inception, the leader of the PVEM has been Jorge González Torres. He has campaigned twice for the presidency, once in 1994 winning only 0.9 percent of the vote, and the second time in 2000, joining with the right-of-center **Partido Acción Nacional (PAN)** under the banner of the Alliance for Change. In 1997, the PVEM gained 14 percent of the vote nationwide and broad support in Mexico City. The PVEM political program centers on defending the **environment** and promoting sustainable development.

Party of the Democratic Center. *See* Partido Centro Democrático (PCD).

Party of the Democratic Revolution. *See* Partido de la Revolución Democrática (PRD).

Paz, Octavio (1914–1998) ☀ Mexico's premier poet, playwright, diplomat, and essayist. His writings cover a wide range of domestic and international topics, including efforts to understand the formative influences on the Mexican personality. His prolific and impassioned writing gained him international fame, and in 1990 he was awarded the Nobel Prize in Literature, the first Mexican to be so honored.

Octavio Paz was born to a distinguished family and raised in Mexico City, but his interest in writing and politics sparked a number of journeys overseas—to Spain, France, the United States, India, and Japan—that had a definitive effect on his work. His lawyer father, Octavio Paz Solórzano, was a veteran of the **Mexican Revolution** of 1910 who fled to the United States to represent the peasant guerrilla leader **Emiliano Zapata**. Between 1932 and 1937 Paz attended the **Universidad Nacional Autónoma de México (UNAM)**; after his university years he married **Elena Garro** in 1937 and then traveled widely (including a two-year period when he lived in San Francisco and New York) before joining the Mexican foreign service in 1945. He maintained his position in the diplomatic service until 1968, when he resigned in protest over the **Tlatelolco massacre**.

Octavio Paz is best known for his surrealist poetry, a style that appealed to him because of its effort to locate a reality beyond the material world. His travels to Japan and India provided an introduction to Oriental philosophy and its view that the real lies outside time and history. In his first important essay, *El laberinto de la soledad* (The labyrinth of solitude, 1950), Paz attempts to find the roots of Mexican psychology and culture in the mix of Spanish colonial and native Indian traditions. This dual cultural heritage—one in which a conquering Spanish father abandons his offspring and an Indian mother turns against her own people—has caused Mexicans to suffer from a life of isolation and defensiveness, hiding behind masks and taking refuge in a "labyrinth of solitude." In his effort to understand Mexican **machismo**, Paz argues that male attitudes toward life (and women) are a mask to conceal his solitude. In dealing with others, Mexican males believe that it is necessary to take advantage of them, lest they take advantage of you: "Screw or be screwed" in the aggressive and violent language of the street. The Mexican macho feels a constant need to project an image of strength and male virility, whether in a business deal or in his treatment of women, with the exception of his saintly mother.

Paz was also a major critic of Mexico's social and political life in a succession of books published after *The Labyrinth of Solitude*. The cultural explanations so important to his essays and poetry are rooted in conflicting traditions—Spanish and Indian—that reinforce a hierarchical and conservative society. These interpretations of Mexican history and politics are found in *El ogro filantrópico: Historia y política, 1971–1978* (1979), *Tiempo nublado* (1983), and *Pequeña crónica de*

Octavio Paz at the Metropolitan Museum of Art, New York, 1994. Credit: AP/World Wide Photos.

nuestros días (1990). In these works he analyzes such topics as **democracy** and totalitarianism, capitalism, pluralism, freedom, and the dilemmas of Mexican modernization. Until his death in 1998, Paz continued to write on poetic themes concerned with love in Western cultures and the essence of Mexican art. Paz's 1990 Nobel Prize in Literature was awarded for his "impassioned writing with wide horizons, characterized by sensuous intelligence and humanistic integrity."

Octavio Paz's moderate political views during the Cold War and his thoughtful evaluation of Mexican culture alienated many Mexican intellec-

tuals, particularly **Carlos Fuentes.** An admirer of leftist causes and a critic of U.S. involvement in Latin America, Fuentes criticized Paz for his bourgeois reformism. Paz continued to defend his views on Mexican politics and economic development, as well as his worldview, despite the censure of his literary peers. When Paz, poet and essayist, died in 1998, it marked the end of an era in which artistic approaches to life in Mexico and beyond define how people identify and interpret their national identity. *See also* Feminism.

SUGGESTED READING

Jorge Aguilar Mora, *La divina pareja: Historia y mito en Octavio Paz* (Mexico, D.F.: Era, 1978); John M. Fein, *Octavio Paz: A Reading of His Major Poems, 1957–1976* (Lexington: University Press of Kentucky, 1986); Yvon Grenier, *From Art to Politics: Octavio Paz and the Pursuit of Freedom* (Lanham, Md.: Rowman & Littlefield, 2001); Octavio Paz, *The Labyrinth of Solitude: Life and Thought in Mexico,* trans. Lysander Kemp (New York: Grove, 1961); Paz, *The Other Mexico: Critique of the Pyramid* (New York: Grove, 1972); José Quiroga, *Understanding Octavio Paz* (Columbia: University of South Carolina Press, 1999); Alberto Ruy Sánchez, *Una introducción a Octavio Paz* (Mexico, D.F.: Joaquín Mortiz, 1990); Jason Wilson, *Octavio Paz* (Boston: Twayne, 1986).

People's Revolutionary Army (ERP). *See* Guerrilla Movements and Counterinsurgency.

Personalismo ☀ One of the many political-historical roots of Mexican society and politics is *personalismo,* or personalism, a cultural trait that emphasizes the individual as the axis of social relationships. Spanish colonialism helped develop a deference to and dependence on individuals and personal authority rather than the state and a constitution with a Bill of Rights. *Personalismo* embodies the Mexican belief that personal dignity supersedes all other considerations in both private and official behavior. This code of behavior means that it is entirely natural for presidents, military chiefs, business tycoons, and all others in positions of power to surround themselves with their kin, friends, and associates and thereafter to use their power to enrich themselves at the expense of the general public. Personalism also means that concepts of law, logic, fair play, equality, and other principles are of lesser importance to individuals in positions of power than protecting family and friends. This personalistic cultural mind-set frequently translates into *whom* you know rather than *what* you know in business and politics. It also means that Mexicans are more sensitive to personal slights and unpleasant personal relationships in the workplace, often refusing to work with people they dislike.

SUGGESTED READING

Roderic Ai Camp, *Politics in Mexico: The Decline of Authoritarianism*, 3d ed. (New York: Oxford University Press, 1999); Glen Dealy, *The Public Man: An Interpretation of Latin American and Other Catholic Cultures* (Amherst: University of Massachusetts Press, 1977); Boye Lafayette De Mente, *NTC's Dictionary of Mexican Cultural Code Words* (Lincolnwood, Ill.: NTC, 1996).

Peso Crisis. *See* Debt Crisis.

Petróleos Mexicanos (PEMEX) ☀ The petroleum industry has been a major part of the Mexican economy since 1904, when U.S. oil magnate Edward L. Doheny opened up the first producing oil field in San Luis Potosí to serve the Mexican Central Railway. The foreign-owned oil industry began to export small amounts of oil in 1911, but with the influx of new technology and further exploration on the Gulf Coast, production increased dramatically. Despite the turmoil of the **Mexican Revolution** after 1911, growing investments in the petroleum industry by an increasing

number of foreign companies helped Mexico become the world's second-ranking oil producer after the United States by 1920. The Mexican oil boom provided employment for thousands of workers—American, Chinese, and Mexican—in the enclave of refineries and terminals along the Gulf Coast around Veracruz during the 1910s. As the oil industry grew, the Mexican **government** took more of an interest in the financial and regulatory aspects of the petroleum economy. When Article 27 of the **Constitution of 1917** overturned the liberal exploration and ownership laws which had encouraged foreign investment in mining and oil, the tradition of state ownership of mineral rights became the law of the land.

This revolutionary change did not go over well with the foreign oil companies, and they soon found themselves in constant conflict with the Mexican government over the interpretation of Article 27. Caught between the topsy-turvy nature of oil prices, the growing number of strikes, and the strength of unionized oil workers, as well as the constant complaining about the host government's efforts to confiscate their property by foreign property owners, the Mexican government nationalized the oil fields. Petróleos Mexicanos (PEMEX) was inaugurated in 1938 after President **Lázaro Cárdenas** nationalized the entire petroleum industry on March 18, 1938.

While the nationalization of the petroleum industry was pleasing to Mexican nationalists, the creation of a state-owned oil firm was not a panacea of the ills that plagued the oil industry. The expropriation of March 1938 led to the necessary reorganization of the petroleum industry, the creation of PEMEX, and the expulsion of British and American oil companies; however, it also increased tensions with the United States over compensation for lost property and an international boycott, and it made the industry more vulnerable to domestic political pressures. For example, the companies responded aggressively to the expropriation by calling their trained engineers and geologists home, calling for a boycott to prevent Mexico from obtaining the necessary equipment for its new industry, and mounting a vicious propaganda campaign in the United States. Subsidized magazines like Standard Oil's *Lamp* and periodicals such as the *Atlantic Monthly* accused the Mexicans of being thieves, debased thugs, fascists, and **communists**. President Cárdenas was alleged to be a captive of the Mexican Communist Party and a supporter of socialist labor organizations critical of foreign capitalists. It was a low point in Mexican–U.S. relations, but eventually the Good Neighbor policy and **World War II** helped the nations get back on a more friendly path.

At the time of nationalization, the Mexican oil industry produced crude oil for export; after nationalization, the industry focused more attention on domestic needs, including asphalt that paved the roads needed to build a national market and fertilizer needed in the development of commercial export agriculture. Following World War II, the oil industry suffered from the lack of adequate knowledge of Mexican oil reserves, particularly in locating new oil fields, and the lack of imported supplies for drilling and refining. Gradually the dependency on foreign petroleum personnel declined as Mexican technicians gained more knowledge of the oil industry. This change to a more nationalist industry was accomplished with the inauguration of the Mexican Petroleum Institute (Instituto Mexicano de Petróleo, IMP) in 1965, with operations under way by 1966. The IMP grew rapidly into a sophisticated research and development center with over 3,000 employees, mostly scientists and technicians with a mission to make the oil industry the cornerstone of Mexican nationalism and economic development.

Although it is considered a parastatal agency within the federal bureaucracy, Petróleos Mexicanos is a state oil (and natural gas) monopoly wholly owned by the federal government. Private domestic or foreign oil companies are forbidden by law to operate in Mexico. PEMEX operates all oil reserves, drilling, transporting, refining, and marketing of oil and leases concessions for retail gas stations. The director of PEMEX is a member of the president's cabinet, which allows him a major voice on the production and export of Mexico's major source of revenue. PEMEX is divided into four subsidiary organizations that concentrate on (1) exploration and production, (2) refining, (3) gas, and (4) petrochemicals.

The world's fifth-largest oil producer, Mexico pumped 2.9 million barrels of crude oil and 1.3 billion cubic feet of natural gas in 2000. Petroleum and petroleum refining is the largest employer (and largest industry by revenue) in Mexico. In 1997 petroleum and derivatives accounted for 10 percent of exports, mostly to the United States. One-third of the government's budget comes from oil exports. In an effort to modernize its economy, hundreds of state-owned companies have been privatized, and since the 1994 peso devaluation there has been added pressure on the Mexican government to denationalize PEMEX, which some consider the heart and soul of national economic development. While these pressures—domestic and foreign—have been successfully resisted by government officials and public opinion prefers that PEMEX remain a state-owned enterprise, it remains a centerpiece of the powerful state sector and an important symbol of Mexican nationalism. With PEMEX vital to the Mexican economy, President **Vicente Fox** insists he will leave the oil monopoly in state hands and work to make the petroleum industry more streamlined and efficient. President Fox's proposed tax reform would allow PEMEX to keep more of the money it makes, but industry and government officials worry about embezzlement and **corruption** among PEMEX officials.

Although Mexico is not a member of the multinational petroleum-producing cartel OPEC (Organization of Petroleum Exporting Countries), founded in 1960, it has observer status and is a major player in the non-OPEC (sometimes referred to as "NOPEC" in the oil industry) oil producers such as Norway and Great Britain. Between 1989 and 1999 world oil prices declined and OPEC found itself again in an unwelcome situation of having to endure low levels of revenue from oil exports. In December 1998, Mexico received less than $8 a barrel for its crude oil, but after price increases propelled by OPEC's cutbacks and the continued economic expansion in the United States and Asia, Mexican oil was selling for close to $25 a barrel in 2000. For Mexico, the drop in oil prices during the decade of the 1990s coincided with a peso devaluation, a stock market crash, an exodus of foreign capital, and the agony of a deep recession. Unable to rely on significant revenues from petroleum exports to bolster the regime's legitimacy, Mexico's ruling party had to face important victories by opposition parties anxious to reap the political benefits from the economic morass.

Despite the fact that Mexico has often supported Third World causes and stressed the importance of nationalism and state sovereignty, the question often arises as to why Mexico has chosen to remain independent of OPEC. Those who run PEMEX cite four reasons for not seeking membership. First, Mexicans feel they have a successful petroleum industry and see no reason to affiliate with an international organization that might compromise its independence. Second, there is some question among policy makers in Mexico City and PEMEX as to whether Mexico satisfies the stated prerequisite of "exporting substantial quantities of oil" found in the OPEC statutes, a nebulous concept that allows for multiple interpretations by oil producers. Third, Mexicans insist that their oil industry is fundamentally different from those of the OPEC members, meaning that Mexico's early oil nationalization and the formation of PEMEX has eliminated the problem of foreign firms setting

oil prices without the endorsement of the host country. Finally, Mexico can obtain higher prices on the world market than any OPEC member because of lower transportation costs to the United States (its major market). It possesses the added advantage of not having to restrict production because of various cartel agreements. Although Mexico is an "independent" oil producer, it often has to walk a tightrope between caving in to world pressure (mainly from Washington) to increase petroleum output when prices are high, and the risk of stirring nationalist political opposition if Mexico City is seen as being too willing to appease the oil-importing nations that are desperate for lower prices.

With the passage of the **North American Free Trade Agreement (NAFTA)** in 1994, PEMEX has gone through several reorganizations aimed at cutting costs, improving efficiency, and making the company more accountable to the Mexican public. Given the need for capital and better technology, NAFTA has changed the role that foreigners can play in Mexico's petroleum industry. For example, a new franchise system allows foreigners to own gas station subfranchises and to have limited foreign participation in the energy sector. NAFTA also opened PEMEX contracts in excess of $250,000 for goods and services and in excess of $8 million for construction activities to foreign participation. The nation's energy secretary has requested legislation that would remove excessive regulation and make PEMEX more of a private operation. To secure the 1995 loan to Mexico from the United States and a few other government entities, Mexico pledged PEMEX oil revenues to guarantee the loan.

The environmental concerns that were incorporated into NAFTA have added domestic pressures on PEMEX to clean up its activities where oil spillage and pollution have been demonstrated to be damaging to the **environment**. When claimants have been able to claim environmental damage attributable to PEMEX operations, the state oil monopoly has promised to comply and pay indemnification to those affected by the activity.

SUGGESTED READING

George Baker, "Petróleos Mexicanos (PEMEX)," in Barbara A. Tenenbaum, ed., *Encyclopedia of Latin American History and Culture* (New York: Scribners, 1996); Jonathan C. Brown, *Oil and Revolution in Mexico* (Berkeley: University of California Press, 1993); George W. Grayson, *The Politics of Mexican Oil* (Pittsburgh: University of Pittsburgh Press, 1980); George D. E. Philip, *Oil and Politics in Latin America: Nationalist Movements and State Oil Companies* (New York: Cambridge University Press, 1982); Laura Randall, *The Political Economy of Mexican Oil* (New York: Praeger, 1989); David Shields, "Mexican Pipeline: The Future of Oil under Vicente Fox," *NACLA Report on the Americas* (January–February 2001); Edward J. Williams, *The Rebirth of the Mexican Petroleum Industry* (Lexington, Mass.: Heath, 1979); Miguel S. Wionczek, Oscar M. Gúzman, and Roberto Gutiérrez, *Energy Policy in Mexico: Problems and Prospects for the Future* (Boulder, Colo.: Westview, 1998); John D. Wirth, ed., *Latin American Oil Companies and the Politics of Energy* (Lincoln: University of Nebraska Press, 1985).

Plaza of the Three Cultures. *See* Tlatelolco Massacre.

Pochos ✸ Mexicans are experienced in creating words that capture the extraordinary influence that the United States has on those who live along the **U.S.–Mexican border**. Words such as *pocho* are often used by Mexicans to refer in a derogatory way to Mexican boys (*pochos*) and girls (*pochas*) who reside along the border and try to imitate Anglos rather than Mexicans. *Pocho* is also a term (literally, someone who is "discolored" or "faded") used in reference to Mexican Americans living in the United States who have embraced North American values and traditions,

do not speak fluent Mexican Spanish, and behave in an arrogant manner when interacting with other Mexicans. As with the term **gringo**, the use of the word *pocho* is gradually undergoing a change in the lexicon of border slang. For many years it was considered totally derogatory, but it is now only slightly derogatory and even on some occasions neutral or laudatory. It is always considered part of the process of **immigration** and assimilation, with multiple meanings on both sides of the border. There is also the creation of border slang (or *pochismos*), words made from a combination of English and Spanish that are used in such a way that non-*pochos* have trouble understanding them. Needless to say, *pochismos* are popular among youth gangs and others who reside in the U.S.–Mexican border region. *See also Pachuco.*

SUGGESTED READING

Boye Lafayette De Mente, *NTC's Dictionary of Mexican Cultural Code Words* (Lincolnwood, Ill.: NTC, 1996); David Maciel, "Pocho," in Barbara A. Tenenbaum, ed., *Encyclopedia of Latin American History and Culture* (New York: Scribners, 1996).

Ponce, Manuel. *See* Chávez, Carlos.

Poniatowska, Elena (1932–) ✸ A feminist journalist, novelist, essayist, and short story writer known for her ability to intertwine fact with fiction in stories concerned with the lives of silent or marginalized Mexicans, particularly lower-class women. Elena Poniatowska was born in Paris in 1932 and moved to Mexico City at the age of nine. She attended the Liceo de México for one year and then studied in the United States, first at the Convent of the Sacred Heart's Eden Hall in Pennsylvania and then at the Manhattanville College in New York City. With a French father of Polish background and a Mexican mother who grew up in France, she developed a distinctive ethnic profile, mixing cultural traditions from Europe and the United States with her adopted Mexico. She spoke French and English and learned Spanish in Mexico, mainly from female domestic servants who worked in her Mexico City home. Her contact with dispossessed segments of Mexican women had a profound impact on her writing style and themes, establishing a bond of solidarity with Mexican language, culture, and politics. Despite her well-to-do European background, she thought of herself as completely Mexican and of Spanish as her native tongue. Once she began to work as a journalist on the newspaper *Excélsior*, Poniatowska learned to interview important literary and political figures along with the most repressed sectors of Mexican society.

As a writer committed to the plight of lower-class women, Elena Poniatowska wrote dialogues that realistically portrayed the lives of the Mexico's marginalized sectors. In *Hasta no verte, Jesús mío* (1969), she has a working-class woman living in the crowded slums of Mexico City tell her life story of oppression and bad luck. At the same time, her heroine, Jesusa Palancares, exhibits her freedom, generosity, and tenacious spirit of survival despite insuperable odds. Many of her novels concern female characters who are controlled by men; double standards abound in a world where women try to do the right thing but in the end lose the men they love and for whom they sacrifice so much.

Some of her novels deal with the position of well-known women in the arts where political activism and artistic achievements collide. Using letters, diaries, photographs, paintings, and personal interviews, Poniatowska weaves a first-person narrative that combines fact with fiction to analyze the feminine existence. In *Querido Diego te abraza quiela* (1978), the author uses personal letters that artist Angelina Beloff sent to **Diego Rivera** after their long love affair ended. In her novel *Tinísima* (1992), Poniatowska examines the political life of Italian American photographer **Tina Modotti**. Although Modotti only lived in Mexico from 1923 until she was deported in 1930, she used her photographic skills to express her political radicalism. Poniatowska's novel of Modotti examines her emotional life alongside her political life (she joined the Mexican Communist Party in 1927 and was good friends with the Mexican muralists: Diego Rivera, **José Clemente Orozco**, and **David Alfaro Siqueiros**) and social activism.

Elena Poniatowska's writings became more historical and political after the 1968 **Tlatelolco massacre** of students, workers, artists, and housewives in Mexico City. Her chronicle of the violence committed by the Mexican military during the bloody event (*La noche de Tlatelolco*, 1971) earned her the Xavier Villarrutia Prize for literature, but she refused to accept it because of her opposition to President **Luis Echeverria**'s policies. Using oral history testimonies, Poniatowska's *La noche* challenges the government's interpretation (and cover-up) of events but also is critical of the student movement. Without decreasing the factual account of the Tlatelolco story, she uses a variety of testimonies, protest literature, and stylistic techniques to create a first-rate piece of literature, one of the most widely read stories in Mexico. She was also awarded prizes for her writing, including the Mazatlán Prize (1970), Revista Siempre Prize (1973), and the National Journalism Prize (1979). Her other chronicles of a current political nature include *Fuerte es el silencio* (1980) and *Nada, nadie: Las voces del temblor* (1988), an account of the survivors of the 1985 Mexican earthquake.

Poniatowska's critical coverage of the events at Tlatelolco helped establish her as a major critic of the **Partido Revolucionario Institucional (PRI)**. In 1984 she helped create *La Jornada*, a daily newspaper that became a severe critic of the PRI. In 1985 *La Jornada* was the only newspaper that published her reports pointing out the government's neglect of those injured in the earthquake and the **corruption** in public construction that exacerbated the natural disaster in 1985. Although Poniatowska's style has been attacked by critics who object to her penchant for treating history as a form of fiction and to her feminist polemics, her chronicles are an excellent source of cultural, economic, and political information about current Mexico and its people. As a prose writer, Elena Poniatowska contributed to 20th-century Latin American literature her testimonial writing, often a complex hybrid of fiction, autobiography, and current documentary.

SUGGESTED READING

Bell Gale Chevigny, "The Transformation of Privilege in the Work of Elena Poniatowska," *Latin American Literary Review* 13, no. 26 (1985); "Elena Poniatowska," in *Encyclopedia of World Biography*, vol. 12 (Detroit: Gale Research Press, 1998); Beth E. Jörgensen, "Elena Poniatowska," in Beth E. Jörgensen, ed., *Spanish American Women Writers: A Bio-Bibliographical Source Book* (Westport, Conn.: Greenwood, 1990); Jörgensen, *The Writing of Elena Poniatowska: Engaging Dialogues* (Austin: University of Texas Press, 1994); Bernardita Llanos, "Poniatowska, Elena," in Michael S. Werner, ed., *Encyclopedia of Mexico: History, Society, and Culture*, vol. 2 (Chicago: Fitzroy Dearborn, 1997); Cynthia Steele, "Testimonio y author/idad en *Hasta no verte, Jesús mío*, de Elena Poniatowska," in Cynthia Steele, ed., *Politics, Gender, and the Mexican Novel, 1968–1988* (Austin: University of Texas Press, 1992).

Popular Socialist Party. *See* Partido Popular Socialista (PPS).

Presidency and Presidentialism. *See* Electoral System/Elections; Government, Mexican National.

Presidential Elections. *See* Electoral System/Elections.

Programa Nacional de Solidaridad (PRONASOL). *See* Salinas de Gortari, Carlos.

Puebla. *See* Geographical Regions.

Querétaro. *See* Geographical Regions.

Quintana Roo. *See* Geographical Regions.

Quintanilla, Luis (1900–1980) Outspoken diplomat and academic political scientist who played a major role in the conduct of Mexican **foreign policy** from the time he joined the foreign service in 1922 to the end of his term as ambassador to the Organization of American States (OAS) in 1958. Critical of how the United States and Europe were conducting the Cold War in Latin America, he often clashed with Winston Churchill, Harry Truman, and **Miguel Alemán** over the nature of ideological hostilities with the **Soviet Union** in the 1940s and 1950s.

Quintanilla was born to a wealthy family in Paris in 1900. His father was an artist who supported the condemnation of revolutionary general Victoriano Huerta by Mexican residents in France. Luis Quintanilla did his undergraduate and graduate studies in philosophy and letters at the Sorbonne, earning a Ph.D. in political science. His formal academic training in political science and international relations followed him in his worldly diplomatic career. Quintanilla became a professor of international organizations and political parties at the **Universidad Nacional Autónoma de México (UNAM)**, followed by academic posts lecturing at Johns Hopkins University, Williams College, the University of Virginia, the University of Kansas, and George Washington University.

Quintanilla joined the Mexican foreign service in 1922, taking diplomatic posts in Guatemala, Brazil, Colombia, and the Soviet Union throughout his long career. Active in international organizations and hemispheric diplomacy, he served as head of the Mexican delegation to the League of Nations (1932), chairman of the Inter-American Peace Commission (1948–1949), delegate to the United Nations Conference in San Francisco (1945), and ambassador to the OAS (1945–1958). As Mexico's ambassador to the OAS, Quintanilla challenged Churchill's call for a special relationship between the United States and Britain, arguing that such a relationship would undermine Pan-Americanism and hemispheric unity. An early critic of the Cold War policies of the United States and Europe, he once told Washington that the best way to defeat **communism** in Latin America was to do something about poverty and underdevelopment in the region. President Alemán tried to disassociate himself from Quintanilla's analysis by reassuring Washington diplomats that Mexico would toe the anticommunist line in the East–West struggle and that Quintanilla did not represent the views of the Mexican government. Toward the end of his career, he served as the director of the National Housing Institute during the *sexenio* of President **Adolfo López Mateos** (1958–1964) and as an adviser to the Center for the Study of Democratic Institutions in Santa Barbara, California. Among the several books he authored, the most widely read is *A Latin American Speaks* (1943).

SUGGESTED READING

Roderic Ai Camp, *Mexican Political Biographies, 1935–1993*, 3d ed. (Austin: University of Texas Press, 1995); Luis Quintanilla, *A Latin American Speaks* (New York: Macmillan, 1943).

Rabasa, Emilio Oscar (1925–) Member of a distinguished family that has been involved in legal, political, and diplomatic affairs stretching back to the 19th century. Rabasa's grandfather was a federal deputy and state governor and represented the Mexican government at the Niagara Falls Conference in 1914. His father, Oscar Rabasa, was a distinguished writer, a professor of constitutional law, and a diplomat in the Mexican foreign service, as well as special adviser to the president of Mexico. Born in Mexico City in 1925, Emilio Rabasa earned a law degree from the National School of Law and then became a professor of law at the same university.

After **World War II** Rabasa built a career as a legal adviser and diplomat. He served as legal adviser for the Ministry of Finance, Ministry of Health, Agrarian Affairs, and the National Bank for **Ejido** Credit. He was appointed ambassador to the United States in 1970 and secretary of foreign relations during the Nixon–Ford years (1970–1975). During the **Luis Echeverría** administration (1970–1976), Rabasa distinguished himself as the leader of those trying to keep President Echeverría from applying increasingly negative policies toward the United States. He was also active in fighting for the creation of the National School of Political and Social Sciences at the **Universidad Nacional Autónoma de México (UNAM)**. His son, Emilio Rabasa Gamboa, was undersecretary of government during the **Carlos Salinas** administration and served as President **Ernesto Zedillo**'s peace negotiator for Chiapas after the **Zapatista rebellion in Chiapas**. *See also* Foreign Policy.

SUGGESTED READING
Roderic Ai Camp, *Mexican Political Biographies, 1935–1993*, 3d ed. (Austin: University of Texas Press, 1995).

Revolución Mexicana, La. *See* Mexican Revolution.

Revolutionary Family or Coalition ☀ For much of the 20th century the power elite of Mexico, made up of an interlocking network of leaders from the federal bureaucracy, the **Partido Revolucionario Institucional (PRI)**, state and local political bosses, organized **labor**, and select members of corporate Mexico. According to Brandenburg (1965), Mexico is ruled by an elite he calls the Revolutionary Family. The Family is essentially an oligarchy that is forged by (1) its dedication to the **Mexican Revolution** and its ongoing struggle to build a better Mexico; (2) friendships developed through schooling, government-bureaucratic service, business connections, and civic affairs, as well as through intermarriages among Family members; (3) self-interest in amassing and retaining power, status, and wealth; (4) fear of political defeat at the hands of an opposition alliance made up of antirevolutionaries that once in power would jeopardize their economic and political achievements; and (5) their dedication to maintaining the status quo as part of the oligarchic setup, thus reducing the risks of disturbing the rewards and benefits of belonging to the revolutionary setup.

While Brandenburg describes the different levels of decision-making power, his assessment of the dynamics of the elite is more closely associated with Mexican politics during the era of **Ruiz Cortines** and **López Mateos** (1952–1964) than the key factors that characterize the ruling elite 50 years later. At the time that Brandenburg wrote his path-breaking study of Mexico's power structure, the political elite was more homogeneous in background and ideology (what he calls the "Revolutionary Creed"). Although the political elite continue to share a number of common social characteristics—education, religion, class, place of birth, and clique membership—political power has shifted in the past 25 years from politicians (*políticos*) who ascended through the ranks as party officials and elected (or appointed) officials to **technocrats** (*técnicos*) who climbed the bureaucratic ladder with little or no electoral experience. Members of the technocratic elite developed careers and built *camarillas* in the economic policy making ministries after earning a first degree at UNAM and then a postgraduate degree (or degrees) in the United States. The new members of the ruling elite tend to be born in the nation's capital and graduate from UNAM and prestigious universities in the United States such as Harvard,

Yale, and Stanford. The rapid ascent of the *técnicos* in the upper ranks of power has caused a split between old-guard politicians (called "the dinosaurs") and the younger technocrats, with the *dinosaurios* accusing the *técnicos* of being arrogant, antirevolutionary, out of step with the grass roots, and too willing to change the existing rules of the political game.

While there is still a great deal of *presidentialismo* (presidential dominance) in the power structure, there is more power sharing between the three major parties than was evident in the period in which Brandenburg made his observations. The self-selecting and self-perpetuating features (*el tapado*, *el verdadero tapado*, and *el dedazo*) of the Revolutionary Family so evident in the early 1960s have vanished with the introduction of primaries and conventions for candidate selection. Clearly, the voter now has more say in the electoral process than was the case 40 years ago. There is greater access to the decision-making process, the media are less censored and more aggressive in challenging the ruling elite over controversial policy decisions, and the authoritarianism of the past has been significantly diluted. The **corporatist** model of governing established by President **Lázaro Cárdenas** in the 1930s has undergone major changes in the past 15 years so that the government must respond to a wider array of demands from interest groups, particularly the growing number of national and international nongovernmental organizations.

While scholars continue to debate the nature of leadership and the dynamics of change in Mexico, the **Revolutionary Family** is still in place, albeit with less corporatism, clientelism, patriarchy, control over the media, and state-guided social and economic policies than prevailed during the second half of the 20th century. Elections are more open and competitive (though not necessarily fair and honest), and a few criminal cases

such as that of **Raúl Salinas de Gortari**, now in jail for politically motivated crimes, indicate that members of the Revolutionary Family are no longer immune from prosecution. In any case, the ruling elite, or Revolutionary Family, still maintains many of its traditional instruments of control—patron–client relationships, cooptation or selective repression of dissidents by police and military forces, *caciquismo*, and a muted labor movement—despite "**democratic**" reforms and troubling economic and political crises of recent *sexenios*. The election of **Vicente Fox** in 2000 is further proof of the erosion of power in the hands of a once powerful elite with few challenges from below. *See also Personalismo.*

SUGGESTED READING

Frank Brandenburg, *The Making of Modern Mexico* (Englewood Cliffs, N.J.: Prentice-Hall, 1965); Wayne A. Cornelius, "Politics in Mexico," in Gabriel A. Almond and G. Bingham Powell, eds., *Comparative Politics Today: A World View,* 6th ed. (Glenview, Ill.: Scott, Foresman/Little, Brown, 2000); Saúl David Escobar Toledo, "Rifts in the Mexican Power Elite, 1976–1986," in Sylvia Maxfield and Ricardo M. Anzaldúa, eds., *Government and Private Sector in Contemporary Mexico* (La Jolla: U.S.–Mexican Studies Center, University of California–San Diego, 1987); Cristina Puga, *México: Empresarios y poder* (Mexico, D.F.: Facultad de Ciencias Políticas y Sociales, UNAM, 1993); Strom C. Thacker, "Big Business, the State, and Free Trade in Mexico: Interests, Structure, and Political Access" (paper presented at the 1998 meeting of the Latin American Studies Association, Chicago, September 24–26, 1998).

Reyes Heroles, Jesús (1921–1985) ☀ An early proponent of electoral reforms after the turbulent events of 1968–1970, associated with the liberal and "humanist" wing of the **Partido Revolucionario Institucional (PRI)**. A writer and public official, Reyes served as a key adviser to all Mexican presidents from the 1940s until the early 1980s. While secretary of government (1976–1979) under President **López Portillo**, he introduced legislation designed to **democratize** elections by increasing majority districts for federal deputies and allocating 100 seats to opposition parties in the Chamber of Deputies.

Born in Tuxpán, Veracruz, Reyes attended public schools in his hometown before earning a law degree from the National School of Law, UNAM, in 1944. He did graduate studies in Argentina and then taught at the National School of Law for close to 20 years (1946–1963). Reyes joined the official party in 1939, beginning a long career in politics and applying his knowledge of law, economics, and public policy. At the National Preparatory School, he befriended **Luis Echeverría** and **José López Portillo**, contacts that later proved valuable in obtaining important government positions. He served as president of the PRI from 1972 to 1975, and was appointed to two cabinet posts in the Echeverría and López Portillo administrations. He was the only member of the original **Miguel de la Madrid** cabinet who held an elective office. His two sons have followed similar career paths, writing books on politics and economics and advising presidents on policy matters. Jesús Reyes Heroles died on March 19, 1985, in Mexico City. *See also* Electoral System/Elections.

Reyes Ochoa, Alfonso (1889–1959) ☀ Prominent author, intellectual, and diplomat who helped internationalize Mexican literary work through his diplomatic travels and friendships with many of the leading intellectuals and artists in Latin America and Europe during the first half of the 20th century. Born in Monterrey (Nuevo León) in 1889, Alfonso Reyes's father, Bernardo Reyes, was a key political figure of late-19th-century Mexico. Alfonso Reyes moved to Mexico City in 1906 and attended the National University and became active in literary circles and advocated for educa-

tional reform. The death of his father during a coup attempt against President Francisco I. Madero in 1913 and his self-imposed exile in Europe before and during World War I influenced his poems, essays, and books throughout his life. He produced important studies of literature, politics, and journalism, drawing on the works of the leading literary figures of the time.

Many of Reyes's important publications were written during the time he was a diplomat in Spain, France, Argentina, and Brazil. During the 1920s President Álvaro Obregón gave him the task of improving Mexico's relations with Spain, damaged during the **Mexican Revolution**. Between 1926 and 1939, Reyes served at various times as ambassador to Argentina and Brazil, completing numerous books of essays, narratives, and poetry while on diplomatic assignments. In Argentina he became good friends with authors Jorge Luis Borges and Victoria Ocampo, and while ambassador to Brazil he developed friendships with leading writers such as Paul Morand, Cecilia Meireles, Manuel Bandeira, and others. The final years of his life were spent in Mexico, where he received the National Literature Prize in 1945 and was appointed director of the Mexican Academy of Language in 1957. As president of the prestigious **Colegio de México** (1940–1959), he contributed to Mexico's academic and intellectual development. Alfonso Reyes was a candidate for the Nobel Prize in Literature and received other awards in Mexico before he died in 1959 at the age of 70. Despite his impressive works of poetry and literature, Reyes is not well known beyond Mexico.

SUGGESTED READING

Roderic Ai Camp, "Reyes Ochoa, Alfonso," in Barbara A. Tenenbaum, ed., *Encyclopedia of Latin American History and Culture* (New York: Scribners, 1996); Héctor Perea, "Alfonso Reyes Ochoa," in Michael S. Werner, ed., *Encyclopedia of Mexico: History, Society, and Culture,* vol. 2 (Chicago: Fitzroy Dearborn, 1997); James Willis Robb, *Por los caminos de Alfonso Reyes* (Mexico City: INBA, 1981).

Río, Dolores del (1906–1983) ☀ One of Mexico's great film stars (born Dolores Asúnsolo y López Negrete) in the 1930s and 1940s who helped Mexico achieve its international reputation during the golden age of Mexican **cinema**. Although Dolores del Río made most of her films in the

United States (only 19 of her 56 films were Mexican), her collaboration with **Emilio "El Indio" Fernández**, **Pedro Armendáriz**, and **Gabriel Figueroa** resulted in several classics of Mexican cinema—notably *Flor silvestre* and *María Candelaria*—in the 1940s, both of which helped establish a European market for the Mexican cinema. Beginning almost by accident in the 1920s, Río had an international film career that spanned over 50 years, both in Hollywood and

Movie still of Dolores del Río and Pedro Armendáriz in *Flor silvestre* (1943), one of the classics of Golden Age indigenist films directed by Emilio Fernández.

Mexico. After making 15 silent films, she learned English and made the difficult transition to sound. Through her beauty and talent, she was successful in Hollywood and later Mexico. At the height of her career she landed a movie contract with United Artists, earning $9,000 a week, a remarkable sum for any actor, Mexican or North American. Some Hollywood photographers considered her more beautiful than any of the famed international film stars of the era such as Greta Garbo or Marlene Dietrich.

Born in 1906 to a well-to-do family from Durango, Río fled to Mexico City in 1911 to escape the turmoil and attend school in the nation's capital. At a young age she developed an interest in dancing, but her high social position prevented her from fully developing her talent. From 1921 until his death in 1928, she was married to Jaime Martínez del Río, a member of the upper classes who helped her develop a career in Hollywood under the encouragement of U.S. film director Edwin Carewe. Her brilliant career began with silent films in Hollywood under the management of Carewe, whose goal was to transpose her into a female version of Rudolfo Valentino. Although she longed to be a light-skinned blonde, Río achieved a good part of her success due to her dark complexion. Her marriage in 1930 to Cedric Gibbons, art director at Metro-Goldwyn-Mayer, was instrumental in making her one of the all-time beauties of Hollywood. An affair with Orson Welles contributed to her divorce from Gibbons and led indirectly to her expulsion from the Hollywood film scene.

During **World War II** Río moved back to Mexico, insisting that she would only work with **Emilio "El Indio" Fernández**, the famous director, with whom she was romantically involved. Under El Indio she helped invigorate the Mexican film industry in the 1940s with such award-winning films as *María Candelaria* (1944), *Las abandonadas* (1944), and *Bugambilia* (1945). At the first Cannes Film Festival in 1946, she won a Golden Palm Award for her performance in *María Candelaria*. After her love affair with Fernández ended in 1945, Dolores del Río took charge of her own career and ventured into theater productions. During the 1950s she was helped by Lewis Riley and after a long friendship they were married in 1959. During this period in the United States, she performed in numerous plays until a spinal illness ended her acting career. Nevertheless, she continued an active life in the arts and social causes until she said farewell to Mexican cinema in 1966.

During the last decade of her life, Río received several awards worldwide, judged film festivals throughout Europe, and was acknowledged by the Organization of American States and U.S. President Jimmy Carter, who gave her a diploma. After a short illness, she died of cancer in 1983, leaving behind a brilliant film career and an important legacy in Mexican cinema.

SUGGESTED READING

Dorothy J. Gaiter, "Dolores Del Rio, 77, Is Dead; Film Star in U.S. and Mexico," *New York Times*, April 13, 1983; Joanne Hershfield, *The Invention of Dolores del Río* (Minneapolis: University of Minnesota Press, 2000); Carl J. Mora, *The Mexican Cinema: Reflections of a Society, 1896–1988* (Berkeley: University of California Press, 1989); David Ramón, *Dolores del Río* (Mexico, D.F.: Clio, 1997); Aurelio de los Reyes, "Del Río, Dolores," in Michael S. Werner, ed., *Encyclopedia of Mexico: History, Society, and Culture*, vol. 1 (Chicago: Fitzroy Dearborn, 1997).

Río, Eduardo del ("Rius"). *See* del Río, Eduardo.

Río Grande del Norte (Río Bravo). *See* Geographical Regions; U.S.–Mexican Border/Boundary.

Ripstein, Arturo (1943–) ☀ One of Mexico's most renowned and controversial film directors. Arturo Ripstein is best known for his iconoclastic approach to the customs of the classic Mexican family melodramas. Following his dictum that "art should be convulsive," Ripstein's films (*The Castle of Purity*, 1972; *Deep Crimson*, 1985) focus on characters trapped in dysfunctional families and impossible, doomed love. In attacking the Mexican family, Ripstein examines authoritarian family structures, **machismo**, homophobia, and other forms of intolerance. His films are often irreverent and pessimistic in tone—characters burdened with guilt and suffering are quite common—with viewers forced to watch scenes that are deliberately and simultaneously painful and pleasurable. Ripstein's filmography includes 23 feature-length films (as of 1999) and scores of short and medium-length film projects.

Born in Mexico City in 1943, Ripstein is a third-generation Mexican Jew of Polish and Russian descent. While a student at the National University of Mexico, the **Colegio de México**, and the Iberoamerican University in Mexico City, he developed an interest in law, art, and history, subjects that he later included in his filmmaking. His father, Arturo Ripstein, Jr., founded Alameda Films in 1948, one of Mexico's prominent film companies. He grew up with constant exposure to commercial film production, watching the Mexican stars of the golden age of **cinema** making their films in his father's studios. Ripstein's mother, Frieda Rosen, was originally from El Paso, Texas, and made sure Arturo mastered English while growing up in a Spanish-speaking home.

Ripstein was influenced by **Luis Buñuel, Emilio Fernández**, John Ford, and Akira Kurosawa and received his theoretical training while taking film classes at the **Universidad Nacional Autónoma de México (UNAM)**. His admiration of Buñuel came from their shared love of the grotesque, the absurd, and the paradoxical in everyday life. Ripstein made his directorial debut at the age of 21 with *Tiempo de morir* (1965), the screenplay written by novelists **Carlos Fuentes** and Gabriel García Márquez. Since making his first film in 1965, Ripstein has collaborated with other famous Latin American novelists and poets. With *El Castillo de la pureza* (1972)—a grotesque family melodrama—he gained international recognition. He directed the first Mexican film to deal with the persecution of Jews in Mexico during the Inquisition (*El Santo oficio*, 1973), and he is one of the few directors to focus on the institutionalized **corruption** of Mexico's political system. Since 1985, he has collaborated with screenwriter Paz Alicia Garcíadiego, who has written all his films since their partnership began.

According to Ripstein, "Normal people are not photogenic, not in my movies. Normal people are just bystanders or secondary figures. I like the great sufferers because they make for great storytelling." Arturo Ripstein has received numerous national and international awards and tributes, including an Ariel for best director (for *Cadena perpetua* and *Imperio de la fortuna*) and the 1999 Akira Kurosawa Award for Lifetime Achievement in Directing.

SUGGESTED READING

Sergio de la Mora, "A Career in Perspective: An Interview with Arturo Ripstein," *Film Quarterly*, Summer 1999; Joanne Hershfield and David R. Maciel, eds., *Mexico's Cinema: A Century of Film and Filmmakers* (Wilmington, Del.: Scholarly Resources, 1999).

Rivera, Diego (1886–1957) ☀ One of the most important painters of the 20th century. Diego Rivera devoted most of his life to monumental murals depicting the important themes to emerge in the aftermath of the world's first great peasant revolution of the 20th century: nationalism, socialism, class struggle, and *Mexicanidad* (Mexicanness). Rivera's art was polemical and propagandistic; he believed the best way to reach the Mexican people was through his murals, which focused on the social and political history of Mexico. He was a quixotic and opportunistic figure who lavishly embellished his own past to augment his political and artistic significance. On returning to Mexico in 1921 after 14 years in Europe, Rivera spent the next three decades painting gigantic murals that covered several thousand square feet of walls.

Rivera joined the Mexican **Communist** Party in 1922, but it was never a comfortable relationship due to his work for the Mexican state, paint-

ing walls in government buildings, and his many capitalist friends. He was eventually expelled from the Communist Party but rejoined in 1954 shortly before his death in 1957.

People tend to undervalue Rivera's artistic achievements because it is almost impossible to capture his significance without actually going to Mexico City to view his works, which adorn many government buildings, particularly the Ministry of

Diego Rivera painting *Detroit Industry* at the Detroit Institute of Arts in 1932. Credit: Fotofest, photo by Detroit Institute of Arts.

Public Education, the Palacio de Bellas Artes (Palace of Fine Arts), the National Palace, and the Ministry of Health. Moreover, his communist ties and anti-American political activism prevented him from receiving the amount of critical acclaim in the United States and Europe that he deserved. His international popularity during the first half of the 20th century made him a global diplomat on par with Spanish artist Pablo Picasso. Today, Diego Rivera's artistic work is officially designated a national treasure of Mexico, protected by the national government. With a boundless artistic talent—he was a genius in his use of line and color—and energy, Rivera became one of the most renowned painters in the Western Hemisphere and one of the most imposing artists of the 20th century.

Diego Rivera was born Guanajuato during the dictatorship of Porfirio Díaz. Both of his parents were educators: his father was a teacher who created rural schools, and his mother taught at local schools before deciding to study obstetrics. When Rivera was seven, the family moved to Mexico City, where Diego studied painting at the Academy of San Carlos. In Europe during the **Mexican Revolution** he studied Western art history, was influenced by cubism, and became friends with Picasso and Georges Braque. It was in Europe that he developed his own artistic identity, particularly the importance of *muralismo* as public art form. The art and architecture of pre-Columbian Mexico—particularly the ancient pyramids constructed by the Aztecs and Mayans—provided Rivera with a formal geometry that became the essential architecture of his mural designs.

Although Rivera was one of the most important painters of the Mexican Revolution, developed friendships with **Tina Modotti** (a photographer and Soviet agent) and **Leon Trotsky** following his expulsion from the Soviet Union and residence in Mexico, and considered himself a communist, his artistic endeavors and philosophy were often full of contradictions: a dedicated Marxist, he painted

for the corporate elite (including **Nelson Rockefeller**) in the United States; a defender of the working class, he possessed a deep fascination with the evolution of technology and machines; a revolutionary artist devoted to the theme of change through revolution, he also painted celebrity portraits and socialites; a pioneer of cubism, he mastered the technique of the large mural devoted to universal images; his murals treat the masses as faceless, anonymous workers, but it is mostly the great heroes and villains who are the main protagonists of Mexican history. The ideology that Rivera expressed in his paintings was more closely identified with the official ideology of the bourgeois elements that emerged triumphant in the aftermath of the Mexican Revolution than a belief system associated with some sort of revolutionary Marxism. Nevertheless, in his murals located at the Ministry of Education (Mexico City) and the chapel at the Universidad Autónoma de Chapingo, Rivera uses explicit communist subjects and symbols. Rivera had an impact on abstract artists in the United States, particularly Jackson Pollock, who took some of Rivera's images and moved then in different directions.

During the early years of the Great Depression (1930–1934), Rivera was commissioned to paint six murals in San Francisco, Detroit, and New York. It is during this period in the United States that he produced some of finest work. Most of his murals in the United States showed a fascination with industrial and architectural technology, emphasizing the notion that social change must come through the use of technology to benefit the working class rather than through social revolution. His New York mural (*Man at the Crossroads*) was a 1,000-square-foot fresco for the great hall of the RCA Building, at the time an important symbol of American capitalism. After it was discovered that Rivera had inserted a charismatic Lenin in his project, Rockefeller asked him to substitute an anonymous figure for the likeness of Lenin, but Rivera adamantly refused. Claiming (falsely) that Lenin appeared in his original drawings, Rivera offered to "balance" Lenin with a great American historical leader such as Abraham Lincoln, but the offer was not accepted. Rockefeller had the scaffolding removed, the offensive portions were covered with a dark curtain, Rivera was paid for the balance of his fee, and the unfinished mural was destroyed by axes several months later. In any case, the fact that a foreign painter, and one with a communist orientation, was paid handsomely ($10,000 for his Detroit mural) for a work of art extolling the virtues of modern industry during the depths of the Depression did not go over well with unemployed factory workers. In the Tim Robbins film *Cradle Will Rock* (1999), the battle between Nelson Rockefeller (John Cusack) and Diego Rivera (Rubén Blades) is portrayed in a screwball leftist comedy about the Depression era.

One of Rivera's assistants, Lucienne Bloch, an acclaimed muralist and hard-line Marxist, managed to slip past the guards with a camera and capture the only visual record of the controversial Lenin sketch before it was ruined. Nine months later, Rivera and his wife **Frida Kahlo**, both disgusted with the United States, returned to Mexico and he started work on a copy to be located on a wall in the second floor of the Palacio de Bellas Artes in Mexico City. However, as Marnham (1998, 265) points out, "There were a few changes: the title was now *Man, Controller of the Universe*; Lenin naturally stands out as the most prominent figure apart from the central controller, a blond, blue-eyed **gringo** looking something like a B-21 bomber pilot." Bloch married Rivera's chief plasterer, Stephen P. Dimitroff, and the couple became an artistic team devoted to murals, photography, and sculpture until her death in 1999 in California.

The healthy commissions that kept Rivera busy painting murals during most of the 1930s ran out in 1941, forcing the great artist to concentrate on painting portraits and Indian themes. This turned out to be only a brief phase in Rivera's career, and he returned to mural painting for the rest of decade.

Diego Rivera's studio homes, designed by architect **Juan O'Gorman**, are now museums where one can view modernist architecture and the creative artistic spaces used by Rivera and his third wife, Frida Kahlo. These include the paired red and blue studios the couple occupied in San Ángel from 1932 until their divorce in 1939; the Blue House (La Casa Azul) in Coyoacán, where they lived from 1940 until Kahlo's death in 1954; and the exotic Aztec-Toltec house-studio Rivera built in Anáhuacalli to house his collection of pre-Columbian objects and works of art, although it was not finished until after his death.

Actively engaged in an effort to express Mexico to Mexicans until he was diagnosed with cancer in the 1950s, Diego Rivera helped define Mexican national identity through his unifying art. In contrast to Rivera's artistic achievements in Mexico that helped define a nation, there are no "great paintings" in the United States with which Americans identify as a nation. Rivera died of heart disease in Mexico City in 1957. Although his will called for his ashes to be mingled with those of Frida Kahlo at the Blue House, he was interred in the Rotunda de Hombres Ilustres along with other national heroes. *See also* Vaconcelos, José.

SUGGESTED READING

Dora Apel, "Diego Rivera and the Left: The Destruction and Reconstruction of the Rockefeller Center Mural," *Left History* (Spring 1999); Eli Bartra, "Rivera, Diego," in Michael S. Werner, ed., *Encyclopedia of Mexico: History, Society, and Culture* (Chicago: Fitzroy Dearborn, 1997); Linda Bank Downs, *Diego Rivera: The Detroit Industry Murals* (New York: W. W. Norton, 1999); Leonard Folgarait, *Mural Painting and Social Revolution in Mexico, 1920–1940: Art of the New Order* (New York: Cambridge University Press, 1998); Joseph Giovannini, "In Painters' Poetic Homes, the Soul of a Nation Emerged," *New York*

Times, March 4, 1999; Pete Hamill, *Diego Rivera* (New York: Abrams, 1999); Laurence P. Hurlburt, *The Mexican Muralists in the United States* (Albuquerque: University of New Mexico Press, 1989); Michael Kimmelman, "For a Chameleon of Modernism, Years of Groping," *New York Times,* March 21, 1999; Anthony W. Lee, *Painting on the Left: Diego Rivera, Radical Politics, and San Francisco's Public Murals* (Berkeley: University of California Press, 1999); Patrick Marnham, *Dreaming with His Eyes Open: A Life of Diego Rivera* (New York: Knopf, 1998); Bertram D. Wolfe, *The Fabulous Life of Diego Rivera* (New York: Stein & Day, 1963).

Rockefeller, Nelson A. (1908–1979) ☀ Born into the wealthy Rockefeller family of New York, Nelson A. Rockefeller was involved in banking, international business, philanthropy, art collecting, and state (governor of New York, 1958–1973) and national (vice president of the United States, 1974–1977) public office. Born in Bar Harbor, Maine, in 1908, the son of John D. Rockefeller, Jr., and grandson of Standard Oil millionaire John D. Rockefeller, Nelson Rockefeller graduated from Dartmouth College in 1930 and then worked for the family oil business. His interest in Mexico and the rest of Latin America developed in the early 1930s, when he hired **Diego Rivera** to paint a large mural for the lobby of the new Rockefeller Center in midtown Manhattan. After Rivera added a portrait sketch of Lenin to his masterpiece in progress, Rockefeller requested that the Russian anticapitalist be replaced with a figure more congruent with capitalist values. Rivera refused the request and Rockefeller held firm; shortly thereafter Rivera was fired, the large mural destroyed, and a more banal art deco design put in its place. After the flap over the Rockefeller Center mural subsided, Nelson Rockefeller decided to mend fences by going on an art-buying trip to Mexico in 1933 for the Museum of Modern Art, the family's favorite cultural project.

The trip to Mexico started Rockefeller's life-long love affair with Mexican pre-Columbian and contemporary art. With the help of friends and artists, particularly **Miguel Covarrubias**, a writer and caricaturist for the *New Yorker*, Rockefeller began amassing a spectacular collection of Mexican folk treasures. With the rise of fascism in Europe beginning to take root in Latin America, Rockefeller believed that the only way to combat the threatening political ideology was to foster closer links between the peoples of Latin America and the United States, using an appreciation of each other's culture as a means of achieving this goal. In a 1940 exhibit at the Museum of Modern Art, *Twenty Centuries of Mexican Art,* under Rockefeller's direction, over 5,000 pieces of ancient and modern Mexican art, borrowed from Mexican institutions, went on display for the New York audience. The New York exhibit was accompanied by other cultural and social events, including a concert by **Carlos Chávez** and Mexican-themed museum parties with Hollywood stars and important writers.

Nelson Rockefeller was a supporter of inter-American cooperation and believed in the social responsibilities of private ownership, a doctrine he practiced as director of Creole Petroleum in Venezuela from 1935 to 1940. Alarmed over Nazi Germany's growing influence throughout Latin America, Rockefeller wrote a memo to President Roosevelt in 1938 urging him to launch a propaganda counteroffensive. As war clouds appeared over Europe, the United States established the first of many "war agencies" in 1940, the Office of Coordinator of Commercial and Cultural Relations between the American Republics, headed by Rockefeller. In 1941 it became the **Office of the Coordinator of Inter-American Affairs (OCIAA)**, with responsibility for promoting inter-American trade, countering Nazi propaganda (using motion pictures, recorded radio programs, local broadcasts, and magazine

Diego Rivera's controversial likeness of Lenin sketch, Rockefeller Center, 1933. Credit: AP/World Wide Photos.

articles), improving relations between the United States and Latin America, and building support among Latin American countries for the war aims of the United States. The dramatic expansion of Mexican film production during **World War II** was due to the direct intervention of Washington; a friendly film industry would counter Nazi propaganda and help promote the war with entertainment propaganda capable of exceeding the limited effectiveness of U.S. "Good Neighbor" films like *Juárez* and others.

Rockefeller's propaganda offensive helped in the development of Mexican radio broadcasting and electronic journalism. The OCIAA Radio Division joined hands with Emilio Azcárraga Vidauretta—who owned almost half of all the radio stations in Mexico at the time—to incorporate its propaganda messages into popular programs based on short dramatizations and Mexican music. The OCIAA also organized Hollywood collaboration with Mexico's filmmaking industry during the war to produce a number of prowar, antifascist propaganda films such as *Soy puro mexicano* (1942). In 1944, Rockefeller was named assistant secretary for American republic affairs, a one-year post in which he focused on diplomatic relations and trade. After his wartime positions with the U.S. government, he continued his travels to the region, in constant search of interesting works of art in local markets.

During the height of the war, Rockefeller's OCIAA asked Walt Disney to make a goodwill tour of Latin America (including Mexico), with instructions to see if Hollywood might be able to help promote the war with entertainment propaganda. In Washington, it was also an attempt to build transnational collaboration, emphasizing the rhetoric of the Good Neighbor policy and Pan-American solidarity during World War II. After returning from Latin America, Disney made two musical films—*Saludos Amigos* (1943) and *The Three Caballeros* (1945)—in which Hollywood

portrayed the people of Latin America (and Mexico) in a positive way, a first for the filmmaking industry. In *The Three Caballeros*, a singing rooster named Panchito (Little Pancho)—dressed like a Mexican *charro*—is a thoroughly likable and fun-loving character who tries to present a positive view of Mexican life through piñata parties, traditional dances and costumes, and popular **music**.

Although Rockefeller played a major role in wartime security and propagandistic media efforts, his major contribution was to create the initial U.S. economic assistance program for Mexico and the rest of the Western Hemisphere. Backed by his family money and political connections, he maintained his influence in Latin American affairs by funding economic and social development projects. He also worked closely with the Central Intelligence Agency (CIA) and ultra-conservative religious organizations to spread American values and interests. He helped launch the career of Harvard professor Henry A. Kissinger by introducing him to Richard M. Nixon in the 1960s.

In 1969 Nelson Rockefeller was appointed by President Richard Nixon to head a fact-finding mission to Latin America, but his entourage was met by anti-American demonstrations and violence, and some of his recommendations for U.S.–Latin American policy paved the way for the rise in military dictatorships. Rockefeller died shortly after his three-year term as vice president under Gerald R. Ford, but his long-term interest in Mexican art remains an important legacy for both Mexico and the United States. Ann R. Roberts, Rockefeller's daughter, chose the Museum of Art in San Antonio, Texas, a location with both a Latino and an Anglo population as the repository of her father's collection of over 3,000 pieces of folk art. After raising millions of dollars to expand their Latin American collection, the Nelson A. Rockefeller Center for Latin

American Art at the San Antonio Museum of Art opened in 1998, a new $11 million museum wing with one of the world's largest Mexican folk art collections.

SUGGESTED READING

Dora Apel, "Diego Rivera and the Left: The Deconstruction and Reconstruction of the Rockefeller Center Mural," *Left History* (Spring 1999); Charles Carreras, "Nelson Aldrich Rockefeller," in Barbara A. Tenenbaum, ed., *Encyclopedia of Latin American History and Culture*, vol. 4 (New York: Scribners, 1996); James Desmond, *Nelson Rockefeller: A Political Biography* (New York: Macmillan, 1964); Seth Fein, "From Collaboration to Containment: Hollywood and the International Political Economy of Mexican Cinema after the Second World War," in Joanne Hershfield and David R. Maciel, eds., *Mexico's Cinema: A Century of Film and Filmmakers* (Wilmington, Del.: Scholarly Resources, 1999); Rick Lyman, "From Mexican Soil to Museum Sanctum," *New York Times,* October 26, 1998; Stephen R. Niblo, *Mexico in the 1940s: Modernity, Politics, and Corruption* (Wilmington, Del.: SR Books, 1999); Joseph E. Persico, *The Imperial Rockefeller: A Biography of Nelson A. Rockefeller* (New York: Simon & Schuster, 1981); Cary Reich, *The Life of Nelson A. Rockefeller: Worlds to Conquer, 1908–1958* (New York: Doubleday, 1996).

President Adolpho Ruiz Cortines. Credit: Benson Latin American Collection, University of Texas at Austin.

Ruiz Cortínes, Adolfo (1889–1973) ☀ Mexico's second postwar president (1952–1958). Following the turbulent years of the **Miguel Alemán** presidency, President Ruiz Cortines offered no political innovations and emphasized conservative economic policies. He worked diligently to restore a sense of unity to the dominant party then divided between followers of **Lázaro Cárdenas** (*cardenistas*) and Alemán (*alemanistas*). It was to be a "balanced revolution" between contending forces of political and economic change. Perhaps his most notable and long-lasting achievement was the final passage of equal political rights for women and his rhetoric praising the importance of women in Mexican society.

Adolfo Ruiz Cortines was born in Veracruz in 1889. Although his studies did not include the university, Ruiz Cortines worked his way into the upper reaches of Mexican politics with his skills as an accountant, first in Veracruz and in Mexico City after he moved there during the first decade of the 20th century. During the **Mexican Revolution** he fought on the side of Venustiano Carranza and earned the respect of many of those who achieved political stature during this period. He filled various appointed positions in the aftermath of the revolution and began his political career in 1937 after being elected deputy for the region of Tuxpan, Veracruz. His close ties with General **Manuel Ávila Camacho** and Miguel Alemán were instrumental in becoming governor of Veracruz and later minister of the interior (*gobernación*). After being handpicked as the PRI candidate for president in 1951, Ruiz Cortines won the presidency in 1952 with 74 percent of the votes.

Faced with dire economic and political circumstances—**corruption**, dishonesty, and overspending—during the Alemán era, Ruiz Cortines set out to solve Mexico's economic development problems with conservative economic policies in an effort to regain the public's confidence in the official party and its policies. Although he continued President Alemán's emphasis on infrastructure expansion, land reform became less of a priority than it had been during the previous three presidential terms. He never had to worry about a recalcitrant Congress or a challenge from opposition parties, since the executive branch maintained tight control over public policy making. Despite advances in agriculture, railroad restoration, and oil exploration, the peso had to be devalued in 1954, leading to labor protests from the working classes.

Ruiz Cortines's **foreign policy** continued the revolutionary ideology of Mexicanism and anti-imperialism. When Lázaro Cárdenas interceded to prevent the impending removal from Mexico of **Fidel Castro**'s small band of Cuban revolutionaries (including Ernesto "Ché" Guevara) planning to overthrow the Cuban government, Ruiz Cortines yielded to the request from the elder statesman. At the 10th Inter-American Conference in Caracas in 1954, the Ruiz Cortines administration opposed a U.S. resolution designed to pressure Latin American governments to fight **communism**. In arguing that communism could be best opposed through economic modernization, Ruiz Cortines once told Vice President Richard Nixon during a visit to a slum in Mexico City, "Look, Mr. Vice President, this [slum conditions] is the most widespread 'ism' in Mexico, 'hungerism,' and this is what I am interested in eradicating so that the 'isms' you worry about will not arise" (quoted in Krauze 1997, 623). When the Falcón Dam on the border between the United States and Mexico was inaugurated, Ruiz Cortines and President Eisenhower met to celebrate the occasion.

Unlike many of his successors, Ruiz Cortines did not end his term of office a wealthy man; however, he did manage to maintain economic growth, balanced the budget, and made advances in curbing corruption. His term of office was characterized by honesty and fiscal integrity; when he left office in 1958 and retired to private life, Ruiz Cortines left a legacy of political moderation, economic growth, and social welfare. His economic moderation, personal integrity, popularity, and relative inertia made him resemble a Mexican Eisenhower. When it came time to select a candidate for the presidential succession of 1958, Ruiz Cortines picked (using the *dedazo*) his successor, **Adolfo López Mateos** (secretary of labor). After retiring to private life in late 1958, Ruiz Cortines lived modestly in Veracruz until his death on December 3, 1973. *See also* Feminism.

SUGGESTED READING

Enrique Krauze, *Mexico: Biography of Power* (New York: HarperCollins, 1997); Cecilia Greaves Laine, "Ruiz Cortines, Adolfo," in Michael S. Werner, ed., *Encyclopedia of Mexico*, vol. 2 (Chicago: Fitzroy Dearborn, 1997); Ward M. Morton, *Woman Suffrage in Mexico* (Gainesville: University of Florida Press, 1962); Juan José Rodríguez Prats, *El poder presidential: Adolfo Ruiz Cortines*, 2d ed. (Mexico, D.F.: Miguel Angel Porrúa Grupo Editorial, 1992); Juana Vázquez-Gómez,

Dictionary of Mexican Rulers, 1325–1997 (Westport, Conn.: Greenwood, 1997).

Ruiz García, Samuel (1924–) ☀ Bishop of San Cristóbal de Las Casas until 1999, known for his outspoken support for the dispossessed and Indian communities in Chiapas and his work as mediator between the Zapatistas and the government after the 1994 uprising in the impoverished southern region. Born in Irapuato, Guanajuato, in 1924 to a conservative religious family of migrant laborers, Ruiz studied at Seminario Conciliar de León and the Gregorian Pontifical University in Rome, where he earned a doctorate in *sagrada escritura* (scripture) in 1951. After returning to Mexico in 1952, Ruiz began to rise rapidly in the Church, teaching theology at the seminary in León before being named bishop of Chiapas (the diocese name was later changed to San Cristóbal de Las Casas) in 1959. At the time of his arrival in Chiapas, he had a reputation as a religious conservative and a staunch anticommunist. However, as he traveled through the remote regions of his diocese in the early 1960s, he encountered a population suffering from systemic poverty and oppression. Bishop Ruiz played an active role in Vatican Council II (1962–1965) and the Second General Conference of Latin American Bishops in 1968, from which grew the process of liberation in Latin America. As a result of his firsthand experiences with the indigenous communities in Chiapas, Samuel Ruiz underwent a profound transformation of his personal and theological beliefs and by the 1990s he had become one of the leading members of the liberal or progressive Church in Mexico.

By building schools, forming cooperatives and credit unions, and providing other forms of assistance to the indigenous communities, Bishop Ruiz worked to establish what he called "an authentic Church," one that would address the critical problems facing the Indian villages. His defense of **human rights** and programs for the downtrodden led to vocal criticism from some government officials, **mestizo** cattle ranchers, members of the military and **government** officials, as well as from an assortment of religious critics, including conservative evangelical Protestants and critics of his activities from within the Catholic Church. With increased violence against Indians, peasants, and church workers, Bishop Ruiz inaugurated a human rights center in 1989 to counter the attacks against the indigenous villages. His devotion to liberation theology and the defense of Indians' human rights led to death threats and verbal attacks. Some referred to him as "Comandante Sam" and the "Red Bishop," while others called for his removal from office because of his alleged use of "Marxist analysis" in defense of the poor.

After the **Zapatista rebellion in Chiapas** on January 1, 1994, Bishop Ruiz became more controversial as worldwide attention focused increasingly on the rebellion and the plight of the Indian majority in Chiapas. While no one had greater credibility within the indigenous population than Bishop Ruiz, he and his pastoral team were blamed for the rebellion and violence. Between his appointment as mediator between the Zapatistas and the Mexican government in February 1994 and 1999, he worked constantly to broker a lasting peace between the government and the indigenous people of Chiapas. After years of controversy and criticism, Bishop Samuel Ruiz, a champion of Indian rights in Chiapas for 40 years, resigned at the age of 75 (Roman Catholic Church regulations require bishops to submit their resignations at this age), ending a long career of serving the poor and oppressed. Pope John Paul II appointed Felipe Arizmendi to replace Bishop Ruiz in March 2000, a decision that many felt would bring an end to the Chiapas conflict because of Bishop Arizmendi's reputation as a force for reconciliation between Zapatistas and the government. *See also* Church and State.

SUGGESTED READING

Thomas Benjamin, "Ruiz García, Samuel," in Michael S. Werner, ed., *Encyclopedia of Mexico: History, Society, and Culture*, vol. 2 (Chicago: Fitzroy Dearborn, 1997); Gary Maceoin, *The People's Church: Bishop Samuel Ruiz of Mexico and Why He Matters* (New York: Crossroad, 1996); John Ross, *Rebellion from the Roots: Indian Uprising in Chiapas* (Monroe, Maine: Common Courage, 1995); Michael Tangeman, *Mexico at the Crossroads: Politics, the Church, and the Poor* (Maryknoll, N.Y.: Orbis, 1995).

Ruiz Massieu, José Francisco. *See* Salinas de Gortari, Carlos; Salinas de Gortari, Raúl.

Rulfo, Juan (1918–1986) ☀ Novelist and short story writer who created the basic characteristics of "magical realism," a form and style of writing that has become a fundamental source of the universal modern novel. As one of the later writers of the **Mexican Revolution**, Juan Rulfo is something of a literary paradox; he displayed exceptional talent as a writer from his childhood, but his literary masterpieces stem from two short books published in a span of two years between 1953 (*El llano en llamas*) and 1955 (*Pedro Páramo*). Both of these works are highly regarded in Latin American fiction due to their portrayal of Mexican village life and memorable characters who were attached to the land on which they lived.

Born in Sayula, Jalisco, where his father was a landowner, Juan Rulfo experienced the aftermath of the Mexican Revolution. His family was ruined—his father was killed in the Cristero war (1926–1928) and his mother died shortly thereafter—by the reaction to the anticlerical reforms of the Mexican Revolution. With the death of both parents, Rulfo was sent to an orphanage and experienced a profound sense of alienation and solitude that later found resonance in his novels. He moved to Mexico City in 1934, studied law at **Universidad Nacional Autónoma de México (UNAM)**, and then found work in the Immigration Department, where his travels brought him in contact with the harshness, poverty, and desolation of the peasant population. He came to know the innermost thoughts of *campesinos* and the local dialects of many rural areas, which he put to brilliant use in his narrative techniques. The 15 short stories that make up *El llano en llamas* portray the way of life and colloquialisms of human beings who are faced with an uncertain, solitary, and bleak existence. There is a universal appeal in the most prevalent themes of Rulfo's work: violence, lack of communication, the power of rich and brutal **caciques** who deceive the masses to enrich themselves while speaking the rhetoric of the revolution, and the portrayal of Catholic religion as fanatical, superstitious, and worthless.

In the novel *Pedro Páramo*, the reader becomes aware that all the characters, including the narrator, are dead and the village they inhabit consists of ghosts and their murmurs caught in a world where both politics and religion have failed the rural masses. Although Juan Rulfo published little in his lifetime, he gained an international reputation for his realist prose and was enormously influential throughout Latin America. In 1970 he was awarded the National Prize for Letters, and in 1983 Spain awarded him its Príncipe de Asturias for his creative writing. He died in Mexico City in 1986 at the age of 67.

SUGGESTED READING

Yvette Jiménez de Baez, *Juan Rulfo: Del páramo a la esperanza* (Mexico, D.F.: Fondo de la Cultura Económica, 1990); Luis Leal, *Juan Rulfo* (Boston: Twayne, 1983); Alicia Llarena Rosales, *Realismo mágico y lo real maravilloso: Una questión de verosimilitud* (Gaithersburg, Md.: Hispanamerica, 1997); Silvia Lorente-Murphy, *Juan Rulfo: Realidad y mito de la Revolución Mexicana* (Madrid: Editorial Pliegos, 1988); Jorge Ruffinelli, "Juan Rulfo, 1918–1986," in Verity Smith, ed., *Encyclopedia of Latin American Literature* (Chicago: Fitzroy Dearborn, 1997).

Sabines Gutiérrez, Jaime (1926–1999) ☀ Popular poet and politician who wrote lyrical hymns about lust and personal loss that left a profound impact on generations of Mexicans. It was not uncommon during Sabines's poetry readings for his audience to chant—word for word—the exact words he was reading to them. His popularity came from his treatment of the travails of the heart, a theme that had special appeal to Mexicans caught between a tradition-bound culture based on close family ties and *compadrazgo* (co-parenthood, or the Mexican tradition of selecting a married couple to serve as godparents for a newborn child) relationships and the turbulent changes brought on by modern life. In *Something about the Death of Major Sabines* (1973), Sabines examines the cry of rage and helplessness made by a child who has suffered the death of a father. In one of his earliest and most quoted poems, "The Lovers" (1950), he treats the passion of love in a plain and intimate fashion that can be understood by anyone. He was awarded numerous prizes for his literary work, including the Premio Chiapas (1959), the Xavier Villarrutia (1972), and the National Prize for Letters, Mexico's highest literary award, in 1983.

Jaime Sabines was born in 1926 in Tuxtla Gutiérrez, capitol of the poor rural state of Chiapas close to Guatemala. The son of Lebanese immigrants, he spent several unpleasant years studying medicine to please his brusque and stern father. He shifted his interests to writing and literature, eventually earning a university degree in language and Spanish literature from the **Universidad Nacional Autónoma de México (UNAM)** in 1949 and then pursuing several years of postgraduate studies. An outcast among Mexican intellectuals for his solitude and conservatism, Sabines decided to try his hand at party politics during his middle years. Representing the ruling party (**Partido Revolucionario Institucional, PRI**), he served two three-year terms as a federal legislator, first in the 1970s and then from 1988 to 1991. However, his service to the dominant party put him at odds with most of the literary and intellectual class in Mexico.

After shattering a hip in a fall, Sabines underwent surgery more than 30 times to correct the joint. The trauma of this accident affected his interest and touch for poetry and he ceased writing after the accident. He died of cancer in Mexico City on March 19, 1999.

SUGGESTED READING

Julia Preston, "Jaime Sabines Gutiérrez, Popular Mexican Poet, Dies at 72," *New York Times,* March 22, 1999; Jaime Sabines, *Pieces of Shadow: Selected Poems of Jaime Sabines*, trans. W. S. Merwin (New York: Marsilio, 1995).

Saínz, Gustavo (1940–) ☀ Novelist and literary critic who is linked generationally with members of a group of writers who came on the scene in the 1960s and broke with existing traditions by writing in a colloquial vocabulary and iconoclastic narrative style. Known as *la onda* (the wave) generation, they were profoundly influenced by the 1968 student movement and the violent events of the **Tlatelolco massacre** and its aftermath, attacking official **corruption**, social injustices, and sexual repression. As part of the **Mexican counterculture** movement, Saínz and his companion writers became well known for their use of popular language to symbolize the problems of the new urban, young middle class in Mexico City.

Born in Mexico City in 1940, Saínz attended the **Universidad Nacional Autónoma de México**

(UNAM) and the **Colegio de Mexico**. After his university training he worked on several literary magazines, contributed to numerous newspapers, and wrote scripts for radio and television. After attending the International Writing Program at the University of Iowa (1968), Saínz was invited to teach at several universities in the United States, including the University of New Mexico, University of Northern Illinois, Washington University, and Indiana University.

Saínz's best known works of *la onda* genre include *Gazapo* (1965), his first novel; *Obsesivos días circulares* (1969); *La princesa del Palacio de Hierro* (1974); *Compadre Lobo* (1977); *Fantasmas aztecas* (1982); *Paseo en trapecio* (1985); *Muchacho en llamas* (1988); *A la salud de la serpiente* (1991); and *Retablo de immoderaciones y heresiarcas* (1992). He was awarded the Xavier Villarrutia Prize in 1974 for *La princesa del Palacio de Hierro*, a narrative account of the life of an anonymous, lower-middle-class woman who works at a Mexican department store called the Iron Palace, and the cultural dichotomy between different generations. He was the recipient of two important fellowships (Guggenheim in 1976 and Tinker in 1980) that allowed him to expand his literary horizons. A master of the intricacies of the historical narrative, Saínz's novels often capture the cultural conflicts and social contradictions of Mexico in its struggle to modernize and meet the demands of a rapidly growing population.

SUGGESTED READING

Salvador C. Fernández, "Gustavo Saínz," in Verity Smith, ed., *Encyclopedia of Latin American Literature* (Chicago: Fitzroy Dearborn, 1997); Raymond L. Williams, "The Reader and the Recent Novels of Gustavo Saínz," *Hispania* 65, no. 3 (1982).

Salinas de Gortari, Carlos (1948–) ☀ Mexico's eighth postwar president (1988–1994). Carlos Salinas spent most of his *sexenio* engaged in the radical transformation of Mexico's political economy. During his administration he put an end to the interventionist state, privatized large numbers of state industries, allowed North American corporations to participate in petroleum exploration for the first time since 1938, implemented policies to draw large amounts of foreign capital to Mexico, tried to restructure the **corporatist** nature of government, and put his stamp on the **North American Free Trade Agreement (NAFTA)**, which went into effect on January 1, 1994.

Once in office, Salinas moved decisively to alleviate the discontent after widespread allegations of fraud during the 1988 presidential **elections**. Salinas's narrow victory margin—he won the presidency with only 50.7 percent of the officially tallied vote—over his main rival, **Cuauhtémoc Cárdenas**, was the lowest figure ever for a winning presidential candidate and a body blow to the ailing PRI. Only 40 years of age, Salinas took charge of the presidency in a dynamic and decisive manner, convinced he could solve Mexico's economic problems with talented young economists possessing graduate degrees from American universities; however, his perestroika (economic restructuring) was never matched by serious political freedom and democratic reforms (glasnost). Salinas argued that the pursuit of meaningful economic reforms would dilute the demands for drastic political reform.

"They were an imperious and impatient group, the new *científicos*, the 'enlightened despots' of the computer age. Like the mode in which they had come to power, their weapons would be quick decisions, the careful selection and manipulation of information, not violence or floods of rhetoric" (Krauze 1997, 773). However, mass arrests of powerful **labor** leaders, tax evaders, drug traffickers, and others set the hard-line tone of his administration. Salinas removed more governors in his first year in office than any president since **Miguel Alemán** (1946–1952). Later, evidence of fraud, corruption, and financial scandals would undermine the legitimacy Salinas so carefully cultivated on the job.

President Salinas was admired in the United States, and *Time* magazine named him the 1993 International Newsmaker of the Year for Latin America because of his success in reversing the Mexican economy's slide. The Mexican press called him *la hormiga atómica* (the atomic ant) because of the frenetic pace he set in his day-to-day activities. He worked hard on his image as a man in constant motion, quick on his feet, with charm and guts (*huevos*) to achieve his stated goals. He was admired by Presidents George H. W. Bush and Bill Clinton, Wall Street investment brokers, and U.S. business magazines like *Forbes* and the *Wall Street Journal*. By joining the **General Agreement on Tariffs and Trade (GATT)** and NAFTA, President Salinas reversed decades in which the state was the driving force of economic growth. He was a champion of international salesmanship, convincing the Mexican political class and Washington policy makers that Mexico was on the move and would soon leave behind its Third World status. He was even hailed in the barrios of Mexico City as an honest president who, many felt, had done many good things for the poor. "More than the great modernizer, Salinas could be likened to the great seducer" (Bussey 1997, 1329). However, his carefully crafted myth of economic prosperity and social stability ended shortly after he left office with a massive devaluation of the Mexican peso and the panicked flight of capital that had poured into Mexico a few years earlier.

Carlos Salinas de Gortari was born in the Federal District in 1948, the second son of Raúl Salinas Lozano and Margarita de Gortari Carvajal. Both were trained economists, and his father had master's degrees from American University and Harvard University. His father was secretary of industry and commerce during the **López Mateos** administration, a position from which he hoped to advance to the presidency, but was passed over by the selection of **Gustavo Díaz Ordaz** in 1963. It was a painful political loss for the Salinas family that motivated Carlos and his older brother, **Raúl Salinas de Gortari**, to prove they could rise to the top with their politically connected father. Carlos Salinas attended public schools in Mexico City and then went on to pursue an economics degree at the **Universidad Nacional Autónoma de México (UNAM)**. After graduating in 1971, he attended Harvard University, earning master's degrees in public administration and political economy and a doctorate in political economy and government (1978).

Carlos Salinas was active in party politics from a young age. At 18 he joined the youth movement of the ruling party. During the 1970s he started working in the Finance Ministry, a post that put him in contact with future Mexican president **Miguel de la Madrid**. When President **José López Portillo** picked de la Madrid to be the PRI candidate for president in 1981, de la Madrid chose

President Carlos Salinas. Credit: *Proceso*, photo by German Canseco.

Salinas to be his campaign director. After de la Madrid was elected president in 1982, Salinas followed him into office with cabinet appointments where he clashed and won several battles with a number of rivals (**Francisco Labastida Ochoa, Jesús Silva Herzog**, Manuel Bartlett Díaz, and Alfredo de la Mazo) before getting the PRI nomination to run for president in 1987 from President de la Madrid.

The 1988 presidential campaign was the first for Salinas, made more difficult by the fact that he did not fit the usual mold of Mexican politicians. He was short in stature, prematurely bald, and extremely sensitive about his physical appearance. As a form of compensation, he always wore elevated shoes while campaigning and demanded that photographers make him appear taller and more handsome than he actually was. His candidacy and the economic policies he represented triggered a split within his party leading to the breakaway candidacy of Cuauhtémoc Cárdenas, heir to the legacy of his famous father. With the Cárdenas candidacy pushing political reforms and populist economic policies, as well as a group of reformers who remained inside the PRI fold, the 1988 presidential election raised the possibility of an opposition party candidate winning the presidency for the first time in the history of the ruling party. When the early returns on election night (July 6, 1988) showed Cárdenas ahead by a large percentage, Salinas instructed his staff to take charge of the vote counting. Needless to say, the allegations of vote tampering quickly led to a national crisis. The next day a visibly shaken Carlos Salinas announced himself the winner after the PRI-controlled Congress declared him president-elect with 50.7 percent of the vote. With no consensus on his fraud-tainted election, Salinas proceeded to restore his personal legitimacy while fulfilling his promises to enact sweeping reforms. It was not the ideal way to win a presidential election, but the ends were what mattered most to the PRI.

The Cold War ended shortly after Carlos Salinas assumed power, giving him the opportu-nity to put some of the conflicts of the 1980s—the debate over Central America and criticisms by U.S. conservatives of shortcomings in Mexico's political system—behind him. Mexican–U.S. relations improved significantly during the Salinas and Bush presidencies. Announcing a "new era of friendship," Salinas stressed the importance of dialogue and negotiations over bilateral differences concerning trade and investment, debt restructuring, **drug trafficking, immigration**, and transborder environmental problems. The "new era" was also driven by the strong showing by the leftist **Partido de la Revolución Democrática (PRD)**, Cárdenas, and the need to reestablish PRI domination in Mexican politics. Washington welcomed the Salinas administration's economic reforms and softer diplomatic language and in return downplayed or ignored complaints dealing with electoral fraud, rampant corruption, and **human rights** abuses. With his eye on passage of NAFTA, Salinas bowed to U.S. interests in the hemisphere by softening Mexico's criticisms of the U.S. invasion of Panama, providing increased oil exports to the United States, abstaining on a UN vote on human rights violations in **Cuba**, and retreating from its desire for a seat on the UN Security Council.

Mexican **foreign policy** under Salinas became more global as Mexico tried to expand its commercial ties with Europe, Japan, Korea, China, and elsewhere in Asia. In order to gain the good graces of the Catholic Church, Mexico improved relations with the Vatican. In hopes of becoming more of a key player in hemispheric affairs, Mexico supported economic integration efforts in Central America, signed a free trade agreement with Chile, and remained active in the Rio Group and the Group of Three (with Colombia and Venezuela). The flip side of Mexican foreign policy was having to respond to international criticism by the Organization of American States (OAS), Americas Watch, the Washington Office on Latin America, foreign news organizations, and various religious groups of its scant progress toward **democratization** and the weak protection of citizen rights. While the above stand out as key components of Mexican foreign policy, Mexico's top priority during the Salinas years was the successful completion of a free trade agreement with United States and Canada. In order to do all of this, Mexico had to balance traditional concerns over national sovereignty and nonintervention with the growing recognition that Mexico's foreign relations still revolve around its relations with the United States, its superpower next-door neighbor.

Carlos Salinas left office the same way he came to power in 1988: amid controversy, denials, and defense of his administration's major accomplishments. Continuing the *dedazo*, the tradition of incumbents handpicking their successors, President Salinas choose **Luis Donaldo Colosio** to be the PRI candidate for the 1994 presidential election. During his last year in office, after toasting the start of NAFTA, Salinas had to face a major peasant insurrection in Chiapas by a group calling itself Zapatistas, the assassination of two top political figures close to him (including PRI candidate Colosio), repeated kidnappings, and financial and political unrest. After Colosio was murdered, Salinas chose **Ernesto Zedillo** to replace him, and the campaign continued. Shortly after Carlos Salinas left office in early December 1994, the peso underwent a devastating devaluation and Salinas's older brother, Raúl (known in Mexico as "First Brother"), was arrested and charged with money laundering and murder. In protest, Carlos Salinas went on a brief hunger strike and then moved to Canada, Cuba, and finally Ireland, where he still remains in self-imposed exile.

From the darling of U.S. editorial pages and the admiration of millions of Mexicans duped by his image as the promoter of free trade, the craftsman of Mexican economic openness, and a Gorbachev-style modernizer, Carlos Salinas quickly became Mexico's most hated former president. With his brother convicted of murder and sentenced to 50 years in prison (later reduced to 27 years) and the enrichment of his family viewed as a national and international scandal, Salinas continues to defend himself and family while a cottage industry in anti-Salinas T-shirts, rubber masks, figurines, and other trinkets flourishes throughout Mexico. The most prevalent image is of Salinas as the Chupacabras—the goatsucker, a mythical beast with fangs and bat wings that sucks blood and makes off with wives and children—a metaphor for the sins committed by the ex-president during his six years in office. The Salinas family continues to take the blame for everything that went wrong in 1994 and 1995, and in presidential campaign politics it is a deep political insult to call someone a *Salinista* (someone who supports Carlos Salinas). *See also* Democracy and Democratization; Zapatista Rebellion in Chiapas.

SUGGESTED READING

Jane Bussey, "Salinas de Gortari, Carlos," in Michael S. Werner, ed., vol. 2, *Encyclopedia of Mexico: History, Society, and Culture* (Chicago: Fitzroy Dearborn, 1997); *Carlos Salinas de Gortari: Biography*, English and Spanish text (Las Cruces: New Mexico State University Joint Border Research Institute, 1988); Jorge G. Castañeda, *La herencia: Arqueología de la sucesión presidential* (Mexico, D.F.: Editorial Alfaguara, 1999); Miguel Angel Centeno, *Democracy within Reason: Technocratic Revolution in Mexico* (Boulder, Colo.: Lynne Rienner, 1994); Stephen D. Morris, *Political Reformism in Mexico: An Overview of Contemporary Mexican Politics* (Boulder, Colo.: Lynne Rienner, 1995); Philip L. Russell, *Mexico under Salinas* (Austin: Mexico Research Center, 1994); Carlos Salinas de Gortari, *México: Un paso difícil a la modernidad* (Barcelona: Plaza & Janés Editores, 2000); José Luis Trueba Lara, *Salinas: El signo de la muerte*, 3d ed. (Mexico, D.F.:

Posada, 1995); John W. Warnock, *Other Mexico: The North American Triangle Completed* (Montreal: Black Rose Books, 1996).

Salinas de Gortari, Raúl (1946–) ☀ Prominent engineer, politician, and notorious elder brother of ex-president **Carlos Salinas de Gortari** (1988–1994). Accused of masterminding the 1994 assassination of José Francisco Ruiz Massieu, secretary-general of the PRI, Raúl Salinas was convicted and sentenced to 50 years in prison (later reduced to 27 years) in 1999. After Carlos Salinas left office in 1994, his brother Raúl and a former high-level government prosecutor, Mario Ruiz Massieu, were found to have pocketed millions of dollars in questionable funds, money widely believed to have originated with the major Mexican drug cartels. Mario Ruiz Massieu, a former deputy attorney general, committed suicide in 1999 while under house arrest in New Jersey.

Born in Monterrey, Nuevo León, Raúl Salinas studied civil engineering at the **Universidad Nacional Autónoma de México (UNAM)** (1965–1969) and taught at the University of Paris (1972–1973) and UNAM (1970–1978). He joined the ruling party and was appointed to its executive committee in 1982, a position that allowed him to advance into important government posts dealing with planning, engineering, and public works. As director of CONASUPO—a bureaucratic agency that distributed subsidized food to the poor—he gained valuable contacts in government and private industry. An investigation of possible embezzlement at the agency by Salinas was halted by President **Ernesto Zedillo** in 1996; however, as a cost-cutting measure, the scandal-plagued agency was closed for good in 1998 after 33 years of operation.

The chronic nature of **corruption**, crime, and tragedy in Mexico gives rise to endless jokes that seem to appear out of nowhere and circulate at a rapid pace throughout the country. One concerns the alleged misdeeds of Raúl Salinas de Gortari

during his brother's presidency, including the accusation that he bought animal feed to resell to the poor for them to eat while he was in charge of CONASUPO. One of the more popular jokes that circulated went as follows: When Raúl Salinas dies and reaches the pearly gates, St. Peter asks for his qualifications to enter heaven.

"I stole 500 million pesos from the poor of Mexico," he says.

"You think this will get you into heaven?" St. Peter asks him.

"Sure!" Salinas responds, adding, "You'll get your cut, don't worry."

There's a flash of bright lightning, and Salinas promptly finds himself in a poor barrio in Mexico

Raúl Salinas de Gortari in jail. Credit: *Proceso*.

City. Satan greets him with "*Buenos días señor, have a warm tortilla.*"

San Andrés Accords ☀ In February 1996, two years after the **Zapatista rebellion in Chiapas**, the Mexican government and the Ejército Zapatista de Liberación Nacional (EZLN) signed the San Andrés Accords, an attempt to bring peace and reconciliation to the poverty-afflicted state of Chiapas. Although never implemented, the accords remain at the center of the conflict between the Mexican state (particularly the Mexican president and the sharply divided Congress) and the Zapatistas. The San Andrés Accords call for a new relationship between the national government and the indigenous communities throughout the country. Its main provisions include respect for the diversity of indigenous municipalities, greater Indian participation in making community decisions and spending public funds, and greater "autonomy" of indigenous communities and their right to "self-determination" within the law. The accords describe a series of steps that, if fully implemented, would radically alter the relationship between the state and Mexico's indigenous peoples.

Much of the pact was written by **Subcommander Marcos**, a non-Indian leftist who is leading the protest against the exploitation of the indigenous population, most recently by the "dictatorial" **Partido Revolucionario Institucional (PRI)** and the negative consequences of neoliberal economic reforms and globalization. The Zapatistas gained an ally with the 2000 election of President **Vicente Fox,** the candidate of the **Partido Acción Nacional (PAN),** who criticized the PRI for its neglect and mistreatment of the indigenous population and vowed in his inaugural address that he would submit the agreement to Congress for prompt consideration. With a narrow election victory, Fox needed to do something about the criticism Mexico was receiving from Europe and the United States over **human rights** concerns and economic and **environmental** neglect in southern Mexico. He allowed Subcommander Marcos and his Zapatista allies to arrange a caravan tour from the jungles of Chiapas to Mexico City in order to lobby the Congress to implement the reforms. Moreover, he overrode his own party's objections to giving the EZLN a national platform to make their case before Congress, withdrew more than 2,000 soldiers from the conflict zone, and freed 84 jailed Zapatistas.

The Mexican Congress was receptive to neither the legislation, known as the Indigenous Rights and Culture legislation, or the lobbying tactics used by Marcos and his followers to achieve their demands. Given the complexity and controversy surrounding the Accords, it seems highly unlikely that the Mexican Congress will bend to such demands, worried that autonomy and self-determination among Indian communities in Chiapas and elsewhere would create a "state within a state," in effect balkanizing the Mexican nation. By the time the Zapatistas returned to Chiapas, President Fox had little to show for his efforts, adding further discord between the executive and legislative branches of **government**, growing discontent within the business community, and increasing frustration among indigenous communities.

SUGGESTED READING

Luis Hernández Navarro and Ramón Vera Herrera, eds., *Acuerdos de San Andrés* (Mexico, D.F.: Ediciones Era, 1998); "San Andrés Accords," trans. Rosaalva Bermúdez-Ballín, http://flag.blackened.net/revolt/Mexico/ezln/San_andres.html (January 18, 1996).

San Luis Potosí. *See* Geographical Regions.

September 11, 2001 ☀ The simultaneous suicide attacks on New York and Washington, D.C., by Middle Eastern terrorists allegedly associated with Osama bin Laden's Al Qaeda network —the deadliest acts of terror by foreign nationals on U.S. soil since **Pancho Villa** attacked Columbus, New Mexico, in 1916—had a profound impact on Mexico and U.S.–Mexican relations.

Estimates place the number of Mexican deaths in the twin attacks on the World Trade Center at 19. However, the federal investigation following the September 11 attacks turned up only one Mexican detainee being held for **immigration** violations by U.S. authorities.

Having a long and porous border with the United States, Mexico figured prominently in the events leading up to the September 11, 2001, terrorist attacks. Two weeks before the attacks, a Mexican magazine reported the Federal Aviation Administration warning that individuals with links to terror networks were planning to fly on U.S. airlines. The FAA memo listed names of suspects (none of whom corresponded with those identified by the FBI as responsible for the skyjackings) and ordered airlines and airports to take measures to prevent them from boarding planes. While it appears that some of the terrorists may have crossed into the United States from Mexico and some of their accomplices may have since fled to Mexico, there is no definitive proof of a Mexican connection.

There are four ways in which the events of September 11, 2001, influenced Mexico and U.S.–Mexican relations. First, the September 11 attacks activated the deeply ingrained principle of sovereignty and nonintervention in Mexico's foreign relations. The effusive pledges of friendship during President Fox's earlier four-day state visit to the United States faded after September 11, forcing the Mexican president to walk a tightrope between domestic political pressures and the commitments he had made to President Bush the week before. Both major opposition parties—the **Partido Revolucionario Institucional (PRI)** and the **Partido de la Revolución Demócrata (PRD)**— warned Fox about the dangers of offering too much to the United States in its military response

to terrorism. The residue of anti-Americanism in Mexico was evident in a postattack poll of 435 Internet users—obviously not representative of the general population (see Appendix A)—who responded by saying, "It is not our fight" and "They [Americans] had it coming for all the things they have done in the rest of the world." While most Mexicans now have a favorable view of the United States, resentment endures because of the loss of territory in the 19th century, a history of U.S. **interventionism** in Mexico, and Washington's penchant to deal with world conflicts through military power.

In the wake of the attacks, President **Vicente Fox** was criticized for not rallying Mexicans to national demonstrations of solidarity and condolence, like those that occurred in Europe. After two weeks of internal political squabbles, President Fox returned to the United States and told President Bush, "We are a friend, we are neighbors, we are partners, and we want to make clear that this means commitment all the way, and that we will keep our commitments." Fox then traveled to New York to tour the wreckage of the World Trade Center with Mayor Rudolph W. Giuliani.

Second, the terrorist attacks contributed to greater U.S.–Mexican cooperation on border-related issues. President Fox offered to help the United States by providing intelligence information on suspected terrorists, tracking the flow of money alleged to be associated with terrorists and **drug traffickers**, and maintaining order along Mexico's international boundary. President Fox also pledged to crack down on people smugglers along the border. The tightened security along the **U.S.–Mexican border** and a dramatic decline in illegal border crossings appeared to put the idea of a blanket amnesty for undocumented Mexicans in the United States on the far back burner. With the border on high alert, people on both sides have restricted their travel. Many experts on border issues argue that this pattern is only temporary and some solution to illegal immigration is still needed.

Shortly after the attack, Mexico apprehended and questioned hundreds of people of Middle Eastern origin, assisting the U.S.-led manhunt for suspected terrorists. Postattack efforts to tighten the border appeared to interfere with President Bush's earlier plans to open the border to more Mexican migration and to create some kind of new "guest worker" program to deal with the status of illegal immigrants. The U.S. response to bin Laden reminded some Mexicans of Pancho Villa's 1916 terrorist attack on Columbus, New Mexico. His *Villistas* (followers of Villa) killed 18 Americans before escaping back across the border. In retaliation, U.S. President Woodrow Wilson sent a 10,000-man punitive expedition force deep into Mexico's northern deserts in search of the elusive Mexican bandit-terrorist. Villa was never caught by U.S. forces, but they did manage to contain the terrorist threat he posed to the United States.

Third, the September 11 attacks altered the prospects for two of President Bush's nominees for key diplomatic posts. By calling on Latin American governments to rally opinion against terrorism and the "evildoers" who carry it out, the president managed to snag his appointments in his own rhetoric. Despite an unsavory record of supporting U.S.-backed death squads while he was President Reagan's ambassador to Honduras in the 1980s, the U.S. Senate approved John Negroponte's nomination on September 14, claiming the United States needed someone in the United Nations immediately in order to handle sensitive diplomatic duties. Many Mexicans saw the Negroponte nomination as a diplomatic reward for someone they considered a terrorist for orchestrating the Contra war against the Nicaraguan Sandinistas during the 1980s.

In another case, Otto J. Reich's long-delayed nomination to be assistant secretary of state for Western Hemisphere affairs was stalled by his close ties with anti-**Castro** terrorist Orlando Bosch, charged with planting a bomb on a Cuban airliner that killed all 73 people on board in 1976. A hero to the Cuban exile community in Miami, Bosch received a presidential pardon from President George H. W. Bush in 1992, despite his illegal entry into the United States and prior convictions related to terrorist charges. Some of Reich's staunchest supporters wanted a recess appointment, requiring no approval by the Senate. However, the Bosch connection bothered many lawmakers in Washington who argued that the Cuban–American nominee did not deserve either a Senate hearing or vote. Ignoring the voice of the U.S. Senate, President Bush resorted to a recess appointment in January 2002 and the controversial Reich assumed the State Department position to oversee Western Hemisphere affairs. Many in Mexico City, and throughout Latin America, were appalled by the negative symbolism and hypocrisy of Bush's determination to push a nominee with close ties to a well-known Miami terrorist in light of the call from Washington for all-out cooperation in the war against terrorism.

Fourth, the events of September 11, 2001, contributed to a flourish of regional solidarity expressed through two related resolutions that were approved by the Organization of American States (OAS). In a speech at OAS headquarters in Washington, D.C. before the terrorist attacks, President Fox said that the hemispheric mutual defense treaty known as the Rio Treaty was "obsolete and useless" and hinted that Mexico might pull out of the agreement altogether. Once the OAS decided to invoke the Rio Treaty in mid-September, something that had not been done in decades, Fox could only reaffirm Mexico's doubts and then go along with the resolution as endorsed by the rest of the member states in large part due to its importance to the United States.

The strains in U.S.–Mexican relations brought about by the terrorist attacks were evident in the way Mexico was forced to walk a fine line between expressions of support for Washington's war on terrorism and its preference for diplomacy and negotiation over military action. While President Bush never requested that Mexico provide troops to join a multinational military coalition, Fox made it clear that Mexico would never commit troops for this purpose. Some argue that it is important for Mexico to stand fast, since cooperating too closely with the United States is equivalent to submitting to it. Others claim that Mexico must become less of a "fair-weather friend" if it wants to maintain its "special relationship" with its northern neighbor. *See also* Foreign Policy.

SUGGESTED READING

Al Kamen, "Afloat in a Sea of Change," *Washington Post*, October 17, 2001; Kevin Sullivan, "U.S. Relations Change Suddenly for Mexico," *Washington Post*, September 21, 2001.

Sexenio ☀ The authority of the Mexican president is enhanced by his six-year term of office, known in Mexican politics as the *sexenio*. The **Constitution of 1917** restricted the presidential term to four years with no reelection. Although this was modified between 1927 and 1933 to allow for reelection after waiting out a term, the current rule of six years and no reelectability became a permanent fixture of Mexican presidential terms of office with the election of **Lázaro Cárdenas** (1934–1940). This fixed six-year term was the Mexican elite's solution to the problem of presidential succession and served as a means of guaranteeing an institutionalized system of elite rotation because of the importance of *camarillas* in the recruitment of political leadership. The continuity of the principle of no reelection has been debated from time to time, but there has not been the political will to initiate legislative reform to put it to rest.

Until 1999, Mexican presidents had the power to choose the next presidential candidate from inside the dominant party. This political ritual, known as the *dedazo*, afforded the president tremendous power over the direction of public policy and the stability of the system. The last year of the *sexenio*—in which public officials associated with the president steal egregiously to protect themselves from an uncertain future—is often referred to as the *año de Hidalgo*, named after the revolutionary priest whose face once adorned the silver one-peso coin. The **personalist** nature of Mexican politics and the insecurity surrounding bureaucratic politics tend to promote **corruption** and nepotism, making it difficult to break the system of rewards that is intertwined with the opportunities for profit and power within the **corporatist** arrangement. President **Vicente Fox** (2000–2006) indicated early in his *sexenio* that he wanted to reduce the opportunities for illicit enrichment within his government, but the tension between the power of the office and limited tenure on the one hand and access to the perks of power on the other made meaningful reform in this area extremely difficult.

Silva Herzog, Jesús (1892–1985) ☀ Prominent economist, author, intellectual, and public figure with close ties to the **Revolutionary Family** for a span of 50 years. Born in San Luis Potosí, the son of a German immigrant mother and a Mexican engineer father, Silva Herzog developed close friendships while completing his studies in economics at the **Universidad Nacional Autónoma de México (UNAM)**.

Silva Herzog completed secondary studies at the Paine Uptown Business School in New York (1912–1914) before returning to Mexico to serve in the **Mexican Revolution** as a reporter (1914–1915). He began his career as a teacher of literature at the National Teachers School in 1919 before moving to UNAM, where he helped establish the National School of Economics in the 1920s. Silva Herzog taught the history of economic thought at UNAM from 1939 to 1959, served as dean of the School of Economics (1940–1942), trained dozens of disciples, and founded and directed one of Mexico's leading magazines, *Cuadernos Americanos*. After serving as Mexico's ambassador to the **Soviet Union** (1928–1930), Silva Herzog advised President **Lázaro Cárdenas** on the labor–management dispute over the petroleum industry. He served as general manager of the National Petroleum Company (before it became known as PEMEX) from 1939 to 1940.

Silva Herzog was sympathetic toward fundamental socialist ideas and supported socialist-inclined reform efforts during the times he served as economics adviser for six Mexican presidents. His writings on political and economic history revealed a liberal interpretation of the Mexican Revolution, namely, that the revolution is best understood as a synthesis of the different revolutionary programs put forth by the major figures such as Francisco I. Madero, Venustiano Carranza, Álvaro Obregón, and **Emiliano Zapata**.

Silva Herzog was awarded the National Prize in Arts and Sciences in 1962. He died in Mexico City in 1985. His son, Jesús Silva Herzog Flores, was secretary of the treasury during the presidency of **Miguel de la Madrid** and ambassador to Spain in the **Carlos Salinas** administration (1991–1993). *See also* de la Madrid, Miguel; Mexican Revolution; Revolutionary Family or Coalition.

SUGGESTED READING

Roderic Ai Camp, *Mexican Political Biographies, 1935–1993*, 3d ed. (Austin: University of Texas Press, 1995).

Sinaloa. *See* Geographical Regions.

Siqueiros, David Alfaro (1896–1974) ☀ One of the most significant artists in 20th-century Mexico. David Alfaro Siqueiros was known for his massive and muscular paintings (he called his combination of painting and sculpture *esculptopintura*), easel paintings, and revolutionary political activities. His murals were known for their innovative techniques—synthetic paint, stencils, and airbrush applications—and a recurrent theme in which he portrays man's progress through the ages and his struggle for social justice. Siqueiros's artistic life and political activities were closely intertwined; he fought in the **Mexican Revolution**, became an officer on the Republican side in the Spanish Civil War, and was part of an unsuccessful attempt to assassinate **Leon Trotsky** at his residence in Mexico City.

Born in Santa Rosalia (today Camargo), Chihuahua, David Alfaro Siqueiros's artistic training began at Academía de San Carlos (today the National School of Fine Arts) in Mexico City and continued in Italy, France, and Spain. Throughout his artistic life he was involved in radical political activities, always using his artistic skills to complement and extend his leftist political views. In 1914 he joined the Constitutionalist Army, which overthrew the regime of Victoriano Huerta, and became the only major muralist to participate in the upheaval. After leaving the army as a captain, Siqueiros traveled to Europe on a state grant, met **Diego Rivera** in Paris, and continued his art studies in France, Spain, and Italy. While living in Barcelona in 1921, he issued a manifesto to the Latin American artists of the region proposing the creation of a public art movement that would synthesize *indigenismo*, universal values, and avant-garde forms of expression. The document appeared in a magazine *Vida Americana* and subsequently became the intellectual/artistic basis for the muralist revival in Mexico.

At the insistence of the new education minister, **José Vasconcelos**, Siqueiros returned from Europe in 1922 to inaugurate the Mexican mural movement, produce a series of allegorical murals, and continue his political activities in support of the Mexican Revolution and populist art. He joined the **Communist** Party in 1923, and the mural movement soon joined hands with the

Mexican intelligentsia, artists, workers, and an assortment of leftists.

From 1930, when he was banished to Taxco as punishment for his radical political activities, Siqueiros concentrated more on politics than art, often going into exile in the United States and Latin America to pursue his painting. While in exile in Los Angeles, he produced a controversial mural (*Tropical America*, 1932) that criticized U.S. imperialism; the following year he was deported from the United States and traveled to Argentina. In 1934, while residing in New York, he set up an experimental workshop that was attended by avant-garde painter Jackson Pollock. It was here that he experimented with the technique of dripping paint in semiabstract compositions such as *Birth of Fascism* (1936) and *Echo of a Scream* (1937).

After fighting in the Spanish Civil War (1937–1938), Siqueiros returned to Mexico in 1939 to begin work on *Retrato de la burguesía* (1939–1940), a monumental mural portraying an epic battle between imperialist capitalism and revolutionary socialism at the Mexican Electricians Union. He broke with President **Lázaro Cárdenas** over asylum for Trotsky and in 1940 was part of a failed effort to assassinate the Russian revolutionary in his heavily guarded compound in Mexico City. He was put on trial and, after being acquitted of homicide, went into exile again, this time in Chillán, Chile, where he painted one of his best-known murals outside of Mexico.

Returning from Latin America to Mexico in 1944, Siqueiros benefited from the postwar construction boom, giving new life to the demand for murals in the capital. Despite his international reputation and the fact that he was working on a mural sponsored by the Mexican government, he was arrested and imprisoned (1960–1964) by the Mexican government for the crime of "social dissolution" during the anticommunist fervor of the **López Mateos** presidency. After his release from

prison, he was commissioned to produce more murals, and in 1966 he received the government's National Prize. In 1968 Siqueiros became president of the Academy of Arts in Mexico City. Among his last outdoor murals was, by his own admission, one of his best works, *Marcha de la humanidad en Latinoamérica* (1966–1973) on the Congress Hall of Mexico City. It was one of the first buildings ever built specifically to accommodate a mural.

Siquieros was an innovator who constantly experimented with technique and form. His best murals stand out because of their bright coloring and dramatic visual impact, often a combination of his ideological drive and love of bold and colorful action. Convinced that the whole concept of revolution required revolutionary art, Siqueiros filled his murals with massive and muscular figures that resemble a sort of imprisoned sculpture. However, in his easel paintings, smaller works that helped him survive financially, he often revealed a different view of humanity, more sensitive and insightful than his best murals. Prior to his death in Cuernavaca in 1974, he was paid a courtesy visit by President **Luis Echeverría** and his wife, a sign that even citizens with deviant ideologies and those considered dangerous to the state deserve recognition for their artistic brilliance and international achievements.

SUGGESTED READING

Leonard Folgarait, *Mural Painting and Social Revolution in Mexico, 1920–1940: Art of the New Order* (New York: Cambridge University Press, 1998); Laurance P. Hurlburt, *The Mexican Muralists in the United States* (Albuquerque: University of New Mexico Press, 1989); Edward A. Riedinger, "Siqueiros, David Alfaro," in Michael S. Werner, ed., *Encyclopedia of Mexico: History, Society, and Culture*, vol. 2 (Chicago: Fitzroy Dearborn, 1997); Desmond Rochfort, *Mexican Muralists: Orozco, Rivera, Siqueiros* (New York: International, 1993); Philip Stein, *Siqueiros: His Life and Works* (New York: International, 1993); D. Anthony White, *So Far from Heaven: David Alfaro Siqueiros* (New York: Cambridge University Press, 1987).

Slim Helú, Carlos (1940–) ☀ Considered the richest man in Latin America, with his family's net worth estimated at over $10 billion in 2001. Carlos Slim studied to be an engineer but then devoted most of his life to the world of business and finance. Born in 1940 in Mexico City, the son of a Lebanese merchant who arrived in Mexico at the age of 12, Slim attended religious schools before enrolling at the **Universidad Nacional Autónoma de México (UNAM)** and graduating with a degree in civil engineering. He also did postgraduate studies in Chile (1963–1964), where he specialized in industrial development. After returning to Mexico, Slim started his business career in 1965 with an interest in construction, mining, and a soft drink bottling plant. By purchasing financially ailing companies, which he turned around through shrewd management and close ties with members of the ruling party, he built his business empire as chairman of Grupo Carso, a conglomerate that owns Mexico's phone giant, Teléfonos de Mexico (TELMEX); a financial company, Grupo Financiero Inbursa; and the Mexican chain of over 40 Sears stores. Unlike most successful Mexican businesses, which are oriented toward the global export market, over 80 percent of Grupo Carso's production is for the domestic market. In 1994 Slim was one of a dozen top business tycoons who attended the "billionaire's banquet" at the home of finance minister **Antonio Ortíz Mena**, arranged to help prop up the ailing PRI for the 1994 presidential elections.

After heart surgery in 1998, Slim began a pattern common in Mexican business of turning his financial empire over to his sons, Carlos Slim Domit and Patrick Slim Domit. He now dedicates his time to Internet and digital communications, a market he feels has tremendous economic potential internationally. This generational shift from father to son among business giants is a common practice in Mexican business: in 1997 Emilio Azcárraga Jean took control of the vast Grupo **Televisa** empire after the death of his father, and Ricardo Salinas Pliego, son of a family of department store owners, is running TV Azteca, the rival television network to Televisa.

Slim's recent financial decisions suggest that he is becoming more interested in the profits that exist in the global marketplace. After watching Philip Morris stock drop for years, Carlos Slim bought $90 million worth of shares in the world's largest cigarette maker in January 2000, a move that gave him a reputation as the Warren Buffett of Latin America. In one of the biggest Mexican purchases of an American business, Slim bought the remainder (he already owned 15 percent of the company) of CompUSA, the Dallas, Texas–based chain of computer stores in January 2000. This bold move is part of a strategy by the Mexican billionaire to transform TELMEX into a dynamic, Web-savvy multinational giant in the Americas and spread his financial empire into the competitive global marketplace. Recognizing another bargain north of the border, in March 2001 Carlos Slim and other family members acquired a 5.9 percent stake in Circuit City Stores, Inc., the second largest electronic chain in the United States.

In February 2001, TELMEX spun off its cellular and international businesses into a new company called América Móvil, already Latin America's largest mobile phone provider. By separating the two giant phone providers, Slim created two businesses with separate administrations, a clever business maneuver that reminded some in the Mexican business world of his earlier financial strategies. Despite the separation into two companies, Carlos Slim remains the chairman and controlling shareholder of each and a major player in Mexican and Latin American telecommunications.

In February 2001, in an effort to transform **Petróleos Mexicanos (PEMEX)** into a more efficient multinational corporation, President **Vicente Fox** appointed three of the richest Mexicans, including Carlos Slim, to a new slate of directors for the PEMEX board. This is a deliberate effort to change the way Mexico's oil monopoly is managed, replacing the political functionaries and high-level bureaucrats who were often accused of **corruption** and mismanagement with more qualified management.

SUGGESTED READING

Graham Gori, "Telmex Completes Spinoff of Two Big Parts of Business," *New York Times,* February 8, 2001; Martha McNeil Hamilton, "Mexico's Slim Buys Stake in Circuit City," *Washington Post,* March 13, 2001; Julia Preston, "Mexican Business Giant Begins Transition to Sons," *New York Times,* October 15, 1998.

Sonora. *See* Geographical Regions.

States and Municipalities. *See* Geographical Regions.

Student Movement of 1968. *See* Tlatelolco Massacre.

Subcommander Marcos (1957–) ☀ In Spanish, Subcomandante Marcos; the guerrilla leader of the Zapatista Army (EZLN) who became a legend after the **Zapatista rebellion in Chiapas** among Mayan Indians in early January 1994. One of eight children of a middle-class furniture store owner in Tampico, Veracruz, Marcos developed a passion for philosophy and a desire to uplift the downtrodden. For brief periods he taught graphic design and communications; he was also a talented actor, humorist, poet, and short story writer. After graduating from high school at age 17, Marcos left for Mexico City, where he attended college and developed an interest in the writings of Marxist French philosopher Louis Althusser. His graduation thesis at the **Universidad Nacional Autónoma de México (UNAM)** was entitled "Philosophy and Education."

In it he offered radical arguments for class struggle and the necessity of a new social order free of capitalist oppression. During the early years of the Sandinista revolution, Marcos worked in Nicaragua as a volunteer. In 1983 he joined the Front for National Liberation (FLN), a guerrilla group that began operation after the **Tlatelolco massacre** in 1968. Although the FLN claimed that its goal was to create a "dictatorship of the proletariat," the Zapatista uprising in 1994 made no mention of socialism or Marxism in its manifesto.

At the time of the Chiapas revolt, Subcommander Marcos emerged from the jungle on horseback and captured the attention of the media with his romantic, modern revolutionary image. Wearing military fatigues, a black ski mask, and a double bandolier across his chest and puffing on a pipe, he became an instant international sensation, acclaimed as a leftist intellectual in charge of an indigenous rebellion of Mayan peasants in favor of social justice, equality, a **democratic** form of **government**, and the removal of "the dictator" (President **Carlos Salinas**) and his federal army. While leading a ragtag, poorly armed band of Indian guerrillas against a powerful government and military, Marcos was an articulate, photogenic, latter-day **Zapata** with his own Web site, ready to lead a rebellion in favor of reforms expanding the rights of Mexico's indigenous people. A master of revolutionary symbolism, Subcommander Marcos's persona is a clever blend of the costumes and props used by Ché Guevara, Emiliano Zapata, Augusto Sandino, and heroes from Mexican movies such as Zorro and the wrestler El Santo.

The effects of President Salinas's reforms—neoliberalism, privatization of major industries, the **North American Free Trade Agreement (NAFTA)**, and a reversal of historic land reform initiatives—helped build a **guerrilla movement** symbolizing Mexico's Indian heritage. By anchoring his struggle in Mexican history, Marcos

As the luster of the Zapatistas faded after years of failed peace negotiations with the **Ernesto Zedillo** administration, hopes of resolving the Chiapas conflict seemed unlikely under PRI rule. The Zapatista rebels agreed to accept the **San Andrés Accords** in February 1996 but seven months later suspended the peace talks, arguing that the government had failed to implement the measures called for in the agreement—measures aimed at providing a remedy for centuries of discrimination against indigenous groups in southern Mexico. Some blamed Subcommander Marcos for the weakness of the rebel movement, particularly his penchant for photo opportunities with luminaries who traveled to his jungle hideout, including film director Oliver Stone, former French first lady Danielle Mitterand, and Mexican American actor Edward James Olmos.

After Subcommander Marcos authored *La historia de los colores* (The story of colors, 1997)—an eye-catching children's book of whimsical tales without references to the Zapatista cause or military tactics—a small publisher of bilingual books in El Paso, Texas, attempted to publish it in an English-Spanish format with the assistance of a small grant from the National Endowment for the Arts (NEA) in the United States. However, the chairman of the NEA abruptly canceled the publisher's award after discovering that the book was linked to the Mexican insurgent, worried about rights payments to the rebels.

After the **Acteal massacre** on December 22, 1997, the government was forced—under national and international pressure—to seek a better solution to the Chiapas conflict. In a package of constitutional and legislative reforms presented by President Zedillo in March 1998, the government hoped by granting the Indians greater rights it could push the Chiapas imbroglio to a satisfactory solution. However, Subcommander Marcos rejected Zedillo's initiative, claiming the reforms did not address the

Zapatista chief Subcommander Marcos. Credit: *Proceso,* photo by Germán Canseco.

believed he could spark a nationwide rebellion and move his army north to Mexico City. However, the Zapatistas were poorly armed and faced a formidable army of 175,000. After the Zapatista revolt, the United States dramatically expanded its security assistance to Mexico. In 1996–1997 Mexico ranked first in military funding from the United States; Mexican personnel dominated those attending the School of the Americas (renamed in 2000 the Western Hemisphere Institute for Security Cooperation, WHISC) and the Inter-American Air Forces Academy.

problems created by numerous paramilitary groups operating in the region and the heavy presence of the Mexican army in Chiapas.

After the election of **Vicente Fox**, the government placed a high priority on settling the dispute with the Zapatistas. To test the intentions of the new government, in early 2001 Marcos organized a march from San Cristóbal de las Casas in Chiapas to the nation's capital to pressure President Fox and Congress to pass legislative reforms that address the needs of Mexico's 10 million Indians. The gathering of Zapatista rebels and their supporters in the nation's capital is the first time guerrilla fighters have taken their movement to Mexico City since **Pancho Villa** and **Emiliano Zapata** captured the city in 1914.

SUGGESTED READING

John Ward Anderson, "Zapatistas' Luster Fades—Along with Hopes for Peace," *Washington Post,* April 19, 1998; John Holloway and Eloina Pelaez, eds., *Zapatista: Reinventing Revolution in Mexico* (London: Pluto, 1998); Elaine Katzenberger, ed., *First World, Ha Ha Ha: The Zapatista Challenge* (San Francisco: City Lights Books, 1995); Subcomandante Marcos, *Shadows of Tender Fury: The Letters and Communiques of Subcomandante Marcos and the Zapatista Army of National Liberation,* trans. Frank Bardacke, Leslie López, and the Watsonville California Human Rights Committee (New York: Monthly Review Press, 1995); Julia Preston, "N.E.A. Couldn't Tell a Book by Its Cover," *New York Times,* March 9, 1998; Ginger Thompson and Tim Weiner, "Zapatista Rebels Rally in Mexico City," *New York Times,* March 12, 2001.

Superbarrio ☀ Since the 1980s, Mexico has experienced a growth of leaders and citizen participation in unconventional political activities, due in large part to the government's incompetence and mean-spirited attitude toward the economic and social problems afflicting low-income neighborhoods. Many of the leaders of these urban protest movements have been inspired by fictional characters designed to change attitudes, foment a popular-cultural renaissance in Mexican urban life, and transform urban slum dwellers into political activists with the means to shape their own destiny. One of the most artistic and colorful leaders of this new type of political mobilization is "Superbarrio," a politically outspoken former street vendor and professional wrestler who became a cult idol for his attacks on the bureaucracy, greedy landlords, and political hacks in the 1980s and 1990s.

Dressed in a mask emblazoned with "SB" (the name Superbarrio is a cross between Superman and *barrio,* a low-income neighborhood), red cape, and gold Spandex wrestling tights (revealing a large paunch), Superbarrio (sometimes referred to as Superbarrio Gómez) has led tens of thousands of people in marches protesting the plight of the urban poor and promising to fight for "what is right" in staged matches against the forces of evil. After the Mexico City earthquake of 1985, he became a sort of political superhero, helping slum dwellers in their disputes with landlords, negotiating with government officials, leading protests and rallies, and in 1987 helping form the Assembly of Barrios (Asamblea de Barrios, AB)—a neighborhood coalition whose goal is to defend the rights of the poor, expand political participation, and redefine citizenship in light of unscrupulous landlords and corrupt authorities.

Superbarrio's flamboyant persona as a defender of the poor gained him national and international media attention, drawing more awareness of the need for housing and the lack of **democracy** in Mexico City. For many years he was a frequent star of political demonstrations in the nation's capital. Working in tandem with the AB, Superbarrio eventually became closely associated with the **Partido de la Revolución Democrática (PRD)** after its founding in 1989.

Superbarrio Gómez. Credit: *Proceso*, photo by Germán Canseco.

He attended many PRD events, symbolizing social justice, bureaucratic effectiveness, and bravery (**machismo**) against difficult odds. With the media in tow, Superbarrio would battle evil characters, popular villains who are portrayed as the personification of social evils. Using his talent as a former wrestler, Superbarrio often stages fights with masked villains such as Cataliño Creel, a greedy and malicious slumlord who appears regularly on a popular television soap opera. However, since the left-of-center PRD won control of the Mexico City government in 1997, Superbarrio has kept a low profile.

Superbarrio's meteoric rise as a defender of the poor also contributed to his speaking tours in the United States as a representative for urban popular movements. After the passage of NAFTA, Superbarrio's heroics generated demands for his services north of the border in order to educate and mobilize people around significant globalization issues. On a "tour" of Los Angeles, Superbarrio took water samples for toxic testing in Mexican labs because a local **environmental** group did not believe the results they received from the U.S. government.

In the meantime, other masked "superheroes" have taken up fights against various forms of injustice of importance to Mexicans. For example, Superbarrio's theatrical efforts spawned social activists to fight against environmental disasters (Super Universal Ecologist), rampant **corruption** (Super Policeman), women's rights (Super Woman), homophobia (Super Gay), and the rights and lives of animals (Super Animal). The superheroes of today will no doubt be followed by artistic and cartoon-like characters symbolizing the need to educate and transform the large numbers of citizens—many of whom have been neglected by government officials—into political activists with the power to address a broad range of issues from income distribution and unemployment to corruption, housing, **labor** rights, and even U.S.–Mexican relations.

The pop culturalization of politics and social mobilization is not limited to Mexico; the press attention and popularity of ex-professional wrestler Jesse "The Body" Ventura—now governor of Minnesota and once a key player in the Reform Party—suggests that people on both sides of the border need "superheroes" to better endure the strains of everyday life, fight for social justice, and put an end to the superficial, elitist, and costly nature of the political process. The power of political theater has proved an effective means of building grassroots support for those who feel that globalization has hurt many workers and farmers in Mexico and that national elites—both public and private—need to pay more attention to those at the bottom of the economic and social ladder. *See also* Barzón, El; Gómez-Peña, Guillermo; Mexican Counterculture.

SUGGESTED READING

Sarah Anderson, John Cavanagh, and Thea Lee, *Field Guide to the Global Economy* (New York: New Press, 2000); Paul Lawrence Haber, "Superbarrio," in Michael S. Werner, ed., *Encyclopedia of Mexico: History, Society, and Culture*, vol. 2 (Chicago: Fitzroy Dearborn, 1997); Michelle Ray Ortíz, "'Superheroes' Take up Fight for Many Causes in Mexico," *Denver Post*, September 17, 1999; Mauricio-José Schwarz, *Todos somos Superbarrio* (Mexico, D.F.: Grupo Editorial Planeta, 1994).

Sustainable Development. *See* Environment and Ecology.

Tabasco. *See* Geographical Regions.

Tamaulipas. *See* Geographical Regions.

Tamayo, Rufino (1899–1991) ☀ Renowned Mexican painter. Rufino Tamayo was born in Oaxaca, where he learned about Indian art and culture and the region's pre-Columbian artistic heritage. He moved to Mexico City in 1910 and studied at the San Carlos Academy of Fine Arts between 1917 and 1920, focusing on Impressionism and native styles of painting. Impressionism awakened Tamayo's devotion to light and color, which influenced his painting throughout his life. Between 1920 and 1934 he worked in Mexico City and New York, where he learned to fuse European styles of Cubism and Surrealism with Mexican subject matter involving figures, still lifes, and animals. In New York (1926–1928) he acquainted himself with the paintings of Paul Cézanne, Georges Braque, and Pablo Picasso. Unlike the Mexican muralists, Tamayo was first recognized in the United States and Europe and only later in his native land. He painted in oils and watercolors and also painted murals in Mexico, France, and the United States.

While working in the Department of Ethnographic Drawing at the National Museum of Anthropology, Mexico City, from 1921 to 1923, Tamayo absorbed more about pre-Columbian art and the national heritage of earlier Mexican cultures. However, he rejected social realist and historical narrative murals made famous by the Big Three of Mexican painting: **Diego Rivera**, **José Clemente Orozco**, and **David Alfaro Siqueiros**. Tamayo and other "antimuralists" rejected the didactic and ideological/propagandistic style of the muralists and instead advocated an easel painting approach that stressed abstract and decorative qualities and stylization of form. His earthy yet vivid colors reflected his attraction to the life and legends of his native land.

In 1936 Tamayo went back to New York, where he thereafter spent his winters, returning to Mexico City for the summers, thus enabling him to maintain contact with both the mainstream New York art world and his Mexican roots. He maintained his New York City–Mexico City residence alternation until 1954, when he and his wife left for Paris. In the United States, Tamayo worked at the Federal Arts Project (FAP) of the Works

Progress Administration (WPA) for a short time before the U.S. Congress barred foreign artists from this work and he was forced to leave. In 1938 Tamayo began a nine-year teaching stint at the Dalton School in New York City. He developed an admiration for Picasso's art, returned to mural painting, and participated in several exhibitions of Mexican art.

By the late 1940s Tamayo was coming to be regarded as one of the outstanding painters of his generation. In 1948 the Palacio de Bellas Artes gave Tamayo his first large retrospective and for the first time he became a recognized painter in Mexico. Tamayo's most creative period occurred during the time he spent in New York and Mexico City, including visits to various European cities. Some of his most famous murals were created during the 1950s, including *Birth of Nationality* and *Mexico Today* for the Palacio de Bellas Artes, *Prometheus Bringing Fire to Man* for the United Nations Educational, Scientific, and Cultural Organization (UNESCO) in Paris, and *Man*, a fresco for the Dallas Museum of Fine Arts.

Tamayo's artistic style of blending scenes of daily life in Mexico with European styles and his own personal touch became the hallmark of his paintings and murals. Tamayo's murals often dealt with cosmic and domestic symbology (cats, women, and the stars) with little interest in the political history of Mexico. His critical attitude toward the work of the propagandistic muralists who tried to link painting with political ideology is what highlights his place in Mexican art history. Tamayo preferred to focus his art on the aesthetics of pre-Columbian art, not in the realm of 20th-century ideas and political struggles. Later in life, he donated his extensive collection of pre-Hispanic art to his native city of Oaxaca, where the Rufino Tamayo Museum of Pre-Hispanic Art of Mexico is located in a restored, 16th-century colonial mansion. In Mexico City's Chapultepec

Park is the Rufino Tamayo Museum, which houses a fine collection of his paintings. When he died at age 92, Rufino Tamayo's artistic contributions were recognized around the world as a major force in the evolution of 20th-century Mexican painting.

SUGGESTED READING

Michael Brenson, "Rufino Tamayo, a Leader in Mexican Art, Dies at 91," *New York Times,* June 25, 1991; Claude Marks, *World Artists, 1950–1980* (New York: Wilson, 1984); Octavio Paz, *Rufino Tamayo: Myth and Magic* (New York: Solomon R. Guggenheim Foundation, 1979); James Vinson, ed., *International Dictionary of Art and Artists: Artists* (Chicago: St. James, 1990).

Technocrats (*Técnicos*) ✹ Mexico's politician-technocrats represent major changes in elite composition and recruitment in the modern period, mainly in their social origins, education, and professional training. During the last 30 years of the 20th century, Mexican political recruitment placed greater emphasis on a new group of elites called *técnicos*, a type of leadership characterized by their technologically sophisticated educations (many with foreign college degrees) and middle- and upper-middle-class backgrounds and by having spent most of their lives in a large urban center, notably Mexico City.

Beginning with the presidency of **Luis Echeverría** (1970–1976), the more traditional elite of *políticos* (this hard-line segment of the elite are widely known in Mexico as "dinosaurs," or *dinosaurios*) began a period of decline while a new generation of leaders found itself in the ascendancy. The rise of a technocratic elite with different career patterns, a different basis for legitimacy, and a different ideology set them apart from the older elite that made up the **Revolutionary Family** reaching back to the founding of the ruling party in 1929. Beginning in the 1970s, Mexico experienced a bifurcation in its leadership structure that came to dominate the politics and policy making process. While it is safe to say that the typical Mexican politician has been a hybrid of the *político* and *técnico*, the rise in technocratic leadership helps explain the attraction to economic liberalization and the growing dissension among Mexican political leadership (dinosaurs and technocrats) in the 1980s and 1990s. With two master's degrees and a doctorate in political economy, **Carlos Salinas de Gortari** epitomized the new group of elites with technical expertise and education.

The pattern of elite university education, intolerance of domestic opponents, relative youth, and limited political experience among the *técnicos* may explain the instability within Mexico's political leadership class. The end of technocratic dominance may be on the horizon, as none of the four major contenders for the **Partido Revolucionario Institucional (PRI)** nomination for president in 2000 could be considered a technocrat. The winner of the November 1999 primary, **Francisco Labastida Ochoa**, was the favorite of the traditional elite and clearly a *dinosaurio* with 37 years of political and bureaucratic experience. Despite his business background, President **Vicente Fox** is not part of the tecnocratic elite that dominated the process of political recruitment used by the PRI since 1970.

SUGGESTED READING

John Ward Anderson, "'Dinosaurs' Clash with Technocrats for Mexico's Soul," *Washington Post,* April 6, 1998; Anderson, "Mexico's 'Dinosaurs' Resurgent," *Washington Post,* May 23, 2000.

Tejano. See Music (Popular).

Televisa ☀ Commercial television broadcasting was inaugurated in July 1950 after the Mexican **government** granted the first license to Rómulo O'Farril to operate Channel 4. The following year the second license was granted to Emilio Azcárraga Vidaurreta to transmit on channel 2. These two individuals represented the titans of the Mexican business community, O'Farril had made his fortune in the **automobile industry** and Azcárraga's financial empire included a monopoly on radio stations, film, and other forms of entertainment that stretched back 30 years. The pattern of private ownership of the broadcast media was established early and has made a significant impact on the symbiotic relationship between television and the Mexican state. As of 1997, Mexico had 236 television broadcast stations, more than 80 percent owned by a single conglomerate—Televisa. Although it must now compete with TV Azteca, privatized in 1993, in reality it faces only nominal competition in the industry.

The competition between O'Farril and Azcárraga during the formative years was ferocious, ultimately leading to a merger and the creation of Telesistema Mexicano (TSM) in 1955 and Azcárraga's dominance over Mexican television for nearly 15 years. After further challenges and financial problems, Azcárraga agreed to another merger leading to a new corporation called Televisa in 1972. With the passing of Emilio Azcárraga Vidaurreta in the same year, his son, **Emilio Azcárraga Milmo,** took over Televisa and it continued its dominance of Mexican mass **communication media.** With his hold on entertainment talent, clout among large advertisers, government policies that protected Televisa from foreign competition, and close ties to the **Revolutionary Family,** Azcárraga was able to maintain the dominant position in Mexican mass communications until 1982.

The long arm of Televisa also reaches into the Spanish-speaking audiences in the United States, where its Univisión television programming network has offered distorted and censored news to a mostly Latino audience since 1961. In what some refer to as "reverse media imperialism," Univisión has grown into the fourth-largest commercial broadcast network in the United States, touching more than 6 million households every day and deliberately selecting news for its North American audience. Spanish-language television in the United States has come under criticism by actors and broadcast personalities for having few African Latinos or indigenous people cast in starring roles. Although part of the problem is rooted in a form of racism—white Hispanic actors dominate popular telenovelas—both Telemundo and Univisión are dependent on Grupo Televisa's programs, which rarely feature darker-skinned people.

One of the greatest electoral advantages of the **Partido Revolucionario Institucional (PRI)** is its favored treatment by the communications media, especially television broadcasting, where the Televisa conglomerate accounts for 85 percent of the nation's television audience and carries close to 90 percent of all lucrative advertising. The pervasiveness of its nightly news program *24 horas* (24 hours) has made its popular anchor, Jacobo Zabuldovsky, Mexico's best-known personality after the Mexican president. The symbiotic relationship between Televisa and the government means that news was selected, and slanted, to support the PRI during its long period of uninterrupted rule, often in return for favors such as new licenses for local stations. In a study of the 1994 election, the PRI candidate received 43 percent of the air time devoted to the presidential race, in contrast with only 12 percent for the PAN candidate and 11 percent for the PRD. With increasing evidence of Televisa's monopolistic position and prejudicial reporting on the presidential elections of 1988 and 1994, critics began demanding that the government make some basic changes in the industry that would help reduce the grip of Televisa's power over television programming.

Despite the creation of a more competitive broadcast environment and modest changes in the way Televisa covers the political scene, television is still a conservative medium dedicated to a progovernment posture, heavy emphasis on commercialism and low-brow entertainment, and very light investigative reporting, if any.

While the current head of Televisa, Emilio Azcárraga Jean, promised to offer more objective and fair reporting on the 2000 presidential campaign, old habits of censorship and media-government symbiosis persisted. In February 2000, Guillermo Ortega—one of the best-known broadcasters at Televisa—was taken off the air after he reported a mock election at a Mexico City school showed **Vicente Fox** winning the presidential election among voting students. Although the evidence is rather blurry, Mexico City's daily *La Reforma* reported that Azcárraga suspended Ortega for one week after being pressured by the PRI, accustomed to slanted coverage in favor of its chosen candidate for president. With such power, government policies that guarantee the right of information and media dependency on government advertising mean very little when the television stations are reluctant to implement such freedoms. In an effort to monitor the media's role in the 2000 elections, *La Reforma* published a weekly breakdown of the amount of electronic exposure received by all the presidential candidates and the amounts of money spent on television advertising.

SUGGESTED READING

Fernando Mejía Barquera, *La industria de la radio y televisión y la política del estado Mexicano, 1920–1960* (Mexico, D.F.: Fundación Manuel Buendía, 1989); Eli M. Noam, ed., *Telecommunications in Latin America* (New York: Oxford University Press, 1998); William A. Orme, Jr., ed., *A Culture of Collusion: An Inside Look at the Mexican Press* (Miami: North-South

Center Press, University of Miami, 1997); Michael B. Salwen and Bruce Garrison, *Latin American Journalism* (Hillsdale, N.J.: Erlbaum, 1991); Raúl Trejo Delarbre, ed., *Televisa: El quinto poder* (Mexico, D.F.: Claves Latinoamericanas, 1985).

Tequila ☀ The robust alcoholic beverage known as tequila is more than a transparent liquor used to make margarita cocktails, a mixed drink popularized in bars and restaurants in Mexican resort areas and throughout the United States. Tequila is a significant part of Mexican history, a symbol of its national character, an important export product, and the world's fastest growing liquor product. Industry officials claim that tequila consumption more than doubled worldwide between 1995 and 2000, leading to shortages in agave, the cactus-like plant from which tequila is distilled, and higher prices for the higher-quality spirits (particularly the 100 percent pure blue agave) that connoisseurs have learned to appreciate and savor. Since 1994, the number of tequila producers in Mexico has tripled and international liquor companies like Seagrams and Heublein have rushed to join the tequila boom, making the beverage the country's leading liquor export in 1998–1999. Even the world's largest brewer, St. Louis–based Anheuser-Busch, has tapped into the tequila-drinking craze with a new product called "Tequiza," a drink composed of beer and tequila flavoring.

Tequila is no longer only a poor man's drink; it has become a sophisticated international product whose quality is controlled by Mexico's Tequila Regulatory Council, a body of experts who guarantee the authenticity of the bottled drink. According to Mexican regulations for tequila production, all tequila must be fermented with at least 51 percent blue agave, a plant that must grow from 8 to 10 years before it can be properly harvested. Today, more than 100,000 acres of blue agave are under cultivation in the tequila region of Mexico, boosting Mexico's annual production to over 55

million liters. With the quality control and international popularity of tequila in the 1990s, the European Union awarded tequila the status of "drink of origin," thereby protecting the authenticity of tequila from its international imitators.

Long before the Spaniards came to Mexico, the technique of cooking the heart of maguey plant (a member of the Agavaceae family, of which there are over 350 species native to Mexico) and fermenting the juices was widely known among the different cultures that populated Mexico. The Mayan culture invented a fermented alcoholic drink called *pulque* (also known as the grandfather of tequila), and the ancient Mexica (Aztecs) considered the maguey (*metl*) sacred because of its commercial value. During the colonial period, the Spaniards began the process of distilling, making it possible to produce a transparent liquor with a higher alcohol content from the maguey. This early drink was called *mezcal,* made from a special type of agave that was harvested after three years, unlike the tequila agave that takes longer to mature.

Tequila became an international drink in the 19th century, when the La Perserverancia Distillery (owned by the Sauza family) bottled and exported it to the United States for the first time. Around 1900, a European botanist named Weber classified the different species of agave, helping to determine that the blue agave was the best suited to the production of quality tequila. The plant grown for tequila production (*agave tequilana*) is a near botanical relative of the maguey, although most Mexicans see no relation between the two plants. The blue agave came to be known as the *Weber tequila,* after Weber's botanical classifications, and is now grown in 124 municipalities in Jalisco and 54 municipalities in four other Mexican states.

The drink we know today as tequila (first called "tequila wine") originated at an exhibition in San Antonio, Texas, in 1910 and the industry grew steadily throughout the 20th century. Today tequila drinkers at trendy bars in Manhattan pay as much as $40 for a *caballito,* or tall shot of premium tequila from Jalisco. Since 1990, the number of brands of tequila in Mexico has increased from 35 to almost 600, a sign of the growing importance of tequila to the Mexican economy.

The main producers and distillers of tequila are located in the Tequila, Amatitán, and Arenal valleys in the state of Jalisco. The tequila made from blue agave is one of only a handful of alcoholic beverages such as champagne and cognac that are produced from a designated region of a specfic country. The process of distilling tequila has improved as demand for a more refined product has influenced the production and marketing process. Depending on the process, there are two kinds of tequila: silver and golden. If the distilled liquid is stored in wooden barrels (usually white oak) for three months or more, the drink is called *tequila reposado* (rested tequila) and is prized for its special flavor. Tequila that is aged one year or longer is called *tequila añejo*, a process that distillers claim improves the taste of the drink. The traditional way to drink tequila in Mexico is straight with a slice of lemon and salt, or occasionally together with sangrita, a drink made from tomato juice, orange juice, spices, and hot sauce. The most common way of consuming tequila in the United States is as a margarita cocktail, blended with orange liqueur and lime juice and served in a salt-rimmed glass.

SUGGESTED READING

Thomas Black, "Volatile Mix: Agave Shortage, Tequila Sales Boom," *Denver Post,* December 24, 1999; Bob Emmons, *The Book of Tequila: Complete Guide* (Chicago: Open Court, 1997); Sandy M. Fernández, "Tequila's Happy Hour," *Time,* March 13, 2000; Rogelio Luna Zamorra, *La historia del Tequila, de sus regiones y sus hombres* (Mexico, D.F.: Consejo Nacional para la Cultura y las Artes, 1991); José María Muria, *Una bebida llamada tequila* (Mexico, D.F.: Editorial Agata, 1996); Arturo Cosme Valadez, "Tequila: The Liquid Heart of Mexico," *Voices of Mexico* (January–March 1999).

Tex-Mex Music. *See* Music (Popular).

Tijuana (City). *See* Geographical Regions; U.S.–Mexican Border/Boundary.

Tlatelolco Massacre ☀ Angered by huge government expenditures on preparations for the 1968 Olympics and the authoritarianism of President **Gustavo Díaz Ordaz**, thousands of students, workers, and homemakers gathered on October 2, 1968, at Tlatelolco, the Plaza of the Three Cultures, for a peaceful protest rally. Their demands emphasized a desire for greater political freedom and their opposition to the nondemocratic regime rather than support for a specific political alternative. After three decades of political stability and economic growth, the government was not prepared to deal with what seemed like a spontaneous event, although it had been preceded by clashes between students and police in Mexico City beginning in July.

The protesters and passersby came to hear the students denounce the army occupation of a university, unaware that the government was determined to eliminate the focus of agitation and preserve the existing system. Shortly after the rally was under way one of two army helicopters dropped a flare into the crowd of 10,000, triggering a volley of fire from hundreds of soldiers hidden among the Aztec ruins of the square. As the crowd panicked and tried to flee, army troops and police quickly turned the plaza into an inferno of carnage and screams. After approximately 30 minutes of gunfire, 2,000 demonstrators were beaten and jailed, hundreds of bodies were trucked away, and fire trucks were instructed to wash the blood from the cobblestones. The government would only concede that 32 people had died, well below the 200–300 figure estimated by most critics of the government.

On October 12, 1968, the **Olympic Games** commenced with thousands of heavily armed soldiers

Panorama of Plaza of Three Cultures (Tlatelolco), Mexico City, 1983. Credit: General Secretariat of the Organization of American States.

protecting Aztec Stadium; after the Games, the protest movement quickly disintegrated. In an effort to maintain control over sensitive information, the government initiated a campaign of cover-ups and lies based on spurious charges of protecting national security.

For the government of Díaz Ordaz, the massacre achieved its immediate objective of dismantling the protest movement and immobilizing the political opposition. Nevertheless, the 1968 student movement sparked the beginning of Mexico's fight for **democracy**, a new literary movement, critical films, and the women's movement. Thirty years after the massacre, opposition politicians managed to uncover

long-secret government files showing that newspaper publishers worked closely with President Díaz Ordáz to present a false version of the events and cover up important facts of the massacre. Despite recent efforts by scholars and journalists to gain access to critical documents, the national government continues to hold on to the most sensitive files, claiming there are "national security" reasons for not releasing the documents.

Since many key documents, including a 35-millimeter film shot by government movie crews during the event, are missing, it is not likely the Mexican people will ever know the truth about Tlatelolco so that the national wound can finally heal.

However, in a new book by Julio Scherer and **Carlos Monsiváis**—*Parte de guerra* (War dispatch)— recently uncovered dispatches from Mexican army officers reveal that government officials and high-level military personnel viewed the students as an enemy army to be vanquished. What happened at Tlatelolco is the result of the anticommunist views of Díaz Ordaz and top civilian and military authorities determined to fight (and win) an imaginary war against students and popular groups thought to be **communist** enemies and severe threats to the state apparatus.

Many of the student strikers who shut down the **Universidad Nacional Autónoma de México (UNAM)** in 1999–2000 were young anarchists who identified with the student protestors of 1968. Because bitter memories of the Tlatelolco massacre continue to haunt the nation, the **Ernesto Zedillo** administration urged university authorities to accede to some of the strikers' demands, reluctant to use force to retake the large campus until there was little choice in the face-off.

Documentary photographs from the deadly 1968 clash between students and Mexican troops mysteriously appeared in December 2001 and were published in *Proceso* magazine. Most of the photos show the work of the Olympia Battalion, a group of plainclothes gunmen that was formed as an antiterrorism force to provide security for the Olympic Games in 1968. The publication of the graphic old photos added pressure on President **Vicente Fox** to fulfill his promise to form a truth commission—something he was reluctant to do because of the residual power of the PRI in Congress and dire warnings from members of this own cabinet—to investigate the **human rights** violations and disappearances that have haunted Mexico for over 30 years. *See also* Poniatowska, Elena.

SUGGESTED READING

Sergio Aguayo Quezada, *1968: The Archives of Violence* (Mexico City: Grijalbo/Reforma, 1998); Sam Dillon, "Anniversary of '68 Massacre Brings Facts to Light," *New York Times,* September 14, 1998; Elena Poniatowska, *Massacre in Mexico*, trans. Helen Lane (New York: Viking, 1975); Julio Scherer García and Carlos Monsiváis, *Parte de guerra* (Mexico, D.F.: Aguilar, 1999); Ginger Thompson, "Flashback to Deadly Clash of '68 Shakes Mexico," *New York Times*, December 13, 2001.

Tlaxcala. *See* Geographical Regions.

Torres Bodet, Jaime (1902–1974) ☀ Diplomat, scholar, and statesman regarded as one of Mexico's outstanding educators during the 20th century. Born in Mexico City, Torres Bodet attended the National Preparatory School before earning his law degree from the National School of Law at the **Universidad Nacional Autónoma de México (UNAM)**, in 1922. He taught for many years at the National Preparatory School and at UNAM including courses on art history, French literature, and philosophy. Torres Bodet belonged to the **Revolutionary Family** in the 1940s, and his career epitomized the generation of Mexican leaders whose lives overlapped the arts and politics.

As a writer (publishing his first book at age 16) and poet, Torres Bodet was part of several literary circles that included many of the most prominent authors of the 1920s and 1930s. He studied under Alfonso Caso at UNAM and was a classmate of **Daniel Cosío Villegas** at the same school. His diplomatic career began in 1929, when he joined the Mexican foreign service and traveled to posts in Spain, France, Belgium, Holland, and Argentina. He served as secretary of foreign relations in the **Miguel Alemán** administration, followed by three years (1949–1952) as secretary-general of UNESCO. As minister of education during the presidencies of **Manuel Ávila Camacho** and **Adolfo López Mateos**, Torres Bodet focused his attention on Mexico's educational shortcomings, particularly the problems of illiteracy and poor wages for teachers. Between 1953 and 1971, he continued to mix government posts with diplomatic activities.

Torres Bodet received the National Prize for Literature in 1966. After his departure from public life in 1971, he worked on his memoirs before committing suicide in 1974 at the age of 72.

SUGGESTED READING

Roderic Ai Camp, *Mexican Political Biographies, 1935–1993,* 3d ed. (Austin: University of Texas Press, 1995).

Tourism ☀ In 1998 Mexico hosted some 20 million foreign visitors who spent almost $8 billion, making Mexico the world's eighth most popular tourist destination. Mexico benefits from its close geographical proximity to the United States, which provides 85 percent of the foreign visitors to its southern neighbor. The tourism industry is the second-largest employer in Mexico and one of the top three earners of foreign exchange. Moreover, Mexico draws nearly 40 percent of all international travelers to Latin America.

Mexico's major tourist attractions include seaside resorts (Acapulco, Puerto Vallarta, Cozumel, Cancún, Ixtapa/Zihuatanejo, Cabo San Lucas, and Huatulco); bustling border cities that offer commercial and service attractions (Tijuana, Ciudad Juárez, Nuevo Laredo, and Matamoros); archeological sites and pre-Columbian ruins from the Aztec, Maya, Mixtec, and Zapotec civilizations (Teotihuacán, Chichen Itza, Palenque, Mitla); scenic canyons (Barranca del Cobre, or Copper Canyon, which includes one of the world's most spectacular railroad journeys); churches, cathedrals, and basilicas (Basilica de Nuestra Señora de Guadalupe, **Metropolitan Cathedral**, and hundreds of others); Mexico City's vibrant nightlife, museums, and architectural achievements, combined with notable features from the Aztec, colonial, and modern periods; magnificent murals from Mexico's 20th-century masters such as **Diego Rivera**, **José Clemente Orozco**, and **David Alfaro Siqueiros**, displayed in public buildings in Guadalajara and Mexico City; and a vast array of handicrafts, including jewelry, masks, pottery, lacquerware, textiles, and leather goods. In 2000 Mexico's receipts from tourism were close to $10 billion, with most visitors arriving from the United States and Canada. For most tourists, Mexico is considered a travel bargain; to enter the interior of Mexico requires only a tourist card, and the cost of spending a week in one of Mexico's resorts is relatively low, in contrast to other tourist destinations in the Americas.

Until the 1940s, Mexico's tourist industry developed slowly, hampered by poor transportation and inadequate tourist infrastructure. During the Prohibition years in the United States (1919–1934), many Americans flocked to Mexico's border towns of Tijuana and Ciudad Juárez to visit the bars, casinos, racetracks, and red-light districts that had sprung up to accommodate foreign tourists. This type of tourism flourished during the Good Neighbor era and **World War II,** when ration-starved American shoppers and U.S. military personnel stationed near the border made frequent visits to the nightlife of the border towns. During the 1920s and 1930s the Mexican government emphasized cultural nationalism and invested in museums, anthropological research, archeological excavations, folkloric presentations, and the rehabilitation of historic buildings. With the creation of National Institute of Anthropology and History (INAH) in 1938, Mexico began to celebrate its cultural past, best symbolized by the creation of the National Museum of Anthropology in Mexico City.

Between 1940 and 1960, the Mexican government shifted the focus of its tourist promotion and investment to emphasize Mexico's beaches, exoticism, and modern tourist services. Mexico City was no longer considered the centerpiece of Mexican tourism. The government invested in costly transportation networks, advertising and marketing, and the creation of government-supported offices in foreign countries to promote travel to Mexico. President **Miguel Alemán** was a prime mover in expanding the tourist industry and served a term as head of the government agency for tourism after he left the presidency. To finance the tourist industry, the government created the Fondo Nacional de Turismo (FONATUR) in 1956, and eventually a cabinet-level ministry was established to underscore the importance of tourism to the Mexican economy.

After 1982, the tourist industry turned away from the state-led pattern of development to one that relied more on private investment, both domestic and foreign. By the 1980s, the success of the Mexican tourist industry had contributed to concern over the ecological damage from millions of visitors to Mexico's most famous sites. The growing interest in **environmental** protection, as well as a recognized potential in promoting ecological tours, compelled the Mexican tourist industry to address the problem of ecological damage and begin promoting ecotourism. With a new political economy in retreat from state-led policies of the past, future expansion of tourism will require more public–private cooperation and foreign investment, as well as greater sensitivity to the costs of ignoring the social and ecological errors of the past.

Over the past four decades, tourism has become a central part of the Mexican economy. Tourism means employment opportunities for over three million Mexicans who work as small vendors, maids, waiters, and cab drivers. Nevertheless, tourism is not without its problems. Narcotics money has permeated the tourist industry as a way of laundering profits while damage to archeological sites and natural attractions is growing. *See also* Virgin of Guadalupe.

SUGGESTED READING

Michael Clancy, "Mexican Tourism: Export Growth and Structural Change since 1970," *Latin American Research Review* 36, no. 1 (2001): 128–50; Nestor García Canclini, *Transforming Modernity: Popular Culture in Mexico*, trans. Lidia Lozano (Austin: University of Texas Press, 1993); Mary Lee Nolan and Sidney Nolan, "Tourism and Economic Growth in Mexico since 1960," *Journal of the West* (October 1988); Alex M. Saragoza, "Tourism," in Michael S. Werner, ed., *Encyclopedia of Mexico: History, Society, and Culture*, vol. 2 (Chicago: Fitzroy Dearborn, 1997); John Wilcock and Kal Müller, eds., *Insight Guides: Mexico* (Boston: Houghton Mifflin, 1996).

Tratado de Libre Comercio (TLC). *See* North American Free Trade Agreement (NAFTA).

Treaty of Tlatelolco ✴ The Treaty for the Prohibition of Nuclear Weapons in Latin America, an international agreement signed by 14 countries in 1967 (in effect in 1968) declaring the Latin American region a "nuclear weapons–free zone." As of 1999, all of the Latin American states except **Cuba** had ratified the treaty and appropriate protocols, and all declared members of the nuclear "club" have agreed to the zone defined in the treaty. Rivals Argentina and Brazil refused to become parties for many years, each waiting for the other to move toward ratification. Argentina made the first move by ratifying it in January 1994 (Chile became a party at the same time), followed by Brazil in May of that year. Although it contains no sanctions against states that violate the treaty, it is considered a milestone in the prohibition of nuclear weapons and a beneficial complement to the Nuclear Nonproliferation Treaty signed in 1968. **Alfonso García Robles**, a Mexican diplomat working in the Ministry of Foreign Affairs, played a key role in bringing about the agreement, an effort that earned him the 1982 Nobel Peace Prize. *See also* Foreign Policy.

Trotsky, Leon (1879–1940) ✴ Born Lev Davidovich Bronstein; a Russian revolutionary, writer, and outstanding historian who clashed with Joseph Stalin after the death of V. I. Lenin in 1924. The son of Russified Jews, Trotsky was educated in the Ukraine. He displayed tremendous intellectual talent, becoming one of the early interpreters of Marxist socialism. Unlike Stalin, who believed in socialism in one country, Trotsky believed in a more utopian version of "permanent revolution" in which the international working class would assume power in capitalist countries. Trotsky argued in his writings that Stalinism betrayed the original intent of the Russian Revolution, which led the Kremlin to expel Trotsky from the Politburo and send him into permanent exile in 1929. He spent the rest of his life seeking a safe haven to write his savage critiques of Stalinist Russia. In addition to his many books on Lenin, Stalin, and the Russian Revolution, he also wrote articles about Mexican politics and U.S. Latin American policies.

After spending years in exile in Turkey, France, and Norway, Trotsky was granted political asylum in Mexico by President **Lázaro Cárdenas** in late 1937. The asylum request came from muralist **Diego Rivera**, one of Trotsky's admirers, who approached the Mexican president with the personal request. After Mexico's oil industry was nationalized in 1937, Cárdenas was criticized for being a puppet of Russian **communism**. He allowed Trotsky to come to Mexico in hopes of proving his independence from the Soviet system. Trotsky's presence in Mexico drove a wedge between Rivera and fellow muralist **David Alfaro Siqueiros**, two artists caught on different sides of a growing ideological divide. Trotsky's arrival on Mexican soil also angered the **Confederación de Trabajadores de México (CTM)**, Mexico's largest **labor** union, and the Communist Party of Mexico, arguing that Trotsky would engage in propaganda against the government of the **Soviet Union**.

Not long after Trotsky settled in Coyoacán, a residential neighborhood of Mexico City, representatives of the Stalin-controlled Comintern and leaders of the Mexican Communist Party began planning to assassinate him. Famous muralist Siqueiros was put in charge of a team with instructions to kill Trotsky. On the night of May 24, 1940, Siqueiros and a group of 30 men wearing police and military uniforms attacked Trotsky's house, firing hundreds of bullets into the room where he was sleeping. Miraculously, Trotsky was not injured, but the failed attempt led to the arrest of Siqueiros and other members of the Mexican Communist Party. Under pressure from the Soviet embassy, President **Manuel Ávila Camacho** pardoned Siqueiros with the proviso that he leave the country for a period of time.

After the failure of the Siqueiros-led attempt on Trotsky's life, Stalin's secret police turned to subterfuge and infiltration to try to assassinate Trotsky. With the backing of Stalin's secret police, a Spanish communist named Ramón Mercader (his real name was Jacques Mornard) gained the confidence of those around Trotsky. On August 20, 1940, he smashed the Russian revolutionary's skull with an ice ax. Trotsky was rushed to a hospital, where he fell into a coma and died on the next day. Mercader was arrested by Mexican police and spent the next 20 years in jail before his sentence was commuted. He returned to Russia and was given the Order of Lenin in a secret ceremony. He moved to **Cuba** after the 1959 Revolution and died there in 1978.

Trotsky's death put an end to the most creative, determined, and forceful enemy of the Stalinist bureaucracy and dashed the hopes of those who envisioned the creation of a worldwide revolutionary organization to fight on behalf of the working class and against capitalism and imperialism. Before his assassination, Trotsky became the defender of the **Mexican Revolution**, but he was critical of Mexico's semicolonial status and the **corporatist** ties of Mexican labor and the peasantry to the capitalist state. Trotsky's writings on Latin America were critical of the Monroe Doctrine, the Good Neighbor policy, and U.S. support of "friendly dictators." While he agreed with the agrarian policies and economic nationalism of *cardenismo*, Leon Trotsky believed in proletarian solidarity in the Americas and once called for the creation of the United Socialist States of Latin America, an inter-American organization that would advocate permanent revolution, but he opposed policies that were built on peaceful coexistence with international capitalism.

SUGGESTED READING

Isaac Don Levine, *The Mind of an Assassin* (New York: Farrar, Straus & Cudahy, 1959); Sheldon B. Liss, *Marxist Thought in Latin America* (Berkeley: University of California Press, 1984); Friedrich E. Shuler, *Mexico between Hitler and Roosevelt: Mexican Foreign Relations in the Age of Lázaro Cárdenas, 1934–1940* (Albuquerque: University of New Mexico Press, 1998); Dmitri Volkogonov, *Trotsky: The Eternal Revolutionary* (New York: Free Press, 1996).

United States and Mexico. *See* Foreign Policy; Mexican American War; Mexican Revolution; U.S.–Mexican Border/Boundary.

Universidad Nacional Autónoma de México (UNAM)

The National Autonomous University of Mexico is located on 800 acres in the southern part of Mexico City. Originally known as the Royal and Pontifical University of Mexico, it was founded in 1551 by special charter from Philip II of Spain. The modern university was created in 1910 and its "autonomous" (free of government control) character was achieved between 1929 and 1933. At first the university was located in the heart of Mexico City, but over the centuries it moved, expanded, and closed down several times before a central campus was started in 1950. When it opened in 1952, in what became known as Ciudad Universitaria (University City), its mosaic-covered modern buildings soon became a showcase for Mexico's modernization and attracted tourists from around the world. Artists and architects worked on the design to incorporate buildings and facilities into the volcanic landscape of the Pedregal area that are still spectacular, despite more than 50 years of use (and hundreds of protests) by students of all social classes.

The most visually striking buildings are the central library (*Biblioteca*) and the administration building (*Rectoría*). The library tower is covered with stone mosaics, colored tiles, and frescoes created by **Juan O'Gorman** to reflect stages of Mexican history, from the pre-Columbian and colonial eras to the artist's vision of the future. The *Rectoría* is dominated by a huge mural by **David Alfaro Siqueiros** designed to emphasize the importance of education. University City also includes faculties, schools, museums, specialized libraries, cultural centers, concert halls, theaters, sports facilities (including the Olympic Stadium used for the 1968 summer **Olympic Games**), and research institutes. Among its various extension and cultural centers are the Educational Center for Foreign Students and two extension schools outside of Mexico, one in San Antonio, Texas, and the other in Hull, Quebec, Canada.

Panoramic view of the new UNAM campus, Mexico City, 1954. Credit: Benson Latin American Collection, University of Texas at Austin.

Today, UNAM is one of the oldest institutions of advanced learning in the Americas and the largest university in Mexico, with 30,000 teachers and 275,000 students. As a source of political recruitment, UNAM has played a key role in the formation of Mexico's political and intellectual elite. The university has also been the source of **labor** strikes, political confrontations, and controversies over tuition, fees, and contrasting philosophies of higher education in Mexico. Students from UNAM were behind the opposition to holding the Olympic Games in Mexico City in 1968, a major strike in 1976–1977 by university

employees that attracted thousands of supporters from the rest of the labor movement, protests in 1987 over tuition hikes and the incorporation of student voices into policy negotiations, and a 10-month strike in 1999–2000 by students demanding the preservation of basically free tuition, open admissions, and some protection from the perceived negative affects from globalization and neoliberal economic policies during the previous two *sexenios*.

The proposal to raise tuition from the equivalent of two cents to $150 set off a nasty strike that began in April 1999 and dragged on through two university presidents, shifting demands from the student protesters, an exodus of students to other universities, and dueling referendums by the administration and strikers. In an effort to avoid a repeat of the 1968 student demonstrations that left hundreds dead after the army fired on students protesting the Olympics, university officials dropped the proposed tuition increase, but students widened their protest to include criticisms of globalization and capitalism. The strike was settled in February 2000, but many troubling questions about education spending in general and the importance of spending more money on university education in particular were left unanswered. The once proud symbol of publicly financed education for the masses deteriorated rapidly as losses in students, research, finance, and academic prominence raised serious questions as to whether the school would be able to recover from the physical damage done by the student-strikers and the significant financial losses. After student protestors rejected the president's plebiscite, refused to move out, and vowed to continue their occupation of UNAM until *all* their demands were met, President **Ernesto Zedillo** ordered police and troops to remove the protesters and reopen the university, ending the months of impasse and public frustration. The UNAM strike added to the woes of the Zedillo administration, faced with an unusually competitive presidential election year and cries of presidential inaction from a citizenry tired of catering to unruly students with unrealistic demands. In the end, the latest UNAM strike achieved very little. The two-cent tuition, in effect since 1948, would remain unchanged for a few years more, regardless of the actual cost of quality education in Mexico.

SUGGESTED READING

Daniel Levy, "National Autonomous University of Mexico (UNAM)," in Barbara A. Tenenbaum, ed., *Encyclopedia of Latin American History and Culture,* vol. 4 (New York: Scribners, 1996); Julia Preston, "University, Mexico's Pride, Is Ravaged by Strike," *New York Times,* January 20, 2000; *The World of Learning 1999,* 49th ed. (London: Europa Publications, 1998).

U.S.–Mexican Border/Boundary ☀ The border between the United States and Mexico runs for 1,951 miles (3,149 km), stretching between the Gulf of Mexico in the east and the Pacific Ocean in the west. The boundary touches Texas, New Mexico, Arizona, and California in the United States and the six Mexican states of Tamaulipas, Nuevo León, Coahuila, Chihuahua, Sonora, and Baja California. The official boundary between the two countries follows both land and river demarcations through deserts and rugged mountains. The eastern section of the boundary follows the Rio Grande River (Río Bravo del Norte) from its mouth on the Gulf of Mexico to a point just upstream from Ciudad Juárez, Chihuahua, and El Paso, Texas, a distance of 1,254 miles (2,018 km). Then the border moves west for a distance of 533 miles (858 km) until it reaches the Colorado River, where it follows the middle of the river north for a distance of 24 miles (38 km). It then moves west for a distance of 140 miles (226 km) until it reaches the Pacific Ocean near Tijuana.

The U.S.–Mexican border region is distinguished by the 15 paired border-crossing cities that engage in agriculture, **tourism**, export-import trade and manufacturing, and a host of other services. The population living in these paired cities and smaller communities close by totals an estimated 7 million (1998). The region where the United States and Mexico come together and overlap is known as Mexamerica, a term that suggests a greater sense of unity and shared traits of both cultures than the series of twin cities that dot the international boundary legally separating the two countries.

The size and close proximity of this region gives rise to a host of transboundary problems related to crime, air and water pollution, **drug trafficking,**

human rights violations, **labor** exploitation, transportation, and industrialization. The U.S.–Mexican borderlands—the 2,000-mile line stretching from Tijuana/San Diego to Matamoros/Brownsville—is the fastest-growing industrial belt in Mexico and the busiest land crossing in the world. It is heavily fortified with agents and inspectors who are part of the U.S. Immigration and Naturalization Service (INS), Drug Enforcement Agency (DEA), and Federal Bureau of Investigation (FBI) presence along the border to handle the growing problems of crime, drugs, and illegal **immigration** that affect the United States. Since 1993, the INS budget has nearly tripled, and the number of Border Patrol agents stationed along the border have doubled. Military and intelligence technology—along with U.S. military personnel—are now being used along the border. Operation Gatekeeper, a program to increase Border Patrol agents along the border with California, has been criticized by human rights activists because it has forced migrants to take more dangerous routes through the deserts, leading to over 450 deaths since the crackdown began in 1994.

The U.S.–Mexican boundary is administered by a binational government agency called the International Boundary Water Commission (IBWC). Its primary responsibility is to see that the numerous boundary and water treaties and related agreements are carried out to the satisfaction of the two governments with authority on both sides of the border. The commission is composed of Mexican and U.S. sections, headquartered in the paired cities of Ciudad Juárez, Chihuahua, and El Paso, Texas. Commissioners on both sides of the border meet frequently to handle day-to-day border problems. Treaty provisions that call for joint action are handled by the U.S. Department of State and the Secretariat of Foreign Relations of Mexico. Projects that require funding are shared by the two governments in proportion to their respective benefits. The wide economic disparity that exists between Mexico and the United States means that illegal crossings are a major issue as Mexicans seeking better paying jobs move north. Although the INS has constructed tall fences to halt illegal crossings in heavily traveled corridors and states such as California have passed legislation denying public welfare, education, and health services to illegal immigrants and their families, the flow of Mexicans into the United States continues unabated.

The U.S.–Mexican border has played a key role in the contrasting patterns of historical development between the two countries. During the 19th century, both nations shared a common desire to populate their frontier, make it economically productive, and subdue (or eliminate) the indigenous inhabitants of the region. Mexico's inability to incorporate its border region with the United States left the area isolated, underpopulated, and subject to attack. With an economic advantage due to its early 19th-century insertion in the world economy, the United States ultimately won control over the region, taking over half of Mexican territory in the **Mexican American War** (1846–1848). The war with Mexico and subsequent cessions of Mexican territory to the United States rearranged the border and displaced many Mexican landowners, leaving the region with angry settlers who resisted U.S. domination well into the 20th century.

The dramatic transformation of the U.S.–Mexican border region in the 20th century is due to small-scale agriculture, cattle ranching, mining, manufacturing, and tourism. Three of the fastest growing metropolitan areas in the United States are along the Texas border, where cities with cross-border transportation links, free trade, and *maquiladoras* have fueled dramatic increases in population during the decade of the 1990s. In response to the rising flood of freight trucks moving goods across the border, creating maddening traffic backups at key crossings, pressures are now building to punch new openings in the border to ease traffic and create new businesses along the border. These new or expanded border crossings, made up of new cross-border communities, are being touted by Washington and Mexico City as a solution to transportation bottlenecks and lagging economic development. *See also* Chamizal Conflict; Environment and Ecology; Geographical Region; North American Free Trade Agreement (NAFTA).

SUGGESTED READING

Peter Andreas, *Border Games: Policing the U.S.–Mexico Divide* (Ithaca: Cornell University Press, 2001); Gideon Biger, ed., *The Encyclopedia of International Boundaries* (New York: Facts on File, 1995); Frank Bonilla et al., eds., *Borderless Borders: U.S. Latinos, Latin Americans, and the Paradox of Interdependence* (Philadelphia: Temple University Press, 1998); Ron Butler, *Dancing Alone in Mexico: From the Border to Baja and Beyond* (Tucson: University of Arizona Press, 2000); Bobby Byrd and Susannah Mississippi Byrd, eds., *Late Great Mexican Border: Reports from a Disappearing Line* (El Paso, Texas: Cinco Puntos, 1996); "Contested Terrain: The U.S.–Mexico Borderlands," *NACLA Report on the Americas* (November–December 1999); Timothy J. Dunn, *The Militarization of the Mexican U.S.–Mexico Border, 1978–1992: Low-Intensity Conflict Doctrine Comes Home* (Austin: Center for Mexican American Studies, University of Texas–Austin, 1996); Claire F. Fox, *The Fence and the River: Culture and Politics at the U.S.–Mexico Border* (Minneapolis: University of Minnesota Press, 1999); Lawrence A. Herzog, ed., *Changing Boundaries in the Americas: New Perspectives on the U.S.–Mexican, Central American, and South American Borders* (La Jolla: U.S.–Mexican Studies Center, University of California–San Diego, 1992); Milton H. Jamail and Margo Gutiérrez, *The Border Guide: Institutions and Organizations of the United States–Mexico Borderlands* (Austin: Center for Mexican American Studies, University of Texas–Austin, 1992); David E. Lorey, *The U.S.–Mexican Border in the Twentieth Century* (Wilmington, Del.: Scholarly Resources, 1999); Oscar J. Martínez, *Border People: Life and Society in the U.S.–Mexico Borderlands* (1994); Ramón Eduardo Ruiz, *On the Rim of Mexico: Where Rich and Poor Rendezvous* (Boulder, Colo.: Westview, 1998); David Spener and Kathleen Staudt, eds., *The U.S.–Mexico Border: Transcending Divisions, Contesting Identities* (Boulder, Colo.: Lynne Rienner, 1999); Luis Alberto Urrea, *Across the Wire: Life and Hard Times on the Mexican Border* (New York: Anchor, 1993).

Valenzuela, Fernando (1960–) Left-handed pitcher from a small village in Sonora who left Mexico in the summer of 1979 to start a career in major league **baseball** in the United States that lasted 15 years. Valenzuela was spotted by Los Angeles Dodgers scout Mike Brito at age 17, and by 1979 he had signed a contract with the Dodgers to play in the minor leagues. The owner of the Los Angeles Dodgers, Walter O'Malley, had long dreamed of bringing a Mexican star to Los Angeles, home of a large and growing Mexican American population. After achieving almost immediate stardom, Fernando Valenzuela became the best Mexican baseball player in the U.S. major leagues between 1980 and 1994.

Fernando Valenzuela pitching for Los Angeles Dodgers. Credit: National Baseball Hall of Fame Library and Archive, Cooperstown, N.Y.

Valenzuela played for a minor league team in Lodi, California, for part of the 1979 season and then moved to Arizona to play winter ball. Between the 1979 and 1980 baseball seasons, general manager Al Campanis sent Dodger pitcher Bobby Castillo—a Latino from the barrios of East Los Angeles—to teach Fernando how to throw a screwball, one of the most difficult pitches in baseball. Valenzuela quickly mastered the art of the screwball and soon became famous for his ability to strike out batters in rapid-fire fashion in minor league play. With the Dodgers in a tight pennant race during the final weeks of the 1980 baseball season, Valenzuela was called to the major leagues as a relief pitcher in an all-out effort to help the Dodgers capture the pennant. In a short span of 10 games at the end of the 1980 season, the Latino community in Los Angeles had a real hero to admire.

After eight consecutive victories on the mound at the beginning of the 1981 season, Valenzuela's pitching prowess started what soon became known as "Fernandomania" or "Fernando Fever." His success on the pitching mound spread Fernandomania to the rest of the country, particularly in cities with large populations of fans of Mexican heritage. Exuberant baseball fans greeted the Mexican left-hander with "Ole!" when he strutted to the mound, and "Fernando, Fernando" after he struck out a befuddled batter with his elusive screwball. The 1981 season was a fabulous year for the rookie pitcher; he earned both the Cy Young Award (the award each league gives to the best pitcher for that year) and the National League's Rookie of the Year, the only player in major league baseball to ever do so. Valenzuela also won games with his bat and glove—in 1981 he was voted a Silver Slugger Award for his batting skills and came close to receiving a Gold Glove Award.

Valenzuela's popularity soared during the 1980s as he achieved international fame as a dependable starter for the Dodgers. From 1981 through 1988, he led the National League in complete games three times and twice in innings pitched. During that period he averaged 255 innings per year and 15 wins per year, including 21 in 1986. In four of those seven years he was one of the top five contenders for the Cy Young Award and was named to the National League All-Star team each year from 1981 to 1986. According to *Sporting News*, each ballpark averaged at least 9,000 more fans when Valenzuela was on the mound. For the 1986 season Valenzuela signed a $5.5 million contract with the Dodgers, making him the highest-paid Latin ballplayer at the time. The same year he became the first Mexican pitcher in major league history to win 20 games or more.

In June 1981 Valenzuela was invited to lunch at the White House with President Ronald Reagan and Mexican President **José López Portillo. Televisa**, Mexico's most influential television network, broadcast every Valenzuela game to Mexican viewers during the 1981 and 1982 seasons. Fernando Valenzuela's popularity and ethnic impact mirrored other baseball heroes of the past whose ethnic heritage engendered considerable pride and sense of accomplishment among those like themselves. Valenzuela's village of Etchohuaquila, where he learned to play baseball, received a community facelift from the Mexican government: a new highway was built and unpaved roads were improved with pavement and street lights. The poverty-stricken community was also honored with a new baseball stadium.

Valenzuela's love of baseball and the impact of his phenomenal success on other Latinos in the United States could not hide the strains of living and working in an alien environment north of the border. After his rookie year he was criticized for asking for too much money in negotiations that brought out the worst in the American press, which failed to understand Latino sensitivities. Negative stereotypes of Mexicans emerged in the portrayals of Valenzuela in newspapers and books and on television. Being depicted as a pudgy, beer-drinking fan of burritos and tortillas angered Valenzuela and his fans, who recognized the arrogance and negativism associated with these demeaning references to ethnic foods and ethnicity. One sports writer in 1982 asked in his column, "Is Fernando a Bandito?" in reference to his salary demands. With the support of ethnic organizations in the United States, Valenzuela's career was not spoiled by the racism and arrogance he faced in America. The growing importance of the Latino community in large cities with major league baseball clubs dampened some of the hostility that he faced. His continual success eventually forced American reporters, players, and baseball management to deal with Valenzuela on his own terms, since he refused to speak English in public throughout his career.

Despite his spectacular career with the Los Angeles Dodgers, Fernando Valenzuela left the team in 1991 and then bounced from one team to another until his finished his career with the Philadelphia Phillies in 1994. His baseball career provided heroism, leadership, and pride to Latino communities in the United States and helped strengthen the bonds between Mexican nationals and Mexican Americans. Until the emergence of Valenzuela, no Mexican of any background had managed to capture the attention of so many Americans in such a positive way. While Fernandomania did not last more than a decade, the young Mexican pitcher may have contributed to a better America for Latinos and greater understanding between the United States and its neighbor to the south. Fernando Valenzuela was more popular among Hispanic communities in the United States than in Mexico, where *fútbol* (soccer) remains the most popular sport throughout the country. *See also* Chicanos.

SUGGESTED READING

William H. Beezley, "The Rise of Baseball in Mexico and the First Valenzuela," *Studies in Latin American*
Popular Culture 4 (1985); S. H. Burchard, *Sports Star: Fernando Valenzuela* (San Diego: Harcourt Brace Jovanovich, 1982); David LaFrance, "A Mexican Popular Image of the United States through the Baseball Hero, Fernando Valenzuela," *Studies in Latin American Popular Culture* 4 (1985); Mark Littwin, *Fernando!* (New York: Bantam, 1981); Michael M. Oleksak and Mary Adams Oleksak, *Béisbol: Latin Americans and the Grand Old Game* (Grand Rapids, Mich.: Masters, 1991); Samuel O. Regalado, "'Image Is Everything': Latin American Ballplayers and the United States Media," *Studies in Latin American Popular Culture* 13 (1994); Regalado, *Viva Baseball: Latin Major Leaguers and Their Special Hunger* (Urbana: University of Illinois Press, 1998).

Vasconcelos, José (1882–1959) ☀ One of Mexico's most distinguished writers, philosophers, and educators. José Vasconcelos gained fame for his devotion to *mestizaje* (racial mixture and synthesis) and numerous essays covering a wide range of intellectual topics. His writings on the vast and complex social issues confronting Latin America—education, race and ethnicity, imperialism, indigenous groups, and **democratization**—became popular throughout the Americas. He often defined his role in society as a "civic missionary" whose responsibility was to influence the course of the **Mexican Revolution** and its aftermath. From 1910, when he helped establish the Ateneo de la Juventud, until his death in 1959, he played an active role in the political, revolutionary, and intellectual life of Mexico. His career followed the trajectory of revolutionary and postrevolutionary Mexico: rector of the National University (1920–1921), secretary of public education (1921–1924), candidate for president (1929), and professor in exile at numerous prestigious universities in the United States (Chicago, Stanford, and Berkeley).

Born in Oaxaca in 1882 to a family in which both parents had a profound influence in his formative years—his father was customs inspector along the U.S.–Mexican border and his mother was well read and served as role model for his interest in literary works—Vasconcelos attended elementary school in Texas but returned to Mexico City to graduate in law from the National University in 1905. He played an active part in the Mexican Revolution from 1910 to 1930, having been a supporter of Francisco Madero (Vasconcelos is reported to have coined the phrase of "effective suffrage, no reelection" that became the banner of the Maderista movement) before Madero's death in 1913 and a follower of influential intellectuals who were clearly prorevolutionary in their orientation. As secretary of public education, Vasconcelos was a strong advocate of using Mexican art (he supported the great muralists of the time who were commissioned to paint indigenous/historical themes on public buildings) and literature to forge a new sense of national identity based on the racial theme of *mestizaje*. In his view, the Indian problem stemmed from ignorance rather than the unjust distribution of land and exploitation.

It was during this period that Vasconcelos wrote his most famous work, "La raza cósmica" (1925), theorizing that the future belonged to the mestizo, not to the Anglo. His idealized sense of the positive features of race and culture motivated much of his civilizing outlook, but despite his role as a romantic civilizer and educator, he was not immune to some of the destructive prejudices (he revealed an admiration for fascist ideologies in 1940–1941) that swept the globe in the 20th century. He was also known as the first opposition candidate to be denied an election due to the electoral fraud of the ruling party in 1929, then known as the National Revolutionary Party (Partido Nacional Revolucionario, PNR).

Forced into exile again because of his electoral "loss," Vasconcelos became more bitter and disillusioned, abandoning his early progressivism and radicalism while moving further to the right. After living abroad for 10 years, he returned to Mexico in 1938, turning his attention to cultural and intellectual pursuits, including the creation of the Colegio de México. Ultimately a tragic figure, José Vasconcelos lived with his social frustrations and recalcitrant political opinions over the last 20 years of his life. He died in Mexico City in 1959.

SUGGESTED READING

Gabriella de Beer, *José Vasconcelos and His World* (New York: Las Américas, 1966); Peter G. Earle, "José Vasconcelos, 1882–1959," in Verity Smith, ed., *Encyclopedia of Latin American Literature* (Chicago: Fitzroy Dearborn, 1997); John H. Haddox, *Vasconcelos of Mexico: Philosopher and Prophet* (Austin: University of Texas Press, 1967).

Velázquez Sánchez, Fidel (1900–1997) ☀ Powerful labor leader known for his close ties to the inner circle of the Partido Revolucionario Institucional (PRI). Fidel Velázquez served as secretary-general of the largest labor confederation in Mexico (the Confederación de Trabajadores de México, CTM) for more than 50 years. One of the founders of the ruling party, he was a fierce defender of the PRI and Mexico's corporatist system of governing.

Born in San Pedro Azcapotzaltongo (today Villa Nicolás Romero), about 20 miles northwest of Mexico City, Velázquez never finished the sixth grade, but this did not hinder his ability to dominate the union movement and exert influence for decades on the PRI. He held numerous low-paying jobs in his early life and then moved to Mexico City, where he got his start in the dairy industry as a union leader. While working in a dairy and observing firsthand the exploitation of farm workers, he helped them organize a union, which soon cost him his job. Velázquez continued his work in the labor field, helping to build the labor movement that he went on to control for decades. In 1929, his Union of Milkmen broke with the Regional Confederation of Mexican Workers

(Confederación Revolucionaria de Obreros y Campesinos Mexicanos, CROM) to form another union. In the same year Velázquez was one of the founders of the Partido Nacional Revolucionario (PNR), later renamed the PRI, the corporatist vehicle for labor representation that would last throughout the century. His cantankerous behavior was formed by hard work, the relative poverty of his early life, union battles, and his abhorrence of the kind of chaos that crippled Mexico during the long period of the **Mexican Revolution**. Velázquez valued stability and order over a system that allowed workers to criticize and challenge those who possessed political and economic power.

In 1936 Fidel Velázquez helped mold what was then a loose confederation of labor unions into the CTM and served as a member of the executive committee of the union until 1941. After wresting control away from the CTM's first secretary-general, **Vicente Lombardo Toledano**, Velázquez controlled Mexico's largest labor union (except when Fernando Amilpa headed the CTM from 1947 to 1950) until his death in 1997. As part of the **Revolutionary Family**, Don Fidel (as he was universally known) also served in the Congress as a deputy and three times as senator (1946–1952; 1958–1964; 1970–1976).

As one of the three sectoral pillars of the ruling party, the CTM is incorporated into the Mexican state itself, giving it a special, and powerful, relationship with the **government**. As the labor movement expanded in the 1950s and 1960s, Mexican presidents came to rely increasingly on Velázquez to keep labor unions in line. When Mexico's economic development model began to show signs of serious problems after 1970, CTM leaders came under fire from both the national government and rank-and-file union members. Despite such criticism, Don Fidel kept the political system together as presidents argued that his leadership was needed to

restrain the working class. As an inner-circle adviser on labor-economic matters for Mexican presidents and the labor sector of the PRI, Velázquez enjoyed the support where it counted the most.

All this began to change in 1986 with neoliberal reforms aimed at fixing the political economy in light of chronic economic difficulties. During the last 10 years of his life, his speeches grew increasingly critical of government policies affecting organized labor; however, his rhetoric was never matched by his deeds, as he favored the government and capital over working Mexicans by signing various "pacts" designed to placate labor, spur production, and restore the power of entrenched elites fearful of losing control because of democratic reforms. Throughout his life, he served as a close adviser to 11 presidents, helping keep the PRI afloat when it appeared to be sinking into oblivion under intense pressures for reform and the growth of opposition parties. The death of such a key figure in the longevity of the official party raised serious questions about the future of the PRI and its relationship to organized labor.

SUGGESTED READING

Javier Aguilar García, "Velázquez Sánchez, Fidel," in Michael S. Werner, ed., *Encyclopedia of Mexico: History, Society, and Culture*, vol. 2 (Chicago: Fitzroy Dearborn, 1997); Agustín Sánchez González, *Los primeros cien años de Fidel Velásquez* (Mexico, D.F.: Editorial Patria, 1997).

Veracruz. *See* Geographical Regions.

Villa, Francisco "Pancho" (1878–1923) ☀ One of the great heroes of the **Mexican Revolution**. Pancho Villa was an outstanding guerrilla leader whose army was a key factor in the military victories in the north that helped drive General Huerta from power in 1914.

Villa was born in Rio Grande, Durango, in 1878 but little is known of his true parentage. After a few years of school, he joined a gang of bandits that roamed the mountains of Durango, learning desert survival and guerrilla warfare techniques. He soon formed his own gang and gave up his birth name, Doroteo Arango, adopting Francisco "Pancho" Villa as his new name. Villa's rapid military success worried Venustiano Carranza, commander in chief of the Revolutionary Forces, and toward the end of 1914 they split into opposing forces: the Constitutionalists, under the leadership of Carranza and Álvaro Obregón, and the Conventionists of Villa and **Emiliano Zapata**, guerrilla leader in the south. The revolutionary conflict then escalated, and these two forces attacked each other in bloody battles in the north-central region of Mexico. After a series of defeats at the hands of General Obregón, Villa retreated to Chihuahua, regrouped his forces, and continued to fight Carranza's troops.

With Villa in retreat throughout 1915, U.S. president Woodrow Wilson recognized Carranza as the de facto government of Mexico and allowed *Carrancista* troops to use U.S. territory to attack Villa's forces. In January 1916, Villa wrote to Zapata in the south alerting him to his military quandary and the existence of a secret deal that Carranza had signed with Washington to make Mexico a protectorate. Villa now believed, according to his sources, that Carranza was joining forces with the United States to defeat him, and he invited Zapata to join his forces to defend Mexican sovereignty. While Zapata declined, Villa continued to fight, attacking a train in Santa Isabel and executing 17 U.S. citizens. Two months later he led an attack on Columbus, New Mexico, killing U.S. citizens on American soil. A week later President Wilson sent a "punitive expedition" of 10,000 troops under the command of General John J. Pershing to capture Villa "dead or alive."

The United States was unable to capture the elusive Villa, despite months of searching the deserts of Chihuahua. To complicate matters further, Carranza considered Pershing's military foray into the northern desert region a violation of Mexican sovereignty, eventually leading to clashes between his forces and those of the United States. Eventually Carranza was able to negotiate an unconditional withdrawal, and Pershing's troops left Mexico for the war in Europe. However, Villa survived the punitive expedition and an assassination attempt by the U.S. State Department and continued to resist Carranza's government. Its forces, which had been created to eliminate Villa, failed to capture the guerrilla leader or win a single battle.

After the assassination of Carranza in 1920, Villa signed a peace treaty with the new president, Adolfo de la Huerta, in which he received four haciendas, a year's salary, and permission to retain his rank as general and a personal guard of 50 soldiers. Villa

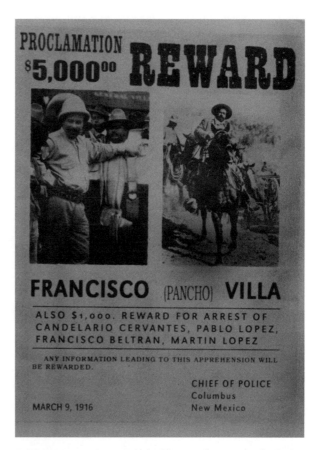

Poster announcing reward of $5,000 for arrest of Pancho Villa after his raid on Columbus, New Mexico, in 1916.

then withdrew from political life and devoted his time to developing his agricultural colonies into prosperous communities. After being wrongly accused of planning to take up arms against Obregón and opposing the presidential candidacy of Plutarco Elías Calles, Villa was assassinated in the city of Hidalgo de Parral on July 20, 1923. His continuing vilification was evident a few years later when his sepulcher was profaned, his corpse decapitated, and his head stolen from his "resting" place.

Decades after his assassination he was recalled as a bloodthirsty bandit by many conservatives. However, by the late 1960s Pancho Villa was transformed into a revolutionary hero, his name placed in gold letters in the Chamber of Deputies, and his bones reburied in the Monument to the Revolution in Mexico City. Villa is the most widely known of Mexico's historical characters, still remembered in *corrido* ballads and stories from the past. In one of the classic films of the Mexican Revolution—*Vámanos con Pancho Villa* (1935)—director Fernando de Fuentes portrays the famous guerrilla leader of the Division of the North as the major icon of the revolution. Villa was a master of public relations, and there were times when he managed to convince the United States of the justness of his cause, despite negative stereotypes of the guerrilla leader and his countrymen in the American press.

Villa's legal widow, Luz Corral de Villa, made a living from the memory and powerful shadow of the slain guerrilla leader for decades. Until her death in 1981, she struggled with what she could make from the mansion-turned-museum (Pancho Villa House) in Chihuahua, full of mementos from the revolutionary period, including the bullet-riddled Dodge touring car in which the former rebel leader and his bodyguard were riding when they were shot in 1923. In a 1913 photograph, Pancho Villa is shown next to his future nemesis, General John J. Pershing. Behind the two men in the photograph stands a young officer who would gain fame in **World War II**, George C. Patton.

A small leftist guerrilla group—Ejército Villista Revolucionario del Pueblo (EVRP)—using Pancho Villa's name was spotted in the state of Morelos in 2000, calling for the replacement of the neoliberal model of development with some variant of socialism.

SUGGESTED READING

Mark C. Anderson, *Pancho Villa's Revolution by Headlines* (Norman: Oklahoma University Press, 2000); Friedrich Katz, *The Life and Times of Pancho Villa* (Stanford: Stanford University Press, 1998); Alan Riding, "In Mexico, Pancho Villa's Widow Guards His Name," *New York Times*, November 23, 1980.

Virgin of Guadalupe ☀ Native American fertility goddess (Tonantzin) in medieval Christian garb. The Virgin of Guadalupe is a national symbol that blends indigenous religious beliefs with the Catholicism of Rome and the Counterreformation. A Roman Catholic icon, the Virgin of Guadalupe is Mexico's patron saint and part of the larger veneration of the Virgin of the Immaculate Conception that originated in Europe. The existence of a brown-skinned, Aztec-speaking Virgin Mary demanding that a church be built on a native religious site is based on a legend that evolved from a Nahua (Aztec) peasant, Juan Diego, who is reported to have seen the Virgin on Tepeyac hill outside Mexico City; a bishop, Juan de Zumárraga, who demanded proof of the apparition; and the existence of a cloak (*tilma*) with the Virgin's image imprinted on it (definitive proof of what Juan Diego saw). Since the appearance of the Virgin in 1531, the story of the Virgin who became known as Guadalupe, has nurtured Mexicans' devout faith in the Catholic Church, especially among the poor.

For the past 200 years, the image and veneration of Our Lady of Guadalupe has played an increasingly important role in the development of a sense

Catholic pilgrims approaching the Basilica of Guadalupe, Mexico City. Credit: General Secretariat of the Organization of American States.

of Mexican national identity. Millions of pilgrims visit Mexico City's massive Virgin of Guadalupe Basilica to celebrate her feast day on December 12. Inside the church, believers gaze with reverence at the cactus fiber cloak—hanging high on a wall inside a glass case—Juan Diego supposedly wore with the miraculous image of the dark-skinned Virgin of Guadalupe. Except for the Vatican, the Shrine of the Virgin of Guadalupe is visited by more people—some 6 million pilgrims arrive annually—than any other religious site in the Christian world.

Many Mexicans consider Guadalupe a maternal symbol, providing comfort, inspiration, and faith in God. Deliberate promotion by the Catholic Church has increased Guadalupe's popularity. She has been viewed as a symbol of liberation (as it is used by independence hero Miguel Hidalgo y Costilla and guerrilla leader **Emiliano Zapata**) and *Mexicanidad*. Those who remain skeptical and hostile to the devotion see the Virgin as a religious figure manipulated by intellectuals and anticlericals to keep people passive. Today, her image appears everywhere in Mexico, including murals, T-shirts, shop signs, car decals, tatoos, and even at political campaign rallies.

There is an ongoing controversy over the apparition, the very existence of Juan Diego, the authenticity of the cloak, Church documents supporting the apparition, and Vatican efforts to canonize Diego. Some claim that the image on the cloak was painted with brushes and that there is no proof that Diego ever existed, despite the Vatican's determination to elevate Diego to sainthood. In 1999 several Mexican priests, all of whom once worked at the Basilica de Guadalupe in Mexico City, wrote a letter to the Vatican objecting to the efforts to name him a saint because there is no empirical proof that the Indian every lived. Pope John Paul II has visited Mexico three times, on each occasion expressing veneration for the Virgin of Guadalupe, and in 1990 he beatified Diego, the first step before a candidate can be considered for sainthood.

While there are dispassionate and scholarly studies of *guadalupanismo* that are part of the controversy, the Virgin of Guadalupe can be seen as a valuable factor in Mexican religious and national life, and a symbol that throughout its history has been manipulated and changed to serve a number of spiritual and worldly goals in society. The Virgin of Guadalupe has a Web site called "Interlupe" and study center. The Center for Guadalupan Studies in Mexico City since its creation in 1972 has devoted itself to research, conferences, publications, and the love and appreciation of Our Lady of Guadalupe. For the past 10 years the center has lobbied for the canonization of Juan Diego. Pope John Paul II initiated a Web site (www.virgendeguadalupe.org.mx) in December 2001 devoted to the Virgin of Guadalupe. It features real-time Masses, a souvenir shop, and a complete history of the controversial appearance in Tepeyac where the Virgin is said to have told Diego to build a church in her honor. *See also* Church and State; Fox Quesada, Vicente.

SUGGESTED READING

David Brading, *Mexican Phoenix: Our Lady of Guadalupe: Image and Tradition across Five Centuries* (New York: Cambridge University Press, 2001); Francisco de la Maza, *El guadalupanismo mexicano* (Mexico, D.F.: Porrúa & Obregón, 1981); Ignacio de la Mota, *Diccionario Guadalupano* (Mexico, D.F.: Panorama Editorial, 1977); Virgil Elizondo, *Guadalupe: Mother of the New Creation* (Maryknoll, N.Y.: Orbis, 1998); Susan Ferriss, "Controversy Surrounds Mexico's Patron Saint," *Austin American-Statesman*, December 11, 1999; Stafford Poole, *Our Lady of Guadalupe: The Origins and Sources of a Mexican National Symbol, 1531–1797* (Tucson: University of Arizona Press, 1995); Jeanette Rodríguez, *Our Lady of Guadalupe: Faith and Empowerment among Mexican American Women* (Austin: University of Texas Press, 1994).

Warman, Arturo (1937–) Social anthropologist best known for his studies of the political economy of rural development, corn production, and the problem of indigenous populations in Mexico. Warman is one of the few anthropologists to be appointed to a cabinet position, having served as minister of agriculture during the presidency of **Ernesto Zedillo** (1994–2000). Born in Mexico City, he studied ethnology at the National School of Anthropology and History (Escuela Nacional de Antropología e Historia, ENAH) between 1960 and 1968. He earned a master's degree from the **Universidad Nacional Autónoma de México (UNAM)** in 1963, and in 1975 a Ph.D. in the same specialty at the Iberoamerican University in Mexico City. Between 1988 and 1992 Warman was director general of the National Indigenous Institute (Instituto Nacional Indígena, INI). He is the author of numerous books on acculturation, corn production, *campesino* life, and the plight of indigenous communities. Warman is a member of the Institute for Advanced Studies at Princeton, New Jersey, and in 1991 he was elected to serve as an adviser for the National Commission for Human Rights. For his work in the field of ethnology, Warman received the National Prize from the Academy of Scientific Investigation in 1976.

Women. *See* Feminism; Machismo.

World War II Although Mexico was more concerned with internal political and economic problems in the 1930s and early 1940s, it eventually joined the Allied cause to combat the hostilities in Europe and Asia during most of the World War II period. Mexico's wartime position was enunciated by President **Ávila Camacho** (1940–1946), who at first had to steer a course between pro-German forces on the right and left and those who supported a pro-Allied course of action. In 1939, the Declaration of Panama produced the first collective effort to confront the Axis powers, proclaiming a "safety belt" of 300–1,000 miles around the Western Hemisphere and an agreement that Latin American armies would only be used to meet an attack until U.S. forces could intervene, not in the status of a combat ally. The Declaration of Panama paved the way for agreements to place U.S. military missions in Mexico and all the other countries of the region, except Bolivia. Following the Japanese attack on Pearl Harbor, Mexico broke diplomatic relations with the Axis powers but avoided the ultimate step of declaring war until German submarines operating in the Caribbean torpedoed and sank two Mexican tankers. Mexico finally declared war on the Axis powers in 1942.

During the period between Pearl Harbor and Mexico's declaration of war, the Ávila Camacho government managed to extract critical concessions from the United States, including a beneficial agreement with U.S. oil companies, modern military equipment, a guaranteed market for all Mexican raw materials during the war, a renegotiation of Mexico's foreign debt, and U.S. financial assistance to overhaul the desolate Mexican railway system. Mexico enjoyed wartime preferences from the United States that were denied other Latin American countries. Wartime collaboration was based on the production and supply of raw materials for the Allied cause and a military alliance that brought Mexican and American troops together for the first time. The skill and expertise of Mexico's wartime diplomatic personnel are also important factors, as their efforts to exploit the contradictions of the war helped improve Mexico's international position.

Beginning in 1940, Mexico embarked on a new economic development strategy based on the need for rapid industrialization in order to become a more developed country. The demands created by World War II supported industrialization policies that were of benefit to Mexico. World War II provided the stimulus for Mexico's industrial development by increasing demands for Mexico's exports—particularly minerals, cotton, and oil seeds—and providing protection from imports. The agricultural sector experienced increased mechanization and greater use of pesticides and herbicides to increase production during the war years. Although Mexico received financial assistance from the United States to build steel mills during the war, these funds turned out to be highly inefficient means of pushing industrialization programs. The policies of Mexico's wartime leadership achieved unprecedented advantages for the Mexican state, but they failed to convert these benefits into significant gains for the majority of the Mexican population. Those who have examined the economic impact of the war argue that Mexico's population suffered hardship due to inflation, an absence of consumer goods, as well as food shortages that contributed to increased hunger, particularly in the countryside.

During the presidency of Manuel Ávila Camacho (1940–1946), a series of measures—tax breaks, selective financing of industries, policies to protect infant industries from foreign competition, and restrictions on the establishment of foreign companies in Mexico—were taken to strengthen Mexican industry. After the declaration of war, the Mexican government moved to confiscate the German chemical industry in Mexico, which added another important industrial sector to its petroleum industry without resorting to expropriation. The war years generated the first large-scale use of **immigrant** farm labor in the United States, partic-

ularly among the states located along the border with Mexico. The *bracero* **program**, created in 1942, provided for the legal, temporary employment of Mexican agricultural workers in the U.S. border region, with over half the contract *braceros* in California agriculture.

The decline in European and American **cinema** during the war years created a new demand for Mexican films—both domestically and throughout the Western Hemisphere—and the need for greater collaboration with the U.S. government. To modernize the Mexican film industry for the benefit of the United States and the war effort, **Nelson Rockefeller**'s **Office of the Coordinator of Inter-American Affairs (OCIAA)** provided funds for the improvement of Mexican film studios in order to have a more authentic source of wartime propaganda for audiences throughout the Western Hemisphere. The United States also manipulated the flow of raw film stock to benefit Mexico and not Argentina, the other major Latin American film producer, due to displeasure over Argentina's pro-Axis foreign policy. The dynamics of U.S. government–coordinated assistance to the Mexican film industry changed with the end of World War II. While the State Department recognized more than ever the important role of motion pictures in fostering its postwar foreign policy agenda, the official rhetoric changed to "free trade" policies wrapped inside the broader ideological goals of U.S. foreign policy. In altering the political economy of film diplomacy, Hollywood's Motion Picture Producers and Distributors of America (MPPDA) replaced the government-run OCIAA, in effect giving Hollywood an "official" role in setting the agenda—facilitating the hegemony of the U.S. film industry throughout the hemisphere—for U.S.–Latin American relations.

Despite opposition from the Mexican left and U.S. military planners, the Mexican military managed to participate actively in World War II.

Presidents Franklin D. Roosevelt and Manuel Ávila Camacho reviewing Mexican troops, Monterrey, Nuevo León, 1943. Credit: General Secretariat of the Organization of American States.

Toward the end of the war Mexico contributed a squadron of airplanes and pilots (the **Escuadrón de Pelea 201**) that fought against Japan from bases in the Philippines in 1945. In addition, over 250,000 Mexicans served in the U.S. military, 14,000 experienced combat as part of the U.S. Army, and 1,000 were awarded with a Purple Heart medal. Diplomatic efforts to strengthen inter-American security during the war succeeded in paving the way for eventual Latin American participation and membership in the United Nations (1945) and the

Organization of American States (1948). Mexican involvement in World War II allowed it to position itself as an important Latin American player in the postwar international political and economic system alongside the winners of the war.

The skill and expertise of Mexico's wartime leadership managed to steer the nation through a major international conflict with a series of domestic gains that would have been impossible in peacetime. Mexico cooperated with the United States during the war without relinquishing its territorial sovereignty or forging agreements that would have allowed the continued presence of U.S. troops on Mexican soil during the Cold War period that followed. Nevertheless, secret German and Japanese espionage aimed at the United States and Canada from Mexico did occur, although neither President **Lázaro Cárdenas** nor President Ávila Camacho was consulted about these nefarious activities of U.S. enemies during World War II.

Although the merits of Mexico's wartime alliance with the United States can be argued, there seems little doubt that by the end of the war Mexico had increased its dependency on the United States. Moreover, the continuation of that alliance after the war also illustrates, according to Fein (1999, 157), one of the central paradoxes of the Mexican state since World War II: "rhetorically nationalist but structurally aligned, both politically and economically, with its North American neighbor." To compete in the global

marketplace and address troublesome binational issues such as immigration, drugs, and crime, Mexico has "softened" its forceful nationalism and anti-Americanism.

SUGGESTED READING

Seth Fein, "From Collaboration to Containment: Hollywood and the International Political Economy of Mexican Cinema after the Second World War," in Joanne Hershfield and David R. Maciel, eds., *Mexico's Cinema: A Century of Film and Filmmakers* (Wilmington, Del.: Scholarly Resources, 1999); Stephen R. Niblo, *War, Diplomacy, and Development: The United States and Mexico, 1938–1954* (Wilmington, Del.: Scholarly Resources, 1995); María Emilia Paz, *Strategy, Security, and Spies: Mexico and the U.S. as Allies in World War II* (University Park: Pennsylvania State University Press, 1997); Friedrich E. Schuler, *Mexico between Hitler and Roosevelt: Mexican Foreign Relations in the Age of Lázaro Cárdenas* (Albuquerque: University of New Mexico Press, 1998).

Yáñez, Agustín (1904–1980) Prolific writer best known for *Al filo del agua* (1947), a classic of Latin American literature that depicts the upheaval of the **Mexican Revolution** in a provincial town in rural Mexico. Yáñez was not only one of Mexico's most important 20th-century novelists but also an erudite journalist, civil servant, statesman, creative essayist, and one of the many intellectuals who molded cultural life in the aftermath of the **Mexican Revolution**. Many of his novels and short stories use social and geographical descriptions of

regional lifestyles to create and consolidate a new national identity. His 1959 novel, *La creación*, was widely read throughout Mexico, and *Al filo del agua* became required reading in the state schools.

Born in Guadalajara in 1904 to a family of peasants, Yáñez grew up in a conservative religious environment in Jalisco, where he studied and taught for part of his long career. He obtained a law degree from the University of Guadalajara (1929) and then continued his studies at the **Universidad Nacional Autónoma de México (UNAM)** in Mexico City, where he taught from 1932 to 1942. As a member of the Mexican Catholic Youth Association, he was sympathetic to the Cristero movement in Jalisco (1928–1929) and later supported the candidacy of **José Vasconcelos** in 1929. After his first bureaucratic appointment as director of radio educational extension programs and then secretary of public education (1932–1934), his career shifted toward politics, diplomacy, and cultural affairs. By the 1930s he had been transformed into an intellectual linked to the political elite, helping to set a pattern for other literary figures (including **Octavio Paz, Carlos Fuentes**, and many others) whose careers dovetailed with important posts in the ruling party (PRI) and the **government**. At the School of Philosophy and Letters at UNAM, Yáñez was a professor of literary theory (1942–1953; 1959–1962) while occupying important political jobs. He was governor of his native Jalisco from 1953 to 1959. During the **López Mateos** presidency, Yáñez served as special adviser to the president (1959–1962) and ambassador to Argentina. During his final years he served as secretary of public education (1964–1970) and president of the Free Textbook Commission (1978–1979).

Agustín Yáñez was best known for his novels of misery and poverty in rural Mexico, and he treated the revolution as a liberating force for the oppressed. But he also achieved a rich and colloquial style that infused his writing techniques. His artistic creativity—mingling well-known celebrities with fictional characters, use of allegory, internal monologues, fragmented time, or juxtaposing various situations—made him a writer who managed to achieve universal dimensions, as well as considerable popularity, while viewing the major transformations taking place throughout rural Mexico. Unlike other Mexican intellectuals, Yáñez did not produce many disciples to carry on his endeavors. Agustín Yáñez died in Mexico City in 1980, shortly after publishing his last novel (*Las vueltas del tiempo*, 1973) and collection of short stories (*La ladera dorada*, 1978).

SUGGESTED READING

John S. Brushwood, *Mexico in Its Novel: A Nation's Search for Identity* (Austin: University of Texas Press, 1966); Claudio Canaparo, "Agustín Yáñez, 1904–1980," in Verity Smith, ed., *Encyclopedia of Latin American Literature* (Chicago: Fitzroy Dearborn, 1997); Richard A. Young, *Agustín Yáñez y sus cuentos* (London: Támesis, 1978).

Yucatán. *See* Geographical Regions.

Zacatecas. *See* Geographical Regions.

Zapata, Emiliano (1879–1919) ☀ A revolutionary whose war cry, "Tierra y Libertad!" (Land and Liberty), drove revolutionary upheaval between 1910 and 1917 for the rural peasantry and proletariat. His legacy still runs deep in modern-day Mexico. The romantic folklore of Zapata's role in the Revolution can still be found in songs, literature, art, and official celebrations throughout Mexico. New **guerrilla movements** of the 1990s, such as the Zapatistas of Chiapas, have adopted

Emiliano Zapata standing with sombrero, gun, and sword. 1912.

hood filled with the tension between villagers and the expanding sugar haciendas of the state. In 1909 he became president of his village council, marking the beginning of life as a leader of the poor and oppressed. With a personal rebellion rooted in disputes over land and social injustice, Zapata's skills as a peasant leader allowed him to forge a wider rebellion with thousands of followers. In response to government claims that his rebel movement was politically illegitimate with no basis of support, he joined with others to produce the Plan of Ayala, a powerful document of the central goals of the rural movement. It demanded basic rights in landownership and accused Francisco Madero of betraying the **Mexican Revolution.** He managed to unify a growing movement and emerge as one of the most prominent leaders of the Revolution. His forces eventually sided with **Pancho Villa**'s forces in the north, facilitating their defeat of the forces aligned with Venustiano Carranza and the capture of Mexico City in 1914. While the capture of Mexico City was a success, the alliance between Zapata and Villa proved too divided to keep Carranza's troops from regaining the initiative, and Zapata's forces were eventually driven out of the capital.

After serious infighting and defections, Zapata's rebel movement weakened as a military force. Five years after riding victoriously into Mexico City with his rebel forces, he was assassinated in an act of betrayal by government forces on April 10, 1919. The original Zapatista movement did not end with Zapata's death, however; his cry for land reform continued, even though it took decades for the reforms mandated in the **Constitution of 1917** to be carried out. The agrarian reform that did take place helped legitimize the new political system that emerged in the 1930s, but the government-sponsored land reform failed to liberate Mexico's peasants from their collective poverty and provide the "liberty" that Emiliano Zapata fought for. Nevertheless, the

Zapata's name and symbols and invoke his spirit with shouts of "Viva Zapata!" **Subcommander Marcos,** the charismatic, pipe-smoking intellectual who leads the Zapatista movement in Chiapas, has taken the name of the earlier revolutionary to champion the cause of disenfranchised Indians in southern Mexico, damaged by Mexico's new economic policies and globalization. Unlike their forerunners, the modern-day Zapatistas conceal their faces, using bandanas or black ski masks to cover everything but their eyes. In Latino communities in the United States, Zapata's struggle is still invoked by protesters demanding better education and health care.

Born into a peasant family in Anenecuilco, Morelos, Emiliano Zapata experienced a child-

legend of Zapata survived, helping to transform him from a founding father of the modern Mexican state into a demigod embodying demands for social justice for peasants and indigenous people. *See also* Zapatista Rebellion in Chiapas.

SUGGESTED READING

Tom Barry, *Zapata's Revenge: Free Trade and the Farm Crisis in Mexico* (Cambridge, England: South End, 1995); Samuel Brunk, *Emiliano Zapata! Revolution and Betrayal in Mexico* (Albuquerque: University of New Mexico Press, 1995); Enrique Krauze, *Emiliano Zapata: El amor a la tierra* (Mexico, D.F.: Fondo de Cultura Económica, 1987); John David Ragan, *Emiliano Zapata* (New York: Chelsea House, 1989); Lynn Stephen, *Zapata Lives: Histories and Cultural Politics in Southern Mexico* (Berkeley: University of California Press, 2001); John Womack, *Zapata and the Mexican Revolution* (New York: Knopf, 1968); Eric Van Young, "Making Leviathan Sneeze: Recent Works on Mexico and the Mexican Revolution," *Latin American Research Review* 34, no. 3 (1999).

Zapatista Army of National Liberation (EZLN). *See* Guerrilla Movements and Counterinsurgency; Zapatista Rebellion in Chiapas.

Zapatista Rebellion in Chiapas ☀ The Zapatista uprising began abruptly when rebels took the colonial tourist town of San Cristóbal de las Casas on January 1, 1994, the same day the **North American Free Trade Agreement (NAFTA)** went into effect and a new electoral year was about to begin. The Zapatista revolt was only one of many violent episodes that plagued Mexico in 1994. While the armed uprising lasted only 12 days, an unofficial cease-fire has held ever since, with forces on each side attempting unsuccessful negotiations to end the Chiapas conflict. The Mexican Army still maintains a large force of between 50,000 and 70,000 troops in the area where most of the con-

flict is centered. The Zapatista Army of National Liberation (Ejército Zapatista de Liberación Nacional, EZLN) has a mere 500–1,000 fighters, backed by a lightly armed militia of perhaps a few thousand. Despite these small figures for a **guerrilla movement**, the Zapatista claim over 500,000 sympathizers in Chiapas and have received the support of numerous **human rights** and peace organizations worldwide. From the beginning of the Zapatista uprising in 1994, the United States increased military aid and training for Mexico's armed forces under the rubric of assistance for drug interdiction, reaching $87 million in 1997. Many Mexicans now believe that the United States is directly supporting the government's counterinsurgency strategy in Chiapas, putting the U.S. government in the awkward position of being seen to support an increasingly unpopular regime in its desperate struggle to retain power at the expense of serious reforms.

The Chiapas conflict is rooted in the growing disparity between the Mexico that is rich, urban, and technologically advanced and the Mexico that is poor, rural, and technologically backward. Many of the indigenous communities in Chiapas still lack electricity, running water, or telephones, and arable land is in scarce supply. On top of these sorrowful quality-of-life indicators, the region is divided along religious, ethnic, and political lines, creating the potential for continuing flare-ups. Agriculture has been devastated in Chiapas and lies at the root of the political crisis: the combination of trade liberalization, the lack of adequate credit and government assistance, and repressive measures taken by state and federal authorities.

The Zapatista leader, **Subcommander Marcos,** claims he is fighting for the same causes that motivated **Emiliano Zapata** 90 years ago: land and liberty for the rural farmers and indigenous communities. However, the original Zapatistas did more fighting than the new version; the modern-day Zapatistas have learned the art of public relations, lobbying, and instant communication in the new global age. The **San Andrés Accords**, a complex set of peace accords that promise fairer treatment and greater recognition of indigenous groups and their cultures, were signed in 1996, but the government has failed to implement them due to what it calls ambiguities in many of the details. In 1998 the **Zedillo** administration sent a new set of proposals for legal changes to Congress, but the legislature did not act on these while he was in office.

With renewed hope because of the election of **Vicente Fox**, the Zapatistas have called for more talks, refused to disarm, and insisted that their original demands (such as removal of the army) be met by the government. What is left after six years of confrontation is a continuation of the struggle by other means, particularly the Zapatista effort to keep international attention focused on Chiapas through various publicity measures. Subcommander Marcos has kept up a steady barrage of interviews and communiqués, and he has even written a controversial children's book to support the Zapatista cause. In response, the government has tried rallying nationalist sentiment by expelling foreign visitors to Chiapas and put a close watch on others who sympathize with the Zapatistas.

With the two sides of the conflict unable to break the impasse that now exists, the **human rights** situation, according to a recent Amnesty International report, continues to deteriorate. Nongovernmental human rights groups claim that a "low-intensity" war is being waged in Chiapas, involving everything from harassment to murder by the police, paramilitary groups, and the army, all with apparent immunity from prosecution for these crimes. To counter the human rights community and build its own political legitimacy, the Zedillo administration spent large sums of money on schools, clinics, and social programs, but for the most part the spending in non-Zapatista areas.

The Zapatista uprising and standoff became an issue in the 2000 presidential campaign; challenger Fox claimed that only he had the wisdom to solve the conflict, and the **Partido Revolucionario Institucional** candidate, **Francisco Labastida**, who ran the Chiapas policy while interior minister in 1998–1999, maintained that the next move is up to the Zapatistas. After taking office December 1, 2000, President Fox submitted a bill to Congress designed to bring peace to the region. In response, Marcos and other rebel leaders emerged from their jungle hideout in February 2001 to begin a "Zapatour" to Mexico City to insist that the national government respond to rebel demands for indigenous rights, **democracy**, and social justice in Chiapas.

Emiliano Zapata's original struggle ended with internal divisions and his assassination by government forces in 1919. It seems obvious that the postrevolutionary reforms that have been carried out in the name of Zapata have not addressed the real needs of the Mexico's large indigenous communities, particularly in the age of globalization and neoliberalism. Zapata's ghost may have contributed to the pessimism among Indian groups who are pressing the government to release all Zapatista prisoners, close military bases near Indian communities, and move forward on legislation for Indian rights before peace talks can be reopened. So far, the San Andrés Accords have not been approved by the Mexican Congress and the Zapatistas who journeyed to Mexico City to lobby for the reforms have returned to their sanctuary in Chiapas. *See also* Acteal Massacre.

SUGGESTED READING

Thomas Benjamin, *Rich Land, a Poor People: Politics and Society in Modern Chiapas* (Albuquerque: University of New Mexico Press, 1996); Pete Brown, "Cultural Resistance and Rebellion in Southern Mexico," *Latin American Research Review* 33, no. 3 (1998); Collier,

"Zapatismo Resurgent: Land and Autonomy in Chiapas," *NACLA Report on the Americas* (March–April 2000); Collier, with Elizabeth Lowery Quarantiello, *Basta: Land and the Zapatista Rebellion in Chiapas,* rev. ed. (Oakland, Calif.: Food First Books, 1999); Michael W. Foley, "Southern Mexico: Counterinsurgency and Electoral Politics," *United States Institute for Peace Special Report* (U.S. Institute for Peace, 1999); Neil Harvey, *The Chiapas Rebellion: The Struggle for Land and Democracy* (Durham: Duke University Press, 1998); Michael Lowry, "Sources and Resources of Zapatism," in Daniel Castro, ed., *Revolution and Revolutionaries: Guerrilla Movements in Latin America* (Wilmington, Del.: Scholarly Resources, 1999); Robert P. Million, "The Struggle of the Zapatistas," in Daniel Castro, ed., *Revolution and Revolutionaries: Guerrilla Movements in Latin America* (Wilmington, Del.: Scholarly Resources, 1999); Carlos Montemayor, *La rebelión indígena de México* (Madrid: Espasa Calpe, 1998); Daniel Nugent, ed., *Rural Revolt in Mexico: U.S. Intervention and the Domain of Subaltern Politics* (Durham: Duke University Press, 1998); Andres Oppenheimer, *Bordering on Chaos: Guerrillas, Stockbrokers, Politicians, and Mexico's Road to Prosperity* (Boston: Little, Brown, 1996); David Ronfeldt and others, *The Zapatista "Social Netwar" in Mexico* (Santa Monica, Calif.: Rand Corporation, 1998); Philip L. Russell, *The Chiapas Rebellion* (Austin, Texas: Mexico Resource Center, 1995); *Shadows of Tender Fury: The Letters and Communiques of Subcomandante Marcos and the Zapatista Army of National Liberation,* trans. Frank Bardacke (New York: Monthly Review Press, 1995); Lynn Stephen, "Pro-Zapatista and Pro-PRI: Resolving the Contradictions of Zapatismo in Rural Oaxaca," *Latin American Research Review* 32, no. 2 (1997).

Zea Aguilar, Leopoldo (1912–) ☀ Leading intellectual historian and philosopher, best known for his important administrative positions, outstanding publication record, and the mentorship of several generations of students, both Mexican and Latin American. Born in 1912 in Mexico City, Zea studied at the **Universidad Nacional Autónoma de México (UNAM),** where he earned undergraduate and graduate degrees. A long-time dean of philosophy and letters at UNAM, his writing established him as one of Mexico's leading nonfiction authors and essayists. While a member of philosopher José Gaos's famous seminar on the study of ideas in Hispanic America, Zea produced his 1943 classic—*El positivismo en México,* a treatise on the importance of Auguste Comte's positivism in 19th-century Mexico, and winner of the annual Book Fair award—and in 1945 *El apogeo y decadencia del positivismo en México.* His most celebrated books were published between 1944 and 1976, dealing with intellectual history, positivism, philosophy, and world cultures. In his 1955 book *América en la conciencia de Europa,* he examines the future role of Latin America as a bridge between Old World and New World cultures. Zea made major contributions to postwar academic historiography in Mexico, helping spark the historiographical renaissance that started with the large number of non-Mexican historians (graduate students and professional historians) who joined Mexican scholars in their pursuits. He helped revive interest in positivism—the idea that society can be improved by the social sciences, provided that it is not corrupted by religion or theology—which dominated 19th-century educational philosophy but declined in influence with arrival of the **Mexican Revolution** in the 1910s.

SUGGESTED READING

Solomon Lipp, *Leopoldo Zea: From Mexicanidad to a Philosophy of History* (Waterloo, Ont.: Wilfrid Laurier University Press, 1980); Mario Sáenz, *The Identity of Liberation in Latin American Thought: Latin American Historicism and Phenomenology of Leopoldo Zea* (Lanham, Md.: Roman & Littlefield, 1999); Gustavo Vargas Martínez, ed., *Biografía de Leopoldo Zea* (Mexico, D.F.: Fondo de la Cultura Económica, 1992).

Zedillo Ponce de León, Ernesto (1951–) ☀ Mexico's ninth postwar president. Ernesto Zedillo's presidency (1994–2000) was the last of a long string of ruling party victories before the defeat of **Partido Revoluciionario Institucional (PRI)** candidate **Francisco Labastida** in the highly competitive (and fair) 2000 presidential elections. Zedillo arrived in power at a crucial time in Mexico's postwar political history. Fate and political tragedy combined to give Zedillo the opportunity to initiate major changes in the Mexican political system during his presidency.

Given his modest background and lack of ties to the **Revolutionary Family**, Ernesto Zedillo was different from previous presidents of Mexico. The son of a lower-middle-class electrician, he was born in Mexico City but grew up along the border in Mexicali, Baja California, where he became familiar with American culture and language. Before moving to Los Pinos, the home of Mexican presidents in Chapultepec Park in 1994, Zedillo lived in a modest middle-class home in Mexico City without servants. His education was typical of Mexican leaders known as *técnicos* (**technocrats**), who studied economics, finance, and public administration. After graduating in economics from the National Polytechnic Institute, Zedillo moved on to Yale University, where he earned a master's degree and doctorate (1974, 1978) in economics. Before entering Yale, he also took courses in finance and economics at Bradford University (England) and at the University of Colorado. Unlike former presidents **Miguel de la Madrid** and **Carlos Salinas**, who came from well-to-do families and could afford to attend private schools, Zedillo had to work hard to be accepted within the close-knit technocratic elite that had dominated Mexican politics since 1982. After several years of teaching at the National Polytechnic Institute and the **Colegio de México** and working as an economist in government agencies, Zedillo served in the Salinas cabinet as secretary of programming and budget beginning in 1988.

President Ernesto Zedillo. Credit: *Proceso*, photo by German Canseco.

After **Luis D. Colosio** died in 1994, Zedillo was picked by President Salinas to be the PRI candidate for the 1994 election. It was a difficult road to the presidency, compounded by the fact that Zedillo had little, if any, charisma, possessed no loyal power base, had never held an elected post (as was the case with his predecessors Salinas and de la Madrid), and knew little about the "game" of winning elections. With little time to get his campaign up and running, Zedillo faced two opponents—**Cuauhtémoc Cárdenas** of the **Partido de la Revolución Democrática (PRD)** and Diego Fernández de Cevallos of the **Partido Acción Nacional (PAN)**—with considerable electoral experience. Furthermore, Zedillo had to carry the weight of the negative impact of the Chiapas insurrection, the failures of the government's record on **human rights** and alleviating poverty, and a poor performance in the country's first-ever televised debates in May 1994. By spending large sums of money and emphasizing the fear of an opposition-controlled government if he lost, Zedillo managed to win while gaining only 48 percent of the vote, the lowest level of popular support of any of the previous PRI presidential candidates. Nevertheless, with thousands of international observers, the 1994 election was the cleanest ever with the largest turnout in the history of Mexico. Few dispute that Zedillo was the clear winner in the presidential election, and many believed that he possessed a number of personal virtues—he is clever, honest, and a quick study—that would help the Mexican presidency.

Upon taking office on December 1, 1994, President Zedillo faced three major challenges to his presidency and the future of Mexico. First, Zedillo had to overcome the widespread perception that he was a weak president, both in terms of experience and his questionable mandate. He needed a power base to consolidate his position by reaching out to more traditional power brokers who could help with his domestic and international goals. Within months he had to confront the ambitions and misdeeds of the two Salinas brothers, ex-president Carlos and older brother Raúl. In February 1995 law enforcement officials arrested and imprisoned **Raúl Salinas** for alleged complicity in the murder of José Francisco Ruiz Massieu, the PRI secretary-general. After a brief protest and hunger strike, Carlos Salinas left Mexico for self-imposed exile abroad. To strengthen his presidency, President Zedillo cultivated more traditional power brokers who could assist with economic and political reform. Consolidating his power proved to be complicated, given the fact that the PRI had dominated the core of Mexican presidential politics for 70 years. Faced with rumors of assassination plots and coup attempts, Zedillo tried to juggle his cabinet (including appointments of opposition leaders) to get the right mix of loyalists to bolster his flagging legitimacy.

Second, within weeks of taking office, President Zedillo faced a liquidity crisis that forced the government to devalue the Mexican currency by 15 percent, triggering events that quickly led to the near financial breakdown of the country. The improper handling of the "peso crisis" sent mixed signals to investors and failed to introduce necessary adjustment measures. The magnitude of the crisis created enormous problems in Mexico, unleashed financial turmoil that had global repercussions, and required a $52 billion rescue package assembled by the Clinton administration and the International Monetary Fund (IMF), World Bank, and other multilateral organizations. The bailout package forced the Zedillo administration to implement one of the most draconian austerity programs in Mexican history, exacting a staggering cost on Mexican citizens. The GDP fell by almost 7 percent, inflation rose to over 50 percent, 15,000 businesses collapsed, and 1.5 million jobs were destroyed. One million people refused to pay money owed to Mexican banks while others left for the United States in search of relief.

The economic and social crisis spawned a multitude of new social movements and violence, kidnapping, **corruption**, robbery, and **drug trafficking** increased dramatically in the major urban centers of Mexico. The **Zapatista rebellion in Chiapas** was joined by a new guerrilla group called the Popular Revolutionary Army (Ejército Popular Revolucionario, EPR) in the state of Guerrero. A nationwide debtors organization (El **Barzón**) was created to offset the strains of indebtedness. President Zedillo became the object of ridicule, like his predecessor, Carlos Salinas, because many believed he lacked the skills to deal with the horrendous suffering.

President Zedillo's third major hurdle was his inaugural commitment to bring about **electoral** reform and greater **democratization**. This proved exceedingly difficult given the resistance of certain elements within the ruling party and the magnitude of the problem of changing the rules of the political game. Within days of taking office, Ernesto Zedillo called a secret meeting of Mexican intellectuals to assist with a plan for political reform. The ideas that materialized from that meeting were later incorporated into wholesale changes in the nation's electoral law. With skill and perseverance, Zedillo managed to reach an agreement on a historic political reform package in 1996 that named an independent national electoral commission, called for the election (not the presidential appointment) of Mexico City's mayor, and tightened accountability in the area of campaign expenditures, equitable access to the media, and public funding of campaigns. The meaning of these democratic reforms became apparent in the July 1997 elections in which the PRI lost its absolute majority in Congress for the first time and PRD candidate Cuauhtémoc Cárdenas was elected mayor of Mexico City, the second most powerful political position after the presidency.

The political reforms and the results of the 1997 elections set the stage for a more competitive election in 2000 with the country's political power split into roughly three equal parts: the ruling PRI, the center-left PRD, and the conservative PAN. After decades of using the *dedazo* to choose PRI presidential nominees, President Zedillo ended the practice by pushing through a series of democratic reforms—the most important being a new primary system open to all voters—that offered the possibility of more lively and open presidential elections beginning in 2000. After casting his ballot in the first presidential primary in November 1999, President Zedillo remarked to reporters: "This finger is a thing of the past," he said, waving the index finger he opted not to use to pick the presidential candidate. "Now we have this one," he added, showing the indelible black ink on his thumb that confirmed he had voted in the primary.

Despite legislative advances that ensure fairer campaigning and impartial election supervision, corruption continues to plague Mexican presidents, regardless of the measures taken to root out bribes, illegal enrichment, and electoral fraud. For example, Mexico's antinarcotics czar, General José de Jesús Gutiérrez Rebollo, was jailed in February 1997 on charges of drug corruption, taking bribes, and facilitating cocaine trafficking for the drug cartel headed by Amado Carrillo Fuentes. High-level corruption has become a campaign issue in Mexico and a source of tension between Mexico and the United States. During his last year in office, President Zedillo had an easier time pushing through his legislative agenda—financial reform and allowing a greater private role in the energy sector—after a failed effort of the opposition to form an electoral alliance for the 2000 presidential election.

Mexican **foreign policy** under Zedillo made strides to cement closer ties with the United States, but without forfeiting the importance of national sovereignty and nonintervention as key values. With the Seattle collapse of the World Trade Organization talks in December 1999, President Zedillo became critical of nongovernmental organizations that have hijacked global trade discussions under the guise of protecting the poor, arguing that old-style free trade works wonders for developing countries such as Mexico. Despite the president's remarks, the enthusiasm that once greeted the **North Atlantic Free Trade Agreement (NAFTA)** in 1994 has diminished, largely because of the difficulty of enforcing **labor** and **environmental** laws and regulations. The success of the PAN in the 2000 elections led many analysts to conclude that Zedillo's zealous political reforms helped bring an end to the long reign of the ruling party, moving the process of democratization farther than anytime in the 20th century. Like Soviet reformer Mikhail Gorbachev, Ernesto Zedillo may be remembered as a leader who did more to undermine the legitimacy of an entrenched party apparatus than address the underlying causes of one-party dominance and the institutionalized perpetuation of power by an old-guard elite.

SUGGESTED READING

Jorge G. Castañeda, *La herencia: Arqueología de sucesión presidential en México* (Mexico, D.F.: Editorial Alfaguara, 1999); Castañeda, *The Mexican Shock* (New York: New Press, 1995); Peter Fritsch and José de Cordoba, "How Zedillo Became a Force for Change in Mexican Politics," *Wall Street Journal,* June 30, 2000; George Grayson, *Mexico: From Corporatism to Pluralism?* (Fort Worth, Texas: Harcourt Brace, 1998); Susan Kaufman Purcell and Luis Rubio, eds., *Mexico under Zedillo* (Boulder, Colo.: Lynne Rienner, 1998); James F. Rochlin, *Redefining Mexican "Security": Society, State, and Region under NAFTA* (Boulder, Colo.: Lynne Rienner, 1997); Donald E. Schultz, "Through a Glass Darkly: On the Challenges and Enigmas of Mexico's Future," *Mexican Studies* (Winter 1996); Judith A. Teichman, *Privatization and Political Change in Mexico* (Pittsburgh: University of Pittsburgh Press, 1996).

SELECTED BIBLIOGRAPHY

Aguayo Quezada, Sergio. *Myths and (Mis) Perceptions: Changing Elite Visions of Mexico.* La Jolla: Center for U.S.–Mexican Studies, University of California–San Diego, 1998.

Aguilar Camín, Héctor, and Lorenzo Meyer. *In the Shadow of the Mexican Revolution: Contemporary Mexican History, 1910–1989.* Translated by Luis Alberto Fierro. Austin: University of Texas Press, 1993.

Aitken, Rob, et al., eds. *Dismantling the Mexican State?* New York: St. Martin's, 1996.

Álvarez, José Rogelio, ed. *Enciclopedia de México.* 14 vols. Mexico, D.F.: Sabeca Investment Corporation, 1998.

Barkin, David. *Distorted Development: Mexico in the World Economy.* Boulder, Colo.: Westview, 1995.

Barry, Tom, Harry Browne, and Beth Sims. *The Great Divide: The Challenge of U.S.–Mexico Relations in the 1990s.* New York: Grove, 1994.

Bruhn, Kathleen. *Taking on Goliath: Mexico's Party of the Democratic Revolution.* University Park: Pennsylvania State University Press, 1997.

Butler, Ron. *Dancing Alone in Mexico: From the Border to Mexico and Beyond.* Tucson: University of Arizona Press, 2000.

Camp, Roderic Ai. *Crossing Swords: Politics and Religion in Mexico.* New York: Oxford University Press, 1997.

———. *Generals in the Palacio: The Military in Modern Mexico.* New York: Oxford University Press, 1992.

———. *Mexican Political Biographies, 1935–1993.* 3d ed. Austin: University of Texas Press, 1995.

———. *Politics in Mexico: The Decline of Authoritarianism.* 3d ed. New York: Oxford University Press, 1999.

Castañeda, Jorge G. *La herencia: Arqueología de la sucesión presidencial en México.* Mexico, D.F.: Editorial Alfaguara, 1999.

———. *Perpetuating Power: How Mexican Presidents Were Chosen.* Translated by Padraic Arthur Smithies. New York: New Press, 2000.

Centeno, Miguel A. *Democracy within Reason: Technocratic Revolution in Mexico.* University Park: Pennsylvania State University Press, 1997.

Cockcroft, James D. *Mexico's Hope: An Encounter with Politics and History.* New York: Monthly Review Press, 1998.

Cornelius, Wayne A. "Politics in Mexico." In Gabriel A. Almond and G. Bingham Powell, eds., *Comparative Politics Today: A World View.* Glenview, Ill.: Scott, Foresman/Little, Brown, 2000.

Cornelius, Wayne A., and Ann L. Craig. *The Mexican Political System in Transition.* La Jolla: Center for U.S.–Mexican Studies, University of California–San Diego, 1991.

Davis, Diane E. *Urban Leviathan: Mexico City in the Twentieth Century.* Philadelphia: Temple University Press, 1994.

DePalma, Anthony. *Here: A Biography of the New American Continent.* New York: Public Affairs, 2001.

Domínguez, Jorge I., and Alejandro Poiré. *Toward Mexico's Democratization: Parties, Campaigns, Elections, and Public Opinion.* London: Routledge, 1998.

Fuentes, Carlos. *A New Time for Mexico.* Berkeley: University of California Press, 1997.

Grayson, George. *Mexico: From Corporatism to Pluralism?* Fort Worth, Texas: Harcourt-Brace, 1997.

Hakim, Peter. "Two Ways to Go Global," *Foreign Affairs,* vol. 81, no. 1 (2002).

Hamnett, Brian R. *A Concise History of Mexico.* New York: Cambridge University Press, 1999.

Hellman, Judith. *Mexican Lives.* New York: New Press, 1994.

Hershfield, Joanne, and David R. Maciel, eds. *Mexico's Cinema: A Century of Film and Filmmakers.* Wilmington, Del.: Scholarly Resources, 1999.

Katzenberger, Elaine, ed. *First World, Ha, Ha, Ha: The Zapatista Challenge.* San Francisco: City Lights, 1995.

Kirkwood, Burton. *The History of Mexico.* Westport, Conn.: Greenwood, 2000.

Klesner, Joseph L. "Political Change in Mexico: Institutions and Identity." *Latin American Research Review* 32, no. 2 (1997).

León, Andrés, ed. *Diccionario Enciclopédico de México.* Mexico, D.F.: Ediciones Pedagógicas, 1989.

Levy, Daniel C., and Kathleen Bruhn. *Mexico: The Struggle for Democratic Development.* Berkeley: University of California Press, 2001.

Levy, Daniel C., and Emilio Zabadúa. *Mexico: The Struggle for Democratic Development.* Boulder, Colo.: Westview, 1997.

MacLachlan, Colin, and William H. Beezley. *El Gran Pueblo: A History of Greater Mexico.* Englewood Cliffs, N.J.: Prentice-Hall, 1994.

Mazza, Jacqueline. *Don't Disturb the Neighbors: The United States and Democracy in Mexico, 1980–1995.* New York: Routledge, 2001.

Meyer, Michael, William L. Sherman, and Susan M. Deeds. *The Course of Mexican History.* 6th ed. New York: Oxford University Press, 1999.

Mora, Carl J. *Mexican Cinema: Reflections on a Society, 1896–1980.* Berkeley: University of California Press, 1980.

Morris, Stephen D. *Corruption and Politics in Contemporary Mexico.* Tuscaloosa: University of Alabama Press, 1991.

———. *Political Reformism in Mexico: An Overview of Contemporary Mexican Politics.* Boulder, Colo.: Lynne Rienner, 1995.

Musacchio, Humberto. *Milenios de Mexico.* Mexico, D.F.: Hoja Casa Editorial, 1999.

Niblo, Stephen R. *Mexico in the 1940s: Modernity, Politics, and Corruption.* Wilmington, Del.: Scholarly Resources, 1999.

Orme, William A., Jr., ed. *A Culture of Collusion: An Inside Look at the Mexican Press.* Boulder, Colo.: Lynne Rienner, 1997.

Pacific Council on International Policy. *Mexico Transforming.* Los Angeles: Pacific Council on International Policy, 2000.

Pastor, Robert A., and Jorge G. Castañeda. *Limits to Friendship: The United States and Mexico.* New York: Knopf, 1988.

Purcell, Susan Kaufman. "Mexico." In Howard J. Wiarda and Harvey F. Kline, eds., *Latin American Politics and Development.* 5th ed. Boulder, Colo.: Westview, 2000.

Purcell, Susan Kaufman, and Luis Rubio, eds. *Mexico under Zedillo.* Boulder, Colo.: Lynne Rienner, 1998.

Quiñones, Sam. *True Tales from Another Mexico: The Lynch Mob, the Popsicle Kings, Chalino, and the Bronx.* Albuquerque: University of New Mexico Press, 2001.

Raat, Dirk. *Mexico and the United States: Ambivalent Vistas.* Athens: University of Georgia Press, 1992.

Rodríguez, Jaime E. *The Evolution of the Mexican Political System.* Wilmington, Del.: Scholarly Resources, 1993.

Rodríguez, Victoria E. *Women's Participation in Mexican Political Life.* Boulder, Colo.: Lynne Rienner, 1998.

Rodríguez, Victoria, and Peter M. Ward, eds. *Opposition Government in Mexico.* Albuquerque: University of New Mexico Press, 1995.

Roett, Riordan. *Challenge of Institutional Reform in Mexico.* Boulder, Colo.: Lynne Rienner, 1995.

Roett, Riordan, ed. *Mexico's External Relations in the 1990s.* Boulder, Colo.: Lynne Rienner, 1991.

Rotella, Sebastian. *Twilight on the Line: Underworlds and Politics at the Mexican Border.* New York: Norton, 1997.

Ruiz, Ramón Eduardo. *Triumphs and Tragedy: A History of the Mexican People.* New York: Norton, 1992.

Schaefer, Claudia. *Textured Lives: Women, Art, and Representation in Modern Mexico.* Tucson: University of Arizona Press, 1992.

Schultz, Donald E., and Edward J. Williams, eds. *Mexico Faces the Twenty-First Century.* New York: Praeger, 1995.

Smith, Clint. *Inevitable Partnership: Understanding Mexico–U.S. Relations.* Boulder, Colo.: Lynne Rienner, 2000.

Smith, Peter H. "Mexico since 1946: Dynamics of an Authoritarian Regime." In Leslie Bethell, ed., *Mexico since Independence.* New York: Cambridge University Press, 1991.

Smith, Verity, ed. *Encyclopedia of Latin American Literature.* Chicago: Fitzroy Dearborn, 1997.

Spener, David, and Kathleen Staudt, eds. *The U.S.– Mexico Border: Transcending Divisions, Contesting Identities.* Boulder, Colo.: Lynne Rienner, 1998.

Suchlicki, Jaime. *Mexico: From Montezuma to NAFTA, Chiapas, and Beyond.* New Brunswick, N.J.: Transaction, 2000.

Teichman, Judith A. *Privatization and Political Change in Mexico.* Pittsburgh: University of Pittsburgh Press, 1996.

Tenenbaum, Barbara A., ed. *Encyclopedia of Latin American History and Culture.* 5 vols. New York: Scribners, 1996.

Toro, María Cecilia. *Mexico's "War" on Drugs: Causes and Consequences.* Boulder, Colo.: Lynne Rienner, 1995.

Weintraub, Sidney. *Financial Decision-Making in Mexico: To Bet a Nation.* Pittsburgh: University of Pittsburgh Press, 2000.

Werner, Michael S., ed. *Encyclopedia of Mexico: History, Society, and Culture.* 2 vols. Chicago: Fitzroy Dearborn, 1997.

Wise, Carol. ed. *The Post-NAFTA Political Economy: Mexico and the Western Hemisphere.* University Park: Pennsylvania State University Press, 1998.

Young, Eric Van, ed. *Mexico's Regions: Comparative History and Development.* La Jolla: Center for U.S.–Mexican Studies, University of California– San Diego, 1992.

ONLINE RESOURCES

The Internet provides a useful source of information on modern Mexico for the professional researcher and the general reader. Online resources are available for basic economic and governmental documents, bibliographies, up-to-date news articles, biographical information on key figures in Mexican history, census data, and election results. Researchers can find Web sites for a wide variety of subjects, including movie stars and entertainers from the past, current political candidates and their parties, famous writers and painters, and a variety of cultural themes of importance to understanding modern Mexico. The following is a selected list of online resources that will complement the conventional bibliography included in this book.

Borderlines. Provides information on U.S.–Mexican borderlands, particularly climate change and water rights, the environment, and human rights. http://www.irc-online.org/bordline/

Cable News Network (CNN). Contains up-to-date material on Mexican politics, electoral analysis, and major candidates. http://www.cnn.com/2000/world/americas/

Cornell University Library, Latin American Government Documents Project. Contains selected summaries—organized by branch of government—of demographic, education, health, economics, housing, communications, and climate from the government agency in charge of Mexico's census. http://lib1.library.cornell.edu/

Corrido Watch. Elijah Wald's Corrido Watch keeps track of *corridos* that appear on current events such as the terrorist attacks on the United States on September 11, 2001. Website includes the lyrics in both Spanish and English. http://www.elijahwald.com/corridowatch.htm/

Federal Electoral Institute (Instituto Federal Electoral, IFE). Contains information on Mexico's electoral institute and data from recent Mexican elections. http://www.ife.org.mx/

Handbook of Latin American Studies, HLAS Online. Provides online access to the handbook's extensive bibliography on Latin America consisting of books, journal articles, and reference books selected and annotated by over 130 scholars in various fields of study. An essential guide to available resources on Mexico in English, Spanish, and other languages. http://lcweb2.loc.gov/hlas/

Hispanic Reading Room, Library of Congress. With access to the Library of Congress catalog for books on Mexico and other Latin American countries, it supplies a comprehensive bibliography and links to other resources. http://lcweb.loc.gov/rr/hispanic/

Incitra. Bibliographic database developed by the Interhemispheric Resource Center. Web site contains information on more than 1,300 books, articles, government documents, and reports on U.S.–Mexican border issues. Database can be searched by title, author, or keyword. http://www.irc-online.org/incitra/

International Monetary Fund (IMF). Contains information on lending programs and economic data on Mexico and other Latin American and Caribbean nations. http://www.monetaryfund.org/

Internet Resources for Latin America. New Mexico State University provides links to many information resources for researchers interested in Latin American studies. http://lib.nmsu.edu/subject/bord/laguia/

Latin America on the Net. Provides information about Mexican geography, culture, politics, and economics, in addition to links to other Web sites. http://latinworld.com/

Latin American Alliance. A project of the World Stewardship Institute, this Web site contains information on protecting biodiversity, sustainable development, habitat protection, ecotourism, and environmental issues facing Mexico and Latin America. http://www.latinsynergy.org/

Latin American Data Base (LADB), University of New Mexico. Professional journalists provide electronic news bulletins about Mexico that are up to date and informative. http://www.ladb.unm.edu/

Latin American Election Statistics: A Guide to Sources. Provides a glossary of election terminology and a chronology of elections since independence at the municipal, state, and federal levels in 19 Latin American countries, including Mexico. The Web site emphasizes sources of statistics and events affecting the particular election, as well as other interesting links to election data and results from a worldwide database. http://dodgson.ucsd.edu/las/mexico/

Latin American Network Information Center (LANIC). Located at the University of Texas, this Web site contains many academic research resources with valuable links to Web sites on Mexican history, anthropology and archeology, government, culture, media, finance, trade, entertainment, education, and recreation. http://http://www.lanic.utexas.edu/la/mexico/

Mexico Online. Contains current information on business, travel, culture, history, and geography. http://www.mexonline.com/

Mexico Web. Contains information about Mexico's history, prominent leaders (e.g., Pancho Villa and Emiliano Zapata), national documents (constitutions), national holidays (e.g., Cinco de Mayo), and indigenous groups. http://mexico.web.com.mx/fhistoria/

New York Times, Americas Directory. Up-to-date news from Mexico and all of Latin America by some of the best foreign correspondents in the news business. http://www.nytimes.com/library/world/americas/

Organization of American States (OAS). Provides flags, words of national anthems, and governmental links for all member states, except Cuba, a nonparticipating member of the inter-American organization. www.oas.org.

Pan American Health Organization (PAHO). Contains information on health programs, diseases, and vital statistics for Mexico and other Latin American and Caribbean countries. http://www.paho.org/

Political Database of the Americas, Georgetown University. Contains information on Mexican politics, including information on elections and political parties. http://www.georgetown.edu.pdba/

Proceso. Contains current articles from the left-leaning political weekly on a wide variety of controversial subjects. http://www.proceso.com.mx/

Reforma. Contains current articles from one of Mexico City's influential and independent daily newspapers. http://www.info-tel.com.mx/reforma/

U.S. Agency for International Development (USAID). Provides information on economic growth, democracy, environment, education, public health, population, and country profiles worldwide, including Mexico. http://www.info.usaid.gov/countries/mx/

U.S. Department of State. Contains background notes for individual countries, including Mexico and other Latin American and Caribbean countries. For each place there is information about the economy, geography, politics, and trade. http://www.state.gov/www/issues/economic/trade_reports/

U.S. Interventions in Latin America. Provides a brief history of U.S. involvement in Latin America, including many of the interventions in Mexico, a timeline, and the complete text of the Monroe Doctrine. http://www.smplanet.com/imperialism/teddy.html/

Virgin of Guadalupe. Vatican site containing information supporting sainthood for Juan Diego as well as real-time Masses, a complete history of the controversial appearance in Tepeyac where the Virgin is said to have told Diego to build a church in her honor, and a well-stocked souvenir shop. http://www.virgendeguadalupe.org.mx/

Washington Office on Latin America (WOLA). Contains publications on Mexico's political parties and elections, human rights, and democratic development. http://www.wola.org/

Washington Post, Americas Regional Coverage. Up-to-date news from Mexico (and Latin America), with implications for U.S. policy. http://www.washingtonpost.com/dyn/world/americas/

World Bank. Contains information on development programs supported by the World Bank, as well as useful economic reports on Mexico and other Latin American and Caribbean nations. http://www.worldbank.org/

APPENDIX A

Mexico and the United States: National Profile Statistics (1999–2000)[*]

	Mexico	United States
Population		
Population (millions)	98,881,000	281,421,906
Population growth (%)	2.1	0.85
Urban population (as % of total)	73	77
Population aged 65 and above (as % of total)	5	12
Gross Domestic Product (GDP) ($)	694.3 billion	8.083 trillion
GDP per capita ($)	7,700	30,200
GDP: Composition by sector (%)		
Agriculture	9	2
Industry	30	23
Services	61	78
Exports (as % of GDP)	15.9	12.1
Imports (as % of GDP)	15.8	13.5
Central government revenues	9.0 (billions)	1.72 (trillion)
Inflation rate (%)	52 (1995)	2
World economic rank (by GDP at PPP)[1]	13	1
Gross receipts from tourism (billions of dollars)	6.9 (1996)	69.9 (1996)
U.S. direct foreign investment (billions of dollars)	34.265	N/A
World Bank income ranking	Middle	High
Billionaires (2001)	12	269
Union membership (as % of workforce, 1995)	42.8	14.2
Politics		
Form of government	Presidential	Presidential
Form of legislative branch	Bicameral	Bicameral
Head of state (2001)	Vicente Fox	George W. Bush
Presidential reelection	No reelection	Two-term limit
Electoral formula for electing president	Plurality	Electoral College

Mexico and the United States: National Profile Statistics (1999–2000) (Continued)

	Mexico	United States
Politics (continued)		
Freedom House ranking[2]		
Political rights	1	1
Civil rights	2	1
Fitzgibbon Democracy Index[3]	6	N/A
Corruption Perception Index ranking[4]	59th	14th
UN voting coincidence with US (%)	54.5	N/A
Women legislators (as % of total)	16.9	12.5
Year women given right to vote	1953	1919
Voter turnout (%, 2000)	60.0	51.0
Military size: Active troops (1998)	175,000	1,448,000
Military cost (% of GDP, 1998)	0.6	3.2
Society		
Adult literacy (as % of total population)	91	95
Life expectancy (years)	73.3	79.7
Birth rate (per 1,000 people)	25.0	14.3
Infant mortality (per 1,000 live births)	34.0 (1993)	6.3
Labor force (millions)	40,606	136,304
Population below poverty line (%)	43 (1996)	13
Personal computers (per 1,000 people)	60.7	580.0
Human Development Index ranking[5]	55th	3d
People per Catholic priest (1998)	7.1	N/A
Percentage Catholic (1998)	90	N/A
Percentage practicing Catholic (1995)	61	N/A
World Bank income distribution (Gini Index)	53.7 (1995)	40.1 (1994)
AIDS cases reported (1997)	2,495	11,388
Per capita costs of medical care, ($, 1997)	240	4,187
Public expenditure on education (% of GDP)	4.9 (1995)	5.4 (1994)

Sources: ECLAC, *Statistical Yearbook for Latin America and the Caribbean*, 2000 (Santiago, Chile: ECLAC, 2001); Michael O'Mara, ed., *Facts about the World's Nations* (New York: Wilson, 1999); James W. Wilkie, ed., *Statistical Abstract of Latin America*, vol. 37 (Los Angeles: UCLA Latin American Center Publications, 2001); Frank L. Wilson, *Concepts and Issues in Comparative Politics: An Introduction to Comparative Analysis* (Upper Saddle River, N.J.: Prentice-Hall, 2002).

*All data are from 1999–2000, except where noted.

[1] This ranking measures per capita GDP at purchasing power parity (PPP).

[2] The Freedom House Survey of political and civil rights defines freedom in both political and civil terms, using definitions that have been traditionally understood in constitutional democratic states. In the ranking system, 1 = most free; 7 = least free. See Freedom House, *Freedom in the World: Political Rights and Civil Liberties*, 1994–2000.

[3] The Fitzgibbon Latin American democracy survey ranks all 20 Latin American countries, using 103 scholars to assess the level of democracy in Latin America at five-year intervals. In 2000, the reputational approach ranked Costa Rica the most democratic and Haiti the least. Mexico ranked sixth behind Brazil (5) and ahead of Venezuela (7).

[4] The Corruption Perception Index (CPI) measures the degree of corruption as seen by businesspeople, risk analysts, and the general public in each country. The CPI ranges between 10 (highly clean) and 0 (highly corrupt). The numbers presented here are the country's CPI rank out of 90 countries throughout the world.

[5] The UN Human Development Index is based on three indicators: longevity, as measured by life expectancy at birth; educational attainment, as measured by a combination of adult literacy and the combined primary, secondary, and tertiary enrollment; and standard of living, as measured by GDP per capita (in purchase power parity).

APPENDIX B

Mexico and the United States: Opinion Surveys on Democracy and Governing

		Mexico	United States
1.	Respondents who believe democracy is better than any other form of government (% who strongly agree)[1]	19	47
2.	Respondents who report "satisfaction" with how democracy is working (%)	41	52
3.	Respondents who report they would be willing to fight for their country (%)[2]	59	77
4.	Citizen views of democracy (%)[3]		
	Liberty/freedom	21	68
	Equality	21	5
	Voting/elections	12	2
	Form of government	14	2
	Welfare/progress	14	1
	Respect/rule of law	13	1
	Don't know/No answer	3	12
	Other	2	9
5.	Levels of confidence in government (%)		
	High	13	N/A
	Medium	41	N/A
	Low	47	N/A
6.	How democratic would you say your country is? (%)[4]		
	Very/somewhat	42	78
	Little/none	53	18
7.	Which system of government do you think is better for your country? (%)		
	Democracy	59	87
	Authoritarianism	28	6
	Other	2	2
	Don't Know	11	6

Mexico and the United States: Opinion Surveys on Democracy and Governing (Continued)

	Mexico	United States
8. Do you agree or disagree with the following statements? (% responding who strongly or somewhat agree)[5]		
The U.S. only pursues its own interests	77	61
The U.S. is a model of democracy for other countries	47	74
The U.S. is a defender of human rights around the world	39	78
9. Voters' perceptions of the effect of having more women in public (political) office (%)[6]		
Better	39	57
Worse	13	17
No difference	33	19
Don't know	15	7

Sources: Wall Street Journal Americas Poll, 1999; Roderic Ai Camp, ed. *Citizen Views of Demcracy in Latin America* (Pittsburgh: University of Pittsburgh Press, 2001); Frank L. Wilson, *Concepts and Issues in Comparative Politics: An Introduction to Comparative Analysis* (Upper Saddle River, N.J.: Prentice-Hall, 2002).

[1] From the 1995–1997 World Values Survey.

[2] From the 1995–1997 World Values Survey.

[3] Question: "In one word, could you tell me what democracy means to you?" Camp, *Citizen Views of Democracy in Latin America*, 17.

[4] *Wall Street Journal* Poll, 1999.

[5] *Wall Street Journal* Poll, 1999.

[6] Gallup Poll, August 1999.

APPENDIX C

Mexican Billionaires, 2001

Billionaires*	Estimated Wealth (in billions)
Carlos Slim Helú	10.8
Emilio Azcárraga Jean	3.0
Ricardo Salinas Pliego & family	3.0
Lorenzo Zambrano & family	2.9
Eugenio Garza-Lagüera & family	2.5
Alberto Bailleres	1.9
Jerónimo Arango	1.8
Carlos Peralta & family	1.5
Alfredo Harp Helú	1.3
Roberto Hernández	1.3
Isaac Saba Raffoul & family	1.3
Germán Larrea Mota-Velasco & family	1.0

Source: "The World's Richest People," *Forbes*, July 9, 2001: 110–118.

Note: At the end of the Carlos Salinas Gortari administration (1988–1994), following years of privatization measures, the number of Mexican billionaires increased to 24. In contrast to Mexico's 12 billionaires in 2001, the United States registered 269, with Bill Gates of Microsoft the wealthiest American with an estimated wealth of $58 billion.

INDEX

The index for the *Encyclopedia of Modern Mexico* was created to be as complete and user friendly as possible. Every effort was made to capture and organize the important ingredients in the index so it would serve as a valuable companion to the rest of book. It is important to keep in mind the following when using this index. First, a full entry (not a blind entry) is paginated using bold face numbers. Second, titles of works that begin within an A, An (or the corresponding Spanish articles) are not inverted, but listed as they appear normally and are alphabetized as if the article is not there. For example, *A Walk in the Clouds* is alphabetized under W, not A. Third, since this reference book consists mainly of short entries, I did not provide subentries for the main entries that appear in the *Encyclopedia*. However, the reader will find that key concepts, organizations, terms, book and film titles, and names that are found *within* each entry are indexed. Finally, the few tables that are found in the book, and some of the data in appendixes A, B, and C, are also indexed for the reader's use.

ABOUT THE AUTHOR

David W. Dent is a professor of political science at Towson University in Baltimore, Maryland. He is the author of *The Legacy of the Monroe Doctrine: A Reference Guide to U.S. Involvement in Latin America and the Caribbean* (1999), the coauthor of *Historical Dictionary of Inter-American Organizations* (1998), and the editor of *U.S.–Latin American Policymaking: A Reference Handbook* (1995) and *Handbook of Political Science Research on Latin America: Trends from the 1960s to the 1990s* (1990). Dent is the author of numerous articles and chapters, including "Ecuador: The Fragility of Dependent Democracy" in Howard J. Wiarda and Harvey F. Kline, eds., *Latin American Politics and Development*, 5th ed. (2000). For the past 26 years he has been a contributing editor for the *Handbook of Latin American Studies*, a biannual reference book published by the Hispanic Division of the Library of Congress in Washington, D.C. He is currently working on the *Historical Dictionary of U.S.–Latin American Relations*.